Library of
Davidson College

Federalism and Regional Development

Federalism and Regional Development

Case Studies on the Experience in the United States and the Federal Republic of Germany

Edited by George W. Hoffman

UNIVERSITY OF TEXAS PRESS
AUSTIN

For reasons of economy and speed this volume
has been printed from camera-ready copy furnished
by the editor, who assumes full responsibility
for its contents.

International Standard Book Number 0-292-73825-0
Library of Congress Catalog Card Number 80-53735

Copyright © 1981 by the Association of American Geographers
All rights reserved
Printed in the United States of America

Requests for permission to reproduce material
from this work should be sent to:
Permissions
University of Texas Press
Box 7819
Austin, Texas 78712

To the importance of international scientific cooperation
and the scholars who strive to make it meaningful

Contents

Preface xix
Acknowledgments xxiii
Abbreviations xxv

1. Central and Federal Legislation and Their Instruments for Regional Development 3
   Die Gesetzgebung von Bund und Ländern und ihre Instrumentarien der regionalen Entwicklung
   KLAUS-ACHIM BOESLER, UNIVERSITY OF BONN

2. Subnational Regional Policies in the United States 41
   Subnationale Regionalpolitik in den Vereinigten Staaten
   NILES HANSEN, THE UNIVERSITY OF TEXAS AT AUSTIN

3. The Federal System of the Federal Republic of Germany 69
   Das Föderative System der Bundesrepublik Deutschland
   PETER SCHÖLLER, RUHR-UNIVERSITY BOCHUM

4. Conceptions and Strategies on Regional Development in the Federal Republic of Germany 95
   Konzeptionen und Strategien zur Raumordnungspolitik in der Bundesrepublik Deutschland
   DIETRICH BARTELS, UNIVERSITY OF KIEL

5. Federal Outlays and Regional Development 125
   Bundesausgaben und Regionalentwicklung
   CLYDE E. BROWNING, UNIVERSITY OF NORTH CAROLINA AT CHAPEL HILL

6. Corporate Organization and Regional Development in the American Federal System: Theory and Policy Perspectives 154
   Unternehmens-Organisation und regionale Entwicklung im bundesstaatlichen System der Vereinigten Staaten: Theoretische und politische Perspektiven
   GÜNTER KRUMME, UNIVERSITY OF WASHINGTON, SEATTLE

7. The Impact of Defense Spending on Regional Industrial Change in the United States   193
   Der Einfluss von Verteidigungsausgaben auf den regionalen industriellen Wandel in den Vereinigten Staaten
   JOHN REES, THE UNIVERSITY OF TEXAS AT DALLAS

8. Federal Housing Policy and Local Housing Markets   223
   Die Wohnungspolitik des bundes und die örtlichen Wohnungsmärkte
   JOHN S. ADAMS, UNIVERSITY OF MINNESOTA

9. Regional Population Development Within the Federal Republic of Germany   254
   Regionale Bevölkerungsentwicklung in der Bundesrepublik Deutschland
   WERNER FRICKE, UNIVERSITY OF HEIDELBERG

10. Federal Policy, Migration and the Changing Geography of the U.S. Population   293
    Die Rolle der Bundesregierung auf die räumliche Bevölkerungsbewegung
    PATRICIA GOBER, ARIZONA STATE UNIVERSITY

11. National Land Use Policies in the United States: Ex Pluribus Nullum   327
    Nationale Landnutzungspolitik in den Vereinigten Staaten: Ex Pluribus Nullum
    RUTHERFORD H. PLATT, UNIVERSITY OF MASSACHUSETTS

12. Programs for Infrastructural Development in Rural Areas   363
    Infrastrukturelle Entwicklungsprogramme in ländlichen Gebieten
    GEORG KLUCZKA, FREE UNIVERSITY OF BERLIN

13. Jurisdictional Issues Regarding Federal and State Policy Regulations: Use and Exploitation of Coastal and Offshore Resources   388
    Gesetzgeberische Ansätze des Bundes und der Staaten über die Nutzung und Ausbeute von Resourcen an der Küste und im Meer
    LEWIS M. ALEXANDER, UNIVERSITY OF RHODE ISLAND

14. National and Regional Influences on the Postwar Development of the West German Inland Waterways (with Particular Consideration of Water Pollution) 415
Bundesstaatliche und regionale Einflüsse auf die Nachkriegsentwicklung der West Deutschen Binnenwasserstrassen (mit besonderen Berücksichtigung der Wasserverschmutzung)
HELMUT W. BREUER, TECHNICAL UNIVERSITY AACHEN

15. The Spatial Distribution of the U.S. Federal Transportation Dollar: Implications for Regional Development 437
Die Räumliche Verteilung des Verkehrs-Dollars des Bundes: Auswirkungen auf die regionale Entwicklung
RONALD BRIGGS, THE UNIVERSITY OF TEXAS AT DALLAS

16. Federal Air Quality Legislation: Implications for Land Use 479
Bundesgesetze zur Luftqualität: Auswirkungen auf die Landnutzung
IAN R. MANNERS AND GUNDARS RUDZITIS, THE UNIVERSITY OF TEXAS AT AUSTIN

17. Federal Impacts on Energy Development and Environmental Management in the American West 528
Der Einfluss der Bundesregierung auf Energieentwicklung und Umweltbewirtschaftung im amerikanischen Westen
MELVIN G. MARCUS, ARIZONA STATE UNIVERSITY

18. The Federal Role in U.S. Wildlife Conservation with Reference to the American Southwest 567
Die Rolle der Bundesregierung in der Wildhege in den Vereinigten Staaten im Bezug auf den Amerikanischen Südwesten
ROBIN W. DOUGHTY, THE UNIVERSITY OF TEXAS AT AUSTIN

19. Regional Development Programs and Their Effectiveness in Areas Along the Eastern Border of West Germany 624
Regionale Entwicklungsprogramme und ihre Wirksamkeit im Bereich des Zonenrandgebiets der Bundesrepublik Deutschland
KARL LENZ, FREE UNIVERSITY OF BERLIN

20. West Berlin and the Federal Republic of Germany 643
Berlin (West) und die Bundesrepublik Deutschland
BURKHARD HOFMEISTER, TECHNICAL UNIVERSITY BERLIN

21. The Postwar Development of Cologne: A Case Study of the Impact of Federal and State Authorities and Assistance Upon a Large Urban Community   665

   Die Nachkriegsentwicklung von Köln: Eine Fallstudie über den Einfluss und die Hilfe von Bund und Land auf eine grosse Stadtgemeinde

   REINHART ZSCHOCKE, TECHNICAL UNIVERSITY AACHEN

22. State Growth Management in a Federal System: The Example of Hawaii   683

   Die Steuerung des Wachstum eines Staates in einem Bundessystem: Der Fall Hawaii

   WILLARD T. CHOW AND ROLAND J. FUCHS, UNIVERSITY OF HAWAII AT MANOA

23. Regional Development Policies by the Federal State of Schleswig-Holstein: The Program North   711

   Regionale Entwicklungspolitik des Landes Schleswig-Holstein: Das Programm Nord

   KARL WEIGAND, EDUCATION UNIVERSITY FLENSBURG AND UNIVERSITY OF KIEL

   Glossary   743
   Notes on Contributors   747

Figures

1-1. Areal units of the Federal Spatial Planning Program   36
2-1. Appalachia: Subregional Boundaries   65
3-1. Existing Federal States, 1980   92
3-2. Revised Federal States (Plan 1972)   93
5-1. Per Capita Federal Outlays—Adjusted, 1976   150
5-2. Sun Belt, West and Core Regions   151
8-1. New Housing Units Started, 1880–1980   249
8-2. Mid-19th Century Housing in Central Baltimore, Illustrating the High Residential Densities of the Pedestrian–Horse Car City   250
8-3. Turn of the Century Minneapolis: Housing Built on Wider Lots in Areas Opened Up by Extending Electric Streetcar Lines   250
8-4. Apartment Houses from the 1920's, Comfortably Spaced Along Transit Lines   251
8-5. Post–World War II Automobile Oriented Suburbia—Housing from the 1950's   251
9-1. Population Development in the Federal States, 1939–1961   283
9-2. Net Migration Change in the Districts of the German Federal Republic, 1950–1961   284
9-3. Population Density in the Districts of the German Federal Republic, 1961   285
9-4. Net Migration Change with Foreign Countries, 1961–1976, per 1,000 Inhabitants   286
9-5. Age Structure of Resident Population in the Historic Core of Mosbach/Baden Württemberg, 1978   286
9-6. Natural Population Change in the Federal Republic of Germany, 1961–1977   287
9-7. Population Development of the German Federal Republic, 1961–1970   288
10-1. Per Capita Defense Contract Expenditures by State, 1977   321
10-2. Spending-Taxes Ratio by State, 1976   322
11-1. Indiana Dunes—1967: Relationship of Federal Port and Park   358

FIGURES

12-1. Regions of Deprived Natural Environment   382
12-2. Backward Areas According to the Recommendations of MKRO of 16 April 1970   382
12-3. Regional Plans of Actions (Status of 1 January 1974)   383
12-4. Areas Threatened by Migration Losses   384
12-5. Retarded Areas Characterized by Particular Structural Inequities   385
13-1. U.S. Fishery Conservation Zone: March 1, 1977   411
14-1. West German Inland Waterways and Projects, Status 1 January 1980   433
15-1. Trends in Federal Assistance for Public Transportation and Passenger Trips by Public Transportation (1962–1977)   465
15-2. Trends in Federal Assistance for Highways: Payments to States by Federal Highway Administration, 1921–1975   466
15-3. Variation Between the 49 Largest U.S. Urbanized Areas in the Receipt of Federal Assistance for Local Public Transportation (1965–1976/77): Per Capita of Their 1970 Population   467
15-4. Variation Between the 49 Largest U.S. Urbanized Areas in the Receipt of Federal Assistance for Local Public Transportation (1965–1976/77): Per Unlinked Passenger Trip in 1972   468
15-5. Ratio of State Apportionments from the Highway Trust Fund to Estimated State Payments into the Highway Trust Fund, Fiscal Year 1957–1976   469
15-6. Federal Highway Expenditures 1965–1975: Per Capita of State Population (1970)   470
15-7. Federal Expenditures for Primary, Secondary, Urban Extension and Urban (ABCD) Highway System 1965–1975: Per Capita of State Population (1970)   471
15-8. Federal Highway Expenditures 1965–1975, per Mile of Highway 1977   472
15-9. Federal Highway Expenditures in Fiscal Year 1975 as a Ratio of Expenditures in Fiscal Year 1957   473
15-10. Federal Highway Funds Committed to Interstate and ABCD Systems July 1, 1956, to December 31, 1977, as a Ratio of Apportionments from Highway Trust Fund, July 1, 1956, to August 31, 1977   474
16-1. Attainment and Nonattainment Areas for Particulate Matter and Sulfur Dioxide   521

FIGURES

17-1. Phases of Environmental Activity in the United States: 1880–1980   564
18-1. Operation of the National Wildlife Refuge System in the Southwest, 1977   612
19-1. Main Industrial Areas of Germany—1928   636
19-2. Interrupted Lines of Transportation in the Border Region   637
19-3. General Orientation of Obersuhl Before and After 1950   638
19-4. Commuters from Obersuhl, 1964   639
19-5. The Eastern Border Region of the Federal Republic of Germany   640
20-1. Rail and Air Traffic Between West Berlin and the Federal Republic of Germany   662
21-1. Cologne: City Borders   679
21-2. Tax Revenue, 1961–1974   680
21-3. Standard Financial Allocation and Grants-in-Aid for Special Purposes: 1961–1974   681
22-1. Federally Owned and Leased Land in the Hawaiian Islands   703
23-1. Public Roads in the Regions North and South of the German-Danish Border in 1954   735
23-2. Program North Area, Location and Extension   736
23-3. Main Roads and Farm Roads in Two Selected Areas North and South of the German-Danish Border   737
23-4. Land Use in Adjoining Communities by Farmers of the Lübke-Koog   738
23-5. Location of the German Development Region and Population Density in the Total Area: Hamburg, Schleswig-Holstein and Denmark   739

Tables

1-1. Federal Regional Policy 32
1-2. Examples of Instruments Applied in Regional Policy 33
2-1. Estimates of the Population of Standard Metropolitan Statistical Areas July 1, 1975, by Population Size Class 48
2-2. Population and Average Annual Change in Regions by Metropolitan Status: 1960 to 1975 (in Thousands) 50
2-3. Poverty Rate for Persons in the United States, by South and Nonsouth Residence, 1959, 1967 and 1976 53
3-1. The Existing Federal States in 1970 76
3-2. The Revised Federal States, 1972 82
5-1. Federal Outlays: Per Capita and as Percent of GNP, 1930–1976 128
5-2. Per Capita Federal Outlays, 1976 (Adjusted) 134
5-3. Location Quotients of Major Functional Budget Categories by Region, 1977 137
5-4. Regional and Subregional Differences by Variables 140
6-1. Winners and Losers Among Headquarter Cities 169
6-2. Regional Dimensions of Senate Decisions: The Lockheed Loan Guarantee Example 178
7-1. Changes in Manufacturing Employment Type by Region, 1947–1976 197
7-2. Government Contracts by Value of Shipment per Region, 1965, 1973, 1976 203
7-3. Government Employment as a Percent of Total Employment per Region 205
7-4. Value of Government Shipments as a Percent of Total Shipments per Region 206
7-5. Regions' Share of Prime Contract Awards in 1965, 1973, 1976 208
7-6. Regions' Share of Subcontracts in 1965, 1973, 1976 209
7-7. Procurement Patterns of Three Large Defense Contractors in Dallas–Fort Worth Area 212
7-8. Backward Linkage Patterns of One Large Defense Contractor Over Time 214

7-9. Defense Firms' Employment Trends in Dallas–Fort Worth Area 216
8-1. U.S. Population, Selected Years and Average Annual Change 230
8-2. U.S. Households, Selected Years, 1930–1978 232
8-3. Average Population per U.S. Household, Selected Years, 1930–1977 233
8-4. Sources and Uses of Mortgage Credit by the End of 1976 236
9-1. Population Development Within the States of the FRG, 1939–1977 258
9-2. Percentage of Unemployed, June 6, 1950 260
9-3. Population Development Within the Federal States, 1950–1961 262
9-4. Percentage of Commuters According to Size of Settlement, 1961 265
9-5. Increase of Commuters in Central Baden-Württemberg from 1900 Until 1961 265
9-6. The Population Development of Cities in the Territory of the FRG (Excluding West Berlin), June 6, 1961 267
9-7. Variation of Age-Specific Fertility Rate in the States Compared to Average of the FRG in 1964 and 1971 274
9-8. Rate of Migration, 1956–1976 276
10-1. Components of Population Change in States, 1960–1975 301
10-2. In, Out and Net Migration Rates for Regions, 1970–1975 and 1975–1978 305
10-3. Components of Population Change in Regions by Metropolitan Area Status, 1960–1975 311
10-4. Apportionment of House of Representatives by State and Region: 1910–1970, Estimates for 1980 316
12-1. Organization of Spatial Development and Regional Planning in the FRG 371
14-1. Total Traffic-Output of the Main Transportation System in the FRG 422
14-2. Rhine Traffic by Sections, 1977 430
15-1. Summary of Section 5 Allocation Formula as Established by the Federal Public Transportation Act of 1978 446
15-2. Federal Expenditures on Assistance to Public Transportation, FY 1965 through FY 1976 452

TABLES   xvii

15-3. Summary of U.S. Federal Aid to Highways   456
16-1. National Ambient Air Quality Standards for Major Pollutants   482
16-2. Prevention-of-Significant-Deterioration Regulations   488
17-1. Federal Land Ownership in Eleven Western States   533
17-2. Number of Printed Pages in Federal Register   546
17-3. Selected Federal Laws Which Significantly Influence Environmental Management and Energy Development   548
17-4. Projected Flow Chart and Timetable for Implementation of RARE II, Federal and Policy Management Act of 1976   558
18-1. Jurisdiction of Principal Federal Wildlife-Related Agencies   572
18-2. Holdings of the U.S. Department of Interior, Fish and Wildlife Service: Budgetary Appropriations, Fiscal Year 1977   578
18-3. Acreage Owned by the Federal Government—1975   584
18-4. Funding Provisions of the Pittman-Robertson Program   598
18-5. Federal Aid to Texas' Wildlife, 1970–1976   604
18-6. Pittman-Robertson Funding for Game Animal Transplant and Restoration in Texas   608
21-1. Residential Houses in Cologne   669
21-2. Assessment of Taxes   669
21-3. Total Expenditures and Grants-in-Aid from the Federation and State Concerning Highway and Street Construction   675
21-4. Number of Projects Subsidized by the Federation and the State Between 1964 and 1975   677
23-1. The Amount of Investments Sanctioned by the Federation and the State for the Special Funds North in the Main Fields Between 1953 and 1978 and for 1979   720
23-2. Results of 25 Years of Land Reallocation and Water Control Conducted by the Program Nord   724

PREFACE

The impact of the federal system on regional development in the United States and the Federal Republic of Germany, two countries with federal systems of government, was the theme of the first German-American geography seminar held in Austin, Texas, September 29 to October 13, 1979. Twenty-four scholarly papers were presented, covering the spatially significant activities of the state as well as the significant sectoral activities and regional case studies. Twenty-three of these papers are included in this volume.

   The selection of both the theme of the seminar and the individual contributors was the responsibility of the two coordinators, Professors Peter Schöller of the Ruhr-University Bochum and George W. Hoffman of the University of Texas at Austin. The selected theme lies in the mainstream of geographic research in both countries, though the approach differs considerably, as can be seen in the papers presented in this volume. The methodology used by American geographers is more statistical-quantitative and process oriented, while German research is more empirical and concentrates more on individual regional case studies stressing planning and development processes.

   The presentations focus on various political geographic issues which have had an impact on federal and sectoral spatial planning acitvities and which have thus become pressing societal issues. This type of approach-which stresses the key planning role of various governmental administrative authorities-may bring a new orientation to political geography, one frequently referred to by German geographers as administrative geography (<u>Verwaltungs-</u>

geographie). While various govermental organs on the federal, state, county, and city levels have become more involved in spatial planning activities, neither of the countries has uniform planning organs nor nationwide spatially oriented development plans.

The purpose of this volume is to present theoretical and empirical studies-from both the American and German perspective-of the spatial activities and constraints of various federal and regional authorities. The essays address the evolution of federal policies and programs in the United States and the Federal Republic of Germany and their impact on a variety of spatial activities on several governmental levels. Evident in most of the essays is the fragmented, conflicting and often inconsistent character of federal developmental efforts, a situation which questions the general assumption that regional development policy is best formulated and implemented by central governmental agencies.

Contributions from some of the United States participants explore selected regional development and policy implications, as well as the relationship between governmental and private systems on the basis of recent United States experiences. The various activities of the federal systems in both countries interact with and are constrained by a variety of multilevel governments and agencies in many different ways. Both governments have only indirect influence on most of these activities, though demands for regional planning activities by numerous authorities are constantly increasing. It is clear that the whole trend in the spatial decision making of the various authorities in both countries is toward more complex political involvement (Politikverflechtung), which is also reflected in a

trend toward a process of increasing centralization which
develops at the expense of individual state authorities.
Both governments have numerous sectoral powers which influence spatial planning policies, but the difference in
the size of the two countries and the density of their populations, differences in the vertical coordination between
various authorities, and differences between both countries
in the meaning of regions often make comparisons difficult.

The relationships analyzed in this volume between the
federal systems of the United States and the Federal Republic of Germany and its spatial impact have thus far not
been studied comparatively. The spatial impacts as well as
a more detailed analysis of the political geographic implications have also been relatively little discussed in the
literature of the United States and hardly at all in the
Federal Republic. It is hoped, therefore, that one result
of this meeting of geographers from both countries and the
publication of these papers-as diffused and fragmented as
they may be to the uninformed reader-will contribute toward
greater comparative efforts jointly undertaken by scholars
from both countries.

The essays in this volume are grouped around three major
objectives: (1) the objectives and organizational forms
of the spatially significant activities of the state, covered by the papers in chapters 1-5, (2) problems of the spatial
potential and spatially significant sectoral activities,
discussed in chapters 6-19, and (3) regional case studies
in chapters 19-23.

It was not the purpose of the meeting at which these
papers were originally presented to seek general conclusions
or to analyze comparatively at this stage the spatial impact
of the federal systems in the two countries. Such an objec-

tive must probably be left to later efforts—perhaps the projected return seminar in Heidelberg in mid-1981. The theme selected, purposely held broad in concept for this first joint meeting of American and German geographers, aimed at introducing the different problems in both countries connected with the evolution of federal policies and programs and their impact on regional development. The seminar with its research presentations and discussions was basically a learning process for the participants and it is to be hoped, for a much wider audience. This experience was further facilitated by numerous formal contacts, especially during the five-day field trip through East and South Texas headed by Professor Robert K. Holz of the Department of Geography of the University of Texas at Austin and several visits and meetings at the conclusion of the seminar in Washington, D.C. The diversity shown by the papers in this volume, it is hoped, is in itself a major contribution to a better understanding of the variety of spatial activities initiated by the central governments of both countries, as well as subnational regional authorities. In the long run this may contribute to our knowledge of an increasingly important area of research for numerous fields of study in both countries.

ACKNOWLEDGMENTS

Credit for making this meeting possible must go to numerous people, both in the Federal Republic of Germany and in the United States. Professors Peter Schöller, Roland Fuchs, and the editor were the initiators and prime movers for such a joint cooperative research effort. Dr. J. Warren Nystrom, then Executive Director of the Association of American Geographers, strongly backed this effort and received the wholehearted support of the Council of the AAG. Professor John Adams worked with the project director in the selection of the American participants; the Division of International Programs of the National Science Foundation, in their program of encouraging greater scientific cooperation between American and foreign scientists, was anxious for American geographers to establish a closer working relationship with their counterparts in the Federal Republic of Germany, and the Deutsche Forschungsgemeinschaft's strong support in making this conference possible was much appreciated.

As far as this volume is concerned, the editor is indebted to numerous German and American participants for assistance beyond their contributions. Professor Klaus-Achim Boesler of the University of Bonn, a member of the Commission of the International Institute for Legal and Administrative Terminology, assisted in the selction of the basic expressions taken from the European Glossary of Legal and Administrative Terminology, volume 18 on Regional Policy (published by Langenscheidt KG in Berlin and Munich, 1973).

Professor W. Fricke wishes to acknowledge the assistance of Drs. Christa Mahn and Wolfgang Herden for the translation into English and many useful comments. Professor R. Doughty is grateful to the personnel of the Texas Parks and Wildlife Department and especially Mr. William Brownless for their helpful comments. Professor G. W. Hoffman wishes to acknowledge the valuable editorial assistance received from several of the participating authors from the United States. The extensive cooperation received from all authors in answering the editor's numerous queries is much appreciated. Ms. Karen Wickline was responsible for the drafting of several maps and Ms. Anita Porterfield did the final typing of the manuscript. The editor's wife, Viola Hoffman, spent untold hours in the detailed English editing of the various manuscripts, thus making a major contribution toward the final product. The whole-hearted assistance by the staff of the University of Texas Press, is gratefully acknowledged.

George W. Hoffman
Austin, Texas
August 1980

ABBREVIATIONS

BROP	Bundesraumordnungsprogram	Federal Regional Planning Program
COMECON	also CMEA	Council of Mutual Economic Assistance
DM	Deutsche Mark or Mark	German Mark, currency
EC, EEC	Europäische Wirtschafts Gemeinschaft	European Communities, European Economic Community
EDA		Economic Development Administration
EPA		Environmental Protection Agency
ERDA		Energy Research and Development Administration
FLMPA		Federal Land Management Policy Act of 1976
FRG (BRD)	Bundesrepublik Deutschland	Federal Republic of Germany (West Germany)
FTC		Federal Trade Commission
GIP	Brutto-Inland Produkt	Gross Domestic Product (GDP=GNP Gross National Product)
GDR	Deutsche Demokratische Republik	German Democratic Republic (East German)
ha	hectares	1 ha = 2.5 acres
HEW		(Department) Health, Education and Welfare
HUD		Housing and Urban Development
MKRO	Minister Konferenz für Raumordnung	Ministerial Standing Conference for Regional Policy

NEPA		National Environmental Policy Act
NSAA		National Aeronautics and Space Administration
NSDAP	Nationalsozialistische Deutsche Arbeiterpartei	Nazi-Party
ROP	Raumordnungspolitik	Regional Planning Policy
ROG	Raumordnungsgesetz	Federal Regional Policy
SMSA		Standard Metropolitan Statistical Area (243 in 1970 in the U.S.)

Federalism and Regional Development

CHAPTER 1

CENTRAL AND FEDERAL LEGISLATION AND THEIR
INSTRUMENTS FOR REGIONAL DEVELOPMENT

DIE GESETZGEBUNG VON BUND UND LÄNDERN UND IHRE
INSTRUMENTARIEN DER REGIONALEN ENTWICKLUNG

Klaus-Achim Boesler

Abstract

In the Federal Republic of Germany policies which have spatial impact are determined by a large number of government entities. A basic distinction must be made in this regard between (a) policies directly affecting spatial organization (for example, spatial regulation, land use planning, and environmental policies) and (b) sector policies, which have spatial impact through affecting the distribution of installations and the determination of maintenance regions.

As far as spatial regulation is concerned, only the federal government has the so-called guidance authority. It has availed itself of this authority through the promulgation of the Federal Spatial Regulation Act and the Federal Spatial Regulation Program. Final authority over spatial regulation, however, rests with the eleven federal states (Länder) that have established the legal basis for spatial regulation by means of state planning laws and have dealt with the content of such regulation by means of state development plans and programs. This application of the basic principle of federalism in regard to spatial regulation has resulted in a situation in which the regulation in the various states differ in their particulars.

Besides federal spatial regulations and state planning, a third level of state activity has spatial impact, that of regional planning. Again, only the states have the authority to regulate regional planning. Finally, the municipalities also have recently established an instrument of community development planning with which they can carry out a comprehensive development plan for their territory in conjunction with the exclusively area-oriented construction planning.

In addition to the spatially oriented planning of the government regarding its corporate area, there exists in the individual spheres of governmental activity, sector planning which has spatial impact. The agencies of the federal government, the states, and the municipalities are involved in planning in accordance with the constitutionally determined distribution of their authority.

The majority of the instruments used in spatial regulation and in those sector policies having spatial impact are based on measures which have their origins in the older disciplines concerned with policy making, especially in economics and finance. This essay attempts to present a taxonomy of the instruments of spatial regulation and to provide concrete examples of them from among the policies of the Federal Republic of Germany (FRG).

Kurzfassung

In der Bundesrepublik Deutschland wird raumwirksame Politik von einer Vielzahl von Trägern bestimmt. Dabei ist grundsätzlich zu unterscheiden:

(a) eine direkt auf die räumliche Ordnung ausgerichtete Politik, wie z.B. Raumordnung, Flachennutzungsplanung und Umweltpolitik.

(b) Eine sektorale Politik, die durch die Verteilung der Standorte von Einrichtungen und die Festlegung von räumlichen Versorgungsbereichen raumwirksam ist.

In der Raumordnung hat der Bund lediglich die sog. Rahmenkompetenz. Er hat sie durch den Erlass des Bundesraumordnungsgesetzes und das Bundesraumordnungsprogramm wahrgenommen. Die Vollkompetenz in der Raumordnung liegt aber bei den elf Bundesländern, die mit den Landesplanungsgesetzen die rechtliche Grundlage und mit den Landesentwicklungsplänen und -programmen die innhaltliche Ausfüllung vollzogen haben. Dieses föderalistische Grundprinzip in der Raumordnung hat zur Folge, daß die Regelungen im einzelnen in den Bundesländern unterschiedlich sind.

Neben diesen räumlichen orientierten Planungen des Staates und seiner Gebietskörperschaften gibt es in den einzelnen Resorts der Staatstätigkeit sektoraler Planungen mit räumlicher Wirkung. Bei der Mehrzahl der in der Raumordnung und in der räumlich wirksamen sektoralen Politik angewandten Instrumente handelt es sich um Mittel, die aus älteren Disziplinen der Politik, besonders der Wirtschafts-und Finanzpolitik stammen. Der Charakter als Mittel der Raumordnung ergibt sich lediglich aus der räumlichen Zielsetzung.

Central and Federal Legislation and Their
Instruments for Regional Development

THE POLITICAL STRUCTURE OF THE
FEDERAL REPUBLIC OF GERMANY

Germany was the last among the larger European nations to gain territorial unity. In general, federal political systems such as the German Reich (up to 1806), the Rheinbund under the protectorate of Napoleon, and the Deutscher Bund (since 1815) are characterized by a confederative element and a weak constitution of the central supreme power. In 1871 a state was organized on a federal basis which has often been called "pseudofederalist." The distribution of power was unbalanced between Prussia and the seventeen other states. Because of Prussia's hegemony there was no chance to develop a true federalism among equal states. In addition, the financial system proved deficient because the Reich was most dependent on the federal states except for customs tariffs. Due to separatist movements in some parts of the Reich, the centralizing forces were much stronger when the Weimar Republic was founded after World War I than in 1871.

The political system of the Weimar Republic was not a federal one but a "decentralized unitary state" (1, p. 197). As a reaction to the centralist unitary state into which the National Socialists transformed the Weimar Republic federalist ideas were extraordinarily strong after World War II. The federal ideas after 1945 were mainly based on a conception of vertical distribution of power.

Therefore, in the FRG today, the federal government and eleven states constitute the body politic. Both the states and the federal government have the characteristics of a state (2). With regard to regional effects this implies several things:

(a) The federal government and the states have a normative, policy-determining structure of supreme governing bodies (legislation, government).

(b) The federal government and the states exercise sovereignty in their territorial domains through institutions of public administration and jurisdiction. Due to the federal structure of the FRG there is no centralized administration. Many state departments have no administrative basis for implementing their political decisions; implementation is carried out by the states on behalf of the federal government (3).

(c) The federal government and the states are responsible for maintaining normal regulations within their territories. This is called the "application area of a judicial norm" or "regional legality" (räumliche Rechtsgeltung) (4).

In the FRG both the federal government and the state exercise their sovereignty within the bounds of the Grundgesetz, i.e., the Constitution of May 23, 1949, also referred to as Basic Law. The federal structure is concerned not only with the matter of territorial sovereignty, but also with the principle of distribution, balance, and control of the supreme power. This principle becomes evident in the participation of the Upper House in federal legislation, as well as in the election of the federal president or the appointment of Supreme Court judges. The same is true for the distribution of administrative responsibility and the constitutional articles on finance.

The federal government and the states exercise their territorial sovereignty through public agencies and autonomous administrative bodies that are legally independent, particularly through local authorities (Gemeinden) and rural districts (Landkreise). Local authorities and rural districts participate in territorial rule because by legislation they are given a wide range of administrative tasks and executive authority (5). Since the local authorities and rural districts are subordinate to the states, the federal government cannot accomplish its plans in direct cooperation with the lower authorities but always must obtain approval from the respective state or states (6). Therefore, a vertical differentiation of power is characteristic of the political system of the FRG.

Formally, the authority to make political decisions is distributed as follows: the federal government (der Bund), 11 states, 25 government administrative districts (Regierungsbezirke), 235 rural districts (Landkreise) and 88 self-governing towns (kreisfreie Städte), and 8,357 local authorities (Gemeinden).

The federal government, states, rural districts, self-governing towns, and local authorities each cover the whole state territory with a net of administrations and directly elected parliaments, whereas the administrative districts have the legal status of subregions dependent on the larger states.

The division of legislative competence between the federal government and the states is laid down in Articles 72 to 75 and in Article 105 of the Constitution. According to Article 73, the federal government is given full legislative competence in domains like foreign affairs and defense, customs and foreign trade enforcement-including tariff policy and the federal railroad, air transport, postal service, and telecommunication. Competing with the states' legislative authority, the federal government is responsible for a large number of additional affairs (Article 74), among which are

the following:
> economic legislation, e.g., laws covering the industrial and energy sector, the generation and peaceful uses of nuclear energy, the establishment and operation of plants for these purposes, the protection against dangers caused by radiation and the disposal of radioactive waste; the transfer of real estate, natural resources, and capital goods into public property or some other type of socially justified expropriation; road traffic, construction, maintenance and repair of long-distance trunk roads; tracks which do not belong to the federal railroad, with the exception of mountain lines; the removal of refuse, the prevention of air pollution and noise.

The federal government has the power to define a framework for state policy (Article 75) concerning affairs such as hunting, the preservation of exceptional natural beauty, landscape conservation, land distribution, regional policy, and water resource management. As in most other federally organized countries, there is a trend toward greater centralization and an eagerness of the federal government to enhance its competence through formal constitutional changes or reinterpretation of existing norms. These competences are generally organized in either of two ways. On the one hand, the planning processes are decided on and carried out independently on their respective administrative levels. On the other hand, the formal independence of each level is increasingly affected by the plans and decisions of superior administrative units, which restrict the freedom of action of subordinate authorities. Significantly, this trend toward more complex political interdependence (Politikverflechtung) goes hand in hand with a process of increasing centralization which develops at the expense of the states and the authority of local autonomy.

What is called Politikverflechtung (cf. 7, 1975 and 1977)

is the complex policy of formal and informal interdependence and vertical and horizontal structures of decision within the politico-administrative system. This complexity applies especially to the local authorities because in regionally relevant decisions they are quite dependent on political partners who decide on locations from a distance and without regard to the individual concerns of the local authority. What the opponents of this policy interdependence criticize most of all is that the factual situation of a region or community and the interests of the people concerned are not respected. They argue that this "deductive planning" lacks considerable knowledge of the facts and familiarity with the citizens' concerns (8). An objection raised against this argument is that the lower levels of political decision and administration usually are not sufficiently qualified to maintain essential autonomy against particular interests such as economic concerns. For this reason local parliaments very frequently must submit to the "logic of economic plan-making processes" (9, p. 231).

Another argument against a larger autonomy of the lower levels of planning is that of the "free-rider principle," a phenomenon noticed quite often. In this case local authorities realize the need for respecting environmental concerns in land use planning but are not willing to commit themselves. Instead, they conceal their preferences and hope for the neighboring community to build a waste incineration plant, sewage treatment plant, and similar facilities so that they can use these facilities without pollution nuisance and financial contributions.

The constitutional reform in 1969 and the definition of joint tasks in Article 91a of the Constitution gave rise to a new means of cooperation between the federal government and the states which particularly applies to the field of regionally significant national policy.

Article 91a of the Constitution of 1969 formulated joint tasks (Gemeinschaftsaufgaben) to be carried out cooperatively by the federal government and the state, namely the construction and expansion of universities, the improvement of regional economic structure and agrarian structure, and coastal protection. In the early seventies the definition of joint tasks was considered an almost perfect solution for coping with the problems in a federal system (cf. 10 and 11). Meanwhile the undermining of the state parliaments' power has been increasingly criticized (12). For these reasons representatives of southern Germany have repeatedly proposed the total abolition of the joint tasks. Still, these proposals-such as a coordination of task planning without joint financing or a political interdependence with the federal government in charge of administering part of the joint tasks on behalf of the state while in complete charge of most of the investment assistance-have no chance of being realized for the time being.

The federal government has extended the influence of its regionally significant national policy since becoming a member of the European Communities. Since that time the EC brought about political obligations, and the federal government must exercise greater control of state policies. In this context the following quotation from a speech by former Minister of Finance H. Apel is very characteristic: "When we point out in international debates, the financial problems resulting from our financial constitution, we do not-and I think, deservedly-encounter understanding. The world politics and their dynamics will not forever pay regard to the particular responsibilities within the German federalism."

(13, p. 3) . The trends of centralization in the "unitary federation" (14), however, can only apply to some fields. In international terms, as well as in the FRG, there are at the same time trends of regionalization, i.e., in France, Italy, and Great Britain.

The developmental possibilities of states and local authorities essentially depend on the financial sources available. The proportional distribution of finances between the federal government and the states is defined in the Constitution (Article 104a to 115). Taxes make up the main sources of revenue when they are distributed in the following way: the financial monopolies (e.g., on matches) and a number of taxes and duties go to the federal government whereas the remaining contributions are taken in by the states. The most important group, however, is composed of the Gemeinschaftssteuern, i.e., income tax, corporate profits tax, and turnover tax, which are collected by both the federal government and the states (15). Each receives 43 percent of the corporate income tax whereas the local authorities are allotted 14 percent on the basis of the yield derived from their inhabitants' income tax. In addition, the local authorities receive a portion of the yield of the Gemeinschaftssteuern (joint taxes) mentioned above-local property tax, part of the local business tax, and the local excise and consumption duties based on Article 106, paragraphs 6 and 7 of the Constitution (16, p. 173).

Actually, the distribution of the turnover tax is a controversial political problem: the proportional share between the federal government and the states is determined at certain intervals by federal legislation which requires the approval of the Upper House. On the other hand, they should complement each other for the purpose of a nationwide equalization of living conditions. Except for the financial equalization by means of the tax distribution, the federal government annually pays an extra block grant of 15 percent of the turnover tax yield to the poorer states, namely Bavaria, Lower Saxony, Rhineland-Palatinate, Saarland, and Schleswig-Holstein as provided by the Gesetz über den Finanzausgleich zwischen Bund und Ländern (Revenue Sharing Act of 1969) promulgated on 28 August 1969. In addition, a horizontal equalization takes place among the states in order to compensate for disparities in financial strength. The local tax revenues of corporation profits, incomes, and wages are split up according to federal regulations on a proportional basis (17, p. 198f).

COMPETENCES AND AUTHORITIES OF REGIONALLY SIGNIFICANT POLICY

German federalism differs from that of other nations in that the material legislative functions and the responsibility for public revenues are mainly held by the federal government whereas the states and local authorities have the main administrative responsibilities and influence on public expenditures, especially public investments. The agencies responsible for regionally significant policy are so numerous that they are referred to as a "conglomerate of institutions relevant to regional policy" (18, p. 51). This multitude of institutions brings about a number of consequences, especially the problem of coordination. In the first place a question arises as to who is entitled to decide goals and measures employed in regionally significant policy, and who is in charge of the execution and control of this policy.

Further impediments to policy with regional implications

result from "tensions within the vertical hierarchy of bodies" (19, p. 404). These tensions apparently grow stronger as more responsibilities are delegated to administrations on lower levels since it involves the danger of under influence of particular local interests.

Apart from this problem, almost all home policy decisions and actions explicitly or unintentionally involve "planning and measures with regional implications" (20). As a consequence, coordination problems come up frequently-for example, the problem that sectoral and regional policy should run parallel or at least not in conflict with each other. This is particularly difficult since the principles underlying the goals and authorities are sectoral in nature. In particular the unintentional regional effects of sector policies on the development of regional structures may lead to additional regional tensions among administrative domains and bodies of equal and/or unequal hierarchic rank. That is to say, there is a problem of coordination between all authorities in charge concerning their technical, temporary, and regional responsibility (18).

Such a coordination of regionally effective policy requires, first of all, that all authorities responsible for regionally relevant decisions and actions accept a legally binding overall concept of regional policy. In other words, a supraregional and a sectoral strategic plan is needed as intended by the Bundesraumordnungsprogramm (Federal Spatial Planning Program) issued in 1975.

HISTORY OF REGIONAL POLICY

The term "regional policy" did not exist in German legislation until 1935. A regional significant policy of some sort, however, had existed long before, the primary initiatives coming from the most densely populated, industrialized cities and agglomerations.

In the Ruhrgebiet industrialization and population density were already alarming at that time. Therefore, in 1910 representatives of all towns and rural districts joined in a commission for the preservation of verdure, the so-called Grünflächenkommission. Out of this commission emerged the Siedlungsverband Ruhrkohlenbezirk (Ruhr Regional Planning Authority) in 1920 with a set of regulations that was later adopted as a law by the Prussian Constitutional Assembly (21). The foundation of this association may be considered the first instance of regional planning in Germany.

The first workshop committes for regional planning were founded in 1929. The planning authorities at that time differed widely in organization, regional responsibility, and planning tasks. Regional planning was still at a pilot stage experimenting with various organization and political models. The authorities in those days were associations, unions, and committes cooperating on a voluntary basis with the exception of the Ruhr Regional Planning Authority mentioned above, the regional planning committee of Hamburg and Prussia, and the regional planning committee of Lower Weser, which were institutionally established by a constitutional law.

In any case, the state was not yet in charge of regional planning at that time. In 1933 and 1934 two laws of great relevance to regional planning were passed. The first was the Wohnsiedlungsgesetz (Housing Development Act) of 1933. According to this law, an economic plan (a so-called Wirtschaftsplan) had to be set up for every larger area of housing activity. These economic plans can be regarded as decisive plans preceding the regional plans of today. The

second law, the Siedlungsordnungsgesetz (Law to Regulate
Regional Structures) of 3 July 1934, demands the registration of larger projects of housing construction and of the
establishment of industrial plants.

The year of 1935 was important since in that year the
Reichsstelle für Raumordnung, the supreme Reich agency for
regional policy, was established. For the first time the
organization was uniform within the whole territory of the
Reich. The states were proclaimed "planning areas," and in
each area a regional planning department representing the
authority of state planning sovereignty was established.
A Landesplanungsgemeinschaft (authorities of a state administration responsible for the preparation of regional
plans) was also founded.

After the breakdown of National Socialism, regional
policy first had to shake off its political burdens, especially the stigma by the general public of being closely
associated with the idea of a state-controlled planned
economy. The length of time this took depended on each
particular state. The first state to establish a regional
planning policy was North Rhine-Westphalia. It passed the
first postwar regional planning act as early as 1950. In
the other states more than a decade went by before they
could establish their own regional planning laws. In
brief, Landesplanung (i.e., the regional policy of a
state) has developed differently in the various states.
In North Rhine-Westphalia the three large Landesplanungsgemeinschaften-Rhineland, Westphalia, and the Ruhr Regional
Planning Authority-continued to exist until 31 December
1975, with their work divided between state administration
and self-government. These Landesplanungsgemeinschaften
had the status of public corporations. Their members were

the self-governing towns and rural districts, tows with more than 30,000 inhabitants but which are administrative parts of rural districts, the Regierungspräsidien (i.e., intermediate authorities on the state level), the Landesbaubehörde (building authority of public works), the Ruhr Regional Planning Authority, and the Landschaftsverbände.

In addition, the initiative of local authorities, especially of those in highly industrialized agglomerations, has contributed to the tradition of regional policy in Germany. All of the activities mentioned can be assumed under the term Regionalplanung (regional planning). Regional planning integrates a good number of town and country land use plans into one (sub)regional plan. This one plan, however, not only comprises existing land use plans but also coordinates and integrates the goals and objectives of the particular plans. Thus regional policy is the connecting link between the regional planning of the states (and the federal government) on one hand and the land use plans of the local planning authorities on the other.

Let me recapitulate briefly. Regional policy in Germany has a tradition of approximately sixty years. It emerged from two sources of exceptional importance in the present distribution of authority and jurisdiction: the Landesplanungsgemeinschaften and Landesplanungsbehörden (the associations of local planning authorities) and the regionale Planungsgemeinschaften (standing conferences for regional planning), which at first were voluntary but later required by law. The present system of regional policy in Germany is derived from both sources; their "descendants" are the Landesplanung and Regionalplanung.

The Bundesraumordnung (Federal Spatial policy), on the contrary, has a far weaker tradition. It is true that there was the Spatial Planning Law of 1935. Yet after World War II a central administrative authority of regional policy could no longer be accommodated in the legal concept of the new constitution, because during the Third Reich the idea of a unitary state was the underlying concept of regional policy. Therefore, a central regional policy seem inappropriate for the planning basis of the federal state established by the new constitution of 1949.

In regional policy the federal government merely issued "framework legislation." What does that imply? The Constitution (paragraph 75:4) gives the federal government the authority to issue regulations which set a legal framework for regional policy, but only if a dispute cannot be legally settled at the state level, or if the regulations of a state government concerning a specific problem should interfere with the interests of the other states or the overall planning concept, or if federal law is needed to maintain equality of laws, economic uniformity, and nationwide homogeneity of living conditions (Article 72:2).

In the discussion preceding the Spatial Planning Act it was never disputed that one or the other condition was satisfied, and consequently federal laws always seemed necessary. The idea of equal living conditions especially required federal legislation. There was less agreement on the definition of "federal framework legislation" and its mandate to frame and limit state legislation. Still, it is generally agreed that regional policy of the state governments, i.e., (sub)regional planning, must be more important than federal legislation. As a consequence a detailed spatial planning policy program for the whole country cannot exist. Since the jurisdiction and responsibility of the federal government for regional policy was not yet clear on the effective date of the Constitution, an expert opinion of the Verfassungsgericht (Constitutional Court) was requested in 1954.

Participation of both the federal and state governments in regional policy is advantageous because centralized comprehensive planning might easily lead to partiality and the neglect of certain regions. It also increases the danger of state control and interference in private investment decisions. In addition, regional, topographic, and climatic conditions, population trends, and any other characteristics vary from place to place. Therefore, different methods and measures are necessary in order to achieve the intended equivalence of living conditions. Apart from that, the fact that representatives of public and private concerns participate in planning almost inevitably leads to subdividing the territory into adequate administrative districts.

One has to take this into consideration when dealing with the Federal Spatial Planning Act of 1965. This law essentially consists of abstract formulations which on further consideration frequently prove to be vague, idle statements. At first sight one disadvantage of such a law lies in the uncertainties that may emerge during the realization of its abstract goals. The advantage on the other hand is its adaptability to new theoretical insights or to changes of the socioeconomic conditions. Above all, this law expresses the constitutional intention of organizing regional policy according to the concept of federal state.

In the Federal Spatial Planning Act of 1965 the legislators distinguished between goals or overall concepts (Ziele or Leitbilder) of regional policy (paragraph 1) and regional policy principles (Grundsätze, paragraph 2). The overall concepts set a "framework" of general directions and at the same time establish criteria to criticize sector planning and measures under the aspect of their regional significance.

RESPONSIBILITY AND PRINCIPLES OF REGIONAL POLICY OF THE FEDERAL SPATIAL PLANNING ACT

The Federal Spacial Planning Act establishes the following responsibility, goals, and overall concept (paragraph 1):

(a) The development of the regional structure should strive to grant everybody the full scope to develop his or her personality within the social community. The natural conditions as well as the economic, social, and cultural requirements must be respected.

(b) The reunification of Germany is to be pursued and its realization advanced. The regional coherence of the areas concerned should be considered and improved.

(c) National regional policy must prepare and encourage the regional qualifications of a Europe-wide cooperation.

(d) The policy concerning particular areas should be an integral part of the nationwide regional policy. The regional policy for the whole country in return should respect the conditions and needs of its component areas.

General principles of regional policy (paragraph 2) are:

(a) The regional structure of areas with intact living and working conditions and balanced economic, social, and cultural conditions are to be preserved and further developed. In areas which lack such a structure measures of structural improvement are to be taken. A provision should be made for transport and public utilities with the purpose of opening up an area to be coordinated with the intended developmental goals.

(b) An agglomeration of housing and employment which contributes to the preservation, improvement or provisions of regional structures with intact living and working conditions as well as balanced economic, social, and cultural conditions is to be sought.

Four years after the passage of the Federal Spatial Planning Act, the federal Parliament decided that the federal government should submit a spatial planning program. Substance and legal form of this program were left open. This decision of Parliament raised some constitutional questions. Apart from the distribution of competences between the federal government and the states, there was uncertainty about how Parliament could participate in governmental planning at all, a problem which has not yet been solved satisfactorily in German law.

A federal spatial planning program, or national interregional plan, should first of all analyze and criticize previous trends of development. This includes, for instance, the issue of whether federal or state grants for infrastructure development have been applied reasonably and effectively. Also, a national interregional plan has to deal with trends of population and employment and with the problem of foreign workers. Apart from economic trends and problems, it should sketch the principles of an energy policy concept. Most of these concerns, however, cannot be covered adequately by a law. Therefore, the legal form of a law of regional policy has never been seriously considered, particularly because the competence of federal laws is restricted to "framework legislation," and hence the efficacy of their regulations is quite limited.

A federal spatial planning program is meaningless unless the state governments join in with their subregional planning. The regional policy authorities at the state level

cannot join independently though, but must cooperate with
the respective agencies of sector planning of their specific
states. In other words, a federal spatial program requires
mutual agreement in three fields: among the federal administrative provinces, among the administrative departments of
each of the eleven state governments, and between the federal
government and the eleven states.

CONTENTS OF THE FEDERAL SPATIAL PLANNING PROGRAM

The Federal Spatial Planning Program is divided into five
parts: definition of subareas, status-quo forecasts, definition of objectives pursued by the regional policy of the
federal government, regionalization of federal resources,
and identification of future issues and priorities.

For the purpose of the Federal Spatial Planning Program
the country has been divided into thirty-eight areal units
(Gebietseinheiten), one of which is Berlin. According to
the concept, these areas are purely statistical, not planning regions. Of course, this decision has one disadvantage. The federal assistance granted thus far and the
future distribution of these financial means will be criticized with reference to these above points. Therefore
in the fifth part of the national interregional plan it is
only natural to define future issues and priorities in terms
of the thirty-eight areal units mentioned above.

The chief goal of the Federal Spatial Planning Program
is to improve the quality of living with the help of long-term strategy of national development. For this purpose it
is necessary to equalize the living conditions throughout
the whole country or, in other words, to abolish the regional
disparity in living conditions. The following measures have

been designed to realize the objectives in the plan: improvement of the infrastructure (including housing), improvement of the physical environment, and improvement of the regional economic structure. These objectives are very difficult to achieve because of the way the thirty-eight areal units have been defined. The underlying demarcation concept is that of balanced functional regions. This implies that on principle the hinterland is added to the urbanized nodal areas for the purpose of forming statistical districts.

The reduction of regional disparity intended by the Federal Spatial Planning Program is only possible among the thirty-eight areal units. That means that the disparity in living conditions can be adjusted only on a large spatial scale. Since it is impossible to make a statistical survey of intraregional disparities in the migration, infrastructural, and employment situation, intraregional disparities are not open to the interference of national policy.

What are the actual effects of the Federal Spatial Planning Program? Its purpose is to achieve a regional "hingejoint" effect for all sector investments and plans, primarily for all departments of the federal government. According to paragraph 3.1 of the Federal Spatial Planning Program (BROG) and Article 65.2 of the Constitution, the federal administrative agencies will strive to adjust their regionally significant plans and measures to the objectives and priorities of the plan. In other words, the plan is not legally binding. The federal agencies are requested to adapt to its objectives, particularly in the joint tasks as indicated in Article 91a of the Constitution, namely the construction of universities, the improvement of regional economic structure, the improvement of agrarian structure, and coastal protection. The federal administration shall also adapt to the objectives of the program in specific tasks carried out with federal assistance. According to Article 104a; 4 of the constitution, these are the <u>Städtebauförderungsgesetz</u> (Urban Renewal and Town Development Act), the <u>Wohnungsbauförderungsgesetz</u> (Housing Development Act), the <u>Krankenhausfinanzierungsgesetz</u> (Hospital Finance Act) and all other activities, measures, and plans having regional implications.

For the states the national interregional plan is not legally binding. Rather, it is a general guideline of legislative framework which can be refined and supplemented by the states.

In the FRG, the full legislative competence for regional policy actually lies with the states. In order to execute their legislative competence, the states have been delegated a much stronger role in regional planning. Examples are: Hessen 1980 (framework plan for 1970-1985); Lower Saxony, April 1973 (state spatial planning program); and Bavaria, May 1976 (state development program). Presently these programs seem to be obsolete and have not been renewed. Simultaneously the sectoral plannings was improved (22, p. 134).

There has been a clear tendency to change the constitutionally defined status of the regional planning programs. "The responsibility of the parliaments to delineate regional policy objectives has increased. Since regional plans are rather abstract and flexible conceptions of the regional development of a state and subject to political accommodation, exceptions and interpretations, they are of limited use as legal regulations." Still, the German state parliaments have succeeded in retaining a wide competence for the practical field of regional policy in spite of their general loss of political influence. Presently the

CENTRAL AND FEDERAL LEGISLATION

constitutionally defined status of the regional policy plans and programs varies among the states as follows:

(a) Bavaria and Rhineland-Palatinate agreed that only a few principles of regional policy should be settled by law. The further planning then is left to the executive. There is one exception though: as a part of the <u>Landesentwicklungsprogramm</u> (land development program), Rhineland-Palatinate has passed a law providing for the demarcation of planning regions (<u>Planungsregionen</u>).

(b) Hessen, Schleswig-Holstein, and North Rhine-Westphalia must still pass laws for their land development program, whereas the implementation of these plans has been left to the executive except for the program of North Rhine-Westphalia, which requires the approval of the state parliament.

(c) In Baden-Württemberg every planning activity requires the parliament's consent to become legally binding.

(d) In Lower Saxony and the Saarland the planning process is the exclusive responsibility of the executive.

Apart from the Federal Spatial Planning Program and the states' regional policy, there is a third level-the so-called regional planning in paragraph 5 of the Federal Spatial Planning Act. According to this paragraph the states provide the legal basis for regional planning. If this seems appropriate for subregions of regional planning the legal basis lies with each federal state (23). This means that the states are authorized to decide: (a) whether they wish to establish regional plans or not (in the <u>Saarland</u> for instance there is no such institution); (b) which authority to put in charge of the regional planning; and (c) what the regional plans are to contain, and for which periods of time they shall be valid. As a consequence, the regulations vary widely from state to state. For instance, the planning regions as defined by the regional planning law differ enormously in size and population. They range in size from 1,200 km^2 or 463 sq. mi. (Southern Palatinate) to 18,850 km^2 or 7,278 sq. mi. (Westphalia), and from 190,000 inhabitants (Western Eifel) to 6,055,000 inhabitants (Rhineland). The following criteria were indicated for the demarcation of the planning regions: (a) consideration of the hinterland of the Oberzentren (the highest central places), (b) consideration of political objectives particularly in those regions which in the opinion of the states require a uniform regional policy because of their close economic, social, and cultural interactions, and (c) consideration of administrative boundaries-for instance, of governmental districts.

Finally, the local authorities also hold important jurisdiction within the system of a regionally significant policy in Germany. Regional planning at the local authority level is entirely based on the 1976 amendment of the Federal Building Law of 1960. The regionally significant policy of the local authorities differs essentially from supralocal regional planning. Regional planning at the local level is town or development planning (Bauleitplanung/städtebauliche Planung) (24). Its intention is to prepare and direct the development within the area of a local authority (paragraph 1:1, Federal Building Law). Town planning includes preparatory Flächernutzungspläne (i.e., land use plans) and the legally binding town or development planning. The land use plan sets out the principle features of the use of land within the entire area of a local authority. Like the regional plans on the level of state and regional planning, the state land use plan is based on a local authority decision and requires the approval of the superordinate administrative agency. The building plan, on the other hand, gives the legally binding regulations for urban land use. These regulations are binding for everybody, including the individual proprietor. The essential difference between development planning and regional policy is that development plans do not include financial planning or specified terms of planning (period of validity), but are legally binding for the individual citizen (25). The local authorities particularly in the cities, have realized since the early sixties that they cannot influence the local development to the extent they intended to. Therefore, many cities have established a kommunale Entwicklungsplanung or Stadtentwicklungsplanung (i.e., local authority or town development planning). At first, town development planning was designed to be a regionally significant planning task that included the dimensions of finances and time period (e.g. the Stadtentwicklungsplan-City Development Plan for Munich, 1963). In the seventies this concept was extended. Today town development planning is the collective term for the entire land use and investment planning. Therefore, city development planning is a planning task which is wholly the responsibility of the local authorities (26, 27). The city of Cologne is a typical example of the task and organization of town development planning. The city council in 1976 decided to establish an agency for town development planning, which would function as an "instrument to optimize plan-making processes of the city council and administration." The individual cases call for a regular mutual adjustment of the concerned agencies, and they come to an agreement in team workshops. These workshops are then dissolved. Thus a flexible system of cooperation is guaranteed which can easily adapt to changing problems

(28).

The system of a regionally significant national policy of the FRG as it pursues regional objectives has been presented. One might call it a system of regionally significant policy. There is also planning for different sectors that is of considerable regional relevance. Sector planning, the planning activities of the ministries (departments) and sector administrations, quite often need space and territory for the realization of their plans. This is particularly true of the planning of railroad and street traffic, waterways, power plants, refuse dumps, hospitals, school and universities, tourist and sport facilities, and defense works. In any of these fields the locations are chosen primarily because of their economic aspect of capacity and efficiency and not for their regional implications (29).

The net sector planning is very finely enmeshed in the Federal Republic. There are sector plannings at the Bund, the Land, and the local authority level depending on the competences. One such example is the planning of the transport network of the so-called Bundesfernstrassen (highways and long distance trunk roads). This plan lays down the exact location of the roads and the order of priority in construction. The network of federal long-distance roads is the general obligation of the federal government's transport policy and budget. In the budget plan of 1976 the Ministry of Transport introduced the following regionally significant criteria: (a) evaluation of accessibility and improvement of communication between remote regions and the large agglomerations, (b) the relation of the construction projects to the interregionally effective transport axes of the Federal Spatial Planning Program, (c) the

CENTRAL AND FEDERAL LEGISLATION

special situation of the development area along the eastern boundary of the FRG (the Zonenrandgebiet), and (d) the characteristic of structural weakness (Strukturschwäche), a criteria of the national interregional plan (30).

A good example of sector planning is transport policy which gives clear evidence of the close interrelation of regional, technical, and political aspects. An example of sector planning at the state level is educational planning. On the basis of their cultural sovereignty the states are in charge of education. The Ministry of Education is the highest supervising authority of education in each state. This board of control decides on the location and type of schools. In the sixties, thousands of elementary and eighth-grade schools were founded in rural areas. Since educational centers have proved to be economic only in central places, the catchment areas of schools have been extended, but so have the school plans for the students. The concentration of schools in a few central places has caused further structural change within the area concerned. As the advantages of central locations increased, this encouraged a further migration from the sparsely populated rural areas to the centers. In general, the small local authorities have lost the political struggle against the concentration of schools. The local authorities have no influence on the choice of location, which is done by the Ministry of Education. They can only decide on the location within the area of local authority and the construction of the school building.

These two examples may indicate that the coordination of regional policy and sector planning is most necessary. In the FRG the vertical structure of regionally significant national policy seems relatively evident and clearly structured by the legislatures, whereas the horizontal relation between regional policy and all the regionally relevant fields of planning is rather vague.

First, a good deal of regionally effective sector planning lacks a subordinate comprehensive plan. Second, there has emerged regionally relevant sector planning which undoubtedly is suprasectoral, part of which could be located somewhere between regional policy and sector planning in its proper sense, e.g., landscape planning and landscape conservation.

TAXONOMY OF REGIONAL POLICY INSTRUMENTS

Finally, let me present a systematic summary of the instruments of regional policy as they are presented in the Federal Republic of Germany. "Instruments" in this context is another term for the politicians' responsibility of action which can be systematized as in Table 1-1.

Most of the material instruments are not specifically of regional policy. Rather, they are instruments of the older political disciplines, particularly of economic and financial policy. The quality of instruments for regional policy is merely due to their regional objectives. Which instruments are to be applied in a specific situation depends on the general political principles, the intended objectives; the discrepancy between the original situation and the intended situation. It further depends on the participants' anticipated reaction to the variety of instruments and finally on the available financial means.

Let me try to summarize and evaluate the application of state instruments in the Federal Republic of Germany with regard to their regional significance:

(a) The regionally significant state expenditures so far have not been sufficiently coordinated. There are differences not only between the administrative units (i.e., be-

CENTRAL AND FEDERAL LEGISLATION

tween the federal government and the states or between the states and the local authorities), but also between sector planning and between sector planning and regional policy (31, 32, p. 197).

(b) Infrastructural state investments, in general, tended to follow the demand. Therefore, roads were built where roads were jammed, and planning was compensative rather than developmental (33).

(c) Only a very small portion of the bulky subsidy budget is regionalized. The vast majority is being spent without respect to regional dispersal. Therefore, financial subsidies are spent efficiently in terms of the particular sector departments but not in terms of regional policy (34).

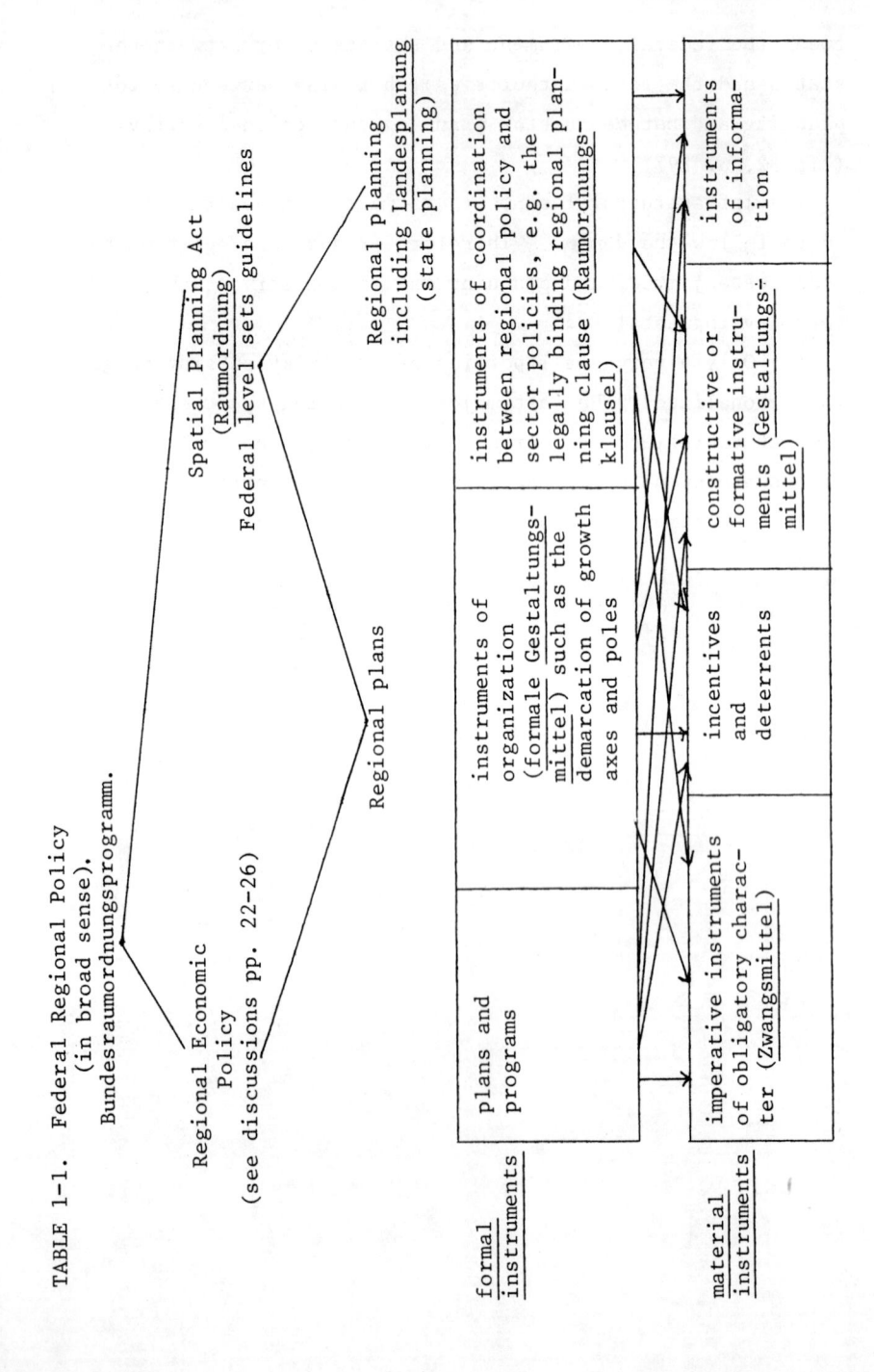

TABLE 1-1. Federal Regional Policy (in broad sense). Bundesraumordnungsprogramm.

```
Federal Regional Policy
├── Regional Economic Policy (see discussions pp. 22–26)
│   └── Regional plans
└── Spatial Planning Act (Raumordnung)
    Federal level sets guidelines
    └── Regional planning including Landesplanung (state planning)
```

formal instruments	plans and programs	instruments of organization (formale Gestaltungsmittel) such as the demarcation of growth axes and poles	instruments of coordination between regional policy and sector policies, e.g. the legally binding regional planning clause (Raumordnungsklausel)

material instruments	imperative instruments of obligatory character (Zwangsmittel)	incentives and deterrents	constructive or formative instruments (Gestaltungsmittel)	instruments of information

TABLE 1-2. Examples of Instruments Applied in Regional Policy.
Beispiele der Instrumente welche in dem Bundesraumordnungsprogramm verwendet werden.

policy \ instrument	regional policy	sector policies, e.g. economic policy
plans and programs	regional policy plan and programs of the Federal Government and the Länder	plans and programs to achieve specific objectives of economic policy such as a decrease in unemployment
instruments of organization (Organisationsmittel)	definition of planning regions, demarcation of settlement and growth axes	instruments concerning the market organization, such as standardization or production and quality control
instruments of coordination (Koordinationsmittel)	introduction of a legally binding regional planning clause into laws with sectoral objectives	optimization of resource consumption through locational policy
incentives and deterrent (Anreiz- und Abschreckungsmittel)	regional differentiation of taxation, direct regional financial assistance, regional assignment of state institutions	

TABLE 1-2. (continued)

policy instrument	regional policy	sector policies, e.g. economic policy
imparative instruments of obligatory character (Zwangsmittel)	public projects, regional differentiation of public transport tariffs	monetary interventions: customs, charge and fiscal subsidies, grant for an expenditure in a particular sector, credits real interventions: demand effects of the budget of state finances, government maintenance of stocks and supplies
	restrictions through the town or development planning of the local authority, interdiction to settle in priority areas of a particular function like nature reserves	(no application)

TABLE 1-2. (continued)

policy instrument	regional policy	sector policies, e.g. economic policy
constructive/formative instruments (Gestaltungsmittel)	infrastructure investments to develop the attractiveness of a region, locational choice of state institutions	provision of growth-oriented infrastructure facilities for specific lines of business
instruments of information	specification of an elaborate catalogue of locational advantages of assisted development areas, regional research (Regionalforschung)	encouragement to investigate the fundamentals and purposes (Grundlagen- und Zweckforschung), state-run model enterprises

——— Borders of areal units

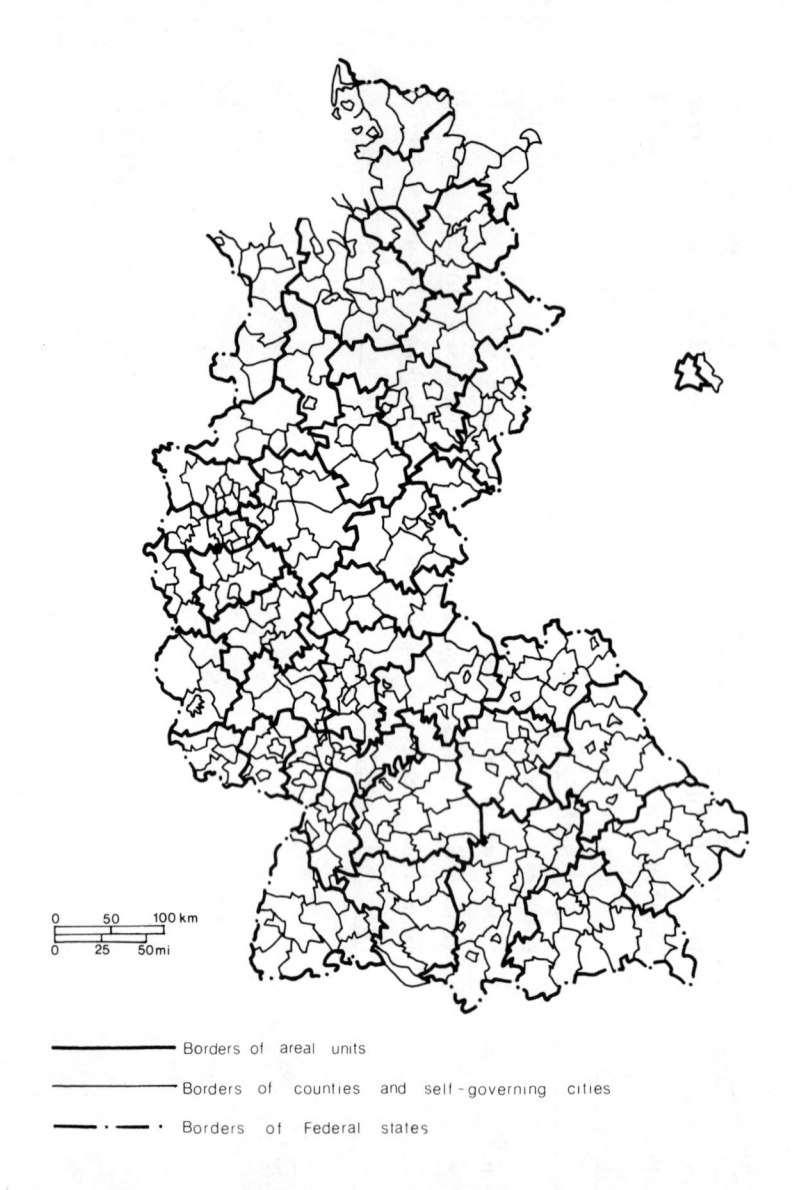

——— Borders of counties and self-governing cities

——·——· Borders of Federal states

FIG. 1-1. Areal Units of the Federal Spatial Planning Program.
            Gebietseinheiten für das Bundesraumordnungsprogramm.

Source: Bundesraumordnungsprogramm. Base map: Kreisgrenzen 1. January 1975, 1:4,000.000.

NOTES

1. Beyme, K. von, Das politische System der Bundesrepublik Deutschland (Munich: Piper Co., 1979).

2. Maunz, Th., Die geteilte Verwaltung im Bundesstaat, in Verwaltungsverfahren Hefte, ed. W. Schmitt-Glaeser (Stuttgart: Kommunalschriften Verlag, 1977).

3. In 1977, 2,529,483 persons were employed in the administration, most of them with the states (1,439,102) and the local authorities (778,694). Only 311,687 persons (excluding soldiers and frontier guards) were officials of the federal government.

4. Maunz, Th., Deutsches Staatsrecht, 19th ed. (Munich, Berlin: Beck, 1973).

5. Loschelder, W., Kommunale Selbstverwaltungsgarantier und gemeindliche Gebietsgestaltung, Vol. 308 (Berlin: Schriften zum öffentlichen Recht, 1976).

6. Wagener, F., Neubau der Verwaltung. Gliederung der öffentlichen Aufgaben und ihrer Träger nach Effektivität und Intergrationswert. 2nd ed. (Berlin: Duncker and Humblot, 1974).

7. Scharpf, F. W., et al., Politikverflechtung. Theorie und Empirie des kooperativen Föderalismus in der Bundesrepublik, 2 vols. (Kronberg: Scripton, 1975; 1977).

8. Grauhan, R. R., "Zur Struktur der planenden Verwaltung," in Mehr Demokratie im Städtebau, ed. L. Lauritzen (Hannover: Rechinger & Co., 1972), pp. 37-57.

9. Muncke, G., "Zur Demokratisierung des kommunalpolitischen Planungs- und Entscheidungsprozesses," Zeitschrift für Parlamentsfragen 2 (1972), p. 231.

10. Tiemann, B., Gemeinschaftsaufgaben von Bund und Ländern in verfassungsrechtlicher Sicht (Berlin: Duncker & Humblot, 1970).

11. Marnitz, S., Die Gemeinschaftsaufgaben des Artikels 91a G. G. (Grundgesetz) als Versuch einer verfassungsrechtlichen Institutionalisierung der bundesstaatlichen Kooperation (Berlin: Duncker & Humblot, 1974).

12. Scharpf, F. W., Politikverflechtung. Theorie und Empirie des kooperativen Föderalismus in der Bundesrepublik, 2 vols. (Kronberg: Scriptor, 1975; 1977).

13. Apel, H., "Wie lange soll Bonn die Zeche zahlen? Die Länder schröpfen den Bund und machen ihn international handlungsfähig," Die Zeit 29 (1977), p. 3.

14. Hesse, K., Der unitarische Bundesstaat (Karlsruhe: Müllers, 1962).

15. Doppler, H., Finanzpolitik und Föderativprinzip (Düsseldorf: Werner-Verlag, 1975).

16. Benznig, A. G., et al., Verwaltungsgeographie (Cologne: Heymanns, 1978), p. 173.

17. Brösse, U., Raumordnung (Berlin: Görschen, 1975), p. 178 f.

18. Hansmeyer, K. H., "Ziele und Träger regionaler Wirtschaftspolitik," in Beiträge zur Regionalpolitik, ed. H. K. Schneider, Vol. 41 (Berlin: Schriften des Vereins für Sozialpolitik, 1968), pp. 36-60.

19. Jürgensen, H., "Animonien in der Regionalpolitik," in Gestaltungsprobleme der Weltwirtschaft. Festschrift für Andreas Predöhl, ed. H. Jürgensen (Göttingen: Vanderhoeck Rupprecht, 1964), pp. 401-413.

20. According to the Bundesraumordnungsgesetz (Federal Regional (Spatial) Policy Act), paragraph 4,1, all those measures are regionally significant which require land or have an impact on the regional development of an area, an attribute which applies to almost all political decisions.

21. "Verbandsordnung des Siedlungsverbandes Ruhrkohlenbezirk," law of May 5, 1920.

22. Hübler, K. H., "Arbeitsorientierte Raumordnungspolitik," in Raumordnung und Raumforschung (1978), pp. 75-78.

23. Akademie für Raumforschung und Landesplanung, Zur Methodik der Regionalplanung, Vol. 41 (Hannover: Forschungs- und Sitzungsberichte, 1968).

24. Löhr, R. P., Die kommunale Flächennutzungsplanung (Siegburg: Rechinger, 1977).
25. Göb, R., et al., Raumordnung und Bauleitplanung im ländlichen Raum, No. 1 (Stuttgart: Schriften des Institutes für Städtebau and Raumordnung, 1967).
26. Siedentopf, H., Gemeindliche Selbstverwaltungsgarantie im Vergleich zur Raumordnung und Landesplanung, 29 (Göttingen: Schriften des Deutschen Städte- und Gemeindebundes, 1977).
27. Hesse, J. J., Stadtentwicklungsplanung, Zielfindungsprozesse und Zielvorstellungen (Stuttgart: Kohlhammer, 1972).
28. Köln (Cologne), Amt für Stadtentwicklungsplanung, ed., Stadtentwicklungsplanung, Gesamtkonzept (Cologne, 1978).
29. Forsthoff, E., and Blümel, W., Raumordnungsrecht und Fachplanungspolitik (Frankfurt am Main: Metzner, 1970).
30. Filter, J. D., Verkehrswegeinvestitionen und Entwicklungspolitik (Berlin: Duncker & Humblot, 1977).
31. Bundesforschungsanstalt für Landeskunde und Raumordnung, ed., Informationen zur Raumentwicklung 1 (1976).
32. Roesler, K., and W. Stürmer, Koordinierung in der Raumordnungspolitik (Göttingen: Schwartz, 1975).
33. Schulz zur Wiesch, J., "Regionalplanung ohne Wirkung," in Archiv für Kommunalwissenschaften, Vol. 17 (1978), pp. 21-39.
34. Scharpf, F., and F. Schnabel, "Durchsetzungsprobleme der Raumordnung im öffentlichen Sektor," in Informationen zur Raumentwicklung, 1 (1978), pp. 29-47.

REFERENCES

Boesler, K.-A., Kulturlandschaftswandel durch raumwirksame Staatstätigkeit (Berlin: Abhandlungen des Geographischen Institutes der Freien Universität Berlin, 1969).

Kisker, G., Kooperation im Bundesstaat (Tübingen: Mohr, 1970).

Kock, H., Stabilitätspolitik im föderalistischen System der Bundesrepublik Deutschland (Cologne: Bund-Verlag, 1975).

Kunze, R., Kooperativer Föderalismus in der Bundesrepublik (Stuttgart: Fischer, 1968).

Laufer, H., Das föderative System der Bundesrepublik Deutschland (Munich: Bayrische Landeszentrale für politische Bildungsarbeit, 1974).

Pinney, E. L., Federalism, Bureaucracy, and Party Politics in Western Germany. The Role of the Bundesrat (Chapel Hill: University of North Caroling Press, 1963).

Ritter, E.-H., "Regionale Entwicklungsplanung zwischen staatlicher Steuerung und Kommunaler Autonomie," in Innere Kolonisation 4(1978), pp. 130-134.

Rudolf, W., "Die Bundesstaatlichkeit in der Rechtssprechung des Bundesverfassungsgerichtes," in Bundesverfassungsgericht und Grundgesetz, ed. Ch. Starck, Vol. 2 (Tübingen: Mohr, 1976), pp. 233-251.

CHAPTER 2

SUBNATIONAL REGIONAL POLICIES
IN THE UNITED STATES

SUBNATIONALE REGIONALPOLITIK IN
DEN VEREINIGTEN STAATEN

Niles Hansen

Abstract

This paper critically discusses the nature and significance of subnational regional policies introduced in the United States beginning in the mid-1960s. The first part examines recent changes in the national distribution of population and economic activity. The influence of public policies and of the federal system on these phenomena is evaluated. At present these influences do not appear to have been decisive. In some instances the presence of federal programs has been a positive factor in development, but the dynamics of regional change have been largely "spontaneous."

The next part briefly deals with current subnational policy issues. For example, some areas still have relatively high levels of unemployment, underemployment, and poverty. Growth also may have undesirable environmental consequences. The final section suggests improvements that might be made in the democratic planning processes of the federal system. Particular consideration is given to the regional commission approach.

Kurzfassung

Dieser Aufsatz erörtert kritisch das Wesen und die Bedeutung der Mitte der sechziger Jahre in den Vereinigten Staaten eingeführten subnationalen Regionalpolitik. Der erste Teil untersucht die jüngsten Änderungen in der nationalen Verteilung der Bevölkerung und der ökonomischen Aktivität. Der Einfluss öffentlicher Programme und des Bundessystems auf diese Erscheinungen wird abgeschätzt. Zur Zeit scheint es, dass diese Einflüsse nicht entscheidend waren. In einigen Fällen war die Anwesenheit von Bundesprogrammen ein positiver Entwicklungsfaktor, aber die Dynamik der regionalen Änderung war weitgehend "spontan."

Der folgende Teil handelt von gegenwärtigen Problemen der subnationalen Politik. Einige Gegenden haben zum Beispiel noch verhältnismässig hohe Arbeitslosigkeit, Arbeitsüberqualifikationen, und Armut. Die Entwicklung kann auch unerwünschte Umweltfolgen haben. Der letzte Teil legt nahe, wie der demokratische Planungsprozess des Bundessystems verbessert werden könnte. Das Vorgehen, das einen Regionalaussschuss in sich schliesst, wird besonders berüchsichtigt.

Subnational Regional Policies
in the United States

Current subnational regional economic development institutions in the U.S. were created for the most part in the mid-1960s in response to regional problems as they were perceived at that time. This paper briefly examines the nature of these institutions and the assumptions underlying regional policy concerns in the mid-1960s. Next consideration is given to the nature and significance of regional economic and demographic changes that have occurred since then, as well as to the degree to which regional policies have influenced these changes. The final section is a critique of regional planning institutions and policies in the light of current regional economic development tendencies. Particular attention is given to the actual and potential roles of regional development commissions.

REGIONAL PLANNING ASSUMPTIONS OF THE MID-1960S

In the mid-1960s it was widely assumed that the nation as a whole would have to adjust to substantial population growth. Moreover, the decline of many small towns and rural areas was accompanied by net migration to metropolitan areas (SMSAs). Nonmetropolitan decline and net outmigration from the South were throught to be causing particular hardship in northern SMSAs. Nevertheless, there seemed to be no end in sight to the growth of the larger SMSAs. In response to these perceptions, increasing pressure was brought to bear on Congress to do something to halt nonmetropolitan decline and to curb the growth of the largest SMSAs. It was even argued that it was in the self-interest of the North's larger cities to improve conditions in the rural South because "the migration streams originating in the rural South form the crucial link in a system of poverty" and that "the magnitude of both Negro and white migration is a measure of the self-interest northern cities have in the rural South" (1, p. 249; 2).

Ever since the mid-1960s, the task of dealing with problems associated with changes in the human settlement system of the U.S. has been approached in terms of attempts to achieve more "balanced" spatial growth. In fact, this vague notion has at one time or another been used to promise something to communities at all levels of the urban hierarchy. For the most part, however, it has been a kind of code expression for using public policy to promote the development of nonmetropolitan areas, especially those experiencing high levels of population outmigration and/or economic stagnation. Unlike France, Great Britain, and some other Western European countries, the U.S. has avoided direct measures to curb the growth of large cities (3). Instead, it has implemented regional development programs intended to improve economic opportunities in the nation's hinterlands, thus indirectly reducing migration to large cities.

REGIONAL DEVELOPMENT INSTITUTIONS CREATED IN THE MID-1960S

Regional development policy in the U.S. has been based primarily on two pieces of legislation passed during the heyday of President Johnson's "Great Society" programs: the Appalachian Regional Development Act of 1965 (ARDA) and the Public Works and Economic Development Act of 1965

(PWEDA).

The ARDA established the Appalachian Regional Commission (ARD) for the purpose of coordinating a joint federal-state development effort--the largest such program yet undertaken in the U.S. The Appalachian program involves thirteen states--stretching from northeastern Mississippi to southern New York--but the only whole state included is West Virginia. Given this vast expanse of territory it is not surprising that the ARC has delineated "three Appalachias," each with its own needs and potentials (Fig. 2-1). The ARC was given specific program and funding authority in nine functional areas, with the highway program being the most significant in terms of resources.

Strictly speaking, the ARC is not a federal agency, but rather a cooperative venture in which the federal government and the relevant states participate as equals. The commission is composed of the governors (or their representatives) of the thirteen states and a federal co-chairperson appointed by the president. The regional, state, and local multicounty development districts have their own responsibilities, but they are supposed to act in concert.

Title V of the PWEDA authorized the Secretary of Commerce to designate, with the cooperation of the states involved, multistate regions with common problems of economic distress or lag that cannot be solved by measures taken within any one state. Once a region has been designated, the relevant states are invited to participate in a regional commission patterned in structure on that for Appalachia. In 1966 and 1967, regional commissions were established for the Ozarks (134 counties in Arkansas, Oklahoma, Missouri, and Kansas), the Four Corners (92 counties in New Mexico, Arizona, Utah, and Colorado), the

Coastal Plains (159 tidewater counties in Georgia and the Carolinas), the Upper Great Lakes (119 counties in northern Minnesota, Wisconsin, and Michigan), and New England, which was the only region comprised of whole states.

During their first six years of operation, federal expenditures for all five of the Title V commissions amounted to a little over $100 million, whereas those for the ARC came to $1.3 billion (through fiscal year 1978 the ARC spent $3.5 billion). Moreover, whereas the ARC was established as an independent agency, the Title V commissions have operated under the Secretary of Commerce. During the 1970s, expansions of previously existing commissions and the creation of six new commissions have led to a situation where part or all of the contiguous forty-eight states now participate in the Appalachian and Title V programs.

In addition to the Title V commissions, the PWEDA created the Economic Development Administration (EDA) to assist the commissions (a role it has never effectively assumed) and to provide assistance in its own right to areas characterized by chronic economic distress. EDA was given a wide range of program tools, including grants and loans for public works and development facilities, industrial and commercial loans, and an extensive program of technical, planning, and research assistance. The EDA has worked primarily through multicounty development districts, which need to prepare an Overall Economic Development Plan in order to qualify for development assistance. Between its inception and 1978, the EDA spent about $3.4 billion on regional development activities, of which two-thirds was allocated to public works projects.

Before commenting on the overall impact of the programs, it is first necessary to identify the major changes that have taken place in the U.S. settlement system in recent years.

REGIONAL CHANGES IN THE DISTRIBUTION OF POPULATION AND ECONOMIC ACTIVITY

The data in Table 2-1 indicate that between 1970 and 1975, the population growth rate in SMSAs was 4.2 percent. This was less than the corresponding nonmetropolitan rate of 6.5 percent. While it is true that there has been net migration from SMSAs as a whole to nonmetropolitan areas during the past decade, this generalization masks more complex processes at work within the urban hierarchy and in interregional migration patterns. For example, between 1970 and 1975, SMSAs with a population over 3 million experienced absolute population decline, and SMSAs with over 2 million persons had net outmigration. However, every SMSA with a population below 2 million had a growth rate exceeding the national average; within this set only the 5000,000-1 million size class had a growth rate (5.7 percent) lower than the 6.5 percent nonmetropolitan growth rate. Thus, with the exception of the larger SMSAs, metropolitan growth is still relatively vigorous.

The data in Table 2-2 show that large SMSA (over 1.5 million) in each of the four major census regions experienced net inmigration between 1960 and 1970. In contrast, the large SMSAs in each region outside the South had net outmigration between 1970 and 1975; net outmigration was particularly pronounced in large SMSAs of the Northeast and North Central regions. In the South, however, large SMSAs with fewer than 1.5 million persons added almost as many people as the large SMSA and nonmetropolitan groups combined.

The general picture then is one of northern big-city

TABLE 2-1. Estimates of the Population of Standard Metropolitan Statistical Areas, July 1, 1975, by Population Size Class.[1]
Schätzung der Bevölkerung von Standard Metropolitan Statistical Areas 1. Juli, 1975, nach Bevölkerung und Grössenklasse.

Size Class	Population July 1, 1975 (provisional)	Population Change, 1970-75 Number	Population Change, 1970-75 Percent	Net Migration, 1970-75 Number	Net Migration, 1970-75 Percent
All standard metropolitan statistical areas (259)[2]	156,097,600	6,271,700	4.2	696,500	0.5
3,000,000 or more (7)	39,848,400	-360,000	-0.9	-1,536,900	-3.8
2,000,000 to 3,000,000 (8)	18,084,500	136,000	0.7	-462,500	-2.5
1,000,000 to 2,000,000 (20)	28,331,200	2,132,600	8.1	1,074,900	4.1
500,000 to 1,000,000 (37)	27,125,200	1,453,000	5.7	437,700	1.7
250,000 to 500,000 (63)	22,725,500	1,477,100	7.0	558,900	2.6
100,000 to 259,000 (97)	16,587,300	1,263,600	8.2	569,800	3.7
Under 100,000 (27)	2,495,600	169,500	7.3	54,700	2.4
Nonmetropolitan areas	56,953,900	3,475,900	6.5	1,770,200	3.3

[1] Population size class of 1970 for SMSAs defined on December 31, 1975.
[2] Numbers in parentheses are the number of SMSAs in each category.

Source: U.S. Bureau of the Census, Data Book for the White House Conference on Balanced National Growth and Economic Development (Washington, D.C.: Bureau of the Census, 1978), p. 22.

decline, widespread nonmetropolitan revival, and continuing rapid growth in small and medium-size SMSAs. The growth of the South--and to a somewhat lesser extent the West--is especially noteworthy. The South accounted for over 54 percent of total national population increase between 1970 and 1975; and all levels of the southern urban hierarchy have participated in the overall regional boom.

The assumptions of the mid-1960s are also inconsistent with what is known today about the nature of interregional migration flows. Even in the 1960s southern white migrants to northern cities substantially improved their economic circumstances, and relatively few were condemned to ghettos or became part of the urban unrest problem (4). As for black migrants, whether one considers poverty status, earnings, or total income, independent studies agree that southern-born blacks have been more economically successful in the North than northern-born blacks (5). Moreover, recent evidence from the Current Population Survey of the Bureau of the Census indicates that the South no longer exports part of its poverty through the interregional migration process. From data on persons who lived in one region in 1975 and another in 1977, it may be inferred that 1.93 million persons moved to the South and 1.47 million moved from the South; the poverty rate for the former group was 16 percent whereas for the latter it was only 12 percent. Education levels of inmigrants to the South were on average less than those of outmigrants from the South. Black inmigrants to the South outnumbered black outmigrants from the South by 183,000 to 166,000. The Northeast region is clearly the least favored by black migrants. Only one in five black southern outmigrants went to the Northeast, and for every black who moved in this direction, three

TABLE 2-2. Population and Average Annual Change in Regions by Metropolitan Status: 1960 to 1975 (In Thousands).
Bevölkerung und durchschnittliche jährliche Veränderungen in Regionen bei Metropolitan Status: 1960 bis 1975 (in 1000).

	Population		
Metropolitan Status	1975	1970	1960
United States	213,051	203,305	179,311
Large metropolitan[1]	82,899	81,472	69,262
Other metropolitan	73,198	68,355	58,676
Nonmetropolitan	56,954	53,478	51,373
Northeast	49,454	49,061	44,678
Large metropolitan[1]	28,569	28,933	26,309
Other metropolitan	13,842	13,548	12,300
Nonmetropolitan	7,043	6,580	6,069
North Central	57,665	56,593	51,619
Large metropolitan[1]	22,612	22,593	20,049
Other metropolitan	17,290	16,815	14,810
Nonmetropolitan	17,763	17,185	16,760
South	68,101	62,812	54,961
Large metropolitan[1]	15,000	13,702	10,232
Other metropolitan	28,546	26,117	22,347
Nonmetropolitan	24,555	22,993	22,382
West	37,831	34,849	28,053
Large metropolitan[1]	16,718	16,244	12,672
Other metropolitan	13,520	11,875	9,219
Nonmetropolitan	7,593	6,720	6,162

[1]Covers 246 standard metropolitan statistical areas and 13 New England County Metropolitan Areas as defined on December 31, 1976. Large metropolitan areas are defined as having 1.5 million or more inhabitants in 1970.

Source: U.S. Bureau of the Census, Statistical Abstract of the United States: 1978 (Washington, D.C.: U.S. Government Printing Office, 1978), p. 18.

Net Change		Average Annual Change		Net Migration	
		Natural Increase			
1970-75	1960-70	1970-75	1960-70	1970-75	1960-70
1,952	2,399	1,456	2,046	496	354
285	1,221	539	804	-254	417
969	968	576	750	393	218
698	211	341	492	357	-281
79	438	218	397	-139	41
-73	262	123	236	-196	26
59	125	63	112	-4	13
93	51	32	49	61	2
217	497	391	567	-175	-68
4	254	171	249	-167	6
95	201	140	188	-45	13
118	43	81	130	37	-37
1,079	785	554	700	525	86
260	347	124	152	136	195
506	377	267	312	239	65
312	61	163	236	150	-174
578	679	294	385	284	293
94	357	122	168	-28	189
309	266	106	139	203	126
175	56	66	78	109	-22

moved from the Northeast to the South (6,7).

It is instructive to consider these migration data in the light of the poverty rate date presented in Table 2-3. In 1976 poverty rates for whites and blacks were higher in the South than elsewhere. However, during both the 1959-1967 and 1967-1976 periods, the poverty rates for both races declined more rapidly in the South, a reflection of the region's rapid growth of economic activity and employment opportunities. It is particularly striking that the black poverty rate outside the South actually increased between 1967 and 1976. In view of these trends it is not surprising that there is now net inmigration of blacks as well as whites to the South. In contrast to the assumptions of the mid-1960s, it would now appear that the South may, in terms of its own self-interest, have a stake in northern urban poverty.

THE IMPACT OF FEDERAL REGIONAL DEVELOPMENT PROGRAMS

The data in Table 2-3 indicate that, with the salutary exception of blacks in the South, poverty rates fell more rapidly between 1959 and 1967 than between 1967 and 1976. This is a remarkable result in view of the fact that the "war on poverty" programs should have begun to have an impact in the late 1960s. Of course, these programs received less than enthusiastic support from subsequent administrations, and the 1976 figures reflect the general stagnation of the national economy in the mid-1970s. But whatever the impact of federal regional development programs on poverty levels, it is at least clear that some of their original policy objectives have been attained. Nonmetropolitan areas over much of the nation have experienced a renaissance.

TABLE 2-3. Poverty Rate for Persons in the United States, by South and Nonsouth Residence, 1959, 1967, and 1976. Armutsverhältnis der Bevölkerung in den Vereinigten Staaten bei südlicher und nichtsüdlicher Ortsansässigkeit, 1959, 1967 und 1976.

	(1) 1959	(2) 1967	(3) 1976	(4) $\frac{1967}{1959}$ x 100	(5) $\frac{1976}{1967}$ x 100
All persons	22.0	14.2	11.8	65	83
South	35.4	22.1	15.2	62	69
Nonsouth	16.0	10.8	10.1	67	94
White	18.1	11.0	9.1	61	83
South	26.8	15.3	10.8	57	71
Nonsouth	14.8	9.4	8.3	64	88
Black	55.1	39.3	31.1	71	79
South	68.5	50.1	33.1	73	66
Nonsouth	34.3	27.3	28.9	80	106

Sources: Columns (1) and (2): U.S. Bureau of the Census, Data Book for the White House Conference on Balanced National Growth and Economic Development (Washington, D.C.: Bureau of the Census, 1978), p. 98. Column (3): U.S. Bureau of the Census, "Money Income and Poverty Status of Families and Persons in the United States: 1976," Current Population Reports, Series P-60, No. 107 (September, 1977), p. 25.

The rural South in particular--excluding those areas with a high proportion of blacks in the total population--is enjoying unprecedented development. And the largest SMSAs are not growing (here policy makers may well reflect on Oscar Wild's contention that one of life's two great misfortunes is to fail to achieve a desired objective; the other is to succeed in attaining it). To what extent have federal regional development programs been responsible for these changes?

The nonmetropolitan areas that have experienced economic and demographic growth in the past decade after relatively long periods of stagnation or decline tend to lie within territories covered by the Appalachian Regional Commission, the Economic Development Administration, and the original Title V regional commissions. These federal initiatives have no doubt been a positive force in some places, by helping to induce growth or by orchestrating growth that has been taking place "spontaneously." However, few observers would go so far as to credit them with the major responsibility for nonmetropolitan revival. The agencies involved have had too little money, too little time, and little in the way of coherent and systematic strategies for development.

While the ARC has been a relatively innovative organization, former Executive Director Ralph Widner has pointed out that few Appalachian states have made much effort to realize the full potential of the program (8). The noncontroversial nature of the ARC has required relatively little gubernatorial attention, and the "roller coaster" aspects of state performance and erratic support from the White House have inevitably affected the quality of administration. Moreover, the states have never clearly defined the responsibilities of the states' regional representative with respect to themselves or the ARC's federal cochairperson. On the positive side, the ARC's greatest successes at coordination have been in functional areas where it had enough of its own funds to be an honest broker, but not so much as to be overwhelmed with operational problems. Housing and education are cases in point. In some states the multicounty development districts have also been effective in fulfilling broad local coordination and development roles. Finally, it is noteworthy that not until ten years after the original ARDA did Congress call upon the ARC to develop a multistate regional development plan for Appalachia to guide ARC investments and to serve as a framework for the states' respective annual development plans. This work is now in progress.

EDA-funded multicounty Economic Development Districts have increased in number from six to 214, which include over 70 percent of the counties in the continental U.S. Recently the EDA administered a $6 billion emergency countercyclical public works program that tended to be of most benefit to the major old industrial states, which experienced particularly high unemployment rates during the last recession. Although this program represents almost two-thirds of the EDA's total outlays throughout its history, it was in reality an untypical function and must be viewed apart from the agency's normal regional development activities. In fact, the EDA's regional development funding capacity has decreased over the years. The result has been a wide scattering of funds in relatively small amounts. The EDA itself acknowledges that its experience "has clearly demonstrated that the piecemeal approach to project funding followed in the past will generally not result in a meaningful increase in the level of an area's economic activity," and that "its resources, even at the substantially increased levels sought, are inadequate to realize economic growth and stability in more than a handful of areas unless maximum use is made of other public and, particularly, of private investment" (9).

In relation to the ARC, the Title V commissions have had less autonomy within the federal structure and much less programmatic authority. Until recently they also have lacked direct linkages with substate economic development districts. The commissions have been primarily "planning" bodies with little in the way of project investment funds to carry out their missions. The commissions are supposed to coordinate the various ongoing federal economic development programs in their respective regions, but there is little evidence of success in this regard. Wilson's evaluation of their performance concludes that "all the commissions have had difficulties producing plans--as well as plan revisions required by 1975 legislation--that are both acceptable and useful" (10). Thus, although some significant initiatives can be credited to the commissions, their overall impact on nonmetropolitan America has been negligible.

In addition to the activities stemming from the 1965 regional development legislation, there are of course a host of other federal government programs related to nonmetropolitan development. These tend to be not only complicated but also compartmentalized and competitive. Section 603 of the Rural Development Act of 1972 directed the Secretary of Agriculture to provide leadership and coordination to the nation's nonmetropolitan development efforts, to establish nonmetropolitan development goals, and to report on progress toward attainment of these goals. In fact this authority has not been used effectively. The responsibility for implementing Section 603 was virtually dumped on the Farmers Home Administration, an agency with a reputation for past inadequacies in policies and in staff and management capabilities. Greater attention has been given recently to upgrading the FMHA's leadership capabilities, and its investment resources--$9 billion in fiscal year 1978--are considerable. Nevertheless, its effectiveness remains to be demonstrated. For the present, as Tweeten and Brinkman remark, "it is apparent that micropolitan [nonmetropolitan] areas have no federal policy at all, only a confused set of piecemeal programs administered by disjointed federal fiefdoms jealous of their narrow self-interests and unable to view micropolitan areas as needing an integrated, systematic policy that is economically efficient and equitable" (4, p. 423).

If federal regional development programs have had only a very limited influence on recent regional and interregional changes in the U.S., it is still possible that the combined effects of all federal programs could have had significant unintended consequences in this regard. For example, it is reasonable to believe that general decentralization of population and economic activity has been facilitated by the completion of the interstate highway system. The economic difficulties experienced in many parts of the Northeast and North Central regions' old industrial areas have in fact frequently been blamed on the geographic incidence of federal taxes and expenditures. However, this contention has not been supported by the available evidence (11, 12).

It also has been argued that net migration to the South may have been only a temporary phenomenon; in this view, the severe economic recession that particularly affected the North's basic industries caused many unemployed workers to return to their places of origin and caused potential migrants from the South at least to delay their moves (13). This position increasingly appears to be inadequate as the evidence mounts that the interregional demographic and economic shifts of the 1970s reflect fundamental structural changes and that the new patterns are likely to persist in the foreseeable future (14, 15). It is noteworthy that similar patterns of change have been occurring in other industrially advanced countries, regardless of whether they have had strong or weak regional development policies. What appears to be taking place is deconcentration of population and economic activity from large metropolitan areas in favor of small and medium-size cities (16, 17). It is tempting to speculate that the cities in a country's urban system may pass through a sequential process wherein concentration and deconcentration are dependent on the country's stage of economic development; however, it is not possible to give adequate consideration to this hypothesis within the scope of this paper.

CURRENT REGIONAL POLICY ISSUES
In the mid-1960s the nation's major regional economic development problems seemed to be clearly delineated, even if there was disagreement about specific strategies for dealing with them. Today the problems themselves appear to be more complex and less precisely defined geographically, despite considerable simplistic rhetoric about the Frostbelt and the Sunbelt. For example, between 1970 and 1975 the rate of population increase in the West (8.5 percent) exceeded that in the South (8.4 percent), and northern California grew more rapidly than Sunbelt California. The widespread

revival of many nonmetropolitan areas has been a result of a number of causes, including the expansion of urban fields from some SMSAs; amenities conducive to recreation, tourism, second homes, and retirement; decentralization of manufacturing and services; and increased employment in primary sector activities involving energy production. In many cases two or more of these factors have been at work simultaneously. But economic growth can be a mixed blessing. In some instances it threatens fragile natural environments. In others, few jobs may be going to unemployed or underemployed persons who end up worse off because of local price inflation. In addition, there remain nonmetropolitan areas that have high levels of underemployment and poverty. These conditions can be found where low-wage, slow-growth industries characterize the local economy, as in many southern counties long dominated by the textile industry (18). And they remain especially evident where the proportion of minorities--blacks, Indians, Mexican Americans--is relatively high. Yet another kind of problem is found in many nonmetropolitan parts of the Great Plains. These areas do not yet possess the resources needed for industrialization or larger-scale urbanization. The agricultural sector is relatively prosperous, but it supports declining and aging populations to whom service delivery is often difficult.

The situation with respect to metropolitan areas is equally complex. The large industrial SMSAs of the old industrial heartland must deal with manufacturing employment losses, plants that frequently are obsolete, and central-city/suburban disparities compounded by the concentration of racial minorities in the inner cities. But even in the Sunbelt some former "boomtown" metropolitan areas that grew when the defense and aerospace industries were flourishing have recently experienced substantial net outmigration. However, in all parts of the country smaller and medium-size SMSAs are growing relatively rapidly, and New England in general is doing better than would be suggested by the Frostbelt wisdom. Indeed, "one of the ironies of current public policy as viewed from a New England perspective is that allocation formulas for public funds and other federal aids for regional economic transitions are becoming more favorable and available to New England just as the worst of its own transition problems may be at an end" (19, p. 114).

THE FEDERAL SYSTEM AND REGIONAL COMMISSIONS
Recent regional and interregional shifts of population and economic activity in the U.S. reflect complex processes whose underlying causes are not yet well understood. The situation could become even more complicated when prices reflect energy scarcities to a greater extent than at present. Thus, it would be inappropriate to make broad generalizations concerning either nonmetropolitan areas, SMSAs, or their interactions. However, it is apparent that the federal system is not well organized to deal efficiently with regional problems. This essay has considered the activities of agencies whose principal mandate is to address regional policy issues. But it has been estimated that there are at least nineteen federal programs with authority to carry on subnational development activities; these programs are administered by five federal departments, two commissions, and an independent agency (20, p. 1). This bureaucratic maze is sprawling, inefficient, and often chaotic. There is no one place in the federal government where one can go to obtain a comprehensive view of programs with significant regional development implications. Congress

does not have sufficient information to evaluate the relative effectiveness of the various programs, and the executive branch also appears unable to come to grips with agencies' overlapping functions and wasteful rivalry and duplication of effort. States and local communities confront such a tangle of cumbersome federal forms and regulations that it is often impossible to put together coordinated plans. In order to obtain federal funds, state agencies have set up direct relationships with counterpart federal agencies, thereby in effect bypassing the governors who might have been able to establish priorities and coordinate programs and projects. As Monroe Newman has pointed out, "If we assume that Federal officials and employees do not intentionally devise cumbersome, illogical, inefficient, frustrating, wasteful programs, the explanation must lie elsewhere. The alternative explanation is that general rules and regulations, designed for 'average' situations, are inappropriate for communities and areas that diverge markedly from the average" (21, p. 2).

Of the various alternatives that have been proposed for bringing more coherency and efficiency into the federal system, multistate regional commissions have probably received the most favorable reaction. Ten years ago I wrote that:

> It is possible, through the vehicle of regional commissions, to have state and local officials and leaders prepare coherent and comprehensive programs that would be federally financed but to preserve a federal veto over projects which are contrary to efficient resource allocation from a national perspective. It would be necessary to divide the entire country into multistate regions (though they would not have to follow existing state boundaries). Moreover, the present regional commissions, with the exception of that for New England, should be redefined to encompass both lagging areas and

> growth centers, in contrast to the present
> policy of defining regions which are made
> up almost entirely of lagging areas. Only
> then will it be possible to relate problems
> of lagging areas and opportunities in genuine
> growth centers within a common framework.
> (22, p. 324)

Although the nature of regional problems and opportunities has altered since then, I still believe that a genuine federal commitment to the regional commission approach could substantially improve the performance of government. Moreover, as a public administration device the commissions would deal with a whole range of issues in addition to "economic development" in the narrower sense. As indicated earlier, the boundaries of existing regional commissions have for the most part been broadened in recent years to include whole states; these changes should constructively enlarge the spatial scope of commission activities. What are needed now are adequately funded commissions that cover the whole country as well as the active cooperation of governments at all levels within the regional framework. For example, although the National Governors Association has endorsed the regional commission approach to federal-state relations, many states could do more even now in this regard. The effectiveness of this approach depends a great deal on the quality of state planning in response to regional needs. The states could insist that intergovernmental programs be coordinated through the governor-designated multicounty development and planning districts that now virtually cover the nation. The problem is not so much a lack of workable proposals (23) as lack of political will. In some instances, governors may fear that strong substate planning areas would be a threat to their authority; thus they readily acquiesce in the proliferation of uncoordinated special districts spawned by rival federal agencies. Nor has the Congress really pushed hard to encourage a greater measure of coordination among the bureaucracy's separate fiefdoms. Indeed, it has tended to discourage planning in some regional programs. The apparent motivation is not so much an ideology favoring the market workings of a "free enterprise" economy as fear that planning of any kind would decrease the opportunities for resource allocation by congressional ad hoc approaches.

Early in 1979, President Carter announced his support for regional commissions and called for greater coordination between the commissions and other elements in the federal bureaucracy. More specifically, the Interagency Coordinating Council was instructed to work with key federal officials and federal cochairpersons of regional commissions to eliminate obstacles to regional development. Federal cochairpersons were made members of the Federal Regional Councils which have been established on a multistate basis to promote greater cohesion among various federal programs. President Carter also specified that the regional commissions' investment programs should be developed from the ground up to reflect substate and state development plans; and he instructed federal agencies to give due consideration to regional commission plans and programs in their own planning processes. However, so much mutual coordination would no doubt leave insufficient time for the effective management of the relevant groups' and agencies' own affairs. It would seem that some organizational streamlining is in order. Moreover, if the regional commissions are to have any hope of achieving quality planning and an impact on federal programs, they will need considerably higher levels of funding (24, p. 127). But so long as macroeconomic problems--especially inflation--continue to receive priority, the regional commissions are likely to receive more good wishes than dollars. Thus, at present it is not clear whether or to what extent the regional commission approach to federalism will ever be seriously implemented.

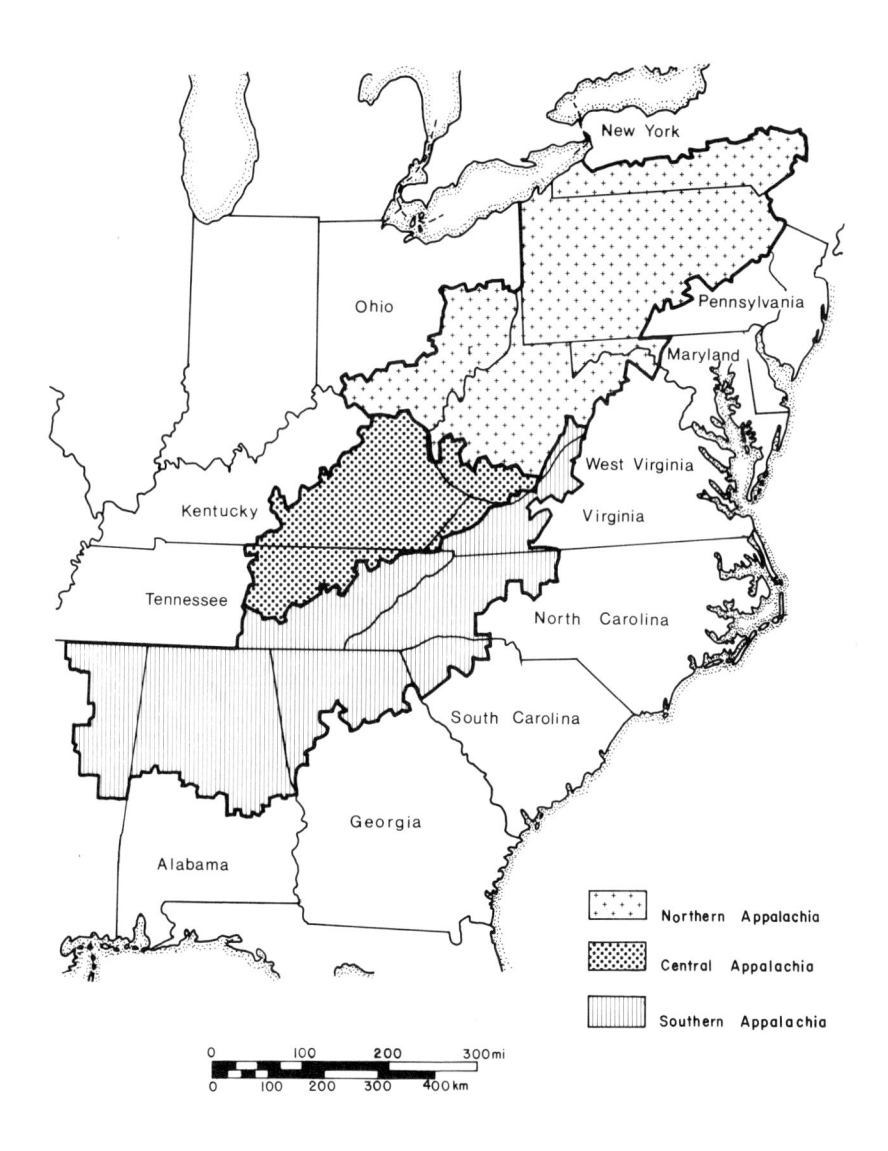

FIG. 2-1. Appalachia: Subregional Boundaries.
         Appalachia: Subregionale Grenzen.

Source: <u>Appalachia-A Reference Book</u>, Appalachia Regional Commission, p. 7.

NOTES

1. Kain, J. F., and J. J. Perskey, "The North's Stake in Southern Rural Poverty," in J. F. Kain and J. R. Meyer, eds., Essays in Regional Economics, ed. J. F. Kain and J. R. Meyer (Cambridge: Harvard University Press, 1971).

2. Advisory Committee on Intergovernmental Regulations, Urban and Rural America: Policies for Future Growth (Washington, D.C.: U.S. Government Printing Office, 1968).

3. Hansen, N., ed., Public Policy and Regional Economic Development: The Experience of Nine Western Countries (Cambridge, Mass.: Ballinger, 1976).

4. Tweeten, L., and G. L. Brinkman, Micropolitan Development (Ames, Iowa: Iowa State University Press, 1976).

5. Long, L. H., and L. R. Heltman, "Migration and Income Differences between Black and White Men in the North," American Journal of Sociology 80 (May, 1975), 1391-1409.

6. Hansen, N., "Does the South Have a Stake in Northern Urban Poverty? Southern Economic Journal 45 (April, 1979), 1220-1224.

7. Long, L. H., Interregional Migration of the Poor: Some Recent Changes, Current Population Reports Special Studies Series p-23, No. 73 (Washington, D.C.: U.S. Bureau of the Census, November, 1978).

8. Widner, R. R., "Evaluating the Administration of the Appalachian Regional Development Program," Growth and Change 4 (January, 1973), 25-29.

9. Economic Development Administration, U.S. Department of Commerce, "The Development Policy," in The White House Conference on Balanced National Growth and Economic Development, Final Report, Appendix Vol. 6 (Washington, D.C.: U.S. Government Printing Office, 1978).

10. Wilson, Leonard U., State Strategies for Multistate Organizations, State Planning Series No. 8 (Washington, D.C.: Council of State Planning Agencies, 1977).

11. Browning, C. E., The Geography of Federal Outlays (Chapel Hill, N.C.: Department of Geography, University of North Carolina, Studies in Geography No.

4, 1973).

12. Peterson, G. E., and T. Muller, "The Regional Impact of Federal Tax and Spending Policies," paper presented at the Conference on Alternatives to confontation: A National Policy Toward Regional Change, Lyndon B. Johnson School of Public Affairs, Austin, Texas, September, 1978.

13. Kain, J. F., "Implications of Declining Metropolitan Population on Housing Markets," in Post-Industrial America: Metropolitan Decline and Interregional Job Shifts, ed. G. Sternlieb and J. W. Hughes (New Brunswick, N.J.: Rutgers Center for Urban Policy Research, 1975).

14. Joint Economic Committee, U.S. Congress, U.S. Long-Term Economic Growth Prospects: Entering a New Era, 95th Cong., 2nd sess. (Washington, D.C.: U.S. Government Printing Office, 1978).

15. Garnick, D. H., "A Reappraisal of the Outlook for Northern States and Cities in the Context of U.S. Economic History," paper presented to the Second Annual Conference on the Economic Future of the Northeast States, MIT-Harvard Joint Center for Urban Studies, Cambridge, 1978.

16. Vining, D. R., Jr., and T. Kontuly, "Population Dispersal from Major Metropolitan Regions: An International Comparison," International Regional Science Review 3 (Fall, 1978), 49-74.

17. Hansen, N., ed., Human Settlement Systems: International Perspectives on Structure, Change and Public Policy (Cambridge, Mass.: Ballinger, 1978).

18. Berentsen, W. H., "Regional Policy and Industrial Overspecialization in Lagging Regions," Growth and Change 9 (July, 1978), 9-13.

19. Meyer, J. R., and R. A. Leone, "The New England States and Their Economic Future: Some Implications of a Changing Industrial Environment," American Economic Review 68 (May, 1978), 110-115.

20. Wise, H. F., Conflicts in Federal Subnational Development Programs (Washington, D.C.: Economic Development Administration, U.S. Department of Commerce, March, 1976).

21. Newman, M., "Whither Multi-State Regional Commissions: Certainly Not Wither," paper presented at the Annual Meeting of the Regional Science Association, Chicago, Illinois, November, 1978.

22. Hansen, N., ed., Public Policy and Regional Economic Development: The Experience of Nine Western Countries (Cambridge, Mass.: Ballinger, 1974).

23. Chinitz, B., "Regional Economic Development Commissions: The Title V Program," Canadian Journal of Regional Science (Autumn, 1978), 107-127.

24. Council of State Planning Agencies, Intergovernmental Strategies, State Planning Series, Vols. 5-9 (Washington, D.C.: CSPA, 1977).

CHAPTER 3

THE FEDERAL SYSTEM OF THE FEDERAL
REPUBLIC OF GERMANY

DAS FÖDERATIVE SYSTEM DER
BUNDESREPUBLIK DEUTSCHLAND

Peter Schöller

Abstract

The first part of this essay delineates the historical development of territorialism and federalism in Germany up to the founding of the Federal Republic in 1949. The organization of the federal system with the division of duties and competencies among the federal government, the states, and the Upper House of Parliament is linked to the problems of regional disparity among the states, which differ greatly as to size and capabilities. Proposals for the restructuring of the federal region as required by statute demonstrate the possibilities for reform and equalization. The refusal to reorganize the states, however, leads to a strengthening of their horizontal financial equalization and thereby to the undermining of federalism. Because of the special status of Berlin and the choice of Bonn as the new federal capital, intended originally as provisional only, the Federal Republic lacks a strong capital city. The principal functions of the entire government are considerably decentralized. Therefore the important regional centers in the federal system are augmented by the lively traditions of German regionalism.

Kurzfassung

Das erste Kapitel behandelt in Hauptlinien die historische Entwicklung des Territorialismus und Föderalismus in Deutschland bis zur Gründung der Bundesrepublik im Jahre 1949. Der Aufbau des bundesstaatlichen Systems (Kapitel 2) mit der Verteilung der Aufgaben und Kompetenzen zwischen Bundesstaat, Bundesländern und Bundesrat führt zu den Problemen regionaler Disparitäten zwischen den sehr unterschiedlich großen und leistungsstarken Bundesländern. Vorschläge zu einer vom Grundgesetz geforderten Neugliederung des Bundesgebietes zeigen Möglichkeiten zu Reformen und Ausgleich (Kapitel 3). Doch die Ablehnung an eine Neuordnung der Bundesländer führt zu einer Stärkung des horizontalen Länder-Finanzausgleichs und damit zu einer Aushöhlung des Föderalismus. Durch den Sonderstatus Berlins und die als Provisorium gedachte Wahl Bonns zur Bundeshauptstadt fehlt der Bundesrepublik eine starke Hauptstadt (Kapitel 4). Die Hauptfunktionen des Gesamtstaates sind in extremer Weise dezentralisiert. Die dadurch bekräftigte Stellung starker Regionalzentren im Städtesystem der Bundesrepublik verbindet sich mit der lebendig gebliebenen Tradition des deutschen Regionalismus .

The Federal System of the Federal Republic of Germany

The United States of America and the Federal Republic of Germany (FRG) represent the same type of federation: a federative state as a community of nonsovereign member states with a separation of power between the federation and the member states. There are some differences, however, in the competence and procedure of the federative system, and some differences between the historical heritage and the geographical background of the two countries.

HISTORICAL NOTES ON THE DEVELOPMENT OF GERMAN FEDERALISM

The tension between a strong and vigorous regionalism and an unstable and discontinuous relationship toward centralized state power is an underlying problem of German history. At a time when other nations-like the French and the British, the Spanish and the Portuguese, but also the Japanese and Koreans-had established their national identity in centralized states, Germany was still a colorful mosaic of small and large territories connected by language, culture, and a more or less idealistic struggle for unity. In spite of several profound changes within the inner structure of the German parts of the Holy Roman Empire of the German nation, the political particularism remained the determining factor in the structure even after the end of the Thirty Years' War. At the Reichstag in Regensburg in 1683, more than 300 territorial sovereigns were present.

More than a century later the Napoleonic Wars and the Vienna Congress in 1815 brought about an important turning point in the territorial development. Even the Deutsche

Bund, which was founded at that time, still consisted of thirty-five states and four free cities. Despite this multiplicity an economic union of the German states, which was an important precondition for developing industrialization, was achieved within the next few decades through economic communities and customs unions. Later, the Prussian annexation in North Germany in 1866 diminished the number of politically autonomous territories and promoted centralization in the North. The reduction of these autonomous territories, however, stressed only the discrepancies in size of the states compared to those in South and Middle Germany.

The Deutsche Reich, proclaimed in Versailles in 1871, still consisted of twenty-two monarchies, three free cities, and the "Reichsland" Alsace-Lorraine. Sixty-five percent of the territory belonged to Prussia where 62 percent of the population of the "Second Empire" lived. Compared with this great power less than one percent of the total territory belonged to seventeen small states. A single Prussian county (Stolp in Pomerania) was larger than twelve states. The population ratio between Schaumburg-Lippe, the state with the lowest population, and Prussia was 1:770. Since the constitution of 1871 was based on the sovereignty of the monarch it did not provide for territorial changes. At the turn of the century some states were still divided into administrative units of various sizes within an empire which had developed into a great industrial and military power. Even in the period between the two world wars individual states still consisted of separated areas and exclaves. Brunswick, for example, was an extreme example. It consisted of twenty-eight separated parts and plots.

The Weimar Republic, following Bismarck's organization of a federal constitution, offered basic elements for genuine reform, but was still strongly characterized by the dualism between Prussia and the Reich. This resulted in a peculiar cooperation between a leading state and a federal union consisting of twenty-five member states of differing size and importance. Influenced by the difficult situation at home and abroad in the early 1920s and because of separatist tendencies, there was a general fear of splitting the strongest link of the federation, the stable body of the Prussian state.

Between 1927 and 1930 the Republic was relieved of its internal pressures and again was able to turn to the question of a new federal constitution. A number of complex plans for reform were under discussion. A constitutional committee representing the states, which was called together in Berlin in 1928, as well as the semipublic Bund zur Erneuerung des Reiches (Federation for the Reconstruction of the State) founded by the former chancellor, Dr. Hans Luther, were important. Combined with the reorganization of functional, financial, legal, and constitutional matters of the Reich and the states, the territorial reform was concerned for the most part with the problem of how Prussia could be integrated without completely destroying the inner links between the various Prussian territories and without radically changing the distribution of votes in the Reichsrat (parliament), the second chamber of the federation.

The great depression at the end of the 1920s and the following crisis in parliamentary democracy soon paralyzed all activities dealing with a political and geographical reorganization. In addition to several consolidations on a lower level and the elimination of exclaves in 1920, Thuringia was united, Saxe-Coburg was combined with Bavaria, and in 1928 Waldeck with Prussia. The Weimar Republic was denied further success other than these unifications.

Although the National Socialist government carried out the unification of the two Mecklenburgs, the long-prepared solution of Greater Hamburg and the integration of Lubeck and Birkenfield (part of Oldenburg) with Prussia, proved it was unable to achieve a constructive reorganization of the Reich. The Nazis united the federal ministries with those of Prussia. This brought about closer connection between the small northern states and the neighboring Prussian provinces. However, the new division into the NSDAP districts, which became more and more important, and into the territories of the defense commissioners resulted in new regions that competed with one another for the power of the party leaders.

According to their constitutions of 1949 both German states, the Federal Republic of Germany (FRG) and the German Democratic Republic (GDR), were considered provisional until the reunification of Germany. But the growing East-West conflict with the integration of both states into two opposing military and economic organizations together with their neighbors' mistrust of an economically strong Germany prevented the reunification of the German people. Since 1961, a complex barrier system against migration of its people across its borders in order to "set itself apart" from the Federal Republic was organized. Nevertheless, the constitution and policies of the Federal Republic still stress as their target a national union of Germany, even though it is agreed that a realization of this aim has almost moved beyond reach because of the continuously diverging two economic and social systems.

THE FEDERAL SYSTEM: STRUCTURE AND JURISDICTION

The Federal Republic of Germany is by its constitution a community of German Länder (federal states) (Figure 3-1 and Table 3-1). Sovereignty is vested in the federation; the federal states do not have the right of secession. The states participate through the Bundesrat (Upper House) in the legislation of the federation. The Constitution divides the state authority between the states and the federation, thus creating a mutual dependence. The states have the right to legislate insofar as the Constitution does not confer power on the federation. Federal law overrides state law. The federal system is regarded as an instrument of democratic control, balance, and influence. It enables the opposition party in the Bundestag (Lower House) to express some of its aims through the Upper House and directly in those states in which it forms the government. Federalism makes for greater participation in politics by the citizen, brings the state closer to the people since it can adapt to local requirements, and takes into account the diversity of historical, cultural, and economic characteristics.

JURISDICTION OF THE FEDERATION

Legislation, for which the federation is solely responsible, covers foreign affairs, defense, questions of citizenship, currency, railway transport, aviation and postal services, as well as parts of the tax law. As far as concurrent legislation is concerned, the states have authority to legislate only as long as the federation does not use its legislative power in the same field; the exception being a genuine need for uniformity throughout the Federal Republic. Areas of concurrent legislation are the economic sphere,

TABLE 3-1. The Existing Federal States in 1970.
Bestehende Bundesländer in 1970.

	Population in mill.	Area 1000 km^2	GNP[1]	Private income[2]	Tax power[3]
1. Schleswig-Holstein	2.49	15.67	84.8	92.7	82.5
2. Hamburg	1.79	0.75	144.3	115.3	154.4
3. Niedersachsen (Lower Saxony)	7.08	47.41	88.8	93.2	83.5
4. Bremen	0.72	0.40	110.8	106.1	120.3
5. Nordrhein-Westfalen (North Rhine-Westphalia)	16.91	34.04	102.0	106.0	104.8
6. Hessen	5.39	21.11	102.3	104.3	107.2
7. Rheinland-Pfalz (Rhineland-Palatinate)	3.64	19.84	95.8	94.0	86.3
8. Saarland	1.12	2.57	83.3	99.6	77.7
9. Baden-Württemberg	8.89	35.75	102.7	100.0	107.5
10. Bayern (Bavaria)	10.48	70.55	97.6	91.0	94.1

[1] Gross National Product in percentage of average of federal states.
[2] Private income per capita of working population in percent of average of federal states.
[3] Taxes of federal states and communities in percent of average of federal states.

the production and use of nuclear energy, state law and housing, shipping and road traffic, waste disposal, and air pollution. Experience, however, has shown that an increasing number of fields of concurrent legislation call for uniform legislation, resulting in a decline in this type of state jurisdiction.

The federation may set a framework of guidelines within which the states can legislate. Such legislation, for instance, comprises university education, nature and landscape conservation, regional planning, and water management. Other tasks included as joint responsibilities according to the Basic Law of 1969 are the extension and building of universities and medical colleges, the improvement of the regional economic structure, the improvement of the agrarian structure, and coastal protection. Most federal laws are implemented by state authorities. The federal president is elected by the federal convention, which consists of the members of the Lower House and an equal number of members selected by the parliaments of the states.

JURISDICTION OF THE STATES

The states have legislative authority in those areas which are not covered by federal laws or are not listed in the Basic Law, namely education, local government, police, and justice. The states strive to coordinate their legislation and administration by interstate or administrative agreement, partly between the premiers of the states or their appropriate ministers. Their responsibility for cultural affairs extends to the entire education system. Although the states have a standing conference of Ministers of Education, coordination in this sector is frequently inadequate, influencing the living conditions and internal migration within the Federal Republic. It would appear from their legislative powers that the states hold a weak position, but this is not necessarily the case. The strength of the states lies in administration and participation in the lawmaking process of the federation. The states are responsible for all internal administration, by which they also implement most of the federal laws and regulations.

The FRG has brought about a state with strong central legislation and a predominantly federal administration. The ordinary citizen feels the effects of federal legislation through the state authorities in the form of numerous regulations. The ministries and agencies of the states, the tax offices, county councils, and police offices act as agents for the federation. Central monitoring of all of the implementing regulations and activities by the Lower House is impossible, and is left to the state parliaments. In addition to their limited legislative power, effective parliamentary control of the administration is one of their main tasks. The states participate through the Upper House in the legislation and administration of the federation.

THE UPPER HOUSE

The Upper House counterbalances the Lower House and the federal government. It is composed of members of the state government, according to the size of the population of the state. Each state has a minimum of three votes. A state with a population of over two million inhabitants has four votes, and with a population of over six million people, five votes. The votes of each state must be cast as a block, which has been decided by the state government beforehand.

The main functions of the Upper House include:

(a) The right to introduce bills.

(b) Any bill introduced by the federal government must first be submitted for comment to the Upper House before being transmitted to the Lower House.

(c) Amendments to the Constitution require a two-thirds majority of the Upper House as well as an equal majority of the Lower House.

(d) Various types of laws and regulations are subject to the consent of the Upper House. These laws concern, in particular, the financial and administrative powers of the states, and joint tasks such as defense.

(e) The Upper House can send any bill (even those not requiring consent) on which it does not agree with the Lower House to a Mediation Committee composed of eleven members of each governing body.

(f) In the case of laws not requiring consent, the Upper House, following the mediation process, can still protest, but the decision can only be overturned by a qualified majority* (see References) of the Lower House.

The history of the Basic Law (Constitution) clearly indicates that the powers of the Upper House have been strengthened constantly since most laws contain administration rules for the states which require their consent for the enactment. The voting of the states in the Upper House is determined not only by the position of the party that forms the respective state government but by the interests of the state. As a result, the federal government and the Lower House, even in the early stages of legislation, must take into account the interests of the states. This does not preclude the possibility that a decision on important legislation, such as social security and tax matters, will not be dominated by party considerations.

In 1979, only four (with West Berlin, five) states shared the same party distribution as the central government: North-Rhine Westphalia, Hessen, Hamburg, and Bremen (the votes of West Berlin are counted separately). The opposition governs in Lower Saxony, Schleswig-Holstein, Rhineland-Palatinate, Saarland, Baden-Württemberg, and Bavaria.

According to the Basic Law, the relationship between the federation and the states is governed by the obligation of mutual loyalty. This principle is especially important in the present political situation. The whole decision making process may be impeded unless there is a minimum of consensus and loyalty to the federation. The many discussions between the federation and the states conducted at the various levels are also aimed at fostering a coordinated policy. Thus, the premiers of the states meet with the federal chancellor several times a year; the ministers and civil servants of the states meet with their counterparts at the federal level. This shows not only the risks and problems inherent in the system of multiple checks and balances, but also the power of democratic control and participation.

DISPARITIES BETWEEN THE FEDERAL STATES

In a geographical context the problem of the division into federal states should be mentioned. Article 29 of the Constitution not only allows for but requires a reorganization of the system of the federal states to be enacted within the war-time occupation zones: "The federal territory is to be reorganized taking into consideration the connection of inner-ethnic ties, the historical and cultural context, economic feasibility, practicability, and the social structure. It is the aim of reorganization to create states capable of adequately fulfilling their tasks according to their size and capability." This constitutional mandate was suspended by an order of the Allied powers; therefore, it was not put into force until the declaration of the full sovereignty of the Federal Republic of Germany of 5 May 1955. Only the urgent reorganization of the Southwest, which was divided into two occupied zones and three federal states, was exempt from this suspension. After a referendum the federal state of Baden-Württemberg was established. Five years later a treaty with France led to a political reintegration of the Saarland after the vast majority of the population had rejected a proposed Saar statute.

On the whole, none of the federal governments since World War II has yet taken a serious initiative for a political and geographical reorganization. By an order of the Federal Constitutional Court there have been several regional referenda concerning regional changes in the state system, and twice, in 1955 and in 1972, committees of experts appointed by the central government submitted proposals with alternatives for reform. But the status quo did not change. Chancellor Brandt received a comprehensive proposal from the second commission on February 20, 1973 (Figure 3-2 and Table 3-2). He suggested a public discussion of the plan before his administration would decide the next steps. But during the public discussion, the energy crisis started, and new economic problems moved to the fore. In 1977 Article 29 of the Constitution was altered with a two-thirds majority in the Upper House, but there are serious questions about the background of this decision.

It was not only the integral power of the federal states

TABLE 3-2. The Revised Federal States (1972).
Neugliederung der Bundesstaaten, 1972.

	Population in mill.	Area 1000 km^2	GNP[1]	Private income[2]	Tax power[3]
1. Nordstaat (A + B)	12.09	64.20	99.0	98.7	96.0
1a. Land Nordost (A)	5.01	24.58	107.8	102.8	106.4
1b. Land Nordwest (B)	7.08	39.62	93.0	95.7	88.5
2. North Rhine-Westphalia	17.11	35.23	102.0	106.0	104.7
3a. Land Mittelwest (C + D)	10.73	43.25	98.4	101.3	96.7
4a. Land Südwest (E)	8.21	35.11	102.2	98.9	108.3
3b. Land Mittelwest (C)	7.27	33.62	98.9	100.8	100.3
4b. Land Südwest (D + E)	11.67	44.82	100.7	99.8	102.5
5. Bavaria	10.38	70.23	97.6	91.0	94.0

[1] Gross National Product in percent of average of federal states.
[2] Private income per capita of working population in percent of average of federal states.
[3] Taxes of federal states and communities in percent of average of federal states.

and the determination of the Hanseatic cities (Hamburg, Bremen) to remain independent that caused a retreat from the reorganization. Some politicians with regional powers also contribute to this retreat. The representation of the federal states' power in the Upper House was at stake because, according to the Constitution, the federal states participate in the legislative process.

Often, during the period after the war, the conflicting political composition of the Upper House and the Lower House required considerable effort for broad political agreement. But even without this reciprocal relation there have been political differences between the majorities in the federation and some federal state governments which could be traced to traditional and social-structural differences. It was this system of broad citizen participation and the distribution of power among the federal states which prevented political predominances and monopolies. Federalism, which in the years immediately following the war was not very popular, today enjoys the broad support of the population. This basic support of federalism, however, does not imply an acceptance of all the shortcomings of the functional delegation of responsibility and the territorial structure. Although state boundaries are not necessarily problematic, the experience of the last decades has proven that they become a problem whenever they cut across conurbations or economically linked areas and whenever they separate important cities such as Hamburg and Bremen from their hinterland.

In the northern part of the Upper Rhine area political boundaries have remained particularly problematic. Three important metropolitan areas are cut politically: the Rhine-Main district between the federal state capitals of Mainz and Wiesbaden, the Rhine-Neckar area around Mannheim,

Ludwigshafen, and Viernheim, and the area around Kalsruhe between Maxau and Worth. Less serious boundary problems exist in the Middle Rhine-Ahr area south of Bonn, on the edges of the Siegerland, around Kassel and Osnarbrück, around Aschaffenburg, as well as in the Middle Main area near Wertheim. The federal state boundaries of Bavaria and Baden-Württemberg make the separation of Ulm and New-Ulm especially bothersome.

More serious than all these local and regional boundary conflicts are the remaining disparities in the structure of the Federal Republic. The German states vary considerably in population and productive capacity. Two of the ten federal states are cities, Hamburg and Bremen; the Saarland is the size of an administrative district, Schleswig-Holstein is the size of a former Prussian province; Hesse and the Rhineland-Palatinate are centered around a mutual central core, and the Rhine-Main area, which includes their respective capitals. Only four federal states, Bavaria, Baden-Württemberg, Lower Saxony, and North-Rhine Westphalia, can be considered large enough and with a sufficient productive capacity and a strong central core of their own.

If we compare the size of the population, the disparity becomes even more obvious. The difference in size between the federal partners ranges from 0.7 million in Bremen to 17 million in North-Rhine Westphalia. We have to bear in mind that experts consider an independent, adequate, and economically effective realization of public services in the federal states as properly secured in the future only when these states have about five million inhabitants. Five of the existing federal states have fewer inhabitants.

Indices of economic and financial capacity accentuate the problems. The degree of industrialization in Schleswig-

Holstein and the Rhineland-Palatinate is below the average of the Federal Republic whereas Baden-Württemberg and North-Rhine Westphalia are well above average. The gross national product taken as a standard of the total economic output achieved in a federal state reveals remarkable differences. In 1970 the gross national product (GNP) of the Saarland, Schleswig-Holstein, and Lower Saxony with 83.3, 84.8 and 88.8 points was considerably below the federal average whereas that of Hamburg was 144.3. The federal states' and municipalities' taxable capacity accentuates the same relations and ranks with even greater extremes.

Since 1970 there has been little change in the differences. A decreased industrial concentration contrasts with unchanged increased discrepancies in other indices of economic capacity. The government is trying to decrease the greatest disparities by means of revenue sharing. North-Rhine Westphalia, Baden-Württemberg, Hesse, and Hamburg, the richer federal states, compensate the relatively poorer states. Revenue sharing is stipulated by Article 107 of the Constitution derived from a constitutional mandate to create similar living conditions in the whole country. In view of this aim federal projects were added to the Constitution in Article 91a. It proposed the participation of the federation in projects within the federal states, i.e., in the expansion and building of universities and university clinics, in the improvement of the regional economic structure, in the improvement of the agricultural structure, and in coastal protection.

In order to reduce the great disparities by improving the infrastructure and the promotion of economy, the conference of the secretaries of regional planning has set up spatial units and indices which reveal the economic stage of development and the federal state's involvement. Again, Schleswig-Holstein, Lower Saxony, the Saarland and, because of their large spatial share, Rhineland-Palatinate and Bavaria stand out in this list. The high percentage of their population in areas which have fallen behind in the general development underlines once more some disparities in the federal structure which have already been pointed out.

An objective appreciation of the situation, however, should not overestimate the regional disparities in the FRG. In comparison with all other countries of similar size, the Federal Republic is quite well-balanced in its regional development. This balance in particular is an advantage for the federal structure. Efforts toward compensation and balance, together with the creation of further federal jurisdiction in new projects, imply the danger of an increased undermining of the federal system itself. Structural dependence of several federal states on the central government and through the states' financial compensation on other states destroys the inner balance of the federal system and leads to a delegation of tasks without giving the citizen a chance for political participation. Thus, the federal states should have a satisfactory economic base. It is certain that general financial aid to compensate for inevitable regional structural differences in the whole federation will never end. But this financial compensation ought to include only those contributions that do not lead to permanent dependency.

This federal responsibility was the justification for reorganization proposals which were submitted in the testimonial of the second committee of experts for a reorganization of the federal territory. Taking into consideration all criteria, the commission proposed two alternatives:

political solutions for North Germany and for the Middle West. For the North, the unification of the two city states and the two federal states, Lower Saxony and Schleswig-Holstein, into one comprehensive northern state was suggested. The second proposal was the creation of two federal states, one in the Northeast including Schleswig-Holstein, Hamburg, and the frontier districts of Lower Saxony south of the river Elbe, and the second in the Northwest with the main areas of Lower Saxony and Bremen. Both solutions would avoid the separation of the Hanseatic cities from their hinterland areas and would create the conditions for a more effective utilization of the economic potential of the northern region. On the basis of a broad development plan this would abolish the gradual economic underdevelopment of North Germany that presently exists.

For the Middle West the commission suggested the unification of Hesse and Rhineland-Palatinate into one federal state. Two alternatives were proposed concerning the integration of parts of this new federal state into Baden-Württemberg. The first plan suggested the unification of Hesse, Rhineland-Palatinate, the Saarland, and the area around Mannhein-Heidelberg. Unification of Baden-Württemberg and Palatinate, the Saarland and the Worms district, resulting in a smaller federal state (Middle West), was offered as a second possibility. Both solutions mean that at the time of the reorganization the new states would have a satisfactory economic base. The abandonment of such possible reorganization schemes since 1974 means that the aim to create states of satisfactory economic base and of a balanced size has been given up. It is still not clear at what time in the future West Berlin will acquire the legal status of a federal state which is desired by its inhabitants. But

since the Eastern side is not yet prepared to accept the
facts and reality of the Berlin case in the same way as the
West has accepted the Oder-Neisse border and the GDR, the
responsibility for Berlin is still vested with the four
occupying powers.

The Berlin Treaty of 1972 has fundamentally improved
the transit traffic from and to West Berlin and visits of the
West Berlin population to East Berlin and the GDR. It
includes two basic statements which are interpreted by both
sides in different ways: (a) West Berlin is not part of the
Federal Republic and is not governed by it. The existing
links with the Federal Republic, however, are to be extended
and further developed. (b) There are no economic or social
differences between the Federal Republic and West Berlin.
In the political sector, West Berlin is represented in the
parliament in Bonn by representatives who do not have a
full vote. A large part of the West Berlin budget is
covered by federal subsidies because the loss of its functions as a capital and its geographical isolation have
caused heavy economic disadvantages, even though West Berlin
is still the largest German industrial city.

CAPITAL AND URBAN SYSTEM

The special situation of Berlin has directly or indirectly
influenced the Federal Republic's problems regarding a
capital. In 1949, when a provisional federal capital was
designated, Bonn was selected because it was believed that
this city would never develop into a really complex capital
with a full spectrum of functions. At that time a reunification of Germany and the reinstatement of Berlin as the
German capital was the unquestioned aim of all Germans in the
West and in the East. This explains why several high-level

federal authorities remained in West Berlin without protest from the East. For this reason, many years after the Federal Republic was founded more civil servants worked in Berlin than in Bonn.

Bonn has remained limited in its importance as a capital. In 1975, 37,800 out of 58,500 government officials worked in other cities. With 8,700 civil servants in ten federal agencies-e.g., the Federal Administration Court, the Federal Health Authority, the Social Insurance and Loan Authority, the Federal Building Administration, the Federal Printing Works, the Federal Environment Authority-West Berlin is still in second place, followed by Frankfurt (Federal Bank, Federal Railways) and Wiesbaden (Federal Statistical Authority, Federal Criminal Investigation Authority). Other Federal authorities are located in Cologne, Hamburg, Munich, Koblenz, Brunswick, Flensburg, and Hannover. Even the highest federal functions are decentralized: The Federal Constitutional Court is in Karlsruhe, the Federal Authority of Employment in Nürnberg, and the Federal Court of Employment in Kassel. This regional dispersion of federal functions is by no means a consequence of Bonn's weak position within the system of cities in the Federal Republic. Decentralization is rooted much deeper and should be considered in the framework of the strong traditional regionalism in Germany, which is only partially represented by the present federal structure.

After the war these large regional centers offered a base for the development of a decentralized system of the highest functions which in the present structure of the states is unequalled in the world. The location of economic organizations, unions, and institutions are not centered around Bonn, but their distribution and grouping points up the leading national centers: Frankfurt/Main is the center of finance and traffic, with the highest number of advertising and travel agencies and the largest airport in Central Europe. Hamburg is the most important export trade and port city. In the Rhine-Ruhr region, Düsseldorf is the center of an increasing number of German and foreign trade associations, exhibitions, and fashion fairs. Other cities have functions which serve the whole counrty. First of all, Munich can rightly be considered the most important cultural center of the Federal Republic with the largest university, serveral research institutions, important theaters, museums, and the motion picture industry. Stuttgart leads in the publishing industry. Hannover has the largest industrial fair and the Academy of Regional Planning, whereas Cologne has the largest number of important insurance companies as well as art galleries, medical organizations, and the headquarters of Lufthansa Airlines.

Summarizing the decentralization of the most important central functions, we can say that there are eight centers with an old and important urban tradition. Three of them were free municipal cities (Hamburg, Frankfurt, and Cologne) and five of them regional capitals of different historical importance (Munich, Stuttgart, Düsseldorf, Hannover, and Bonn). All eight leading cities are now cities of important central functions, as well as regional centers, while industrial conurbations such as the Ruhr region could not acquire important urban functions for the whole federal territory. It is important, however, to avoid viewing the distribution of functions among eight centers as locally isolated and static.

A closer look at this development reveals a tendency toward increased concentration around four regional capitals: the capital region Bonn-Cologne-Düsseldorf, Frankfurt, Munich, and Hamburg. The elevation of Bonn to the new political center of the Federal Republic is certainly the most important modern development. Since the end of World War II, Frankfurt also has strengthened its position as a center of finance and organization. In the 1960s Munich had the greatest increase in importance because of the sheer force of its cultural functions and rising international reputation as a congress and Olympic city. Hamburg had more difficulties. The future of the Hanseatic City is mainly influenced by its supraregional integrative power in North Germany.

The development does not reveal over-concentration on one single leading center but a balance and cooperation among several important centers and regions. It would be wrong to overstate such an interplay because the minor importance played by Bonn as a city when compared to Paris, London, Brussels, Rome, and Vienna has disadvantages. Bonn is not an intellectual and cultural center. It is not a leading capital of a highly developed modern industrial and urban society. It lacks satisfactory infrastructural facilities for international conferences and congresses. Specialized urban services, diplomatic obligations, and capital functions can only be fulfilled in combination with the neighboring centers of Cologne and Düsseldorf. Yet, even these disadvantages reveal only a lively regionalism, its balanced democratic distribution of power, and the close structural links with German history which the Federal Republic acknowledges.

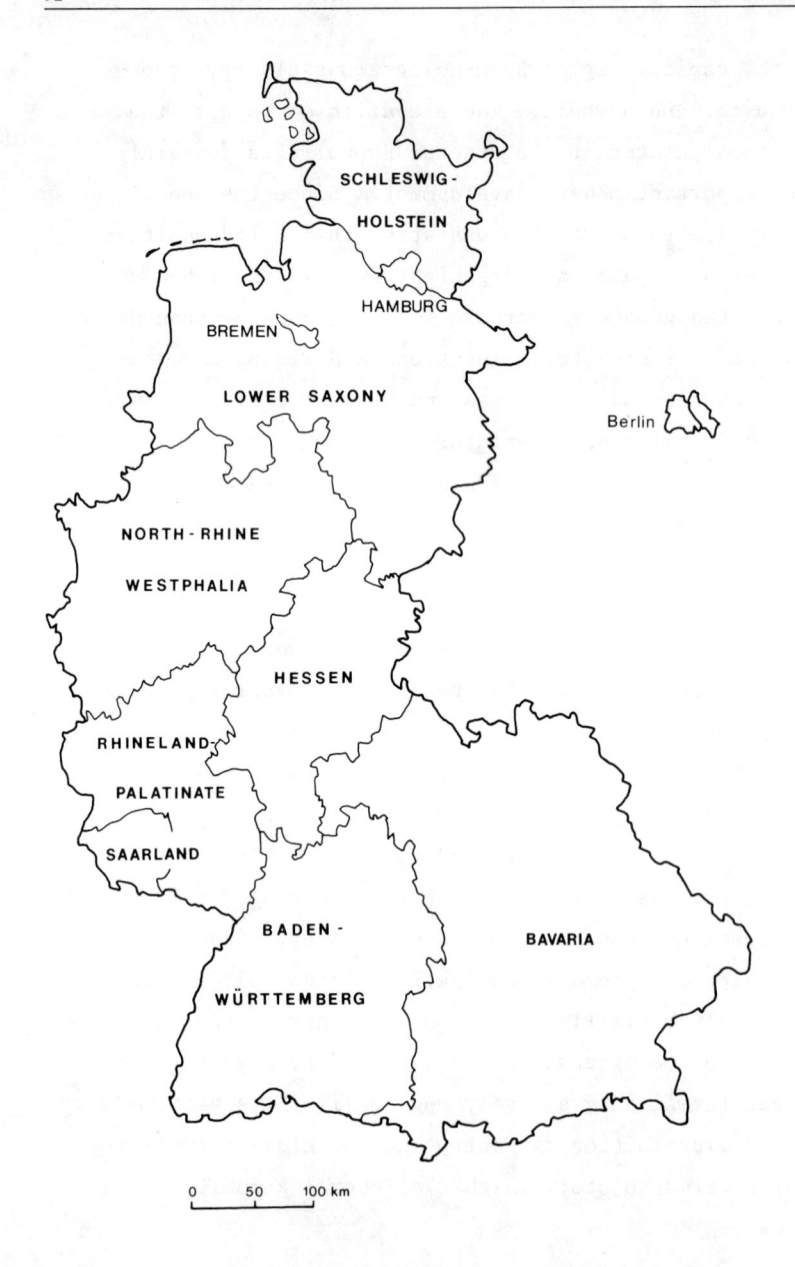

FIG. 3-1. Existing Federal States, 1980.
Bestehende Bundesländer, 1980.

FEDERAL SYSTEM OF THE FRG 93

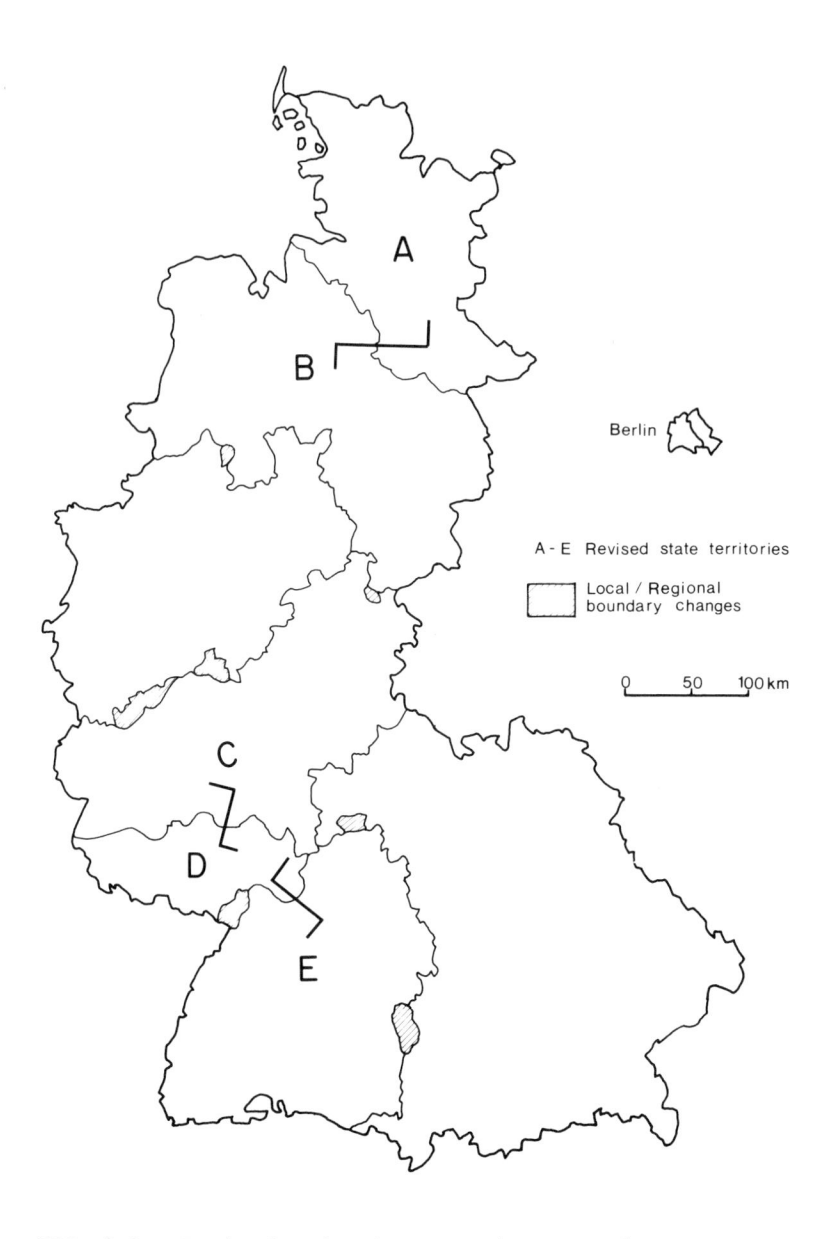

FIG. 3-2. Revised Federal States (Plan 1972).
Neugliederung der Bundesländer (Plan 1972).

REFERENCES

Presse und Informationsamt der Bundesregierung, "Federal Republic of Germany: Federalism," <u>Information</u> 10 (Bonn, 1978).

Sachverständigenkommission für die Neugliederung des Bundesgebietes, <u>Vorschläge zur Neugliederung des Bundesgebietes gemäss Artikel 29 des Grundgesetzes</u> (Bonn, 1972).

Schöller, P., et al., <u>The Settlement System of the Federal Republic of Germany</u>. Report to the Commission on Settlement Systems of the International Geographical Union (Bochum, 1978).

Schäfer, F., <u>Aspects of the Federal System of the Federal Republic of Germany</u>, Sonderdienst SO 3-75 (e) (Bonn-Bad Godesberg: Inter Nations, 1975).

---

*(see p. 79).
 The "qualified majority" is an expression used for the definition under which the Lower House can reject an objection of the Upper House in the procedure concerning adopted bills (see Basic Law, Article 77, paragraph 4). A bill can be adopted by the majority of the members of the Lower House who are present at the time of voting. This is the so-called simple majority (einfache Mehrheit). Parliament is competent to pass bills if more than half of its members (248) are present. A bill can therefore pass the Lower House if there is no objection of the Upper Shouse with a simple majority of 125 votes, where an objection of the Upper House can only be rejected by the Lower House with the "qualified majority" of 249 votes.

CHAPTER 4

CONCEPTIONS AND STRATEGIES ON REGIONAL DEVELOPMENT IN THE FEDERAL REPUBLIC OF GERMANY

KONZEPTIONEN UND STRATEGIEN ZUR RAUMORDNUNGSPOLITIK IN DER BUNDESREPUBLIK DEUTSCHLAND

Dietrich Bartels

Abstract

Since the sixties, the incapacity of a pure free-enterprise economic system has led to increasing demand for regional planning activities by the authorities of Bund and Länder (federation and states).

The distribution of responsibilities between them, however, as provided for by constitutional law, has proven to be inexpedient and has resulted in ineffectual compromise. This situation has been aggravated by the party-political constellation between the governments of Bund and Länder since 1968, which has changed the normally expected division of preferences between the objectives of general national growth and interregional balance. Thus a clear formulation of well-balanced and practicable conceptions for regional planning policies has been hampered.

In this essay an attempt has been made to point out (a) which approaches have been pursued under the circumstances of this strained cooperation between Bund and Länder, (b) that the actual national development has increased the spatial disparities and that by 1990 the interregional equilibrium can be expected to shift increasingly, and (c) which instruments of regional policy are being discussed at present to solve these problems.

Kurzfassung

Die Mängel reiner Marktwirtschaft als Vehikel zur ausgleichenden Steuerung räumlicher Polarisationsprozesse (oder auch die Mängel einer Marktwirtschaft mit starken staatlichen Interventionen ohne Koordination ihrer Raumeffekte) haben in der Bundesrepublik Deutschland zeit den 60er Jahren zu wachsenden Forderungen nach Raumordnungsaktivitäten bei Bundes-

und Länderbehörden geführt. Deren gemäß Grundgesetz gegebene Kompetenzenverteilung erwies sich in dieser Politik jedoch als unzweckmäßig und hat zu unwirksamen Kompromißstrategien geführt.

Diese Situation wurde verschärft durch die parteipolitische Konstellation bei Bundes- und Länderregierungen seit 1968 mit ihrer Umkehrung der an sich zu erwartenden Akzenteverteilung zwischen Gesamtwachstums- versus Gleichverteilungszielen und der damit gegebenen Blockierung der Ausformulierung klar abwägender Zeilkonzeptionen für die Raumordnungspolitik.

Es soll in diesem Beitrag gezeigt werden, (a) welche Ansätze in der spannungsreichen Zusammenarbeit von Bund und Ländern verfolgt worden sind, (b) daß die tatsächliche nationale Entwicklung unterdessen die räumlichen Disparitäten weiter hat wachsen lassen und bis 1990 stark zunehmende Verschiebungen des interregionalen Gleichgewichts zu erwarten sind, und (c) welche Instrumente staatlicher Politik zur Problemlösung gegenwärtig diskutiert werden.

Conceptions and Strategies on Regional Development
in the Federal Republic of Germany

THE CARDINAL PROBLEM OF NATIONAL REGIONAL PLANNING POLICY

Owing to the real spatial immobility of numerous primary or derived production factors, a pure free-enterprise economy results in spatial polarizations of economic development and, consequently, of the general welfare of a nation. These polarizations-contrary to the anticipation of neoclassical regional economic theory--nowhere show the expected long-term tendency toward reduction but rather entail, for the present, unjustifiable social disparities. This holds true both in countries in which the regional equilibrium of development has been gradually suspended and in nations which, while expanding their territory, have included a periphery to complement their existing pole regions. The consequence has been a call for national regional planning policies to compensate for this defect of free-enterprise economics and to harmonize or prevent regional disparities. In the Federal Republic of Germany (FRG) this call became so urgent by the late 1950s that it could no longer be disregarded.

Theoretically the cardinal task of such national regional planning can be formulated as an optimization problem:

$$\Delta W = \sum^{n} \sum^{m} \Delta w_z^r \longrightarrow \text{Max.} \qquad (1.1)$$

subject to the restriction:

$$\sum^{m} \left(w_z^r + \Delta w_z^r \right) \geq a \frac{\sum^{n} \sum^{m} \left(w_z^r + \Delta w_z^r \right)}{n} \qquad (1.2)$$

with: W = national welfare;
     w = elements of welfare (per capita, as a rule) for particular needs 1 ... z ... m, and regions

1 ... r ... n;
= increase within a certain planning period;
a = crucial control parameter (e.g., a = 0.9).

The fundamental conflict between the two basic goals of raising the national general welfare and creating interregional balance is expressed here by the contrast of the objective function with its constraint. A logical equivalent can be conceived by reversing the assignment of the basic goals to the two elements of the models:

$$\sum^n \frac{\sum^m (w_z^r + \Delta w_z^r)}{\sum^n \sum^m (w_z^r + D w_z^r)} \longrightarrow \text{Min.} \qquad (1.1^*)$$

subject to the restriction,

$$\frac{\Delta W}{W} \geq g \qquad (1.2^*)$$

where g = control parameter (e.g., g = 0.04).

Operationalizations of such attempts to identify the cardinal task of national regional planning could be found in German literature on the subject as early as about 1965, but with a reduced definition of general welfare involving concepts of national income only (1):

$$\Delta Y = \sum^r \sum^p \Delta y_i^r \longrightarrow \text{Max.} \qquad (2.1)$$

subject to the two constraints:

CONCEPTIONS AND STRATEGIES

$$\sum_{i}^{p}(y_i^r + \Delta y_i^r) \geq B \cdot \sum_{i}^{n}\sum_{i}^{p}(y_i^r + \Delta y_i^r) \qquad (2,2)$$

$$\sum_{i}^{p} \Delta y_i^r \geq C \qquad (2,3)$$

with: Y = gross national product;
y = shares in the gross national product of economic sectors 1 ... i ... p, and regions 1 ... r ... n;
b,c = crucial control parameter (e.g., b = 0.85; c = 0.0).

If we assume that the gross national product is generated by land, labor, and capital, then the respective increase of the total regional product is composed of:

$$\sum_{i}^{p} \Delta y_i^r = \sum_{i}^{p}\left(\frac{\partial y_i^r}{\partial F} \cdot \Delta F_i^r\right) + \sum_{i}^{p}\left(\frac{\partial y_i^r}{\partial A} \cdot \Delta A_i^r\right) + \qquad (3)$$
$$\sum_{i}^{p}\left(\frac{\partial y_i^r}{\partial C} \cdot \Delta C_i^r\right)$$

with: F, A, C = investment units in the production factors of land, labor, and capital respectively;
a/a = marginal productivity (differential quotient).

The production factors in this simple model can be further disaggregated, or complemented by, for example, factors indicative of the spatial settlement structure or of the spatial situation of the respective region within the national territory.

If the sectoral/regional production functions for the

specific production factors can be estimated with sufficient accuracy, and if calculations are made, for example, over annual periods of planning, then implementation of the cardinal objective of general regional planning policy (or of its subset, economic regional policy (see 2.1), is revealed as the task of directing the location/allocation of mobile production factors across the sectors (including infrastructure domains) and the regions in such a manner that the increase of the gross national product is maximized, without neglecting the other objectives of interregional balance and avoidance of regional shrinkage. If alternative paths of development during a period of several years are included in the model, it should be possible to identify an optimal long-term strategy, which might either achieve the intended interregional balance immediately, maximize national product, or seek a combination of both. Besides the development potential available, other real or normative restrictions (such as limitations on regional land uses or limitations on population migration rates) may be introduced into the model as additional constraints. These bring the model closer to reality, and are applicable as long as the algorithm provides positive solutions with regard to the objective function in mind. Apart from the gross national product, other elements of welfare may also be introduced as well as interregional transfers. The latter can compensate (at least up to some preestablished maximum) for marked interregional differences which may have to be tolerated in favor of a high general level of national development.

Approaches of this type, based on an area division of the FRG into thirty-eight regions, have been available since the beginning of the seventies in the first drafts of a

Bundesraumordnungsprogramm or Federal Regional Planning Program (BROP). We shall not discuss in detail the practical problems involved with real application, which range from the identification of existing regional factor potentials and their spatial mobility, through the estimation of regional production functions, to weighing the different degrees of fulfillment of the partial welfare demands. It should be emphasized, however, that the actual application of rationalized formulations of the cardinal goals of national planning policy, with their theoretically clear quantification of the opportunity costs between alternative models of general spatial organization, have encountered grave difficulties. These are typical of the FRG as a federal political system, but also occur in a similar form in other countries with pluralistic interests. For this reason approaches of this kind have not been pursued until now in the FRG.

THE INSTITUTIONAL AND POLITICAL CONSTELLATION IN THE FRG

A free-enterprise economy, as mentioned above, did not exist in the FRG during the era of Ludwig Erhard, nor has it existed since. Rather, the government has been, and continues to be, involved in many economic (and infrastructural) activities, whether in the form of state enterprise management or structural or business cycle policies and their public financing. Indeed, public expenditures and transfers in the FRG, which presently stand at nearly 40 percent of the gross national product, have perhaps reached a critical point for the economic system. However, until a short time ago, little was known about the regional effects of these government activities and in the last twenty years a considerable number of independent and poorly coordinated regional programs have been developed by various government departments responsible for particular fields of intervention. Their goals were at best aimed toward optimizing only partial aspects of the regionalized general welfare objective for such sectors as transportation, agriculture, or full employment. It has been impossible to put this political reality into a coordinating location-allocation model of the type outlined above because of the absence of a generalized view of the situation. A unifying conception of Raumordnungspolitik (ROP)-large scale regional planning policy-particularly failed on the level of the federation, as well as on the level of the individual states within the FRG, because of the weakness of the rather young departments of ROP compared with the sectoral planning authorities, which were already well established and much better equipped with planning instruments and financial funds. The institutionalized (although not yet fully programmed) boards of regional economic structural policy within the economic ministries of the federation and states are the best examples of this.

On the other hand the FRG is not a unified state, but a federation of ten states (not including Berlin), which have hardly been willing to embark on a coherent federal ROP as long as they could expect to advance the general welfare (or, at least, the total gross national product) of their own territory-with the instruments and potentials at their disposal-more autonomously and effectively than would be possible in a national framework.

Thus, for the strategy of ROP to be pursued by a single state, the basic model given above by equation 1.1 must be converted as follows:

$$\Delta W^R = \sum_z^n \Delta w_z^R \longrightarrow Max. \qquad (4.1)$$

subject to the restruction:

$$W^R + \Delta W^R = h \cdot \frac{\sum^n (W^r + \Delta W^r)}{n} \qquad (4.2)$$

with:

W^R = general welfare of state R as a part of the national territory

h = parameter corresponding to the threshold of the federation's and state's tolerance of eventual development advantages in state R.

As long as the margins of action of an individual state within the national framework have not been fully utilized or even defined, obviously the state has no interest in seeing its own development concerns treated as a lateral minimum condition rather than a core objective function. In the FRG this is particularly true since the Constitution assigns to the states, as compared to the federation, a higher degree of competence and consequently more instrumental power for implementing their intentions. This power, however, is limited by the development potential which is available in the respective state, and this normally is greatest in the most developed states.

For these reasons a coherent ROP with homogeneous objectives for the FRG as a whole depends on the good will and common sense of all authorities involved in the horizontal and vertical cooperation of their departments. Generally, the need for this must be stressed by the central institutions of the federation. However, there are many political problems vying for attention in the FRG, and ROP is only one of those. The federal government and Parliament are not strongly disposed toward ROP (a fact to be explained later), yet a concern is essential to begin the indispensable but complicated coordination of the sectoral departments (for example, under the auspices of the planning staff of the special board of the federal chancellor, which is largely inactive). And the antagonism between federation and states, which is anchored in the Constitution, has increased considerably over the last few years since it has become associated with the permanent confrontation between the two major political parties in the FRG.

Since 1968 the federal government has been led by the SPD (Social Democrats) in conjunction with the FDP (Liberals), whereas the majority of states-including those economically more dominant-are governed by the CDU (Christian Democratic Union). The result has been that the Upper House often acts as a decisive government in addition to the government of the Federal Republic. Because both political parties operate on the federal level as well as on the state level, the SPD in particular is compelled to consider its own electoral chances in the states. This means that the SPD is not able to advocate and influence on the federal level an appropriate ROP aimed toward general national growth. This would not fit well with the political program of the SPD, which emphasizes social justice, including interregional balance. On the contrary, a growth objective for ROP harmonizes much more with the program of the CDU, which is based on the idea of free enterprise, providing only subsidiary social relief of interregional balance within the territory of the federation or the respective states.

It would exceed this essay's limits to explain the much more complicated distribution of special interests within the political climate of the FRG. But this division of roles between CDU and SPD results, of course, in some rather remarkable conflicts which would be impossible if ROP had succeeded in becoming an overall societal concern with a consistent strategy for solving its problems. For example, as a CDU-dominated state, the comparatively poor Schleswig-Holstein at the periphery of the FRG has to remain a protagonist of increasing spatial polarization within the national territory, whereas Hamburg, an SPD-dominated state, must defend this highly developed city-state against interregional equalization with the "foreign" surroundings of its agglomeration.

THE FEDERAL SPATIAL PLANNING PROGRAM (BROP)

Despite these circumstances, many ROP activities have been carried out over the last twenty years, and in 1975 the federal government, after a long wrestling period with its partners, approved a Federal Spatial Planning Program. However, under the conditions described above, initial intentions have been reduced, in many cases to the smallest common denominator to avoid a political fiasco. Accordingly, the BROP remains extremely vague and without practical stipulations as to its future implementation. Nevertheless, it contains some basic intellectual approaches which are of interest for analytical work in regional science in the FRG.

The BROP aims at creating the preconditions for "equal chances of life" in all parts of the nation. Thus, equal social conditions are the chief goal. To secure this goal, the ROP emphasizes avoiding interregional differences by improving the infrastructure, the quality of the environment, and the economic structure in all regions. As a fourth, supplementary objective, an efficient settlement structure is considered necessary in order to guarantee in all parts of the nation both minimum agglomeration economies and reasonable maximum distances between places providing residential, employment, service, and recreational opportunities.

By coordinating the investment of all funds of the federation and states affecting spatial structure (the goal of these funds is understood as the "development potential available"), the BROP is to influence the planning and the measures of all departments and boards, particularly those implementing regional economic support and infrastructure policies. This involves improving the structure of those regions whose development is furthest below the national average, and counteracting undesirable trends of national spatial differentiation. In particular it is desirable to avoid depleting low density areas that are particularly deficient, which would result in social discrimination of the remaining population.

The implementation of these objectives is especially to prevent five large areas, because of the deficiencies of their structures, from being depleted with increasing speed. The result will be that within their boundaries social discrimination of the remaining population will grow.

These main objectives, however, do not assume concrete form in the BROP, as may be illustrated by five examples which constitute the principal statements of the BROP.

(a) The first priority of the BROP is evidently not to maximize total national growth but to create interregional equality of life. However, it says nothing about how to operationalize this goal, especially in regard to the well-known theoretical problems of the admissibility of substitutions between conflicting elements of the general "quality of life" concept, such as between income and environmental pollution. In 1976, however, the federal government adopted a proposal of its Beirat für Raumordnung (the legal advisory board for ROP) to specify minimum standards for each objective of the BROP. These standards include maximum distances to various opportunities and minimum services to be provided by central places, as well as complete equilibrium of interregional population migration. However, this declaration of numerous unalterable and constant minimum values for all regions does not solve the problem of substitutions between elements of overall "life quality" and leaves ROP without any direction over and above these minimum standards, such as policies for a spatial organization more in favor of total national growth (except where the minimum indicators are formulated dynamically as negative differences compared with the federal average). The advisory board also left open the problem of weighing the indicators and, accordingly, of ranking the priorities for reaching the minimum standards in particular regions.

(b) Insofar as the BROP provides actual or normative information for individual regions, it relies on a set of thirty-eight Gebietseinheiten (areal units). However, internally these are very spatious and heterogeneous. Therefore the entire set is de facto impractical for planning. In addition, the areal units are not congruent with the set of sixty-nine planning regions which the states have embodied by law and which are much more important and practical in applied regional planning. However, this situation seems to be the intention of the federation, in order to avoid any direct judgment on the adequacy or inadequacy of current development programs. Therefore "the retarded regions with structural inequities" identified by the BROP are units of little informative value.

(c) As a spatial organization concept aimed at overcoming large-scale disparities, the BROP proposes that Entwicklungszentren (development centers) be designated and supported within those retarded regions. Although this is obviously intended to go beyond basic central-place concepts to a theory of spatial economic development, there are no references to growth pole theory or practice (2). No attempt is made to specify the motor units or the agglomeration economies of these development centers or the expected spillover effects to the respective hinterlands. On the contrary, the BROP only discusses very simple pragmatic concepts of general spatial concentration favoring certain larger places with a minimum threshold population. The population is only referred to obliquely, but may conform to the standards of 100,000 to 250,000 inhabitants as recommended by the research literature.

(d) As far as the interregional equality of life priority will allow, certain functional differentiations between regions of higher and lower population density are permitted. Vorrangfunktionen (areas with priority functions) may be declared for such functions as agriculture, water supply or recreation, although only in sparsely populated areas. However, nowhere is this idea thoroughly pursued in the BROP.

(e) Compared with the customary procedure of elaborating objective conceptions of ROP without any time line or financing plans-a practice the Great Hessenplan of 1971 was the first to break-BROP represents remarkable progress inasmuch as the accomplishment of its objectives is conceived, at least in principle, in relation to the already mentioned development potential available to the federation and the states. But how this potential is to be distributed optimally among different development measures and regions according to a strategic time frame is not considered by the BROP. That is, all references of a strategic nature are lacking.

SPATIAL ORGANIZATION CONCEPTIONS IN ACTUAL REGIONAL SUPPORT PROGRAMS

The support programs of the federation and states which are explicitly understood to be a part of ROP activities, apart from the BROP which has not yet been put into direct action, include some with purely pragmatic political motives, but also a number with theoretical spatial organization concepts. The most important are as follows:

(a) The oldest and until today the most important is the central-place model, which has gone beyond its classical function of explaining actual settlement structure and has assumed the normative role of directing measures to enlarge numerous aspects of infrastructure as well as exercising a certain control over spatial population distribution in the form of land use and building supervision. In 1968, the Ministerkonferenz für Raumordnung (MKRO, a board to coordinate ROP between the federation and the states) passed a model of a four-level system of central places. Subsequently, however, this has been differentially interpreted by the individual states. The minimum population thresholds for "superior," "medium," "inferior," and "mini" centers and their references either to actual or to normative future conditions vary. The lists of central-place installations and capacities to be created or safeguarded are different. Also, the maximum distances within the hinterlands and certain regulations which allow for exceptions have been applied much differently in order to fit into the historical structure in the different parts of the nation. Because the principles behind support policies for developing the designated central places also vary from state to state, the importance of this concept for actual ROP in the FRG over the last ten to fifteen years can be emphasized only in a general sense.

(b) Playing a supplementary role to that of central-place theory is the conception of spatial <u>Entwicklungsachsen</u> (growth axes). This emerged in 1964 in the first development program of the state of North Rhine-Westphalia and some time earlier in the regional planning of Greater Hamburg. There it referred to the problem of avoiding uncontrolled spatial agglomeration expansion around the big cities, a problem which should be managed by diverting agglomeration development in the form of "axes" extending along main traffic arteries. Since the spatial pattern of central places, even in its normative future version, entailed excessive travel distances and was incomplete in the peripheral regions, the conception of development axes, however, provided a means to complement the intended central-place structure through the declaration of development axes as rails for the expansion of agglomeration cores into peripheral regions. However, the processes of transmission implicit in this hypothetical model have never been clarified. Thus, a certain euphoria, and without consideration of the actual development potentials, a great number of development axes forming a hierarchical system were generously incorporated into regional plans until about 1972.

Identification of these axes was primarily the responsibility of the states, as documented rather distinctly by the collage of uncoordinated normative spatial patterns for the individual networks of central places and development axes of the states.

The main criticism of the central-place concept as a basis for ROP refers primarily to the known assumptions of the Christaller model merely as an explanatory approach. Moreover, it is inadvisable to favor the present central-place pattern, inherited from preindustrial times, as the normative plan to meet the spatial organization needs of a society which will be divided largely along functional lines by the beginning of the twenty-first century. This criticism refers, above all, to the under-dimensioning of the central places and to the overly specific division of hinterlands. In addition, it has become illusory to hope to attract more trade and industry to the central places of sparsely populated areas and to anticipate strong spillover effects into their hinterlands simply by improving the general infrastructure. Much capital has been invested in prestigous projects without creating long-term benefits or inducing dynamics. Nevertheless, in fifteen years of central-place support activities by the federal government, much progress has been made toward providing the population with adequate infrastructures. In some respects one can speak today of a ubiquitous level of infrastructural development within the FRG.

(c) One fundamental goal of ROP has been and is to bring underdeveloped areas (zurückgebliebene Gebiete) and rural areas (ländliche Gebiete) up to the level of densely populated areas (Verdichtungsräume), as the federal Law on Regional Planning of 1965 has labelled the three main types of regions within the nation. However, until now the rural areas have not been defined, and the delimitations of underdeveloped areas have been debated and revised again and again.

For a certain number of regional support programs covering retarded regions in all parts of the national territory, a fifty-fifty division of the financial costs between the federation and the states has been in effect, in spite of the much larger implementing competence of the states. Generally, an agreement on one or the other of these joint tasks of ROP could not be achieved unless the program provides that all states will share in the federal funds in a manner proportional to their general size and not, unfortunately, to their respective degree of underdevelopment. Since the comparatively poorer states often have trouble contributing their half of the support costs, they tend to restrict the volume of the total program. Thus, many common development programs do not focus their main efforts on the least developed areas in the nation.

This is particularly true for the joint tasks for improvement of the regional economic structure. Programs within this framework created or safeguarded more than 1 million jobs between 1971 and 1979, at a total expense of about DM 8 billion. This was primarily spent to subsidize industrial capital investment. It has contributed to retarding spatial polarization, but at a rather high price. The program, which initially applied to no less than twenty-one underdeveloped regions (called Regionale Aktionsprogramme) with weak infrastructures in all states, now covers 61 percent of the entire national territory and includes 36 percent of the population of the FRG.

Some improvements have gradually occurred in the spatial

units used by this program. By 1972 economic development efforts had already become concentrated on 327 Schwerpunktorte (focal places), and by 1975 a total reorganization had been effected in favor of the cores of weakly structured Arbeitsmarktregionen (labor market regions). Since 1975 a set of 175 labor market regions has covered the entire national territory and has been declared the specific regional basis of reference for economic regional policy, with its main objective being to achieve quantitatively and qualitatively "equal" regional labor markets. These regions were organized, however, without any reference to the previously constructed normative network of central places and their hinterlands. And since other planning authorities rely on other sets of regionalizations, the famous coherence of federal ROP, which is more invoked than prescribed in the BROP, does not exist at this time, even with regard to the spatial partitions.

THE TURNING POINT

Since 1975 a Trendwende or turning point in the development of ROP is often spoken of in the FRG. This expression refers to at least three factors, of which only the first shows a real change in trend.

(a) Planning fatigue. Since the first laws on ROP were promulgated at the federal and state level at the beginning of the sixties, regional planning in the FRG has developed into an extremely perfect instrument. There is hardly another field of public administration which has developed such detailed ideas about the processes of planning and implementation of plans and has legitimized all its steps through laws and decrees. Even the defects of not having linked ROP to time lines and financing perspec-

tives have been at least realized since the beginning of
the so-called "midterm financial planning" of the federation
and states and will gradually be eliminated as priorities
are set. However, compared with the perfection of this apparatus, the success in carrying out the plans and in approaching the chosen objectives of ROP has been very slight. The
poor results of the actual ROP have had a sobering effect,
and there has been wide-scale dissillusionment about the
number and type of planning instruments and potentials
available to the government. Paralleling the big economic
recession of 1974, all this has led to a lasting resignation
about the chances of ROP affecting all planning institutions
of the FRG. The lack of individual responsibility for
the so-called "common tasks" is an additional critical
point.

There is an old quotation from Bertolt Brecht which has
a rather modern application in the present context:

Ja mach nur einen Plan,	Yes, only make a plan
sei nur ein grosses Licht	only be a great light
Und mach dann noch 'nen zweiten Plan:	And then make a second plan
geh'n tun sie beide nicht	neither will function

(From <u>Lied von der Unzulänglichkeit menschlichen Strebens</u>,
"Song of the Inadmissibility of Human Struggle.")

(b) <u>Decline in the number of places of employment</u>. Projections of the employment structure in the FRG up to 1990
have indicated that structural adjustment to alterations in
the international division of labor, the diminishing rate of
economic growth, and major technological changes will cause
not only a decline in the total number of jobs, but also
extremely disadvantageous shifts in their spatial distribution. There are indications, for example, that the more

qualified jobs will be concentrated in a few areas of agglomeration.

(c) <u>Rise in the number of potential workers</u>. Simultaneously, a considerable decrease in the total German population has been predicted for the first time, a decrease which will continue at an ever more rapid pace until the turn of the century. In contrast, a big rise in the number of potential workers is to be expected during the next ten years, which will not be reduced to its present level again before 1990. Regional projections have shown that the mean natural decrease in population of about 5 percent until 1990 will have an above average effect on the agglomeration areas, whereas the increase in employment potential will occur particularly in the peripheral rural areas. Assuming there is no out-migration, this may result in unemployment rates of 10 percent and more, even if full employment in the densely populated areas is assumed.

To this "turning point period" belongs a growing awareness of the problems of migration from the cores to the border zones of the agglomerations with their consequences of desolation of the old cores and excessive demands for new infrastructures in the suburbs, which are endangered by settlement disarray. Furthermore, an increasing perception has emerged of eventual problems involved in providing sufficient energy and of ecological balance in the environment. All this has contributed to the sense of a turning point in ROP, but will not be discussed here in more detail.

PRESENT DISCUSSION OF THE OBJECTIVES OF ROP

On behalf of the federal government between 1971 and 1977 an independent commission to study economic and social change compiled a report on future general societal policies, including some rather distinct proposals for a reorientation of ROP. While the report retained the formula of "equality of life in all parts of West Germany," it pleaded for (a) accommodation of the existing settlement structure to modern life requirements and not for its mere conservation, (b) a more pronounced allocation of special functions to the individual regions by differentiating the regional objectives of ROP in order to increase the total national growth and welfare, (c) within the scope of this interregional division of functions the FRG must make allowances for comparatively high interregional migration, (d) rather large interregional financial transfers are indispensable in order to compensate for inevitable differences in infrastructure and productive capacity. Altogether the report, which has been the subject of considerable discussion, documents a distinct withdrawal from what it calls "old-fashioned ideas of equilibrium."

Until now this impulse to reconsider and specify the objectives of ROP has hardly been considerate, at least not at the federal level. Although it was admitted immediately after publication that an official extrapolation of the 1975 BROP was urgently needed, little was done. Contrary to the above-mentioned report of the commission, the Raumordnungsbericht (report on present regional structures) of the federal government in 1978 emphasized distinctly the continued validity of the established objectives of avoiding large-scale interregional migration, attaining living conditions as equal as possible across the nation, and accordingly, placing a regional labor market policy in the foreground of future ROP in order to obtain equal changes of employment. However it seems "indicative that this report

CONCEPTIONS AND STRATEGIES

is now to be submitted every four years instead of every two years. Also the claim of the former BROP total coordination of all spatially relevant planning activities by the federation and the states is clearly diminished by the 1978 report."

Current thinking on ROP contains the following comparatively new elements:

(a) Tacit renunciation of further support for the numerous "inferior" and "mini" central places formerly designated but having no special "economizing spatial strategies" beyond the thinning out of infrastructure supply as decreasing population figures perhaps might suggest.

(b) Renunciation of the interpretation of designated development areas beyond their real communication function, as future concentration axes, but the planning of supplementary axes of communication (so-called <u>Querachsen</u> traverse axes) between smaller places within peripheral regions in order to strengthen or develop cooperative spatial production systems between these places by linking together comparatively dispersed basic industries within rural regions.

(c) Comparative intensification of the development potential of peripheral rural areas by the gradual creation of new localization economies through the concentration of specified branches with nationwide or at least large-scale market areas. This idea of creating specific localization economies in appropriate places, each specializing in its own way, supplements earlier ideas which have become rather unrealistic: those of developing efficient general urban economies in the inferior centers of even the sparsely populated areas, which as a matter of fact will never be able to exceed certain size limits.

(d) Deliberations about supporting a few solitary cities on the periphery as development centers of between 200,000 and 300,000 inhabitants in regions which lack superior centers within the normative central-place network. The declared norm is one superior center in every 7,000 km^2, which are also to act as cores of the specified regional labor markets, such as in the Emsland or in the region of Frankenberg. In this process, the planning authorities hope to profit from the observed appeal of such solitary cities to one group of migrants or another.

(e) More emphasis on the ecological reserve capacities which are only available in certain retarded regions through reducing minimum environmental standards in densely populated areas. The supposition is that the adverse environmental effects of shifting jobs to the periphery may be worse than expanding employment within the already densely developed areas.

(f) First attempts to come to terms with the political movement of environmentalism (the so-called "green lists"), which, beyond its primary intention of environmental protection, pleads for the reduction of the interregional division of labor, which is thought to have been pushed to extremes, and for the restitution of small, autonomous "cellular" living spaces with an interregionally balanced supply of all of life's needs. This discussion should result in a more detailed and clearer conception of balanced regions—between spatial units which are too large and those which are too small—within a hierarchical system of distinctly defined overall functional regions.

PRESENT DISCUSSION OF THE INSTRUMENTS OF ROP

The growing perception of the limited success of ROP as hitherto practiced has generated considerable effort to construct more efficient planning instruments. Emphasis has been on instruments which do not increase only the supply and productive capacities in the retarded areas, but also and above all raise the private and public demand occurring in these regions, or which do not directly refer to the peripheral regions, but are aiming at a slowing down of continued concentration of development in densely settled areas. However, controlling land use and building activities, as has been attempted around most major European metropolitan areas, is judged less appropriate because it is ineffective.

The current discussion in the Beirat für Raumordnung (the advisory council for ROP) unpublished thus far but already welcomed by the federal government, proposes supplementing the present ROP support programs of the federation and states by:

(a) A special agglomeration tax in the densely populated areas which might take the form of a tax covering productively employed land, (with the least possible mutual substitution effects) labor, and capital, and/or a regionally differentiated motor vehicle tax, and/or a sewage duty. All of these taxes should correspond to the comparatively high social costs within the agglomeration areas which today are borne by the federal government and other public organizations.

(b) The regional differentation of wage taxes (as a distinct part of income taxes) aimed at a comparative rise in available income of employees and thus a rise of consumption demand in the retarded areas. Currently existing discounts of 30 percent on the wage tax in West Berlin and the differentations in the Cantonal income taxes in Switzerland are cited as evidence for the practicability of this measure.

(c) The decentralization of the location of certain federal and state boards and administrations which do not require personal contacts with the public in order to shift their direct or indirect effective demand potentials to the retarded areas. The direct and indirect impact on the respective regional gross products is expected to be much greater than the additional costs that decentralization will generate within these administrations. The possible volume of these shifts may involve as many as half a million employees.

(d) The adjustment of financial transfers between communes in favor of sparsely populated retarded areas.

Some of these new measures could really have a greater impact on the evolution of the spatial structure of the FRG than we have seen from all the efforts of ROP over the last ten years. However, the power of the federation, as limited by the Constitution and by the political situation, to bring these new instruments into action must be viewed with considerable scepticism.

THE PRESENT DISCUSSION OF THE POLITICAL SCOPE OF ROP IN THE FRG

In addition to the above discussions of the objectives and instruments of ROP which are to be modified, the "turning point" has generated a number of more fundamental criticisms regarding the general political dilemma of any ROP in the FRG. The suggestions for reform, resulting from these criticisms, may be summarized as four main models:

(a) <u>Further development of engineering planning</u>. Advocates of this model are convinced of the potential for success through updating and perfecting the existing system of nationwide regional planning by expanding and detailing the implementation regulations. The necessity for improving horizontal and vertical coordination of the boards involved is pointed out, as well as the inadequate specificity of planning objectives, the lack of effective instruments, the waste of support funds because of badly delimited regional units, and the unproven basic assumptions of cause and effect within a spatial economic and social system. Above all, changes in the organization of the departments and a redistribution of their diverse responsibilities are recommended, if necessary, by alteration of the Constitution.

(b) <u>Neoclassical restoration of the economic system</u>. This line of criticism, advocated for example in 1977-1978 by the "<u>Sachverständigenrat</u>" (a council of experts to judge on general economic development) emphasizes the priority of productivity-oriented national growth. This would be attainable only by the restoration of free markets for productive factors. Like all government interventions in the mechanism of market-controlled factor-allocation, ROP is considered incapable of recognizing and enforcing optimal allocations in a sufficient manner. Accordingly, micro-interventions by decentralized small sector planning authorities should at most be tolerated, rather than extensive and rigid federal systems capable of being steered. ROP therefore should be restricted to furnishing regional data to orient the markets and to social short-term bottlenecks.

(c) <u>Regional planning and policies aimed at humanizing the world of labor</u>. This position, initiated by the trade-union movement, has a criticism of the objectives of present economic regional policy at its core. This system is said to be directed above all toward increasing capitalistic economic capacity. Thus national production is based less and less on labor as a production factor and more and more on mobile capital which, in the FRG, can be reinvested at a rate of at least DM 150 billion per year (thus allowing reexamination of the respective production locations). These locational decisions, it is argued, are made only in the interests of the optimal exploitation of capital and no longer in favor of the welfare of working people at the places of residence. The secondary transfer of some portion of the gross national product to peripheral regions is considered insufficient to compensate for the unredeemable right to jobs worthy of human beings wherever they choose to live. Thus, a regionalized "revitalization of the world of labor" should be declared the main goal of ROP.

(d) "Activist" regional policies. Exponents of this view, who are found particularly in political science, argue that the limited impact of ROP (i.e., the deadlock situation of ROP) results from its failure to compete successfully with other societal objectives (3). Compared with many political goals, which involve the specialized interests of a small constituency, ROP requires broad overall public support. Because such broad participation can seldom be attained, the complex ROP problem has become a typical "nondecision sector" of politics, and the actual evolution of the spatial structure of the nation has become the passive result of decisions made in all the other sectors of society.

The solution, according to this perspective, is to open up ROP by identifying those groups of individuals who are the true "victims of space," such as employees in rural areas, inhabitants of city cores endangered by social erosion, or the petty bourgeois of declining small boroughs. These groups should be mobilized by politicizing their claims and demands. The resulting formations of regional political interests should far exceed the spontaneous and momentary actions of local protest groups (Bürgerinitiativen). By means of appropriate political alliances to counter existing spatial-dominant centers of political power, this should lead to a new "activist" ROP which will be based on regional interests instead of being mastered by bureaucrats.

In summary, national regional planning and policy in the Federal Republic is not a comparatively strong theme in federal politics. It has relatively limited influence, especially compared with its objectives, which are very broad but still rather vaguely defined. Generally, it has not utilized the finding regarding spatial processes which regional theory and empirical regional science has provided or tried to offer. Considering the forecasts for significant changes in the spatial structure of the FRG, this situation is not satisfying.

NOTES

1. Thoss, R., "Ein Vorschlag zur Koordinierung der Regionalpolitik," *Jahrbücher für Nationalökonomie und Statistic* 182 (1969), 490-529.

2. Uhlmann, J., "Die 'Entwicklungszentren' des Bundesraumordnungsprogramms: Wachstumszentren oder pragmatische Verdichtungskonzept?" *Schriftenreihe IREUS*, Vol. 2 (Stuttgart, 1979).

3. Naschold, F., *Alternative Raumpolitik* (Kronsberg: Athenäum, 1978).

REFERENCES

Bachrach, P., and M. S. Baratz, *Power and Poverty* (Baltimore: Oxford University Press, 1970).

Beirat für Raumordnung, *Empfehlungen von 16.6.76*, edited by Bundesminister für Raumordnung, Bauwesen und Städtebau (Bonn: Presseamt Bundesregierung, 1976).

Bundesforschungsanstalt für Landeskunde und Raumordnung, *Informationen zur Raumentwicklung*, 6 issues per year (Bonn).

Bundesraumordnungsbericht 1978 der Bundesregierung und Materialien hierzu. Schriftenreihe des Bundesministers für Raumordnung, Bauwesen und Städte bau, No. 06.040 (Bonn, 1979).

Bundesminister für Raumordnung, Bauwese und Städtebau, ed., *Bundesraumordnungsprognose 1990*, Schriftenreihe No. 06.012 (Bonn, 1977).

Bundesraumordnungsprogramm 1975 (BROP), Schriftenreihe des Bundesministers für Raumordnung, Bauwesen und Städtewesen, No. 06.002 (Bonn, 1975).

Buttler, F., et al., *Grundlagen der Regionalökonomie* (Reinbek: Rowolt, 1977).

Kommission für wirtschaftlichen und sozialen Wandel, *Wirtschaftlicher und sozialer Wandel in der Bundesrepublik Deutschland*, Gesamtgutachten (Göttingen: Schwartz, 1977).

Stiens, G., "Vorausgesagte Entwicklungen und neue Strategien für den ländlichen Raum," *Informationen zur Raumentwicklung* 6 (1977), 139-152.

CHAPTER 5

FEDERAL OUTLAYS AND REGIONAL DEVELOPMENT

BUNDESAUSGABEN UND REGIONALENTWICKLUNG

Clyde E. Browning

Abstract

The emergency of regional rivalries has become a striking aspect of American geography in the last decade. Much of the rivalry centers on the distribution of federal funds. Until ten years ago, the geographical allocation of federal funds was largely unknown; but now, annual reports give the federal spending by program for states, counties, and cities over 25,000. This essay reviews the background of the regional rivalry that has centered on the claim of Northeastern spokesmen that the growth of the Sunbelt has been financed by federal dollars from their region. The distribution of federal outlays is examined by state, region (the Sunbelt, the U.S. Core Area, and the West), and major budget categories. The main conclusion is that the regional debate has been misleading. If there is a split between the have and have-not regions in terms of federal spending, it is an East-West rather than North-South alignment. The essay also discussed the difficulties of working with outlay data and measuring the economic impact of federal spending, the conclusions of some previous studies on the subject, and a brief case study of the impact of federal spending using the example of Washington, D.C.

Kurzfassung

Im vorigen Jahrzehnt wurde das Hervortreten regionaler Konkurrenzen ein auffallender Aspekt der amerikanischen Geographie. Viel dieser Konkurrenz konzentriete sich auf die Verteilung der Bundesmittel. Bis vor zehn Jahren war die geographisch differenzierte Zuweisung von Bundesmitteln grösstenteils unbekannt, aber jetzt stellen jährliche Berichte die Bundesauslagen nach Programmen für Staaten, Landkreise und Städte mit mehr als 25,000 Einwohnern dar. Dieser Aufsatz blickt auf die Vorgeschichte der regionalen Debatte zurück, unter-

sucht die Verteilung der Bundesausgaben, erläutert die
Probleme einer solchen Analyse, und führt den Fall von Washington, D. C. als Beispiel der Wirkung der Bundesausgaben.

Federal Outlays and Regional Development

The role of the federal government in the affairs of individuals, institutions, and regions in the United States has assumed an unprecedented importance. Almost every facet of our lives is increasingly affected in some way by the actions and authority of the federal government. It is appropriate, therefore, that we examine the regional aspect of the increasingly important role of the federal government. We are not the first to confront the topic. Never before in our nation's history has there been such interest and controversy over federal involvement at the regional level. This essay will examine primarily the impact of federal outlays on regional development.

THE BACKGROUND

A century ago the current controversy over federal spending on the regional level would have been unheard of because of the size of the federal establishment. The budget was small ($268 million in 1880), the number of employees modest, and the largest item in the budget was the post office. By 1940, however, the federal government was on the threshold of an enormous expansion (Table 5-1). Even when allowance is made for inflation and the growing importance of insurance trust funds (chiefly social security) the thirty-six-year increase in spending has been impressive.

I began a study of the geography of federal outlays eight years ago with the assumption that the consequence of these trends was the increasing ability of the federal government to shape the economic geography of the United States (1).

TABLE 5-1. Federal Outlays: Per Capita and as Percent of GNP, 1930-1976.
Bundesausgaben: Pro Kopf und als Perzent des GNP, 1930-1976.

Year	Federal Outlays*	Per Capita Federal Outlays	Outlays as a Percent of GNP
1930	3.3	27	3.1
1940	9.5	72	10.0
1950	42.6	282	16.1
1960	92.2	512	18.5
1970	196.6	968	20.5
1976	358.9	1677	22.8

*Billions of Dollars

Source: U.S. Bureau of the Census, Statistical Abstract of the United States (Washington, D.C.: U.S. Government Printing Office, 1978), Table 403, p. 247.

The traditional economic geographies reviewed the production of pigs, iron and steel, and retailing but ignored the increasing important role of federal spending in contributing to local economies. The classical location economists were no better; their theories were formulated before the advent of large-scale government spending. At the conclusion of the study I found the original assumption had not been confirmed by the analysis. There were low correlations between federal outlays, population growth, and per capita incomes. High per capita federal outlays were not necessarily a prerequisite for growth or high income levels, nor their presence an assurance of the occurrence of growth and high incomes. The complexity of the federal programs, the heterogeneity of the areal units employed (especially some states), and the broad categories often used combined to make generalizations difficult: some large states had high per capita outlays, but so did some small states; some rich states had high per capita outlays but so did some poor states; some agricultural states had high per capita outlays but so did some nonagricultural states, etc.

Yet, despite the low correlations, I was not ready to dismiss the federal outlays as unimportant in regional and local economic development. The periphery of the country (excepting the northern boundary) has enjoyed considerable growth the past thirty years, and in part this growth has been a consequence of massive federal government spending. Undoubtedly growth would have occurred in the periphery but I doubt if it would have reached anything like its present level without the federal outlays: e.g., Boeing in Seattle, the California defense aerospace complex, the Southwest, or to a lesser extent, Florida. We are meeting in an area impacted by federal outlays. Austin, as a state and university center, was destined to grow, but it was boosted by 5,000 additional federal jobs during Lyndon Johnson's presidency. Some state employees are funded by federal money. Grants and other support are received by the University, and private employers like Tracor, Inc., have defense contracts.

REGIONAL RIVALRIES
As the size of federal spending has grown and its distribution has become better known, the rivalry between regions for a share of federal spending has become more intense. In particular, the United States core area (often called the Snowbelt) during the last recession awoke to the realization that its traditional economic dominance could no longer be taken for granted. In fact, the area had declined relative to other regions, and many of its spokesmen claimed its economic vitality was being sapped by the Sunbelt. It was strongly argued that the core had been bankrolling the expansion of the Sunbelt by the taxes it paid.

Sale (2) wrote a book in 1975 which was widely and favorably reviewed in the East; his book savaged the Sunbelt and seemed to generate a series of alarmist articles whose titles stressed regional conflict. Business Week started this emphasis in 1976 with its cover article, "The Second War Between the States" (3). U.S. News and World Report followed with "The Pork-Barrell War Between The States" (4). The theme was continued in 1978 with a cover article in the Saturday Review, "Sunbelt vs. Frostbelt: A Second Civil Way" (5).

An example of an extreme position is that of Richard S. Morris's passionate defense of New York and the East (6):

> So massive is the shortchange in federal spending, so pervasive the imbalance between federal spending in the Northeast and federal tax collections from it, that one must go well beyond considerations of justice or fairness. Indeed, the federal government is guilty of pursuing two diametrically opposite fiscal policies. Toward the Northeast it offers a rigid, restrictive policy, taxing far more than it offers in spending, taxing wealth out of the region's economy depleting consumer buying power. Toward the Sun Belt, it offers a policy of massive pump-priming and deficit spending, taking far less in taxes than it puts back in spending. (6, p. 111)

> If Keynes was at all right in his assertion that an excess of government taxes over government spending tends to retard economic growth, then the economic problems of the Northeast are truly explainable by federal fiscal policies. The Sun Belt is booming, not because of its supposedly vaunted qualities of enterprise and capitalist initiative, but because it gets $36 billion more in federal money than it has to pay in taxes. Similarly, the Northeast is slumping not because of its climate, labor unions, crime, pollution, minority groups or its liberalism, but because it is paying $44 billion more in federal taxes than it gets in federal spending. (6, p. 137)

> The federal government is not an equal opportunity employer, at least when it comes to providing jobs for Americans regardless of their geographic location. The federal government is a Sun Belt employer and one of that region's key sources. But precious few federal jobs find their way to the Northeast and its cities. (6, p. 142)

The outpouring of magazine articles, newspaper accounts, and editorials was accompanied by the formation of many organizations designed to further various regional interests (7). A few of the organizations' names may convey the mood: Coalition of Northeastern Governors, Southern Growth Policies

Board (established in 1971), New England Congressional Caucus, Midwest Governors Conference, and the Federation of Rocky Mountain States. Many of these organizations have substantial budgets and work closely with members of Congress to get legislation passed or allocation formulae revised which will favor their region. A White House conference on balanced growth and development in which the main theme seemed to be a "poorer-than-thou" sectionalism (8) was convened in January, 1978.

The purpose of this essay is not to review fully the origin and nature of the regional rivalries or to assess carefully how equitable the federal funds are distributed. These topics, however, cannot be ignored in reviewing regional development and the federal system because they have generated widespread attention to the topic (much of it unfortunately biased) and have become highly politicized subjects of debate.

The debate over the regional distribution of federal spending has occurred in part because of the availability of data which show where the federal money is spent. Beginning in 1968 yearly reports on the geographic distribution of federal spending were issued by order of President Johnson, who was acting upon the request of some of the state governors (9). In the decade since, the outlay reports have been refined and revamped with an improvement in their utility and accuracy. They are not, however, entirely reliable principably in two aspects. Military contracts are listed by the address of the prime contractor rather than by job site. A good example of the misleading information which can result is the case of American Motors. This corporation, headquartered in South Bend, Indiana, sells millions of dollars worth of jeeps to the government each year. South Bend is the location assigned this contract, but in reality the jeeps are made in Toledo, Ohio. Another distortion arises from the use of proration procedures by some agencies to geographically allocate spending. The outlay volumes--there is one issued for each state--have codes which indicate for a program which proration technique was used, if any. They are generally prorated on the basis of population, the distribution of the client population, or employment in a given activity. Another problem is the assignment of some federal funds to the state capital from which they are allocated throughout the state. Some critics have maintained these distortions gravely flaw the data, but for most programs--especially at the state level--the outlays are reasonably accurate. In any event they are the only source of the spatial distribution of federal spending.

THE DISTRIBUTION OF OUTLAYS

The 1976 federal outlays will be examined here in the light of the regional controversy. They have been rank ordered by the per capita amount which has been "adjusted" by subtracting the categories of interest, retirement, and post office (Table 5-2). The impact of interest payments is highly problematical; generally these payments are assigned to the big New York City banks. Retirement payments are non-discretionary, and the post office allocations are population-oriented (although the fit is not perfect). An index number is provided for easier comparison (it is set as equal to 100 for New Mexico because of the special cases of Alaska and Hawaii).

The distribution of the adjusted per capita federal outlays by quintiles is seen in spatial perspective (Fig. 5-1). The "have" and the "have not" states are generally found

TABLE 5-2. Per Capita Federal Outlays, 1976 (Adjusted)*.

Bundesausgaben pro Kopf, 1976 (Angepasst)*.

Rank	State	Per Capita Outlays	Index Number**
1	Alaska	$3574	207
2	Hawaii	2098	122
3	New Mexico	1723	100
4	Virginia	1600	93
5	Washington	1565	91
6	Maryland	1501	87
7	California	1465	85
8	Colorado	1361	79
9	Nevada	1355	79
10	North Dakota	1355	79
11	Missouri	1328	77
12	Mississippi+	1305	76
13	Arizona	1242	72
14	Connecticut	1200	70
15	Utah	1169	68
16	Vermont	1169	68
17	Massachusetts	1146	67
18	Wyoming	1142	67
19	Tennessee+	1133	66
20	Montana	1120	65
21	Oklahoma+	1107	64
22	Maine	1089	63
23	Georgia+	1055	61
24	Alabama+	1049	61
25	South Carolina+	1039	60
26	Kentucky	1028	60
27	Texas+	1015	59
28	South Dakota	1004	58
29	Idaho	985	57
30	New York	985	57
31	Rhode Island	977	57
32	New Hampshire	976	57
33	Florida+	923	54
34	Louisiana+	911	53
35	Minnesota	886	51
36	North Carolina+	882	51
37	Oregon	874	51
38	Arkansas+	872	51
39	Kansas	855	50
40	Illinois	828	48

TABLE 5-2 (Continued).

Rank	State	Per Capita Outlays	Index Number**
41	New Jersey	$ 794	46
42	Delaware	791	46
43	Pennsylvania	743	43
44	Nebraska	715	41
45	West Virginia	699	41
46	Ohio	686	40
47	Michigan	649	38
48	Indiana	622	36
49	Iowa	616	36
50	Wisconsin	595	35

*Without the following categories: Retirement, Interest, Postal

**New Mexico = 100

+Sunbelt-South state

Source: Community Services Administration, Federal Outlays, (Springfield, Va.: The National Technical Information Service, 1977).

in distinct regional groupings. All of the lowest quintile states are in the Midwest with an extension eastward to Pennsylvania, New Jersey, and Delaware. Only Illinois breaks the East-West band, and it is ranked fortieth. Conversely, the top quintile states are all in the western United States except for North Dakota, Maryland, and Virginia, which are special cases due to the spillover of federal agencies from the District of Columbia.

Three major regions are employed in the analysis with each one divided into two subregions (Fig. 5-2). The Sunbelt is used not because it is adequate as a region but because it is constantly referred to in discussions of the regional rivalry. The Snowbelt, sometimes called the Frostbelt or the Northeast, is quite similar to the old Manufacturing Belt or the United States core. Since the core concept is part of the existing body of the theory of regional development it is the preferred term. The West includes the Census Mountain and Pacific regions. Note that seven states in the Great Plains-Midwest are not included in the regional division.

The outlays are given in Table 5-3 by major functional budget categories which are listed according to their importance in the budget. Income Security (social security, unemployment insurance, and public assistance) is over $123 billion, while General Science and Space is about $5 billion. The numbers given are location quotients, a quotient of 100 indicating that the share of a region's population and outlays are the same. If the number is below 100, the outlays are less than expected on the basis of population, and if over 100, more than expected.

The most striking aspect of Table 5-3 is the marked difference between the subregions, especially within the

TABLE 5-3. Location Quotients Of Major Functional Budget Categories By Region, 1977. Schwerpunkt der Staatsausgaben, aufgeteilt bei Regionen, 1977.

| | Sunbelt ||| Core ||| West ||||
	Total	South	West	Total	East	West	Total	South	North
Income Security	94	93	97	99	101	91	94	96	92
National Defense	119	93	175	67	86	43	156	170	111
Health	87	80	104	115	119	111	94	100	71
Education and Manpower	99	93	111	95	104	84	112	110	121
Veterans	109	110	109	82	87	76	107	107	108
Commerce and Transportation	84	85	91	88	100	72	95	94	100
Agriculture	87	105	50	41	40	43	77	56	150
Revenue Sharing	96	86	116	107	117	96	112	113	111
Law Enforcement	89	79	109	73	89	54	100	104	84
General Science and Space	170	86	347	57	71	41	259	323	34
All Outlays	100	91	119	88	98	76	116	117	114

Source: Community Services Administration, Federal Outlays (Springfield, Va.: The National Technical Information Service, 1977).

Sunbelt and the Core. For most of the categories, the Sunbelt-West has a substantially higher quotient than the Sunbelt-South. Put another way, quite often the South is equated with the Sunbelt, which is clearly misleading in the case of federal outlays. Note the lower quotient of the All Outlays category for the Sunbelt-South compared to the Core-East, which has some of the most vociferous critics of the unfair advantages of the Sunbelt-South.

Another way of looking at the federal outlay picture is to consider the grant outlays; they made up about 18 percent of the total 1976 outlays ($64 billion of $359 billion). Government agencies greatly differ in the importance of grants. Such major agencies as the Department of Defense, the Civil Service Administration, the Department of Energy, NSAA, and the Veterans Administration have little or no grants. On the other hand, 92 percent of EDA, 83 percent of HUD, 72 percent of the Department of Labor, 57 percent of the Department of Agriculture, and 21 percent of HEW budgets were grants.

The per capita grant outlays in 1976 by region were:

Region	Amount Per Capita
Sunbelt	279
Sunbelt-South	266
Sunbelt-West	305
Core	285
Core-East	314
Core-West	248
West	302
West-South	302
West-North	304

Note the rather low position of the Sunbelt South, significantly lower than the Core-East and lower than the other subregions except the Core-West, which is lowest in most categories. The states are not shown, but unlike the total

FEDERAL OUTLAYS AND REGIONAL DEVELOPMENT

outlays there is little regional grouping except for some cluster of states in New England and New York. The low-ranked states are in the Middle-West: Ohio, Indiana, Illinois, Iowa, Kansas, and Nebraska. There is no obvious rationale to the overall ranking except the lowest-ranked states seem to share a general fiscal conservatism which may be manifest in a reluctance to participate fully in many grant programs, especially those requiring matching monies.

A final empirical example of federal outlays at the broad regional level is taken from a study recently completed on the adequacy of the Sunbelt as a region (10). A limited number of variables related to the Sunbelt discussion were incorporated in the analysis. They are listed, along with their abbreviations, in Table 5-4.

For easier regional comparisons the values for the variables have been converted to index numbers with the Sunbelt set at 100. The fourth column, per capita federal outlays, should be compared with the other variables: columns 2 and 3 are population-related; 5, 6, and 7, the federal government, and 8, 9, and 10, economic performance. The final column is the score on a factor analysis and may be considered an index of Sunbelt characteristics, the higher the number the more the region is presumed to have Sunbelt characteristics. Special emphasis should be given to the comparison of the per capita outlays with the government and economic variables. Although there is a fairly close correspondence with the federal civilian pattern, the importance of federal grants by region is not often the same as the outlay pattern. There is also a frequent dissimilarity with the economic variables.

The foregoing sets of data give an approximation of the relation between regional development and the distribution of

TABLE 5-4. Regional and Subregional Differences by Variables (Sunbelt = 100).
Regionale und Unterregionale Verschiebungen, bei Variabilität.

	SUN	POP	MIG	PCO	DEF	CIV	FGS	PCI	POV	UPL	SCR
Sunbelt	100	100	100	100	100	100	100	100	100	100	100
Sunbelt South	94	69	84	90	90	89	96	95	106	91	33
Sunbelt West	119	244	110	127	128	130	111	113	83	124	283
Core	85	27	-18	78	73	81	92	120	54	109	-130
Core East	85	27	-11	89	93	96	104	123	53	119	-84
Core West	84	27	-29	59	39	58	83	118	55	95	-204
West	103	204	112	112	101	131	110	110	66	110	155
West South	113	242	134	122	125	148	108	110	72	108	252
West North	88	160	85	100	72	110	113	110	59	91	38
Snowbelt	88	75	18	88	83	97	103	111	61	92	-45

Sunbelt   South: NC-SC-GA-FLA-TN-AL-MS-AR-LA-OK-TX
          West: NM-AZ-CA-NV

Core   East: MA-CT-RI-NY-NJ-PA-MD-DE
          West: OH-IN-MI-IL-WI

West   South: CO-UT-AZ-NM-CA-NV
          North: MT-WY-ID-OR-WA

Snowbelt All non-Sunbelt states-33 states

SUN Percent of possible sunshine
POP Population change 1970-1976
MIG Net Migration rate 1970-1976
PCO Per capita federal outlays
DEF Location quotient, federal defense spending, 1976
CIV Location quotient, federal civilian employment, 1975
FGS Per capita federal grants, 1975
PCI Per capita income, 1976 (percent of U.S. average)
POV Percent of families below poverty level, 1975
UPL Percent unemployed, 1976
SCR Score on Factor 1 - Sunbelt Characteristics Index

federal outlays. It is, however, considerably short of measuring the relative importance of federal outlays. To my knowledge this has never been attempted, let alone successfully accomplished (the literature on federal outlays has been growing, but much of the work has been not widely circulated-consisting, for example, of a staff report of one of the regional interest groups or perhaps a congressional report).

As previously mentioned, there are often crosscurrents operating in this area, and simple, easy-to-measure relationships are rare. There are formidable difficulties to be surmounted. Greater precision and understanding would be obtained by working at the program level rather than the overall total or major functional or cabinet categories. Yet there are more than a thousand different programs. The geographic level of major region and/or state is too gross. As in the case of the programs it would be helpful to be not only program-specific but area-specific as well. A logical case can be made for disaggregating outlays and using a finer areal grain in the analysis, but this procedure involves the problem of seeing the trees and not the forest.

There is another problem which is important but not easily recognized. The impact of federal outlays varies because a dollar spent on one kind of program is not the same in its local or regional impact as a dollar spent on another kind of program. In the terminology of the economic base, the multiplier effect differs for different kinds of programs. Consequently dollar amounts alone will not reveal the actual impact.

The idea was expressed somewhat differently by Auletta (11) who strongly indicts the gross mismanagement of New

FEDERAL OUTLAYS AND REGIONAL DEVELOPMENT 143

York fiscal affairs. In his chapter "Is Washington to Blame?" he reviews the federal role and in the course of the discussion he writes:

> One has to be careful to distinguish between soft federal dollars-direct grants, CETA funds, countercyclical aid, community development funds-which tilt toward New York and hard federal dollars-highways, home loans, military and space expenditures, dams, water projects-which tilt toward the Sun Belt (11, p. 138).

Essentially the hypothesis is that different federal outlays will have different multiplier effects on the local economy. Or to phrase it differently, the potency of a given amount of federal money will vary with the type of program. Ten million dollars in food stamps will not likely cause the local supermarkets to hire additional staff or build more stores. Welfare payments and social security payments to those who have had low life-time earnings would probably have a similar overall result. Ten million dollars in military contracts or for personnel in a research center, like the National Center For Communicable Disease in Atlanta, would help sustain a new boutique, a health food store, or a studio of ballet.

THE WASHINGTON, D.C., METROPOLITAN AREA

The methodology needed to disentangle the effects of federal spending upon a local economy and to further gauge the multiplier effects of different federal programs is unknown. There have been, however, a number of discussions or studies that have addressed the question, and they are briefly reviewed in the following paragraphs.

In the early 1970s, a study was prepared by the Economic Development Division, Economic Research Service of the Department of Agriculture, The Distribution of Federal Outlays Among U.S. Counties. As a part of a series of studies under the general heading "Economic and Social Condition of Rural America in the 1970s," it was commissioned by the U.S. Senate Committee on Government Operations (12). The initial conclusion, boldly set forth in capital letters, succinctly expresses the principal finding of the study, "RURAL AMERICANS DO NOT SHARE PROPORTIONATELY IN PROGRAMS FUNDED BY THE FEDERAL GOVERNMENT." Quite clearly the agency conducting the study and the committee sponsoring it were biased in favor of agriculture and rural areas, so there may have been axe-grinding. Nevertheless, the data indicate that rural areas receive less per capita federal money. Although the study was done on a rural-urban continuum, regional differences can also be perceived (there were six categories of counties classified on the basis of the percent of the urban population and the population density).

Federal Activities Affecting Location of Economic Development was another study conducted about the same time by the Economic Development Administration of the U.S. Department of Commerce (13). The study was primarily concerned with the economic impact of various assistance programs, thus the limited scope of this study should be kept in mind. The basic conclusion was that federal assistance programs have relatively little impact on the process of economic development and its geographic distribution. The federal assistance programs were selected from the departments of Agriculture; Commerce; Health, Education and Welfare; Housing and Urban Development; Labor; Office of Economic Opportunity; and the Small Business Administration. Among other conclusions were (a) aids to business investments had the most immediate effect of stimulating additional economic development; (b) aids to public infrastructure may remove barriers to economic progress, but they do not stimulate the process initially; and (c) investment in human resources has little demonstrable economic impact. The type of programs reviewed in the study would generally be considered as *soft* federal dollars according to the previous discussion.

More recently, the Rand Corporation conducted a large-scale study on the Urban Impacts of Federal Policies (14). Rather than generate new empirical analysis, the report attempted to conceptualize, organize, and synthesize the existing literature. As the title implies, the study was primarily concerned with urban impacts; but these were also viewed on a regional level, thus its conclusions are germane to this discussion.

The Rand study found the process of economic growth and development to be complex; and it acknowledged the difficulty of trying to measure the importance of the factors that determine the development. A major finding was the limited knowledge about the effects of federal policies on urban economic development and the lack of data to conduct an analysis. On a regional level, the report concluded:

> . . . the relatively rapid growth in areas outside the Northeast and Midwest appears to be the result of underlying social and economic changes. The most important federal influence has been through the construction of national transportation networks, which cannot be reversed. Among federal policies that have exerted regional biases but could be reversed if it were desired to assist in the economic recovery of the Northeast, the most important are the distribution of federal expenditures and the regulation of transport and energy prices. (15, p. xiii)

Given the formidable difficulties of assessing the role

of government spending and policies on economic development, how does one proceed? It would seem that a case study, while not providing the kind of specific numerical answers which are ultimately desired, would provide an opportunity to explore this further, and that the Washington, D.C., metropolitan area would provide the quintessential example of the federal impact upon a local area.

In previous work with federal outlay data the Washington metropolitan area has been deliberately excluded from the analysis because it was considered exogenous to the question of regional equity in the distribution of federal funds. In other words, the national headquarters function was not open to allocation to other regions so it was considered outside the framework for assessing regional equity. Yet no place has been influenced more by federal funds, and thus it was thought that Washington, D.C. would exhibit the most dramatic multiplier effect.

It is not necessary to make a strong case for considering Washington as having been created by the federal government. The economy is either directly or indirectly affected by the federal government, but the largest other "basic" activities such as tourism and the newly developing lobby industry are closely tied to federal activities. For such a large area Washington has very little manufacturing or wholesaling. These functions seem to be supplied, in part, by other nearby cities in Megalopolis.

No other capital of a large industrialized country appears to have such a high concentration in government or government-related activities as Washington. All the other large capitals of industrialized countries such as London, Moscow, Tokyo, Paris, and Rome are less specialized than Washington (Bonn may be the interesting exception due to its

FEDERAL OUTLAYS AND REGIONAL DEVELOPMENT

role in a divided Germany and as a reluctantly designated successor to Berlin.)

Washington is unusual among large metropolitan areas (those of 2,000,000 or over in 1960) in its ability to keep growing in the face of a general decline in the growth of other large metropolitan areas. It grew rather rapidly in the decade of the 1950s, but so did a number of other large metropolitan areas. By the 1960s, however, most of the large metropolitan areas began to stagnate while Washington became the clear leader in growth. In the 1970s, when many of the other large metropolitan areas actually lost population, the Washington area continued to grow, although more slowly.

The recent sustained growth of the nation's capital has been surprising in the sense that the growth of federal employment leveled off in the 1970s; the Washington area gained just 11,000 new workers from 1970 to 1977. The increase in trade associations has filled the gap. These trade associations, e.g., the Aluminum Association, were often formerly located in a business center such as New York City or a convenient location such as Chicago. As the power and influence of the federal government expanded and its regulations became more far-reaching and numerous, these associations chose to locate near the new seat of power in America, Washington, D.C., rather than Wall Street. There are more than 1,800 of these associations in Washington employing more than 40,000 persons; new associations arrive almost weekly. The American Society of Association Executives is constructing its own headquarters; a fifteen-floor, $14.5 million office building. Nonprofit organizations are relocating there as well. It is no accident that the headquarters of the Association of American Geographers is in

Washington. The increasingly legalistic nature of American society has spawned a rapidly growing corps of high-priced Washington law firms.

In addition to its growth in numbers and power, Washington has also grown in wealth. The Department of Commerce estimated that Washington had the highest per capita income in 1977 among the major metropolitan areas (16). Sales and Marketing Management magazine estimated that Washington had an after tax income per household of $24,806 in 1978 (17). This was substantially above New York ($19,090), Los Angeles ($19,767), and Chicago ($22,391). Washington has few very wealthy families like the Du Ponts of Delaware to boost the average income. It has instead large numbers of well paid jobs. In 1978, in the white-collar category (General Schedule employees) there were 19,418 employees with a mean salary over $41,748 and 120,000 over $19,000. These figures do not include employees of the legislative and judicial branches, among the highest paid federal employees. Many of the staff members of the various associations are well paid. Households with two working members can easily have an income over $50,000.

This account of Washington is suggestive of the impact of federal money, but it is an extreme rather than a typical example. Other communities would not have the same characteristics of growth, power, and affluence, but in-depth case studies of the impact of federal money are needed to supplement the work on specific programs and the total spending pattern.

CONCLUSIONS

It has only been a decade since the first federal outlay data were made available on a geographic basis. For part of this time they went unnoticed until the regional debate over federal funds brought them into prominence. We still do not know the accuracy of the data, the pitfalls in their analyses, and how they can best be put to use in answering such questions as how equitable their distribution and their impact upon local and regional economies is. Disentangling their role in regional development is no small task. It may never be fully realized, but it is certainly a challenge well worth meeting.

Unfortunately much of the work utilizing federal outlay data is done to serve the purpose of advancing some region's goal or interests. Objective analysis and comments are rare, and there is often a deliberate bias or, at the very least, a tendency to overly dramatize the results on the part of the media.

The thrust of this essay has been to provide a background for the regional debate, to examine briefly the distribution of outlays, and to discuss some of the problems inherent in federal outlay analysis. There are difficulties in selecting the level of disaggregation of the programs, the areal units, and in reconciling the differing multiplier effects of individual types of outlays. We may be able to more fully understand the impact of federal outlays by intensive studies of selected areas. In this regard the Washington metropolitan area may be a good place to begin.

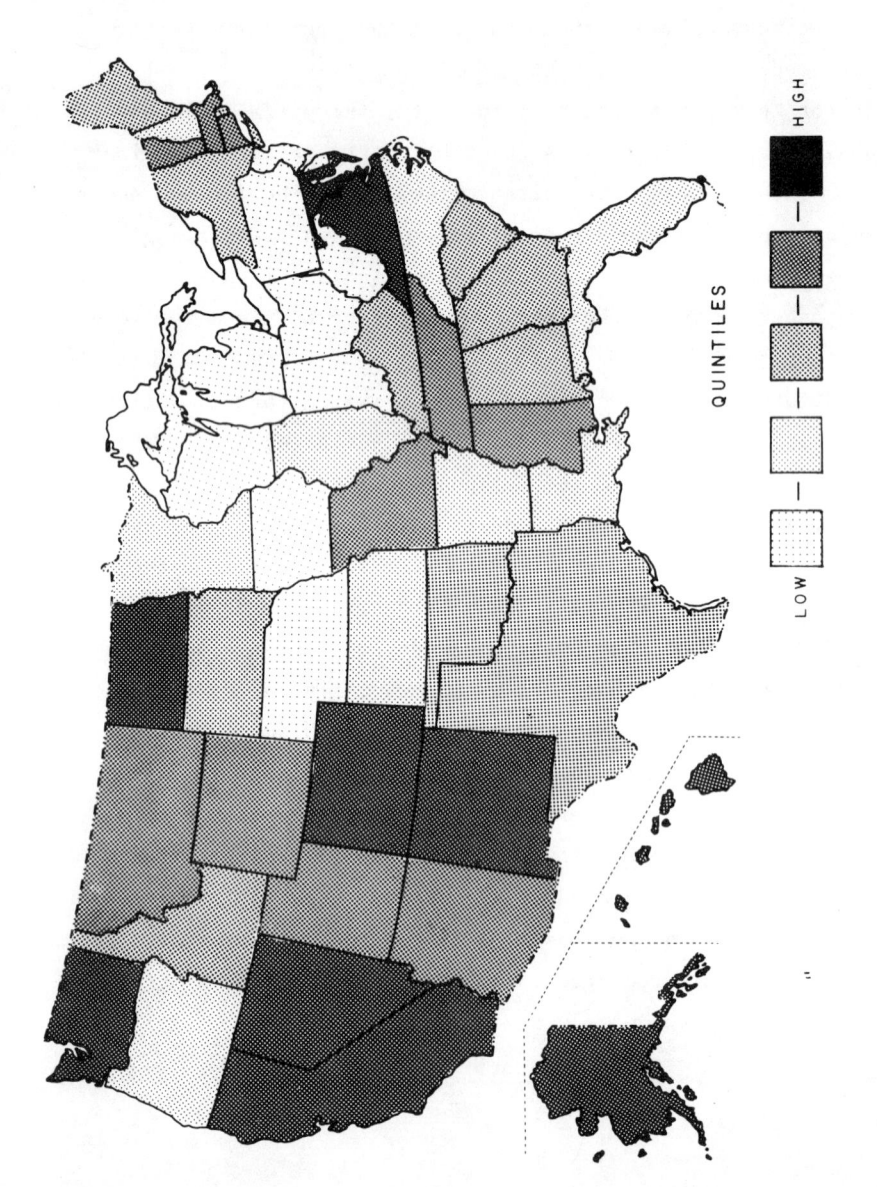

FIG. 5-1. Per Capita Federal Outlays-Adjusted, 1976. Bundesauslagen pro Kopf der Bevölkerung-angepasst, 1976.

FEDERAL OUTLAYS AND REGIONAL DEVELOPMENT 151

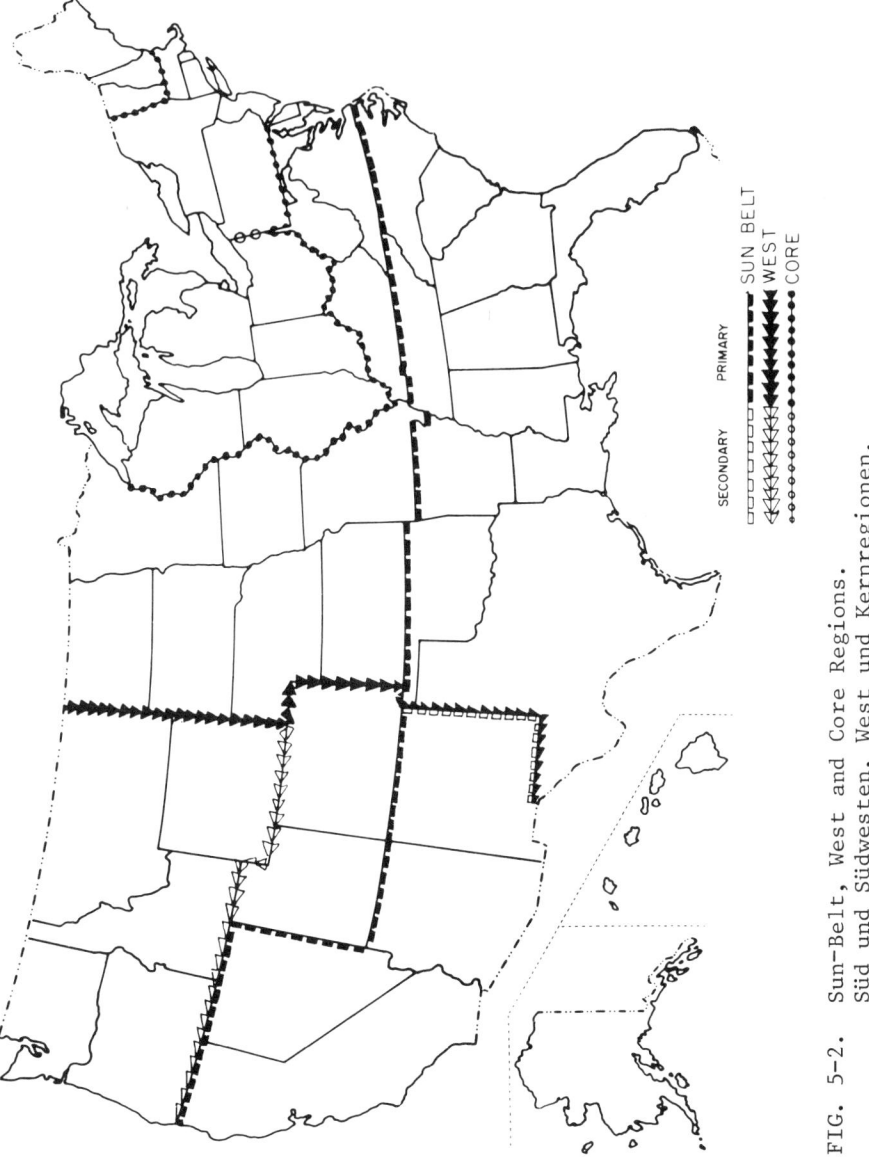

FIG. 5-2. Sun-Belt, West and Core Regions.
Süd und Südwesten, West und Kernregionen.

NOTES

1. Browning, C. E., The Geography of Federal Outlays, Studies in Geography, No. 4 (Chapel Hill, N.C.: Department of Geography, University of North Carolina at Chapel Hill, 1973).

2. Sale, K., Power Shift: The Rise of the Southern Rim and Its Challenge to the Eastern Establishment (New York, Random House, 1975).

3. Business Week, May 17, 1976.

4. U.S. News and World Report, December 5, 1977.

5. Saturday Review, April 15, 1978.

6. Morris, R. S., Bumrap on America's Cities (Englewood Cliffs, N.J.: Prentice-Hall, 1978).

7. Rafuse, R. W., Jr., "The New Regional Debate: A National Overview," prepared for the National Governor's Conference Center for Policy Research and Analysis, Washington, D.C., 1977.

8. Time, February 9, 1979.

9. Community Services Administration, Federal Outlays, Summary volume and one for each state, the National Technical Information Service, 1977.

10. Browning, C. E., and W. Gesler, "The Sun Belt-Snow Belt: A Case of Sloppy Regionalizing," The Professional Geographer 31 (February, 1979), 66-75.

11. Auletta, K., The Streets Were Paved With Gold (New York: Harper and Row, 1979).

12. Economic Development Division, U.S. Department of Agriculture, The Distribution of Federal Outlays Among U.S. Counties, Committee on Government Operations, U.S. Senate, (Washington, D.C.: U.S. Government Printing Office, 1971).

13. United States Department of Commerce, Federal Activities Affecting Location of Economic Development, (Washington, D.C.: U.S. Government Printing Office, 1970).

14. Vaughan, Roger J., The Urban Impacts of Federal Policies: Vol. 2, Economic Development (Santa Monica, California: the Rand Corporation, 1977).

15. ------, op. cit. p. xiii (see footnote 14).

16. U.S. Department of Commerce, Survey of Current Business (April, 1979), p. 29.
17. "New Evidence of Area's Economic Strength Due," Washington Post, July 22, 1979, p. F-6.

CHAPTER 6

CORPORATE ORGANIZATION AND REGIONAL DEVELOPMENT
IN THE AMERICAN FEDERAL SYSTEM: THEORY
AND POLICY PERSPECTIVES

UNTERNEHMENS-ORGANISATION UND REGIONALE ENTWICKLUNG IM
BUNDESSTAATLICHEN SYSTEM DER VEREINIGTEN STAATEN:
THEORETISCHE UND POLITISCHE PERSPEKTIVEN

Günter Krumme

Abstract

The fact that patterns of economic development of communities and regions are directly influenced by organizational and corporate characteristics of underlying economic activities has only recently been fully recognized by regional development theorists. This significance rests, for example, on different local employment impacts of different corporate forms and different interregional corporate linkages accommodating flows of materials, capital, personnel, information, know-how, power, and influence. In federal systems such as the United States, multidivisional and multilocational corporate activities interact with and are constrained by a variety of multilevel governments and agencies in many different ways, reaching from the acceptance of governmental authority, laws, and regulations, via lobbying activities and the exchange of taxes and subsidies, to military procurement contracts. This essay explores selected regional development and policy implications of some of these relationships between governmental and corporate systems on the basis of recent examples from the United States.

Kurzfassung

Die Tatsache, dass die wirtschaftliche Entwicklung von Gemeinden und Regionen unmittelbar von unternehmens-organisatorischen Zusammenhängen und Gegebenheiten der zugrundeliegenden Wirtschaftsbeziehungen beeinflusst wird, ist erst in letzter Zeit von Regionalwissenschaftlern voll anerkannt worden. Diese Bedeutung basiert zum Beispiel auf unterschiedlichen lokalen Beschäftigungsauswirkungen verschiedener Betriebs- und Unter-

CORPORATE ORGANIZATION AND REGIONAL DEVELOPMENT 155

nehmensformen und verschiedener interregionaler, zwischenbetrieblicher Beziehungen in Bezug auf Materialfluss, Kapitalbewegungen, Personal-Wanderungen, Austausch von Informationen und Know-How, und Machtausübung und organisatorische Einflussnahme. In bundesstaatlichen Systemen wie dem der Vereinigten Staaten werden diese Zusammenhänge dadurch kompliziert, dass Grossunternehmen mit vielen Unternehmensbereichen und Standorten vielseitige Beziehungen mit wiederum sehr verschiedenen Regierungen unterhalten, Beziehungen, die von der Anerkennung der jeweiligen Regierungsautorität, über Versuche der Beeinflussung von Gesetzgebung und den Austausch von Steuern und Subventionen hin bis zu militärischen Lieferverträgen reichen. Dieser Vortrag beschäftigt sich mit ausgewählten regionalwirtschaftlichen und -politischen Auswirkungen solcher Zusammenhänge zwischen Regierungen und Unternehmen an Hand neuerer, amerikanischer Beispiele.

Corporate Organization and Regional Development In the American Federal System: Theory and Policy Perspectives

The United States economic system is often considered a "mixed economy" containing elements of both capitalist-free market economies and socialist-planned economies. Clearly, this dualistic simplification is in many ways inadequate, since the larger part of the American "real world" is neither a "free market" nor a "planned" economy; not even a simple mixture of the two. Rather it appears to be a world in which a plethora of multilevel governmental and corporate-organizational bureaucracies interfere with economic processes in endless, often conflicting, and largely uncoordinated ways, yielding to an unending stream of special interests: regional, governmental, corporate, industrial, labor-oriented, and environmental. The lack of focus, goals, and a precise definition of the role of government appears to subject government institutions to stifling bureaucratization and to make Congress particularly vulnerable to organizational and regional lobbyists, resulting in often haphazard, uncoordinated regional allocation of federal funds. A case in point is the Department of Energy with 20,000 employees and a $11 billion annual budget unable to correct a situation which the president described just two years ago as "a horrible conglomeration of confusion in the energy fields" (1).

Equally complex and unintelligible is the "private" segment of the economy. An ever increasing component of the economy is withdrawn from the "market" disappearing behind corporate and conglomerate walls. It is not merely the size of the individual corporate organization which curtails the workings of a free-market economy in many industrial sectors but also its organizational and locational complexity which shields corporate operations and interactions from the public eye and democratic control. The multiregional presence of firms and their ability to shift resources, personnel, and tax responsibilities between communities and states; to engage in transfer pricing, income shifting, and regulation-circumventing behavior; to practice large-scale political lobbying on different governmental levels and to apply corporate-level political and economic power in a concentrated and localized manner; and, finally, to control individual lives in terms of careers, residential locations, or exposure to unhealthy environments are aspects which make terms such as "private sector" or "free-enterprise economy" misnomers (2). The focus of this essay, therefore, will be on the expanding "grey area," or what Galbraith called the technostructure, between the private-entrepreneurial and the public-governmental sectors in the context of the U.S. federal system and its concern or lack of concern for matters of regional development at the federal level.

In federal systems in which the federal level does not assume responsibility for its role as goal and guideline setter, interregional coordinator for federal programs and allocations, and mediator between subnational governmental units, de facto regional policy consists of uncoordinated ad hoc concessions to regional interests and wasteful competition between regions for federal funds and industrial plants.

Such a situation tends to result in:

(a) giving inappropriate executive powers to regional representatives and senators in Congress and in inordinate amount of influence to (among others) lobbyists for nonterritorial, organizational (corporate) interests who flexibly and opportunistically align themselves with regional representatives to gain legislative favors via amendments and intergovernmental and interpersonal logrolling. Indeed, it does not seem overstated to say that federal regional policy consists of a few specific acts and an unending list of more or less obscure, largely ad hoc, regional amendments to nonregional legislation.

(b) interregional competition and inequitable tax abatements and other concessions to industrial corporations at the subnational level reducing the benefits and increasing the cost of industrialization.

The apparent consequences of such tendencies are, first, that governments at all levels act like Simon's "satisficing" (nonoptimizing) private firms with rather narrow and short-term goal sets, using the fire department's crisis management procedures and aligning themselves with constantly changing coalitions in rather uncoordinated ways similar to the unstable oligopolistic marketplaces, and, second, that business, particularly large and multiregional corporations, assumes governmental roles by filling in the vacuum left by federal inaction (formulating goals, designing new weapon systems, organizing political coalitions, and taking other political initiatives). In a way, they act as "interregional governments" representing their own interregional and multiregional interests in a world of territorially oriented state and local governments and a federal government which lacks the will and muscle to accept the interregional dimension of its mandate.

REGIONAL POLICY IN FEDERAL SYSTEMS
It is no accident that many more studies are available on regional policies in Britain and France than on Germany and

the United States. Independent of how much substantive regional policy actually exists in these countries, there simply "happens" more at the national level in centralized countries than in federal systems in terms of goal formulation, coordination, and implementation (3). Data collection and institutional and policy analysis are simply easier, "neater," and more comprehensive where authority is centralized than where it is spread between a complex hierarchy of semiindependent governments, with much of the actual policy implementation occurring at the local and regional level.

Indeed, superficial evaluations of regional policies at the national level in the United States frequently come to the conclusion that either a regional policy does not exist or that it is not sufficiently coordinated to deserve such a lable. While such criticisms have substantial merit, one nevertheless should also consider the following opposing arguments. First, the scale of the country, the widely different population and employment densities, economic structures, cultural backgrounds, and political philosophies tend to favor decentralized approaches to regional problems. As a result, considerable legislative and executive powers--which in other, even federally organized, countries are centralized at the national level--lie in the United States in the hands of local and state governments or other subnational agencies. Consequently, the federal government has less scope for formulating comprehensive and well-coordinated regional policies. Perhaps more importantly, many programs and policies exist at the national level which are regional in nature and which are used as such, without being designated and emphasized as "regional policies" for reasons which may include the wish to avoid the appearance of regional favoritism or the need to justify a particular measure on regional grounds and to compensate other regions. Finally, there may be--ceteris paribus--less need for an explicit and visible "regional policy" in federal systems than in centralized countries simply because the federal governmental system may have prevented the type of polarization which gives rise to interregional inequalities or because the constitutional or political mandate for regional policies may simply not be powerful enough.

The history and institutional aspects of "regional policy" in the United States from the New Deal programs via the Appalachia Regional Development Act of 1965 to the activities of the Economic Development Administration (EDA) have been reviewed elsewhere and will not be repeated here (4). Suffice it to say that "organizational" or "corporate" dimensions can hardly be detected in these policies or their implementations. The reason for this neglect lies presumably in the lack of conceptual constructs which could have assisted in assigning roles to corporate characteristics and processes, both in policy legislation and its implementations as well as in posterior evaluations. This situation is astounding considering that "from the very beginning of the developing of regional policies within Western Europe and North America, there has been a close association between strategy and the role of industry. In fact, the association became so intertwined as to lead one to believe that regional policies in most countries were, de facto, industrial development policies" (5).

ORGANIZATIONAL PERSPECTIVES OF GOVERNMENTS
AND CORPORATE SYSTEMS

In the perspective of this essay, society organizes itself in complex sets of largely hierarchical, organizations, formal and informal, in order to meet the needs and requirements of governance and of cultural, social, and economic relationships. While all of these relationships occur in space, not all are equally sensitive to space as a barrier to interaction, a condition which tends to have a direct bearing on the spatial and hierarchical structure of an organization.

In addition, the extent to which such functional relationships within and between organizations at different levels of their respective hierarchies are or can be regionalized in meaningful ways differs widely and depends on factors such as society's attitudes toward public and private property rights, the desirability of territorial monopolies or control over relationships, available means of communication and production technologies-in short, the areal extent and overlaps of different functional relationships. In this sense, this essay focuses attention not only on the complementarities and interdepencies but also on the geographic differences between two types of dominant organizational forms in Western countries, namely (a) governmental institutions with given authority over specifically delineated territories, and (b) large industrial corporations which operate at more than one location and have generally weak associations with specific regions. For most corporations, terrestrial space is flexibly organized and subject to constant strategic and competitive change in response to altered situations. Their organization is functional in nature, consisting of multiple and functionally differentiated nodes which are linked to each other and to other organizational systems (6).

The Western World has witnessed an unparalleled growth of multilocational corporate systems, much of which has occurred since World War II. There are many explanations for such growth, some of which can be related to the existence of territorial spatial organizations. In the United States, private corporations have had a long history of contributing to the political, social, and economic integration of the country via the improvement of industrial and communications linkages (such as railways, telephone, airlines). On the other hand, private corporations have also benefitted from the emerging unity and interregional integration of the country and have grown and specialized to a degree which would have been impossible otherwise. Such processes of growth and structure rationalization thus had both organizational and spatial dimensions:

> With improved transportation and communication, the mechanisms of territorial integration have become increasingly organizational in character. The growth of large-scale organization, operating alike in economic and non-economic sectors, has spanned distances with many strands of interdependence and has woven a dense network of connections. (7)

It is not clear, however, whether and in what precise ways such processes of growth and rationalization have benefitted from the federal governmental structure of the United States. On the one hand, national integration and corporate expansion are favored by a centralized political structure due to the lack of state boundaries and the potentially greater utilization of scale economies. However, in general we observe that countries with centralized goverenments tend to have a more severe problem with unintegrated peripheries and the unwillingness of private firms to expand into the periphery without financial incentives. Thus, the spatial economic structure of a federal country could be expected to benefit from the political decentralization if such decentralization went hand-in-hand with economic and corporate decentralization. It seems fair to say that a centralized government system in the U.S., unless it pursued a vigorous decentralization policy, would have led to appreciably more economic concentration in cities such as New York than what actually occurred, not the least due to the powerful role states play in the chartering and regulation of banks and other financial institutions.

Emery and Trist (8) have suggested that organizations grow in response to environmental uncertainty as a way to "internalize" such environments. Much of the relevant uncertainty arises from the world's division into politically independent "containers" pursuing their own policies and imposing different and changing regulations for business operations, a situation which may require a corporate presence in many different territories.

Organizations may also grow due to the need to reinvest retained earnings or to recycle knowledge and experience related to growth per se. Such growth would eventually be constrained by territorial boundaries. Territorial governments may find excessive size and monopolistic domination of markets by any one corporation undesirable and thus favor expansion into other territories. However, not only antitrust considerations of territorial governments may promote such diffusion; firms themselves often want to avoid creating "states within states," preferring the independence and mobility of territorially more diversified corporate systems which can tap resources and supply markets in different territories in a flexible manner (9).

Such an interterritorial flexibility, however, may in turn have grave repercussions for territorial governments in that it lends additional bargaining power to the corporation in negotiation for territorial concessions such as tax abatements. "The flexibility, fluidity and bargaining power of multi-regional corporations then tend to cause regional authorities to concentrate their regulative and revenue-generating energies unduly on those activities which lack this spatial flexibility" (10).

The concentration of economic power practically beyond the influence of individual regional or state governments will, in turn, tend to promote countervailing power and regulatory bureaucracy at the higher, federal level or prevent otherwise desirable deconcentration of governmental authority to lower levels of government.

REGIONAL DEVELOPMENT THEORY AND THE CORPORATE DIMENSION

Regional development theory as formulated over the past two decades has been highly abstract and aggregate in nature, largely ignoring institutional and organizational constraints, idiosyncracies, and impulses. Yet there is no doubt that both governmental and corporate organizations have become dominant factors in regional growth, declines, and interregional economic differentiation.

It is generally acknowledged that the impulses for a region's development originate either on the demand side, particularly in the form of changes in the demand for a region's exports, or on the supply side in the form of productivity changes resulting from technological or organizational progress or the discovery of new resources. It is no secret that developmental impulses which bring about continuous modifications of regional comparative advantages and which result in long-term interregional structural changes as well as short-term shocks and interregional differences in the severity of booms and recessions, are based on and comprised of patterns of individual behavior, corporate decisions, and governmental responses and initiatives.

Leibenstein has recently observed that while in most sciences there are changes of scale in the object of investigation in both directions, the movement "toward the detailed study of smaller and more fundamental (micro) units has predominated" (11). It appears that this observation is valid for the field of regional economic development as well. Only twenty years ago, the conceptualization had not significantly progressed beyond the macroeconomic Keynesian export-base multiplier model. Many writers felt obliged to deride conventional location theory as adding little to the explanation of regional change.

Progress was made during the era of growth-pole conceptualizations and its many attempts to illuminate the development role of the "lead firm" or "firme motrice." The impetus came largely from Francois Perroux who acknowledged the role of such firms in capital expansion, innovation, and the backward integration and domination of smaller firms. Today, micro-scopic, inter- and intraorganizational, as well as location-behavioral and decision making theories and approaches offer widely accepted perspectives to the regional development theorist (12). On the other hand, it must be conceded that there are still substantial difficulties in the translation of insights between different scales and that there is at present no sign of a unified and coherent theory of spatial behavior of organizations which could contribute in a more direct way to a micro-oriented regional development theory (13).

THE GEOGRAPHY OF CORPORATE ORGANIZATION

Over the course of the late 1960s and the 1970s a growing number of industrial geographers have recognized the spatial significance of the modern industrial corporation and searched for tools and concepts to gain a better understanding of the way in which organizational characteristics and decision making processes impact the evolution of economic landscapes (14). Among the topics which have been considered in conceptual and empirical studies we find:

- spatial corporate structure within systems of cities;
- location patterns of specialized corporate functions (headquarters, R&D facilities);
- characteristics and performance of branch plants;
- external control of corporate functions within regions;
- acquisitions, mergers and relocation activities of firms;
- location decision processes within corporate organizations;
- characteristics of corporate decision environments;
- dominant firms in local and regional labor markets; and
- intra- and intercorporate linkage patterns (contacts, input-output).

All of these topics are in some way pertinent in a regional development and policy context. However, only the issue of branch plants and external control will be discussed here in view of recent regional industrialization processes in the United States, particularly the establishment of manufacturing plants in small towns and rural areas ("nonmetropolitan industrialization") and the industrial growth of selected regions in the South, (the "Sunbelt phenomenon") (15).

One of the more controversial topics relates to the characteristics and roles of branch plants in the industrialization of rural, low-income or high-unemployment areas. It has been recognized that large multiplant firms operating at different locations and possibly in several different industries are likely to be in a better position to accumulate the resources and know-how needed to operate modern industrial plants at a satisfactory scale in relative geographic isolation. "Multinational and multiregional firms are better able to bridge the distance to peripheral areas" (16).

However, the very mobility and superior access to many locations and resources may also impose limitations on the contributions of such corporations and their branch plants to the economic and social welfare of a region. In this context, the "external control" of such plants, their frequently unbalanced and relatively inferior occupational structure, their relative lack of local linkage and multiplier effects, their occasionally observed relatively high sensitivity to closure during economic recessions, and their possibly high capital intensity have been cited, particularly in the British literature, as potentially undesirable characteristics. Recent empirical investigations in the United States related to organizational characteristics of industrialization processes generally support the British findings (17, 18, 19, 20, 21). Policy suggestions resulting from this research include the proposition that development agencies should concentrate their strategies on the support of "homegrown," already existing firms rather than less stable newcomers and branch plants and, in the absence of such indigenous firms, on assisting in the adaptation of the local population to the high turnover of factories for the short-run, and improvement of local skill levels as a long-term policy.

REGIONAL DEVELOPMENT IN THE U.S.:
A ZERO-SUM GAME?

One of the issues in the discussion of the Sunbelt/Frostbelt development differences has been the question of whether or not the "South" has benefitted at the expense of the "North." This question has been discussed on at least two fronts, namely with respect to allegedly unfair allocation of federal funds between the North(east) and the South (22), and with reference to the question of external control and organizational dependence of the recent employment growth in the South. For the latter issue, two contrasting perspectives can be identified. The "Northern" point of view would argue that:

> Industry is turning away from the Northern quadrant to avoid the higher costs of union shops, taxes, and the other expenses that go with maintaining plant operations in the older and more antiquated industrial corridor. At the same time, the banking community has begun to turn off the vital flow of finance capital in a a regional 'redlining' campaign that is effectively blocking any further economic development in this already hard-pressed area of the country. (23)

Others in the "North" point to the migration of corporate headquarters from northern cities to southern metropolitan areas: Coca-Cola (from New York to Atlanta), Shell Oil (New York to Houston), Mobil Oil (New York to Fairfax, Virginia), National Gypsum (Buffalo to Dallas), and, most recently, American Airlines (New York to Dallas) and Georgia Pacific (Portland, Oregon, to Atlanta). This trend is shown in Table 6-1.

In contrast, the Southern perspective questions the interdependence between the northern decline and southern growth and attributes the latter largely to indigenous stimuli. Given the fact that the northern share of industrial employ-

TABLE 6-1. Winners and Losers Among Headquarter Cities.
Gewinner und Verlierende zwischen Zentralstädten.

Cities (including suburbs)	Number of Corporate HQs of 500 Largest U.S. Corporations		
	1975	1965	Change
Losers:			
New York	152	167	-15
Chicago	42	51	- 9
San Francisco	15	21	- 6
Philadelphia	21	23	- 2
Winners:			
St. Louis	13	5	+ 8
Houston	11	7	+ 4
Washington	7	3	+ 4
Miami	4	–	+ 4
Dallas	12	9	+ 3
Denver	4	1	+ 3

Source: Rand McNally, 1977 Commercial Atlas and Marketing Guide, p. 69.

ment has decreased since 1970, then, many authors contend, the South would have benefitted from the Northern decline if migration of plants or firms had played a major role in this shift. But only 1.5 percent of the North's employment losses between 1969 and 1972, for example, were due to outmigration of firms, and only 1.2 percent of the employment gains in the South were due to firm inmigration. Yet over 50 percent of the employment losses were due to the demise of firms in the North, and 64 percent of the employment increase in the South was due to expansion of existing firms. Thus, the argument cannot possibly hold (24). Rees likewise states that "in the South the primary cause of increasing employment has been the expansion of existing firms and the birth of new ones." An unpublished 1975 study by Allaman and Birch, which was based on the Dun and Bradstreet national directory for the period 1970-1972, indicates that the Northern decline was based largely on closures of firms rather than relocation.

Rees's conclusion that the process of regional economic growth in the U.S. is not a zero-sum game situation and that "growth in the South does not necessarily imply decline in the Northeast" is shared by other authors as well, all of whom seem to rely heavily on the same empirical study (25).

It should be pointed out that modern corporate reality supplies an endless array of other ways of shifting real and monetary capital, entrepreneurial and other human resources, know-how, and "control" between regions where such shifts may well be statistically recorded as "closure" or "death" in one region and "birth" or "expansion" of existing facilities in another instead of "relocation." "Births" and "death" drawn from Dun and Bradstreet entries give little or no indication of the underlying behavioral and organizational processes involved and imply an independence between actions which may in fact not exist. Such processes may be interrelated in complex, interregional ways, involving indirect ownership patterns, hidden conglomerations, investment policies of major banks, pension funds, and other organizations which make the concept of "local" ownership or control a rather tenuous proposition (26).

Thus, while there is every indication that, in the future, southern industrialization will be more locally and regionally "owned" and "controlled," due to past and present relocations of headquarters to the South, it appears questionable that the degree of indigenousness has reached the levels implied by some of the cited authors. Therefore, in the opinion of this author, the question of "on what kind of micro-scopic and organizational characteristics the relative growth of the South was built" has not been answered. Indeed, it may be an excellent example of the inadequacy of existing data and statistics in this field of inquiry and the need for more initial case studies which could explore the full range of possible organizational processes involved in such interregional changes.

FEDERAL INFLUENCES ON CORPORATE AND REGIONAL DEVELOPMENT

Selected topics and issues which relate more specifically to the American governmental system and their interdependencies with regional and corporate developments are explored on the following pages.

Unlike the situation in the United Kingdom, the federal government in the United States has no direct influence on industrial location decisions through permits or other means (27). Nevertheless, in one way or the other, corporate spatial behavior is influenced by all types of government involvement in economic affairs. These include:

(a) Tax exemptions for industrial bonding financing;

(b) Operation of federally owned production facilities, particularly for the manufacturing of military hardware;

(c) Antitrust legislation and enforcement;

(d) Environmental legislation and enforcement;

(e) Financial support of research and development activities;

(f) Financial backing of large private corporations deemed necessary for national security or local employment reasons (Lockheed, 1971; Chrysler, 1979);

(g) Federal government contracts with private firms for the supply of items such as rockets, airplanes, office desks, and pencils;

(h) Countless items of legislation and executive orders which have an overt or hidden regional dimension.

THE CORPORATE ELEMENT IN THE CONCENTRATION OF DEFENSE EXPENDITURES

Two interrelated factors appear to have contributed most to the concentration of defense and space expenditures in newer industrial areas outside the traditional manufacturing belt. First, due to the characteristics of modern ordinance products, "new" industries (such as aerospace and electronics) located in California, Texas, and Washington, are drawn upon more than older industries and industrial areas. Second, the complexity and size of modern weapon systems favor large corporations for the integrative stages, i.e., as final assembly and "prime" contractors. Such prime contractors are highly concentrated in specific metropolitan areas (28). Obviously, spatial diffusion of federal military and NASA procurement funds does occur as a result of the allocation of contract performance within corporations, and the awarding of subcontracts and the existence of ordinary supply linkages to other firms. However, neither type of these diffusion channels significantly contributes to a wider spread of Pentagon dollars as one would expect, at least not during the very early rounds of the indirect linkage relationships (29).

STATE AND LOCAL LEVEL PROCUREMENT IMPACTS AND INSTABILITY

While at the state level, the dependence on large-scale procurement contracts is most significant from a budgetary point of view; the impact at the local and metropolitan levels is most visible in terms of trends in employment and unemployment. Here, the resulting "regional" problem is aggravated by the spatial concentration of high direct employment levels and the "compactness" of employment and income multiplier effects.

Such patterns may be further reinforced by a particular region being linked to such military programs through only a single corporation. Thus it depends on the quality of a single body of management, its access to capital, and its ability to generate new and competitive technology. Among the important cases of regional concentration of federal procurement contractors are the following: Boeing Corporation (Seattle-Everett, Washington; Wichita, Kansas); Lockheed (Burbank, California; Marietta, Georgia); General Dynamics (San Diego, California; Dallas, Texas; Groton, Connecticut); McDonnel Douglas (St. Louis, Missouri; Long Beach, California); Hughes Aircraft (Los Angeles, California; Tucson, Arizona); Martin (Denver, Colorado); Grumman (Bethpage, Long Island, New York); Ingalls Shipbuilding Co. (Litton, Mississippi); United Aircraft (Connecticut).

While military procurement demand has occasionally been used to counter regional unemployment problems, either overtly or through congressional bargaining, such shifts are generally difficult if not inappropriate due to the specialized nature of the production involved, the spatial concentration of the industry, and the small number of firms involved. In addition, military procurement is required by law to be based on other than local or regional economic conditions (30). However, there have been cases where these Armed Services Procurement Regulations and the restrictions in the Defense Appropriations Act have been bypassed, for example by transferring defense funds to the Small Business Administration for their subsequent contracting (31).

The point which has to be stressed, however, is that the instability of military procurement activities and their large volume and degree of specialization tend to create their own regional employment problems. This may have several implications. First, the instability as such may--for national security or social reasons--require follow-up orders, possibly on a less than competitive basis, thus generating further concentration and regional dependence on the federal government. Second, the cumulative, noncompetitive dependence on federal contracts results in poor management and work habits which "rapidly infects entire communities. There is a growing body of opinion which asserts that this situation is one of the root causes of a national productivity problem which threatens our competitive position in world markets and, hence, our balance of trade " (32). Finally, due to such considerations, military procurement firms may not be the best agents of industrialization in disadvantaged regions.

Clearly, these implications do not apply only to large military contractors, but to large corporations (in cyclically sensitive industries) with large individual plants (in sensitive labor markets) as well, as the case of the U.S. automobile manufacturing industry and Chrysler's recent plea for government financial support amply demonstrates. Some military contractors (such as Boeing) who successfully reduced their dependence on government contracts were less successful in getting a grip on the cyclical investment goods characteristics of their new commercial markets.

CORPORATE POLITICAL POWER

Writers such as Pred and Friedmann (33) have extensively explored spatial and locational ramifications of different types of job control and power relationships, both from a cross sectional and developmental point of view, in unitary as well as decentralized governmental systems. Following Friedmann, one would have to interpret the present situation in the United States as one characterized by a high percentage of nonproduction personnel and the ability of large corporations to separate headquarters and other administrative functions from manufacturing locations. While one might expect corporations to use this opportunity to move headquarters into the immediate proximity of political power, namely into the national capital, Friedmann suggests that at this advanced stage of industrialization, "the extreme dependency of business on governmental power may have waned relative to the rapidly growing requirements for inter-industry contracts " (34). Since these contracts are relatively dispersed but nevertheless accessible, corporate headquarters are free to locate at a larger number of central locations. Corporate representation in Washington is then left up to occasional executive visits and to the thousands of "representatives," "corporate liaison officers," or simply "lobbyists."

The large military contractors are not the only ones maintaining lobbyists in Washington, D.C., but their activities may be ethically most questionable. In 1972, there were more than 5,000 lobbyists in the capital (35). The army of lobbyists may be the most important part of the "informal" segment of today's governmental organization. Its purpose is to insure that the goals of the lobbying organizations are met and included in legislation. Their geographic proximity and professional expertise allow them to communicate more directly with members of Congress than constituents are able to do. They maintain and cultivate the influence which, according to writers such as Galbraith, modern corporations have over governmental goal-setting procedures and legislative activities, an influence quite different from the direct, pecuniary influence which the entrepreneurial firm used to exert (and frequently still does) in order to gain specific favors from legislators or government officials (36). In this sense, the modern corporation does not buy power directly, but, since it cannot live without it, needs other ties and links to insure and cultivate it. Campaign financing of elected officials through "private" contributions by well paid corporate executives is the most direct financial way to open congressional doors for subsequent lobbying activities. Corporate collaboration with labor unions with their independent power base in Congress, their formidable political campaign chests, and their interest in employment stability at corporate locations may be the most intriguing example from a regional point of view, not least because of the North-South decay in the unions' spheres of influence (37).

To this writer's knowledge, only very little systematic insight has been gained about regional dimensions of congressional decision making patterns. Clearly we would like to know more about it than what the Wall Street Journal suggests:

> On an economic issue that will have a direct or minus impact back home, a Senator naturally votes the interest of the folks who elected him. (38)

Over the past few years, Congress had to vote on many issues which concerned directly a specific corporation and, as a result, specific regions within which these firms, or firms linked to them, were located. The Senate decision on Lockheed's federal loan guarantee is a case in point (Table 6-2). The successive funding and termination decisions for the SST and B-1 bomber constitute other examples. In all of these cases, substantive issues related to the primary "mission" of the projects were overshadowed by a variety of regional economic considerations and externalities which generated changing coalitions in Congress. The idea of modelling the development of congressional seniority and power is intriguing and may contribute to a better understanding of the dynamic, cyclical nature and regional implications of governmental decision processes (39).

It has also been suggested that as Senators gain seniority and gradually move their way up the committee structure, they remove themselves "ever farther from the public pressures that reflect the public cognizance" (40). While this

TABLE 6-2. Regional Dimensions of Senate Decisions: The Lockheed Loan Guarantee Example.
Regionale Dimensionen bei Senat Entscheidungen: Lockheed Loan Guarantee Beispiel.

Senate Decision	Affected Corporations	Affected States	Votes	Competing States	Votes[1]
HR 8432 Emergency Loan Guarantees	Lockheed Aircraft Company	California	Y Y	Washington (Boeing Co.)	N _[2]
Passage (49:48) of bill to authorize federal guarantee of $250 million in bank loans for failing major businesses (Lockheed Aircraft Corporation)		Georgia	Y Y	Missouri (McDonnell-Douglas)	N N
		Louisiana (rumors that Lockheed promised to reopen plant)	Y Y	New Mexico (General Electric parts plant for competing DC-10 engines)	N N
August 2, 1971	Avco Corporation, Nashville (contract for Lockheed-Trister wing assemblies)	Tennessee	Y Y		

[1] Votes of two senators; Y = "yea," N = "nay"

[2] Washington's junior senator had decided to make a run for the U.S. presidency in 1972 and, according to the Wall Street Journal, not only had to worry about his home state but about the California primary as well. "Mr. Jackson evidently could see only one way out: He didn't show up for the vote" (WSJ, August 5, 1971).

Sources: Congressional Quarterly, 92nd Congress, Senate Vote No. 164, HR 8432, p. 28-S; Wall Street Journal, "Anatomy of a Vote," August 5, 1971, p. 1.

argument would speak in favor of increased detachment from narrow regional interests, it is also clear that the increased seniority, familiarity with the Washington bureaucracies, and direct influence as committee and subcommittee chairpersons would increase the senator's value to the state he or she represents.

In addition to the direct influence a committee member or chairperson can have on legislation or budgetary allocations in powerful committees such as Appropriations, Armed Services, Ways and Means, or Finance, there are the modern forms of political bribery by which the Pentagon rewards favorable votes with allocations of military installations (e.g. veterans hospitals) or procurement contracts to the senator's home state.

> On the occasion of the first public display of the C-5A Transport in Marietta, Georgia, the President of the United States publicly accorded warm credit to the skill with which Senator Russell had exacted such reward from the public bureaucracy. (41)

The question arises in this context whether corporations increase their congressional clout by manipulating the corporate spatial structure. Two opposing hypotheses are plausible. A corporation gains power by concentrating its activities in one state or a small number of state(s) in order to account for a relatively strong economic impact within that state. On the other hand, a dispersion over many states would increase the congressional delegation representing corporate locations. Which of these hypotheses is valid will depend on, inter alia, the size of the corporation as a whole and of its individual units, its labor intensity and employment structure, the extent to which congressional delegations of different states with a corporate presence belong to "camps" with homogenous voting behavior, the extent to which the direct corporate impact upon any one state may be substituted by an indirect impact via important and "visible" subcontracting relationships, and the relative actual or perceived significance of any one corporation or its subsidiary among other corporations within the state or legislative districts (42).

THE ROLE OF SUBNATIONAL GOVERNMENTS

This discussion of the organizational element in federal regional policy remains incomplete since much of the relevant policy happens on a subnational or state level. Thus, the extent to which national governments tolerate regional independence and interregional economic competition appears to be an important characteristic in an evaluation of differences among federal systems.

Descending from the federal to the state and local level adds considerable differentiation to the regional policy landscape in the form of aspects as general as the state and local "business climate" or as specific as local anti-trust ordinances, environmental regulations, taxes, and zoning provisions. These territorial constraints will tend to have a different impact on firms which are operating solely within such territories and those which are or could potentially be operating in many different jurisdictions (and thus be better able to adjust their operations to the constraints of individual political territories).

Little is known about the effect of such differences in regional attractiveness on location decisions and inter-corporate resource and investment shifts in the United States. Earlier studies concluded overwhelmingly that tax differences played little or no decisive role in location decisions. Today, such findings have to be seen in a new light: we are concerned not merely with new location decisions but with a variety of organizational shifts between regions; industries, firms, and, particularly, activities within corporations have become increasingly more "footloose" as a result of changes in transportation and resource dependence, improvement in communications, and changes in industrial technology. As a result, other nonmaterial-resource-oriented location factors have become relatively more important, even though it appears that no single such location factor has yet gained the dominance which "transport cost" represented in the past. A variety of intracorporate, organizational phenomena could be considered among those "new" location factors; the preference for amenities of various kinds is often suggested to be another. Finally, state and local economic and political climate has been emerging as an important force in location decisions (43).

The shift in the weight of location factors has, in turn, brought about a change in the relationship between the location-searching corporation and the industry-searching community or state. Appreciating the extent to which both state or community government and corporations can benefit from each other, government development agencies are actively recruiting attractive industrial corporations by using a whole palette of different incentives, while corporations compare locations much more in terms of political and economic "climate" and in terms of how much they "are wanted" than was previously the case:

> It would appear that a new era has indeed emerged, at least for the more progressive communities, in which industry and community recognize each other's goals and needs and seek to achieve these in a compatible framework or perhaps not at all. (44)

Thus, one may suggest, that, analogous to the well-known Tiebout proposition, firms choose within a relevant group of states and communities, that state and that community which best satisfies its preferences for public goods, including (or in addition to) industrial climate and a package of incentives (45). Given the general outlines of such a corporate-community/state "mutual attraction" model, a large number of more specific topics need to be discussed. Among these are the following:

(a) Costs and benefits of granting local financial concessions to new industrial firms and branch plants of various kinds (and presumably not to established ones);

(b) Appropriateness and regional repercussions of using federal income tax-exempt industrial bonds for financing local and state industrialization;

(c) The effectiveness of state and local financial concessions as a location factor in attracting new "footloose" industries and corporations with different organizational and spatial structures;

(d) The jurisdictional dimension of corporate spatial and interregional structure and the distribution of corporate political power (including interstate patterns of tax avoidance by multistate corporations; congressional representation; and lobbying activities in state capitals);

(e) Issues concerning the roles which are most appropriately performed by corporations with different organizational and spatial structures in the industrialization process.

CONCLUSIONS

Some years ago, John Cumberland (46) concluded his review of U.S. regional development policy with a call for a more deliberate policy with revised goals and new priorities: "It must be a truly federal program, based upon full recognition of the federal, state and local governments as well as private interests" (46, pp. 138-139). Cumberland felt that the appropriate role for the federal government would lie in the provision of leadership in analyzing the problem, identifying consensus goals, designing guidelines, establishing rules for interregional competition, assisting local governments in implementing programs, coordinating activities between governmental levels, and continually monitoring the results.

In light of intermittent inaction and today's policy needs, Cumberland's mandate for the federal government has not lost its relevance. Granted, the public has become weary of additional federal bureaucracies and authorities, and there has been even a tendency among regional policy theorists to acknowledge that the national scale may not be the most appropriate level for many regional policy concerns:

> If the role of government were more precisely defined, the government could be smaller in size. To a great extent, the plethora of bureaucracies results from a lack of focus and comprehension--an ironic bit of fallout from the old notion of the limited state. With greater awareness of what needs to be done it will be possible to consider more fruitfully which issues are best left to local action, to regional planning, to centralized coordination, and which transcend the nation-state to require a more global approach. (47)

In addition, the Security and Exchange Commission and congressional post-Watergate investigations have revealed misuses of corporate power in the United States and the lack of coordination between the very few federal corporate control mechanisms which do exist, largely those administered

by the Department of Justice (antitrust) and the SEC. It
appears that in light of the multijurisdictional presence
of large industrial corporations, additional and simpli-
fying mechanisms are needed at the federal level, particularly due to the fact that the traditional intercommunity
competition for industries of earlier years has been supplemented increasingly by rather vigorous competition between
states for the nationally shrinking number of industrial
jobs. New policy concerns and newly emerging policy goal
antinomies (i.e., energy versus environment) have strong
regional and interregional corporate dimensions which
ought to be addressed as such and not left to the interregional logrolling procedures of Congress, particularly
in light of the corporate structure of the affected industries (e.g., energy and automobile manufacturing). Unfortunately, the same still applies to the creation and
allocation of the federal military budget.

The fact that large, multiregional industrial corporations dominating local or regional labor markets are, in
many ways, "public" institutions rather than "private"
firms has to be acknolwedged in a broader, long-term policy
context and not only at the time when management asks government for a "bail-out" funds to avoid massive lay-offs and
unacceptable regional unemployment levels.

If the large business corporation continues to plead
"that on moral questions it is 'value neutral' [and that]
as a corporation, its [sole] obligation is to seek the best
return on investment" (48), then it is the role of government
to establish these moral constraints, successively adjust
them to changing requirements, and enforce them. The concept
of corporate responsibility, particularly corporate social
and regional-economic responsibility (49) is appealing but

inadequate in scope. If one defines such responsibility as the margin which a firm yields beyond what is institutionally and legally required in the pursuit of public goals, then it appears that the size of this margin should not be determined by the profit levels in monopolistic or oligopolistic markets or by the whims of corporate decision makers who are generally rewarded on the basis of factors quite unrelated to their concerns for local and regional economic and social well-being.

NOTES

1. Time, July 23, 1979, p. 29.
2. The many ironies of bureaucratic, corporate capitalism and the lack of comprehension of proper relationships between the private and the public sector belong to our daily diet. Here is simply one example in the form of quote from an Exxon executive justifying his company's use of tax-exempt bonds for financing pollution control investment (Wall Street Journal, July 8, 1974, p. 20):

   > We're opposed in principle to this sort of thing. Exxon in general feels that private enterprise should finance on its own. We've gone this route because the bonds have been authorized by Congress and used by a number of corporations. Not to take advantage of the bonds would put us at a competitive disadvantage.

3. Townroe, P., Industrial Movement: Experience in the U.S. and the U.K. (Westmead, Hants: Saxon House, 1979), Ch. 1.
4. Cameron, G. C., Regional Economic Development: The Federal Role (Washington, D.C.: Resources for the Future, 1970); Hansen, N. M., "Regional Policy in the United States," in Regional Policy and Regional Economic Development: The Experience of Nine Western Countries, ed., N. M. Hansen (Cambridge, Mass.: Ballinger, 1972) pp. 271-303; Martin, C. H., and R. A. Leone, Local Economic Development (Lexington: Heath, 1977).
5. Hewings, G. J. D., "Industrial factors in the development of regional systems," paper presented at the Polish-American Seminar, University of Pennsylvania, April, 1979, p. 27.
6. Soja, E. W., The Political Organization of Space, Association of American Geographers Commission on College Geography, Resource Paper No. 8 (Washington, D.C., 1971), p. 13; Mc Nee, R. B., "A systems approach of understanding the geographic behavior of organizations, especially large corporations," in Spatial Perspectives on Industrial Organization and Decision-Making, ed., F. E. I. Hamilton (London: Wiley, 1974), p. 48.

7. Hawley, A. H., Urban Society: An Ecological Approach (New York: Ronald Press, 1971), p. 236.
8. Emery, F. E., and E. L. Trist, Towards a Social Ecology: Contextual Appreciation of the Future in the Present (New York: Plenum Press, 1973).
9. Krumme, G., "The interregional corporation and the region," Tijdschrift voor Econ. en Soc. Geog. 6 (1970), 318-333.
10. Krumme, G., and R. Hayter, "Implications of corporate strategies and product cycle adjustments for regional employment changes," in Locational Dynamics of Manufacturing Activity, ed. L. Collins and D. F. Walker (London: Wiley, 1975), p. 330.
11. Leibenstein, H., "A branch of economics is missing: Micro-micro theory," Journal of Economic Literature 17 (1979), 477.
12. Erickson, R. A., "The lead firm concept: An analysis of theoretical elements," Tijdschrift voor Econ. en Soc. Geog. 63 (1972), 426-437" Stöhr, W., and F. Todtling, "An evaluation of regional policies," in Human Settlement Systems, ed. N. M. Hansen (Cambridge, Mass.: Ballinger, 1978), 85-119; Thomas, M. D., "Explanatory frameworks for growth and change in uninational and multinational firms," Economic Geography 56 (1980), 1-17. Here it should be emphasized that, at the regional level, the traditional "micro" and "macro" scale frequently converge inasmuch as the large corporate presence in a region or community may constitute a significant component of total employment or total regional production (Krumme, op. cit., (note 9); Lever, W. F., "Company-dominated labour markets: The British Case," Tijdschrift voor Econ. en Soc. Geog. 69 (1978), 306-312.
13. Keeble, D., Industrial Location and Planning in the United Kingdom (London: Methuen, 1976), 4.
14. Hamilton, F. E. I., ed. Spatial Perspectives on Industrial Organization and Decision-Making (London: Wiley, 1974).
15. Summers, E. F., Industrial Invasion of Nonmetropolitan America (New York: Praeger, 1976); Lonsdale, R. E., and H. L. Seyler, eds., Nonmetropolitan Industrialization (New York: Wiley, 1979);

Jusenius, C. L., and L. C. Ledebur, <u>A Myth in the Making: The Southern Economic Challenge and Northern Economic Decline</u> (Washington, D.C.: Economic Development Administration, 1976); Weinstein, B. L. and R. E. Firestine, <u>Regional Growth and Decline in the United States: The Rise of the Sunbelt and the Decline of the Northeast</u> (New York: Praeger, 1978); and Beyers, W. B., "Contemporary trends in the regional economic development of the United States," <u>Professional Geographer</u> 31 (1979), 39-44.

16. Stöhr and Tödtling, op. cit., (note 12), p. 9.

17. Erickson, R. A., and T. R. Leinbach, "Characteristics of branch plants attracted to nonmetropolitan areas," in <u>Nonmetropolitan Industrialization</u>, ed. R. E. Lonsdale and H. L. Seyler (New York: Wiley, 1979), Ch. 4.

18. Rees, J., and B. L. Weinstein, "Industrial components of change: Structural and organizational trends in the southwestern United States," paper prepared for IGU Commission on Industrial Systems, Rotterdam, June, 1979.

19. Rees, J., "Manufacturing change, internal control and government spending in a growth region of the USA," in <u>Industrial Change: International Experience and Public Policy</u>, ed. F. E. I. Hamilton (London: Longman, 1978), 155-74.

20. Barkley, D., "Plant ownership characteristics and the locational stability of rural Iowa manufacturers," <u>Land Economics</u> 54 (1978), 92-99.

21. Klimasewski, T., The Significance of Manufacturing Activity in a Rural Area in East Tennessee, Ph.D. dissertation, University of Tennessee, Knoxville, 1974.

22. "Federal spending: The North's loss is the Sunbelt's gain," Special Report, <u>National Journal</u>, June 26, 1976, 878-891; Jusenius and Ledebur, op. cit., (note 15); Bingham, R. D., et. al., <u>The Politics of Raising State and Local Revenue</u> (New York: Praeger, 1978); and Weinstein and Firestine, op. cit., (note 15), p. 30ff.

23. Rifkin, J., and R. Barber, <u>The North Will Rise Again: Pensions, Politics and Power in the 1980s</u> (Boston: Beacon, 1978).

24. Bingham, et. al., op. cit., (note 22), p. 189.

25. Rees, op. cit., (note 19), p. 159; Weinstein and Firestine, op. cit., (note 15); Choate in The Declining Northeast: Demographic and Economic Analyses, ed. B. Chinitz (New York: Praeger, 1978), p. 64.

26. The same point was recently made by Barry Bluestone and Bennett Harrison ("Capital Mobility and Economic Dislocation," mimeographed, October, 1979).

27. Townroe, op. cit., (note 3).

28. "Although it may furnish a misleading picture of the distribution of defense production, it does show the regional pattern of final assembly. This is important because the firms involved in final assembly may be more specialized and thus find adjustment to shifts in demand more difficult. Parts and materials suppliers, on the other hand, may be more versatile their products being more like the components in products needed to satisfy civilian demand." (Bolton, R., Defense Purchases and Regional Growth (Washington, D.C.: Brookings Inst., 1966), p. 17f.; Krumme, G., "Comments on interregional subcontracting patterns and bilateral feedbacks", Journal of Regional Science 10 (1970b), p. 237f).

29. See Karaska, G. J., "The spatial impacts of defense-space procurement: An analysis of subcontracting patterns in the United States," Papers, Peace Research Society International 8 (1967), 109-122; Weidenbaum, M. L., The Economics of Peacetime Defense (New York: Praeger, 1974).

30. Cumberland, J. H., Regional Development Experiences and Prospects in the United States of America (The Hague: Mouton & Co., 1971), p. 19.

31. Fitzgerald, A. E., "Defense waste and the industrial engineer," in The War Economy of the United States: Readings in Military Industry and Economy, ed. Seymour Melman (New York: St. Martin's Press, 1971), p. 104.

32. Fitzgerald, op. cit., (note 31), p. 103.

33. Pred, A., City Systems in Advanced Economies (New York: Wiley, 1977); Friedmann, J., "The spatial organization of power in the development of urban

systems," in Systems of Cities, ed. L. S. Bourne and J. W. Simmons (New York: Oxford University Press, 1978), 328-340.

34. Friedmann, op. cit., (note 33).

35. Larson, C. J., and S. R. Nikkel, Urban Problems: Perspectives on Corporations, Governments, and Cities (Boston: Allyn and Bacon, 1979).

36. Galbraith, J. K., The New Industrial State, 3rd ed. (Boston: Houghton Mifflin, 1978), p. 318.

37. A recent example was provided by Chrysler Corporation and the United Auto Workers, both trying to convince the government that the firm should receive a $1 billion tax concession. The union's president Fraser was quoted, "We are afraid for Chrysler. Specifically we are afraid for the 135,000 families that depend on a Chrysler paycheck to buy groceries and pay the rent. It is too callous to kiss off one-third of the Big Three." He also suggested that, in return, the government, the union and the public interest ought to be represented on the board of directors, and he indicated that the union would exercise temperance in upcoming contract negotiations in order to assist the firm to become competitive with GM and Ford (Seattle Times, August 6, 1979).

38. Wall Street Journal, "Anatomy of a Vote," August 5, 1971.

39. Treas, Judith, "A life table for postwar Senate careers: A research note," Social Forces 56 (September, 1977), 202-207; and Johnston, R. J., "The geography of federal allocations in the United States: Preliminary test of some hypotheses for political geography," Geoforum 8 (1977), 319-326; It may also help to appreciate the dilemma which the State of Washington is increasingly facing. Having benefitted over several decades from accumulating power of its two "Senators from Boeing," chances are now increasing that the state may lose this accumulated clout during a relatively short period of time. Both were long-term House members before being elected to the Senate, Magnuson (now seventy-four years old) in 1944 and Jackson (sixty-seven) in 1952.

40. Galbraith, J. K., Economics and the Public Purpose (Boston: Houghton Mifflin, 1973).

41. ------, op. cit., (note 40); according to Proxmire, W., Report from Wasteland: America's Military-Industrial Complex (New York: Praeger, 1970), 102-103, Lyndon Johnson praised his political ally in the Senate in these words:

> I would have you good folks of Georgia to know that there are a lot of Marietta, Georgias, scattered throughout our fifty states. All of them would like to have the pride that comes from this production. But not all of them have the Georgia delegation.

42. "...the president can offer huge government contracts to IBM, and AT&T and Fairchild and Texas Instruments and General Motors and Lockheed and Boeing--all the great states of Christendom. No wonder they fall over themselves to anticipate his wishes; like Douglas Aircraft making sure that plenty of their subcontractors were in depressed areas when preparing their bid for the TFX contract," (Jay, A., Management and Machiavelli: An Inquiry into the Politics of Corporate Life (New York: Holt, Rinehart & Winston, 1967), p. 47.

43. Stafford, H. A., Principles of Industrial Facility Location (Atlanta, Georgia: Conway Publications, Inc., 1979), Ch. 5; Krumme, G., "Making it abroad: The evolution of Volkswagen's North-American production plans," in Spatial Analysis, Industry and Industrial Environment, Vol. II, ed. F. E. I. Hamilton and G. Linge (London: Wiley, forthcoming).

44. Hunker, H. L., Industrial Development: Concepts and Principles (Lexington, Mass.: D. C. Heath, 1974), p. 150.

45. Tiebout, C. M., "A pure theory of local expenditures," Journal of Political Economy 64 (October, 1956), 416-424.

46. Cumberland, op. cit., (note 30), 138-139.

47. Walton, C., The Ethics of Corporate Conduct (Englewood Cliffs: Prentice-Hall, 1977), p. 95.

48. Bell, Daniel, The Coming of Post-Industrial Society (New York: Basic Books, 1976), p. 291.

49. Chinitz, B., "Regional development," in _Social Responsibility and the Business Predicament_, ed. J. W. McKie (Washington, D.C.: Brookings Inst., 1974), Ch. 10.

CHAPTER 7

THE IMPACT OF DEFENSE SPENDING ON REGIONAL INDUSTRIAL CHANGE IN THE UNITED STATES

DER EINFLUSS VON VERTEIDIGUNGSAUSGABEN AUF DEN REGIONALEN INDUSTRIELLEN WANDEL IN DEN VEREINIGTEN STAATEN

John Rees

Abstract

Despite the importance of the defense budget in the economic growth of the United States, the regional impact of defense spending has been a relatively neglected research topic. After addressing the methodological problems implicit in assessing the impact of any type of government policy on regional change, this essay focuses on the interregional impact of defense procurement policy. Particular attention is paid to the differing spatial patterns of prime contracts as opposed to subcontracts. Following this, the implications of changes in defense spending on the economic health of a growing urban-industrial complex is examined in the Dallas-Fort Worth area. Industrial linkage patterns of large military-industrial firms are examined over time, and the impact of the military spending cycle on employment trends are also investigated. A positive relationship is seen between rising unemployment rates and the increased birth rates of new firms. Interregional investment allocations by the federal government become more important at a time of slower economic growth nationally; it is advocated that interregional impact statements accompany the passing of federal legislation.

Kurzfassung

Trotz der Bedeutung des Verteidigungsaushaltes für das wirtschaftliche Wachstum der Vereinigten Staaten, waren die regionalen Einflüsse von Verteidigungsausgaben ein relativ vernachlässigtes Forschungsthema. Diese Arbeit untersucht zunächst methodische Probleme, die für die Beurteilung des regionalen Einflusses jeder Art von Regierungspolitik typisch sind; danach wird der interregionale Einfluss der Verteidigungsbeschaffungspolitik behandelt. Besondere Aufmerksamkeit ist den verschiedenen Arten regionaler Einflüsse der wichtigsten Direktaufträge im Vergleich zu Unteraufträgen gewidmet. Im Anschluss daran werden die Auswirkungen der sich ändernden Verteidigungsausgaben auf die wirtschaftliche Situation eines wachsenden städtisch-industriellen Komplexes in der Dallas-Fort Worth Region geprüft. Untersucht werden sowohl der industrielle Verbund zwischen grossen militärisch-industriellen Unternehmen über einen speziellen Zeitraum hinweg als auch der Einfluss militärischer Ausgaben-Zyklen auf die Beschäftigungsentwicklung. Wachsende Arbeitslosigkeit verhält sich positiv zur steigenden Geburtsrate neuer Betriebe. Die interregionale Zuteilung von Regierungsinvestitionen wird in einer Zeit verlangsamten wirtschaftlichen Wachstum an Wichtigkeit gewinnen; schliesslich wird vorgeschlagen dass eine Erklärung, die die interregionalen Auswirkungen betrifft, der jeweiligen Bundesgesetzgebung beigefügt werden sollte.

The Impact of Defense Spending on Regional Industrial Change in the United States

During the course of the 1970s geographers in the United States have become increasingly concerned with public policy analysis and policy evaluation. This stems partly from the changing focus of geography as a discipline, from its dominant concern with methodology in the 1960s to a policy focus in the 1970s. More important, it is also a reflection of the policy makers' increasing concern with regional issues and the geographical allocation of federal resources. This stems in turn from a realization that, as national population growth rates decline, the interregional shifts in population take on an increasingly important dimension. Likewise, in an era of relatively slow national economic growth, interregional factor mobility and the growth and stagnation of regions become relatively more important issues in Washington. Furthermore, an impending presidential election in 1980 together with a post-1980 shift in regional representation in Congress can only heighten this new regional focus among decision makers in the American federal system.

This increasing regional awareness among policy makers is taking place at a time of considerable change in the American space economy, epitomized by the economic growth of states in the South and West and the revival of nonmetropolitan America. The determinants of these changes seem to be a major issue of concern. Are these changes the result of the "theory of national demand" or are they the result of "the theory of planned adjustment," as regional scholars chose to call such debates some time age (1)?

Structural changes have taken place in the American

economy recently which clearly affect the location of economic activities. These structural changes are represented by faster growth rates in the service sector as opposed to manufacturing (at least in terms of employment), and the dominance of certain high-technology sectors within manufacturing: electronics, chemicals, and aerospace-related industries in particular. These structural changes, particularly the growth of high-technology industries like electronics, are the result of higher innovation potentials and productivity increases, as suggested by the theory of national demand. They represent market mechanisms at work and are not by any means restricted to the United States (2). They have gradually led to the spatial decentralization of industrial activity in the U.S., a process which started long before the 1970s. As Table 7-1 shows, the spatial decentralization of production workers away from the Manufacturing Belt has been underway in the U.S. at least since 1947. The link between structural changes and locational changes in American industry has been shown elsewhere (3, 4), however, and will not be dealt with further in this essay.

The focus of this essay will be one aspect of "planned adjustment" in the U.S. and the extent to which the federal government reveals a regional bias in its procurement patterns, at least through national defense policy. National defense allocations will be examined over time in order to assess to what extent they can be related to the regional changes taking place. Following this, defense spending will be examined at a more micro level in the way it can influence regional economic health at the level of a metropolitan area.

TABLE 7-1. Changes in Manufacturing Employment Type by Region, 1947-1976.
Veränderungen in 'Manufacturing' Beschäftigungstypus bei Regionen 1947-1976.

Region	1947-1963			1963-1976		
	Change in Total Employment	Change in Production Workers	Change in Non-Production Workers	Change in Total Employment	Change in Production Workers	Change in Non-Production Workers
New England	- 50.2	- 205.7	155.5	- 85.7	- 141.9	56.2
Mid Atlantic	121.3	- 399.1	520.4	- 573.9	- 568.6	-5.3
East North Central	160.9	- 333.8	494.7	301.9	90.0	211.9
Manufacturing Belt	232.0	- 938.6	1170.6	- 357.7	- 620.5	262.8
West North Central	228.3	78.9	149.4	237.9	161.2	76.7
South Atlantic	600.9	320.3	280.6	609.7	397.3	212.4
East South Central	252.3	153.8	98.5	407.8	291.2	116.6
West South Central	313.8	169.3	144.4	488.2	327.4	160.8
Mountain	143.2	80.6	62.6	154.4	98.4	56.0
Pacific	884.4	444.8	439.6	266.0	182.4	83.6
Periphery	2422.9	1247.7	1175.2	2164.0	1457.9	706.1

Source: Census of Manufactures.

PROBLEMS IMPLICIT IN ASSESSING THE IMPACT OF GOVERNMENT POLICY ON REGIONAL INDUSTRIAL CHANGE

Before addressing more explicitly the impact of defense spending on regional industrial change in the U.S., a cautionary note is needed. Assessing the impact of government policy generally if fraught with methodological difficulties, not the least of which is comparing the supposed results of policy with what might have happened in the absence of such policy. Another is the problem of measuring the benefits as well as costs of federal policy and regulation. Some of the problems of policy evaluation were recently addressed by Julius Allen for the Joint Economic Committee (5) as well as by Weidenbaum and others (6). "The cost imposed on the American economy by federal regulatory activities in 1976 totaled $66.1 billion. This estimate comprises $3.2 billion in administrative costs and $62.9 billion in compliance costs" (6, p. 6). This represent 4 percent of the gross national product, $307 per person living in the U.S., 18 percent of the federal budget, and so on. Let's assume that these total estimates are nearly perfect, that they are 99 percent correct. Then the estimates would only be off by $661 million!

Some of the problems involved specifically in measuring the impact of government policy on various regions of the country (not only states but also cities and counties) have been addressed recently by Hines and Reid of the U.S. Department of Agriculture (7). Since the late 1960s detailed annual reports on federal spending in small areas have been available in the Federal Outlays series initiated by the Community Services Administration and also analyzed by Browning in this volume. Earlier editions suffered from serious deficiencies in completeness and accuracy until 1975 when program identification was improved by using the system in the Catalog of Federal Domestic Assistance. However, there is still the problem of assessing whether the county where a federal payment was received was the place where that money was spent, and its subsequent multiplier effect. The multiplier effect of federal outlays will undoubtedly vary from one program to another, while research shows that the tendency of federal dollars to migrate across regional boundaries may be very high (8).

Another problem is of a taxonomic nature, i.e., one has to differentiate between policies that have a direct, indirect, and induced impact on various regions. The kinds of policies that have an explicit, direct impact on regional industrial change are: (a) taxation policy, though most of the literature rates this to be minimal (9); (b) defense procurement policy; (c) EDA policy toward distressed areas, an agency that has hardly enough financial resources to have any major impact on development, having only one-tenth of one percent of total federal outlay (10); and (d) EPA policy and HUD's $3.3 billion Community Development Block Grant program. Other policies have a more indirect effect on regional change, e.g., the interstate highway system, the investment tax credit, deregulation in the transportation sector, and FTC classifications of mergers and acquisitions. The rest of this essay will be concerned with the impact of defense procurement policy, a form of policy that can have a large impact on regional industrial patterns, given that DOD accounted for 23 percent of total federal outlays in 1976.

THE IMPACT OF DEFENSE PROCUREMENT POLICY
ON A MACROREGIONAL SCALE

One of the major topics of contention in the recent debate on regional change in the United States is the differential effect of federal procurement policy, specifically involving national defense. Defense procurement, it has been alleged, is biased against the northeastern part of the country. "The 16 states of the Northeast and Midwest have lost a disproportionate share of the defense dollar since the 1950s and now receive a lower level of military expenditure than any other area of the country. The pattern of declining defense expenditures has increased unemployment in the sixteen state study area, exacerbating economic problems while the shift of expenditures to other areas has helped fuel those area's economic boom," claims a report by the Coalition of Northeastern Governors and Northeast Midwest Research Institute. The current North-South debate is only about the fifth time that the "Conspiracy Theory" has raised its head, but this time in the opposite direction (11).

This is not the first time that the impact of defense purchases on regional growth has been the subject of debate in the United States. It was the subject of considerable academic study by Bolton (12), Karaska (13), Tiebout (14), Leontief (15), and others in the 1960s. The Leontief study used his now-famous input-output approach to simulate the direct and indirect effects of a defense cutback in various parts of the United States. His results showed that certain Western states, Colorado, New Mexico, and California in particular, would be hard-hit together with states on the East Coast. More recently, Bezdek (16) carried out a similar study of the regional and occupational shifts in defense spending by the year 1980. He found that for the nation as a whole decreases in defense spending would likely increase aggregated employment, but again regional variations would be great. Using an admittedly rigid input-output model where he assumed changes in national output would be distributed proportionately across all industries without any allowance for interregional multiplier effects, he shows that defense spending (assuming it was transferred to domestic programs) would tend to increase total employment within the traditional Manufacturing Belt. The Western states on the other hand, including California and Texas, would suffer the greatest employment decreases, though New England and the South generally would not be very sensitive to changes in defense spending.

Other studies that have played a role in the current debate on regional defense expenditures have lacked the methodological rigor or even the proper concern for data before making their recommendations. The major data problem in many of these studies, particularly those using federal outlays, is the assumption that states receiving prime contracts are also the locations where all the work was performed. Back in the early 1960s Tiebout (15) and others had shown that roughly 50 percent of a defense prime contract was subcontracted, in many cases out of state. One source of information on subcontracting that has not been used by studies reviewed for this essay is the Bureau of Census' annual survey of defense-oriented manufacturing companies (Current Industrial Reports: Shipment of Defense Oriented Industries). State data have been reported since 1965 on subcontract as well as prime contract work. A comparison of these census data with federal outlays data indicates that the latter understate the fraction of direct federal expenditures from military procurement going to states in the Northeast, North Central, and West census regions and substantially overestimate the fraction of military procurements going to state in the Southern census region. Data on the shipments of defense-oriented industries by subcontractor as well as prime contractor were examined for selected years, and the findings are shown in Tables 7-2 through 7-6.

The years chosen for study were 1965 (when the data were first available), 1969 (the height of the Vietnam War), 1973 (when the defense budget had been cut as a proportion of GNP), and 1976 (the latest available data). The data from the 1960s therefore include an era when defense spending was at its highest while the data from the 1970s reflect defense cutbacks that may have had a regional impact. The data are based on a large sample of companies in ninety-four industries that undertake government contracts and account for 80 to 90 percent of all federal procurement. The results are aggregated at the census region level, with three regions making up the Manufacturing Belt (the Northeast, Mid-Atlantic, and East North Central regions). The Periphery has been disaggregated here to isolate the impact of the Pacific region, particularly California, on the national pattern of defense spending. The areally vast but relatively unimportant defense-oriented Mountain region has also been excluded so that the Periphery corresponds with the South census region and the West North Central region.

One would expect the Manufacturing Belt to receive a larger absolute amount of government contract work than the Periphery either in terms of employment or value of shipments. There is a greater absolute level of manufacturing activity in the three regions of the Manufacturing

TABLE 7-2. Government Contracts by Value of Shipment Per Region, 1965, 1973, 1976.
Regierungsaufträge nach dem Wert der Versendung bei Regionen, 1965, 1973, 1976.

(Amount in $ Millions)

REGION	1965 Amount	1965 % of U.S.	1973 Amount	1973 % of U.S.	1976 Amount	1976 % of U.S.
Manufacturing Belt		41.7		37.4		37.3
New England	2985.2	10.4	3258.6	10.8	5192.7	11.8
Middle Atlantic	5488.4	19.1	4284.0	14.2	5963.7	13.6
East North Central	3504.1	12.2	3740.7	12.4	5213.8	11.9
Periphery		26.5		29.1		28.7
West North Central	2102.2	7.4	2361.0	7.9	3604.5	8.2
South Atlantic	2642.3	9.2	3032.5	10.1	3712.0	8.4
East South Central	841.8	2.9	1274.5	4.2	1960.9	4.5
West South Central	1997.9	7.0	2083.6	6.9	3332.0	7.6
Other						
Mountain	892.6	3.1	1132.4	3.8	1676.1	3.8
Pacific	8306.4	28.9	8911.6	29.6	13351.0	30.3
United States	28758.9	100.0	30079.0	100.0	44008.8	100.0

Source: Current Industrial Reports: Shipments of Defense Oriented Industries.

Belt than in the four regions of the Periphery as defined here. The value of shipments of government contracts, mostly to DOD, but also NASA, ERDA, and other agencies, is broken down by region for selected years in Table 7-2. It shows that in 1965 nearly 42 percent of all government contracting was carried out in the Manufacturing Belt, 27 percent in the four census regions of the Periphery, and 29 percent in the Pacific census region alone. By the mid-1970s the proportion of government contracting in the Manufacturing Belt was down to 37 percent while the Periphery contributed 29 percent and the Pacific region stayed constant at the high rate of 30 percent. The image of the Pacific region, particularly California, as the largest government contractor in the nation is clearly evident from Table 7-2. The Manufacturing Belt, as expected, received a greater proportion of government contracts than the Periphery throughout the 1960s and 1970s.

When the same data are examined in a different light, from a relative perspective, a different pattern tends to emerge (Tables 7-3 and 7-4). From these tables it can be seen that government employment as a proportion of total employment in the defense-oriented industries and also the value of government shipments declined consistently for the nation as a whole between 1965 and 1976 (from 34 to 20 percent in the case of employment, and 27 to 14 percent in the case of value of shipments). Table 7-3 shows that over this eleven-year period the number of employees on government contracts as a proportion of total employment in these defense-oriented industries was consistently higher in the Peripheral regions than in the Manufacturing Belt, though the Pacific region once again displayed the largest proportion of government employees. Table 7-4 shows value of

TABLE 7-3. Government Employment as a Percent of Total Employment Per Region.
Regierungsbeschäftigung als Perzent der Gesamtbeschäftigung bei Regionen.

REGION	1965 %	1969 %	1973 %	1976 %
Manufacturing Belt	26.3	26.5	17.1	17.3
New England	35.7	35.4	25.4	25.7
Middle Atlantic	29.0	26.9	17.3	18.0
East North Central	14.2	17.2	8.7	8.1
Periphery	39.2	42.2	26.1	22.3
West North Central	38.7	41.7	25.2	22.7
South Atlantic	46.4	50.9	33.9	24.4
East South Central	37.2	33.7	23.0	25.1
West South Central	34.6	42.5	22.4	16.8
Other				
Mountain	51.0	38.8	27.9	25.6
Pacific	63.9	49.6	41.4	36.9
United States	33.9	33.5	22.2	20.4

Source: Current Industrial Reports.

TABLE 7-4. Value of Government Shipments as a Percent of Total Shipments Per Region.
Wert der Regierungssendungen als Perzent der Gesamtversendungen bei Regionen.

REGION	1965 %	1969 %	1973 %	1976 %
Manufacturing Belt	23.1	24	12.5	14.2
New England	33.0	33.7	16.7	24.4
Middle Atlantic	24.1	24.2	12.8	11.6
East North Central	12.1	14.2	8.0	6.7
Periphery	29.8	31.5	17.1	13.5
West North Central	33.3	32.7	19.4	18.0
South Atlantic	42.5	41.4	23.3	16.3
East South Central	25.9	25.1	16.0	13.2
West South Central	17.4	26.8	9.5	6.3
Other				
Mountain	38.7	30.8	22.6	18.0
Pacific	53.7	42.2	33.7	27.8
United States	27.2	17.4	16.7	13.8

Source: Current Industrial Reports.

shipments data which reflect a similar trend. An important characteristic here, however, is the lesser differential between the relative amount of government-oriented shipments that originate from the Manufacturing Belt compared to the Peripheral states. From 1965 to 1973 the government-oriented manufacturers in the Periphery shipped a relatively higher proportion of total shipments to government sources, but by 1976 the data show a slight reversal. Whether such a reversal continues or is just an anomaly has to await further reporting.

Tables 7-5 and 7-6 show the proportions of government shipments allocated to prime contracts and subcontracts by region over the 1965-1976 period. The Manufacturing Belt was consistently a larger receiver of prime contract awards compared to the Periphery, though the gap between the two regions decreased to within 2 percentage points by 1976. The largest single receiver of prime contracts throughout the period was the Pacific census region once again. Table 7-6 is more significant for the purposes of this essay since it shows the consistent dominance of the Manufacturing Belt relative to the Periphery as the location of subcontracting work carried out for the prime contractors. The Manufacturing Belt produced over 50 percent of the subcontracts in 1965, though this had fallen to 48 percent in 1976. The Periphery only accounted for 18 to 22 percent of the subcontracting work over the 1965-1976 period, an amount substantially less than that carried out in the Pacific region.

The inference that can be made from Table 7-6 is that many of the prime contracts let in the Periphery are subcontracted to the companies in the Manufacturing Belt. It tends to confirm the high degree of interregional industrial linkages between key growth centers of the Southwest and the

TABLE 7-5. Regions' Share of Prime Contract Awards in 1965, 1973, 1976.
Regionalle Anteile der Zuerkennung von wichtigen Verträgen in 1965, 1973, 1976.

(Amount in $ Millions)

REGION	1965 Amount	1965 % of U.S.	1973 Amount	1973 % of U.S.	1976 Amount	1976 % of U.S.
Manufacturing Belt		38.4		34.9		33.7
New England	2113.0	9.9	2438.2	10.5	3837.3	11.7
Middle Atlantic	3900.1	18.2	2987.1	12.8	4029.7	12.3
East North Central	2192.1	10.3	2700.6	11.6	3172.7	9.7
Periphery		29.1		31.3		31.8
West North Central	1681.6	7.9	2082.5	9.0	3012.3	9.2
South Atlantic	2196.7	10.3	2343.2	10.1	2982.7	9.1
East South Central	661.7	3.1	1090.8	4.7	1697.5	5.2
West South Central	1676.7	7.8	1737.8	7.5	2723.8	8.3
Other						
Mountain	639.7	3.0	794.2	3.4	1170.1	3.6
Pacific	6325.1	29.6	7097.1	30.5	10138.9	30.9
United States	21386.7	100.0	23271.3	100.0	32764.9	100.0

Source: U.S. Current Industrial Reports.

TABLE 7-6. Regions' Share of Subcontracts in 1965, 1973, 1976.
Regionalle Anteile von Unteraufträgen in 1965, 1973, 1976.

(Amount in $ Millions)

REGION	1965 Amount	1965 % of U.S.	1973 Amount	1973 % of U.S.	1976 Amount	1976 % of U.S.
Manufacturing Belt		51.1		46.5		47.5
New England	872.2	11.8	820.5	12.1	1355.6	12.1
Middle Atlantic	1588.3	21.8	1296.9	19.1	1934.1	17.2
East North Central	1312.0	17.8	1040.1	15.3	2041.1	18.2
Periphery		18.5		22.0		19.5
West North Central	438.6	6.0	278.5	4.1	592.2	5.3
South Atlantic	445.6	6.0	689.3	10.1	729.3	6.5
East South Central	180.1	2.4	183.7	2.7	263.5	2.3
West South Central	301.2	4.1	345.8	5.1	608.2	5.4
Other						
Mountain	242.9	3.4	338.2	5.0	506.0	4.5
Pacific	1982.3	26.9	1814.5	26.7	3212.1	28.6
United States	7373.8	100.0	6807.5	100.0	11243.8	100.0

Source: Current Industrial Reports.

more established manufacturing areas of the country as suggested by other research carried out in the Dallas-Fort Worth area, the second largest SMSA responsible for government shipments in 1976 (17).

The patterns discussed so far are descriptive and do not explain the role of defense policy in the changing regional geography of the United States. But this first stage of scientific endeavor, examining the regional patterns, has already led to a host of unsubstantiated inferences about regional biases in federal spending. This cursory examination shows that the relative dependence of state economies on federal defense spending is greater in the peripheral growth areas of the U.S. than is the case in the Manufacturing Belt throughout the 1960s and early 1970s. The data confirm the fallacy of assuming the location of prime contract work to be the location of subcontracting. This section also shows that census data, the most reliable available to researchers, do not substantiate the accusation that states of the South and Southwest obtain a disproportionate share of federal defense dollars.

DEFENSE SPENDING AND INDUSTRIAL CHANGE AT THE MICRO LEVEL

To further examine the impact that defense policy can have on regional industrial trends, one has to dig deeper to a more micro level that encompasses individual metropolitan areas and the behavior of specific companies. This reveals that a relatively small number of companies are responsible for a relatively large share of defense contracts. From a detailed survey of manufacturing companies in the Dallas-Fort Worth area, where the growth industries sell most of their output to the Department of Defense (Texas Input-

Output Model 1972, 1978) one can draw inferences about the effect of defense spending on the urban-regional scale by examining industrial linkage patterns and cyclical employment changes at the company level.

SPATIAL PROCUREMENT PATTERNS OF LARGE DEFENSE CONTRACTORS IN THE DALLAS-FORT WORTH AREA

As a part of a larger study that examines the impact of branch plants, acquisition, and firm births on employment, linkages and technology changes (17) data on the spatial procurement patterns (backward linkages) of five large defense contractors in the Dallas-Forth Worth area were examined for 1975. All five companies employed more than 4,000 people each in the Dallas-Fort Worth area, and each supplied between 35 and 100 percent of their output to the Department of Defense. The geographical procurement pattern of five of these firms is shown in Table 7-7, which only includes states contributing one percent or more of the total plant procurement in 1975. Total purchasing amounts varied between $50 and $700 million for this sample in 1975.

Despite the large geographical scatter evident in Table 7-7, the backward linkage patterns of these three companies show a high degree of reliance on the leading manufacturing states in the country and tend to confirm the hypothesis postulated in the first part of this essay: that the spatial pattern of prime defense contractors differs considerably from that of subcontractors. All three companies are dependent in their procurement of materials produced in the traditional Manufacturing Belt, the "American Ruhr" of the Northeast and Midwest, an area that showed an absolute decline in manufacturing employment between 1967 and 1975.

TABLE 7-7. Procurement Patterns of Three Large Defense Contractors in Dallas-Fort Worth Area.*
Beschaffungsmodelle von drei grossen Verteidigungs Verträgern in der Dallas-Fort Worth Region.

STATE	PERCENT PROCUREMENT			1975 PRIME MILITARY CONTRACTS
N. Hampshire	1.0	.14	.25	100
Massachusetts	1.5	2.1	2.5	1,781
Connecticut	1.9	1.3	1.0	2,642
New York	27.5	7.3	4.8	2,785
New Jersey	2.2	3.3	3.5	968
Pennsylvania	1.1	2.1	4.7	1,307
Ohio	1.6	.4	1.7	994
Indiana	.2	.14	1.9	748
Illinois	1.5	.7	4.1	456
Minnesota	.6	1.2	1.1	408
Missouri	6.0	.9	.3	296
Kansas	.1	.4	1.6	1,373
Maryland	1.1	.21	.3	743
Virginia	.16	5.3	2.3	953
Tennessee	.02	1.0	.6	329
Alabama	.1	2.0	.03	336
Oklahoma	.2	1.2	.3	170
Texas	18.3	45.0	46.0	1,914
Colorado	.12	.5	1.8	239
New Mexico	.02	3.3	.01	103
California	31.0	16.0	17.0	6,917

*Only includes states where firms bought 1 percent or more of total procurement. Data compiled from company sources.

Among the nation's leading manufacturing states, California, New York, Connecticut, Texas, and Massachusetts received the greatest amount of prime military contracts per capita from the Department of Defense in 1975, but these are not all growth states. This again questions the argument that the states receiving the greatest amounts of defense contracts per capita were the growth states, i.e., that the spatial allocation of the defense budget has subsidized the recent interregional growth and decline in the U.S. Because a considerable amount of covariation seems to exist between the procurement patterns of this sample of three companies, an inverse distance decay effect was found, as was the case in an earlier study of defense subcontracting from Philadelphia (13).

Given the procedures by which defense contracts are allocated, it is also important to consider geographical procurement patterns over time, as it is possible for large fluctuations in federal outlays to have disequilibriating tendencies within urban industrial complexes. The stability or lack of stability of industrial linkages over time can have important influences on regional development, but little is known about temporal changes in spatial linkage patterns. Table 7-8 shows the changes in the geographical procurement patterns of one of the largest defense-oriented companies in the Dallas-Fort Worth area between 1973 and 1975, with such changes amounting to large investment reallocations (around $100 million per year) between states. Company purchases varied by 8 percent in Texas itself in two consecutive years, whereas procurement from California increased by 27 percent and that from Connecticut decreased by 23 percent. These reallocations are based on total purchases of $237 million and $393 million in two years, pre-

TABLE 7-8. Backward Linkage Patterns of One Large Defense Contractor Over Time.*
    Komponenten Lieferant Modelle von einem grossen Verteidigungsverträger.

	PERCENT PROCUREMENT		
STATE	1975	1974	1973
Vermont	.7	1.2	8.0
Massachusetts	.8	1.5	.5
Connecticut	1.1	5.1	28.0
New York	1.5	2.8	2.0
New Jersey	1.3	2.1	2.1
Pennsylvania	.7	1.5	.6
Ohio	5.3	9.2	5.1
Indiana	2.4	4.8	3.2
Illinois	.5	1.3	.9
Michigan	.8	1.5	1.5
Wisconsin	.5	1.1	.9
Missouri	.5	1.3	.7
Kansas	3.2	4.8	3.4
North Carolina	2.1	.2	.2
Oklahoma	.1	1.5	.3
Texas	30.5	36.6	28.2
Arizona	1.0	2.6	.9
Utah	1.4	1.0	.04
Washington	1.5	.7	.04
California	42.0	15.0	12.0

* Includes states where 1 percent or more of total supplies purchased.

sumably affecting numerous job opportunities. The same company disclosed that these changes involved intracompany purchases amounting to 9 percent of the total procurement in 1973, 10 percent in 1974, and 16 percent in 1975, involving other company divisions in Texas, California, and New York State. In 1973 the Texas division of the company supplied 9 percent of the intracompany purchases, 43 percent in 1974, and 40 percent in 1975. The California division on the other hand supplied 32 percent of intracompany purchases in 1974 and 47 percent in 1975, whereas the New York division supplied 24 percent in 1974 and 13 percent in 1975. This shows that defense budget changes can have a differential effect on intracompany purchases as well as intercompany transactions. One company division does not necessarily buy the products of another division even when they are available if another company can supply them at cheaper rates. Companies may have policies that encourage strong competition between the divisions, and it is not necessarily the case that large companies always prefer and subsidize their own units. Such competitive pressures between units of the same company as well as between separate companies can have disturbing effects on regional economies, particularly when defense contracts fluctuate so much on an annual basis.

EMPLOYMENT CHANGES IN MILITARY-INDUSTRIAL FIRMS

Constant changes in defense budgets and their concomitant interregional multiplier impacts through procurement patterns can have major repercussions on regional employment trends (17). Table 7-9 shows the large magnitude of employment changes over time in five of Dallas-Fort Worth's largest

TABLE 7-9. Defense Firm's Employment Trends in Dallas-Fort Worth Area. Beschäftigungs Trend von Verteidigungsauftragnehmern in der Dallas-Fort Worth Region.

					DFW UNEMPLOYMENT PERCENT
1965	10,500	6,500	9,000	13,750	17,000	4.4
1966	10,500	6,500	9,000	16,568	18,000	3.3
1967	10,600	6,500	15,000	23,376	18,000	2.7
1968	10,500	6,700	22,000	28,847	24,000	2.3
1969	10,600	6,300	23,300	27,847	30,000	2.2
1970	10,900	6,300	21,000	25,589	22,500	3.6
1971	8,800	4,500	15,000	15,818	23,500	4.4
1972	7,300	3,500	12,000	11,230	28,000	4.0
1973	6,800	4,000	12,000	9,233	32,000	2.7
1974	7,500	4,300	11,000	7,080	32,000	3.5
1975	9,600	5,300	12,000	7,054	28,000	5.3
1976	10,000	4,700	12,000	7,050	27,000	4.3

military-industrial manufacturers relative to the region's overall unemployment rates. When defense spending as a proportion of the GNP declined in the early 1970s, this translated itself into employment layoffs in most of the region's leading defense companies. The cuts in the smallest employer were not as severe, while the larger employer (which also had large commercial markets for its diverse range of products) actually increased between 1970 and 1976 after a sharp cut between 1969 and 1970. As these defense cutbacks took place, the unemployment rate increased accordingly. But these unemployment rates would have been much higher had it not been for the diverse economic base of the Dallas-Fort Worth area generally, which has a large financial and nondurable producing sector as well (17).

When aggregate data on manufacturing trends in the Dallas-Fort Worth area are examined, a healthy picture can emerge (17). But the details behind this broad picture are not so healthy, given the sensitivity of numerous plants and companies to the military-industrial funding cycle. Such dependence on military contracts could have initiated a "Boeing type" of recession experience as in Seattle in 1969 if it were not for two counterbalancing forces. One was firm adaptation to uncertain environments, and the ability of the Dallas-Fort Worth manufacturers to reorient themselves to commercial and international marketing opportunities. The other process was a seedbed effect taking place in the region, with an increase in firm births taking place during the time of employment layoffs.

When the birth rate of new manufacturing companies is examined in the Dallas-Fort Worth area even in the 1965-1976 period, it shows a positive relationship to the local unemployment rate. This suggests, contrary to expectations in this case, that recessionary periods, or at least downturns caused by the military spending cycle, are opportunistic times for the birth of new firms. In this case, the military recession of the early 1970s enabled risk-taking entrepreneurs with available capital to tap laid-off, skilled labor pools and to start their own companies. This tendency was confirmed by interviews with personnel managers of new firms in the Dallas-Fort Worth area. Though one may expect such "spin-offs" to be more prevalent during times of prosperity, a recessionary period in this case led to the spawning of new industrial growth. Little support for such a trend has been found in other areas, though this tendency may be implicit in what Schumpeter (18) meant by the process of creative destruction.

This section has therefore shown that through what Pred (19) termed nonlocal multiplier mechanisms, few large employers heavily dependent on military contracts in one metropolitan area can have a major impact on the economic health of other urban-industrial complexes around the country. Furthermore, large-scale annual changes in the purchasing patterns of such companies have the potential for having drastic effects on the economic welfare of their regions. This is an induced impact on regional economies that is often underestimated when government contracts are allocated. Yet such impacts could easily be anticipated if interregional impact statements were a mandatory part of federal policy making, in the way that inflation impact statements may become mandatory on all future federal policy that involves the regulation of industry. This section also shows that despite the instability that can be introduced into specific labor markets via federal procurement policies, regional recessions induced by cutbacks in military spending can be an opportunistic time for the birth of new firms, at least in growth areas. It is doubtful whether this would also be true of recessions which may be caused by other factors or in less healthy economic regions.

CONCLUSIONS

This essay has described the interregional pattern of defense spending in the 1960s and 1970s, and the effect that linkage and employment fluctuations in a few military-oriented firms can have on the economic health of urban economies. The patterns outlined should shed some light on a topic that has gained considerable attention in the media and from policy makers--mostly as a result of what has been called Newton's Third Law of Journalism where every overreaction leads to an equal and opposite overreaction.

An examination of the patterns outlined in this essay should also confirm the notion that the federal government, through its procurement policies, is a forum for planned adjustment in the U.S. regional system in a de facto if no de jure sense. However, this still leaves unanswered the complex question whether such federal policies, either by design or by accident, played a more important role than national demand or technological change in the major changes that have taken place in the U.S. space economy in the 1960s and 1970s. These regional changes may never be answered in such simple terms, given the incrementalism implicit in such change and given the myriad of complex interdependencies between the causal factors behind such changes. The research and development intensive nature of military products and the growing innovative capacity of the peripheral regions of the U.S. provide a complementarity of processes that make the accumulation of causal relationships more important as explanatory factors than any one single cause.

NOTES

1. Rees, J., Government Policy and Industrial Location in the United States, Special Study on Economic Change, Joint Economic Committee (Washington, D.C.: U.S. Congress, Governmental Publication Office, 1980).
2. Hamilton, F. E. I., "Aspects of Industrial Mobility in the British Economy," Regional Studies 12 (1978), 153-165.
3. Norton, R. D., and J. Rees, "The Product Cycle and the Spatial Decentralization of American Manufacturing," Regional Studies 13 (1979), 141-151.
4. Rees, J., "Technological Change and Regional Shifts in American Manufacturing," Professional Geographer 31 (1979), 45-54.
5. Allen, J. W., Costs and Benefits of Federal Regulation: An Overview (Washington, D.C.: Congressional Research Service, 1978).
6. Weidenbaum, M. L. and R. DeFina, The Cost of Federal Regulation of Economic Activity, Reprint No. 88 (Washington, D.C.: American Enterprise Institute, 1978).
7. Hines, F. K., and J. M. Reid, "Using Federal Outlays Data to Measure Program Equity: Opportunities and Limitations," American Journal of Agricultural Economics 59 (1977), 1013-1019.
8. Bahl, R. W. and J. J. Warford, "Interstate Distribution of Benefits from the Federal Budgetary Process," National Tax Journal 24 (1971), 169-176.
9. Advisory Commission on Intergovernmental Relations, "Study of Interstate Competition for Industry," preliminary report, 1978.
10. Miernyk, W. H., "The Tools of Regional Development Policy: An Evaluation," paper presented to Regional Science Association, 1978.
11. Danhof, C. H., "Four Decades of Thought on the South's Economic Problems" in Essays in Southern Economic Development, ed. M. L. Greenhut and W. T. Whitman (Chapel Hill: University of North Carolina Press, 1964), 7-68.

12. Bolton, R. E., *Defense Purchases and Regional Growth*, (Washington, D.C.: The Brookings Institution, 1966).

13. Karaska, G. J., "Inter-regional flows of defense-space awards: the role of subcontracting in an impact analysis of changes in the levels of defense awards upon the Philadelphia economy," *Papers, Peace Research Society* 5 (1966), 45-62.

14. Tiebout, C. M. and R. S. Peterson, "Measuring the Impact of Regional Defense-Space Expenditures," *Review of Economics and Statistics*, 46 (1964), 421-428.

15. Leontief, W., et al., "The economic impact-industrial and regional-of an arms cut," *Review of Economics and Statistics* 47 (1965(, 217-234.

16. Bezdek, R. H., "The 1980 Economic Impact--Regional and Occupational--of Compensated Shifts in Defense Spending," *Journal of Regional Science* 15 (1975), 183-198.

17. Rees, J., "Manufacturing change, internal control and government spending in a growth region of the USA," in *Industrial Change: International Experience and Public Policy*, ed. F. E. I. Hamilton (London: Longman, 1978), 155-174.

18. Schumpeter, J. A., *Capitalism, Socialism and Democracy*, (New York: Harper and Row, 1942).

19. Pred, A. R., "The interurban transmission of growth in advanced economies: empirical findings versus regional-planning assumptions," *Regional Studies* 10 (1976), 151-171.

CHAPTER 8

FEDERAL HOUSING POLICY AND LOCAL HOUSING MARKETS

DIE WOHNUNGSPOLITIK DES BUNDES UND DIE ÖRTLICHEN WOHNUNGSMÄRKTE

John S. Adams

Abstract

The supply of United States urban housing has expanded annually as private builders erected annual rings of new construction around the edges of the existing stock. New demand for housing has depended on net household formations, which depend in turn on birth rates of a generation earlier. Almost all new housing in America is occupied first by upper middle income families. Low and moderate income families improve their housing by moving into housing discarded by wealthier households. Federal housing policy works through federal and state regulated financial institutions, and through state and local governmental units and agencies. Policy goals are (a) to stabilize normal fluctuations in housing construction, (b) to promote mortgage lending by minimizing risk to financial institutions, (c) to try to insulate the mortgage market from the rest of the money market so as to ensure a steady flow of mortgage funds, and (d) to promote subsidy programs for low and moderate income families. Experience shows that elements of federal policy are often blunt instruments when applied to the realities of local housing markets.

Kurzfassung

Das Angebot an Wohnhäusern in den Städten wird jährlich erweitert, indem private Baufirmen jährlich Ringe neuer Bauten um den vorhandenen Bestand herum errichten. Der neue Bedarf an Wohnungen hängt von den Nettohaushaltsbildungen ab, die selber von der Geburtenrate der vorigen Generation bestimmt wird. Neue Wohnungen werden in Amerika zum grössten Teil für Familien der oberen Mittelklasse gebaut. Familien mit niedrigem und mittleren Einkommen verbessern ihre Wohnsituation dadurch, dass sie in die Häuser, die von wohlhabenden Familien verlassen wurden, einziehen. Die Wohnungspolitik der Bundesregierung bezweck durch die Aktivitäten der von der Bundesregierung und dem Staat geregelten Finanzinstitute und der Staats- und Ortsbehörden (1) den Ausgleich der normalen Schwankungen im Wohnungsbau, (2) die Förderung der Hypotheksleihen durch Verringerung des Risikos für Finanzinstitute, (3) die Absonderung des Hypothekenmarkt von dem Rest des Geldmarkts, um einen ständigen Strom der Hypothekengelder zu sichern, und (4) die Beförderung der Subventionsprogramme für Familien mit niedrigem und mittleren Einkommen. Die Erfahrung beweist, dass die Elemente der Bundespolitik oft stumpfe Instrumente sind, wenn sie auf die Wirklichkeit der örtlichen Wohnungsmärkte angewandt werden.

Federal Housing Policy and Local Housing Markets

There is no better way to illustrate the distinctive features of public policy within a federal structure than to focus on the relations between housing supply, housing demand, financial institutions, and related federal policies and programs. On the supply side, one set of forces regulates the rate of new house construction. Other factors regulate the demand, which depends on the birth rate and net household formations. Financial institutions accumulate funds and provide the credit needed by house builders and house buyers. The federal government attempts to define and implement policies that advance the interests of the participants in the process. Let us examine each topic in turn.

HOUSING CONSTRUCTION HISTORY IN THE U.S.:
1889-1978

Housing construction rates in the United States have varied widely during the past century, from lows of a few hundred thousand units per year, to highs of over two million (Figure 8-1). The annual construction rates of new housing tend to rise to high levels during times of peace and prosperity, then drop sharply to low levels in times of war, economic recession, or periods of tight money, high interest rates, and general business uncertainty.

New housing built during a boom period in the construction cycle is normally placed at the edge of the existing housing stock. It has been an American tradition that most new houses are built on a speculative basis by small private builders who later sell them to middle and upper middle income households. Relatively few houses are custom built, and almost no new housing has traditionally been provided for low and moderate income households. Instead, lower income households have improved their housing by moving into used housing as it is vacated by middle and upper income families moving up to better housing.

New housing is customarily built at lower density (that is, fewer housing units per square miles) than older housing closer to the city center. Most Americans prefer low-density living and have moved to higher density locations only when journey to work requirements and urban transportation opportunities demanded those densities. The older northeastern pedestrian and horsecar cities that grew to large size before the electric streetcar was introduced in the 1880s were left with high-density cores as they entered the twentieth century (Fig. 8-2). The development of city streetcar systems between the 1880s and the 1920s meant that older cities would expand by adding lower density streetcar suburbs, while newer smaller cities could build at low densities throughout (Fig. 8-3).

After World War I the middle and upper middle classes who comprised the main market for new houses were the same groups that were buying and using private automobiles, so the added rings of new housing were built at even lower densities than those built during the streetcar era (Fig. 8-4). The net result of cities maturing at different times is that a large, old city like New York had 26,343 persons per square mile in 1970 (101 per hectare), compared to 13,936 (53) in Boston, 15,175 (58) in Philadelphia, and 15,136 (58) in Chicago. Density was lower still in newer cities like Minneapolis, with 7,884 (30 per hectare), Los Angeles with 6,060 (23), or Austin with 3,492 (13). The consequence of placing desirable, low-density housing on the suburban margins is that lower income households improve their housing and living environments by moving outward, thereby reducing the populations of older city neighborhoods and raising the population in newer suburban areas. This relocation process reached a peak in the 1960s and continues today. The majority of the new housing constructed in the United States in the twentieth century has been placed in what has become the Standard Metropolitan Statistical Area, that is, aggregates of contiguous counties (towns in New England) that include the central cities, their suburbs, and surrounding commuter hinterlands. Until 1960, about three-quarters of the annual housing starts during the twentieth century had been in the form of single-family detached houses, the style thought to be preferred by the middle and upper middle class buyers. Since 1960, the percentage of single units has dropped to half or two-thirds of annual production. In addition, since the mid-1960s, one-quarter to one-third of the singles have been mobile homes. The remaining new housing units are apartments for rental or owner-occupancy (condominiums), and most of them were built in the suburbs to house young people leaving home to form households of their own (1, pp. 12-15, 447-452).

The housing construction industry is one of the country's major industries, producing $26-43 billion worth of product each year since 1960. Its aggregate national level of activity fluctuates sharply with varying economic conditions, especially those affecting loan availability and mortgage interest rates. But the industry is geographically so dispersed, the local variations in construction activity can be so extreme, and it uses such a wide range of construction materials, transportation services, business services, and specialized labor services, that gyrations in the level of housing construction activity are immediately felt in most other sectors of the local and national economy. Stability in the housing construction industry therefore has become a serious matter of public concern (2, 13).

THE DEMAND FOR HOUSING AND THE FORCES THAT INFLUENCE IT

Each housing unit in the U.S. is a bundle of three packages. First, is the house or apartment unit itself, offering floor area, room volume, and interior and exterior furnishings. Second is the location of the house in terms of access to water, sewer, electricity, recreation, schools, fire and police protection, and other essential or desirable services and amenities. Third, the housing bundle includes a social setting among neighbors whom the residents want to be near and perhaps to become more like. When a household buys or rents a housing unit, it acquires simultaneously the entire bundle.

When individual tastes and needs for housing are aggregated and focused within a geographically defined housing market at the neighborhood, city, or metropolitan level, three of the basic influences on housing demand are: population size; population location; and average household size and composition. Population size affects housing demand because an increase in population must be accommodated within certain limits with a corresponding increase in housing.

Households require that their housing bundles be provided at the locations within urban areas where they want to live. With the minor exceptions of mobile homes that are truly mobile, housing is highly immobile and must be used where it is built. The mere existence of housing at an undesirable location is no guarantee that people will want to use it.

Finally, the housing bundle should match approximately the needs of the household living in it, but often what the household has and what it needs are badly matched. An elderly single person may have requirements different from those of a single young person. Both will have needs different from those of a couple with young children.

The U.S. population has risen steadily through history, although in recent decades the rate of increase has slowed (Table 8-1). The U.S. population varies because of births, deaths, immigration and outmigration. In recent decades, the most volatile of these has been the pattern of births (Figure 8-1). Variations in births during the past two generations have stimulated several kinds of instabilities in the housing market and will continue to do so for years to come.

Since 1910, the U.S. birth rate has varied from a twentieth-century low in 1933 to an all-time high in 1957. From the point of view of eventual impact in housing, the most significant elements of the birth record are the generation born before 1945 (1924-1944) and the generation born right after the war (1945-1965). Persons born in the late 1920s and 1930s reached adulthood, formed their households, and entered the housing market in the 1950s and early 1960s. It was a small generation entering a healthy economy offering high wages, low prices, and cheap abundant housing. This postwar experience set a high standard of expectations that was hard for the later generation to achieve.

That later generation was born after the war and has been reaching adulthood since the mid-1960s. It is a huge generation that entered the unhealthy economy of the 1970s,

TABLE 8-1. U.S. Population, Selected Years, and Average Annual Change.
Bevölkerung der Vereinigten Staaten, ausgewählte Jahre und durchschnittsjährliche Veränderungen.

(millions)

Year	Population	Average Annual Change
1978	217.6	
		+ 1.7
1970	203.8	
		+ 2.4
1960	180.0	
		+ 2.8
1950	151.9	
		+ 1.9
1940	132.5	
		+ .9
1930	123.1	

Source: 15, p. 6.

an economy plagued with lagging productivity, rapid growth of the public sector, exploding energy prices, and high levels of inflation brought about in part by too many dollars pursuing too few goods and services. The postwar generation is currently putting an excruciating strain on the existing housing stock, and generally lacks the productivity or purchasing power sufficient to buy or to elicit enough new housing to satisfy what are felt by them to be justifiable expectations.

The new demand for housing can be described either in raw numbers of people or in numbers of new households. In 1933, the birth low point, there were 2.3 million births. The high point in 1957 and for several years beyond was 4.3 million per year--almost twice as many. As the postwar generation left their parents' homes to form their own households, they had to be housed. As they entered the housing market in the late 1960s a gap developed between vacant housing units available and the number of housing units desired, so prices started rising at rapid rates. The gap had two sides to it, a supply side and a demand side. Production rates were fairly high, but volatile in the early 1970s when market demand was strong and the economy was ready to absorb many more new housing units than were produced. The other side of the gap was the number of new households, which have risen recently at an increasing rate (Table 8-2).

But the increase in new household formations comes from smaller average household size as well as larger populations of young people. In the last half-century the average household size in the U.S. has dropped by almost 30 percent, from 4.11 to 2.91 (Table 8-3). Thus, although the U.S. population went up 6 percent between 1970 and 1977, the number of house-

TABLE 8-2. U.S. Households, Selected Years, 1930-1978.
Vereinige Staaten Haushaltungen, ausgewählte Jahre, 1930-1978.

(millions)

Years	Total Households	Net New Households Formed
1977	74.1	
		10.7 in 7 years
1970	63.4	
		10.4 in 10 years
1960	53.0	
		10.1 in 10 years
1950	42.9	
		8.2 in 10 years
1940	34.9	
		5.0 in 10 years
1930	29.9	

Source: 15, p. 43.

TABLE 8-3. Average Population per U.S. Household, Selected Years, 1930-1977.
        Durchschnittsbevölkerung pro U.S. Haushaltungen, ausgewählte Jahre 1930-1977.

Year	Average Household Size
1977	2.91 persons
1970	3.20 persons
1960	3.38 persons
1950	3.52 persons
1940	3.77 persons
1930	4.11 persons

holds rose 17 percent.

A large share of the expanded demand for housing can be traced to a disproportionate rise in the number of one-person households, mainly young and elderly, but including all ages. There were under 5 million such households in 1950, but 15.5 million by 1977.

The consumer price index for housing rose 70 percent from 1970 to 1978, a rate exceeded only by food (82 percent), and well ahead of apparel (38 percent), transportation (63 percent), health care and recreation (58 percent), or the average for all consumer prices. Despite the price, the expanded housing demand by singles and by other new households has been fueled by prosperity, relatively low cost (by world standards) for quality housing and mortgage credit, and an increased desire for independence and self-indulgence.

In the face of housing supply gyrations due to economic forces and demand fluctuations due to demographic history and changes in life styles, public policy makers have intervened to smooth out the discontinuities and to improve equity in housing. Their policies and programs have taken diverse forms, but all have worked directly or indirectly with the system of mortgage lending institutions that has developed within the U.S. federal system.

MONEY SUPPLY AND MORTGAGE FINANCE INSTITUTIONS

To understand the process by which resources become available and are then allocated to housing construction and maintenance, it is necessary first to survey how lending capacity is created and how savings are collected by various institutions that will invest in mortgage loans (3, 8). After the mortgage loan is completed, the mortgage instrument is a marketable asset that is often sold to a long-term investor so that the financial institution can gain liquidity to allow it to originate additional mortgage loans. The most important of these institutions in terms of total assets controlled are commercial banks. In the U.S. commercial banks are private, investor-owned corporations. They receive their charters either from the federal government (national banks) or from a state government (state banks). Residential mortgages represent less than 20 percent of commercial bank assets, but those assets are so huge that the small percent makes them one of the largest holders of residential mortgages in the U.S. (Table 8-4). Commercial banks invest mainly in loans to corporations and individuals and in securities. Commercial banks have six times the assets of mutual savings banks.

The savings and loan associations operate in all states, under federal or state charter, and may be mutual associations owned by depositors or stock companies owned by investors. Federally chartered associations must be mutually owned and must belong to the Federal Home Loan Bank System. State-chartered associations are free to join, and are sometimes forced by state law to join. The Federal Home Loan Bank provides banking services for its members.

Many associations were started by local businessmen who were interested in promoting population growth and business development in a particular locale that lacked a nearby savings institution that could make mortgage loans. During the 1920s and 1930s, the savings and loan associations were generally smaller than savings banks. Loan standards during early days were sometimes inadequate, which led to instability in the 1930s. Major federal controls in the 1930s put the savings and loan associations

TABLE 8-4. Sources and Uses of Mortgage Credit by the End of 1976.
Quellen und Verwendung von Hypotheken, am Ende 1976.

(Billions of dollars)	Long terms loans held on: 1-4 family homes	Multi-family homes	Total loans originated in 1976
Savings and loan associations	$253.1	$26.9	$59.6
Commercial banks	73.0	4.3	16.7
Mutual savings banks	52.9	13.8	6.0
Life insurance companies	15.5	18.4	.4
Private, non-insured pension funds	.6	.5	*
State and local government retirement funds	2.7	2.2	.2
Mortgage companies	4.2	.1	15.0
Mortgage investment trusts	.2	1.0	.1
State and local government credit agencies	4.5	5.2	.4
Federal credit agencies	37.4	13.0	2.5
Federally supported pools (financed by securities guaranteed by GNMA, FHLMC, FMHA)	39.5	1.9	.6
State chartered credit unions			

(*negligible)

Source: 12, pp. 115-124.

on a stable footing and by the 1950s they were growing at a rate much faster than savings banks.

The savings and loan associations are the third largest group of financial intermediaries in the U.S. today, after commercial banks and insurance companies. The savings and loan associations are the largest single originator and holder of home mortgages (Table 8-4). Over 80 percent of their collected assets are invested in residential mortgages, compared to about 70 percent for mutual savings banks. The savings and loans held about half the mortgages in the U.S. in the mid-1970s. As competition for savings has sharpened in recent years, and as the demand for credit for nonresidential purchases and investment has risen sharply, savings and loans are caught in periodic squeezes as the demand for mortgage loans rises beyond what they are able to supply.

The mutual savings banks have state charters. There is no federal law permitting the chartering of mutual savings banks. These banks originated in the early nineteenth century as working class and artisan families began to save money. Their purpose was safeguarding the savings of families of modest means and providing them with a regular return. The bank then invested the savings of depositors in mortgages and bonds. The assets of these banks are owned by depositors. Mutual savings banks were founded first in New England and the Middle Atlantic states and today are found principally in those areas. With later mid-western settlement and industrialization beyond Indiana, commercial banks successfully fought the introduction of mutual savings banks. At the end of 1975 the assets and resources of over 14,000 U.S. commercial banks were $975 billion, while those of the 476 mutual savings banks stood at $121 billion. Unlike the commercial banks which may join the Federal Reserve System whether they are chartered by the state or federal government, the mutual savings banks are not allowed to join and are restricted from certain commercial banking functions such as checking accounts holding demand deposits. They may join the Federal Home Loan Bank, and the Federal Deposit Insurance Corporation (FDIC), which insures deposits up to $40,000 per account.

As a condition to writing the insurance, FDIC inspects the mutual savings banks and has had the right to set ceilings on the rate of interest that can be paid on different types of accounts. As it sets its ceilings, FDIC has been aware that the Federal Reserve Board has placed a ceiling of zero interest that commercial banks are allowed to pay on money left in demand deposits. In 1966, direct federal regulation of all interest paid by commercial banks, mutual savings banks, and savings and loan associations was established for the first time. The regulations provide that commercial banks may not pay a rate of interest as high as mutual savings banks and savings and loan associations. This rule protects the deposit growth or stability of what are called the thrift institutions (mutual savings banks and savings and loan associations) from the competition of the commercial banks. In return, the commercial banks are permitted to charge higher interest rates for their loans. Because most of the deposits in mutual savings banks and savings and loan institutions end up in the residential mortgage market, it is theoretically the supply of money to the mortgage market that gains from the higher interest paid to savers by those institutions. In each of the savings bank states there is an intense competition between the mutual savings banks and the commercial banks. Each side wants rules that will encourage maximum deposits, with restrictions on the competitor. The right to open branch banks is another hotly debated question at the state level.

There is heavy and persistent pressure on mutual savings banks and savings and loan associations to invest their mortgage funds in local, or at least instate, mortgages. Some pressure reflects an impatience with conditions in the cities where the banks are located. Critics argue that a fair share of the impressive resources of the bank should be devoted to the improvement of local housing, especially low-income housing. Other pressure comes from the bank's trustees, reflecting their interest in the bank's immediate surroundings and the city where it is located.

There are contrary pressures at work to prove to the Congress and the national banking authorities that mutual savings banks are national institutions, benefitting the entire country in their operations. The banks argue that in 1970, 39 percent of their mortgage loans were on out-of-state properties, and only one-fourth were made to other states where savings banks are legal.

In 1969, 1970, and 1973 when credit was tight due to gaps between supply and demand at existing interest rates, plus deliberate federal policy, interest rates rose, and depositors were eager for higher returns. But in 1969 withdrawals from savings banks exceeded deposits, despite a savings rate of 6 percent of national income. The savings banks failed to attract their share of the savings. As a result, many people seeking mortgage loans from savings banks were disappointed.

A second problem was created by the shift of U.S. population toward the southern and western states and away from the states having most of the savings banks. The higher growth and productivity of newly settled states was increasingly remote from older settled regions of continued demand for mortgage funds.

<u>Life insurance companies</u> are the second largest financial intermediary for savers in the 1970s. They are the fourth most important investor in residential mortgages, behind the mutual savings banks' investment. A high fraction of their loans are for nonresidential, income-producing property.

A fifth type of lending institution is the <u>mortgage company</u> or mortgage banker. Mortgage companies do not, as a rule, accept savings from the public and invest them. Instead, they perform as intermediaries for savings institutions, especially life insurance companies and the federal government, to place into long-term residential mortgages funds already saved by savers. They help borrowers and investors by originating mortgages, using their own or borrowed money. They service mortgages for lengths of time before forwarding them to the long-term lender at a time convenient to the lender.

<u>State and local public agencies</u> are a sixth source of residential mortgage money. This idea took shape in New York in 1955 with a bill authorizing the establishment of a limited profit housing company, authorizing loans of 90 percent of the value of properties and authorizing the sale of local government revenue bonds to provide the funds needed by the company. The bonds are issued by local governmental units such as cities, metro governments, or counties, or by separately chartered local housing and redevelopment agencies. Local government bonds are attractive to private investors because the interest is not subject to federal and state income taxes. The bonds are also attractive to the public agency because they sell at higher

prices than bonds with taxable interest. In the current environment of tight money and high interest rates, increasing numbers of cities large and small have expanded their sales of tax-exempt bonds to pump new, lower priced loans into the mortgage market. The recent expansion of such bonded indebtedness has elicited some sharp response from members of Congress who view it as a program option running out of control and threatening an unstable bond market instead of curing a chronic problem in the mortgage market. Nevertheless, many cities view municipal bonds as a potent device for stimulating central-city rejuvenation. Thus, the economic redevelopment of declining middle income neighborhoods has been given a strong boost from a federal tax provision that was designed for entirely different reasons (6, 8, 5, 14). The revival of interest by middle class house buyers in older middle class housing areas previously headed for decline has triggered interest by cities in providing easier mortgage financing. The city realizes that luring middle income families back into middle class inner city neighborhoods will rescue local businesses, schools, and municipal services that could not otherwise be maintained (11).

By the late 1960s energy and materials prices had begun inflating rapidly the cost of new suburban construction, while young home buyers continued to transfer their housing demand outward from the city center. Prices of older, center-city houses softened badly in real terms and sometimes in money terms. By the end of the 1960s housing abandonment was becoming widespread near the cores of the active housing sectors of many older cities. The combination of rapid inflation, slowed wage increases, concerns over energy prices and availability, and the extraordinary rise in household formations—well beyond the rate of net new-house construction in some years—meant that the old, inner-city houses, hitherto near obsolescence, began to look like good buys.

To summarize, the supply of new and used housing in each locale is controlled by a variety of historical and contemporary economic factors in that locale. The demand for housing in the locale depends on population size, household competition, and the purchasing power of households. As households enter the housing market to buy, access to mortgage loans is the key to completing most purchases. The major institutions that originate the loans or that end up holding mortgage instruments as long term investments include: commercial banks, mutual savings banks, savings and loan associations, insurance companies, mortgage bankers, state public agencies, and local public agencies.

The latest major thrust of federal policy is the Housing and Community Development Act of 1974, which has as a primary goal the reduction of the isolation of income groups within communities and geographical areas and the promotion of an increase in the diversity and vitality of neighborhoods through the spatial reconcentration of housing for persons of lower income. This law is the most recent in a series of federal measures that focus on money for housing as a key policy for urban development. Over the years it has increasingly become the policy of the federal government to channel a steady flow of mortgage money at moderate rates of interest into the money market. Several policies have been pursued and major programs have resulted (10, 12). Analysts dispute some of the results of these policies (3, 9).

FEDERAL RESIDENTIAL CREDIT POLICIES TO AID LOCAL HOUSING MARKETS

There are six main ways in which the federal government has tried to aid the stable expansion of residential mortgage credit and to insulate it from strains and fluctuations within the general money market (4). They include: interest rate subsidies, direct loans, mortgage insurance and guarantees, secondary market support, tax expenditures, and regulation of mortgage lending institutions.

Three methods are used to provide <u>interest rate subsidies</u>. The government may pay part of the interest on private loans (Section 235 Loans), make direct loans bearing interest rate subsidies (Farm Home Administration Loans), or purchase below market interest mortgages made by private lenders, paying prices that provide a slightly higher than market return (Government National Mortgage Association Tandem Loans). The focus of the 235 programs is to assist lower income families to become homeowners, and to increase construction of new housing for such families in each locale.

The <u>direct home loan</u> programs are basically aimed at providing adequate housing in rural areas, not in countering construction cycles. The GNMA Tandem program was designed to mitigate cycles in housing construction, especially to induce construction when interest rates are high and construction is declining. It appears that this program has served mainly high income borrowers who would have bought new houses without assistance.

A fourth program of housing assistance is not a credit program, but state or municipal aid programs to stabilize demand in the rental market. The Section 8 Housing Assistance Payment Program, covering new construction and units undergoing substantial rehabilitation, provides money for housing assistance payments to families whose income does not exceed 80 percent of the area median so that they can obtain standard new or rehabilitated housing at rents they can afford. The program pays the difference between the rent for a unit and 25 percent of the family's income.

Under the direct loan programs the federal government makes loans directly to certain classes of borrowers who cannot find mortgage credit elsewhere. These programs were popular during the 1950s when the federal government had frequent budget surpluses. The Section 502 Homeownership Loans are made to low and moderate income house buyers in rural areas. Money comes from sales of Farm Home Administration notes. Veterans Administration Direct Loans are made to veterans from a revolving fund for new purchases, construction, and home improvement. Section 312 Rehabilitation Loans are granted for substantially rehabilitated properties in locales that have been specifically defined as "uninsurable, high-risk, and in serious decline." There are additional small loan programs aimed specifically at the elderly and handicapped citizens and physical disaster loans.

There are four main federal mortgage insurance and guarantee programs. The Federal Housing Administration (FHA) has 40 mortgage insurance programs covering mortgage balances due to the lenders if the borrowers default. The Veterans Administration (VA) guarantees mortgage loans taken out by eligible veterans. Under the GNMA mortgage-backed securities program, GNMA guarantees securities issued by private lending institutions and backed by government-insured or guaranteed mortgages. The purpose is to attract additional funds into the mortgage market using existing loan portfolios as collateral. Finally, the Federal Home Loan Mortgage Corporation guarantees securities issued by savings and loan associations that are members of the Federal Home Loan Bank System. Again, the securities are backed principally by government-insured or guaranteed mortgages. And again, the purpose is to attract additional funds into mortgage markets.

Secondary market support means the purchase of mortgages from primary lenders and the subsequent resale or refinancing of them by federal credit agencies. The purchase of the mortgages from the primary lenders puts loanable funds back into the mortgage market. The purpose is to induce mortgage lenders at the local level to continue making mortgage loans, especially on high-risk housing designed for federally subsidized low-income occupants. The other purpose is to offset cyclical declines in private mortgage credit supplied to house buyers.

Probably the largest method of federal assistance to the local house buyer is the provision in the federal income tax law that permits the house buyer to deduct mortgage interest payments and real estate taxes from gross income in calculating net taxable income. The federal tax savings to the home owner and loss to the federal treasury from interest deductability alone in 1976 was about $5 billion. Most states with income taxes also permit deductability of interest and property taxes from gross income in calculating taxable income. Finally, the federal government regulates mortgage lending institutions to ensure a steady flow of mortgage money and to protect the stability of the private financial institutions. The main forms of control include:

(a) ceilings on deposit interest rates to control competition among lenders.

(b) limitations on investments by thrift institutions to

ensure their emphasis on mortgage loans.

(c) limitations on services provided by thrift institutions to promote their attention to the mortgage market.

(d) ceilings on FHA-insured and VA-guaranteed loan interest rates to promote house purchases and to keep interest costs down for the buyers, especially those of lower income.

(e) state usury laws, which prohibit mortgage interest rates in excess of the legal maximum, usually 8, 9, or 10 percent. If market rates rise above the legal limit, a serious decline in lending follows until the state legislature raises the ceiling.

(f) federal prohibition of discrimination against individuals in mortgage lending. The Home Mortgage Disclosure Act of 1975 requires lending institutions to report the loans they make by census tract, which will permit analysis of whether discriminatory lending policy has been practiced against entire locales.

SUMMARY AND CONCLUSIONS

Federal housing policy aims to provide a decent home for every household. But federal policies are difficult to refine for application at each locale. Moreover, the needs of earlier decades are often different from those of recent years (7, 17). At the end of the decade of the 1970s, house prices have been inflating faster than the earning power of many households. Even though inflation is a new experience for Americans, they have learned quickly that in an inflationay environment, buying a house is the best investment for them and delay costs them money. One man bought a house in the booming city of Dallas in 1977 for $47,900. By 1978 it was worth $67,000. In Danville,

Indiana, a house bought for $25,000 in 1973 sold for $50,000 in 1978. In Louisville, one family built a house for $37,000 in 1975. It was worth $65,000 in 1978.

One finance innovation that permits buyers of modest means but promising futures to buy houses is the graduated mortgage, which permits lower monthly payments in earlier years and higher payments later. This method allows a buyer a maximum early purchase in the expectation that his or her income will later rise with inflation faster than the mortgage payment.

A second major contemporary concern centers not in how to arrange a purchase for moderate income families, but where in the local market they should live. The American system of urban housing that puts the older and cheaper housing near the center of the city and the newer, more desirable, more expensive housing at the edge means that income groups tend to be geographically segregated in each local market. In addition, since racial minorities are on the average poorer than majority households, segregation by income promotes segregation by race and ethnicity. In response, some metropolitan planning agencies are encouraging suburban municipalities to encourage the creation of housing for low and moderate income families in areas that formerly were exclusively middle and upper income (16). Encouragement is provided by withholding metro government support for suburban participation in various other federal programs if the suburb will not cooperate. Such support is often an essential condition for federal approval of grants to local governments. In this way the metro government promotes federal policy at the local level.

But there are at least two sides to the debate that the poor should or should not be dispersed to the richer suburbs, just as there is a debate whether the middle income families should be welcomed back to the older central cities. The rapid return to the city of middle income households may put pressure on the poor, raise their rents, and perhaps displace them to less satisfactory housing. On the other hand, relocating the poor to the suburbs puts pressure on the middle and upper middle classes already there. The relocation of the poor may separate them from transit and other services they need. It disperses their political clout and dilutes community cohesiveness. Some even argue that dispersal of the poor to the suburbs is a bad thing because it makes their problems and the general fact of inequality in America less visible than it otherwise would be. The matter is far from settled as federal policy continues to unfold and as families continue to make their way in local housing markets.

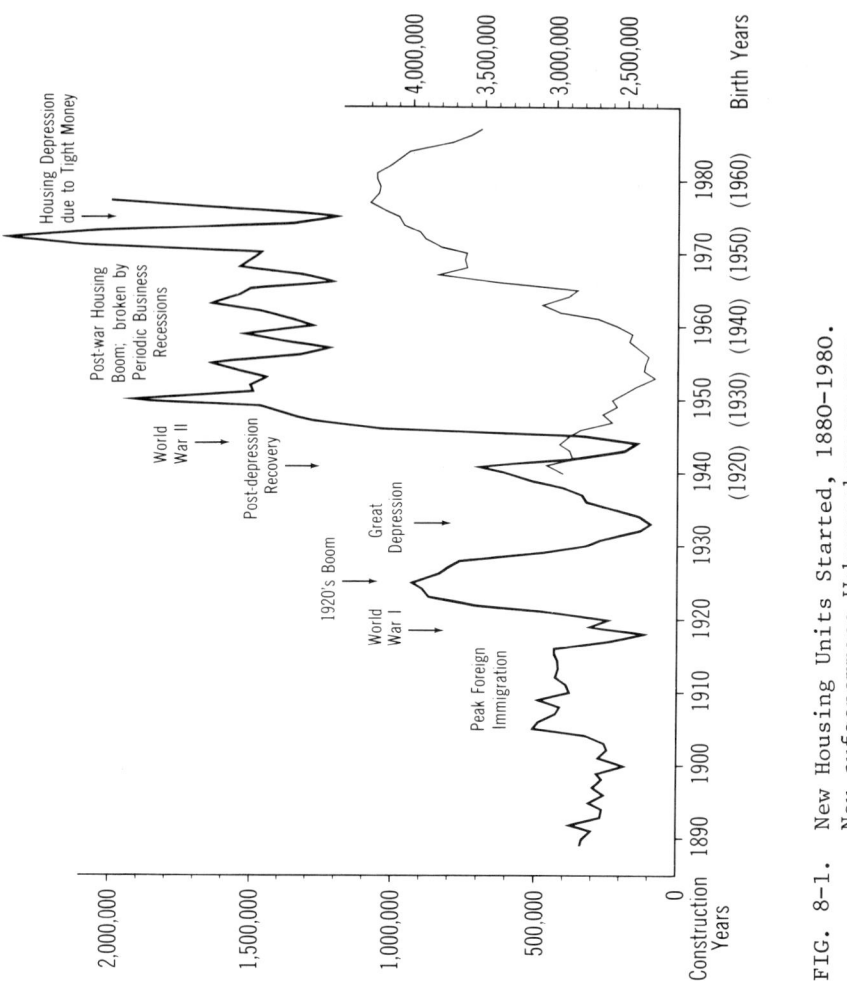

FEDERAL HOUSING POLICY AND LOCAL HOUSING MARKETS 249

FIG. 8-1. New Housing Units Started, 1880–1980.
Neu aufgenommene Wohnungsbauprogramm.

FIG. 8-2. Mid-19th Century Housing in Central Baltimore, illustrating the High Residential Densities of the Pedestrian-Horse Car City.
   Mitte 19 Jahrhundert Wohnungsanlagen im Zentrum von Baltimore welche die hohen Residenz-Densitäten der Fussgänger-Pferd Auto Stadt anzeigt.

FIG. 8-3. Turn of the Century Minneapolis, Housing Built on Wider Lots in Areas Opened Up By Extending Electric Streetcar Lines.
   Minneapolis Mitte des Jahrhunderts mit Wohnungsanlagen auf grösseren Parzellen in Gegenden die bei der Erweiterung des Strassenbahnnetzes aufgeschlossen wurden.

FEDERAL HOUSING POLICY AND LOCAL HOUSING MARKETS 251

FIG. 8-4. Apartment Houses From the 1920's, Comfortably Spaced Along Transit Lines.
 Apartments in den 1920 Jahren, mit genügend Raum entlang Durchgangslinien.

FIG. 8-5. Post-World II Automobile Oriented Suburbia--Housing From the 1950's.
 Automobile orientierte Vorstädte nach dem zweitem Weltkrieg--Wohnungen von 1950's.

NOTES

1. Abler, R and J. S. Adams, A Comparative Atlas of America's Great Cities: Twenty Metropolitan Regions (Minneapolis: University of Minnesota Press, 1976).

2. Aaron, J., Shelter and Subsidies (Washington, D.C.: The Brookings Institution, 1972).

3. Buckley, R. M., et al., Capital Markets and the Housing Sector: Perspectives on Financial Reform (Cambridge: Ballinger, 1977).

4. U.S. Congress, Congressional Budget Office, Housing Finance: Federal Programs and Issues (Washington, D.C.: U.S. Government Printing Office, September 23, 1976).

5. Downs, A., Federal Housing Subsidies: How Are They Working? (Lexington, Mass.: Lexington Books, 1973).

6. Follain, J., and R. Struyk, Homeownership Effects of Alternative Mortgage Instruments (Washington, D.C.: The Urban Institute, 1977).

7. Housing and Community Development Amendments of 1978. Hearings before the Subcommittee on Housing and Urban Affairs, of the Committee on Banking, Housing, and Urban Affairs. 95th Congress, 2nd Session (Washington, D.C.: U.S. Government Printing Office, 1978).

8. Kain, J. F. and W. C. Apgar, Jr., Simulation of Housing Market Dynamics and Evaluation of Housing Allowances. Discussion Paper D77-7 (Cambridge: Harvard University, Department of City and Regional Planning, 1977).

9. Mandelker, D. R., and R. Montgomery, Housing in America: Problems and Perspectives (Indianapolis: Bobbs-Merrill, 1973).

10. Minnesota Housing Finance Agency. Minnesota Housing Needs, Housing Resources, and Housing Resource Distribution Plans (St. Paul, Minnesota: October, 1976).

11. Paul, A., and K. Baker, Economic Investment and the Future of Neighborhoods (New York Commission on Human Rights: April, 1977).

12. President of the United States, Ninth Annual Report on National Housing Goals. 95th Congress, 1st Session. House Document No. 95-53 (Washington, D.C.: 1977).

13. Starr, R., Housing and the Money Market (New York: Basic Books, 1975).

14. Third Annual Report of the Housing Assistance Supply Experiment. The Rand Corporation. R-2151-HUD, February, 1977. Analysis of whether a national program of direct cash assistance to low-income households is feasible and desirable.

15. U.S. Bureau of the Census, Statistical Abstract of the U.S.: 1978 (Washington, D.C.: U.S. Government Printing Office, 1978).

16. U.S. Department of Housing and Urban Development, 1976 Statistical Yearbook (Washington, D.C.: U.S. Government Printing Office, 1977).

17. U.S. Department of Housing and Urban Development, The President's 1978 National Urban Policy Report (Washington, D.C.: U.S. Government Printing Office, August, 1978).

CHAPTER 9

REGIONAL POPULATION DEVELOPMENT WITHIN THE FEDERAL REPUBLIC OF GERMANY

REGIONALE BEVÖLKERUNGSENTWICKLUNG IN DER BUNDESREPUBLIK DEUTSCHLAND

Werner Fricke

Abstract

The population development of the FRG can be characterized by the enormous increase of 43 percent since 1939. Until 1950, federal states with a predominantly rural structure gained the highest number of evacuees from the cities, mainly refugees from Eastern Germany. At first this caused a more even distribution than in 1939 or today. Resettlement and migration to the more industrialized regions led to a concentration in the West and southwest of the FRG. The process of accelerated urbanization is shown in 1961 by the city regions where 56 percent of the population lived on 17 percent of the territory. The period after 1961 was dominated by the inmigration of foreign labor replacing the German population of the city center, which moved to the suburbs. The migration losses of rural areas, especially in the north and east of the FRG continue and are not compensated for by a natural increase as in former periods because of a general decline in the birth rule. Because of the independent policy of municipalities and economic forces the federal structure seems not as important for regional planning and population development.

Kurzfassung

Die Bevölkerungsentwicklung der Bundesrepublik Deutschland wird durch die sehr hohe Zunahme von 43% gegenüber dem Vorkriegsstand gekennzeichnet. Bis 1950 haben die durch eine vorherrschende Agrarstruktur gekennzeichneten Bundesländer den stärksten Zuwachs, bedingt durch Evakuierte aus den Großstädten und Flüchtlingen und Vertriebenen aus Mittel- und Ostdeutschland sowie aus Osteuropa. Hierdurch bestand gegenüber 1939 eine höhere regionale Gleichverteilung. Umsiedlungen und Wanderungen in die industrialisierteren Regionen führten

zu einer Konzentration der Bevölkerung im Westen und Süden
der Bundesrepublik. Bis 1961 verstärkte sich auch die Ver-
städterung: in den Stadtregionen lebt 56% der Bevölkerung
auf 17% der Fläche. Die Periode danach ist durch die Einwanderung ausländischer Arbeitskräfte gekennzeichnet, die besonders die deutsche Bevölkerung der Stadtkerne ersetzte, die
in die suburbane Zone abwandert. Die anhaltende Abwanderung
aus den ländlichen Gebieten der nördlichen und östlichen
Teile der Bundesrepublik wird nicht mehr wie in den früheren
Perioden ausgeglichen, da auch dort die Geburtenrate rück-
läufig ist. Infolge der Planungshoheit der Gemeinden lassen
sich in der Bevölkerungsentwicklung mehr der Einfluß wirtschaftlicher Kräfte als der der Planung nachweisen.

Regional Population Development Within the Federal Republic of Germany

INTRODUCTION

During the four decades from 1939 to 1977, the population of the Federal Republic of Germany increased from 43.0 million to 61.4 million or by 42.8 percent (Table 9-1). When West Berlin is included in the figure, the increase is almost 48 percent. This compares to a growth rate in the United States of 47.3 percent, in Great Britain of 14.7 percent, and 25.0 percent in France.

The impact of the federal structure on regional population change cannot be assessed easily. The aim of the federal Constitution (<u>Grundgesetz</u>) is to eliminate disparities in living conditions between regions and states and within the different states. It is the aim of the numerous state and federal regional development programs to promote an even distribution of population growth. Actual population redistribution has been related to forces beyond those of official government programs. This essay will focus attention on the pattern of population change in different postwar periods and will suggest some of the socioeconomic forces that have brought them about.

POSTWAR POPULATION INCREASE: THE DOMINATION OF REFUGEE INMIGRATION

<u>Pre-1950 Pattern of Refugees</u>

Prior to 1950, population redistribution was dominated by two main processes: the reverse migration of evacuees into the cities and, more important, the inmigration of refugees from the East.

Between 1939 and 1950 refugees from the eastern parts of prewar Germany, Eastern Europe and Middle Germany, and the territory of the German Democratic Republic (GDR) accounted for a population increase of 8.4 million or 20.9 percent of the territory of the FRG (1, p. 130; 2 [1963], p. 4). This is remarkable when one considers the sizable war casualties that were suffered by the region. Initially, the distribution of refugee destinations was fairly even; small communities attracted refugees because of the potential for accommodation in undamaged farmhouses and dwellings of the nonagricultural population. Cities (in Germany municipalities) with more than 100,000 inhabitants where there was emphasis on employment in the secondary and tertiary sectors accounted for 39.6 percent of the refugees. By 1950 refugees constituted 16.5 percent of the population of the FRG (excluding West Berlin). Major regional concentrations included: Schleswig-Holstein with 33.0 percent, Lower Saxony with 27.2 percent, Bavaria with 21.1 percent, and Hesse with 16.7 percent. Refugees accounted for only 5.1 percent of the population in Rhineland-Palatinate because it was in the French-occupied zone where the influx of refugees was prohibited until 1949. Moreover, the lack of employment opportunities restricted the relocation of refugees in some states, and this is evidenced by differential rates of unemployment in 1950, which is displayed in Table 9-2.

Overall, the 1950 population in the FRG was more balanced than at any other time since the beginning of industrialization and urban growth.

TABLE 9-1. Population Development Within the States of the Federal Republic of Germany 1939-1977.
Bevölkerungsentwicklung innerhalb der Länder der FRG 1939-1977.

	1939	%	1950	%	Net increase %	1961	%	Net increase %
Schleswig-Holstein	1589.0	3.7	2594.6	5.2	63.3	2317	4.1	-10.7
Lower Saxony	4539.7	10.6	6797.4	13.4	49.7	6641	11.8	- 2.3
North Rhine-Westphalia	11935.3	27.8	13197.0	26.0	10.6	15902	28.3	20.5
Hesse	3479.1	8.1	4323.8	8.5	24.3	4814	8.6	11.3
Rhineland-Palatinate	2960.0	6.9	3004.8	5.9	1.5	3417	6.1	13.7
Baden-Württemberg	5476.4	12.7	6430.2	12.7	17.4	7759	13.8	20.7
Bavaria	7084.1	16.5	9184.5	18.1	29.6	9515	17.0	3.6
Saarland	909.6	2.1	944.7	1.9	3.9	1073	1.9	13.8
SUBTOTAL	37062.7	86.2	46474.4	91.5	22.8	51438	91.6	10.7
Hamburg	1711.9	4.0	1605.6	3.2	-6.2	1832	3.3	14.1
Bremen	562.9	1.3	558.6	1.1	-0.8	706	1.3	26.4
Federal Republic	40248.0	93.6	48641.2	95.8	20.9	53976	96.1	11.0
West Berlin	2750.5	6.4	2147.0	4.2	-21.9	2197	3.9	2.7
TOTAL	42998.5	100.0	50778.2	100.0	18.1	56175	100.0	10.6

Sources: 1939, 1950, 1961: Statistiches Jahrbuch Für Die Bundesrepublik Deutschland 1963, p. 33.

1970: Statistiches Jahrbuch Für Die Bundesrepublik Deutschland 1972, p. 25.

1977: Statistiches Jahrbuch Für Die Bundesrepublik Deutschland 1978, p. 50.

1970	%	Net increase %	1977	%	Net increase %	1939-1977	Net increase %	1950-1977	Net increase %
2494	4.1	7.6	2582.7	4.2	3.6	993.7	62.5	-11.9	-0.5
7082	11.7	6.6	7226.9	11.8	2.1	2687.2	59.2	429.5	6.3
16914	27.9	6.4	17032.2	27.7	0.7	5096.9	42.7	3835.2	29.1
5382	8.9	11.8	5538.4	9.0	2.9	2059.3	59.2	1214.6	28.1
3645	6.0	6.7	3649.0	5.9	0.1	689.0	23.3	644.2	21.4
8895	14.7	14.6	9119.3	14.9	2.5	3642.9	66.5	2689.1	41.8
10479	17.3	10.1	10804.3	17.6	3.1	3720.2	52.5	1619.8	17.6
1120	1.8	4.4	1089.0	1.8	-2.8	179.4	19.7	144.3	15.3
56011	92.4	8.9	57041.8	93.0	1.8	19979.1	53.9	10567.4	22.7
1794	3.0	-2.1	1698.6	2.8	-5.3	-13.3	-0.8	93.0	5.8
723	1.2	2.4	710.0	1.2	-1.8	147.1	26.1	151.4	27.1
58528	96.5	8.4	59450.0	96.8	1.6	19202.0	47.7	10808.8	22.2
2122	3.5	-3.4	1950.7	3.2	-8.1	-799.8	-29.1	-196.3	-9.1
60650	100.0	8.0	61401.0	100.0	1.0	18402.5	42.8	10622.8	20.9

TABLE 9-2. Percentage of Unemployed (June 6, 1950).
Perzentsatz der Arbeitslosen (6.Juni, 1950).

	Population %	Labor Force %	Refugees %	Rest of Population %
Schleswig-Holstein	7.8	24.3	12.6	5.2
Lower Saxony	5.2	16.5	8.0	4.2
North Rhine-Westphalia	1.7	5.0	2.2	1.7
Hesse	3.0	9.4	5.1	2.6
Rhineland-Palatinate	2.1	8.0	6.6	2.0
Baden-Württemberg	1.3	4.1	3.0	1.0
Bavaria	3.9	12.9	7.7	2.9
Hamburg	5.9	14.1	2.3	6.2
Bremen	4.2	11.1	4.9	4.2
Federal Republic of Germany (excluding West Berlin)	3.2	10.0	6.6	2.6

Source: Statistiche Berichte 1955.

Growth Between 1950 and 1961

Between 1950 and 1961 the population increased at a rate of 10.6 percent. The major forces underlying this growth were a natural increase and continued influx of people from the GDR and East Berlin (Table 9-1) (3, p. 18). The central forces shaping the regional composition of the population between 1950 and 1960 were internal migration and resettlement programs supported by state and federal governments. These programs aimed to spread the social costs of resettlement and rehabilitation and to enable the occupational integration of at least the younger generation. By the end of 1961, the resettlement of 1.1 million people had been accomplished (1, p. 134). In Schleswig-Holstein alone 429,000 refugees were resettled, 349,000 in Lower Saxony, and 272,000 in Bavaria. Professionally qualified younger refugees moved on their own initiative to regions with better employment opportunities and were, therefore, less dependent on resettlement programs.

The second major force underlying population redistribution between 1950 and 1961 was internal migration. This involves interregional movement among the indigenous population as well as migration on the part of refugees who sometimes moved from state to state before they found permanent residence.

Nearly 35 million persons moved from one community to another and 10 million moved from one state to another between 1950 and 1960. This represents a rate of between 60.7 and 66.0 per thousand inhabitants for intercommunity migration and between 17.1 and 19.3 per thousand for interstate migration (4, p. 245). During the period 1950-1961 the net migration gain amounted to only 2.8 million. Table 9-3 shows that the number of births exceeded the deaths by

TABLE 9-3. Population Development Within the Federal States 1950-1961.
Bevölkerungsentwicklung innerhalb der Bundesländer 1950-1961.

	Census Population 13.9.1950	Surplus of Births (+) Deaths (−)	Surplus of In-(+) or Out-migration (−) Total	Surplus of In-(+) or Out-migration (−) Within the Federal Republic of Germany	Surplus of In-(+) or Out-migration (−) Outside the Federal Republic of Germany	Population increase (+) or decrease (−)	Population increase or decrease per 1000 persons	Population Census 6.6.1961[2]
		1000	1000	1000	1000	1000		
Schleswig-Holstein	2,579.9	+ 102.0	− 365.2	− 422.3	+ 57.1	− 263.3	− 102	2316.6
Hamburg	1,568.5	− 6.8	+ 270.7	+ 129.6	+ 141.1	+ 263.9	+ 168	1832.4
Lower Saxony	6,750.2	+ 422.9	− 531.6	− 862.9	+ 331.3	− 108.7	− 16	6641.4
Bremen	546.6	+ 22.1	+ 137.6	+ 103.4	+ 34.2	+ 159.7	+ 292	706.4
North Rhine-Westphalia	12,986.0	+ 914.4	+ 2001.3	+ 915.9	+ 1085.4	+ 2915.7	+ 225	15901.7
Hesse	4,257.0	+ 216.1	+ 341.2	+ 96.0	+ 245.2	+ 557.4	+ 116	4814.4
Rhineland-Palatinate	2,946.7	+ 267.6	− 202.8	− 31.7	− 171.1	+ 470.4	+ 160	3417.1
Baden-Württemberg	6,328.8	+ 531.3	+ 899.0	+ 438.3	+ 460.6	+ 1430.3	+ 226	7759.2
Bavaria	9,118.5	+ 555.8	− 160.5	− 429.6	+ 269.1	+ 395.3	+ 43	9513.9
Saarland	955.4	+ 85.6	+ 31.4	—	—	+ 117.2	+ 122	1072.6
German Fed Rep. (excluding Berlin)	48,037.7	+ 3111.0	+ 2826.9	—	—	+ 5937.9	+ 124	53975.6
West Berlin	2,147.0	− 136.4	+ 187.1	—	—	+ 50.7	+ 24	2197.6
German Fed Rep. (including Berlin)	50,184.7	+ 2974.6	+ 3013.9	—	—	+ 5988.5	+ 119	56173.2

1) Saarland: census from 14.11.1951
2) Preliminary census figures

Source: Statistiches Jahrbuch für die Bundesrepublik Deutschland 1962, p. 43.

3.1 million, but this was not as important as the migration for the regional population trends in the states (Figure 9-1).

The highest rates of positive net migration occurred in states that had little growth in the past. Figure 9-2 shows that the north, east and southeast regions of the FRG exhibited large net outmigration (in excess of 10 percent), whereas the western states of North Rhine-Westphalia (on the Lower Rhine axis-Bonn-Cologne-Dinslaken) and the east-west axis (Aachen-Hamm, the coal mining and industrial districts), reached a net inmigration of more than 10 percent. The average net migration of the FRG was about 5 percent.

Viewed in the context of population density, there was a general tendency for outmigration in the less dense regions and inmigration in the denser regions (Figure 9-3). The trend toward urbanization and industrialization has created employment centers, and they are by their very nature relatively high in density. During the 1950s, these regions experienced a net inflow of people to take jobs in the expanding industrial sector.

In terms of net migration rates, less dense, rural regions of the FRG were adversely affected by Germany's entrance into the European Economic Community (EEC). In order to maintain economic viability, existing family farms had to expand the amount of area under cultivation. The maintenance of small farms became increasingly uneconomic. Between 1949 and 1961, the number of farms decreased by 410,600 or 20.3 percent. This decline was particularly acute among very small farms with areas between two and ten hectares; they decreased by 256,000 or 26.7 percent (2 [1963], p. 159).

The decline in agricultural employment and the integration

of refugees was not always accompanied by migration, but it often led to increased commuting, a common substitute for more permanent migration. Table 9-4 shows that the percentage of labor force that commuted to work was extremely high in small communities (under 2,000 inhabitants) and in small provincial towns (with less than 20,000 inhabitants). Commuting was also pervasive in communities in and around city regions where the percent of the labor force that commuted exceeded 35 percent (Table 9-5).

Permanent relocation was necessary in regions where commuting was not possible. As a result, population growth was restricted to less than 6 percent in large parts of Schleswig-Holstein, southern Lower Saxony, areas bordering the GDR, and in remote western regions.

THE DEVELOPMENT OF CITIES AND CITY REGIONS
BEFORE 1961

The number of cities in the FRG increased steadily from the period of rapid industrialization (1871 to 1905) to 1939. In 1871 there were only four cities with more than 100,000 inhabitants comprising a total population of 340,000. By 1939, this number had increased to forty-three with a total population of 13.3 million.

In spite of a population decline in cities of 12.5 million or 5.4 percent for the period 1939 to 1950, the number of cities increased to 52 by 1961. This represented a population of 16.6 million and amounted to 30.5 percent of the population of the FRG (5, p. 331). Growth was caused by an increased concentration of industrial employment and a parallel growth in the tertiary sector. An excellent example of this is Mannheim, where the number of industrial jobs increased by 23.9 percent between 1954 and 1961. In

TABLE 9-4. Percentage of Commuters According to Size of Settlement, 1961.
Perzent von Pendlern nach der Grösse der Ansiedlung, 1961.

Size of Community (inhabitants)	Percentage of people employed in agriculture.	Percentage of commuters among gainfully employed
2000	40%	20.5%
2000	20-40%	35.0%
2000	20%	48.2%
2000- 20000		36.1%
20000-100000		17.2%
100000		5.2%

Source: K. Schwartz, op.cit., (note 1), p. 268.

TABLE 9-5. Increase of Commuters in Central Baden-Württemberg, 1900 until 1961.
Wachstum der Pendler in Zentral Baden-Württemberg, 1900 bis 1961.

Commuters employed in another community:

1900:	6.6%
1910:	8.0%
1925:	10.1%
1939:	13.8%
1950:	17.9%
1961:	25.4%

Source: K. Schwartz, op.cit., (note 1), p. 261.

1961 Mannheim had 313,000 inhabitants and 212,000 jobs of which 58 percent were in the manufacturing sector (6, p. 41).

Table 9-6 shows a breakdown of the components of population change for cities in the FRG. Net migration accounted for over six times more population increase than natural increase for the period between 1950 and 1960. Natural increase was low because birth rates in numerous cities were below average for the FRG. Major causes of low birth rates were age structures that contained a large proportion of old people, biased sex ratios, and a general reduction of fertility evidenced by a decline in the average number of children per family.

For cities themselves, the peak population increase had passed by the mid-1950s. Growth had diffused into neighboring communities and the urbanized zone where population continued to increase (7, p. 35). Reasons for growth in peripheral suburban regions include central-city flight and inmigration from outside areas. Growth of this type placed additional stress on existing transportation networks since 56.8 percent of the employed population commuted from their places of residence to working places in the cities (8).

The major reason for attracting migrants to city regions was the concentration of jobs in the secondary and tertiary sectors. On an average, 51.6 percent of the employed population in city regions were involved in the secondary sector compared to 48.8 percent for the FRG as a whole. The tendency for city regions to have large manufacturing employment is especially marked in the industrial district of the Rhine-Ruhr region where 58.8 percent of the workers were employed in the secondary sector and also in smaller city regions that developed around isolated industrial locations

TABLE 9-6. The Population Development of Cities in the Territory of the Federal Republic (Excluding West Berlin), June 6, 1961.
Die Bevölkerungsentwicklung von Städten in der Bundesrepublik (ausschliesslich West Berlin) bis 6.Juni, 1961.

Subject	Unit	Total	Male	Female
Resident population (May 17, 1939)	1.000	13,996.8	6,738.5	7,258.3
Decrease until 1950	1.000	518.4	421.0	97.4
	%	3.7	6.2	1.3
Resident population (Sept. 13, 1950)	1.000	13,478.5	6,317.5	7,160.9
Births	1.000	2,218.0	1,144.0	1,074.0
Deaths	1.000	1,803.3	949.5	858.8
Natural Increase	1.000	409.7	194.5	215.2
Net migration gain	1.000	2,714.0	1,237.1	1,476.9
Total population increase	1.000	3,123.7	1,431.6	1,692.1
	%	23.2	22.7	23.6
Resident Population (June 6, 1961)	1.000	16,602.1	7,749.1	8,853.0

Source: Wirtschaft und Statistik, 1961, op.cit., (note 5), p. 322.

mostly in the southern half of the FRG (9, p. 31). On the other hand these industrial cities show a deficit of employees in the private field of the tertiary sector. The percentage lies below 15 percent, whereas an average of 20.6 percent has been computed for all city regions amounting to 20.2 percent for the FRG. The high average for the city regions is the result of the economically most dynamic cities such as Hamburg and Bremen in the north and Frankfurt in the south. Munich is an important center for both private and public tertiary employment.

Urban development, then, can be summarized as a process of compaction until the mid-1950s followed by a process of spatially expansive or suburban growth, especially after 1961.

POPULATION REDISTRIBUTION IN THE 1960S

Important developments during the 1960s caused changes in the population distribution of the FRG. These include the end of the inmigration from the GDR, the inmigration of foreign labor, and differential decline in the birth rate.

End of Inmigration from the GDR

By the late 1950s and early 1960s, inmigration from the GDR had reached sizable proportions; it amounted to 226,300 in 1958; 1,973,800 in 1959; 225,400 in 1960, and 223,400 in 1961, whereas inmigration from foreign countries in 1953 amounted to only 99,000. In addition to their large size, the migrating population tended to be younger and better-educated than the population of the GDR in general. Whereas only 34 percent of the 1961 population of the GDR was between 14 and 40 years of age, 53 percent of the migrating group fell into this prime labor force age category. Migrants also were drawn disproportionately from professionally qualified and high school educated groups (10, p. 588; 11, p. 6).

On 13 August 1961 this influx came to an abrupt halt with the erection of the Berlin Wall. This effectively ended the large-scale inmigration of young and well educated persons from the GDR into the FRG.

Inmigration of Foreign Labor

A second process that affected population growth and distribution during the 1960s was the inmigration of foreign workers and their families. The significant flow of foreign residents into the FRG began around 1961 when there were 624,000 foreign residents in the FRG, of which 88 percent were gainfully employed. This figure was three and one-half times higher than the 1958-1959 figure (10, p. 588). In 1966 the number of foreign residents reached an initial peak of 1.3 million, but by January, 1969, this number had decreased to 900,000 due to the recession of 1967.

A second peak was reached in 1974 when the number of foreigners totaled 4.13 million and represented 6.65 percent of the FRG's population. Thereafter, the number declined because of the affects of the 1973 recession and the 1973 ban on the entry of foreign workers from non-EEC nations (Figure 9-4). This affected all major groups with the exception of the Italians since Italy is a member of the EEC. By 1977 the number of foreign residents had decreased somewhat to 3.95 million.

After 1960, the proportion of foreign residents who were gainfully employed decreased as foreign workers brought their families with them to live in the FRG. This is evidenced by the fact that only 11 percent were 16 years of age and under in 1960 as compared to 23 percent in 1973.

In 1974, the average duration of foreigners' residence in the FRG was four years, but this varied across national groups. While 23 percent of the Italian population had lived in the FRG for more than ten years, comparable figures for the Turkish population were 6 percent and 7 percent for the Yugoslavs. The latter groups entered the FRG in the large migration wave of the late 1960s and were not, as a result, as well integrated into the economy by 1974.

Destinations for foreign workers were not evenly distributed but were concentrated in the four federal states of North Rhine-Westphalia, which contained 29.1 percent of the foreign labor force in 1974, Baden-Württemberg with 22.1 percent, Bavaria with 17.8 percent, and Hesse with 10.7 percent. Within these states, the foreign worker population was concentrated in rapidly growing city regions of the Rhine axis from Düsseldorf to Mannheim and in the districts of Stuttgart and Munich. In Munich, foreign workers represented a full 19 percent of the total city population (12, p. 813).

Within the city regions themselves, there was a tendency for the spatial concentration of workers in older sections to lead to a ghettoization process. Two such areas in the Heidelberg region have been studied by the Department of Geography at the University of Heidelberg. In older sections, foreigners represented around 15 percent of the population, which is double that of the rest of the city. In the nearby provincial town of Mosbach in the Neckar Valley foreigners encompass 27 percent of the older section of the town as against 9 percent in the rest of the city. A similar relationship can be observed for German citizens over fifty years of age (Figure 9-5). Ghettoization, which results in the social and cultural isolation of foreigners, is a result of the speculative use of older housing in the zone of transition bordering the Central Business District (CBD), and it is reinforced by heavy inmigration of foreign workers from peripheral regions. Weak industrial growth in these regions results in salaries that were 20 to 28 percent lower than in the core industrial region. Economic differentials give rise to internal migration, especially among the foreign worker population. Personal information from fellow compatriots is particularly important in this process since migrants possess a very limited range of information about the dispersion of alternative destinations available to them. This information process leads to the concentration of national groups in the same area. It also evolves from the practices of large companies who prefer to employ workers from the same country of origin. An example is the concentration of 66.6 percent Turks in Salzgitter (13, p. 19).

Decline in the Birth Rate

A third factor in population change in the FRG involves decline in the birth rate, a trend displayed in Figure 9-6. The number of births per thousand population or crude birth rate reached a peak of 18.3 per thousand in 1963 due, in part, to the entry of a large cohort (a group of persons who were born at the same point in time) into prime reproductive age. Since then, the crude birth rate has steadily declined. In 1970 the crude birth rate was 13.4 per thousand, and the surplus of births over deaths was 1.3 per thousand, which translates into an annual rate of natural increase of .13 percent (14 [1952], p. 36; 2 [1972], p. 43). In addition, the very small surplus of births over deaths was primarily a result of high fertility among foreign workers rather than a result of the reproductive behavior of the indigenous population.

After 1971 there was no longer a surplus of births over deaths in the population of the FRG. By 1977 the crude birth rate had declined to 9.5 per thousand, and it resulted in a natural decrease of 2 per thousand or .2 percent (2 [1978], p. 67). The obvious cause was a reduction in the family size. In 1966 there were 218 children per 100 marriages, and this is about the number needed to maintain a stable population. By 1972 this figure had dropped to 151, and to 138 in 1975. Between 1966 and 1975 the number of first children declined by 13.5 percent; the number of second children decreased by 26.5 percent, the third-born by 49.4 percent, and the fourth-born by 63.4 percent. The fact that the largest declines occurred in the higher birth orders indicates that the impact of people having smaller families was more important than the impact of fewer people choosing to have families at all (15).

Regional and Social Factors Influencing Birth Rate

Reasons for the decline in fertility rates are threefold: rising expectations of married couples, greater educational and vocational training, and greater participation of women in the work force. There is a strong inverse relationship between social class and fertility rates such that women in lower socioeconomic groups tend to have families that are above average in size. This has been documented for farmers and laborers (16).

Regional differentials in fertility rates tend to run along religious lines. Areas that contain large Catholic populations have traditionally had higher than average fertility, but these predominantly Catholic areas have experienced significant reductions in fertility in recent years. In the Saarland, which is predominantly Catholic (73.4 percent in 1950), the crude birth rate fell from 20.1 in 1961 to 8.8 in 1976. In Schleswig-Holstein, which is mainly Protestant (88 percent in 1950) comparable figures were 17.4 in 1961 and 9.6 in 1976. In the Saarland, the decline in the birth rate was caused by a transition from a predominantly mining economy with little participation of women in the work force to a more mixed economic structure with high female employment and by the outmigration of younger age groups. Age-selective outmigration left the area with fewer than normal numbers of people in prime reproductive ages.

In contrast, Schleswig-Holstein had a strong agricultural structure with a small outmigration, and, in fact, the state experienced inmigration especially in the hinterland of Hamburg. This involved primarily young families who moved into the suburban zone which developed outside the border of the city state. Discrepancies in age structure have been eliminated in Table 9-7 which presents interstate differentials in fertility.

The correlation between the specific birth rate, denomination, and rural or urbanized structures has already been shown on the district level. In general, the specific birth rate of rural districts was 25 percent above those in urban districts in 1970. Rural Catholic districts, e.g., in Lower Saxony, had a significantly higher figure: Osnabrück, 34 percent, and Emsland, 50 percent above average. This tendency can also been seen if one compares the specific birth rates on the district level for 1961 and 1970. A linear regression based on the district confirms a high posi-

TABLE 9-7. Variation of Age-Specific Fertility Rate in the States Compared to Average of the Federal Republic of Germany in 1964 and 1971.
    Veränderungen der Altersbedingten Fruchtbarkeitsrate in den Länder im Vergleich zum Durschschnitt der FRG in 1964 und 1971.

State	Number of Births Average of Federal Republic of Germany = 100		Increase (+) or Decrease (−) 1964-1971
	1964	1971	
Schleswig-Holstein	106	106	−−
Hamburg	78	76	− 2
Lower Saxony	108	112	+ 4
Bremen	89	90	+ 1
North Rhine-Westphalia	98	98	−−
Hesse	96	95	− 1
Rhineland-Palatinate	109	104	− 5
Baden-Württemberg	104	103	− 1
Bavaria	102	100	− 2
Saarland	103	91	−12
West Berlin	72	76	+ 4

Source: Wirtschaft und Statistik, 1973, op. cit., (note 17), p. 292.

tive correlation coefficient of the specific birth rate in 1961 and 1970 with r = 0.85. Besides the general decline in the birth rate during this period, the rural districts with still high birth rates, had a relatively greater decrease (minus six to minus seven per thousand), than the densely populated and urbanized districts (minus one to minus five per thousand). The regression analysis proved that the decline in the birth rate, starting from a lower level, was less in absolute numbers in densely populated areas than in thinly populated agrarian districts with a higher specific birth rate (17, p. 295).

More detailed studies of the suburbanization process on the municipality level reveal the effect of time on the rise or fall of the crude birth rate in general. Between 1961 and 1967 the crude birth rate declined from fifteen to twenty per thousand, to ten to fifteen per thousand in already suburbanized municipalities of the Frankfurt city region, whereas municipalities affected most recently by the suburbanization process showed an increase to more than twenty per thousand resulting from the inmigration of young couples (18, p. 22). Thus regional differentials in fertility then can be largely attributed to religious and urbanization effects.

POST-1961 MIGRATION TRENDS

Since 1961 the magnitude of intercommunity migration decreased. This trend is evidenced in Table 9-8. The rate of internal migration had declined from 65.7 in 1956 to 47.9 per thousand in 1976. Table 9-8 also shows the trend in international migration which largely includes the impact of foreign workers which was discussed in an earlier section of this essay.

TABLE 9-8. Rate of Migration, 1956-1976
(per 1,000 inhabitants).
Rate der Zu-und Abwanderung, 1956-1976
(per 1,000 Einwohnern).

	1956	1960	1966	1970	1973	1976
International migration -	11.3	11.7	22.8	25.9	24.9	17.4
Internal migration -	65.7	60.7	62.6	60.4	59.3	47.9
Total -	77.0	72.4	85.6	86.3	84.2	65.3

Source: Statistisches Jahrbuch der Bundesrepublik Deutschland 1962, 1972, 1978, op. cit., (note 2).

During the 1960s and 1970s there has been a general southward migration of the German population. The states of Hesse, Baden-Württemberg, and Bavaria experienced a net population gain from internal movement (19, p. 554).

For the period 1961 to 1970 only seven out of thirty-eight planning regions experienced positive internal net migration gain (including Germans and foreigners). With the exception of Hamburg and Munich, these were densely populated areas along the Rhine axis from Düsseldorf to Mannheim. In general, their economies were experiencing significant growth in employment in the service sector (20). Nearly all planning regions along the eastern border of the FRG which includes a large part of Lower Saxony and the Ruhr area experienced negative net migration for both Germans and foreigners between 1966 and 1971. This negative net migration, in part, can be explained by the regrouping of the economy from mining to manufacturing.

Areas with positive net migration of Germans but losses of foreigners included the regions of Lüneburg Heath and the Upper Rhine Valley-southern Black Forest. In these areas pensioners were attracted by high recreational potential. This trend has also occurred in the Alpine Foreland in conjunction with inmigration of working-age population (21, p. 51).

THE PROBLEM OF THE CITY REGION: POPULATION DECREASE IN THE CENTRAL CITY

Decline in the Concentration Process

Between 1961 and 1970 city regions grew at a rate of 8 percent, but this growth was differentially distributed between central cities and suburban areas. While suburban areas grew at a rate of 22 percent, central cities experienced growth of population of only 1 percent. The tendency for the greatest amount of growth to occur at the outskirts of the urban area is representative of the process of suburbanization.

Since local communities in the FRG must finance public services from local taxation, there is competition between central cities and suburban municipalities for the attraction of secondary and tertiary activity. Central cities have found themselves in a disadvantageous fiscal position because of the decentralization of population and manufacturing. The lack of growth in population has meant that central cities have received a reduction in the proportion of revenue from private persons. Revenue from industry has also decreased because of decentralization into suburban areas where cheaper land as well as additional land for expansion is available. All this has also meant an increased competition between the central city and the neighboring municipalities within a city region.

Exodus from the Central City

Although the influx of foreign workers partially compensated for the outmigration of the German population from central cities, the growing concentrations of foreign workers reinforced the social and economic differentiation between central cities and suburbs. Upper classes had left the central cities and had moved into amenity-rich surrounding municipalities (suburban areas) soon after the beginning of individual motorization in the early 1950s (22, p. 48). Education disparities have been documented in the Munich area where the proportion of persons with a university education living in residences near the forest and lakes in the vicinity of Munich is nearly double that of the central city districts of Munich itself (23, p. 105).

There are also demographic differences between central cities and suburban areas such that younger persons with young children are more prevalent in outlying areas (24, p. 66). In 1970, 14.5 percent of the population of Frankfurt was sixty-five years of age or older. Those fifteen years of age and under comprised only 15.9 percent of the total population. Comparable figures for the state of Hesse are 13.3 percent and 22.1 percent respectively. The disparities in age structure would have been greater in Frankfurt if it were not for the influence of the foreign workers who tend to fall into economically active age categories (25, p. 127). The percentage of persons sixty-five years of age and older in all central cities was 14.1 compared to 13.2 percent for the FRG as a whole, and the proportion of those fifteen years and under was 19.6 compared to 23.2 percent for the whole country. A similar age structure distribution also has begun to take place in towns with a population between 20,000 and 100,000.

Intra-Urban Processes and Suburbanization

In addition to migration from the central city to suburban areas, there is mobility within central cities and suburban areas. In general, central cities have higher rates of mobility than suburban areas, and this is, in part, a result of their large foreign populations (18, p. 36). Districts in which housing is particularly old or the residential amenity is low have been abandoned by the German population. There are also examples of dwelling units in neighborhoods of the Central Business District that have high residential amenity but have been abandoned by German residents because of speculation on the part of realtors.

Inmigration in suburban zones can be differentiated according to the influence of public and private development. Such inmigration is not only the result of a different social status of the population, but also strongly influenced by the age structure of the population and the financing of housing available. In addition, this process is supported by the inmigration as well as by the local population which has lost permanently its agricultural employment opportunities (26, p. 79). In the 1950s and 1960s municipalities were eager to attract as many people as possible so they built new residences in the form of medium to high-rise apartment complexes. Unfortunately, this type of housing did not meet the expectations of the middle class who tended to move into publicly assisted housing. The middle class preferred detached homes with gardens that were privately constructed. Currently central city municipalities are trying to reduce further outmigration from cities by offering detached two-story houses, but only a small amount of land is available for that type of development within the borders of central cities.

Urban renewal of historic cores is aimed at halting the formation of ghettos that contain foreign workers and attracting middle and upper classes back to the central city. However, the potential for attracting higher socioeconomic groups to return to the city may be limited by the underlying residential preferences of that population. In a survey of environmental preference, only 15 percent of the suburbanites would be inclined to move back to the central city even if housing of comparable quality and price were available (24, p. 69). These survey results may be flawed by the fact that they report the preferences of only a small number of potential city-dwellers (27, p. 123).

REGIONAL IMBALANCES AND POPULATION REDISTRIBUTION

The basic components of regional population change in the FRG are summarized in Figure 9-7. Trends indicated for the 1961-1970 period have continued into the 1970s. Because of the overall lack of coordination in regional planning in the FRG, population redistribution evolves primarily from the operation of the space economy. Economic forces operate differently at small and large geographic scales. At the regional scale, the supply of new employment opportunities has affected the flow of internal migration and has impacted the destination choices of foreign migrants. At a subregional scale, the forces of supply and demand in the housing market have operated to promote a decentralization of people and economic activity in Germany's city regions.

In areas adjacent to city regions, urban decentralization has resulted in the conversion of prime agricultural land into built-up areas. This process is symptomatic of "urban sprawl," and it should be prevented by governmental policy. Appropriate actions include the renewal of small towns and villages within city regions and by a redevelopment or recycling of older suburbs.

SUMMARY

The purpose of this essay is to outline the basic forces of population change in the FRG and to evaluate the role of regional development planning in affecting population redistribution. The essential elements of population change included the inmigration of refugees from the East, the inmigration of foreign workers, and a decline in the birth rate. Internal migration operated to concentrate growth and development in major city regions, and specifically in the suburban areas, the neighboring municipalities of these city regions.

Population redistribution has created a number of problems which should be addressed by regional planning efforts. These problems include the outmigration from the subsequent decline of central cities, the formation of foreign worker ghettos, the conversion of prime agricultural land into urban-related uses, and population decline in more isolated rural regions.

REGIONAL POPULATION DEVELOPMENT 283

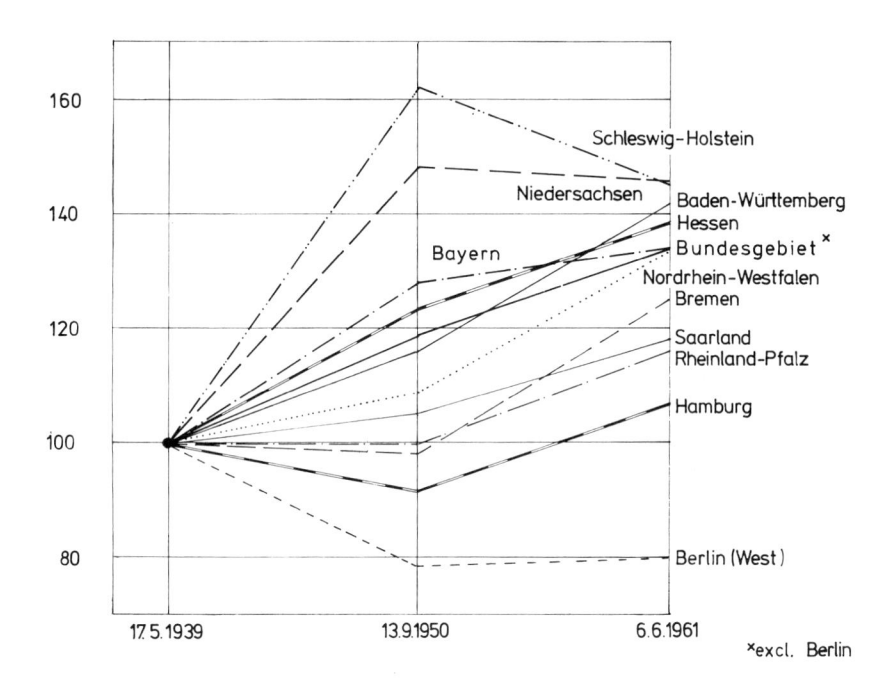

FIG. 9-1. Population Development in the Federal States
1939-1961 (Census Population 1939 = 100).
       Bevölkerungsentwicklung in den Bundesländern
1939-1961 (Zensus Bevölkerung 1939 = 100).

Source: Statistisches Bundesamt 2227, in Wirtschaft und Statistik, 1961, p. 253.

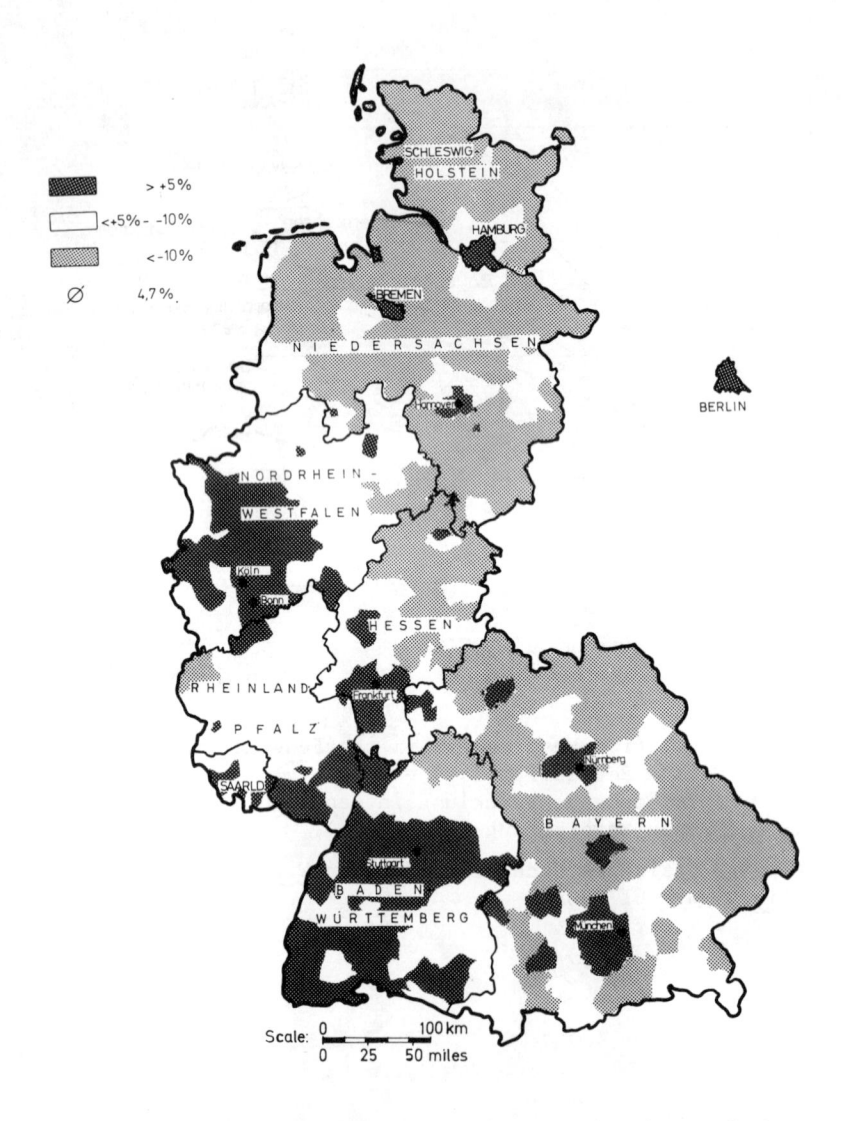

FIG. 9-2. Net Migration Change in the Districts of the German Federal Republic 1950-1961.
   Netto Einwanderungs Veränderungen in Bezirken der Deutschen Bundesrepublik 1950-1961.

Source: Generalized from *Atlas der Bundesrepublik Deutschland* 3131/2.

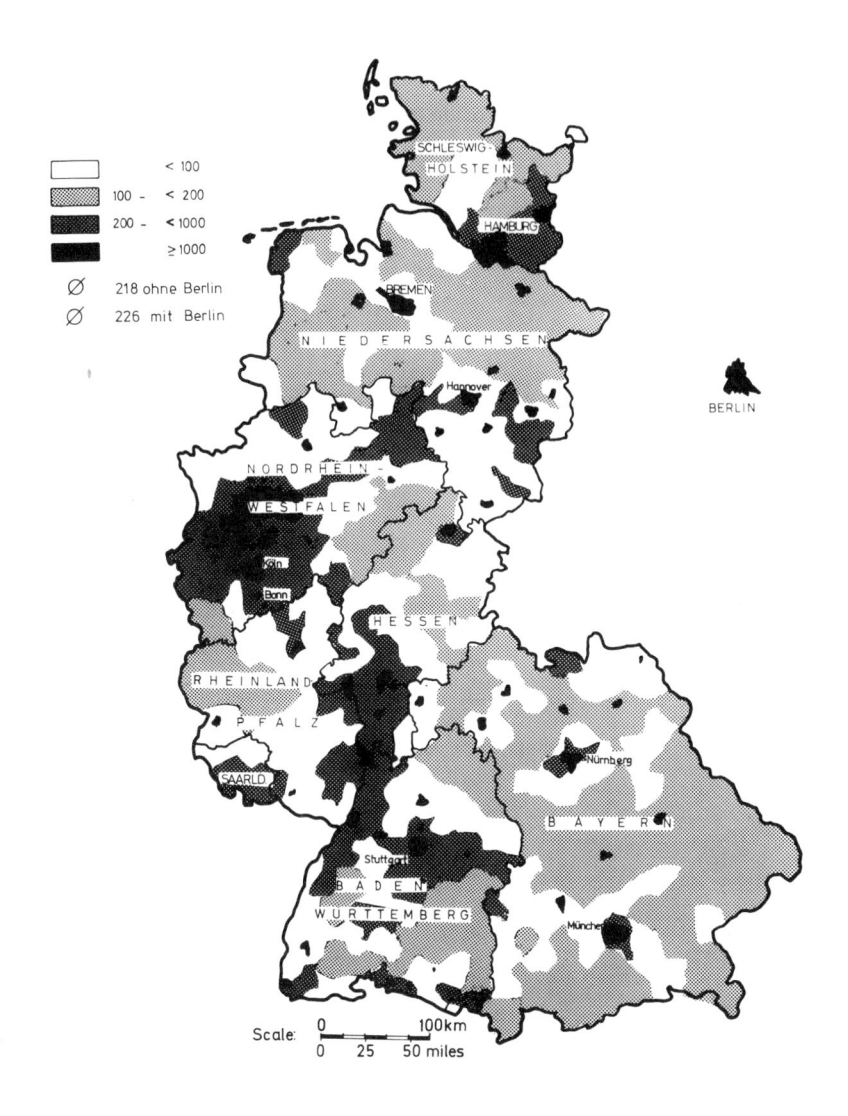

FIG. 9-3. Population Density in the Districts of the German Federal Republic 1961.
    Bevölkerungsdichte in Bezirken der Bundesrepublik 1961.

Source: Generalized from Statistischen Bundesamt 2230, in Wirtschaft und Statistik, 1961, p. 256.

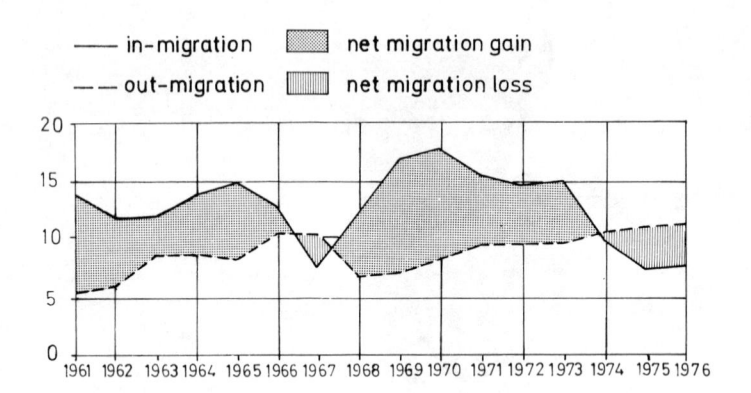

FIG. 9-4. Net Migration Change with Foreign Countries 1961-1976 per 1000 Inhabitants.
　　　　Netto Einwanderungsveränderungen mit fremden Ländern 1961-1976 per 1000 Einwohnern.

Source: Statistische Jahrbücher der BRD 1963, 1972, 1978.

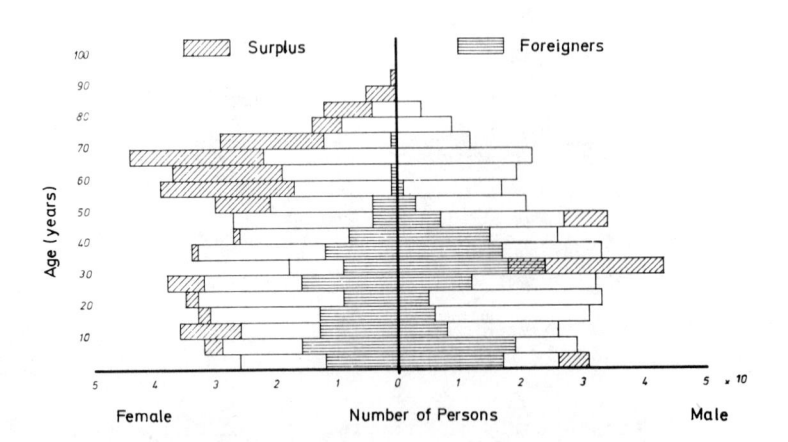

FIG. 9-5. Age Structure of Resident Population in the Historic Core of Mosbach/Baden Württemberg, 1978.
　　　　Struktur des Lebensalter der wohnhaften Bevölkerung im geschichtlichen Kern Mosbach/Baden Württemberg, 1978.

Source: K.-D. Roos, personal communication.

REGIONAL POPULATION DEVELOPMENT

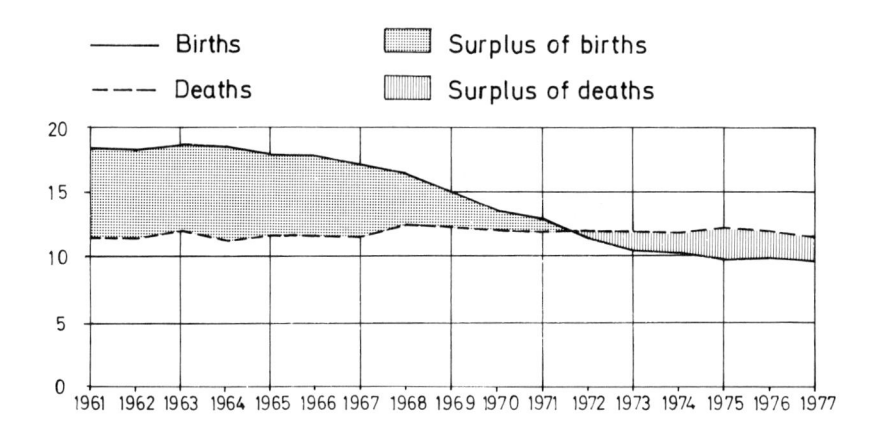

FIG. 9-6. Natural Population Change in the Federal Republic of Germany 1961-1977.
   Natürliche Bevölkerungs Veränderungen in der Bundesrepublik Deutschlands 1961-1977.

Source: Figures from Wirtschaft und Statistik 1978, p. 426.

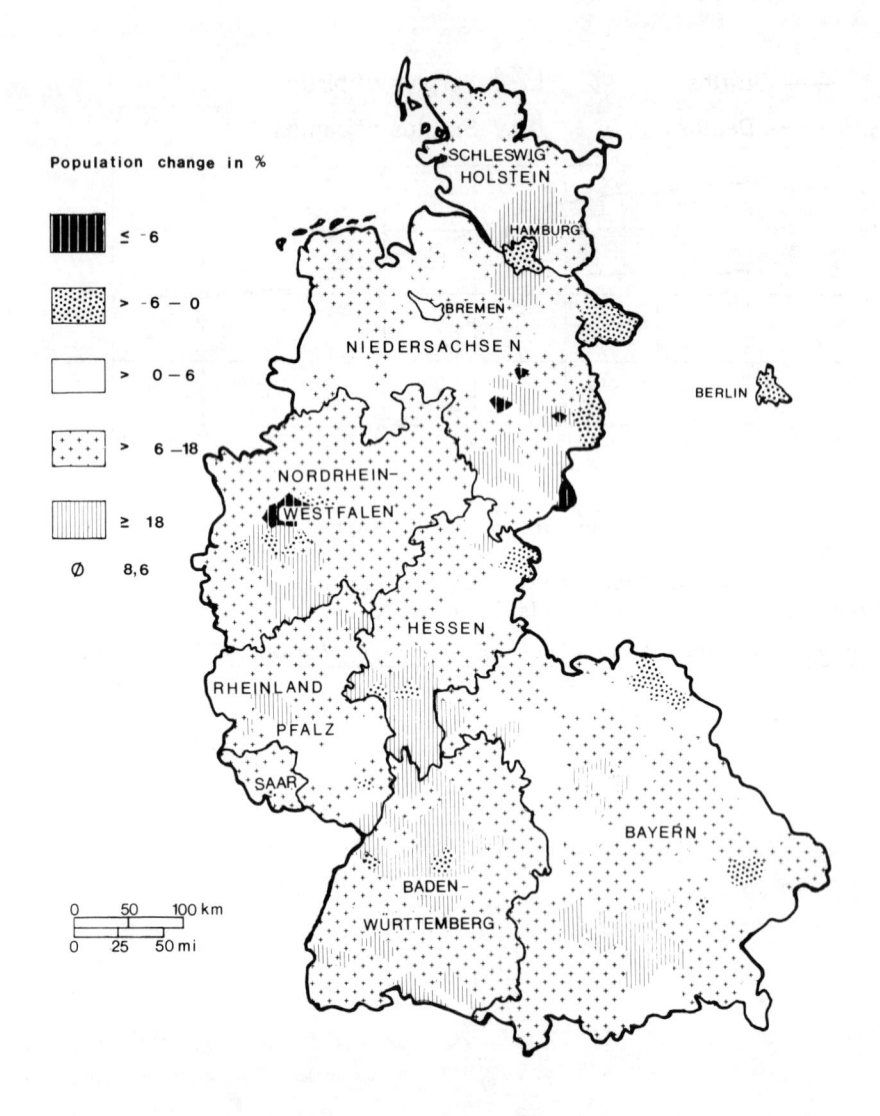

FIG. 9-7. Population Development of the German Federal Republic 1961-1970.
Bevölkerungsentwicklung der Bundesrepublik Deutschland 1961-1970.

Source: Generalized from Atlas zur Raumentwicklung, 4, Bevölkerung, Map 4.01, op. cit., note 38.

NOTES

1. Schwarz, K., Analyse der räumlichen Bevölkerungsbewegung. Abhandlungen Vol. 58 (Hannover: Veröffentlichungen der Akademie für Raumforschung und Landesplanung, 1969).

2. Statistisches Bundesamt/Wiesbaden, ed., Statistisches Jahrbuch der Bundesrepublik 1962, 1963, 1972, 1978 (Stuttgart and Mainz: Kohlhammer).

3. Statistisches Bundesamt/Wiesbaden, ed., "Bevölkerungs-, Kultur-, und wirtschaftsstatische Ereignisse 1954 bis 1966," Vertriebene und Flüchtlinge, Serie 4 (Stuttgart and Mainz: Kohlhammer, 1967).

4. Schwarz, K., Demographische Grundlagen der Raumforschung und Landesplanung, Abhandlungen Vol. 64 (Hannover: Veröffentlichungen der Akademie für Raumforschung und Landesplanung, 1972).

5. Statistisches Bundesamt/Wiesbaden, ed., "Wohnbevölkerung in den Gemeinden nach der Volkszählung vom 6. Juni 1961," Wirtschaft und Statistik (Stuttgart and Mainz: Kohlhammer, 1961), pp. 329-332.

6. Fricke, W., "Bevölkerung und Raum eines Ballungsgebietes seit der Industrialisierung. Eine geographische Analyse des Modellgebietes Rhein-Neckar," in Die Ansprüche der modernen Industriegesellschaft an den Raum -dargestellt am Beispiel des Modellgebietes Rhein-Neckar, Forschungs-und Sitzungsberichte, Vol. 111 (Hannover: Veröffentlichungen der Akademie für Raumforschung und Landesplanung, 1976), pp. 1-68.

7. Schwarz, K., "Stand, Entwicklung und Struktur der Bevölkerung," in Stadtregionen in der Bundesrepublik Deutschland, Forschungs-und Sitzungsberichte, Vol. 32 (Hannover: Veröffentlichungen der Akademie für Raumforschung und Landesplanung, 1968), pp. 1-50.

8. City regions (Stadtregionen) consist of central cities (Kernstädte) and their commuter zones. The central zones (Kerngebiet) are formed by the central city and the neighboring municipalities (Ergänzungsgebiet). Central zones are characterized by a population density of more than 500 persons per km^2 (square kilometer) in 1950 and 1960 and less than 10 percent employed in agricul-

ture. Urbanized zones (verstädterte Zonen) are defined as municipalities in which the agricultural population is less than 30 percent and at least 30 percent of the employed are commuters, 60 percent of these commute to the central city. The outer zones (Randzonen) are formed by municipalities in which more than 30 percent, but not more than 65 percent, of the employed work in agriculture, and at least 20 percent of the inhabitants commute. Olaf Boustedt, "Die Stadtregionen in der Bundesrepublik Deutschland im Jahre 1961," in Stadtregionen in der Bundesrepublik Deutschland 1961 Forschungs-und Sitzungsberichte, Vol. 32 (Hannover: Veröffentlichungen der Akademie für Raumforschung und Landesplanung, 1967), pp. 1-24; reference p. 9.

9. Beutel, J., Konzentrations-und Verstädterungstendenzen in der Bundesrepublik Deutschland. Raumwirtschaftstheoretische Analyse und raumordnungspolitische Strategien der Entlastung für Verdichtungsräume. Schriften zur wirtschaftswissenschaftlichen Forschung, Vol. 106 (Meisenheim an der Glan: Hain, 1976).

10. Statistisches Bundesamt/Wiesbaden, ed., "Wanderungen über die Grenzen des Bundesgebietes 1961," Wirtschaft und Statistik (Stuttgart and Mainz: Kohlhammer, 1963), pp. 587-689.

11. Statistisches Bundesamt/Wiesbaden, ed., "Statistische Unterlagen zur Beurteilung der Bevölkerungsstruktur und Wirtschaftskraft der Bundesländer," Statistische Berichte 1955 (Arb. No. II/6/6).

12. Statistisches Bundesamt/Wiesbaden, ed., "Wanderungen der Ausländer zwischen dem Ausland und dem Bundesgebiet nach Altersgruppen 1968 bis 1973," Wirtschaft und Statistik (Stuttgart and Mainz: Kohlhammer, 1975), pp. 813-815.

13. Selke, W., "Räumliche Entwicklungschancen und Ausländerwanderung," Geographische Rundschau, Vol. 31 (1977), pp. 310-314.

14. Statistisches Bundesamt/Wiesbaden, ed., Statistisches Jahrbuch der Bundesrepublik Deutschland 1952 (Stuttgart and Mainz: Kohlhammer).

15. Statistisches Bundesamt/Wiesbaden, ed., "Gründe des Geburtenrückganges 1966 bis 1975 und für 'Nullwachstum' erforderliche Kinderzahl der Ehen," Wirtschaft und Statistik (Stuttgart and Mainz: Kohlhammer, 1977), pp. 374-378.

16. Statistisches Bundesamt/Wiesbaden, ed., "Ehen im April 1977 nach dem Einkommen des Mannes, Ergebnisse des Mikrozensus," Wirtschaft und Statistik (Stuttgart and Mainz: Kohlhammer, 1979), pp. 170-174.

17. Statistisches Bundesamt/Wiesbaden, ed., "Der Rückgang der Geburtenhäufigkeit in regionaler Sicht," Wirtschaft und Statistik (Stuttgart and Mainz: Kohlhammer, 1973), pp. 290-296.

18. Fricke, W., "Sozialgeographische Untersuchungen zur Bevölkerungs-und Siedlungsentwicklung im Frankfurter Raum," in Untersuchungen zur Bevölkerungs-und Siedlungsentwicklung im Rhein-Main-Gebiet, Vol. 71 (Frankfurt: Rhein-Mainische Forschungen, 1971), pp. 1-75.

19. Statistisches Bundesamt/Wiesbaden, ed., "Wanderungen 1975," Wirtschaft und Statistik (Stuttgart and Mainz: Kohlhammer, 1976), pp. 549-554.

20. Bundesforschungsanstalt für Landeskunde und Raumordnung, Atlas zur Raumentwicklung, Part I: Arbeit, map 101 and 1.02.4; Part 4: Bevölkerung, map 4.01 (Bonn, 1976).

21. Selke, W., Die Ausländerwanderung als Problem der Raumordnungspolitik in der Bundesrepublik Deutschland. Eine politische-geographische Studie. Vol. 55, Bonner Geographische Abhandlungen (Bonn, 1977).

22. Geipel, R., Die regionale Ausbreitung der Sozialschichten im Rhein-Mainz-Gebiet, Vol. 125, Forschungen zur Deutschen Landeskunde (Bad Godesberg, 1961).

23. Maier, J., "Sozialräumliche Kontakte und Konflikte in der dynamisch gewachsenen Peripherie des Verdichtungsraumes; Beispiele aus dem westlichen Umland Münchens," Tagungsbericht und wissenschaftliche Abhandlungen, 41. Deutscher Geographentag Mainz 1977 (Wiesbaden: Steiner, 1978), pp. 114-115.

24. Fricke, W., et al., "Ergebnisse quantitativer Untersuchungen zur mesoregionalen und mikroregionalen Bevölkerungsgeographie des Rhein-Neckar-Raumes," Tagungsbericht und wissenschaftliche Abhandlungen, 41. Deutscher Geographentag Mainz 1977 (Wiesbaden: Steiner, 1978), pp. 45-71.

25. Tharun, E., "Wohnungsbaudisparitäten in der Verstädterungsregion Untermain," Tagungsbericht und wissenschaftliche Abhandlungen, 41. Deutscher Geographentag Mainz 1977 (Wiesbaden: Steiner, 1978), pp. 125-138.

26. Fricke, W., "Lage und Struktur als Faktoren des gegenwärtigen Siedlungswachstum im nördlichen Umland von Frankfurt," in Geographische Studien aus dem Rhein-Mainischen Raum, Vol. 50 (Frankfurt: Rhein-Mainische-Forschungen, 1961), pp. 45-83.

27. Höllhuber, D., "Zurück in die Innenstädte? Gründe und Umfang der Rückwanderung der grossstädtischen Bevölkerung in die Stadtzentren," Tagungsbericht und wissenschaftliche Abhandlungen, 41. Deutscher Geographentag Mainz 1977 (Wiesbaden: Steiner, 1978), pp. 116-124.

CHAPTER 10

FEDERAL POLICY, MIGRATION AND THE CHANGING GEOGRAPHY OF THE U.S. POPULATION

DIE ROLLE DER BUNDESREGIERUNG AUF DIE RÄUMLICHE BEVÖLKERUNGSBEWEGUNG

Patricia Gober

Abstract

Although the federal government does not have an official migration policy, many federal activities impact population distribution and migration. Almost all policies have territorial consequences, and, therefore, they differentially affect regions and communities. At a regional level the patterns of federal spending and military installation location, immigration policy, and retirement migration have reinforced ongoing processes of population growth and inmigration in Sunbelt regions. At a subregional scale, migration flows have shifted in the direction of nonmetropolitan areas; relevant federal actions are in the areas of energy, transportation, and retirement.

Change in the nature and direction of migratory flows will necessitate a reorientation in traditional policy-oriented research. Specific issues include the process of metropolitan population decline, the evolution of energy-related boom towns, the social-psychological impacts of movement from metropolitan areas to small towns, migration of elderly persons, and the consequences of their spatial segregation in retirement communities.

Kurzfassung

Obwohl die Bundesregierung keine offizielle Wanderungspolitik verfolgt, beeinflussen viele ihrer Aktivitäten die Verteilung und Umsiedlung der Bevölkerung. Fast alle Aktivitäten der Bundesregierung haben territoriale Folgen, deswegen wirken sie unterschiedlich auf Regionen und Gemeinden ein. Die Regionalgliederung der Aufgaben, die Standortwahl militärischer Einrichtungen, die Einwanderungspolitik der Bundesregierung sowie auch die Pensionärswanderung verstärken die gegenwärtigen Prozesse des Bevölkerungswachstums und Zuwanderung in die "Sunbelt" Regionen. Innerhalb der Regionen hat sich die Richtung der Wanderung umgekehrt und ist nicht mehr auf die Großstädte gerichtet; die wirksamen Bundesaktivitäten liegen auf den Gebieten der Energie, der Verkehrsmittel und des Ruhestandes.

Die Änderungen in der Natur und in der Richtung der Wanderungen machen eine Umorientierung der traditionellen Forschung über den Einfluß von Bundesprogrammen nötig. Spezielle Schwerpunkte bilden: der Prozeß des Rückganges der Großstadtbevölkerung, die Evolution der durch Energieindustrie sich schnell entwickelnden Städte, die sozial-psychologischen Wirkungen des Wandels von der großstadtorientierten zur kleinstadtorientierten Wanderung, die Umsiedlung älterer Menschen und die Folgen ihrer räumlichen Absonderung in geplanten Ruhestandsgemeinden.

Federal Policy, Migration and the Changing
Geography of the U.S. Population

In recent years, population redistribution in the U.S. has taken a number of forms. The first of these involves the emergence of the South as a vital economic force and as a magnet for migrants from the North. On a subregional level, reversal in traditional migration patterns has resulted in movement away from large metropolitan areas, the traditional foci of national growth and development, into nonmetropolitan America. What is perhaps most significant about this trend is that inmigration and population growth have not been confined to nonmetropolitan counties that border SMSAs but have occurred in more isolated rural regions as well.

Although these changes have been underway for some time, it is only recently that they have attracted interest in the popular press and scientific community. As a result, little attention has been directed to their policy ramifications. It will be argued that changing migration patterns will require a reanalysis of government's role in relation to population redistribution. Traditional concern with overconcentration in large metropolitan areas and population decline and its attendant problems in small towns and rural areas will change to an emphasis on metropolitan decline and how to accommodate rapid growth in nonmetropolitan communities.

Another intriguing facet of contemporary population redistribution involves the growing number of persons who move for nonjob-related reasons. Traditional views of migration as a labor market mechanism are inadequate to explain the growing numbers of retired migrants and the sizable number of people who claim to move for "quality of life" reasons.

It is perhaps misleading at this point to imply that there is such a thing as migration policy in the United States, for there is not now, nor has there ever been, a conscious comprehensive national migration policy. However, this is not to say that federal policy does not affect population redistribution and migration. One can even go so far as to say that all policy has territorial implications and, therefore, impacts where people live. The most obvious type of federal policy that affects migration is in the area of regional development, but interactions also occur in defense spending, transportation, energy, and the environment.

The enormous scope of migration-related policy is made even more complex by the problem of scale. In that spatial patterns and hence population distributions are scale-specific, a policy that consciously promotes decentralization at one scale may well lead to greater concentration at another scale. Growth-center strategies in distressed regions are a good example of this. In trying to stimulate growth and development in declining regions, they operate, at least in the short run, to concentrate growth in a few high-potential areas.

In a migration context, scale boundaries are fuzzy at best, but three levels of aggregation emerge in studies of population redistribution. They include regional movements such as Sunbelt migration, intraregional movement like the recent SMSA to nonmetropolitan migration, and local level movement from central city to suburb. Emphasis in this essay will be on the first two levels although discussion will necessarily overlap into the third.

This essay will outline general issues in migration

policy. Recent migration trends in the U.S. will be summarized with emphasis on movement to the Sunbelt, nonmetropolitan migration, and the migration of the elderly. Federal policy that has contributed to the evolution of these trends will be identified, and the policy consequences of recent migration shifts will be explored.

CONCEPTUAL ISSUES IN POPULATION AND MIGRATION POLICY

Definition

In recent years, it has become fashionable for social scientists to discuss the policy implications of their research. Unfortunately, the term policy has taken on different meanings to different people. Herein, population policy is defined as action by government which affects the size, rate of growth, composition, or distribution of its population. Action may be of a formalized nature or it may be intended for other purposes but has an indirect effect on population characteristics. Naturally, migration policy relates primarily to population distribution, but size, growth, and composition policies may also affect migration. For instance, Hoover (1) predicts that slower national population growth will lead to an older population which may, in turn, stimulate additional migration to the Sunbelt.

Five components of an idealized population policy include (a) awareness of a problem, (b) goal formulation, (c) goal adoption, (d) choice of appropriate instruments to meet goals, and (e) an evaluation or monitoring procedure (2). In the absence of a normative view of what the distribution of population should look like, it is common for planners and government officials to follow a problem-specific approach such as in response to excessive outmigration from distressed areas. As a result, programs exist outside of the context of goals concerning what the pattern of population distribution should look like or what is a desirable organization of inter- and intraregional migration flows (2, 3). Even when goals are stated, they can be so general as to lack utility in the process of policy formulation. Take, for example, the aims of the Commission on Population Growth and the American Future (4, p. 120):

> To promote high quality urban development in a manner and location consistent with the integrity of the environment and a sense of community.
>
> To promote a variety of life style options.
>
> To ease the problems created by population movement within the country.
>
> To increase freedom in choice of residential location.

A meaningful set of programs could not possibly evolve from this noncommittal list of goals. Are we looking for centralization or decentralization, and at what scale? What happens when a person pursues a life style option that is inconsistent with the integrity of the environment? Programs need to fall into a set of national purposes regarding population distribution, but with the exception of the nineteenth-century goal of settling the continent, the federal government has never really had clear and consistent objectives regarding population distribution or migration patterns.

Justification

Justification for explicit or implicit governmental intervention into the migration process makes two critical assumptions: that uncontrolled movement leads to social, economic, or other kinds of problems and that action at the federal level can alleviate these problems (3). The first assumption can be supported with evidence that people make less than optimal decisions regarding whether or not to move and where to move, and this creates problems for themselves and for the places where they live. Potential migrants are influenced by personal preferences, the location of friends and relatives, and imperfect information about employment opportunities in destination regions (5, 6). Governmental intervention in the form of human resource development or job information is justified if it leads to higher incomes or greater satisfaction for the people involved.

Disadvantageous impacts of migration on places evolve from the effects of negative externalities (7, 8). Individuals don't pay all the costs associated with their behavior, in this case their movement. Instead, they impose costs like greater congestion and pollution on the destination or the underutilization of public and private services on the origin (1). The public, then, is justified to step in to correct the imbalance between individuals' well-being and the public good.

The second assumption about the potential success of federal policy in alleviating the problems of migration is more controversial than the first. Promising evidence has been reported in a federally sponsored pilot program designed to provide relocation assistance to unemployed or potentially unemployed persons (9, 10), but generally there are few barometers of success in migration-related programs. The viability of federal development programs associated with the Appalachian Regional Commission or the Economic

Development Administration in stemming outmigration from distressed areas is very difficult to assess, especially in the light of recent changes in migration trends.

While it is probably reasonable to accept that migration creates problems for people and places, the viability and political acceptability of federal intervention into the migration decisions of individuals is debatable. Therefore, an official national policy regarding population redistribution has never existed nor is it forthcoming. There is, however, no shortage of federal policy that inadvertantly impacts migration patterns. In the following section, recent migration trends will be related to the territorial effects of federal policies in the areas of energy, defense spending, transportation, and retirement.

MIGRATION TRENDS

Regional Patterns

The most well publicized of recent migration trends involves the southward migration of population to regions euphemistically called the "Sunbelt." Actually, the origins began several decades ago, but did not attract widespread attention until recently. Watkins (11) has shown that growth in Sunbelt metropolitan areas was well underway during the 1950s and 1960s.

How, then, can one account for the recent burst of interest in Sunbelt growth? Prior to 1970 natural increase compensated for net outmigration in large northern states like New York, Pennsylvania, Ohio, and Illinois, and growth in the Sunbelt was concentrated in Florida, Texas, California, Colorado, and Arizona. Table 10-1 shows the absolute magnitude of population growth and the relative importance

TABLE 10-1. Components of Population Change in States, 1960-1975.
Komponenten der Bevölkerungsveränderungen in den Ländern, 1960-1975.

	NET CHANGE		NATURAL INCREASE		NET MIGRATION	
	1960-1970	1970-1977	1960-1970	1970-1977	1960-1970	1970-1977
New England	1338	394	1022	358	316	37
Maine	24	91	94	39	-69	52
New Hampshire	131	111	62	33	69	78
Vermont	55	39	40	20	15	18
Massachusetts	541	93	466	143	74	-51
Rhode Island	90	-15	78	24	13	-39
Connecticut	497	76	282	98	214	-22
Mid-Atlantic	3034	-175	2976	1057	59	-1232
New York	1458	-318	1509	555	-51	-873
New Jersey	1101	158	614	234	488	-76
Pennsylvania	475	-16	853	267	-378	-283
East North Central	4028	791	4180	1988	-153	-1197
Ohio	946	44	1072	507	-126	-464
Indiana	531	135	548	281	-16	-146
Illinois	1033	132	1076	514	-43	-382
Michigan	1052	248	1025	495	27	-247
Wisconsin	466	233	461	191	4	42
West North Central	930	557	1529	657	-599	-100
Minnesota	391	169	417	179	-25	-11
Iowa	68	54	250	97	-183	-43
Missouri	358	123	355	156	2	-33
North Dakota	-15	36	86	34	-94	1
South Dakota	-14	23	81	33	-94	-11
Nebraska	72	76	145	67	-73	10
Kansas	70	77	201	90	-130	-13

TABLE 10-1 (continued).

	NET CHANGE 1960-1970	NET CHANGE 1970-1977	NATURAL INCREASE 1960-1970	NATURAL INCREASE 1970-1977	NET MIGRATION 1960-1970	NET MIGRATION 1970-1977
South Atlantic	4700	3627	3367	1527	1332	2100
Delaware	102	34	64	29	38	5
Maryland	822	215	437	175	385	42
Virginia	682	483	540	250	141	233
West Virginia	-116	115	149	66	-265	49
North Carolina	526	441	620	299	-94	142
South Carolina	208	285	357	187	-149	98
Georgia	646	460	596	316	51	144
Florida	1838	1661	511	183	1326	1478
South Central	3125	3409	3465	2059	-740	1351
Kentucky	181	238	208	166	-153	72
Tennessee	357	373	402	196	-45	178
Alabama	177	245	410	196	-233	49
Mississippi	39	172	306	160	-265	13
Arkansas	137	221	208	193	-71	128
Louisiana	386	277	516	257	-130	19
Oklahoma	238	251	217	119	13	133
Texas	1617	1632	1471	871	146	760
Mountain	1429	1741	1122	756	307	985
Montana	20	67	78	39	-58	27
Idaho	46	144	88	65	-42	79
Wyoming	2	74	42	26	-39	49
Colorado	453	409	238	160	213	249
New Mexico	65	173	195	99	-130	74
Arizona	470	520	243	163	228	358
Utah	169	209	180	167	-11	42
Nevada	203	145	60	36	144	108

TABLE 10-1 (continued).

	NET CHANGE		NATURAL INCREASE		NET MIGRATION	
	1960–1970	1970–1977	1960–1970	1970–1977	1960–1970	1970–1977
Pacific	5328	2683	2780	1487	2547	1196
Washington	556	245	307	160	249	85
Oregon	323	285	164	94	159	191
California	4236	1925	2123	1107	2113	817
Alaska	76	105	60	42	16	62
Hawaii	137	125	127	84	11	40

Source: U.S. Bureau of the Census, "Preliminary Intercensal Estimates of States and Component of Population Change, 1960 to 1970," Current Population Reports, Series P-25, No. 460, June, 1971.

of its natural increase and migration components for U.S. states and census regions between 1960 and 1977. During the 1960s northern regions (New England, Mid-Atlantic, East North Central and West North Central) experienced sizable population growth in spite of net outmigration or very small net inmigration.

During the 1970s fertility dropped below replacement levels, and as a result, natural increase was no longer large enough to compensate for net outmigration in the North. Moreover, inmigration diffused from its foci in Florida and Texas such that all states in the South Atlantic and South Central regions experienced net inmigration during the 1970s. A similar situation occurred in the West where inmigration diffused from California, Arizona, and Colorado into other Mountain and Pacific Coast states.

Table 10-2 depicts net migration rates by region and race for the 1970s; it shows that the Northeast and North Central regions lost while the South and West gained population. A particularly interesting element of this is for blacks to be leaving the North and moving in the direction of the West. In the South, large-scale black outmigration which characterized the postwar period came to an end, and the region experienced small gains in black population as a result of the migration process. This trend along with sizable white inmigration contributed to rapid overall population growth in the South.

In any discussion of migration to the Sunbelt, the operation of climatic favorability cannot be ignored. In several studies, climatic variables have successfully explained interstate variations in migration rates (12, 13). In addition, high rates of employment and income growth in the region appear to have induced inmigration. Because of the inter-

TABLE 10-2. In, Out and Net Migration Rates for Regions, 1970–1975 and 1975–1978.
In, Zu und Netto Abwanderung nach Regionen, 1970–1975 und 1975–1978.

	1970–1975			1975–1978		
	In	Out	Net	In	Out	Net
Northeast	2.3	5.3	-3.0	1.9	3.3	-1.4
Whites	2.3	5.3	-3.0	1.9	3.2	-1.3
Blacks	3.0	4.6	-1.6	1.5	5.3	-3.8
North Central	3.3	5.6	-2.3	2.7	4.0	-1.3
Whites	3.3	5.7	-2.4	2.6	4.0	-1.4
Blacks	3.5	4.7	-1.2	3.3	3.4	-.1
South	6.6	3.7	2.9	4.4	2.8	1.6
Whites	7.5	3.9	3.6	4.8	3.0	1.8
Blacks	2.7	2.6	.1	2.2	2.0	.2
West	6.8	4.7	2.1	5.1	4.1	1.0
Whites	7.0	5.0	2.0	5.1	4.3	.8
Blacks	8.0	2.7	5.3	8.5	4.0	4.5

Source: U.S. Bureau, the Census, "Geographic Mobility of the Population, 1970–1975," Current Population Reports, Series P-20, No. 285, October, 1975; U.S. Bureau of the Census, "Geographic Mobility of the Population, 1975–1980," Current Population Reports, No. 331, November, 1978.

dependent nature of the relationship between migration and economic change, inmigration, in turn, stimulated further growth in employment and income (14, 15).

The role of the federal government in stimulating inmigration to the South and West is manifest in a number of forms. The most publicized of these involves the territorial bias associated with federal spending (16, 17, 18). Federal expenditures include defense contracts, payrolls to military and nonmilitary personnel, highway and sewer programs, welfare (medicaid, aid to families with dependent children, food stamps, supplemental security income, grants to states of social service programs, and unemployment compensation), federal retirement programs, and the maintenance of public lands. Large and significant regional variations occur in the area of defense spending where, at best, activities are allocated on the basis of cost effectiveness and, at worst, their location reflects pork barrel whims of members of Congress seeking favors for local districts. In either case, the distribution of federal defense monies has occurred without concern for its regional development consequences or its impact on population distribution or migration trends.

Figure 10-1 depicts the regional distribution of per capita defense contract expenditures during 1977. The largest favorable impacts occurred in the Pacific region where all states except Oregon experienced massive infusions of federal defense expenditures. The South also faired well in the allocation of defense dollars. The biggest regional loser was the East North Central region comprised of Ohio, Michigan, Illinois, Indiana, and Wisconsin, whose share of federal defense monies averaged only $153 per capita.

In order to provide a more complete picture of spending in the context of federal taxation, Figure 10-2 presents statewide variation in the spending-taxes ratio (the amount of money spent for every dollar of tax money paid). The largest outflows occurred in the Mid-Atlantic and East North Central regions, which together experienced a net loss of more than $30 billion. The East North Central states were particularly disadvantaged by the pattern of federal spending as evidenced by the fact that they received in federal spending only 70 percent of what was collected taxes.

The main benefactors of geographically biased federal spending were the South Atlantic, South Central and Western regions of Mountain and Pacific states. In the South net inflows that occurred in Maryland and Virginia were undoubtedly due to their proximity to Washington, D.C., the center of federal employment, but other states in the region like Georgia, South Carolina, Kentucky, Tennessee, Alabama, and Mississippi were also favored with large inflows of federal dollars. In the West, the largest share of federal net inflows of money occurred in California, but other states like Arizona, New Mexico, Alaska, and Hawaii had higher spending taxes ratios.

The aforementioned taxation-expenditure patterns reflect a long-term federal spending bias which has favored the South and West. Recognizing this, how can one contend that federal spending has played a role in the turnabout in migration patterns? One plausible explanation is that federal activities in the South traditionally reduced what would have been even larger outmigration. Presently, it operates to reinforce ongoing processes of growth and inmigration.

The distribution of military installations has special relevance for the migration process. Migrants possess a very narrow range of information about potential destinations, and many are dependent on information obtained from visiting other places or from friends and relatives who visit or live elsewhere. As a result of their military service, men and women have become acquainted with what it is like to live in the South and West. After completing their military obligation, many return to work in schools, small businesses, or industries that are spawned by the initial military establishment. Post-World War II inmigration to Phoenix has been related to the proximity of Luke Air Force Base, one of the nation's largest air bases. Gordon (19) has outlined the role of the military installation as a nucleus for the development of ancilliary businesses and industries which attract people with military experience. If one is willing to accept the special significance of military service to long-run migration decisions, then the consequences of geographically biased military installation location will be far-reaching.

Generous benefits by the federal retirement system and increasingly stringent regulations over private plans set forth in the Pension Reform Act of 1974 have made retired persons more financially secure (20, 21). As more retired persons possess the financial means to change their residence, they have sought locations with climates conducive to a leisure-centered life-style.

Federal policy governing the number and origin of foreign immigrants has also affected the regional balance of population growth. Although foreign immigrants cannot be thought of as interregional movers in the usual sense, they are certainly regional inmigrants, and they represent a form of growth. The imprint of Cubans in the Miami area and Orientals in San Francisco and along the West Coast is documented in the literature (22). The lax policy regarding Mexican farm workers has contributed to inmigration in California, Texas, and Arizona. Although they are not included in official counts, illegal aliens represent a form of migrant whose economic, social, and political presence must be recognized.

Another provocative issue involves federal action toward Southeast Asian refugees. In June, 1979, monthly quotas were increased from 7,000 to 14,000, and Congress approved $231 million in refugee assistance for 1979 and $371 million for 1980 (23). Settlement is great in the Los Angeles and Gulf Coast regions since many refugees prefer residence in temperate environments. Sunbelt regions will surely receive a large portion of future refugees as friends and relatives join those who have already established residences. The overall effect is to reinforce the indigenous process of growth and inmigration in the Sunbelt.

Government action benefitting the South and West was hardly designed for that purpose. Policies in the area of federal spending, military installation location, retirement, and immigration were not meant to deal with migration directly, but nevertheless, they have had profound territorial consequences. In an era when the Northeast and Midwest were experiencing rapid population and economic growth, these consequences were overlooked, but times have changed, and federal dollars moving in the direction of greatest growth has become a source of discontent or, at least, concern in the North.

Subregional Patterns

After years of decline, America's nonmetropolitan areas have recently experienced rapid rates of population growth largely as a result of positive rates of net migration. Beale (24) was the first to identify the turnabout in traditional growth patterns; he found faster growth rates in nonmetropolitan counties than in metropolitan ones. Between 1970 and 1973 SMSAs grew at a rate of 2.9 percent while nonmetropolitan counties adjacent to SMSAs grew by 4.7 percent, and nonadjacent ones increased by 3.7 percent. More recently, geographers, regional scientists, rural sociologists, and others have displayed an avid interest in the process of nonmetropolitan growth and migration, its causes and consequences (24, 26, 27, 28, 29, 30).

Examination of Table 10-3 provides an overview of the nonmetropolitan growth experience and its various components. Absolute population change is given for SMSAs exceeding 1.5 million inhabitants in 1970, smaller SMSAs, and nonmetroplitan areas. Between 1960 and 1970 population growth in the U.S. was largely metropolitan in character; net migration was positive in metropolitan areas and negative in nonmetropolitan areas. The 1970s witnessed a reversal in these patterns such that net migration became positive and quite substantial in size in nonmetropolitan areas. The largest declines occurred in large metropolitan areas.

Table 10-3 also provides a breakdown of these trends by major census regions. Substantial growth in large metropolitan areas of the Northeast and North Central region in the 1960s changed to declines or very slow growth during the 1970s. Although small metropolitan areas continued to grow during the 1970s, nonmetropolitan areas accounted for most of the population increase. In the South and West growth during the 1970s was predominantly metropolitan in character although nonmetropolitan areas still exhibited population increase.

TABLE 10-3. Components of Population Change in Regions by Metropolitan Area Status, 1960-1975. Komponenten der Bevölkerungsveränderungen in Regionen nach Ballungsräumen, 1960-1975.

	NET CHANGE 1960-1970	NET CHANGE 1970-1975	NATURAL INCREASE 1960-1970	NATURAL INCREASE 1970-1975	NET MIGRATION 1960-1970	NET MIGRATION 1970-1975
United States	2399	1952	2046	1456	354	496
Large metropolitan	1221	285	804	539	417	-254
Other metropolitan	968	969	750	576	218	393
Nonmetropolitan	211	698	492	341	-281	357
Northeast	438	79	397	218	41	-139
Large metropolitan	262	-73	236	123	26	-196
Other metropolitan	125	59	112	63	13	-4
Nonmetropolitan	51	93	49	32	2	61
North Central	497	217	567	391	-68	-175
Large metropolitan	254	4	249	171	6	-167
Other metropolitan	201	95	188	140	13	-45
Nonmetropolitan	43	118	130	81	-87	37
South	785	1079	700	554	86	525
Large metropolitan	347	260	152	124	195	136
Other metropolitan	377	506	312	267	65	239
Nonmetropolitan	61	312	236	163	-174	150
West	679	578	385	294	293	284
Large metropolitan	357	94	168	122	189	-28
Other metropolitan	266	309	139	106	126	203
Nonmetropolitan	56	175	78	66	-22	109

*Large metropolitan areas are those having 1.5 million inhabitants or more in 1970.

Source: U.S. Bureau of the Census, "Estimates of the Population of Counties and Metropolitan Areas: July 1, 1974 and 1975," Current Population Reports, Ser. P-25, No. 709, September 1977.

Morrison (6) outlined three dimensions of recent growth and inmigration in nonmetropolitan areas. The first involves decentralization of metropolitan economic activity into surrounding nonmetropolitan areas. This represents a leakage or spillover effect and is associated with improvements in transportation in such a way that business can be efficiently conducted at greater distances from the central city. The second dimension involves a large-scale change in the geography of economic opportunity such that industry filtered down into nonmetropolitan areas, and energy extraction created employment and population growth in heretofore declining regions of Appalachia and the West. Change in the American life-style represents the third and perhaps most significant dimension of nonmetropolitan growth. An increase in retired persons who are free from employment-related concerns, and a growing emphasis on quality of life considerations among people of all ages made nonmetropolitan areas more attractive to migrants (31).

Residential preference surveys show that a majority of Americans desire residence in small towns and rural areas (32, 33). When asked about the reasons, people list quality of life attributes such as clean air and water, a nice place to raise children, and freedom from perceived urban ills like congestion and crime. With increased incomes and leisure, a growing number of people are able to realize their residential preferences by moving to nonmetropolitan areas.

If people are, in fact, realizing the preferences that they have had all along, then what part has the government played in the process of nonmetropolitan migration? The government did not set about consciously to stimulate a "rural renaissance" or "nonmetropolitan resurgence," but its actions played a facilitating role. By making nonmetropolitan areas more accessible to national markets and population, the federal interstate system improved their desirability for industrial and recreational purposes. In addition, freeways promoted residential development beyond the official margins of SMSAs in adjacent nonmetropolitan areas.

Improvements in the federal retirement system or federally induced improvements in private plans enable retired persons to seek residences in places where they can use their leisure time more productively. In northern Michigan, many retired persons have transformed long-time vacation homes into year-round residences (34). In so doing, they stimulated service activity and created regional multiplier effects.

Federal energy policy favoring greater self-sufficiency and emphasizing coal production has contributed to the evolution of a growing number of "boom towns." Although rapid inmigration associated with energy exploitation is initially welcomed as a symbol of prosperity and a welcome relief from selective outmigration, its consequences are frequently disruptive to the social and political balance of community life (35, 36, 37).

Gilmore and Duff (38) conducted an in-depth study of the impacts of rapid population growth due to inmigration in Sweetwater County, Wyoming, an important coal-producing center in the West that has attracted attention in the news media due to reports of local corruption and the infiltration of organized crime. Due to expansion in coal mining activities, county population grew from 18,391 in 1970 to 36,900 by the end of 1974 representing an annual growth rate of 19 percent. Besides the crime problem, Gilmore and Duff reported that labor productivity in the mines had declined due to high turnover and labor shortages, and the overall quality of life deteriorated because of the inability of local institutions to provide adequate housing, health services, schools, and retailing. Other boom towns have sprung up in areas adjacent to mineral resources in the nonmetropolitan West. Each has a set of unique problems, but in all cases, they are the direct result of the inability of formally stable communities to accommodate relatively large numbers of newcomers in a short period of time. Cortese and Cortese (39) have compiled an excellent bibliography of boom towns in the West.

At this time, not much is known about the mechanisms that underlie inmigration in nonmetropolitan areas, much less about their policy ramifications. It is clear, however, that nonmetropolitan growth and inmigration entail a whole new set of policy questions. While there is a rich literature dealing with the rural inmigrant's adjustment to urban life, very little is known about the psychological and social problems attendant in moving from metropolitan areas into small communities. Public attitude surveys have been geared primarily to assessing people's willingness to stimulate growth in small communities and to control growth in large metropolitan areas. The emphasis has shifted to a concern with what people think about aiding declining metropolitan areas and slowing unorderly growth in nonmetropolitan communities.

POLICY CONSEQUENCES OF MIGRATION

Although the focus of discussion has been on policy as the causal factor and changing migration patterns as the outcome, it can be argued that migration affects the regional balance of population and population characteristics and this, in turn, affects federal, regional, and local policies. Migration and policy then, can best be regarded as interdependent processes.

The most obvious consequence of migration-induced regional shifts in population will be the reapportionment of congressional representatives after the 1980 Census. The Constitution provides that representatives are apportioned among states according to population and that each state must have at least one representative. Since 1921 a base of 435 seats has been used in all years except between 1960 and 1962 when the number was increased to 437 to accommodate the inclusion into the Union of Alaska and Hawaii. Table 10-4 shows the historical distribution of representation among regions and states and an estimate of post-1980 changes. The Mid-Atlantic and East Central regions will be major losers while the West and South will experience the largest gains. Western regions will pick up a few seats, but these gains will be small in comparison to those in the South. Not surprisingly, the reallocation of representation and hence power is worrisome to many Northern politicians. In a speech before the White House Conference on Balanced Growth and Economic Development, Senator Daniel Patrick Moynihan (40) of New York warned of increased regional rivalries and factionalism. He was, of course, making a plea for reorientation of federal expenditures and loan guarantees for New York City.

A related issue involves federal programs like revenue sharing whose funding formulas use population as one input. Morrison (6) points out that regions or communities that are unable to show population gains or even population stability may experience decreases in program support. Declining regions that need aid the most may very well lose federal

TABLE 10-4. Apportionment of House of Representatives by State and Region: 1910-1970, Estimates for 1980.
Zuteilung des Unterhauses bei Läandern und Regionen: 1910-1970, Schätzung für 1980.

	1910	1930	1940	1950	1960	1970	1980	Estimated Change 1970-1980
New England								
Maine	32	29	28	28	25	25	25	0
New Hampshire	4	3	3	3	2	2	2	0
Vermont	2	2	2	2	2	2	2	0
Massachusetts	2	1	1	1	1	1	1	0
Rhode Island	16	15	14	14	12	12	12	0
Connecticut	3	2	2	2	2	2	2	0
	5	6	6	6	6	6	6	0
Mid-Atlantic								
New York	91	93	92	87	83	79	73	-6
New Jersey	43	45	45	43	41	39	35	-4
Pennsylvania	12	14	14	14	15	15	15	0
	36	34	33	30	27	25	23	-2
East North Central								
Ohio	86	90	87	87	88	86	82	-4
Indiana	22	24	23	23	24	23	21	-2
Illinois	13	12	11	11	11	11	11	0
Michigan	27	27	26	25	24	24	22	-2
Wisconsin	13	17	17	18	19	19	19	0
	11	10	10	10	10	9	9	0
West North Central								
Minnesota	57	47	44	42	37	35	34	-1
Iowa	10	9	9	9	8	8	8	0
Missouri	11	9	8	8	7	6	6	0
North Dakota	16	13	13	11	10	10	10	0
South Dakota	3	2	2	2	2	2	1	-1
Nebraska	3	2	2	2	2	2	1	-1
Kansas	6	5	4	4	3	3	3	0
	8	7	6	6	5	5	5	0

Delaware								+5
Maryland	6	6	6	7				0
Virginia	10	9	9	7	8	8	9	+1
West Virginia	6	6	6	10	10	10	10	0
North Carolina	10	11	12	12	5	4	4	0
South Carolina	7	6	6	12	11	11	11	0
Georgia	12	10	10	6	6	6	6	0
Florida	4	5	6	8	10	10	10	+4
					12	15	19	
South Central	80	79	79	74	70	69	72	+3
Kentucky	11	9	9	8	7	7	7	0
Tennessee	10	9	10	9	9	8	9	+1
Alabama	10	9	9	9	8	7	7	0
Mississippi	8	7	7	6	5	5	5	0
Louisiana	8	8	8	8	8	8	8	0
Arkansas	7	7	7	6	4	4	4	0
Oklahoma	8	9	8	6	6	6	6	0
Texas	18	21	21	22	23	24	26	+2
Mountain	14	14	16	15	17	19	20	+1
Montana	2	2	2	2	2	2	2	0
Idaho	2	2	2	2	2	2	2	0
Wyoming	1	1	1	1	1	1	1	0
Colorado	4	4	4	4	4	5	5	0
New Mexico	1	1	2	2	2	2	2	0
Arizona	1	1	1	1	3	4	5	+1
Utah	2	2	2	2	2	2	2	0
Nevada	1	1	1	1	1	1	1	0
Pacific	19	29	33	43	52	57	59	+2
Washington	5	6	6	7	7	7	7	0
Oregon	3	3	4	4	4	4	5	+1
California	11	20	23	30	38	43	44	+1
Alaska	x	x	x	x	1	1	1	0
Hawaii	x	x	x	x	1	2	2	0

x Was not a state in that year.

Source: U.S. Bureau of the Census, Census of Population: 1970 - Characteristics of the Population, vol. pt. 1, U.S. Summary, 1973, U.S. Bureau of Economic Analysis, Population, Personal Income and Earnings by State: Projections to 2000, October 1977.

support making it more difficult for them to prevent future outmigration if, indeed, that is their goal.

Increased decentralization outside official SMSA limits into adjacent nonmetropolitan areas will almost surely involve increased commuting and more automobile travel. Implications in the area of energy policy are considerable. Large-scale ex-urban development as a form of nonmetropolitan growth and migration is inconsistent with national efforts at more frugal energy utilization.

Retirement-related migration is a factor in both Sunbelt and nonmetropolitan migration, and the changing distribution of the elderly can potentially have enormous implications for the regions and communities involved. Older persons impact politics in their destinations by electing representatives who are in tune with their views. The high voter registration and turnout among elderly persons make them a potent political force in destination regions.

This impact is accentuated by the growing trend for elderly persons to concentrate in retirement communities. Sun City, Arizona (in the Phoenix metropolitan area), is a prime example of a community whose political clout is recognized by local politicians and those interested in the political process. In 1977 the population of Sun City was 43,000 and represented a seemingly small relative proportion of the total county population of almost 1.3 million. When one considers that virtually the entire population of Sun City is of voting age and, more importantly, falls into age and socioeconomic categories in which the propensity to vote is very high and that in the county as a whole there are only about 900,000 persons of voting age, many of them young adults and minorities who tend not to vote, the impact of 43,000 spatially concentrated elderly persons is large.

Sun City residents play an important role in determining the character of local, state, and national representation and, indirectly, the kinds of decisions that are supported by those representatives.

CONCLUSION

Although the federal government does not have an official migration policy, many federal decisions impact population distribution and migration. Almost all policies have territorial consequences and, as such, they affect certain locales and regions more than others. At a regional level, federal spending, immigration, and retirement migration have reinforced ongoing processes of population growth and inmigration in Sunbelt regions. At a subregional scale, migration flows have shifted such that nonmetropolitan areas are experiencing high rates of population growth. Relevant federal actions involve areas of transportation, energy, and retirement.

Governmental interference in the migration process may be justified on the basis that uncontrolled migration is deleterious to people and/or places. While it is apparent that massive inmigration to small communities in nonmetropolitan areas has detrimental consequences, the impact of outmigration on large metropolitan areas in declining regions is more difficult to assess. Certainly, sizable outmigration causes problems in maintaining local services and market-oriented industries, but from a broader perspective, outmigration may reflect the capacity of people to adjust to changes in the national geography of economic opportunity.

It is obvious that a great deal of information is needed in order to make rational decisions concerning future population distribution and migration patterns. Migratory shifts necessitate a reorientation in traditional policy-oriented research. Specific issues include the process of population decline in large metropolitan areas, the evolution of energy-related boom towns, migration of elderly persons, and the consequences of their spatial segregation in retirement communities.

Although prospects for a comprehensive national migration policy are dim, it is increasingly necessary to understand the geographic impacts of government policy. Seemingly unrelated activities may have far-reaching and sometimes unwanted consequences in terms of population distribution and migration. Recognition of the geographic qualities of government activity is a prerequisite to the efficient planning and manipulation of future population growth and its spatial distribution.

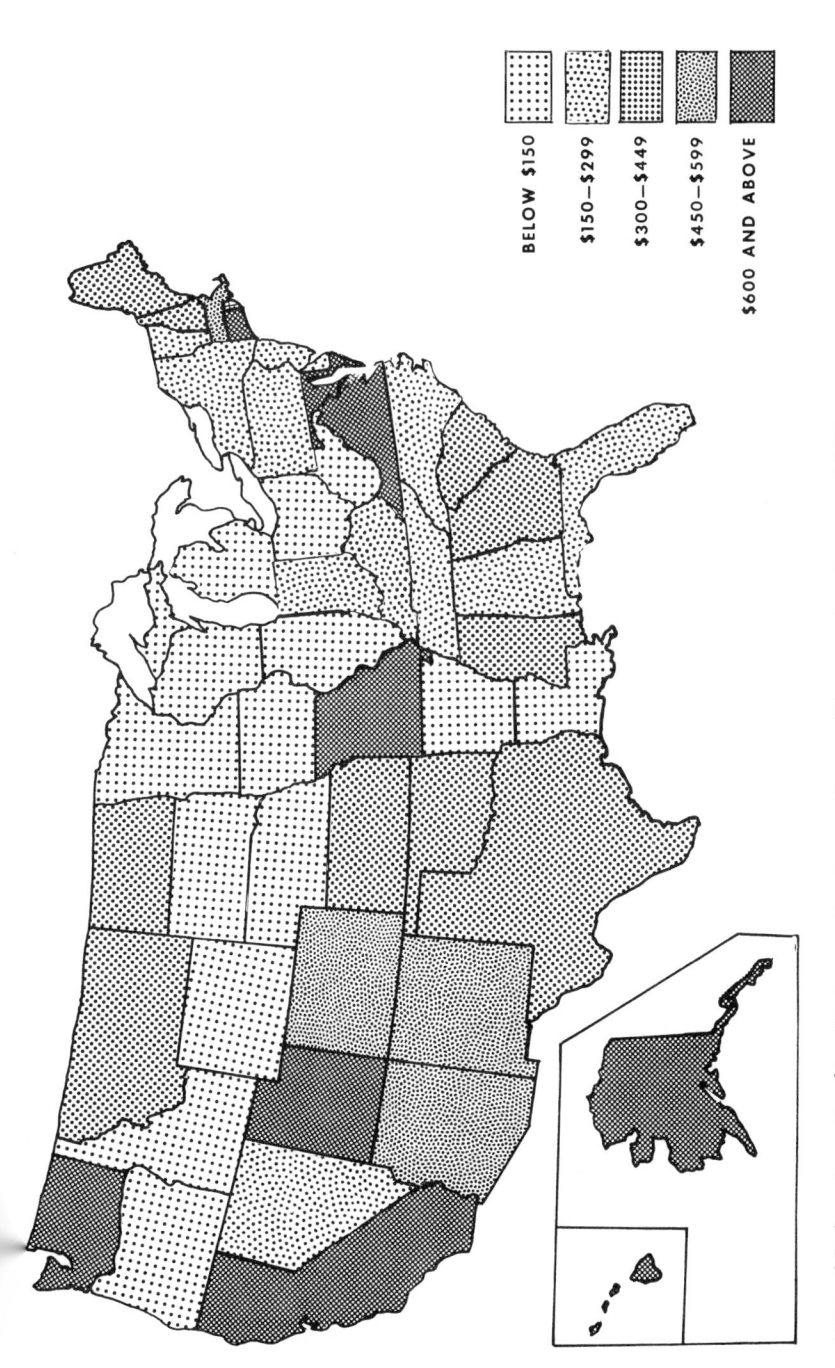

FIG. 10-1. Per Capita Defense Contract Expenditures by State, 1977. Verteidigungsausgaben pro Kopf der Bevölkerung der amerikanischen Bundesländer, 1977.

Source: U.S. Department of Defense, Office of the Secretary, Prime Contracts by State, 1977.

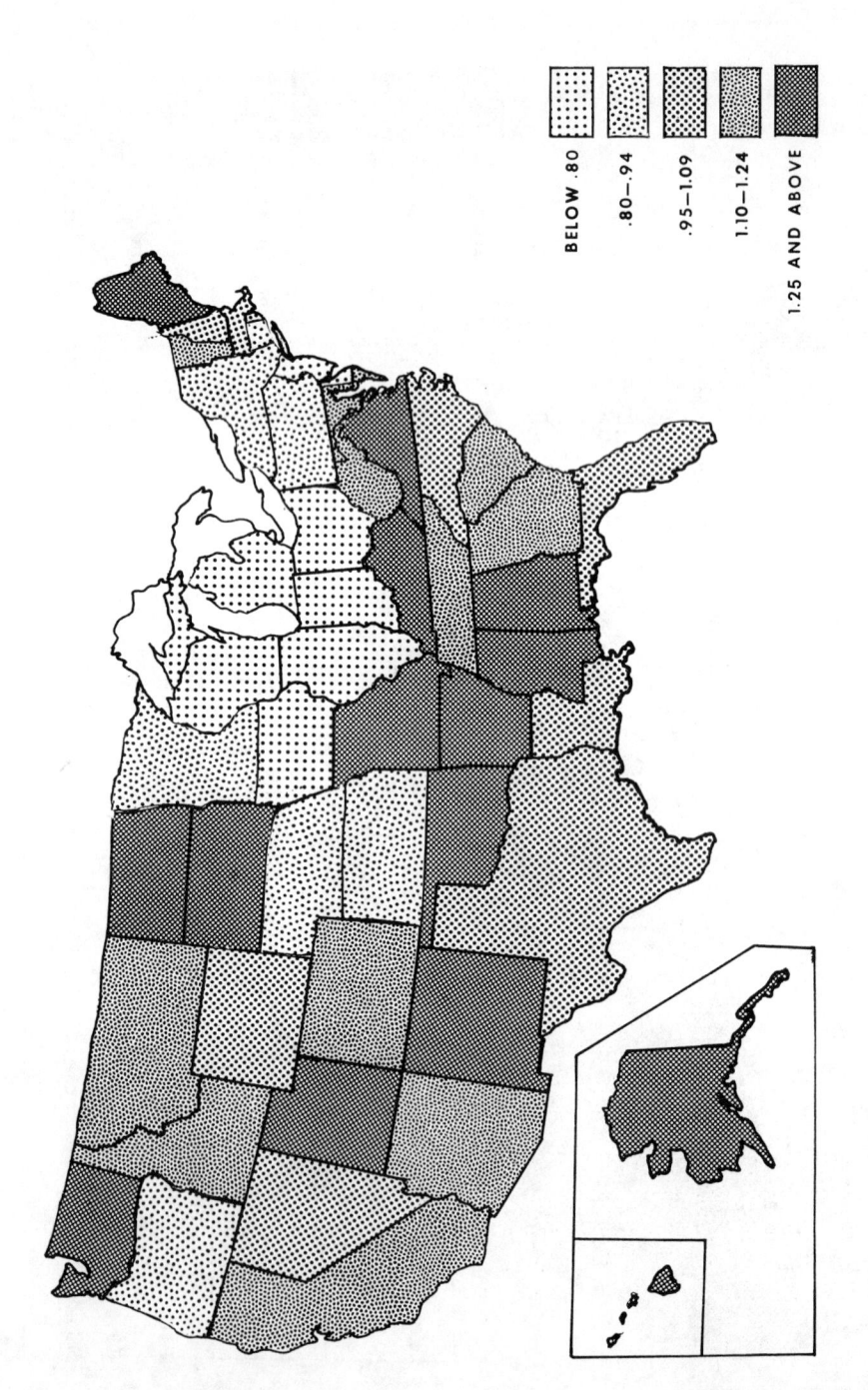

FIG. 10-2. Spending-Taxes Ratio by State, 1976.
Ausgaben-Steuer Ratio bei Bundesstaaten, 1976.
Source: Government Research Cooperation, Washington, D.C. National Journal, July 2, 1977.

NOTES

1. Hoover, E. M., "Reduced Population Growth and the Problems of Urban Areas," in Population, Distribution and Policy, ed. S. M. Mazie (Washington, D.C.: U.S. Government Printing Office, 1972).

2. Demko, G., "Population Redistribution and Migration Policy in the U.S. Urban Context," in Urban Development in the U.S. and Hungary (Budapest: Publishing House of the Hungarian Academy of Sciences, 1978).

3. Reid, W. J., "Federal Migration Policy: Present Reality and Future Alternatives," in Migration and Social Welfare, ed. J. W. Eaton (New York: National Association of Social Workers, 1971).

4. Population and the American Future, Report of the Commission on Population Growth and the American Future (Washington, D.C.: U.S. Government Printing Office, 1972).

5. Morrison, P. A., "Population Movements and the Shape of Urban Growth: Implications for Public Policy," in Population Distribution and Policy, ed. S. M. Mazie (Washington, D.C.: U.S. Government Printing Office, 1972).

6. ------, Emerging Public Concerns Over U.S. Population Movements in an Era of Slowing Growth, Rand Paper Series No. P-5873 (Santa Monica: Rand Corporation, 1977).

7. Mills, E. S., "Economic Aspects of City Sizes," in Population Distribution and Policy, ed. S. M. Mazie (Washington, D.C.: U.S. Government Printing Office, 1972).

8. Cameron, G. C., "The Relevance to the United States of British Regional Population Strategies, with a Note on the French Experience," in Population Distribution and Policy, ed. S. M. Mazie (Washington, D.C.: U. S. Government Printing Office, 1972).

9. U.S. Department of Labor, Worker Relocation: A Review of U.S. Department of Labor Mobility Demonstration Projects (Washington, D.C.: C. K. Fairchild, E. F. Shelby and Company, Inc., 1970).

10. Hansen, N. M., "The Case of Government-Assisted Migration," in Population Distribution and Policy, ed. S. M. Mazie (Washington, D.C.: U.S. Government Printing Office, 1972).

11. Watkins, A. J., "Intermetropolitan Migration and the Rise of the Sunbelt," Social Science Quarterly Vol. 59 (1978), 553-561.

12. Greenwood, M. J., "An Analysis of the Determinants of Labor Mobility in the U.S.," Review of Economics and Statistics 51 (1969), 189-194.

13. Schwind, P., "A General Field Theory of Migration: United States, 1955-60," Economic Geography 51 (1975), 1-16.

14. Okun, B., "Interstate Population Migration and State Income Inequality: A Simultaneous Equations Approach," Economic Development and Cultural Change 16 (1968), 297-311.

15. Gober-Meyers, P., "Interstate Migration and Economic Growth: A Simultaneous Equations Approach," Environment and Planning A 10 (1978), 1241-1252.

16. Rudquist, B. S., et al., "The Impact of Defense Cutbacks on Employment and Migration," in Population Distribution and Policy, ed. S. M. Mazie (Washington, D.C.: U.S. Government Printing Office, 1972).

17. "The Second War Between the States," Business Week, April 17, 1976, pp. 92-98.

18. Sutton, H., "Sunbelt vs. Frostbelt: A Second Civil War?" Saturday Review, April 15, 1978, pp. 28-37.

19. Gordon, L., "Social Issues in the Arid City," in Urban Planning for Arid Zones, ed. G. Golany (New York: Wiley, 1977).

20. Stoeber, E. A., Pension Reform Act Explained (Cincinnati: The National Underwriter, 1974).

21. Greenough, W. C., and F. P. King, Pension Plans and Public Policy (New York: Columbia University Press, 1976).

22. Alonso, W., "Problems, Purposes, and Implicit Policies for a National Strategy of Urbanization," in Population Distribution and Policy, ed. S. M. Mazie (Washington, D.C.: U. S. Government Printing Office, 1972).

23. "Indochinese Refugee Plight," Congressional Quarterly, June 30, 1979, p. 1331.
24. Beale, C. L., The Revival of Population Growth in Nonmetropolitan America, Economic Development Division, Economic Research Series No. 65 (Washington, D.C.: U.S. Department of Agriculture, 1975).
25. Morrison, P. A., "Rural Renaissance in America?" Population Bulletin 31 (1976), 3-26.
26. Tucker, J. C., "Changing Patterns of Migration Between Metropolitan and Nonmetropolitan Areas in the United States: Recent Evidence," Demography 13 (1976), 435-443.
27. Roseman, C. C., Changing Migration Patterns Within the United States, Resource Papers for College Geography No. 77-2 (Washington, D.C.: Association of American Geographers, 1977).
28. Sternlieb, G. and J. S. Hughes, "New Regional and Metropolitan Realities of American," Journal of the American Institute of Planners 42 (1977), 227-241.
29. Wardwell, J. M., "Equilibrium and Change in Nonmetropolitan Growth," Rural Sociology 42 (1977), 156-179.
30. McCarthy, K. F., and P. A. Morrison, The Changing Demography and Economic Structure of Nonmetropolitan Areas in the 1970s, Rand Paper Series No. D-6062 (Santa Monica: Rand Corporation, 1978).
31. Williams, J. D., and A. J. Safranko, Migration Motivations for Population Turnaround in Nonmetropolitan Areas, Department of Agricultural Economics, Illinois Agricultural Staff Papers No. 78, S-4 (Champaign: University of Illinois, 1978).
32. Zuiches, J. J., and G. V. Fuguitt, "Residential Preferences: Implications for Population Redistribution in Nonmetropolitan Areas," in Population Distribution and Policy, ed S. M. Mazie (Washington, D.C.: U.S. Government Printing Office, 1972).
33. Fuguitt, G. V., and J. J. Zuiches, "Residential Preferences and Population Distribution," Demography 12 (1975), 491-504.
34. Marans, R. W., and J. D. Wellman, The Quality of Nonmetropolitan Living: Evaluations, Behavior and

Expectations of Northern Arizona Residents (Ann Arbor: University of Michigan Survey Research Center, 1978).

35. Cortese, C. F., and B. Jones, "The Sociological Analysis of Boom Towns," Western Sociological Journal, (1977), pp. 76-90.

36. Ploch, L. A., "The Reversal in Migration Patterns-Some Rural Development Consequences," Rural Sociology 43 (1978), 292-303.

37. Schwarzweller, H. K., "Migration and the Changing Rural Scene," Rural Sociology 44 (1979), 7-23.

38. Gilmore, J., and M. Duff, Boomtown Growth Management: Rock Springs-Green River Wyoming (Boulder: Westview Press, 1975).

39. Cortese, C. F., and J. A. Cortese, The Social Effects of Energy Boomtowns in the West: A Partially Annotated Bibliography, Exchange Bibliography No. 1557 (Monticello, Illinois: Council of Planning Librarians, 1978).

40. Moynihan, P. A., "How to Politicize the Economics of Growth--And Why Not To," address before the White House Conference on Balanced Growth and Economic Development in Washington, D.C., 1978.

CHAPTER 11

NATIONAL LAND USE POLICIES IN THE UNITED STATES: EX PLURIBUS NULLUM

NATIONALE LANDNUTZUNGSPOLITIK IN DEN VEREINIGTEN STAATEN: EX PLURIBUS NULLUM

Rutherford H. Platt

Abstract

The dilemma of national policy in the United States was epitomized in the outcome of a fifty-year controversy involving the Indiana Dunes on Lake Michigan. Congress approved both a national park and a federally constructed harbor in close proximity to each other resulting in mutually harmful externalities. This and similar situations prompted a quest for a single "national land use policy" which would resolve such conflicts in the future. A review of past and present land policies suggests that such an exercise may be futile. American history is interlaced with diverse policies and counterpolicies affecting both directly and indirectly the use of land. Some of these relate to the disposition or management of the public domain. Others influence the use of nonfederal land through public works programs, financial subsidies, regulations, and taxation. It is suggested that national land policy is too complex to be encompassed by a single enactment. Instead, the land use implications of alternative federal actions should be better recognized. NEPA and the Coastal Zone Management Program facilitate this objective.

Kurzfassung

Das Dilemma der Innenpolitik in den Vereinigten Staaten wurde durch das Ergebnis einer Fünfzig Jahre währenden Kontroverse um die Dünen von Indiana am Michigansee kurz dargestellt. Der Kongress hatte sowohl einen Nationalpark als auch einen von der Bundesregierung gebauten Hafen in direkter Nachbarschaft zu einander gebilligt, was zu gegenseitigen schädlichen Beeinträchtigungen führte. Diese und ähnliche Situationen verlassen ein suchen nach einer einzigen "nationalen Landnutzungspolitik," die solche Konflikte in Zukunft lösen sollte.

Ein Überblick über vergangene und gegenwärtige Landnutzungsprogramme lässt darauf schliessen, dass ein solcher Versuch vergebens sein dürfte. Die amerikanischen Geschichte ist von verschiedenen Programmen und Gegenprogrammen durchwoben, die sowohl unmittelbar als auch mittelbar die Landnutzung beeinflussen. Einige dieser Programme beziehen sich auf die Disposition und die Bewirtschaftung von Staatsgut. Andere beeinflussen die Landnutzung ausserhalb des Staatslandes durch öffentliche Arbeitsprogramme, finanzielle Beihilfen, Verordnungen und Besteuerung. Es wird daraus geschlossen, dass die nationale Landpolitik zu komplex ist, um durch ein einziges Gesetz erfasst zu werden. Statt dessen sollten die Landnutzungsauswirkungen alternative Bundesunternehmungen besser erkannt werden. NEPA und Coastal Zone Management Program (<u>Küsten Zonen Programm</u>) erleichtern dieses Ziel.

National Land Use Policies in the United States:
Ex Pluribus Nullum

THE INDIANA DUNES CASE: NATIONAL POLICIES IN CONFLICT

Lake Michigan, the second largest of the Great Lakes of North America, extends 350 miles (564 km) from south to north, connecting the U.S. agricultural and industrial heartland centered in Chicago with the timber and mining regions of the northern tier. In the course of 12,000 years since withdrawal of the Wisconsin stage of glaciation, prevailing winds and winter storms have lined the eastern and southern shores of Lake Michigan with fine sandy beaches and sand dunes extending in places up to a mile from the water's edge. These littoral features attain their greatest height and width at the lake's southern tip where the longest fetch of wind and waves have created a natural province known as the Indiana Dunes after the state of Indiana in which it principally lies.

Before the arrival of Caucasian settlements, this duneland phenomenon extended from the Calumet marshes (now in the southeastern corner of the city of Chicago), around the foot of the lake and northwards on what is now the Michigan shoreline (Figure 11-1). The poet Carl Sandburg once referred to the Indiana Dunes as the "Grand Canyon of the Midwest." While not "grand" in scale, they were a region of topographic, ecologic, and scenic diversity in dramatic contrast to the generally monotonous prairie terrain of the upper Midwest.

For centures the Indiana Dunes region was avoided and ignored. Unsuited to farming and difficult to traverse, the area was bypassed by settlers heading for more fertile lands in Illinois, Iowa, and Minnesota (1). Drainage of the marshlands south of the Dunes opened up northern Indiana to agriculture in the mid-nineteenth century. With the growth of Chicago to a city of a million in 1870, and the development of rail, highway, and steamer routes along the Indiana shoreline, the Dunes region itself began to attract attention.

Interest in, and ultimately competition for the use of the dunelands assumed at least four different forms (2). First, recreation was early established as a natural function of the Dunes. In the 1870s, Chicagoans began to make a summertime hegira out of their smoke-polluted city to the sandy beaches of the Dunes. Recreational use of the Dunes was encouraged in 1923 by the establishment of the Indiana Dunes State Park encompassing 2,180 acres and 3.3 miles of shoreline (3, p. 508). Construction of the Chicago, South Shore, and South Bend Interurban Railroad provided convenient access from downtown Chicago to several points in the Dunes. This heralded a second wave of interest in the form of summer-home dwellers and eventually year-round residents. While these users of the Dunes were drawn by the same amenities as the recreationists, the former's interest in privacy and exclusivity was to clash with a wider interest in public use of the beaches.

Meanwhile, a third and quite different claimant to the Dunes was emerging in the form of heavy industry, especially steel manufacturing. The southern tip of Lake Michigan offers waterborne access to the iron deposits of the Mesabi Range along Lake Superior, as well as train or barge communication with coalfields in southern Indiana and Illinois. With a market close at hand in Chicago (and later in Detroit), steel mills appeared along the Michigan shore at

South Chicago in 1888 and at Gary, Indiana, in 1908 (3). The latter involved extensive excavation and removal of the natural dunes to accommodate the U.S. Steel Corporation works and the planned industrial city of Gary. By 1920, the western portion of the Dunes in Indiana was entirely obliterated by one of the world's major complexes of steel mills, refineries, and associated industries.

A fourth claim to the Indiana Dunes emanated from a growing public interest in the protection of natural areas as habitats for native flora and fauna. This interest in the Dunes was aroused by the studies of Professor Henry Cowles, a University of Chicago botanist, who in the late nineteenth-century undertook pioneering studies of plant succession there. By comparing the species of plants in relation to the age of successive dune landforms, he established the Indiana Dunes as the "birthplace" of the science of ecology (4). Preservation of remaining natural portions of the duneland for scientific study and environmental education has been widely championed.

Thus four distinct and largely incompatible land uses-public recreation, private residence, heavy industry, and nature preserve-have vied for decades over control of the remaining Dunes. By 1960, the area of natural dunes left to be allocated amounted to an area of only about 7,000 acres, extending twelve miles along the shore and a mile inland. This was the scene of the "Battle for the Indiana Dunes."

The "battle" actually turned on the outcome of two competing proposals for action by the U.S. Congress. As early as 1916, Stephen Mather, the first director of the National Park Service, recommended that the Indiana Dunes be established as a national park. This concept lapsed with the creation of the state park in the 1920s but was revived in the 1950s at the urging of a private organization known as the "Save the Dunes Council." A competing proposal offered by a coalition of Indiana businessmen and politicians sought federal construction of an artificial harbor to allow industrial expansion into the remaining dunelands.

Both the park and port concepts were pressed with growing vigor during the late 1950s and early 1960s. Although both concepts related to approximately the same land, each was expressed in a separate series of bills and underwent hearings before different committees of the U.S. Congress. The pros and cons of each were, therefore, not directly debated. The national decision process in effect lacked any opportunity to weigh the contrasting proposals against each other or against other possible alternatives.

The remarkable outcome was adoption of both proposals, albeit in modified form as to the land to be included in the park. The Bethlehem Steel Company in 1963 had bulldozed the portion of the Dunes which it owned, thus eliminating this area from consideration for the park. Conservationists reluctantly settled for other, less auspicious tracts of beach, dunes, and inland terrain. The park bill was adopted 21 June 1965. Congress then approved federal construction of a harbor to serve Bethlehem Steel and another steel firm. This industrial complex would be surrounded by the scattered fragments of the newly authorized Indiana Dunes National Lakeshore Park.

Subsequent experience has sustained predictions that these would be unhappy neighbors. The steel plants impose a variety of harmful externalities upon adjoining park areas in the form of air and water pollution, traffic, and visual blight. The park, meanwhile, preempts land which in the view of the steel companies is needed for supporting facilities. By straddling the issue, Congress achieved a result satisfactory to no one. The park consists of scattered tracts of uneven quality and low capacity for public use. Meanwhile, the comptroller general of the U.S. has determined that the federal port has not fulfilled Congressional requirements that its economic benefits exceed its cost to the U.S. taxpayers (5). Ironically, this failure results in part from the presence of the park which occupies land otherwise usable for additional industrial expansion to be served by the port.

Lessons of the Indiana Dunes

The Indiana Dunes episode on its face involved a clash between two competing land use policies-promotion of economic growth and development on the one hand and protection of significant natural areas for public enjoyment on the other. Each of these is a long-standing and oft-stated objective of national policy in the United States. But where these objections conflict, which frequently happens, the outcome is left to the political process. The haphazard and unsatisfactory outcome of the Dunes case is typical of national decision making in land use matters.

Several elements in the Indiana Dunes experience suggest practical obstacles to the establishment of a national land use policy. The first factor is the institution of private ownership of land, a direct legacy of the English common law. Ownership of land in this country bestows upon the owner broad rights to use one's land as one sees fit, subject only to reasonable limitations by public authorities in the interest of protecting the public health, safety, and welfare. Preparation of a site for development is a recognized prerogative of the owner in the absence of proven harm to adjoining property owners or distinct physical hazard. Thus Bethlehem Steel exercised its right as a private landowner to bulldoze its portion of the Indiana Dunes without restraint by any governmental authority (6).

A second factor closely related to the first is land speculation, the ancient practice of buying land cheaply in the expectation that a change in circumstances will yield a sharp increase in its value. Many speculators were involved with the dunelands. There was much evidence of conflict of interest in the ownership of interests in land by persons or firms in positions to influence the ultimate authorization of the federal port (7). Needless to say, the influence of speculators tended to distort a balanced consideration of the merits of the port proposal in Congress.

A third complicating factor is federalism, the doctrine which establishes the relative roles of the federal and state governments under the U.S. Constitution. Where land use is concerned, federalism is construed to assign whatever power the public may exercise over private land use to the state in which the land is located. The state in turn usually assigns its land use powers to local governments. Thus the issue as to whether Bethlehem Steel and its neighbor Midwest Steel could utilize their land for industrial purposes lay with the State of Indiana and those local and county governments having jurisdiction over the land. Neither the U.S. government nor the State of Illinois could interfere in the policy of these authorities that industrial use was appropriate (except through federal acquisition of the land in question for park purposes).

Finally, a fourth factor which has historically distorted

national land use decisions is the Congressional tradition of the "pork barrel" or "logrolling." These terms refer to the practice of approving federal public works expenditures, especially pertaining to navigation and flood control, which benefit the district of particular members of Congress. Legislators, knowing their own turn will come, support their colleagues' favorite projects. Furthermore, projects tend to be approved according to the seniority of their patron rather than on the basis of their actual merits. Sponsorship of a federal harbor for the Indiana Dunes by Charles Halleck, former Majority Leader of the U.S. House of Representatives greatly influenced the bill's ultimate adoption.

The Search for a Single "National Land Use Policy"

Indiana Dunes and similar debacles in national land use decision making prompted widespread public outrage in the late 1960s. This was a part of a larger concern for environmental protection which emerged at this time in the United States and other developed countries. A loose coalition of activist organizations, academics, students, housewives, and politicians wielded considerable influence in federal, state, and local government during the period between 1968 and 1974 (ending roughly with the Arab oil embargo). Significant new laws dealing with air and water pollution, pesticides, solid waste, and other environmental concerns were adeopted at each level. A prevailing theme of the movement was the need for "national policies" on the environment and land use.

The first objective was signed into law on January 1, 1970, as the National Environmental Policy Act (NEPA).

NEPA declared a national policy:

> . . . which will encourage productive and enjoyable harmony between man and his environment; to promote efforts which will prevent or eliminate damage to the environment and biosphere and stimulate the health and welfare of man. . . . (P L 91-190, Sec. 2)

This broad objective was backed up by a requirement that all federal agencies prepare an "environmental impact statement" prior to undertaking any "major federal action significantly affecting the quality of the human environment." As of 1978, this requirement has elicited some 10,000 statements dealing with a broad spectrum of federal activities including highways, water resource projects, and airports, as well as federal assistance to state and local governments and federal regulatory programs (8). While the scope of this act is very great, there is reason for concern that the policy objectives of NEPA have been lost in the sea of paperwork which it has generated (9).

NEPA was never viewed as an adequate expression of a "national land use policy" since most land-related decisions are nonfederal in origin and therefore outside of NEPA's scope. The effort to achieve a national land use policy act continued in the early 1970s, most notably under the aegis of Senator Henry Jackson of Washington. Between 1970 and 1973, over 320 land-use related measures were introduced in Congress (10, p. 3). The goal in most cases was to legislate a policy declaration which embraced all land-related decisions, not merely federal ones.

The effort proved fruitless except for the passage of the Coastal Zone Management Act of 1972, which adopted the national land use concept in "watered-down" form (11). Opponents maintained that land use was traditionally a matter of state and local prerogative in which the federal government must not interfere. This romantic view of course overlooks the intimate involvement of the national government in the distribution and utilization of land since the very founding of the United States.

Perhaps equally naive, however, is the view of some proponents of a "national land use policy" that a single Congressional enactment, no matter how well intentioned, could repeal and nullify the accumulated doctrines, dogmas, and policies which determine the use of land in the United States. The history of land use in this nation has been one of the conflict between opposing interests, policies, and philosophies. As in the Indiana Dunes cases cited above, sub-rosa factors play major roles in shaping the outcome of both public and private land use decisions. National land use policy cannot be created in a vacuum; rather it must be forged in a cauldron. The balance of this essay will review some of the conflicts which have characterized national land use policies in the past. The clash of opposing policies and counterpolicies may be expected to continue in the future whether or not national land use policy legislation is ever adopted.

LAND USE IN THE U.S.: A HISTORY OF DISCORD

Foreign observers have always been intrigued with the sheer abundance of land in the United States. According to the British land use authority Delafons (12):

> Land has never been a scarce resource in America. Its great abundance has been a powerful influence on American attitudes toward the land, its development, and attempts by government to control its use. The total area of the United States (excluding Hawaii and Alaska) is 1,904 million acres. England and Wales, with a poulation of about one quarter that of the United States, have a land area of less than 2 percent of this.

In an early Congressional debate on public land policies in 1796, Gallatin remarked that 'If the cause of the happiness of this country was examined into, it would be found to arise as much from the great plenty of land in proportion to the inhabitants, which their citizens enjoyed, as from the wisdom of their political institutions.'

Plentiful though it may be, land has also been the source of strife as well as happiness throughout the nation's history. At the federal level, this has been most pronounced in the administration and disposition of lands owned by the national government, the "public domain." Of more recent vintage are issues relating to indirect federal influence upon the use of nonfederal lands through a multitude of grant-in-aid programs, regulatory measures, and policy guidelines, many of which conflict with each other. Issues relating to federal and nonfederal land are considered separately in the discussion which follows.

Federal Lands

At the time of its founding, the national government of the United States was faced with literally an embarrassment of riches in the form of land. As described by Treat (13, p. 7):

It seems paradoxical on the face of it that a Congress too poor to own and maintain a capital, too weak to protect itself from the insults of a band of ragged mutineers, should yet be concerned with the disposal of a vast domain of over 220,000 square miles of the richest of virgin soil.

The public domain originated in the cession by seven states to the national government of lands totalling 236 million acres claimed by them extending west to the Mississippi River. (The cessions were made in settlement of Revolutionary War debts owed by the states). The public domain was trebled in size in 1802 by the purchase of 530 million acres west of the Mississippi from France. Further acquisitions eventually yielded a total of 1,837 million acres owned at one time or another by the federal government, more than two-thirds of the entire land area of continental United States and Alaska (14, Table 2).

The fate of this vast empire of unsettled land was substantially influenced by a policy established before the United States formally came into existence. The initial state cessions of 1784-1786 raised the issue as to what, if anything, should be the nation's policy as to such land. According to Morrison (15, p. 297), the Confederation (which served as the national government until ratification of the federal constitution in 1789) wrestled with such questions as:

> Should white settlement in the Indian country be encouraged or discouraged, and how? Should Congress anticipate a long-term colonial status for the West to protect Indians and fur traders, or encourage white settlement, abandon the Indians, and promise eventual admission of the West to the Union?

The result of this debate was expressed in the Land Ordinance of 1785, possibly the most important declaration of land policy in the nation's history (16). If for no other reason, the ordinance is renowned for establishing the federal land survey system. In place of the "metes and bounds" form of survey used in the original thirteen states, the 1785 ordinance prescribed a strict grid system whereby the western lands would be divided into square townships, six miles on each side. Each township was in turn divided into square-mile "sections." This rectangular system provided a convenient means of establishing title to land which proved immensely valuable to eventual settlement.

Morphologically, the federal survey system was responsible for the rectilinear landscape visible from the air over most of the nation's territory between the Appalachians and the Rocky Mountains.

The Land Ordinance of 1785 thus prepared the way for a policy of disposition and settlement in preference to retention of the public domain in federal ownership. Yet this in turn triggered a much more heated debate as to the terms under which disposition should occur. Two schools of thought were advanced, championed respectively by Thomas Jefferson and Alexander Hamilton: disposal free or for a very low price to promote settlement and agriculture versus disposal at a significant price to augment the nation's treasury. The debate was further complicated according to Treat by a schism within the "settlement" school between those advocating the New England pattern whereby towns were settled incrementally on the edge of the already consolidated territory versus the more expansive southern practice of loosely claiming large tracts with only crude surveys.

The 1785 Land Ordinance compromised between these conflicting views. The settlement objective, on the New England plan, was served by the requirement that land be precisely surveyed prior to sale, and that it be available in parcels of 640 acres, reasonably suited to settlement by a family or group of families. The revenue objective was served by a requirement that land be sold at public auction with a "substantial" minimum price of $1 per acre (raised in 1796 to $2).

The disposition question, however, was by no means settled by this apparently equitable solution. According to Hibbard (17), the land disposal situation in 1800 was vastly complicated by several factors: (a) granting of free lands to veterans of the Revolutionary War as promised upon their enlistment; (b) conveyance of large blocks of federal land to private companies for resale to settlers; (c) speculation by persons who bought land cheaper from each of the preceding recipients and resold it below the prevailing federal price. These factors tended to undermine the revenue policy since relatively little land was purchased directly from the federal government.

An additional complication was the prevalence of illegal "squatters" who entered and settled federal land without any legal title. Technically law-breakers, these pioneers epitomized the westward movement. During the early decades of the nineteenth-century, support increased among the northern and the "western" states to grant a right of "preemption" to such settlers, i.e., to allow them to buy their land for a token price without competition from speculators. The southern states through their spokesman Henry Clay opposed preemption on the ground that it would reward illegal conduct (and incidentally promote settlement from nonslave sections of the country). The Preemption Act of 1841 awarded the right to purchase 160 acres of land at $1.25 per acre without competition. While technically still a revenue measure, it further undermined the principle of sale to the highest bidder. Furthermore it allowed the settler three years in which to pay, a significant departure from prior practice (17, pp. 156-170).

Pressure for abolishing the revenue policy altogether was exacerbated by Congressional gifts of land to many classes of recipients in the mid-nineteenth century. Foremost among such grants were those to promote public improvements-canals, roads, and railroads-totalling 125 million acres, and those to states for various purposes totalling 140 million acres. Grants to railroads in particular foreshadowed the federal monetary grant programs of the past thirty years. Land was conveyed in a checkerboard pattern with alternate sections retained by the federal government. It was expected that the latter would become more valuable for future sale as a result of settlement promoted by the railroad. This proved to be a miscalculation; most settlers bought directly from the railroad company or from speculators rather than the federal government. Once again, the realization of income from public lands, even indirectly, proved illusory.

The revenue policy was substantially repealed in the Homestead Act of 1862. After decades of debate, the act was finally adopted upon the secession of the southern states from the Union. It provided that settlers would receive clear title to 160 acres upon filing their claim and living on the land for a period of five years. The new policy was claimed as a victory by western states who foresaw a massive influx of new settlers.

Statistically, the Homestead Act indeed promoted the settlement of the West. In the decade 1870-1880, some 140,000 claims were filed involving 16 million acres of land (17, p. 396). Altogether, 300 million acres have been conveyed under the Homestead Act by the federal government to private settlers.

But Gates (18, pp. 316-317) warns that the Homestead Act should not be viewed as providing the nation with an all-encompassing new land use policy:

> The Homestead Law has been considered the capstone of an increasingly liberal land policy, and to it has been ascribed the rapid settlement of the West and the large percentage of farmer-owners in the United States. It has also been regarded as providing an outlet for

the discontented and surplus labor of the East,
with the result that, as compared with European
countries, high wage rates have prevailed in that
section. The influence of free land has been
blithely discussed by writers who have never taken
the time to examine the facts with which they dealt
so lightly.

To the contrary, Gates notes that during the decade following adoption of the Homestead Act, Congress granted 127 million acres of land to railroads, five times the total of the previous twelve years. This land was thereby foreclosed to homesteaders except upon purchase from the railroads. Potential homestead sites were perforce removed to areas remote from rail lines. Furthermore, since 160 acres was wholly inadequate to support a family in the arid west, homesteaders were forced to obtain additional land through purchase or under the terms of a different act. In Gates's view (18, pp. 316-317): "The Homestead Law did not completely change our land system, . . . its adoption merely superimposed upon the old land system a principle out of harmony with it and . . . until 1890 the old and new constantly clashed."

A clash of a different order was soon to emerge. From 1785 to 1860 there seemed to be unanimity on at least one aspect of national land policy, namely that federal land should be conveyed to nonfederal parties. The policy of disposition, however, was to experience growing challenge in light of widespread abuse of the nation's resources by mining, timber, ranching, and other interests. As recounted in Stewart Udall's book The Quiet Crisis, the "barbecue" of the nation's animal, vegetable, and mineral wealth in the mid-nineteenth century was to inspire an intellectual foundation for conservation. The works of Thoreau, Marsh, Emerson, Parkman, Bartram, and Audubon were particularly influential. The creation of urban parks under the direction of Frederick Law Olmstead aroused interest in more remote national parks. The first of these, Yellowstone Park, was established in 1872.

Despite this symbolic bow to conservation sentiment, land continued to move out of the public domain during the last nineteenth century at an incredible pace. Of 1.3 billion acres in the public domain in 1850, about 40 percent was distributed to individuals by 1909 either for a price or as a free grant. Another 11 percent was granted to states for various purposes (17, p. 529). Accompanying this massive change of ownership there was ample evidence of fraud and misuse of lands obtained for particular purposes. Lands conveyed upon condition of physical improvement by the recipient in the form of drainage, irrigation, or timber planting were frequently never utilized as specified.

While conservation is not necessarily synonymous with retention in federal ownership, this concept was widely viewed as a necessary response to the situation. In 1891 Congress enacted what proved to be its most significant antidisposal measure in terms of acreage ultimately affected. The Act authorized the President to withdraw certain forests from active lumbering and to retain them as "forest reservations." Presidents Harrison, Cleveland, and Roosevelt set aside 132 million acres under this provision including the bulk of today's total of 187 million acres in national forests. The National Park Service was established in 1916 at the height of the conservation movement. The national park system today includes 25 million acres, much of which has been repurchased from the private sector.

Accommodation between the counterpolicies of disposition and retention was no more tranquil than the transition from revenue to free land. Gates (18, p. 340) again is skeptical:

> The Act of 1891 was the first fundamental break with the underlying philosophy of our land system—the desire to dispose of the lands and hasten their settlement. The conservationists had now convinced the country that a part of our natural resources must be retained in public ownership and preserved for the future. Unfortunately, conservation when first adopted was embedded in an outworn "laissez faire" land system of a previous age, just as the free homestead plan had been superimposed upon a land system designed to produce revenue. In both cases the old and the new clashed with disastrous results.

Inevitably, the advocates of public land retention have divided on the issue of management. The extreme positions are preservation of public lands as pristine wilderness versus maximum exploitation of their natural resources under leasing arrangements with private enterprise. The doctrine of "multiple use" has been legislated for national forests. In national parks, mining and lumbering are normally forbidden. But the possible acceptance of mining in Death Valley National Park could set a precedent for encroachments elsewhere. National parks inevitably are subject to continuing strife concerning the degree of public access permitted versus preservation of natural values (19).

Thus no constant discernible policy may be detected in the history of the nation's public domain. Although it once exercised total rights of ownership over two-thirds of the nation's land area, the federal government has at best fumbled from one compromise posture to another. The ambiguous state of official thinking on the key question of retention versus disposition is perhaps summarized in the following statement by the Public Land Law Review Commission (20, p. 1):

> . . . we urge reversal of the policy that the United States should dispose of the so-called unappropriated public domain lands. But we also reject the idea that merely because these lands are owned by the Federal Government, they should all remain forever in Federal ownership.

Nonfederal Lands

As with the public domain, federal policies concerning the remainder of the nation's land resources have been at cross purposes. To cite some flagrant examples, between 1944 and 1964 about 22.5 million acres were brought into production through federally assisted reclamation programs. During the same period the Department of Agriculture spent approximately $4 billion annually to <u>remove</u> agricultural land from production. In 1968 President Johnson declared a national goal to build or renovate 26 million dwelling units during the succeeding decade. During the three years following 1968 the urban renewal program displaced 55,000 families eligible for public housing—i.e., too poor for private housing—yet only 12,000 new units of public housing were completed in connection with urban renewal projects (21, p. 332).

The very nature of the federal role with respect to nonfederal land is ambivalent. The Constitution clearly limits the direct powers of Congress to dealing with federal land:

> The Congress shall have power to dispose of and make all needful rules and regulations respecting the territory <u>or other property belonging</u> to the United States. (Art. IV, Sec. 3: Emphasis added)

No such mandate defines the relationship of the federal government to land owned by states and their subdivisions and private land. The Tenth Amendment is sometimes considered to deny any role to Congress as to such areas:

> The powers not delegated to the United States by the Constitution, nor prohibited by it to the States, are reserved to the States respectively, or to the people.

Congress has nevertheless influenced land use, directly or indirectly, through activities authorized under several provisions of the Constitution, such as Article I, Section 8:

> Congress shall have power:
>
> 1. To lay and collect taxes . . . and provide for the general welfare;
>
> 3. To regulate commerce . . . among the several states;
>
> 7. To establish post-offices and post-roads . . .
>
> 18. To make all laws which shall be necessary and proper for carrying into execution the foregoing powers.

Other provisions relate to the federal spending power (Art. I, Sec. 9, Clause 7), and the federal power of eminent domain (Fifth Amendment to the Bill of Rights). The implications of these sparse phrases could scarcely have been anticipated by their authors in 1787. But as the nation grew and perception of public needs changed, the Constitution has proven succinctly flexible.

Congress before 1970 seldom undertook to directly set goals and policies for the use of nonfederal land. Land use implications of proposed measures and programs were examined neither before nor after the fact. Land has been viewed as a dependent variable, simply one factor needed to achieve a particular result such as housing or food production. And the seeming inexhaustibility of land especially in the western states continues to obfuscate the need for more explicit consideration of land as a scarce and destructible resource.

But for better or worse, the land of the United States has been profoundly altered by federal policies, measures, and programs of many kinds. For purposes of discussion, these may be classified in four categories: (a) public works and improvements undertaken directly or indirectly by federal agencies; (b) fiscal subsidy and guarantee measures which influence the private sector in its investment and location decisions; (c) regulation of the private sector; and (d) taxation of personal and corporate income. Detailed consideration of these areas of activity obviously exceeds the scope of this essay. Points of conflict and inconsistency, however, may be briefly noted.

Public Works

Promotion of economic development through public works dates back at least to the era of "internal improvements" beginning with construction by the federal government of the National Road through Cumberland Gap in the Appalachian Mountains in 1811. The opening of the Erie Canal in 1825 inaugurated the "canal era" which in the 1850s yielded to the railroads. While many of the canal and road building projects of the 1830-1840 period were state enterprises, the federal government in some cases provided grants of land or money. Federal land grants as already mentioned were instrumental in the construction of the western railroads following the Civil War. (Reluctance of Congress during the mid-twentieth century to revive this practice of subsidies to private railroads has led to the near collapse of passenger rail service and its direct assumption by the government at great cost to the federal taxpayer).

NATIONAL LAND USE POLICIES

Water resource development has long been a major concern of Congress with profound implications for the use of land in affected areas. The Supreme Court decision in Gibbons versus Ogden (1824) declared that Congress may exercise primary authority over the nation's navigable waterways under the insterstate commerce clause of the Constitution. This led initially to a wave of navigation and harbor improvement projects. With establishment of the Mississippi Valley Commission in 1879, federal responsibility for navigation gradually encompassed flood control as an additional objective. Under the Flood Control Acts of 1936 and 1938, federal activity in that area eclipsed navigation per se. During the past four decades, the United States government has spent some $14 billion dollars on flood control dams, reservoirs, dikes, levees, seawalls, and channelization projects (22, p. 10).

Land use implications of water resource projects have generally been considered only in terms of specific project "benefits:" flood control, irrigation, water supply, recreation, and so forth. Detailed analysis of the land use implications of a project throughout the region it serves is seldom performed. An example to the contrary has been the Tennessee Valley Authority, established by Congress in 1933. TVA has sought to utilize basinwide water resource management as a tool for upgrading the social and economic well-being of the region. This effort has involved erosion control, floodplain zoning (by local municipalities), and related measures to guide the use of private land within the Tennessee Valley.

In water resources, as in public lands, contradictory policies have emerged. Beginning with studies conducted by the National Resources Board (23) during the administration of Franklin D. Roosevelt, increasing criticism has been directed at the "structural" approach to flood loss control. The geographer Gilbert F. White (24, 25, 26) has been especially influential and persistent in pointing out the importance of combining engineering measures with "nonstructural" responses to floods, e.g., land use controls, land acquisition, flood warnings, insurance, and disaster assistance. As a result of White's advice, Presidents Johnson and Carter have each issued executive orders directing federal agencies to avoid undertaking or sponsoring any unnecessary encroachment in floodplains (27). In 1968, Congress adopted the National Flood Insurance Act under which local communities must adopt floodplain management regulations as a condition to becoming eligible for federally subsidized flood insurance. Despite these substantial steps toward a "nonstructural" response to floods, Congress continues to approve the construction of dams, dikes, and levees, some of dubious economic merit.

A parallel situation exists in the water quality field. As part of the 1972 amendments to the Federal Water Quality Act, Congress authorized $12 billion for construction of sewage treatment plants. As in flood control, doubts have arisen concerning the purely engineering approach to water pollution control. An alternative approach has been the development of "land disposal" systems, notably at Muskegan, Michigan, where partially treated sewage is applied as a source of nutrients to farmlands (28). In 1977 Congress approved the use of federal funds for land disposal systems at the option of local governments (29).

Perhaps the most important federal public works contribution to land use change has been the construction of the $50 billion interstate highway system. This system extends more than 41,000 miles and connects every U.S. city of more than 50,000 population. Cutting through undeveloped areas as well as through central city neighborhoods, federal-aid highways have generated probably more hostility among affected residents and property owners than any other activity of the U.S. government. To ameliorate some of the opposition, Congress in 1966 established a limitation that federally assisted highways should not be constructed through public parks and open space preserves unless no feasible alternative exists (30). This "counterpolicy" did not extend to the protection of established urban neighborhoods whose residents often suffered extreme economic and social disruption for the benefit of highway users. Congress has thus given higher priority to the preservation of undeveloped open land than to existing developed neighborhoods in which people may have invested much work and savings. The plight of the latter is addressed only by a 1970 statute which guarantees certain financial payments to persons relocated by any federally funded activity (31).

Subsidy and Guarantees

The role of the federal government as a source of economic incentives for many public activities is well known. The land use implications of these efforts is less recognized. Space permits mention of only one outstanding example, namely federal incentives to the private homebuilding industry.

Like the federal flood control program, the impetus to the establishment of a national housing program was the Great Depression. Congress adopted the National Housing Act of 1934 to stimulate the construction industry and thereby to create jobs. An incidental purpose was to upgrade the housing stock of the nation. Its basic approach was to provide federal insurance for mortgages so as to encourage the financial community to invest in new home construction. Between 1934 and 1976, the Federal Housing Administration (FHA) insured mortgages covering 12 million single family homes and 2.2 million apartment units, amounting to an aggregate value of $207 billion (32, p. 46). The overwhelming majority of these new units have been located outside of central cities on previously undeveloped land. This has resulted from the policy of FHA to insure only "sound" investments. The result of this policy has been massive "urban sprawl" since World War II. Metropolitan population increased by 26 percent from 1950 to 1960 and by 16 percent in the following decade. The proportion of persons living within metropolitan areas outside central cities increased from 41 percent in 1950 to 49 percent in 1960 to 53 percent in 1970. The spatial extent of metropolitan areas (33) nearly doubled from 207,000 to 387,000 square miles between 1950 and 1970. This growth reflects the influence of both the federal housing and highway assistance policies.

By 1960, there was increasing dismay with the dreary and wasteful land use patterns of these emerging metropolitan regions. An outpouring of professional and popular literature documented the loss of open space, farmland, scenery, and small-town atmosphere due to suburban sprawl (34, 35, 36, 37). Federal policies promoting low density urban sprawl were widely questioned.

As usual, instead of removing the source of the problem by substantially modifying its housing and highway policies, Congress launched new policies and programs to counteract them. During the 1960s these took the form of two programs of federal matching grants to states and local governments to acquire and improve open space (38). In 1970 the National Environmental Policy Act finally lent some authority to the demand for consideration of land use impacts of major federal funding decisions. Nevertheless, urban growth and open space objectives of Congress continue to operate on a mutually conflicting basis. Pitting antidevelopment measures against prodevelopment policies, the objectives of each are thwarted or at least made more expensive to accomplish (26, p. 337).

Regulation

The decade of the 1970s may well be viewed by resource historians as the era of regulation. Reflecting the increasing strength of the federal governments vis-a-vis state and local authorities, Congress in the past ten years has delegated wide-ranging powers to federal agencies dealing with such fields as economic competition, consumer protection, health and safety measures, and environmental quality. Within the latter category are found extensive federal regulations dealing with air and water pollution, noise, pesticides, and energy. In many respects these new programs for the betterment of the American people closely skirt the controversial area of federal intervention in land use.

Regulation has been widely employed as a makeweight to the deleterious effects of federal construction and financial assistance programs, especially where water is involved. The National Flood Insurance Program (NFIP), for instance, establishes minimum federal standards for local management of flood plains. If and when these standards are fully adopted and enforced, they should reduce the tendency of federal flood control projects to generate new development in floodplains.

In both the NFIP and the Coastal Zone Management Program, Congress approaches land use regulation indirectly through federal standards to be met by state and local governments. Incentives for the adoption of such regulations are the availability of federal flood insurance and of federal planning and program grants to coastal states.

Reversal of long-standing federal policies through regulation is perhaps nowhere more dramatic than with respect to wetlands. Under the Swamp Land Acts of 1849 and 1950, nearly 64 million acres of public domain land were granted to states for purposes of drainage and improvement for agriculture (17, p. 274). Although much of this land was never so utilized, the national purpose clearly was to convert "worthless" wetlands into productive resources. Disposition of land for this purpose continued into the 1920s. The Report of the National Resources Board (23, p. 131) documented a total of 91 million acres of "drainable" wetlands which it recommended as suitable for farming. These were predominantly the coastal marshes of the Southeast and Gulf and the inland wetlands of the Mississippi Valley.

A contrary policy was declared in Section 404 of the 1972 Federal Quality Act Amendments. Thenceforth, private owners of wetlands related to navigable waters were required to obtain a permit from the Army Corps of Engineers for any drainage or alteration of the site in question. While not fully effective to date due to administrative difficulties, Section 404 represents a sharp break with prior federal policy. It remains to be seen whether the new view of wetlands as resources in their natural state will prevail against the long-standing policy which considers them to be wastelands.

Taxation

The federal Internal Revenue Code is the terra incognita of national land use policies. Through labyrinthine provisions concerning capital gains, exemptions, deductions, tax credits, depletion allowances, and so forth, the federal income and estate tax law exerts vast and largely unknown influence upon private investment decisions. To cite a familiar example, interest on home mortgages and local property taxes are deductible from personal income, and no federal income tax need be paid on such amounts. This effectively provides the private homeowner with a federal subsidy varying in amount according to his or her tax bracket. No such subsidy is available to persons who rent their homes or apartments since rental payments are not deductible (39). The land use impact of this disparity between the costs of owning and renting a home clearly favor ownership, and the building market has responded accordingly. Sixty percent of all dwelling units in the United States in 1976 were "owned units" (32, p. 272). Since these are mostly single-family, whereas rental units are largely multiple, vastly more land is devoted to housing the owner component of the nation's population than the tenants.

Another land-related federal tax provision is the deduction for the value of land contributed to public or private nonprofit organizations for open space purposes. It has been estimated by the New York Regional Plan Association (36) that one-third of the public open land in the New York region has been contributed by private owners. On the other hand, much development of shopping centers and residential construction has been prompted largely by tax considerations (40).

Federal tax provisions variously affect most land-consuming activities: agriculture, mining, recreational development, forest products, and energy development. Through the tax law, Congress is an implicit partner in practically any land-related investment venture. The geographic consequences of diverse tax policies have scarcely begun to be seriously considered.

CONCLUSION

Land-related policies of the United States are found to be numerous, confusing, uncoordinated, and often at cross-purposes. This results historically from the perception of land as an inexhaustible resource. It also relates to the ongoing conflict between the institution of private property on the one hand and expanding public needs on the other. Federalism, the division of authority between the federal government and the states, has tempered the federal role as to nonfederal land. Finally, the balance of power between the president and Congress has obstructed serious attempts to achieve rational land use policies.

No single national policy can resolve the many and varied land use conflicts which arise in the United States. Efforts to legislate a "national land use policy" are doomed to futility if the desired result is simplification of the land use decision process. Land use conflicts over shorelines are, for example, more intense than ever since the advent of the Coastal Zone Management Program (CZMP).

But the CZM Program and the National Environmental Policy Act (NEPA) have achieved notable improvement in land use policy in one respect, namely the identification and analysis of land-related implications of alternative public decisions. At last, natural wetland values are receiving consideration along with economic development, recreation, and other public needs. The CZM and NEPA might not have saved the Indiana Dunes, but they would have focused more systematic attention upon the alternatives at stake. The political process might then have responded more rationally.

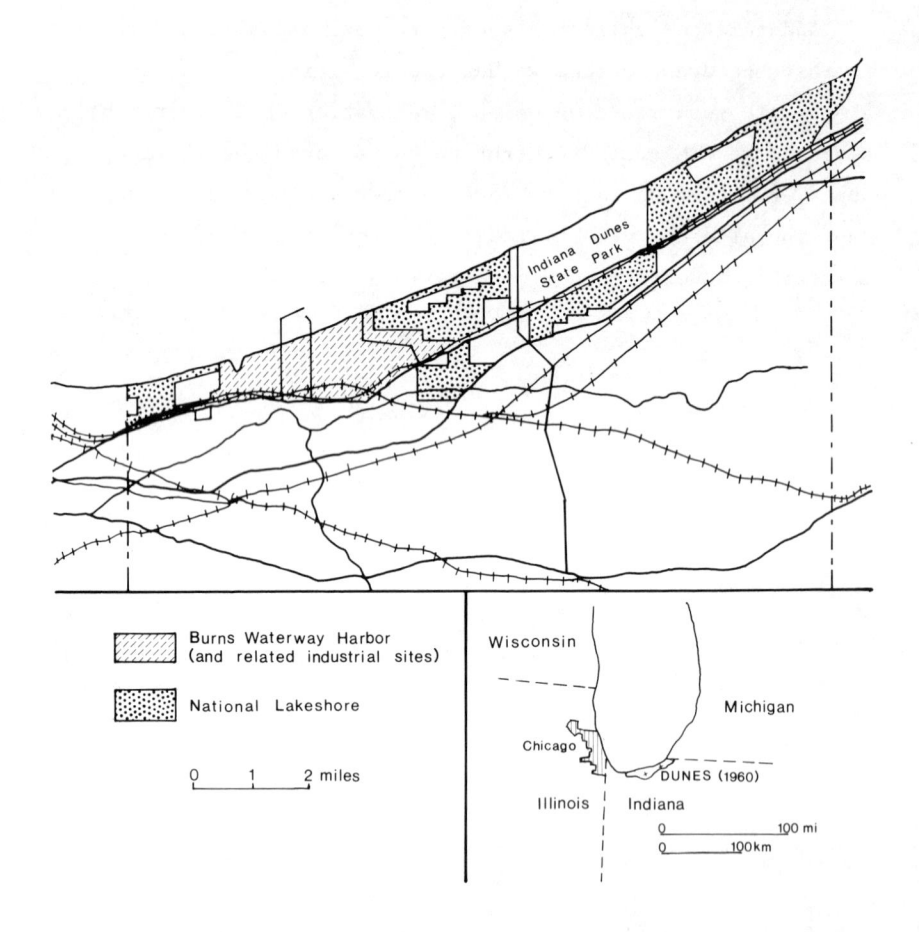

FIG. 11-1. Indiana Dunes-1967: Relationship of Federal Port and Park.
Indiana Dünes-1967: Verhältnis von Bundeshafen und Parkanlage.

NOTES

1. Meyer, A. H., "Circulation and Settlement Patterns of the Calumet Region of Northwest Indiana and Northeast Illinois," Annals of the Association of American Geographers 44 (1954), 245-74.

2. Platt, R. H., The Open Space Decision Process, Paper No. 142, (Chicago: University of Chicago Department of Geography Research Series, 1972).

3. Mayer, H. M., "Politics and Land Use: The Indiana Shoreline of Lake Michigan," Annals of the Association of American Geographers 54 (1964), 508-523.

4. Cowles, H. C., "The Ecological Relations of the Vegetation on the Sand Dunes of Lake Michigan," Botanical Gazette 27 (1899), 1-30.

5. General Accounting Office, Environmental and Economic Problems Associated with the Development of The Burns Waterway Harbor, Indiana, Report No. B-160199 (Washington, D.C.: Office of the U.S. Comptroller General, 1971).

6. This could be modified today under the Coastal Zone Management Program and other recent enactments.

7. Peeples, W., "The Indiana Dunes and Pressure Politics," Atlantic Monthly, Feb., 1963, pp. 84-88.

8. Council on Environmental Quality, Environmental Quality, 1978 (Washington, D.C.: U.S. Government Printing Office, 1978).

9. Fairfax, S. K., "A Disaster in the Environmental Movement," Science (February 17, 1978), 743-748.

10. U.S. Congress, National Land Use Policy Legislation, 93rd Congress: An Analysis of Legislative Proposals and State Laws, Senate Committee on Interior and Insular Affairs (93rd Congress, 1st Session), (Washington, D.C.: U.S. Government Printing Office, 1973).

11. Platt, R. H., "Coastal Hazards and National Policy: A Jury-Rig Approach," Journal of the American Institute of Planners 44 (1978), 170-180.

12. Delafons, J., Land-Use Controls in the United States (Cambridge: M.I.T. Press, 1969).

13. Treat, P. J., "Origin of the National Land System under the Confederation," in The Public Lands, ed. Vernon

Carstenson (Madison: University of Wisconsin Press, 1962).

14. U.S. Department of the Interior, Public Land Statistics, 1975 (Washington: U.S. Government Printing Office, 1975).

15. Morison, S. E., The Oxford History of the American People (New York: Oxford University Press, 1965).

16. Pattison, W. D., Beginnings of the American Rectangular Land Survey System: 1784-1800 (Columbus: Ohio State Historical Society, 1970).

17. Hibbard, B. H., A History of the Public Land Policies (Madison and Milwaukee: University of Wisconsin Press, 1965). The public domain today comprises about 700,000 acres, including Alaska.

18. Gates, P. W., "The Homestead Law in an Incongruous Land System" in The Public Lands, ed. Vernon Carstenson (Madison: University of Wisconsin Press, 1962), pp. 315-348.

19. Conservation Foundation, National Parks for the Future (Washington, D.C.: The Foundation, 1972).

20. Public Land Laws Review Commission, One Third of the Nation's Land, (Washington, D.C.: U.S. Government Printing Office, 1970).

21. Platt, R. H., "The Federal Open Space Programs: Impacts and Imperatives," in Urban Policymaking and Metropolitan Dynamics: A Comparative Geographic Analysis, ed. John S. Adams (Cambridge: Ballinger Publishing Co., 1976), pp. 331-377.

22. U.S. Water Resources Council, Estimated Flood Damages: Appendix B-Nationwide Analysis (Washington, D.C.: U.S. Water Resources Council, 1977).

23. National Resources Board, Report (Washington, D.C.: U.S. Government Printing Office, 1934).

24. White, G. F., Human Adjustment to Floods, Paper No. 29 (Chicago: University of Chicago Department of Geography Research Series, 1945).

25. White, G. F., et al., Changes in Urban Occupance of Flood Plains in the United States. Paper No. 57 (Chicago: University of Chicago Department of Geography Research Series, 1958).

26. White, G. F., Flood Hazard in the United States: A Research Assessment (Boulder: University of Colorado Institute of Behavioral Science, 1975).
27. E. O. 11296 (1966) and E. O. 11988 (1977).
28. U.S. Environmental Protection Agency, Land Treatment of Municipal Wastewater Effluents: Case Histories (EPA-625/4-76-010) (Washington: EPA, 1976).
29. ee USC Sec. 202 (a) (3).
30. Department of Transportation Act of 1966, 49 USC Sec. 1653 (f).
31. Uniform Relocation Assistance and Real Property Acquisition Policies Act of 1970, P.L. 91-646 (1970).
32. U.S. Department of Housing and Urban Development, 1976 Statistical Yearbook (Washington, D.C.: U.S. Government Printing Office, 1976).
33. The number of Standard Metropolitan Statistical Areas established by the Bureau of the Budget increased from 169 in 1950 to 243 in 1970. Some SMSAs were enlarged to reflect changes in development pattern. It should be noted however that SMSAs are defined according to county boundaries and thus contain much underdeveloped land.
34. Editors of Fortune, The Exploding Metropolis (Garden City: Doubleday Anchor Books, 1958).
35. Outdoor Recreation Resource Review Commission, Outdoor Recreation for America (Washington, D.C.: U.S. Government Printing Office, 1962).
36. New York Regional Plan Association, The Race for Open Space (New York: The Association, 1960).
37. Whyte, W. H., The Last Landscape (Garden City: Doubleday and Co., 1968).
38. These were the Open Space Land Program of the Department of Housing and Urban Development which functioned from 1961 until 1972 and the Land and Water Conservation Program of the Bureau of Outdoor Recreation, established in 1965 and still the mainstay of federal open space assistance.
39. Aaron, H. J., Shelter and Subsidies (Washington: The Brookings Institution, 1972).

40. Slitor, R. E., "Taxation and Land Use," in *The Good Earth of America*, ed. C. Lowell Harriss (Englewood Cliffs: Prentice-Hall, 1974), pp. 67-87.

CHAPTER 12

PROGRAMS FOR INFRASTRUCTURAL DEVELOPMENT IN RURAL AREAS

INFRASTRUKTURELLE ENTWICKLUNGSPROGRAMME IN LÄNDLICHEN GEBIETEN

Georg Kluczka

Abstract

In the Federal Republic of Germany there is no generally accepted definition and no nationwide delimitation of rural areas. The planners' term "infrastructure" is equally vague. Since the founding of the Federal Republic, however, attempts have been made to define the various rural problem areas for development purposes. The 1965 Federal Spatial Planning Act for the first time contains uniform national concepts for infrastructural development. As a result the Regional Planning Ministers' Conference (MKRO) passed a central-place program specially aimed at rural area development. The 1975 Federal Spatial Planning Program (BROP) envisages a changed regional aid concept covering the whole Federal Republic using a system of indicators to establish in particular those regional units with infrastructural development below the federal average. These are to receive increased aid. The question remains whether infrastructural conditions in the mostly rural problem regions can really be improved.

Kurzfassung

In der Bundesrepublik Deutschland gibt es keine allgemein akzeptierte Definition und Abgrenzung der ländlichen Gebiete. Ebenso vage ist das Wort "Infrastruktur" der Planer. Seit der Gründung der Bundesrepublik hat man jedoch die verschiedenen ländlichen Problemgebiete für Entwicklungszwecke zu bestimmen versucht. Das 1965 verabschiedete <u>Bundesraumordnungsgesetz</u> (Federal Regional Planning Act) enthält zum ersten Mal einheitliche Auffassungen für infrastrukturelle Entwicklungen auf Bundesebene. Die Folge war, dass die <u>Minister-Konferenz für Raumordnung -MKRO</u> (ministerial standing conference for regional policy) ein besonders auf ländliche Entwicklung gerichtetes örtliches Zentralprogramm verabschiedete. Das 1975 verabschiedete Bundesraumordnungsprogramm -BROP (Federal Regional Planning Program or national interregional plan) berücksichtigt durch ein verändertes Konzept der regionalen Unterstützung die ganze Bundesrepublik, wobei ein System von Indikatoren benutzt wird, um insbesondere jene regionalen Einheiten mit unterdurchschnittlicher infrastruktureller Entwicklung festzustellen. Diese werden erhöhte Unterstützung bekommen. Die Frage bleibt, ob die infrastrukturellen Zustände in den grösstenteils ländlichen Problemgebieten wirklich verbessert werden können.

Programs for Infrastructural Development in Rural Areas

WHAT ARE RURAL AREAS?

In the past the rural areas of the Federal Republic of Germany (FRG) have been the target of governmental activity with respect to agricultural conditions. They were to be modernized so that sufficient staple food could be produced and agriculture would remain an independent sector of the overall economy. The integration of German agriculture into the European Community (EC) market has not affected this objective. There have been and still are many and varied measures that stabilize and consolidate agriculture. These include the modernization of agricultural technology, land consolidation, and village renewal. Agriculture is among the leading recipients of state subsidies.

The question of what rural areas are may well have been answered already. Are they the areas whose external appearance is characterized by agricultural and forestry land use, roads, and settlements? Are they areas where population is employed principally in agricultural production or in related trades and services? Perhaps all that is lacking is suitable measuring criteria backed up by statistical data which will enable us to define rural areas as primarily agricultural areas.

To pursue this question further, let us take a look at a handbook which is much read by students and scientists and is also of topical interest. Here we are told that rural areas comprise "all areas outside agglomerations" (1). This seems to contradict our first tentative definition, or does it? Is there a direct connection as far as regional planning is concerned between the twenty-four officially designated agglomerations of industry and population in the FRG and the rural areas, a link so direct that it justifies defining rural areas indirectly, so to speak, from outside?

Here we have two approaches which seem to conflict but, like structure and function, can well complement each other. They also mark the different tasks of, on the one hand, departmental agricultural policy and, on the other, interdepartmental coordinating regional policy-what in Germany is called <u>Raumordnung</u> (regional or spatial policy). Relatively independently functioning sector-related agricultural planning competes with the more comprehensive concept of developing mutually complementary functional areas. The latter concept seems to assign to the rural areas a complementary and compensatory function with regard to agglomeration areas.

In this role, the agglomerations have assumed the leading position. Their special status is due to the fact that regional growth theories have recently become firmly established in German regional policy, and it is owing to the influence of these theories that a further definition of rural areas is possible: the combination of all those areas which, despite their heterogeneity, have in common a "lack of agglomeration advantages" (2). One can hardly imagine a lower common denominator. Nevertheless, the 1964/1966 spatial classification of the whole of North Rhine-Westphalia seems to interpret rural areas in the following sense: the category "rural zones" appears alongside two categories of agglomeration (cores and marginal zones) (3). However, a generally accepted definition of rural areas still does not exist, nor is there a corresponding delimitation valid for the whole Federal Republic.

WHAT IS INFRASTRUCTURE?

What do we understand by the term infrastructure? There is no simple answer to this question. Since the economic crisis of the sixties, this term has been firmly established in the theory and practice of German regional planning. Almost overnight it became the magic spell which would solve all planning difficulties. This is particularly true of a regional policy oriented toward structurally weak rural areas. This situation can be traced back to the influence of A. O. Hirschman on the infrastructure discussion in Germany, although we know Hirschman himself does not use the term. His theory of social overhead capital, of basic functions as prerequisites for the primary, secondary, and tertiary sectors of an economy, was conceived with reference to lesser developed or as yet undeveloped countries. However, he restricts himself to the field of transportation and power supply, i.e., the narrow material basis from the viewpoint of development theory (4).

In the German-speaking countries, the leading figures in the infrastructure discussion are F. Boesler, R. Jochimsen, and the Swiss authors J. Stohler and R. L. Frey. Their discussions have produced a variety of diverging opinions (5). The best known attempt at a definition was made by Jochimsen, who distinguished three fields of infrastructure: material, institutional, and personal infrastructure.

Material infrastructure, or social overhead capital (4) includes the total stock of buildings, machinery, etc., which serve to supply power, transport, telecommunications, communication systems, and conserve natural resources.

Institutional infrastructure refers to natural and

created norms, organizational institutions and procedures providing the framework for the preparation and implementation of economic plans.

Personal infrastructure, or human capital, covers the number, capacities, and abilities of people insofar as they contribute to the level and integration of overall economic development.

Thus, infrastructure "describes the basic functions of the overall economy which are necessary for growth, integration, and public utilities" (6). Infrastructure is seen as the sum of publicly provided social, institutional, and human capital.

This comprehensive definition attempts to integrate various approaches. At the same time other authors use other criteria, depending on their line of research; e.g., consumptive-productive infrastructure, or production and household-oriented infrastructure.

This last approach will be discussed in more detail. It was logical that the generally accepted importance of infrastructure for economic growth led at first to an almost exclusively production-related regional policy. Production-oriented infrastructure was promoted because it was assumed that it was the sole factor influencing regional development. The importance of production-oriented infrastructure as a decisive determinant of economic growth is indisputable. However, we now regard it as the necessary but not the only precondition of regional development. The supply aspect as well as the growth aspect must be considered, i.e., public expenditure on household-oriented infrastructure must be increased.

F. Fischer made precisely this distinction, basing his concept of complementary production and household-oriented infrastructure on the utilization aspect (7). By production-oriented infrastructure he means cost-saving services for enterprises, such as the development and allocation of industrial sites; by household-oriented infrastructure he means those services consumed by private households. Fischer includes here the provision for cultural, educational, health, welfare, and leisure facilities within a region, as well as supply facilities in the more restricted sense, such as shopping centers and central services (8). The theoretical discussion of this question may be summed up as follows: as in the case of "rural areas" there is no generally accepted definition for "infrastructure." However, this concept, originally borrowed from economic terminology, has taken a firm foothold in the vocabulary and instrumentation of regional policy and regional planning. It will be shown that great importance is attached to infrastructure as far as the spatial development of rural areas is concerned.

SPATIAL EFFECTS OF INFRASTRUCTURE

Apart from the question of terminology, there is another aspect that is important: what spatial effects are likely to result from infrastructural improvements? It can be said immediately that there is a dearth of scientific analyses on this point. The planning theorist Brösse distinguished between the effects of land use, settlement structure, growth, incentive, income, supply, mobility, and stabilization and self-creation (9).

Growth, settlement structure, and supply effects are particularly relevant for the problem of rural areas. Efforts to achieve growth effects have a long history here, especially indirect productivity effects to help boost regional economic growth. Typical examples of these are infrastructure expenditure on road building in order to minimize transportation costs for local industry. As an example, settlement structure effects are achieved by concentrating expenditure on selected sites and transport routes. In this way a desired settlement pattern may be obtained. Within a thinly populated rural area this is just as important as the availability of infrastructural amenities. The latter are brought about by concentrated support of infrastructure facilities for consumption purposes. Such an expenditure can prove necessary in the case of considerable disparities in available services in neighboring areas.

In the following sections, a selection of examples will be used to show which infrastructure-related programs or programmatic statements for the development of rural areas exist at present in the FRG. Special emphasis will be placed on programs directed at the spatial effects of infrastructure in the above-mentioned sense, i.e., growth, settlement structure, and/or supply effects. For pragmatic reasons the term infrastructure will be understood in its most comprehensive sense.

WHAT THE ROG HAS TO SAY ON DEVELOPMENT POLICY FOR RURAL AREAS

It seems inevitable that whenever German planning problems are mentioned, the starting point is always the Federal Planning Law of 1965 (known as ROG) (Table 12-1). This essay is no exception (10).

The ROG contains the first programmatic statements on the infrastructure and development of rural areas with reference to the federal territory as a whole. However, it

INFRASTRUCTURAL DEVELOPMENT IN RURAL AREAS 371

TABLE 12-1. Organization of Spatial Development and Regional Planning in the Federal Republic of Germany.

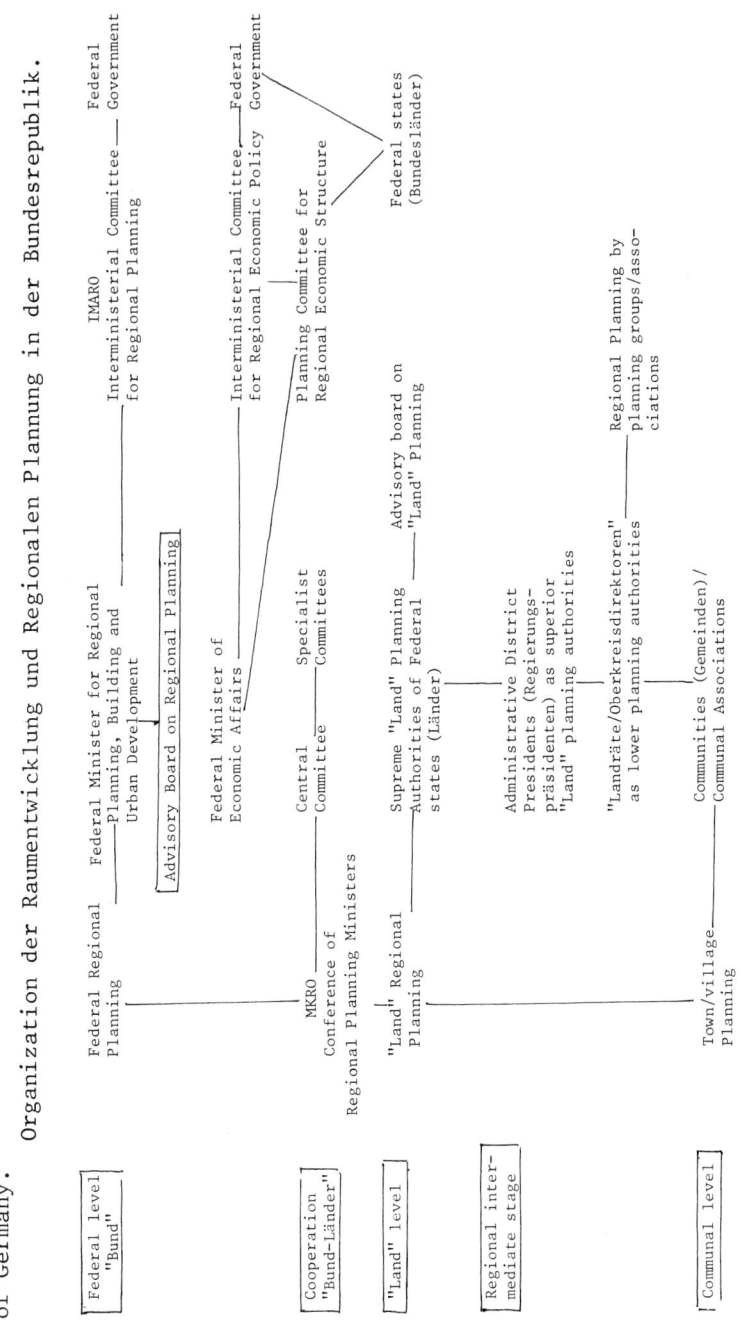

Organization der Raumentwicklung und Regionalen Plannung in der Bundesrepublik.

Federal level "Bund"

- Federal Regional Planning
- Federal Minister for Regional Planning, Building and Urban Development
- IMARO — Interministerial Committee for Regional Planning — Federal Government
- Advisory Board on Regional Planning
- Federal Minister of Economic Affairs — Interministerial Committee for Regional Economic Policy — Federal Government
- Central Committee — Specialist Committees
- Planning Committee for Regional Economic Structure — Federal states (Bundesländer)

Cooperation "Bund-Länder"

- MKRO Conference of Regional Planning Ministers

"Land" level

- "Land" Regional Planning
- Supreme "Land" Planning Authorities of Federal states (Länder)
- Advisory board on "Land" Planning

Regional intermediate stage

- Administrative District Presidents (Regierungspräsidenten) as superior "Land" planning authorities
- "Landräte/Oberkreisdirektoren" as lower planning authorities
- Regional Planning by planning groups/associations

Communal level

- Town/village Planning
- Communities (Gemeinden)/Communal Associations

took another ten years for the ROG to be followed by a Federal Planning Program (1975) (11). In its regional planning principles rural areas are mentioned in several respects: directly as an independent category of areas primarily for agricultural and forestry use, indirectly as the main component of those problem areas with an unhealthy and unbalanced spatial structure, and indirectly as the main component of those special problem areas where living conditions as a whole fall short of the federal average. Another essay in this publication will deal with the predominantly rural Zonenrandgebiet (border zone) as a special spatial category.

Assuming favorable conditions for production, rural areas should be preserved as a separate regional category and as areas primarily for agricultural and forestry use. They should continue to receive aid as described in the beginning of this essay. After all, agricultural land today accounts for about 55 percent of the economic area of the FRG. With an additional 29 percent of forest area, this means that 84 percent of the total economic space of the Federal Republic is used for agriculture and forestry, a remarkably high proportion for a densely populated industrial state which has correspondingly high spatial requirements for the secondary and tertiary sectors. However, the percentage of people employed in the primary sector has decreased in the last ten years alone by 40 percent to the present (1978) figure of 6 percent of the working population.

The ROG has established the following requirements for rural areas as a separate regional category: agricultural and forestry land should be preserved, possibly even given priority; local culture should be promoted; there should be an adequate population density; economic efficiency should be the goal; and jobs must be created both in and outside agriculture and forestry. These basic requirements are to be taken into consideration and stipulated also by the states in their programs and plans.

Two points do not fall within the framework of the agricultural and forestry sector: an adequate population density and additional jobs outside agriculture and forestry. They represent a reaction to the increase of outmigration from rural areas in the sixties and at maintaining the population level necessary for an efficient economy and an adequate supply of amenities. Both of these problem areas, the so-called structurally weak areas and the underdeveloped areas, are to be assisted in attaining the general level of economic, social, and cultural conditions. The essential point of the ROG's programmatic statements is that this goal, the improvement of living conditions, is to be attained by developing communities that are important as central places, i.e., the central places themselves.

RURAL PROBLEM AREAS IN THE FEDERAL REPUBLIC

Even before the ROG was passed an attempt had been made to determine rural problem areas and to classify them for subsidy purposes. These are the "naturally underprivileged areas" (Figure 12-1), whose classification was based on a resolution passed by the Lower House of Parliament. Since 1961 this designation has applied to farming and forestry areas having the following characteristics: poor soil, extreme climatic conditions, and unfavorable location (height or slope). To be included in this category the crop yield had to be below the average for the FRG. The Federal Minister for Food, Forestry, and Agriculture was responsible for the categorization, not the planners. The promotion of these areas was therefore only partial. It was the agricultural sector which was subsidized by measures of land consolidation, transfer of population, construction of farm roads, and drainage. From Figure 12-1 it can be seen that areas with poorer natural conditions occur more often in southern Germany than north of the Main River. On the other hand, the most northerly federal state, Schleswig-Holstein, accounts for more than 50 percent of the agriculturally utilized area.

The ROG introduced what was called the regional category of the "backward areas" (Figure 12-2). It described those areas "in which the conditions of life as a whole are significantly below the federal average or where a retardation is to be feared" (12). As in areas with poor natural resources, the federal average has again been chosen here to determine the position within a category. Soon after the first delineation of the special agriculture-related areas of poor natural resources, members of the Institute for Planning in Bad Godesberg turned their attention to the generally backward areas. They considered the structural characteristics of density of population, industrialization, taxable capacity, and gross domestic product. When the ROG was passed, these areas, later officially designated as "backward areas," accounted for 34 percent of the surface area (84,400 km^2 or 32,587 square miles) and 12 percent of the population (7.2 million) of the Federal Republic. With only 5 percent of the total number of industrial employees, these were clearly predominantly agrarian areas (13).

A delineation of the underdeveloped areas by the MKRO was more realistic. In 1970 the MKRO dispensed with the above-mentioned criteria and described the following threshold values (14):

Balance of migration	1961	67: ± 0
Population density	1968	100 inhabitants per km^2
Industrial density	1968	70 employees per 1000 inhabitants
GDP	1966	DM 6,080 per capita of the economic population
Taxable capacity	1967	DM 118 per capita

It was necessary for at least three of these characteristics to be included in the category of a "backward area."

The procedure was complicated by the fact that these regional categories were added to those areas in which, according to the ROG, a retardation was to be feared. Here are the additional characteristics that were taken into account (alternations 1961-1968): industrial density: 4 employees per 1000 inhabitants; GDP: DM 1,890 per capita of the economic population; taxable capacity: DM 36 per inhabitant. The map of backward areas in this essay shows the largest contingent areas to be in northern Germany, in the Rhineland-Palatinate, and in Bavaria, still the main agrarian regions of the Federal Republic. At the same time, these are the regions of poor natural resources. The previously mentioned categorizing procedures can do limited justice only to the rural problem areas. Because of the applied methods of threshold-values, no comparison between individual subareas is possible. They do not concretely describe regional deficiencies because the necessary specific measures of development cannot be introduced.

A decisive step toward a coordinated view of the structurally weak and retarded regions and their specific promotion by the federation in the states was taken in 1969 by the initiation of so-called "regional plans of action" (Figure 12-3) for the improvement of the economic structure.

They affect those regions where economic strength is, or tends to be, considerably below the federal norm. Since 1971, plans have been outlined for extending the present twenty regional action areas, which are illustrated according to the position in 1974 (15). Their spatial distribution pattern resembles both of the previously mentioned categories. The structurally weak agrarian areas are, at the same time, employment development areas. Within the regional action areas, industrialists receive investment grants, loans, low interest rates, etc., if new jobs are created by the establishment or there is an extension of industrial enterprises or if they carry out rationalization aimed at securing jobs. If necessary, subsidies can be given to jobs in the tourist sector, making land accessible for industry, communal infrastructure, and training establishments. The declared aim of such possible measures is to abolish spatial imbalance in order to achieve equality of opportunity and quality of life in all regions of the FRG.

THE CENTRAL PLACE PROGRAM OF THE MKRO

The Conference of Germany's Regional Planning Ministers (MKRO) as coordinator between federation and states passed two resolutions (in 1968 and 1972) as a step toward endorsing the ROG's demand for the further development of central places (16). In the opinion of the MKRO an adequate infrastructure should be guaranteed throughout the Federal Republic. This is to be achieved by means of a system of central places with surrounding areas dependent upon them. This system is divided into three classes: major centers with amenities for specialized luxury requirements for the population of a major area; medium-sized centers with facilities providing high-quality requirements for the population of a medium-sized area having more than 20,000 inhabitants in thinly populated areas (otherwise 40,000 inhabitants and over); and minor centers and small centers with basic amenities for the population of a small local area with over 5,000 inhabitants. The last two classes generally differ only in that the minor centers offer more services. The MKRO envisages minor and small centers possessing <u>Mittelpunktschule</u> (central elementary school of a rural area) and a <u>Hauptschulen</u> (upper division of elementary school), play and sports grounds, a doctor and pharmacist, as well as retailers, skilled workers, and other services. Access by public transport should not take longer than half an hour.

Special amenities are expected in the medium-sized centers. Here the MKRO decided on a list of the minimum facilities required for education, health, sport, commerce, banking, and communications. Only one example from each sector is given: grammar school, hospital, indoor swimming pool, a wide choice of shopping facilities, and direct access to the federal highway network. These and other amenities must be accessible to the population if an intermediate area is less than an hour's traveling time by public transport. In order to obtain settlement structure effects, the rural area outside the medium-sized center should have the same (or a higher) number of inhabitants using the facilities as the center itself. The concentration of infrastructure services in a system of central places, which in turn are concentrated on lines or axes of communication, is intended to achieve a further effect. It should attract those industries whose production is not dependent on location. When new government offices are to be set up they too should be located in central places, preferably in medium-sized centers. It is the task of the states to designate central places and their catchment areas in official programs and plans.

The experience of the last ten years has shown that the central-place program has not lived up to expectations from the point of view of supply and development. There are two main reasons for this:

(a) The standard values of at least 5,000 inhabitants for small areas and 20,000 for medium-sized areas were far too low to permit the creation/preservation of the necessary infrastructure for basic high quality services. Today, these minimum values would have to be doubled.

(b) In the last decade both public administration and private industry have been engaged in spatially concentrating their infrastructures and have thus contributed to the withdrawal of important service facilities from rural areas.

THE FEDERAL REGIONAL PLANNING PROGRAM (BROP)

Exactly ten years after the ROG, the Federal Regional Planning Program represents the first attempt to apply a system of indicators to test and classify the regions of the entire federal territory according to available infrastructure and job opportunities (employment structure) with the aim of providing state aid to reduce the deficits. Compared to the analysis of employment structure, which tried to establish gross domestic product and income, the BROP's infrastructure analysis is fairly comprehensive. It uses the following indicators:

Sector:	Indicators:
Education	Secondary modern and grammar school pupils and university students
Health	Doctors in private practice, hospital beds for emergency cases, hospital beds within the norm (subsidized)

Social Services	Nursery schools, space in retirement homes
Sport and Recreation	Gyms and indoor sports facilities, indoor swimming pools, and teaching pools
Housing	Living space, apartments with bathroom, toilets and central heating
Communications and Transportation	Federal highways and nonfederal highways; time-schedule of long-distance federal railways; cruising speed on long-distance federal railways; commuters using public transport
Technical Supply and Removal Systems	Public sewage systems and sewage disposal

Indicators of infrastructure and employment structure were tested throughout the federal territory in a total of thirty-eight areal units which possessed spatial characteristics and a suitable field of reference to the problems at hand. This regionalization was based on functional characteristics and, as such represented an innovation because most of the previously mentioned regional planning classifications of the FRG were delineated as homogenous areas according to structural characteristics.

Which parts of the Federal Republic show by the analysis of the BROP a particular lack of quality of life? The BROP speaks here of "retarded areas characterized by particular structural inequities" (Figure 12-4). Even at first glance the appended illustration shows a clear conformity with the well-known picture of regions deprived by nature and lagging behind the general level of development.

A current rural problem area with an extensive lack of infrastructure institutions and employment structure once more predominates in wide areas of northern Germany, from Schleswig-Holstein across the lower Weser to the Ems River district. An equally clear impoverished picture is presented by traditional problem areas of northern and eastern Bavaria, and those of the Eifel and west Palatinate. In addition, as can be seen from the illustration, there are problem areas with population loss (Figure 12-5). At the time of the last population census in 1970, there were more than 7.5 million people living in these extremely depressed areas alone. How can planning help them to achieve a better quality of life?

BROP's answer is that it intends-enabled by the recognition of this program-to give aid to specific key areas. A number of centers of development and large regionally important axes were especially created for this purpose but can only become effective if the states governments make use of them. This is the crux of the matter. But even from the planning theory approach, and considering recent alterations in the framework of economic conditions, it is doubtful whether the planning instrumentation devised for large areas can solve the problems of structurally weak areas.

The recommendation of the Commission of the Federal Ministry of Regional Planning, Building, and Urban Development made on June 16, 1976, a year after the publication of the BROP, rightly points to the fact that the opportunities for development of many peripheral areas have grown significantly worse because the importance of the industrial factors of production has changed. To summarize: the favorable position of many towns, situated in rural problem areas but at the focus of an efficient communications network, as a result of the latest concentrations in both the "secondary" and the "tertiary" sector, has become much less favorable in relation to the large centers and central regions.
The declared goal of improving employment and income structure in rural problem areas is incapable of being fulfilled

in the foreseeable future. At the same time, the willingness to move elsewhere and the resulting exodus of skilled labor from these problem areas will certainly continue. Additionally, two factors suggest that within the infrastructure sector a similar negative development has already begun. First, the effects of centralization as a result of communal reform have generally led to an increased travel time cost expenditure, particularly for the inhabitants of rural areas. This is especially true regarding the availability of governmental administration and education. Furthermore, the declining revenue from trade and other taxes and, at the same time, increasing costs inevitably lead in structurally weak regions, to a decline in investment in the infrastructure sector. We will have to wait for the next federal program.

FIG. 12-2.

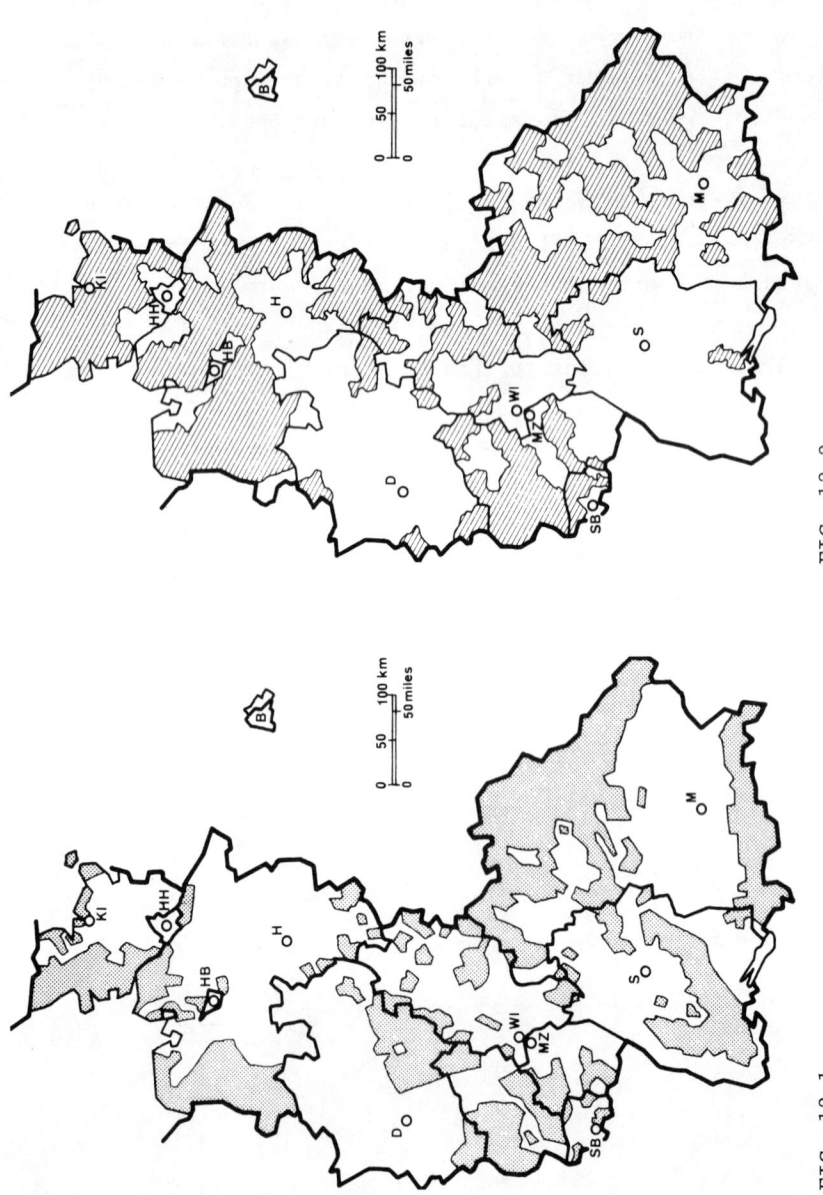

FIG. 12-1.

FIG. 12-1. Regions of Deprived Natural Environment. Naturbenachteiligte Gebiete.

Source: Friedrich Malz, Taschenbuch der Umweltplanung (Munich 1974).

FIG. 12-2. Backward Areas According to the Recommendations of MKRO of 16 April 1970. Hinter der allgemeinen Entwicklung zurückgebliebene Gebiete gemäss Empfehlung der MKRO vom 16 April 1970.

Source: Friedrich Malz, Taschenbuch der Umweltplanung (Munich 1974).

FIG. 12-3. Regional Plans of Action (Status of 1 January 1974). Regionale Aktionsräume (Stand 1. Jänner 1974).

Source: Friedrich Malz, Taschenbuch der Umweltplanung (Munich 1974).

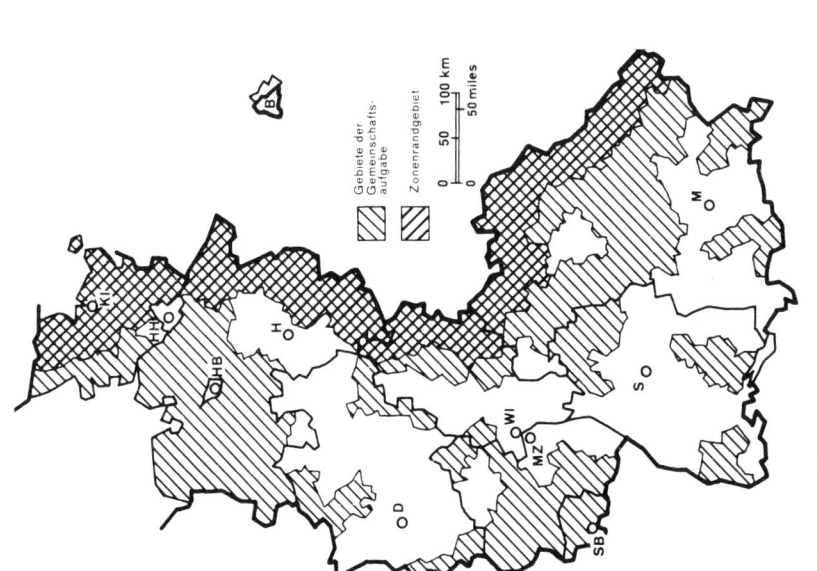

FIG. 12-3.

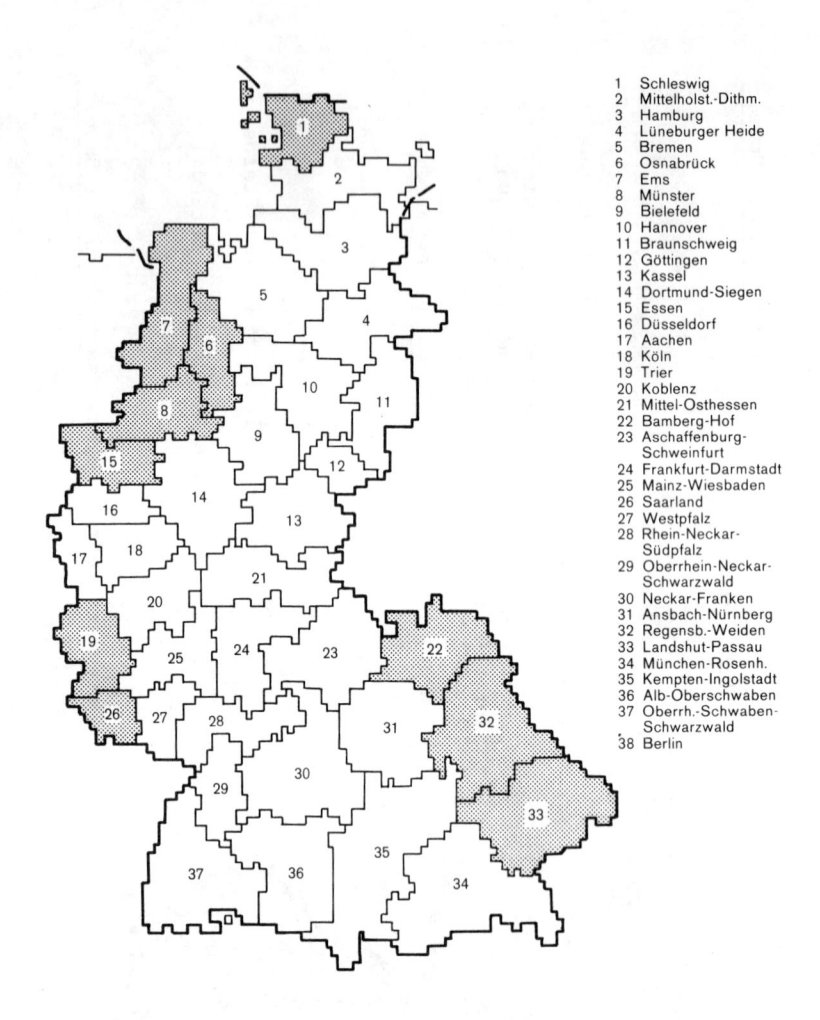

1 Schleswig
2 Mittelholst.-Dithm.
3 Hamburg
4 Lüneburger Heide
5 Bremen
6 Osnabrück
7 Ems
8 Münster
9 Bielefeld
10 Hannover
11 Braunschweig
12 Göttingen
13 Kassel
14 Dortmund-Siegen
15 Essen
16 Düsseldorf
17 Aachen
18 Köln
19 Trier
20 Koblenz
21 Mittel-Osthessen
22 Bamberg-Hof
23 Aschaffenburg-Schweinfurt
24 Frankfurt-Darmstadt
25 Mainz-Wiesbaden
26 Saarland
27 Westpfalz
28 Rhein-Neckar-Südpfalz
29 Oberrhein-Neckar-Schwarzwald
30 Neckar-Franken
31 Ansbach-Nürnberg
32 Regensb.-Weiden
33 Landshut-Passau
34 München-Rosenh.
35 Kempten-Ingolstadt
36 Alb-Oberschwaben
37 Oberrh.-Schwaben-Schwarzwald
38 Berlin

FIG. 12-4. Areas Threatened by Migration Losses.
Abwanderungsgefährdete Räume.

Source: BROP 1975.

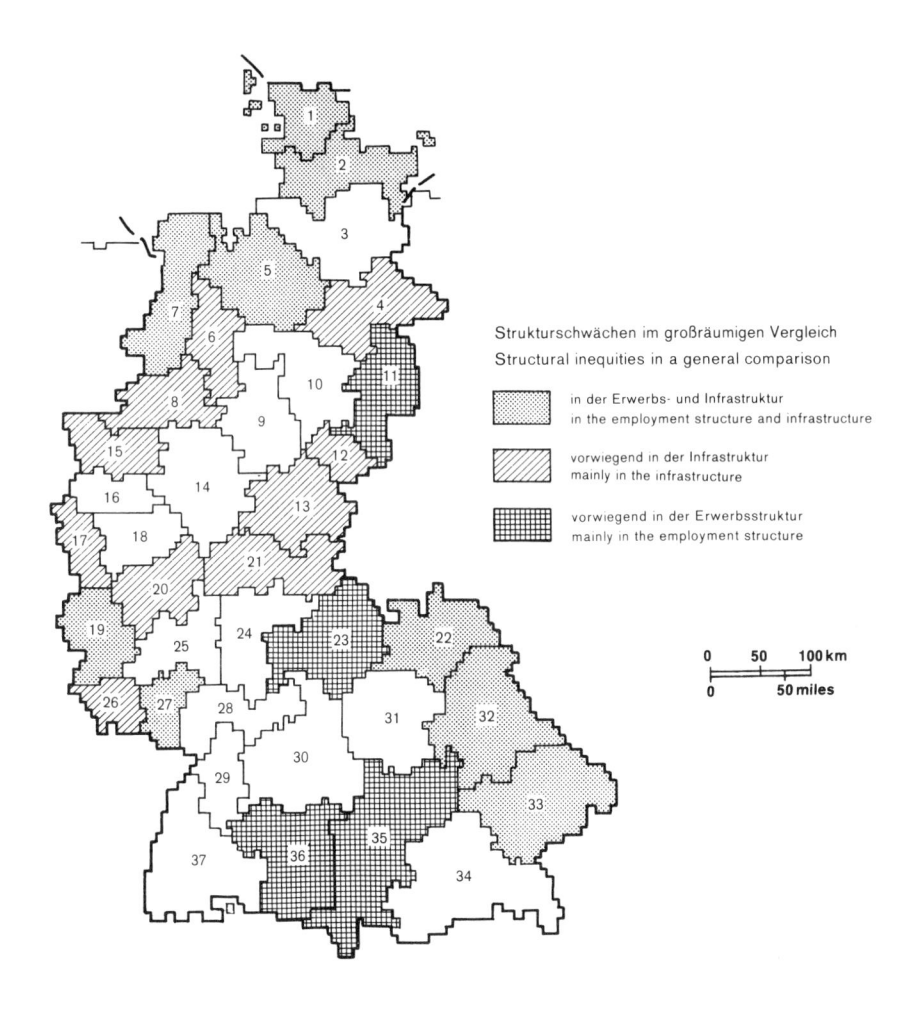

INFRASTRUCTURAL DEVELOPMENT IN RURAL AREAS 385

FIG. 12-5. Retarded Areas Characterized by Particular Structural Inequities.
    Schwerpunkträume mit besonderen Strukturschwächen.

Source: BROP 1975.

NOTES

1. Boesler, K. A., Fischer Länderkunde, Vol. 8: Europa (Frankfurt A.M.: Fischer Taschenbuch Verlag, 1978), p. 340.

2. Fischer Länderkunde, op. cit., p. 340 (see note 1).

3. Landesentwicklungprogramm ('Land' Development-Program) of North Rhine-Westphalia of 8.7.1964, MB.1. NW p. 1205-1217, and Landesentwicklungsplan 1 ('Land' Development Plan) NW of 11.28.1966, MB1. NW p. 2263 (revised version of both now valied).

4. Hirschman, A. O., The Strategy of Economic Development (New Haven: Yale University Press, 1958); printed in German translation as Die Strategie der wirtschaftlichen Entwicklung (Stuttgart: Gustav Fischer Verlag, 1967).

5. Compare the following: Boesler, F., "Infrastruktur," in Handwörterbuch der Raumforschung und Raumordnung, 1st ed. (Hannover: Verlag Zänecke, 1966), column 768; Jochimsen, R., Theorie der Infrastruktur. Grundlagen der marktwirtschaftlichen Entwicklung (Tübingen: Verlag F. C. B. Mohr, 1966); Jochimsen, R., and K. Gustafsson, "Infrastruktur," in Handwörterbuch der Raumforschung und Raumordnung, 2nd ed. (Hannover: Verlag Zänche, 1970), column 1318-1335; Stohler, J., "Zur rationalen Planung der Infrastruktur," Konjunkturpolitik, No. 5 (1965), pp. 279-308; Frey, R. L., "Probleme der statistischen Erfassung der Infrastruktur," Schweizerische Zeitschrift für Volkswirtschaft und Statistik, No. 7 (1967), pp. 235-256, and Simonis, U. E., ed., Infrastruktur, Theorie und Politik (Cologne: Verlag Kiepenheuer and Wirtsch, 1977).

6. Jochimsen, R., and K. Gustafsson, op. cit., (see note 5), column 1318.

7. Fischer, G., Praxisorientierte Theorie der Regionalforschung (Tübingen: Verlag F. C. B. Mohr, 1973).

8. Fischer, G., op. cit., (see note 7), pp. 243-244.

9. Brösse, U., Raumordnungspolitik (Berlin: Verlag Walter de Gruyter, 1975).

10. Raumordnungsgesetz (ROG) of 4-8-1965. Bundesgesetzblatt

I, p. 306.

11. Raumordnungsprogramm für die grossräumige Entwicklung des Bundesgebietes (Federal Regional Planning Program of February 14, 1975), Publication Series "Regional Planning" 06.002 (Bonn: Federal Ministry of Regional Planning, 1975).

12. ROG, op. cit., (see note 10), paragraph 2, section 2, No. 3.

13. Federal Government's Regional Planning Report 1966 (Bonn: Deutscher Bundestag 1966), V/1155.

14. "Areas lagging behind in their general development," Recommendation of the Conference of Ministers for Regional Planning, April 16, 1970.

15. At the present time the Achter Rahmenplan der Gemeinschaftsaufgabe Verbesserung der regionalen Wirtschaftsstruktur (8th Joint Skeleton Plan on the improvement of regional economic structure for the period 1979-1982) is valid.

16. Central places and their linkage areas 2.8.1968, ROB 1968 (Bonn: Deutscher Bundestag, 1969) V/3958, p. 149; Central place linkage areas of intermediate order in the Federal Republic of Germany, 6-15-1972, ROB 1972 (Bonn: Deutscher Bundestag, 1972), VI/3793, p. 146.

CHAPTER 13

JURISDICTIONAL ISSUES REGARDING FEDERAL AND STATE
POLICY REGULATIONS: USE AND EXPLOITATION OF
COASTAL AND OFFSHORE RESOURCES

GESETZGEBERISCHE ANSÄTZE DES BUNDES UND DER STAATEN
ÜBER DIE NUTZUNG UND AUSBEUTE VON RESOURCEN
AN DER KÜSTE UND IM MEER

Lewis M. Alexander

Abstract

A variety of uses occur within United States coastal and offshore waters, including the exploitation of living and nonliving resources, nonresource uses of ocean space, and various activities taking place along and inland from the shoreline. Three levels of government-national, state, and local-have various forms of authority with respect to these activities, and federal legislation is moving in the direction of identifying more clearly the divisions of authority and of providing for the initiation of comprehensive management programs, particularly with respect to coastal zone areas and to fisheries.

The essay focuses on three important pieces of national legislation-the Submerged Lands Act, the Coastal Zone Management Act, and the Fishery Conservation and Management Act-as illustrative of the complexities of federal/state relationships involving the marine environment. It suggests that pressures for expanded state authority will develop, and indicates that greater coordination of agencies at the state level concerned with marine-related regulations is needed.

Kurzfassung

Eine Vielzahl von Nutzungen tritt an Küsten und küstennahen Gewässern der Vereinigten Staaten einschließlich der Ausbeutung von lebender und toter Materie sowie der Benutzung des Meeresraumes auf, ebenso finden die verschiedensten Aktivitäten längs und auch innerhalb der Küstenlinie statt. Die drei Regierungsebenen - Bundes-, Staaten- und Gemeindeverwal-

JURISDICTIONAL ISSUES 389

tungen - haben unterschiedliche Formen der Befugnis hinsichtlich dieser Aktivitäten. Die Bundesgesetzgebung bewegt sich in Richtung einer klareren Aufteilung der Befugnis und Bereitstellung eines geschlossenen Bewirtschaftungsprogramms besonders für die Küstenzone und die Fischerei.

Der Aufsatz konzentriert sich auf drei wichtige Teile der Bundesgesetzgebung - der "Submerged Land Acts," der Coastal Zone Management Act" und der "Fishery Conservation and Management Act" - die die Komplexität der Beziehung zwischen Bundesregierung und den Staaten hinsichtlich der marinen Umwelt veranschaulichen. Wir nehmen an, daß der Druck für eine sich erweiternde Autorität der Staaten zunehmen wird und weist darauf hin, daß eine stärkere Koordination aller auf der Staatenebene mit meeresbezogenen Verordnungen befassten Behörden nötig ist.

Jurisdictional Issues Regarding Federal and State Policy Regulations: Use and Exploitation of Coastal and Offshore Resources

One of the more illuminating aspects of federal/state relationships in the United States concerns the use of coastal and offshore waters and the exploitation of their living and nonliving resources. By almost any form of measurement, the entities involved are impressive. The United States has the fifth longest coastline of any country in the world, the fourth largest area of continental shelf (measured out to the 200-meter isobath), and the largest expanse of ocean space of any country within its 200-mile exclusive fisheries limits (1). There are abundant oil and gas reserves on the adjacent continental margin, and within the U.S. exclusive fisheries zone is perhaps one-fifth of the estimated commercial fisheries potential (excluding Antarctic krill) of the world ocean. Twenty-four of the nation's fifty states border on the ocean (2).

It is the purpose of this essay to discuss, first, the nature of United States coastal and offshore resources and the federal/state issues concerning their use; second, to consider administrative structures involved in the regulation of these resources; and, third, to emphasize three pieces of federal legislation which have strong federal/state relationships-the Submerged Lands Act, the Coastal Zone Management Act, and the Fishery Conservation and Management Act.

COASTAL AND OFFSHORE RESOURCES
Utilization of the marine environment is generally considered under the following three headings: (a) exploitation of

living resources, (b) exploitation of nonliving resources, and (c) nonresource uses. Each form has its own particular regulatory problems. So far as the terms coastal and offshore are concerned, there are no standard definitions. For the purposes of this essay, coastal will be used in terms of the "coastal zone," a belt which, for the most part, comes under state jurisdiction and includes the shoreline, the area behind the shoreline defined as the shoreland (3), and the adjacent territorial sea extending out to three nautical miles from the coastline (4). By contrast, the term offshore will refer to the waters and underlying continental shelf (the "outer continental shelf") beyond the coastal zone.

Exploitation of Living Resources

The U.S. commercial fishing industry annually harvests between 2.4 and 2.7 million metric tons of fish. Of this, approximately 91 percent by volume comes from U.S. coastal waters (5). Considering the recent restrictions placed on the operations of foreign fishing vessels within the U.S. exclusive fisheries zone, the volume of domestic catch within that zone is expected to grow.

The two principal regulatory problems associated with commercial fishing are (a) which agency sets and enforces fisheries standards within a coastal state's jurisdictional belt, and (b) which agency establishes standards in the offshore waters out to the 200-mile limits. A related issue in both instances is the potential conflict between U.S. commercial and sports fishermen, the latter an increasingly large and politically vocal group.

Fishing interests are also concerned with coastal pollution of various types, a problem which, in addition, affects the efforts of a particular segment of the fishing industry, the people associated with aquaculture, particularly along the coasts. Additional regulations may be necessary to protect their concerns.

    Fisheries are taken here to include shellfish as well as mammals, such as whales. Currently, the only whaling carried on in the United States is by the Eskimoes, who have had their problems conforming to the regulations of the International Whaling Commission. Other living marine resources include seaweed and kelp, which are found largely in areas within coastal state jurisdiction.

Exploitation of Nonliving Resources

The principal items here are offshore hydrocarbons (oil and gas) which represent both considerable investments and considerable returns. The issues of federal versus state ownership are long and complex, and are considered later in this essay. So, too, is the problem of interstate boundaries on the shelf. An additional question, which has considerable impact, is that of conflict of interests between offshore oil and gas operations and other marine-related phenomena, including fishing. If offshore oil and gas facilities are set on the shelf beyond the limits of state jursidiction, what steps may the state take to protect itself against the dangers of pollution (as occurred in the Santa Barbara channel off California)?

    Other nonliving marine resources include sand, gravel, and shells (taken mostly from within state waters), sulphur derived from the subsoil of the shelf, metalliferous sands (e.g., titanium, gold), and salt, iodine, and other products from seawater. It is questionable whether manganese nodules will be found in commercial quantities on the U.S. continental margin, but there have been suggestions that nodules derived from the eastern Pacific seabed may be processed on U.S. coasts (particularly the island of Hawaii). One "resource" of the oceans which may before long be utilized is the strong thermal differences in certain areas close to the coast, which could be utilized in OTEC plants to produce energy.

Nonresource Uses

A principal nonliving resource use is navigation. Another is utilizing the oceans as a site for waste disposal. It is also a site for marine scientific research, for recreational boating and swimming, for naval activities, and for communications, inasmuch as submarine cables and pipelines are laid on the ocean floor.

Navigational uses are perhaps less contentious, so far as federal/state relationships are concerned, than are many other issues, in part because of the U.S. government's authority with respect to the nation's "navigable waters," but there is the problem of establishing superports in waters beyond state jurisdiction, and the 1974 Deepwater Port Act permits a state adjacent to the site of a proposed deepwater port to veto the federal license for the port, even if there is a demonstrable national need for that facility. To date, the only deepwater port being constructed off the United States is LOOP (Louisiana Offshore Oil Port), installed in the Gulf of Mexico, eighteen miles off the Louisiana coastline.

The use of the ocean as a dumping ground is, of course, a serious problem, not only at the federal/state level but also between states. What effects, for example, will the dumping of New York City refuse in the New York Bight have, over time, on the New Jersey beaches? Or, at the national level, can the U.S. Department of Defense continue dumping noxious chemicals on the outer portions of the continental shelf?

Coastal and offshore shelf areas can also be used as storage sites and as marine sanctuaries. In the former instance, there are already examples in the Persian (Arabian) Gulf region where large oil storage facilities have been located on the seabed, and there seems little reason why this could not also happen off the United States. So far as marine sanctuaries are concerned, the Marine Protection, Research, and Sanctuaries Act of 1972 requires that in the designation by the federal government of such sanctuaries not only are federal/state approvals necessary but also, within the federal government itself, interagency support must be obtained.

It goes without saying, since the ocean medium is multi-dimensional, that inasmuch as activities take place simultaneously on the water surface, within the water column, and on and beneath the seabed (as well as in the superjacent air space), many ocean-related activities interact with one another. And, through the medium of the coastal zone, they interact with events on land as well. Thus, regulation of activities in coastal and offshore waters is a highly complex phenomenon, one which is constantly in the process of evolution, particularly as a result of the growing concern in the United States with problems of environmental pollution.

REGULATORY STRUCTURES CONCERNED WITH MARINE RESOURCE USE

There are four levels of government involved in marine resource activities in the United States-international, national, state, and local. Each has its particular form of input.

At the international level, a primary moving force concerns the negotiations associated with the Third United Nations Conference on the Law of the Sea. The conference has been underway since December, 1973, with representatives of virtually every independent nation of the world in attendance. The second meeting of the eighth session was held in New York City in July and August, 1979. From the conference have emerged a series of Negotiating Texts, representing positions which, in the opinion of conference officials, come closest to consensus support. The last major Negotiating Text was the Informal Composite Negotiating Text (ICNT), which was issued in July, 1977. This has been somewhat modified by Revision 1 (RICNT), issued in April, 1979.

Some revision of the RICNT may eventually be adopted as a new oceans treaty. Should a bill approving the new treaty pass the U.S. Congress and be signed by the president, the United States will have a new body of regulations regarding the oceans to which it must adhere. Other than issues of deep-seabed mining, there is relatively little in the articles of the RICNT as they now exist which would require changes in U.S. domestic legislation (6).

At the national (federal) level the United States has already moved toward closer coordination of its regulatory agencies associated with the oceans through the creation of the National Oceanic and Atmospheric Administration (NOAA) within the Department of Commerce. In 1969 a presidentially-appointed Commission on Marine Science Engineering, and Resources (the Stratton Commission), after two years of study, recommended the establishment within the federal structure of an independent body, the National Oceanic and Atmospheric Agency. This agency would include the agencies now in NOAA (which is an administration, not an agency), as well as the U.S. Coast Guard, the U.S. Lake Survey of the Corps of Engineers, the Bureau of Sport Fisheries and Wildlife, and several small programs financed by the National Science Foundation. While the agency itself did not evolve, NOAA is a reasonably close approximation. But other federal agencies are also vitally concerned with ocean affairs, among them the Maritime Administration, the Bureau of Land Management (which handles offshore leasing for oil and gas), the Environmental Protection Agency, the Coast Guard, and the Army Corps of Engineers. For a time in the late 1960s there was within the federal government a National Council on Marine Resources and Engineering Development, headed by the vice-president and composed of the heads of marine-related departments and agencies within the government. Despite the considerable success which the council demonstrated during its short period of existence, it was permitted to terminate and no analagous organization has since been established. As a result, the handling of federal/state relationships with respect to the marine environment is, at the federal level, often cumbersome.

The coastal states vary considerably among themselves with regard to the management of coastal and offshore problems. Some handle such issues through their departments of natural resources and/or the environment. A number have enacted coastal zone management programs, requiring designated agencies for program implementation. Ports and shipping are often administered within a special department. For some states (e.g., New Hampshire, Alabama), the coastline is very limited, as are the offshore resources, with the result that ocean issues have a relatively low priority within the state government. For other states, such as Hawaii, Alaska, California, and Florida, the coastal environment is of great importance. But few coastal state officials perceive marine-related issues in the sense of comprehensive trade-offs-yielding on fisheries issues, for example, in order to gain on marine recreation, or accepting limitations on U.S. support for shoreline development in order to win marine pollution control concessions.

At the local level the principal issue is zoning. States vest zoning regulations in the local communities, be they townships, counties, parishes, municipalities, or other agencies. Although both the state and federal governments have certain powers of condemnation of shoreline or coastland space, it generally rests with the local communities to determine permissible uses. But such zoning powers stop at the water's edge. To date, no zoning appears to have taken place offshore-even in bays, coves, and estuaries-although the local communities and/or the states generally have jurisdiction over such areas.

LIMITS OF JURISDICTION: THE
SUBMERGED LANDS ACT

Two federal/state problems have emerged regarding ownership of offshore areas: (a) whether the individual states or the United States government (hereafter referred to as "United States") owns the seabed and superjacent waters of the territorial sea; and (b) where the baseline is along the coast from which the breadth of the territorial sea is measured. Both issues arose initially with respect to offshore oil and gas, but they subsequently included fisheries as well.

Exploitation of offshore oil resources began off the coast of California in 1897 with drilling from wharves extending over the sea. During subsequent years coastal landowners in California granted mineral leases to oil companies, but in 1921 the California legislature adopted an exploration and leasing act applying to all minerals and power fuels in lands belonging to the state, a provision which applied also to the submerged lands off the coast. Later, both Texas and Louisiana passed legislation indicating their purported ownership of offshore areas.

In September, 1945, President Truman issued a presidential proclamation asserting the claim of the United States to the exclusive right of exploitation of the natural resources of the seabed and subsoil of the continental shelf appertaining to the United States. The following month the United States filed action in the United States Supreme Court against California seeking a declaration of U.S. rights as against the state in the submerged lands of the territorial sea out to three nautical miles from shore.

In the United States v. California decision (1947) the Supreme Court ruled in favor of the United States. Ownership of coastal areas by the individual states was limited to bays, estuaries and other "inland waters" behind the baseline from which the territorial sea is measured. But once the ruling had been handed down, the U.S. Congress initiated legislation specifically awarding ownership of the seabed out to three miles to the states. Eventually Congress passed, and President Eisenhower signed into law, the Submerged Land Act of 1953 (Public Law 83-31), under which the United States relinquished to the coastal states all of its rights in the submerged lands immediately off the coast (7). Subsequently, the Court found, because of historic rights, that the boundaries of Texas and of Florida in the Gulf of Mexico extended to nine nautical miles from the coast (8).

The Submerged Lands Act did not resolve the question of the coastline from which a state was to measure its offshore boundary. The act simply provided that the term <u>coastline</u> means the line of ordinary low water along that portion of the coast which is in direct contact with the open sea and the line marking the seaward limit of inland waters. In the years since the act was passed the United States has repeatedly contested state claims to particular baselines from which to measure offshore areas, among the most difficult situations involving California (9), Louisiana (10), and Texas (11). Along many parts of the U.S. coast the "official coastline" is still a matter of federal/state contention. The United States has traditionally followed a conservative approach to defining the coastline under the terms of the 1958 Geneva Convention on the Territorial Sea and the Contiguous Zone. More specifically, the government has refused to permit the adoption of a "straight baseline" regime, as provided for in Article 4 of that convention, even though portions of the coast, particularly in southeastern Alaska and in Maine, conform to the definitions contained in the convention.

The principal basis for federal involvement in determining the exact "coastline" from which the breadth of the territorial sea is measured is the fact that the outer limits of the territorial sea have international ramifications. The same is true, of course, in the case of lateral maritime boundaries with Canada and Mexico, these boundaries out to three nautical miles from the coast (12) being both the limits of national and of state-owned maritime space. The various Negotiating Texts which have emerged from negotiations at UNCLOS III permit the breadth of the territorial sea to be as much as twelve nautical miles. In years to come the United States may elect to extend its own territorial limits from three to twelve miles; should this occur, the question arises whether there will be pressure for the offshore boundaries of the coastal states then to be extended from three to twelve miles from shore.

One final delimitation issue concerns the lateral seaward boundaries between the coastal states themselves. In some cases (e.g., Florida/Georgia, Florida/Alabama, Oregon/Washington) adjacent state governments have concluded compacts delimiting their common offshore boundaries. But there was little impetus from the federal government for a movement in this direction until the enactment in 1976 of an amendment to the Coastal Zone Management Act establishing a Coastal Energy Impact Program. One aspect of the program is the issuance of various grants, loans, and guarantees to coastal states; the percentage of the total annual funds available to each state will be proportional to the amount of outer continental shelf acreage which is adjacent to the state, and has been newly leased by the federal government. The legislation calls on the states to determine their offshore boundaries by agreement. In the absence of agreement, the federal government will determine the lateral seaward boundaries, such determination being subject, of course, to judicial challenge by either or both of the affected states.

THE COASTAL ZONE MANAGEMENT ACT (CZMA)

The concept of the coastal zone as a discrete management unit was first proposed in the 1969 report issued by the Stratton Commission (13). The report suggested that the coastal zone include the territorial waters of the U.S., and that each coastal state be authorized to define the landward extent of its coastal zone for itself. The report recommended "that a Coastal Zone Management Act be enacted that will provide policy objectives for the coastal zone and authorize Federal grants-in-aid to facilitate the establishment of State Coastal Zone Authorities empowered to manage the coastal waters and adjacent land" (14). The 1972 Coastal Zone Management Act (Public Law 92-583) reflected closely this recommendation.

The act declares that it is the national policy "to encourage and assist the states to exercise effectively their responsibilities in the coastal zone through the development and implementation of management programs to achieve wise use of the land and water resources of the coastal zone" and "to encourage the participation of the public, of Federal, state, and local governments and of regional agencies in the development of coastal zone management programs." The act defines the coastal zone as "the coastal waters (including the lands therein and thereunder) and the adjacent shorelands (including the waters therein and thereunder), strongly influenced by each other and in proximity to the shorelines of the several coastal states, and includes transitional and intertidal areas, salt marshes, wetlands, and beaches. . . . Excluded from the coastal zone are lands the use of which is by law subject solely to the discretion of or which is held in trust by the Federal Government, its officers or agents."

The act provides for federal assistance and advice to the coastal states (including those bordering the Great Lakes) in the development and implementation of each state's coastal zone management program. The programs must be comprehensive, and be approved by the Secretary of Commerce (within whose department is located NOAA, with its Office of Coastal Zone Management). Approval by the Secretary can occur only after adequate consideration has been given to the views of other federal agencies affected by the management program on the proposed activity. As an added incentive to coastal states to develop and implement coastal zone management programs, the act includes a "consistency" provision which holds, in effect, that after a state program's approval and implementation, any action taken with respect to the state's coastal zone by federal agencies shall, to the maximum extent possible, be consistent with the approved state management program.

Several coastal states have had their proposed programs accepted by the Department of Commerce and thus have become eligible for administrative grants from the federal government. And already amendments to the act have been necessary, in part because new federal/state complications have arisen over the impacts within the coastal zone of activities carried out in the area of the continental shelf beyond the limits of state jurisdiction. Coastal states are becoming increasingly concerned, for example, about potential environmental damage occurring along their coasts as a result of oil and gas developments on the adjacent outer continental shelf and the 1976 amendments (Public Law 94-370) to the CZMA state that any exploration or development on the outer continental shelf must, once a coastal state has an approved management program, be consistent with that program (15).

The Coastal Zone Management Program is an experiment both in federal/state relationships and in regional management of what may seem to be a loosely defined geographical area. One difficulty with the coastal zone management concept is that the managers themselves must serve two major constituencies with often opposing interests. These two are, first, the "environmentalists," who seek to preserve and protect the coastal environment, particularly from irreversible damage. Second, the "developers" also must be served, including those associated with providing energy, be it in the form of oil terminals, offshore wells, shoreside nuclear power plants, etc. State coastal zones management programs must be carefully worded and implemented in order to fit in with other forms of regulatory process (e.g., land use planning, waterway development, fisheries management) and to accommodate as much as possible the environmental and development aspects of coastal interests.

THE FISHERY CONSERVATION AND MANAGEMENT ACT (FCMA)

Traditionally, the United States has pursued an oceans policy which favored maximizing the extent of area of the high seas which are free to the use of all nations. U.S. fishermen were able to harvest the living resources off other countries' coasts beyond narrow territorial limits, and vessels from foreign states could do the same off the United States. Conservation efforts were carried out within the framework of multilateral or bilateral fisheries arrangements to which the U.S. was a party (Figure 13-1).

In 1966 the United States enacted its first extrateritorial protective fisheries legislation by unilaterally proclaiming an exclusive fisheries zone between three and twelve miles from shore. Two years prior to that, when the 1958 Geneva Convention on the Continental Shelf (to which the U.S. was a party) went into effect, the United States acquired exclusive rights with respect to the "living resources" of the adjacent shelf. No precise identification had ever been made of the particular species covered by the "living resources" provision (16), and the United States later found itself confronting other countries, particularly the Japanese, as to whether or not a particular type of living resource was actually covered by the provision (17).

The advent in the late 1960s of increasingly larger numbers of foreign vessels, particularly off the northeast coast of the United States, led to growing pressures for greater fisheries protection by the U.S. government. Finally, in 1976 the Fishery Conservation and Management Act (Public Law 94-265) was signed into law, and the United States unilaterally established a 200-mile exclusive fisheries zone. Along with protection for U.S. fishermen against foreign competitors, the act also provided for a new and unique form of federal/state cooperation in management of the fisheries within the 200-mile zone.

Section 302 of the FCMA provides that there be established eight Regional Fishery Management Councils covering the coastlines of the United States and its territories. All but two are multistate councils (18). Membership on the councils includes both representatives of the member states and of the federal government (19). The major function of the councils is to prepare and implement fishery management plans affecting both domestic and foreign fishermen within the U.S. exclusive fisheries zone. These plans are to be drawn up (and when necessary revised) according to the best available biological, social, and economic data. Input to the councils comes from the National Marine Fisheries Service, state fisheries agencies, the fishing industry itself, public and private institutions, and other sources.

Since the councils are newly formed, they have operated up to now only on the basis of preliminary fishery management plans. The principal charge to these councils in the FCMA is to "achieve and maintain, on a continuing basis, the optimum yield from each fishery." The term optimum with respect to the yield from a fishery means the amount of fish "(A) which will provide the greatest overall benefit to the Nation, with particular reference to food production and recreational opportunities; and (B) which is prescribed as such on the basis of the maximum sustainable yield from such fishery, as modified by a relevant economic, social or ecological factor." Once a management council has determined the optimum yield of a fishery within the area under its jurisdiction, it must then set the total allowable level of foreign fishing, this being that portion of the optimum yield which will not be harvested by vessels of the United States, as determined by the council. The federal government then allocates among foreign nations their annual portion of the total allowable level of foreign fishing in the area under the council's jurisdiction.

Not only are federal/state relationships involved insofar as the councils are concerned, but so too are council/state relations. Regulations set by the councils can be enforced only for stocks of fish harvested outside state waters, unless the actual fishing activity for the stock is carried out "predominantly" in areas seaward of the offshore limits of state authority. This bifurcation of state and council responsibilities could, in the absence of genuine cooperative efforts, have serious repercussions. At least 50 percent of the domestic commercial harvest and 80 percent of the recreational catch spend at least a part of their life cycle within estuaries, wetlands, and other near-shore waters under state jurisdiction. Yet a state is not required, under the FCMA, to implement the provisions of council-approved fishery management plans within its own waters.

One of the more lucid summaries of federal/state relationships with respect to the councils is provided by a 1979 report by the comptroller general of the United States (20), which reads in part:

> The act (FCMA) created a system of resource management in the form of a partnership consisting of the Secretary of Commerce, the States, and the eight regional fishery management councils. This system emphasizes local development of fishery management plans by the councils and approval and implementation of the plans by the Secretary of Commerce.
>
> The councils are federally supported through the Department of Commerce. The Secretary of Commerce has provided program, administrative, and technical support to establish the councils, processed budget requests and funding, and provided guidance on operation to councils.
>
> The State appointees act as liaisons between the councils and the States. The NMFS representative performs a similar role between the councils and the NMFS. Individual members selected from the Governor's lists generally include commercial and recreational fishermen, processors, and consumers; therefore, they represent those groups to the council. Non-voting members include Federal, State, and local representatives and others with an interest in fisheries management.
>
> The act also provides for Federal funding through the Secretary of Commerce for council staff. Each council can appoint and assign duties to an executive director and other full- and part-time administrative employees. Council staff are responsible for preparing budgets, financial management, procurement, coordinating planning efforts, maintaining council records, corespondence, and preparing required council

reports.

THE INTERACTION OF FISHERIES AND COASTAL ZONE MANAGEMENT PLANS

At both the federal and the state levels, various aspects of fisheries and coastal zone management issues are not necessarily handled administratively in ways which insure efficiency of accommodations. Within the federal government, the National Marine Fisheries Service and the Office of Coastal Zone Mangement are both in the same administration (NOAA), but recreational fishing is handled by the Bureau of Sports Fisheries and Wildlife in the Department of the Interior.

It is within the areas under state jurisdiction that many of the problems associated with sport/commercial fishing competition develop. Here also are the sites for aquaculture. And it is here that potential conflicts between the interests of fishermen and those associated with coastal zone management occur. One group of interests within a coastal state will be working toward the development of a long-range coastal zone management plan (which presumably includes the interests of existing and potential aquaculturists), while another group will be involved with the Regional Fishery Management Council and will be seeking ways of protecting and promoting the state's fishing interests in its coastal waters in the light of any long-range management programs the council may develop. One future direction for coastal state administrative policy would seem to point toward greater coordination of its various marine efforts, much as the federal government has done with NOAA, with the addition within the state organization of recreational fishing and other interests.

Another future direction may be for the expansion of

certain aspects of state jurisdiction beyond the current limit of state waters. One avenue of approach to this may lie through the Office of Coastal Zone Management. The office is already seeking some forms of jurisdiction beyond territorial limits through the establishment and administration of marine sanctuaries, some of which may lie wholly or partly beyond the offshore limits of state authority. Coastal states may also, in time, challenge fishery management councils' decisions as to which coastal stocks are fished "predominantly" beyond the limits of state waters, and thereby fall within the purview of the councils, so far as management programs are concerned. In coming encounters between the states and agencies of the federal government, so far as jurisdiction in marine areas is concerned, it will be instructive to watch the attitudes both of Congress and of the Executive Office of the President, as well as the decisions of federal courts involving states' rights.

SUMMARY OF FEDERAL/STATE RELATIONSHIPS RELATIVE TO THE MANAGEMENT OF MARINE AREAS

In the coastal and offshore areas of the United States the federal government has paramount rights and responsibilities with respect to external relations of the U.S. to the resources of the outer continental shelf, and to fisheries conservation and management within the exclusive fisheries zone. It also has certain rights regarding commerce, navigation, defense, and other activities within the coastal zones of the littoral states. There are, for example, large areas of federally owned lands along the U.S. coast, and the total areal extent of these lands expands and contracts over time. There is even a clause in the CZMA relating to state coastal zone management programs which notes: "The management program [must provide] for adequate consideration of the national interest involved in the siting of facilities necessary to meet requirements which are more than local in nature" (21). Such facilities might be defense or energy-related.

Upon assuming jurisdiction over the living resources of the 200-mile exclusive fisheries zone, the federal government initiated an ambitious management program, involving federal, regional, and state administrations in a complex process, the results of which are not yet clearly observable. It is the federal government's responsibility to coordinate the work of the councils and to accommodate conflicting positions arising as a result of overlap of councils' jurisdictions. It is incumbent upon the states to cooperate with the provisions of the councils' long-range fishery management programs, once these have been approved and implemented.

State governments have title over the waters of the territorial sea and of the submerged lands underlying them. Under the provisions of the CZMA, the federal government has been employing a "carrot and stick" approach toward the planning and adoption by the coastal states of comprehensive coastal zone management programs. Again, it will be up to the federal government to coordinate, where necessary, elements of the management plans of adjacent states.

There are other pieces of federal legislation affecting marine areas which also impact federal/state relationships. Among these are the Deepwater Port Act, the Federal Water Pollution Control Act, the Fish and Wildlife Coordination Act, and the National Environmental Policy Act. On the other hand, the Federal Port and Waterways Safety Act, which establishes a comprehensive federal scheme for regulating the operation, traffic routes, pilotage, and safety design specifications for tankers specifically has excluded state participation and regulatory authority.

During the past two decades "cooperative federalism," as it applies to the U.S. marine environment, has grown exceedingly complex. A whole cadre of experts (many of them with legal training) has been trained to handle federal/state interactions in the coastal and offshore areas. With the continually growing concerns of U.S. citizens over energy, environmental protection, and the costs of government in an inflationary cycle, all that can be said is that much of what is written today may be out of date within a few years because of amendments, deletions, and changes in federal legislation, and because of changing practices on the part of coastal states as they seek to adjust to evolving conditions.

FIG. 13-1. U.S. Fishery Conservation Zone: March 1, 1977.
Vereinigte Staaten: Fisch Erhaltungszonen, 1. März, 1977.

NOTES

1. Figures from the U.S. Department of State, Office of the Geographer, "Sovereignty of the Sea," (Geographic Bulletin no. 3, 1969); and "Theoretical Allocations of Seabed to Coastal States. . . ." (International Boundary Study, Series A, Limits in the Seas, no. 46, August 1972).

2. The United States Government considers the U.S. coastline to include areas bordering the Great Lakes. In this case, six additional U.S. states are also "coastal."

3. The 1972 Coastal Zone Management Act, in defining the landward boundary of the "shoreland," notes: "The [coastal] zone extends inland from the shorelines only to the extent necessary to control shorelands, the uses of which have a direct and significant impact on coastal waters." The act left it up to the individual coastal states to define for themselves the landward limits of the shoreland. See Robinson, J. M., and Hershman, M. J., "Boundaries of the Coastal Zone: A Survey of State Laws," Coastal Zone Management Journal 1 (1974), 305-332.

4. In the cases of Texas and the Gulf coast of Florida, state jurisdiction extends seaward to three leagues (nine nautical miles) as explained later on. For a discussion of the official "coastline" from which the breadth of the territorial sea is measured, see the section of the essay on limits of jurisdiction.

5. The principal "distant-water" catches are tuna from the west coast of South America, shrimp from the Gulf of Mexico/Carribean and off the northeast coast of South America, and rock lobster from the Bahamas.

6. One issue may be the outer limits of the legally-defined "continental shelf." U.S. domestic legislation is silent on this issue, although the definition at present conforms with the "exploitability" criterion of the 1958 Geneva Convention. The RICNT places the limit at the "outer edge" of the continental margin, with certain modifications.

7. The act refers to all lands beneath navigable waters within state boundaries. It then defines the area in terms of state boundaries "as they existed at the time a state became a member of the Union,

or as heretofore approved by Congress," not extending seaward from the coast of any state more than three geographical miles in the Atlantic and Pacific oceans, or three marine leagues in the Gulf of Mexico. At approximately the same time as the Submerged Lands Act became law, Congress passed and the president signed the Outer Continental Shelf Lands Act, establishing U.S. jurisdiction and control over the "outer continental shelf," that area of the shelf beyond the limits of state jurisdiction.

8. In the case of Texas, the Court's rationale was based on the conditions under which Texas, as the Lone Star Republic, was admitted to the Union. For Florida, the reasoning was founded on the terms of that state's constitution in 1968, the date at which Florida (which with other states had seceded from the Union to form the Confederacy) had been readmitted to the Union.

9. United States v. California (1965).

10. United States v. Louisiana (1960).

11. United States v. Texas (1967).

12. Except for three leagues in the case of the eastern (Gulf of Mexico) extension of the U.S.-Mexican border.

13. Our Nation and the Sea: A Plan for National Action. Report of the Commission on Marine Science, Engineering and Resources (Washington, D.C.: U.S. Government Printing Office, 1969).

14. Ibid., p. 57.

15. See "Legislative History of the Coastal Zone Management Act of 1972, as Amended in 1974 and 1976 with a Section-by-Section Index," U.S. Senate Committee on Commerce Print, 94th Congress, 2nd Session (Washington, D.C.: U.S. Government Printing Office, 1976).

16. Article 2(4) of the convention refers to "living organisms belonging to sedentary species, that is to say, organisms which, at the harvestable stage, either are immobile on or under the seabed or are unable to move except in constant physical contact with the seabed or the subsoil."

17. A principal dispute concerned U.S. rights to the Alaskan king crab, harvested on the adjacent continental shelf by both Alaskan and Japanese fishermen. The U.S. claimed the king crab qualified as a "sedentary species," according to the definition of "living resources of the shelf," as set out in the 1958 convention; the Japanese Government disagreed. Eventually, the disagreement was negotiated.

18. There are councils for the following areas: New England, Mid-Atlantic, South Atlantic, Caribbean, Gulf of Mexico, Pacific, North Pacific, and Western Pacific. The Caribbean Council consists only of the Virgin Islands and the Commonwealth of Puerto Rico. The Western Pacific Council has but one state, Hawaii: it also comprises American Samoa and Guam.

19. Voting members include (a) the principal fishery management official in each state in the council's region; (b) the NMFS regional director; and (c) individuals selected by the Secretary of Commerce from lists submitted by governors of the states in the council's region.

20. <u>Progress and Problems of Fisheries Management Under the Fishery Conservation and Management Act: Report by the Comtroller General of the United States</u> (Washington, D.C.: United States General Accounting Office, January 9, 1979).

21. Sec. 1455(c)(8).

CHAPTER 14

NATIONAL AND REGIONAL INFLUENCES ON THE POSTWAR DEVELOPMENT OF THE WEST GERMAN INLAND WATERWAYS (WITH PARTICULAR CONSIDERATION OF WATER POLLUTION)

BUNDESSTAATLICHE UND REGIONALE EINFLÜSSE AUF DIE NACHKRIEGSENTWICKLUNG DER WEST DEUTSCHEN BINNENWASSERSTRASSEN (MIT BESONDEREN BERÜCKSICHTIGUNG DER WASSERVERSCHMUTZUNG)

Helmut W. Breuer

Abstract

With the exception of the Danube all the important navigable rivers in Germany run relatively close to each other in an essentially south-north direction. In the lower courses of the rivers the mutual watershed areas are low; since early times it has been technically possible to build linking canals across them. Historically, the rivers which are usually navigable throughout the year formed the lines of direction for urban development in Germany.

The setting up of borders after World War II means a significant truncation and reorientation of the West German waterway network, especially since the navigable sections of the larger West German rivers do not run entirely within the boundaries of the Federal Republic of Germany. The inclusion of the Federal Republic in the European Common Market is considered to be especially important as a basis for development. One must understand, then, the international as well as national and regional viewpoints which, as is shown, are often not in agreement.

Among numerous factors, the national and regional influences on both the previous and the planned development of the West German waterways are pointed out. These influences are well illustrated by the Saar canalization and the Rhine-Main-Danube canal, the Elbe lateral canal, the development of shipping on the Rhine, as well as other past and present expansion projects.

The observable results of development, the alternative possibilities and especially the ever-growing significance of the role of the waterways as conduits for drinking water, industrial cooling water, general use water, and sewage disposal are discussed as a superregional problem using the Rhine as an example.

Kurzfassung

Mit Ausnahme der Donau verlaufen alle wichtigen schiffbaren Flüsse Deutschlands in relativ geringer Entfernung voneinander im wesentlichen in Süd-Nordrichtung. Schon früh wurden sie durch Kanäle verbunden. Historisch bildeten die meist ganzjährig schiffbaren Flüsse wichtige Leitlinien städtischer Entwicklung in Deutschland.

Die Grenzziehungen nach dem 2. Weltkrieg bedeuteten eine wesentliche Beschneidung und Umorientierung des westdeutschen Wasserstrassennetzes, zumal keiner der grossen Flüsse Deutschlands in voller schiffbarer Länge in der BRD verläuft. Die Einbeziehung der Bundesrepublik in die EWG ist dabei als besonders wichtige Entwicklungsgrundlage zu berücksichtigen. Daher sind sowohl internationale als auch nationale und regionale Gesichtspunkte, die oftmals nicht übereinstimmen, zu erfassen.

Unter den Faktorengruppen natürliche Eignung, wirtschaftliche Erfordernisse, technische Möglichkeiten und, insbesondere, politische Absichten werden an Beispielen die Staatlichen und regionalen Einflüsse auf die erfolgte und geplante Entwicklung der westdeutschen Wasserstrassen aufgezeigt. Der beobachtete Erfolg der Entwicklung, alternative Möglichkeiten und besonders auch die immer bedeutender werdende Rolle der Wasserstrassen als Trink-, industrielle Kühl und Brauchwasserleitungen sowie als Abwassertransportwege werden am Beispiel des Rheins als überregionales Problem diskutiert.

National and Regional Influences on the Postwar Development of the West German Inland Waterways (With Particular Consideration of Water Pollution)

TOPOGRAPHIC AND HISTORICAL BASES

All the important navigable rivers in Germany with the exception of the Danube run relatively close to each other in an essentially southeast-northwest direction. In the lower courses of these rivers, after passing the German uplands, the mutual watersheds are very low. Since early times, therefore, people have tried to overcome these watersheds and to link river systems by navigable canals at places of important economic activity. Insofar as this was impossible or of minor economic importance, a linking of river systems by a series of navigable canals near their estuaries in the North, near the Baltic Sea, was always possible (1).

Historically, most of these rivers could be used throughout the year and accommodated the normal ship-size at that time (2). They became important guidelines for the urban development of all of Germany. This is also true for most of the other northwest European river basins. Crossing sites, so-called Furt-lagen (e.g., Frankfurt/Main or Frankfurt/order), confluence sites, so-called Konfluenz-lagen (e.g., Koblenz/Rhine-Moselle), and fortress sites, so-called Festungs or Etappenplätze (e.g., Magdeburg/Elbe) were usually the initial settlement centers which later became important German towns.

The industrialization of the nineteenth century, the introduction of steamship navigation, and a corresponding increase in the actual size of ships since the mid-century (to compete with the railroad) diminished navigation rather sharply. With the exception of the Rhine, the majority of the German rivers could save their navigability only by canalization or at least by certain river regulation works. On numerous upper and middle courses freight traffic came to an end. On the other hand, new shipping arteries were built in fast-growing industrial areas, i.e., in the Ruhr area and in Upper Silesia. Strategical reasons and efforts toward national self-sufficiency (in regard to ocean connections) encouraged creation of new canals during the last decade of the nineteenth century, e.g., the Dortmund-Ems Canal (1899) and the Kaiser Wilhelm Canal (1895), today named the North-Baltic Sea Canal (Figure 14-1).

During this century there have been many reasons why keeping inland navigation competitive is of extraordinary importance: (a) overcoming larger grade sections during flood periods in the upstream direction, (b) insufficient navigable depth during low-water periods in summer, (c) shortening of numerous meanderings as well as the completion of a dense and continuous waterway network, and (d) construction of large-sized locks, especially with increased lifting heights. The introduction of ship-lifting devices were most important milestones during that evolution.

When the Middleland Canal was completed (1938) as a connecting canal between the shipping arteries of the Rhine and Elbe rivers, continuing via the German capital region of Berlin to the Oder system, there was a continuous west-east waterway network in northern Germany, but individual sections have different capacities.

In contrast to this development, southern Germany did not have a comparable waterway network. The Danube navigation downstream was restricted to a small section below Regensburg. The only navigable waterway linking the northern and southern parts of the country was the Rhine River, which

reached southwest Germany at the Swiss border near Basel.
The Rhine lateral canal on French territory was also of great
importance. New borders after World War I and, particular,
certain rights given to France by the Versailles Treaty (1919,
paragraph 358) diverted water out of the Rhine and limited
Germany's full authority on the river to Karlshruhe and
upstream.

SPATIAL CONSEQUENCES OF WORLD WAR II

Boundary demarcations after World War II imposed an even more
important orientation change on the West (and East) German
waterway network. None of the large German rivers any longer belonged in their whole navigable length to the FRG (if
we omit the Weser, which is definitely of less importance in
its whole length).

It is particularly important to recognize, considering
various transportation factors and the broader economic
picture, that the demarcation line between the two Ger-
manies since World War II resulted in two different economic
systems and blocs, e.g., between members of the European
Community for Coal and Steel (ECCS, 1951), the European
Economic Community (EEC, 1958) and the European Community
(EC, since 1970)-which have always included the Federal
Republic, and between the members of COMECON-CMEA (since
1949), which includes the GDR. Berlin occupies a special
position with regard to navigation because West Berlin
is part of the economic unit of the FRG, even though it does
not belong to the territory of the Federal Republic. Due
to this separation, Germany's North Sea ports, especially
Hamburg, are located in a very negative periphery site
within the Federal Republic. At the same time economic
linkages between West Germany and the other members of the

European Community developed very favorably and resulted in international freight traffic.

The industrial reconstruction after World War II first began in the Rhine-Ruhr area and in the Rhine-Main region around Frankfurt. It then expanded to the metropolitan areas of Munich and Stuttgart. This latter development therefore chanced the economic focus of the Federal Republic more and more to the southwest, which at the same time meant further from the West German North Sea ports. The reintegration of the Saar (1957) with the FRG provided another strengthening effect in the same direction. These political events have thus been the basic influence on the FRG's actual inland waterway network and today's traffic pattern. Regional, federal, and-in a growing proportion-international influences and measures (existing or actually planned) can only be understood by consideration of these developments.

POSTWAR DEVELOPMENT OF THE WEST GERMAN TRAFFIC
AND TRANSPORTATION SYSTEM

The effective postwar development of West German inland waterways may be explained under three causative complexes. The different federal and regional influences, together with measures taken, can easily be related to these fields: (a) enlargement, completion, extension, and modernization of existing navigable waterways according to rapidly changing economic demands in one or several regions, (b) junction of existing economic areas which lost their hinterland after World War II or had never had such links, and (c) measures of modernization on a European scale corresponding basically to paragraphs 74-84 of the ECC treaty, e.g., related to international agreements and demands of border traffic crossing.

Arguments in favor of certain improvements are based on one of the three mentioned groups and are influenced according to different spheres of interest. The opposite national and regional points of view are mentioned first. But mutual agreement of different traffic systems and carriers, especially between inland navigation, railroad traffic, and pipeline transports, also are seen distinctly. In this connection it is very important to consider public or private ownership and participation in traffic.

In the FRG, it is important to notice that all navigable waterways are under federal administration, as are the highways and the railroad network of the Deutsche Bundesbahn (German Federal Railways). Also, whereas highway traffic, pipeline transports, inland and sea navigation (and aviation) are served by various companies (sometimes state-owned companies, i.e., Lufthansa), the railroad freight traffic virtually has a federal monopoly; i.e., the German Federal Railways which taxpayers support with several billions of marks annually. This must have had some influence on the traffic policy of the federal government as a whole.

A short survey of traffic development in the territories of today's FRG since 1926, with regard to the main transportation systems, is helpful. Table 14-1 shows two characteristics: (a) total traffic output (in ton/km product) has risen remarkably since the FRG was established, and (b) the share of inland navigation remained essentially unchanged. The transport of goods by rail, on the other hand, lost much of its importance due to the fact that long-distance transport by van or truck has multiplied ten times during the last two decades.

TABLE 14-1. Total Traffic-Output of the Main Transportation System in the Federal Republic of Germany. Gesamt Verkehrsertrag der Haupt Verkehrsmittel in der FRG.

TRANSPORTATION SYSTEM	RAILROAD		INLAND NAVIGATION		ROAD LONG-DISTANCE TRAFFIC		TOTAL	
Year	billions tkm	%	billions tkm	%	billions tkm	%	billions tkm	%
1936*	46	67.6	20	29.4	2	3.0	68	100
1950*	48	65.7	17	23.3	8	11.0	73	100
1960	65	50.4	40	31.0	24	18.6	129	100
1970	86	48.6	49	27.7	42	23.7	177	100
1977	56	31.8	49	27.8	71	40.4	176	100
1978	57	30.8	53	28.6	75	40.6	185	100

* Without Saarland.

Sources: Bundesminister für Verkehr, 1965, p, 41; Statistiches Bundesamt/Wiesbaden, ed., Statistisches Jahrbuch der Bundesrepublik 1960 (Stuttgart and Mainz: Kohlhammer).

TYPES OF INLAND WATERWAY DEVELOPMENT

For the three different influences mentioned earlier one can cite some very characteristic examples from a geographic point of view. Therefore, it becomes clear from the different spheres of interest, different sizes, and different economically structured areas which claim either federal or local and more and more also international influences. Even if there are no differing concurrent traffic interests, a growing difference has become noticeable lately with respect to industrial use of the inland waterways, water on the one side and water pollution control on the other. This will be discussed later in this essay using the Rhine River as an example.

(a) <u>Enlargement, completion, extension, and modernization of existing navigable watersways</u>. This group covers a great variety of projects that were completed after World War II, i.e., enlargement of the middle and upper parts of the Rhine, enlargement of the Dortmund-Ems Canal for the so-called Europa-Shiff (Europe Ship) of 1,350 tons by 1963, (3), canalization of the middle Weser by 1960, extension of the Neckar navigation to Stuttgart (1961) and further to Plochingen (1968), as well as the further canalization of the Main River to Bamberg (1962) (Figure 14-1). Although the question of the upper Rhine enlargement has merit for international as well as ecological aspects, they will not be discussed here due to the limited focus of this essay.

(b) <u>Junction of existing economic areas</u>. Examples of this category are the Elbe lateral canal (Figure 14-1), which was in an earlier phase of planning named the North-South Canal, and the canalization of the Saar, a tributary of the Moselle. The Elbe lateral canal has been completed since 1976, and after a one-year interruption due to a dam breaking has been in full service. The canalization of the Saar was begun very recently.

The Saar canalization may be a good example of different regional, federal and even international impacts on waterway construction in the FRG today. When the Saar region was returned to Germany and became a federal state of the FRG in 1957, better traffic connections between the Saar, predominantly a region of heavy industry, and the other parts of the FRG had to be provided. For a long time an entirely new canal link was discussed, the so-called Saar-Palatinate Canal (Figure 14-1, No. 1). As a link of the Saar mining and steel district with other parts of the FRG and at the same time as a considerable meliorizaion of the freight traffic situation within the economically backward Palatinate area (Rhineland-Palatinate), this canal was regarded as the best solution for several years. In connection with the Saar's return to the FRG, the government agreed with France on a Moselle canalization, which was signed as the so-called International Moselle Treaty in 1956 (also for 1,350-ton ships). Construction work was undertaken during the period 1958-1964. France as well as Luxembourg had a strong interest in the Moselle canalization because they needed a good waterway link with the Rhine system and the seaports for exporting their steel mill products, as well as for receiving their coal and coke supply from upstream. For the German section of the Moselle, which is basically without industrial sites (especially heavy industry), this canalization is not given a high priority regarding freight traffic. In effect, transit traffic on the 150-mile-long German section of the Moselle is predominant. Up to the present time approximately 80 percent of the traffic, which totals 11-12 million tons annually, is transit.

The Germans had two serious doubts about the success and advantage of the canalization for the FRG. Vineyards and tourism in the Moselle valley would be hidden by such a freight traffic canal, and some people feared that there would be a massive transfer of traffic from rail to water and consequently a big traffic loss for the railroad.

Both fears proved to be basically unfounded. Reverse tourism even gained by the introduction of passenger navigation and by improvements of water-oriented sport facilities. Traffic output of the railroad increased also due to a more competitive position for the heavy industries in Luxembourg and along the French Moselle. Moreover, most of the German Moselle Valley communities obtained a complete sewer installation for the first time. When the Moselle canalization was completed as far as France, it became obviously cheaper to jointly develop a Saar canalization than the proposed Saar-Palatinate Canal. The federal government of Germany therefore decided to promote the canalization of the Saar instead of proposing construction of a new canal. Since 1974, the Saar canalization has been under construction between the confluence of the Saar and the Moselle and the state's capital, Saarbrücken. Initially work should be finished by 1983, but technical difficulties may cause a delay of perhaps several years (4). At any rate, the originally forseen improvement of the traffic infrastructure in the Palatinate region failed.

The Elbe lateral canal (Figure 14-1) had its roots in the inner German border demarcation after 1945-1949, as already cited. There are some other questionable aspects regarding this canal; i.e., hydrographic data shows some low-water periods of the Elbe during summer that will affect regular full-tonnage navigation. This natural obstacle finally has resulted in the lateral canal becoming a "West European modernization project" within the EC that can be funded under EC regulations rather than just on a national level. (The most remarkable building within the canal is the ship elevator near Luneburg, which has a 126-foot elevation difference).

In connection with further enlargement of the Middleland Canal, until 1993 the Elbe lateral canal provides an important link between Hamburg, the most important German seaport, and the Rhine-Westphalian manufacturing centers (Figure 14-1). There seems to be a strong national interest in this waterway, but as preliminary traffic figures demonstrate, the Elbe lateral canal can serve only in a restricted way as a Hamburg-Ruhr-Rhine junction. The most important consequence of the opening of the canal was a stimulation of industrial settlements and production in the Lower Saxonian border areas of the GDR. This finally also had a positive effect on the port development of Hamburg.

(c) <u>Measures of modernization</u>. The Moselle canalization was mentioned earlier as a European modernization project. The navigable link between the Rhine and the Danube basin, which is regarded as another example, obviously is a much larger European project (Figure 14-1). For a long time the relatively short distance between these two large and important basins has been of considerable interest for several countries in Europe. Strategy experts as well as regional planners share their interest in this so-called European southeast-northwest axis, but sometimes their enthusiasm is without regard for the potential traffic demand, especially the consequences for other navigable areas. (Historically, it is of interest to remind the reader that earlier canal projects have been discussed since Charlemagne in the ninth century. Plans partially materialized when the Ludwig-Danau-Main Canal was completed in 1846 comprising more than 100 locks and a 100-ton maximum tonnage per ship).

The actual Rhine-Main-Danube Canal, which in essence is a Main-Danube Canal (Figure 14-1) was started in 1924 and is expected to be completed in 1984. The equivalent enlargement of the Danube downstream to the Austrian frontier will require additional time. The German federal government has clearly stated in all international councils that the Main-Danube Canal (not the Rhine-Danube link) is to be regarded as a national waterway (5). This is at first considered to be a very meaningless statement. But really it contains a dubious feeling about the construction of this canal, because international, national, and regional aspects converge here with remarkable impact. When this canal is completed there will be not only a connection between the southern German Danube area that has existed since 1972, but also between the Nurnberg economic region with the Rhine-related German waterways. There also will be an opportunity for all Danube-related countries, especially for the COMECON countries (as well as for Yugoslavia, which is associated with the COMECON), to participate with their own fleet, via the new canal connection, in the international Rhine traffic. The Rhine River is by far the most heavily used European waterway. On the side of the EC countries bordering the Rhine, there is a deep fear that the COMECON countries basically are not interested in the Main-Danube Canal or in traffic to and from their home countries, but rather in an opportunity to compete with low fare (paid in strong currency) in the entire Rhine traffic in order to earn foreign money by offering low tariffs (6). The estimated traffic volume between the Rhine and the COMECON countries which could be transported on the Rhine-Main-Danube Canal is quite low. If the Rhine-Main-Danube Canal is declared an international waterway like the Rhine, all Danubian traffic would be allowed to participate in the Rhine traffic without restrictions. The German federal government therefore insists on a national authority for this canal, which thus would be under regional jursidiction, an essential aspect for the progress of some parts of Bavaria. Thus far it has not been involved in and linked with Rhine navigation, and therefore backs the canal construction because of Bavarian interests and is less concerned in the other questions mentioned earlier. It is uncertain whether the federal government will be able to resist the internationalization of the canal because there are possible pressures on the waterways linking West Berlin through the GDR, a member of COMECON.

The same points of view could be made in another possible junction between the waterway systems of the Rhine and the Danube by a projected (Rhine-) Neckar-Danube Canal (Figure 14-1, No. 3). A natural disadvantage is that the Danube is not navigable downstream from Ulm. This minimizes the chances for that project. In Figure 14-1, a third canal project is indicated (No. 2), the Maas-Rhine Canal, which has not yet been started and very probably will not be under construction in the foreseeable future. Nevertheless this project could also serve as an example for these discussions.

THE RHINE RIVER: TRAFFIC, INDUSTRY, AND WATER POLLUTION-A CRUCIAL POINT OF WEST EUROPEAN ECONOMIC DEVELOPMENT

Even though several different waterway projects, either realized or under construction, were cited previously, there is no doubt that the Rhine River is of the greatest importance as Europe's shipping artery and has the largest amount of traffic. More than 80 percent of all goods shipped on West German waterways in 1977 used the Rhine to some extent. As Table 14-2 demonstrates, the heaviest traffic concerns the lower sections of the German Rhine below Cologne (Köln) and especially below the Ruhr area starting with Duisburg, Europe's largest inland port (Figure 14-1). The Wesel-Datteln Canal and Rhine-Herne Canal are two important canals of the Ruhr area.

Altogether in 1977, 68.8 percent of the FRG inland waterway traffic utilized the Rhine and an additional 11.9 percent used its navigable tributaries the Moselle, Main, and Neckar rivers. These figures correspond to those shown above for the volume of freight traffic in Table 14-1. Generally, there is a strong concentration of all West German traffic on both sides of the Rhine Valley, because the main highways and railroads are laid out along this route. This creates a vulnerable concentration of the nation's traffic arteries from a strategic point of view.

In addition to this possible strategic danger, rarely perceived by the public, there are numerous other problems which are based on a so-called "use concurrence" (Nutzungskonkurrenz) of the Rhine waterway. These negative factors have reached such dimensions and influenced the areas bordering the Rhine to such an extent that finally it has become necessary to control the uses of the Rhine River. Under the theme of this conference we must stress regional as well as national and multinational influences and aspects of this question. In addition to its function as a navigable waterway, the Rhine River is of central importance today as a source of drinking water for many millions of people (e.g., in North Rhine-Westphalia, which is the most

TABLE 14-2. Rhine Traffic by Sections, 1977.
Rhein-Verkehr nach Abschnitten 1977.

Rhine section	Transported goods (in millions of tons)
Rheinfelder-Strassbourg	12.2
Strassbourg-Neuburgweier	29.5
Neuburgweier-Mannheim	50.6
Mannheim-Bingen	59.3
Bingen-Lülsdorf (south of Cologne)	66.3
Lülsdorf-Orsoy (north of Duisburg)	133.2
Orsoy-Dutch border	139.5
Rheinfelder – Dutch border total [+]	192.2

[+]Due to transit multiple-count addition is difficult.

Sources: Statistiches Bundesamt/Wiesbaden, ed., Statistisches Jahrbuch der Bundesrepublik, 1979 (Stuttgart and Mainz: Kohlhammer), p. 286.

populated state of the FRG, there are still in 1979 some 3.5 million inhabitants who have to drink purified Rhine water daily).

A growing number of industrial plants within the manufacturing corridors along the river use the Rhine water for cooling and processing purposes. A large number of nuclear power plants, already installed or under construction, increase the heat of the river water substantially. The critical heat limit of the Rhine, which averages some 64° F., is being surpassed during certain periods in several sections of the river (8). (Originally, average water temperature before industrialization was around 55° F.)

The emission of quantities of damaging ingredients into the river, a third problem burdening the Rhine, starts first in the upper Rhine section when French salt is added from the potash mines in Alsace. On the German side there are at regular distances other inputs, so that even during very favorable water levels, there is very serious pollution of the water. Since none of the emission places are affected by the pollution due to the fact that they are located upstream, a solution to these problems is very difficult and extremely expensive. North Rhine-Westphalia, which borders the lower parts of the Rhine, is greatly affected by water already polluted to a high degree. The Rhine transports, among other substances, 30,000 tons of salt freight every day; although, as mentioned earlier, there are many inhabitants of that state who have to drink the water and the state government and local authorities have paid some two billion dollars during the last decade for sewer plants and water purification, additional pollutants will be added to the Rhine River in the same state, which consequently will not please the Netherlands.

In 1976 the FRG, France, Switzerland, Luxembourg, and the Netherlands signed a treaty, the so-called Rhine Water Convention. The main goal of this treaty was to fix maximum quantities of pollution and establish pollution standards for the Rhine water. For example, a 200-milligram-per-litre maximum of calcium chloride was established, but the average measured at the German-Dutch border during September, 1979, was 300 milligrams (9). More serious is the fact that the French parliament obviously could not find a majority in favor of that treaty. Therefore, the French government withdrew the treaty at the end of 1979. This caused serious diplomatic difficulties between France and the Netherlands (10).

It seems to be very clear that in the future, much more investment in antipollution measures will be necessary than in canal construction for navigation purposes in the FRG and the EC. This also forecasts more trouble between local, regional, federal, and international authorities.

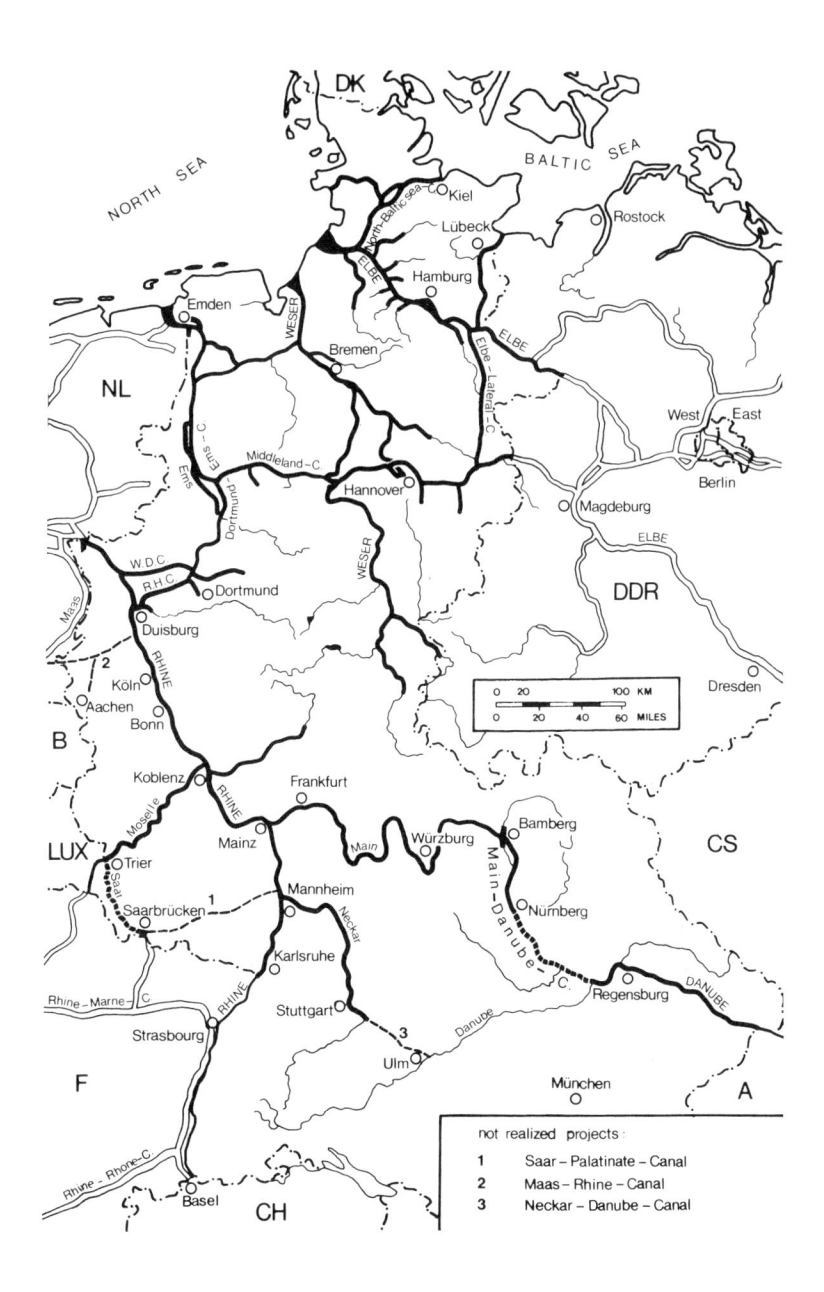

FIG. 14-1. West German Inland Waterways and Projects, Status 1 January 1980.
West Deutschland Inland Wasserstrassen und Projekte, Stand 1. Jänner, 1980.

NOTES

1. Kellenbenz, H., "Landverkehr, Flus- und Seeschiffahrt im europäischen Handel (Spätmittelalter - Anfang des 19 century)," in Les grandes voies maritime dans le monde - XV-XIXe siecles; report presented at the 12th International Congress of Historical Sciences (Vienna, 1965), pp. 65-175, and (Paris, 1965).

2. Hagedorn, B., Die Entwicklung der wichtigsten Schiffstypen bis ins 19 Jahrhundert, Vol. I (Berlin: Veröffentlichungen des Vereins für Hamburgische Geschichte, 1914).

3. One of the most important and successful decisions of the EEC was the agreement on a prototype of an inland ship of 1350-ton tonnage as minimum capacity for all European inland waterways with highest traffic importance (category I).

4. Information of the Federal Waterway Administration from October, 1979; there are technical problems in the weir and lock construction in the loser Saar.

5. Annual report of the Federal Minister for Traffic Affairs 1977 (Bonn, 1978), p. 26.

6. Experience with the tariff-system for the Danube navigation (Bratislava agreement, 1956) strengthen these fears.

7. In order to obtain a tons x miles product, the tkm figures are to be multiplied by 0.62.

8. Many maps in modern German atlases demonstrate these facts already, e.g., Alexander Weltatlas (Stuttgart, 1976), p. 107.

9. Official Dutch information, October, 1979.

10. The Dutch Government withdrew its ambassador in France temporarily.

REFERENCES

Beyer, P., Wasserstrassen aus der Sicht der Verkehrs-und Wirtschaftspolitik (Duisburg, 1960).

Breuer, H., "Die Maas als Schiffahrtsweg," Aachener Geographische Arbeiten, Heft 1 (Wiesbaden, 1969).

Bundesminister für Raumordnung, Bauwesen und Städtewesen, "Empfehlungen zur Europäischen Raumordnungspolitik," Schrifterreihe Raumordnung, Heft 9 (Bonn, 1975).

Bundesminister für Verkehr, "Die Verkehrspolitik in der Bundesrepublik Deutschland 1949-1965," Schriftenreihe des Bundesminister für Verkehr, Vol. 29 (Hof, 1965).

Bundesminister für Verkehr, Jahresberichte 1977 und 1978 (Bonn, 1978, 1979).

Bundesminister für Verkehr, Mitteilungen aus dem Bundesverkehrsministerium, ed., Die Investitionen des Bundes im Verkehrsbereich der Länder (one single number for each of the states) (Bonn, 1978), annually.

Deutscher Kanal- und Schiffahrtsverein, e.V., ed., Entwicklungsachse Donau (Nürnberg, 1978).

Deutscher Kanal- und Schiffahrtsverein, e.V., ed., Das Tor zum grösseren Markt (Nürnberg, approximately 1978).

Doni, W., "Die Binnenschiffahrt in der europäischen Integration," Beiträge aus dem Institut für Verkehrswissenschaft der Universität Münster, Heft 34 (Göttingen, 1965).

Internationale Moselgesellschaft, ed., Der Ausbau der Mosel (Trier, 1964).

Körber, J., Bibliographie zur Binnenschiffahrt Mitteleuropas 1937-1960, Berichte zue deutschen Landeskunde, Sonderheft 5 (Bad Godesberg, 1961).

Most, O., ed., Die deutsche Binnenschiffahrt, II (Bad Bodesberg: Berichte zur deutschen Landeskunde, 1964), II.

Müller, J. H., Die Binnenschiffahrt im Gemeinsamen Markt, Schriftenreihe 7, Handbuch für Europäische Wirtschaft, Fol. 28 (Baden-Baden, 1967).

Otremba, E., "Die Rhein-Main-Donau Linie im Rahmen des Europäischen Wirtschaftsraumes," Geographische Rundschau, Vol. 16 (Braunschweig, 1962), pp. 56-63.

Stang, F., Die Wasserstrassen Oberrhein, Main und Neckar - Häfen und Hinterland, Forschungen zur deutschen Landeskunde, Vol. 140 (Bad Godesberg, 1963).

Wasser- und Schiffahrtsdirektion Mitte, Die Verkehrsbedeutung des nordwestdeutschen Wasserstrassennetzes (Hannover, 1978).

Wasser- und Schiffahrtsdirektion Nord, ed., Schiffshebewerk Lüneburg in Scharnebeck (Hamburg, 1976).

Wasser- und Schiffahrtsdirektion Südwest, Ausbau der Mosel, Ausbau der Saar, Materialsammlung (Mainz, 1979).

CHAPTER 15

THE SPATIAL DISTRIBUTION OF THE U.S. FEDERAL TRANSPORTATION
DOLLAR: IMPLICATIONS FOR REGIONAL DEVELOPMENT

DIE RÄUMLICHE VERTEILUNG DES VERKEHRS-DOLLARS DES BUNDES:
AUSWIRKUNGEN AUF DIE REGIONALE ENTWICKLUNG

Ronald Briggs

Abstract

Three themes characterize the geographical literature on the role of federal governments in the space economy. One explores the impact of federal funds on the recipient region, a second examines the causal factors underlying the spatial distribution of federal funds, and a third inquires how policy should be written in order to ensure the most appropriate geographical targeting of monies. This essay examines the legislative factors behind the spatial distribution of federal mass transit and high aid and the implications of the resulting funding pattern for regional development. It suggests that legislative provisions have had little effect on the spatial distribution of mass transit aid, consequently there is marked variability between cities in the receipt of aid. This implies considerable potential for differential urban development, but it is too soon to assess actual effects. Legislative provisions have affected the spatial distribution of highway aid, and there is some reason to believe that highway aid, in conjunction with other factors, has affected current regional development patterns.

Kurzfassung

Drei Themen charakterisieren die geographische Literatur über die Rolle der Bundesregierung in der Raumökonomie. Eines erforscht den Einfluß der Bundes-Fonds auf die Empfänger-Region, ein zweites untersucht die für die räumliche Verteilung von Bundesgeldern maßgeblichen Gründe, und ein drittes fragt nach den notwenigen politischen Maßnahmen, um die angemessenste geographische Verteilung des Geldes zu erreichen. Dieser Aufsatz untersucht den Einfluß der Gesetzgebung auf die räumliche Verteilung der Bundeszuschüsse für Massenverkehrsmittel

und Autobahnen und die Auswirkungen der Mittelverteilung auf
die regionale Entwicklung. Er vermutet, daß die legislativen
Bestimmungen nur einen geringen Einfluß auf die gerechte
räumliche Verteilung der Zuschüsse gehabt hat, so daß es
hinsichtlich des Empfangs von Hilfen auffällige Unterschiede
zwischen Städten gibt. Dies bewirkt ein bemerkenswertes
Potential für unterschiedliche Stadtentwicklung, wobei es
aber noch zu früh ist, die tatsächliche Wirkung abzuschätzen.
Gesetzliche Bestimmungen haben auf die räumliche Verteilung
der Autobahn-Zuschüsse eingewirkt und es besteht einiger
Anlaß dafür anzunehmen, daß die Autobahnzuschüsse - in
Zusammenwirken mit anderen Faktoren - das gegenwärtige
regionale Entwicklungsmuster beeinflußt haben.

The Spatial Distribution of the U.S. Federal Transportation Dollar: Implications for Regional Development

Three themes characterize the geographical literature on federal expenditure policy (1). One seeks the causal factors underlying the spatial distribution of federal funds, a second explores the impact of federal disbursements on the recipient region, and a third inquires how policy should be written in order to ensure the most appropriate geographical targeting of monies. This essay encompasses all three of these themes. Specifically, it examines the legislative provisions underlying the geographical distribution of federal mass transit and highway aid in the United States and the resulting patterns in the spatial distribution of these funds. Its goals are to (a) provide a general understanding of federal mass transit and highway transportation assistance policy in the the U.S., (b) assess the role of legislative provisions as a factor influencing the spatial distribution of federal funds, (c) examine some of the implications of federal transportation expenditure policy for regional development, and (d) offer some comments on the appropriateness of current mechanisms for spatially distributing transportation assistance.

A SPATIAL PERSPECTIVE ON U.S. PUBLIC FINANCE

Comprehension of the issues involved in the spatial distribution of federal funds, for transportation or any other purpose, is aided by a clear understanding of the mechanisms and associated terminology used by the U.S. government to exact programs and distribute funds. Federal programs are begun, continued, or modified by authorizing legislation which usually specifies maximum amounts of monies--<u>authorizations</u>--which may be used for the program in future fiscal years (2). In most cases (federal aid to highways being a notable exception), authorized funds cannot be spent until they have also been appropriated during the annual budget cycle for a particular fiscal year. These <u>appropriations</u> may be available for spending during that year only, for several years thereafter, or even indefinitely. However, they can never exceed and indeed may often be less than the authorization for the fiscal year concerned. Immediately following appropriation (or authorization in the more unusual case of highways), if called for in the authorizing legislation, funds are apportioned among states and/or local governments using the formula or rules specified in the legislation. These <u>apportionments</u> form legislatively mandated ceilings on the total amount of federal funds a particular state or local government may receive. When funds do not have a legislatively mandated distribution formula, <u>allocations</u> may be made to state and local governments by the federal agency administering the program. Once funds have been apportioned (or allocated) they are available for commitment or obligation to a particular project. <u>Obligations</u> are agreements by the federal government to pay the federal share of a particular project or expense. The actual payment, usually made on completion of the project and/or following the incurrence of an expense by state or local governments, which may be many years after the obligation, is termed a federal <u>expenditure</u>, outlay, or disbursement. Only at this point does federal money change hands. Finally, apportionments, obligations, and expenditures are only for the federal share of costs. In many cases state and/or local funding sources must provide a local match which is usually a fixed percentage, specified in the authorizing legislation, of the total costs of a project.

For geographical purposes, four types of programs can be recognized based upon similarities in the spatial distribution of apportionments (or allocations), obligations, and expenditures (3):

(a) Entitlement determined programs (for example, social security pension payments) obligate the federal government to make payments to individuals who meet certain preestablished criteria, such as age. Here, obligations equal expenditures, apportionments are not relevant, and the spatial distribution of funds is a simple reflection of the location of persons having the preestablished criteria.

(b) Formula determined programs (for example, general revenue sharing) automatically transfer funds to a local or state government based solely on their formula determined apportionment, the only exception being where a government declines its allotment, usually because of the real or perceived regulatory burden accompanying any federal funds. Here, apportionments equal expenditures, and the spatial distribution of funds is a function of national political processes which establish the formula.

(c) Formula influenced programs (for example, community development block grants) apportion funds on the basis of a legislatively established formula, but state and local governments must apply for them on a project-by-project basis. Apportionments, obligations, and expenditures are not necessarily equal since some governments may not seek their entire apportionment, for one reason because the local match may not be available, for another because eligible projects may not exist to absorb all of the apportionment. The formula simply places a ceiling on the maximum amount of funds a state or local government may receive, but does not determine the actual amount. Consequently, the spatial distribution of funds is a function of both the national political process which established the formula and the political and socioeconomic conditions of the recipient government.

(d) <u>Discretionary</u> programs (for example, the urban renewal program prior to 1974) have no legislatively mandated apportionment formula. State and local governments make applications on a project-by-project basis, and funds are awarded at the discretion of the federal agency administering the program, although guidelines regarding the nature of eligible projects invariably exist in the lesiglation, as may restrictions regarding the geographical distribution of funds. Consequently, the spatial distribution of funds is primarily a function of political and socioeconomic conditions in the recipient governments, which will determine the entities making application for the funds, but program guidelines established at the national level may also exert a strong influence.

SPATIAL ASPECTS OF TRANSIT FUNDING LEGISLATION

Clearly, federal programs differ regarding legislative provisions for the geographical distribution of funds. How is federal assistance to local transit handled in the United States, and what legislative provisions apply to the spatial distribution of funds? This question is explored in this section; likewise the following section examines the same question for highway aid.

Federal assistance for urban mass transportation began

with a loan and demonstration program enacted as part of the Housing Act of 1961 (4). However, a clear federal commitment to a local public transportation assistance program was not made until the Urban Mass Transportation Assistance Act of 1964 (P.L. 88-365), which remains the basic authorizing statute for the current program (5). The latest amendments to the program were made by the Federal Public Transportation Act which became law November 6, 1978, as a part of the omnibus Surface Transportation Assistance Act (P.L. 95-599). However, even before the major changes made by the 1978 act, the program was considerably modified by four key pieces of legislation--the Urban Mass Transportation Assistanct Act of 1970 (P.L. 91-453), the Federal Aid Highway Act of 1970 (P.L. 91-605), the Federal Aid Highway Act of 1973 (P.L. 93-87), and the National Mass Transportation Assistance Act of 1974 (P.L. 93-503). From these various acts four major sources of federal funds have emerged which are currently available for urban public transportation. These are commonly referred to as Section 3, Section 5, Interstate Transfer, and Urban System monies. Each is legally distinct with its own set of legislated requirements for the distribution of monies to local areas.

Section 3 of the Urban Mass Transportation Assistance Act of 1964 is a discretionary program which provides monies to public agencies for the purchase of capital equipment, providing various comprehensive planning requirements are met and a "local match" of 20 percent is available. These monies have been the cornerstone of the urban mass transportation assistance program since its inception. Funding levels were moderate to small at first, but they took a major leap in magnitude with the passage of the Urban Mass Transportation Assistance Act of 1970 and again in 1974 with passage of the National Mass Transportation Assistance Act (Figure 15-1). Over the same period, planning requirements were substantially tightened, and the local match was changed by the Federal Aid Highway Act of 1973 from its original value of one-third, set in the 1964 act, to its current value of 20 percent.

Although Section 3 is a discretionary program, one provision (Section 12 in the original 1964 act, Section 15 following the 1966 amendments) restricted the total grants made in any one state to 12.5 percent of the national total. Its significance (and perhaps its very existence) lies in the fact that some 40 percent of all transit trips in the U.S. occur in New York City alone (6). This provision was repealed in 1974. A second legislative provision affecting the spatial distribution of funds was a $500 million set-aside in the 1974 act (covering fiscal years 1975-1980) which earmarked funds for smaller urban areas with populations below 50,000. Although such places were not excluded under the provisions of earlier acts, since the definition used for "urban" was very general (see Section 12(c)4 of the act as currently amended), Congress felt that larger cities were preempting smaller cities in the receipt of funds and added this provision.

Section 5 funds, first authorized by the National Transportation Assistance Act of 1974, are intended to help local transit agencies meet their operating expenses by providing funds for day-to-day operations as well as for the replacement and improvement of capital equipment. As with Section 3, the receipt of funds is subject to various comprehensive transportation and land use planning requirements, and a local match of 20 percent for capital equipment and 50 percent for operating funds is necessary.

Unlike Section 3, Section 5 funds are apportioned on a formula basis to urbanized areas only. Under the 1974 act each city received an apportionment based upon its population and population density, the precise dollar amount being given by:

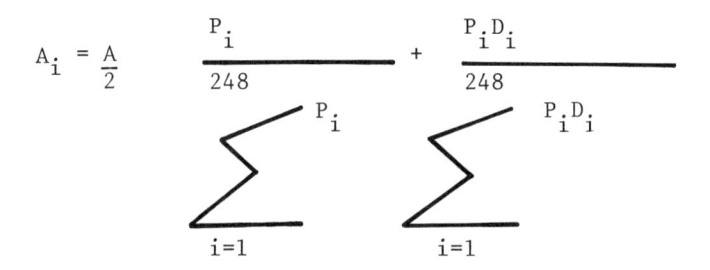

$$A_i = \frac{A}{2} \left[\frac{P_i}{\sum_{i=1}^{248} P_i} + \frac{P_i D_i}{\sum_{i=1}^{248} P_i D_i} \right]$$

where A_i is an annual apportionment for the ith urbanized area, P_i is the population of that area, D_i is its population density, and A is the total amount to be allocated nationwide for the fiscal year (7). The 1978 act made a major change in this apportionment methodology by introducing a "second tier" program over and above the basic population/density formula established in the 1974 act. One element of the second tier program directed general capital and operating assistance monies to the largest U.S. cities (those over 750,000), a second element directed capital and operating assistance to cities with fixed guideway transit (including commuter rail), and a third element directed capital assistance to cities with bus transit systems only. Each of these elements has its own apportionment methodology (Table 15-1), although the bus transit formula is the same as that for the general, first-tier program (8). The 1978 act also introduced a completely separate formula-based program to apportion capital and operating assistance funds to nonurbanized areas. Appor-

TABLE 15-1. Summary of Section 5 Allocation Formula as Established by the Federal Public Transportation Act of 1978.
Kurzfassung der Sektion 5 Zuteilungsformular gemäss des Federal Public Transportation Act von 1978.

Type of Allocation	Amount Authorized to be appropriated
1. General or First-Tier Allocation	1979 - $850 million 1980 - $900 million 1981 - $900 million 1982 - $900 million
2. Second Tier Allocation for Large Cities (operating and capital expenses)	1979 - $250 million 1980 - $250 million 1981 - $250 million 1982 - $250 million
3. Second Tier Allocation for Fixed Guideway Transit (operating and capital expenses)	1979 - $115 million 1980 - $130 million 1981 - $145 million 1982 - $160 million
4. Second Tier Allocation for Bus Transit (capital expenses only)	1979 - $300 million 1980 - $300 million 1981 - $370 million 1982 - $455 million

The Bases for a Particular Urbanized Areas's (U.A.'s) Allocation

$$\frac{1}{2} \left(\begin{array}{c} \text{Total Funds to be} \\ \text{distributed nation-} \\ \text{wide} \end{array} \right) \left(\frac{\text{Population of U.A.}}{\text{Total Population of all U.A.s}} \right)$$

$$\text{plus } \frac{1}{2} \left(\begin{array}{c} \text{Total Funds to be} \\ \text{distributed nation-} \\ \text{wide} \end{array} \right) \left(\frac{\text{Population of U.A. x Density of U.A.}}{\text{Sum of Densities x Population for all U.A.s}} \right)$$

-85% of the funds go to urbanized areas with populations over 750,000: the same formula as in the first-tier allocation is used except that totals are only taken over the cities receiving the allocation.

-15% of the funds go to urbanized areas with populations less than 750,000; the same allocation method is used as above.

-2/3rds of the funds go to cities based upon the presence of commuter rail systems:
  - 1/2 of this is based on the proportion of commuter <u>train</u> miles serving the urbanized area relative to total commuter train miles in all urbanized areas;
  - 1/2 is based upon commuter route miles serving the urbanized area relative to total commuter route miles in all urbanized areas;
  - no one state's part of an urbanized area can receive less than 1/2% or more than 30% of the total amount apportioned.

-1/3 of the funds go to cities based upon the presence of fixed guideway systems other than commuter rail;
  - allocations are based upon the proportion of fixed guideway route miles (other than commuter rail) in an urbanized area relative to total fixed guideway route miles in the U.S.
  - no one state's part of an urbanized area can receive more than 30% of the total amount apportioned.

-for fiscal 1979 and 1980 allocations are made to all urbanized areas using the same formula as for First Tier allocations
- for future years a new methodology is expected to be enacted based upon the results of a study called for in the act.

tionments are made to each state for distribution to local areas on the basis of the proportion of the nation's non-urbanized population which lives in that state. This made operating assistance available to smaller places (below 50,000) which hitherto had been restricted to capital funds from Section 3.

Urban System monies, first authorized by the Federal Aid Highway Act of 1970, are highway funds which cities were initially permitted to use for "highway-related public transit facilities" such as bus pull-outs and dedicated bus lanes. The 1973 Federal Aid Highway Act made use of these funds for public transit far more flexible, permitting capital investment in any type of public transit (including the purchase of buses and rail equipment as well as the construction of fixed mass transit facilities such as rail lines) in lieu of building highways. A local match of 25 percent is required (lowered by the Surface Transportation Assistance Act of 1978 from 30 percent in the original legislation), the same figure as for highway construction. As with Section 5 monies, Urban System funds are distributed by formula, but the formula is based upon highway needs (see below).

The use of Interstate Highway Transfers for public transportation capital investment was authorized by the Federal Aid Highway Act of 1973. Under the legislation which established the interstate system (the Federal Aid Highway Acts of 1944 and 1956), the interstate system comprises a network of 42,500 miles of limited access highway. Cities can petition the Secretary of Transportation for the deletion of portions of this system lying within their boundaries which are not "essential to the integrity of the overall Interstate system." They can then spend on public transportation an amount equal to the estimated cost of the withdrawn interstate segment. However, a 20 percent local match is required rather than the 10 percent which would have been necessary if the original freeway had been constructed. Again, interstate funds are distributed on a formula basis, but the critical factor determining the monies available for public transportation is the mileage of the interstate system within a particular city and the extent to which construction has already been undertaken. Cities cannot "double-dip": monies already spent on the construction of a freeway segment cannot be spent a second time around on mass transit.

While the above sources account for the large majority of federal investment in local public transportation in dollar terms, there are many additional sources of federal funds used in public transportation, some of which are formula-based, others of which are discretionary. Under the provisions of the Urban Mass Transportation Assistance Act itself, as amended through 1978, funds are available for nonprofit organizations to provide transportation for the elderly and handicapped (Section 16(b)2), for technical studies (Section 9), for managerial training (Section 10) and for research, development, and demonstration projects (Section 6). The Regional Rail Reorganization Act of 1973 and the Rail Revitalization and Regulatory Reform Act of 1976 provide assistance for commuter railroad operations. Several cities have used general revenue sharing and CETA (Comprehensive Employment and Training Act) monies to support their public transit systems. There are also a multitude of human service programs, primarily under the auspices of the Department of Health, Education and Welfare, which provide transportation assistance (9). Finally, it should not be forgotten that federal transit funds, although the major source of assistance for capital equipment, provide only 14 percent of the transit industry's revenue for operating needs. States and local governments provide 31 percent as a national average (10), but this figure varies considerably from state to state and from city to city.

An indication of the relative importance of the four major sources of funding is given by Table 15-2. Section 3 has clearly provided the bulk of federal assistance for public transportation over the past twelve years. However, this mix is changing rapidly. Authorizations for Section 5 under the 1978 act exceed those for Section 3 ($1,515 million versus $1,375 million), the reverse of the expenditure situation hitherto. Also, the 1978 Federal Public Transportation Act requires that all other sources of funds be utilized prior to the use of Section 3 monies for bus transit, the relevant mode for the great majority of cities. Consequently, in the future the majority of funds will be distributed under formula apportionments rather than as discretionary, grant-in-aid programs.

SPATIAL ASPECTS OF HIGHWAY FUNDING LEGISLATION

The modern era of federal assistance for highways began with the Post Office Appropriations Act of 1912 which appropriated $500,000 for states to improve roads used for postal deliveries (11). The principles which are still used today for federal assistance to highways were established in the Federal Aid Road Act of 1916 and the Federal Highway Act of 1921. The four principles are (a) state or local government ownership, construction, and maintenance of highways, (b) federal government payment of a percentage of construction costs only, (c) apportionment of funds by formula, and (d) restriction of assistance to a designated system of highways known as the federal aid system. Critical legislative acts since that time were the Federal Aid Highway Acts of 1944 (the first to make urban roads formally eligible for federal assistance), of 1956 (which funded the Interstate Highway System and established the Highway Trust Fund), and of 1973 (which realigned the federal aid highway system along functional lines). The Federal Aid Highway Act of 1978, a part of the omnibus Surface Transportation Assistance Act, made the most recent changes, the most significant of which permitted federal funds to be used for certain maintenance purposes. Currently, there are four major categories of federal assistance--the interstate, primary, secondary, and urban system programs--as well as a miscellaneous group (12).

The <u>interstate highway system</u> consists of 42,500 miles of limited access highways linking major cities nationwide. Since the system was first designated (primarily under the provisions of the 1956 Federal Aid Highway Act, although its earliest origins go back to the 1944 act), the federal government has paid 90 percent of its construction costs with funds being apportioned to states essentially on the basis of the ratio which the costs of completing the system in a particular state bears to the estimated costs of completing the system nationwide. In essence, the federal government pays states to build the interstate system.

The federal aid <u>primary system</u> consists of the more important main roads including "urban extensions" into and through urban areas. It was established in 1921, with urban extensions being added in 1944, although for apportionment purposes these were treated as part of a separate "urban

TABLE 15-2. Federal Expenditures on Assistance to Public Transportation, FY 1965 through FY 1976.

Bundesausgaben für finanzielle Unterstützung an den öffentlichen Transport 1965 bis 1976.

	Grants (in $000,000) 1965-1976	% of Total
Section 3 (grants-in-aid for capital improvement)	6,950	74%
Section 5 - Capital (formula grants for capital improvement)	81	1%
Section 5 - Operating (formula grants for operating assistance)	1,126	12%
Urban System (capital improvements)	116	1%
Interstate Transfers (capital improvements)	1,062	11%
Section 16 (b) 2 (elderly and handicapped)	32	<1%
TOTAL	9,367	100%

Note: Section 5 monies began in FY 1975.
Urban System and Interstate Transfer grants began in FY 1974. Data are through FY 1977.
Section 16 (b) 2 began in FY 1975.
Interstate Transfer monies have been used by: Philadelphia, Boston, and Washington.
Urban System monies have been used by: New York, Los Angeles, Chicago, San Francisco, St. Louis, Minneapolis, Houston, Cincinnati, Buffalo, and Portland.

DISTRIBUTION OF TRANSPORTATION DOLLAR 453

Comparisons:

1. 7,616 million trips were made by transit in 1977. Federal grants over the period 1965-1977 represent an investment of:

    $1.23 per trip

2. Over the period 1956-1977 total federal aid highway expenditures (for the Inter-state and ABCD Systems) amounted to $88.1 billion. In 1969, 163 billion person trips were made in private motor vehicles. Federal expenditures amount to:

    $0.54 per trip

Sources:

Urban Mass Transportation Administration, UMTA Capital Grants, FY 1977 (Washington, D.C.: U.S. Department of Transportation, undated mimeo).

American Public Transit Association, '77-78 Transit Fact Book (Washington, D.C., 1978), p. 26.

Motor Vehicle Manufacturers Association, Motor Vehicle Facts and Figures '77 (Detroit, 1978), p. 48.

U.S. Department of Transportation, News Release, March 6, 1978.

extension" system until 1973. The secondary system, consisting of major collector highways in rural areas, was established in 1944. Urban extensions were added in 1954, but these were placed under the urban system program by legislation in 1973. The federal aid urban system, estab- in 1970, comprises major roads providing intraurban movement as distinct from urban extensions of the primary system which are oriented toward interurban flows (13). Apportionments for these systems are very different from those for interstates, being based upon a combination of land area, population, and highway mileage measures. The details of the formula are given in Table 15-3. Most striking is the fact that, except for relatively minor changes, the formulas in use today were established as early as 1916. This suggests that models which attempt to explain the spatial distribution of federal funds in terms of current political processes at the national level are likely to have little success in the highway transportation area (14).

There are also a series of other programs, both within the Department of Transportation and in other agencies of the federal government, which provide assistance for highways. They vary greatly in nature, with some being apportioned on a formula basis and others being discretionary. Although these have tended to proliferate in recent years, it is expansion in the basic federal aid programs which accounts for the marked increases in federal highway assistance over time (Figure 15-2). However, mass transit assistance (Figure 15-1) is rapidly catching up with highway aid, and the latter is decreasing in real dollar terms. Finally, as with mass transit, federal assistance is not the only source of government aid. In fact, in fiscal year 1976 total government spending for highways nationwide (exclud-

DISTRIBUTION OF TRANSPORTATION DOLLAR

ing police and safety) was $26.6 billion, of which the federal government provided $6.5 billion, which is only 24 percent (15).

Until 1956 funding for highways came from general federal revenues. However, the Federal Aid Highway Act of that year established a Highway Trust Fund which receives most federal taxes imposed on highway users, and in turn is the source of all funds for the interstate, primary, secondary, and urban systems. Other highway programs draw variously from this fund and from the general revenue fund. Initially dedicated to highways alone, beginning in 1970, some limited use of these monies for mass transit purposes was permitted. Although this use has been broadened somewhat since that time, it remains limited (16). The source of receipt by the Highway Trust Fund has its own spatial distribution which is independent of, and often quite different from, the spatial pattern of apportionments or expenditures from the fund (see below).

THE SPATIAL DISTRIBUTION OF FEDERAL TRANSIT ASSISTANCE: CITY-TO-CITY VARIATION

The above overview of transit and highway assistance programs shows that most fall into "formula-influenced" or "discretionary" categories. In these types of programs legislative provisions, such as apportionment formulas, place ceilings on the maximum amount of federal funds a state or local government can receive but do not necessarily determine the actual amount. This raises the question of the extent to which state or local governments expend up to their legislatively established ceilings, and hence the degree to which legislative provisions determine actual expenditure patterns. This section, and the one which

TABLE 15-3. Summary of U.S. Federal Aid to Highways.
Kurzfassung der U.S. Bundeshilfe für den Fernstrassenbau.

Program	Apportionment Bases to States
Interstate construction	Ratio of the estimated cost of completing interstate system in each state to the estimated cost of completing the whole system.
Interstate Resurfacing, Restoration and Rehabilitation (3R)	75% of funds on the ratio of the number of lane miles in a state to total lane miles nationwide. 25% of funds on the ratio of vehicle miles on interstates in a state to total vehicle miles on interstates nationwide.
Primary System (including extensions into urban areas)	2/3rds of funds as follows: 1/3 on the ratio of state population to total U.S. population. 1/3 on the ratio of state land to total U.S. land area. 1/3 on the ratio of motor vehicle mail route miles in state to the total for U.S. (prior to 1973 all funds were distributed on the above basis). 1/3 of funds according to ratio of urban population in state to U.S. urban population, with no state to receive less than 1/2% of each years apportionment.
Secondary System (rural areas)	Same as the 2/3 portion of the Primary System, except that rural population used as a factor instead of total population.
Urban System (now includes extensions of secondary system into urban areas)	Ratio of the population in urbanized areas (over 50,000 population) in a state to the total U.S. urbanized population.
Extensions of Primary and Secondary System into Urban Areas (not used since July 1, 1976)	Ratio of population in places over 5,000 to total of this for the U.S.
Other DOT highway programs	Various
TOTAL	

Note: Total authorization for public transportation for 1979 was $3,175 million.

Source: Title 23, United States Code, <u>Highways</u>, 1976 and Federal Highway Administration, <u>The Surface Transportation Assistance Act of 1978</u>. Washington, D.C.: U.S. DOT.

DISTRIBUTION OF TRANSPORTATION DOLLAR

Federal Share	Federal-Aid Highway Act Creating Program	Authorizations For FY1979 $ millions	%
90%	1944 1956		
		3,550	47%
75% (90% 1976-1978)	1976 1978		
75% (1978 Act)	1916 1921	1,550	21%
70% (1970 Act)	Urban Extension 1944		
50% (1916 Act)			
See Primary	1944	500	7%
See Primary	1970	800	11%
See Primary	primary 1944 Secondary 1954 Transferred 1973		
Various	Various	1,078	14%
		7,478	100%

follows, examines these questions for mass transit and highway funding respectively, and explores the impact of the federal assistance received on regional development.

Figures 15-2 and 15-3 show capital assistance received over the entire span of the urban mass transportation assistance program from FY 1972 through FY 1976 (FY 1977 for Interstate Transfer and Urban System monies) for the four major federal assistance programs (Section 3, Section 5, Interstate Transfer, and Urban System) for the forty-nine largest urbanized areas in the U.S. Data are given for expenditures per capita of the 1970 population and per unlinked passenger trip in 1972 (17). Clearly, there is substantial variation from city to city in per capita or per trip expenditures, some of which can be explained by the three categories into which the cities have been classified.

"New rail" cities were without significant rail transit prior to the 1960s but have completed, or are advanced in the development of, such systems at present. Per capita or per trip expenditures are substantially higher here than for cities in other categories except for a few cases discussed below. This is a simple reflection of the very high fixed costs involved in rail transit. "Old rail" cities had some form of rail transit (commuter rail, heavy rail, or light rail) in existence prior to the 1960s which continues to operate today. Most noticeable for these cities is the high level of federal investment on a per capita basis (Figure 15-3), contrasting with the relatively moderate level on a per trip basis (Figure 15-4). Despite the high fixed costs involved in rail transit these cities have received fewer funds per trip than many of the bus transit dependent cities in the "no rail" category--a point which has not been ignored by critics of the federal subsidy program, especially those from "old rail" cities (18). Boston is the stand-out case in this group with high subsidies on both a per capita and a per trip basis.

By far the largest number of cities are in the "no rail" category, depending exclusively upon buses for their public transportation. However, even within this category the extent to which cities have received federal assistance is extremely varied. Of particular note are the twelve cities which have received above-average sums on both a per capita and a per trip basis: St. Louis, Minneapolis, Dallas, Seattle, Cincinnati, Kansas City, Denver, Portland, Dayton, Sacramento, Omaha, and Toledo. Of these, Seattle and Portland stand out. However, no immediate explanatory pattern appears to emerge. The list of cities with above-average expenditures contains both large and small urbanized areas within the spectrum of city size which is represented; it contains newer, low-density cities of the Southwest and West, as well as older, higher density cities of the Midwest; it contains cities where regional transit authorities exist (such as Denver), and those where they do not (Dallas); cities substantially similar in many respects (such as Dallas and Houston) are not on the list.

While differentiating between new-rail, old-rail, and no-rail cities explains some of the grossest variability between cities in federal assistance for mass transit, it is far from a complete explanation. We might ask why the new-rail category contains the cities it does, why there is almost as much variability within the no-rail category as between it and the rail category, and why cities such as Boston, Portland, and Seattle have received so much more funding than other cities in their categories. It is certainly apparent that legislative provisions regarding the spatial allocation of funds do not provide the answer to these questions. Except for New York, no state even approaches the 12.5 percent expenditure limit in force for most of the period covered by the data. Differential responses to the federal assistance programs by recipient governments, rather than federally mandated distribution provisions, appears to be the major factor underlying the spatial distribution of mass transit assistance. However, in the future, as funding increasingly comes under the Section 5 formula program rather than the Section 3 discretionary program, which provided most of the monies covered by this data, this variability between cities may be reduced.

The marked variability between cities in their receipt of mass transit aid suggests a potential for differential impact on regional development. Will cities which stand out in terms of federal transit aid, such as Atlanta, Portland, and Seattle, substantially benefit in terms of social and economic development? Will they retain more viable downtowns, will inner-city unemployment be reduced, will erosion of central-city population, jobs, and income to the suburbs be ameliorated, will they attract industry from other, automobile-choked cities (19)? A definitive answer will only be possible in the long run. In the short run Briggs has shown that federal assistance has impacted mass transit ridership, although in a very limited way (20). It certainly could be argued that even heavy investment in mass transit will provide relatively few trips in comparison to the automobile, thus major impacts on regional development are unlikely.

THE SPATIAL DISTRIBUTION OF FEDERAL HIGHWAY ASSISTANCE: STATE-TO-STATE VARIATION

The primary feature in the spatial distribution of highway aid is the redistribution of funds from the more populous to the less populous regions of the nation. If the dollars apportioned to a state for each dollar the state's residents contribute to the Highway Trust Fund are examined, there is a spatial redistribution of funds from the more populous Eastern and Central states to the less populous West and Mountain states (Figure 15-5). The same pattern emerges for expenditures per capita of the population (Figure 15-6). An argument to support this redistribution is that highways, particularly interstates, passing through the West link the more populous Pacific and Eastern portions of the nation, thus these areas should contribute financially. However, essentially the same redistributive pattern emerges if interstate funds are excluded (Figure 15-7). Federal highway policy is clearly oriented toward aiding lower density regions. However, this conclusion should be viewed in light of Figure 15-8. Federal aid per mile of highway is still less in the West than the East, despite the higher level of funding on a per capita basis. Also, in terms of trends, increases in urban highway programs have resulted in a far faster growth of federal assistance in the East compared to the West. This is apparent in Figure 15-9, which maps the ratio of federal highway expenditures in 1975 to expenditures in 1957.

To what extent have these expenditure patterns been determined by legislative apportionments as opposed to actions by recipient governments, as was the case for mass transit aid? For the most part, states have spent federal highway funds exactly as apportioned (Figure 15-10). Although interstate highway funds were distributed essentially on a cost reimbursement basis, funds for the primary, secondary, and urban systems were formula-based. The formula used is deceptively simple, essentially apportioning funds one-third on the basis of land area, one-third on the basis of population, and one-third on the basis of postal route mileage. However, it is not easy to assess its appropriateness, which is perhaps the reason it has remained virtually unchanged throughout this century. Obviously, population, land area, and postal route mileage have some relationship to highway needs, but, as the formula implies, is this relationship linear and should each of the three factors be given equal weight? There is virtually no research to answer this question. Also, the formula takes no account of the fiscal capabilities of each state, nor does it make allowances for climatic and topographic differences which clearly effect highway construction and maintenance costs. Thus, while legislative apportionments have determined highway expenditure patterns, questions can be raised concerning the appropriateness of the apportionment formulas themselves.

What are the implications of the spatial patterning of highway aid for regional development? Although federal aid has redistributed highway transportation dollars, variability in aid between recipient regions is less than for mass transit aid. Consequently, the potential impact on regional development is perhaps less. However, without the redistributive effect of federal aid, the highway system of the West would be considerably less developed than it is, which might have reduced the degree of population and economic development currently occurring there. Even more interesting is the possible effect of the interstate highway system, essentially a federal project, on current regional development trends. To what extent has this sytem, by linking the "periphery" of the U.S.--the West, Southwest, and South--to the traditional industrial "heartland" of the Midwest and Northeast (21), contributed to the current resurgence of the periphery (22)? Certainly, it is only part of a cluster of changes, but the availability of high quality linkages must have aided the growing interdependency between the heartland and the periphery. A related question is the impact of the interstate system on growth rates in nonmetropolitan regions which now exceed, for the first time ever, growth rates in metropolitan areas (23). Since the trend is not unique to the U.S. (24), freeway development cannot be the sole explanation, but some effect would be expected. Unfortunately, the few studies which address this question do not permit a definitive answer.

For example, studies by the Federal Highway Administration (25) show that nonmetropolitan counties with freeways experience higher population growth rates than those without. However, Humphrey and Sell and Fuguitt and Beale show that these places were experiencing faster growth before freeways were constructed (26). Controlling for pre-freeway growth rates, a later FHWA study confirmed their own earlier findings and concluded that (27):

> While the differences (in growth rates) are not necessarily caused by freeways, it should be noted that the chance of these nonmetropolitan counties being crossed by freeways occurs almost randomly, since the Interstate System was located primarily to connect metropolitan areas.

However, Hansen points out that counties bordering SMSAs have a higher chance of being crossed by a freeway since freeways focus on metropolitan centers (28). In his study of counties in six regions of the U.S., he concludes it is adjacency to SMSAs which accounts for the higher growth rates of freeway counties. Wheat, in a study of 106 city pairs (freeway-located cities matched by similar nonfreeway-located cities), concludes that freeway cities grew faster, but only in areas where traffic flow along regular highways is seriously impaired (29). Bohm and Patterson conclude that interstate location appears to be of some significance, especially in regions where past highway investment has lagged (30). Research to provide more definitive answers to these questions is currently underway (31).

CONCLUSION

This essay has examined the spatial distribution of federal transportation funds as a potential force in regional development. It has shown that there are legislative provisions which can spatially direct federal funds. In the case of mass transit aid, these provisions have had little impact on the spatial pattern of federal aid, and there is great variability from city to city in the amount of federal aid received. This suggests considerable potential for differential development, but it is not possible at this time to ascertain actual impacts. In the case of highway aid, legislative provisions have had a clear effect on the spatial distribution of funds. The funding pattern appears to have affected regional development, at least as a part of a cluster of change at an aggregate level, although the exact nature of this impact is not definitive at present.

DISTRIBUTION OF TRANSPORTATION DOLLAR 465

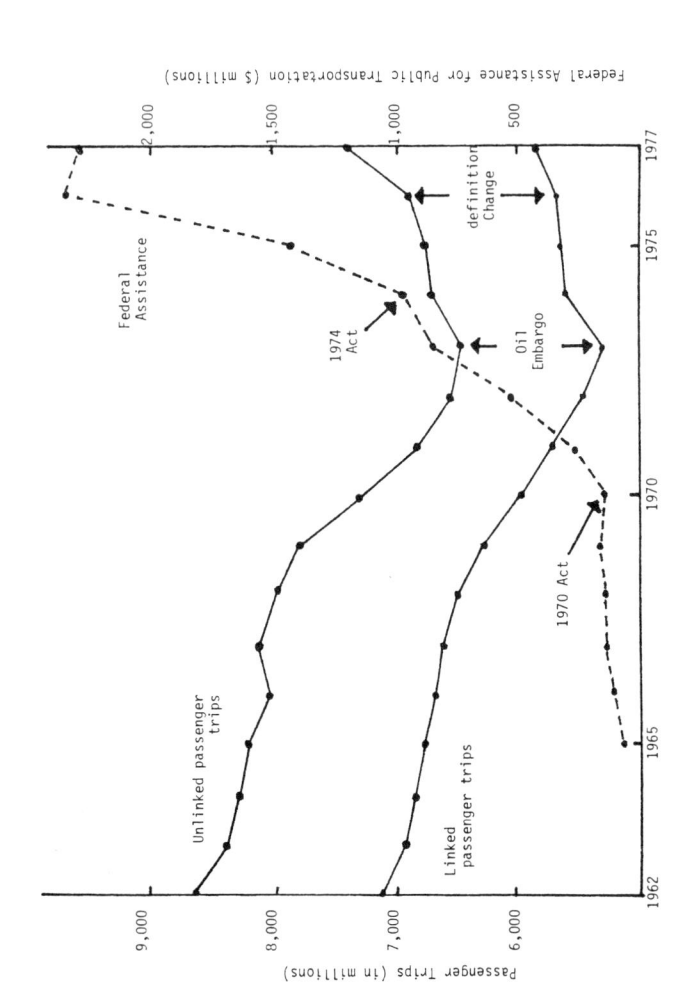

FIG. 15-1. Trends in Federal Assistance for Public Transportation and Passenger Trips by Public Transportation (1962-1977).
Trends der Bundeshilfe für öffentliche Verkehrsmittel (1962-1977).

Source: American Public Transit Association, Transit Fact Book, '78, Washington, D.C.: Tables 8, 9 and 19; and, Urban Mass Transportation Administration. UMTA Capital Grants, FY1977 (Washington, D.C., U.S. Department of Transportation, undated mimeo) for Urban System and Interstate Transfer monies.

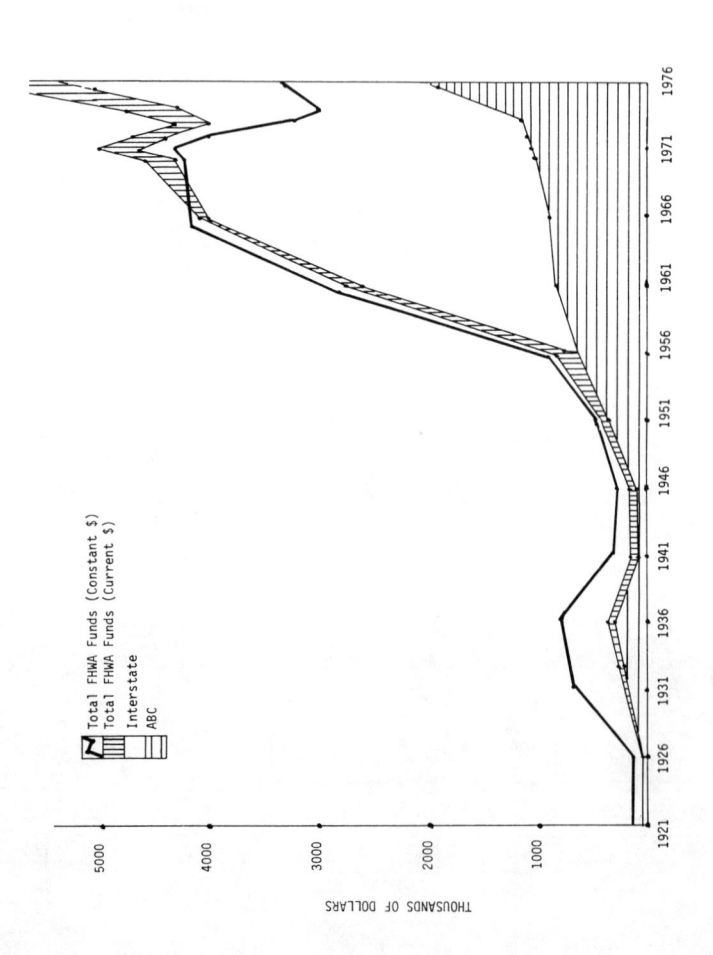

FIG. 15-2. Trends in Federal Assistance for Highways: Payments to States by Federal Highway Administration, 1921-1975.
Trends der Bundeshilfe für Bundes-Fernstrassen: Zahlungen an die Bundesstaaten durch die Bundesfernstrassen Verwaltung, 1921-1975.
Source: Federal Highway Administration, Highway Statistics: Summary to 1975. Washington, D.C.: U.S. Government Printing Office, 1976, Table FA 205, p. 155.

DISTRIBUTION OF TRANSPORTATION DOLLAR 467

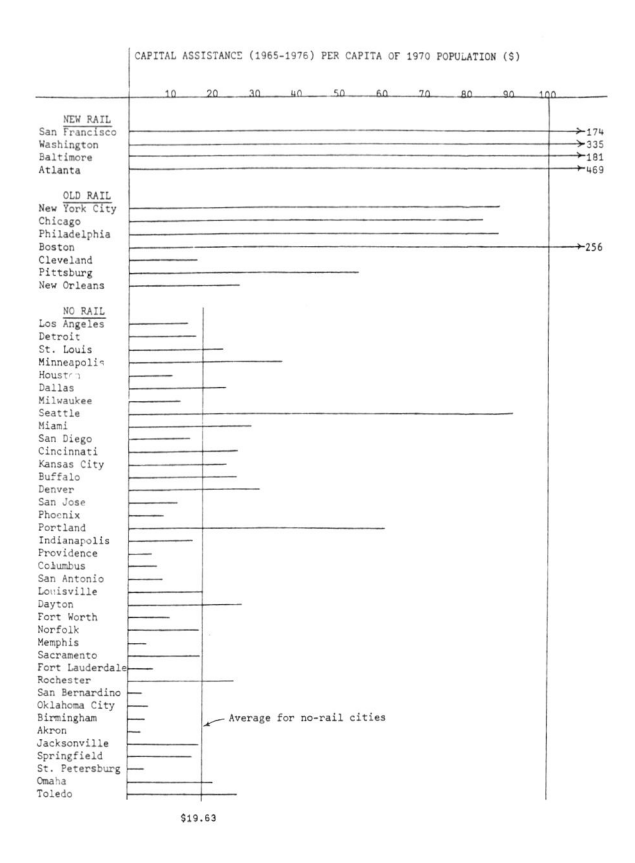

```
CAPITAL ASSISTANCE (1965-1976) PER CAPITA OF 1970 POPULATION ($)
           10    20    30    40    50    60    70    80    90   100
NEW RAIL
San Francisco                                              →174
Washington                                                 →335
Baltimore                                                  →181
Atlanta                                                    →469

OLD RAIL
New York City
Chicago
Philadelphia
Boston                                                     →256
Cleveland
Pittsburg
New Orleans

NO RAIL
Los Angeles
Detroit
St. Louis
Minneapolis
Houston
Dallas
Milwaukee
Seattle
Miami
San Diego
Cincinnati
Kansas City
Buffalo
Denver
San Jose
Phoenix
Portland
Indianapolis
Providence
Columbus
San Antonio
Louisville
Dayton
Fort Worth
Norfolk
Memphis
Sacramento
Fort Lauderdale
Rochester
San Bernardino
Oklahoma City
Birmingham      ← Average for no-rail cities
Akron
Jacksonville
Springfield
St. Petersburg
Omaha
Toledo
             $19.63
```

FIG. 15-3. Variation Between the 49 Largest U.S. Urbanized Areas in the Receipt of Federal Assistance for Local Public Transportation (1965-1976/77): Per Capita of Their 1970 Population.
   Veränderungen zwischen den 49 grössten urbanisierten Räumen in dem Empfang der Bundeshilfe für den Nahverkehr (1965-1976/77): Pro Kopf der Bevölkerung von 1970.

Source: Urban Mass Transportation Administration, Statistical Summary (Washington, D.C.: UMTA Office of Public Affairs, 1977); Urban Mass Transportation Administration, UMTA Capital Grants FY1977 (Washington, D.C.: U.S. Department of Transportation, undated mimeo); U.S. Department of Transportation, 1974 National Transportation Report, Urban Data Supplement (Washington, D.C.: U.S. Department of Transportation, 1976), Table D-23 for passenger trips.

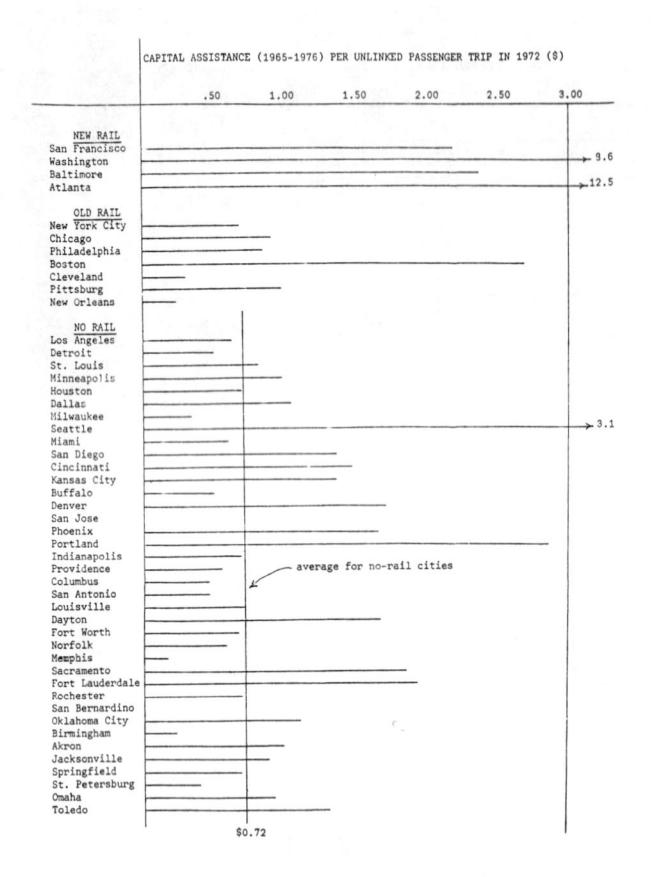

```
CAPITAL ASSISTANCE (1965-1976) PER UNLINKED PASSENGER TRIP IN 1972 ($)

                    .50      1.00     1.50      2.00     2.50     3.00

NEW RAIL
San Francisco
Washington                                                          → 9.6
Baltimore
Atlanta                                                             → 12.5

OLD RAIL
New York City
Chicago
Philadelphia
Boston
Cleveland
Pittsburg
New Orleans

NO RAIL
Los Angeles
Detroit
St. Louis
Minneapolis
Houston
Dallas
Milwaukee                                                           → 3.1
Seattle
Miami
San Diego
Cincinnati
Kansas City
Buffalo
Denver
San Jose
Phoenix
Portland
Indianapolis
Providence              ← average for no-rail cities
Columbus
San Antonio
Louisville
Dayton
Fort Worth
Norfolk
Memphis
Sacramento
Fort Lauderdale
Rochester
San Bernardino
Oklahoma City
Birmingham
Akron
Jacksonville
Springfield
St. Petersburg
Omaha
Toledo
                   $0.72
```

FIG. 15-4. Variation Between the 49 Largest U.S. Urbanized Areas in the Receipt of Federal Assistance for Local Public Transportation (1965-1976/77): Per Unlinked Passenger Trip in 1972.

       Veränderungen zwischen den 49 grössten urbanisierten Räumen in dem Empfang der Bundeshilfe für den Nahverkehr (1965-1976/77): Pro "unlinked" Passagier Reise in 1972.

Source: Urban Mass Transportation Administration, <u>Statistical Summary</u> (Washington, D.C.: UMTA Office of Public Affairs, 1977); Urban Mass Transportation Administration, <u>UMTA Capital Grants FY1977</u> (Washington, D.C.: U.S. Department of Transportation, undated mimeo); U.S. Department of Transportation, <u>1974 National Transportation Report, Urban Data Supplement</u> (Washington, D.C.: U.S. Department of Transportation, 1976), Table D-23 for passenger trips.

DISTRIBUTION OF TRANSPORTATION DOLLAR 469

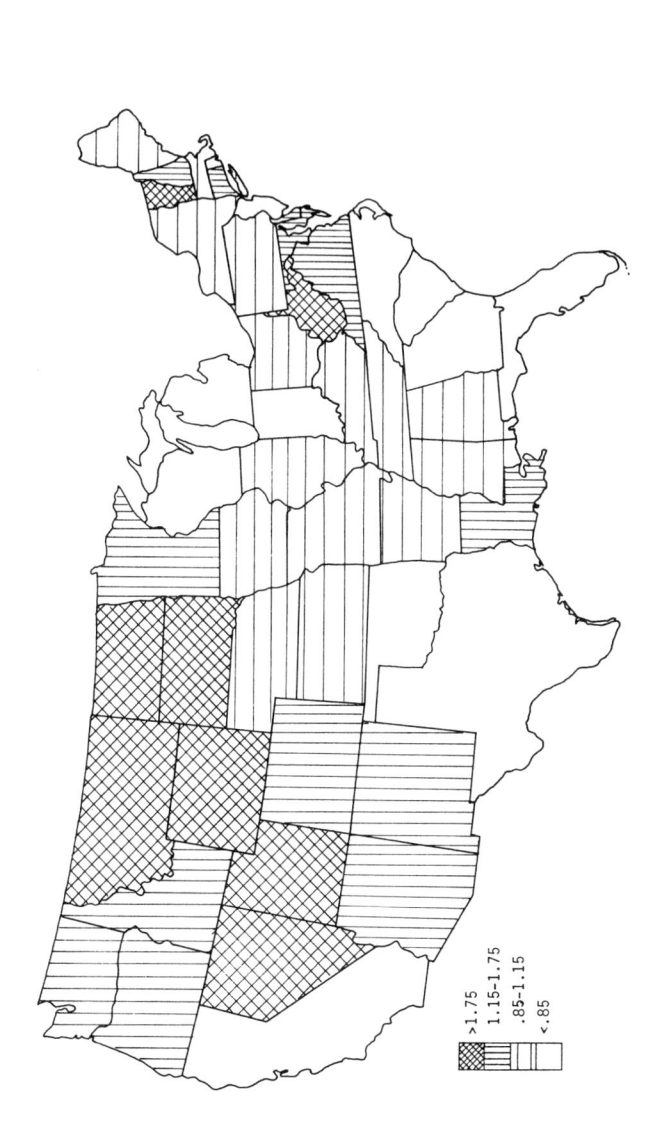

FIG. 15-5. Ratio of State Apportionments from the Highway Trust Fund to Estimated State Payments into the Highway Trust Fund, Fiscal Year 1957-1976.
Ratio der Bundeszuteilung vom Fernstrassen Trust Fund zu den schätzungsweisen Landeszahlungen in den Fernstrassen Trust Fund, Fiskal Jahr 1957-1976.

Source: Federal Highway Administration, Highway Statistics, Summary, to 1975 Washington, D.C.: Government Printing Office, 1976, Table FE 221, p. 98.

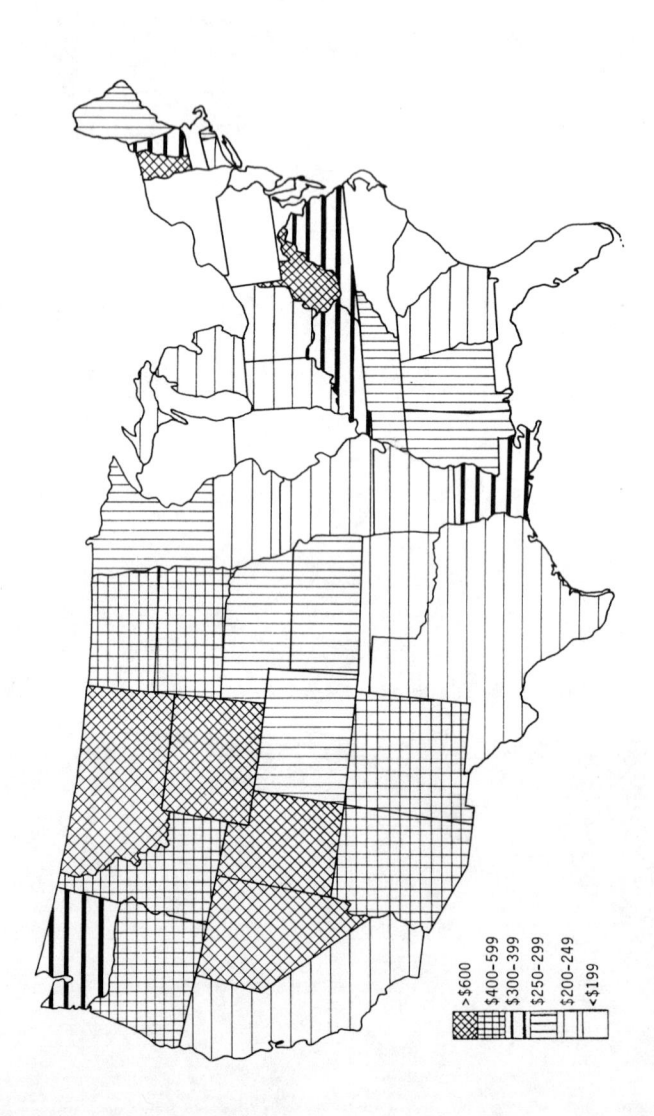

FIG. 15-6. Federal Highway Expenditures 1965-1975: Per Capita of State Population (1970). Ausgaben für die Bundesfernstrassen 1965-1975: Pro Kopf der Bundesstaatlichen Bevölkerung (1970).

Source: Clifford W. Woodward, Trends in Federal Domestic Transportation Programs, Revenues and Expenditures, Washington, D.C.: U.S. Department of Transportation, 1978, Appendix.

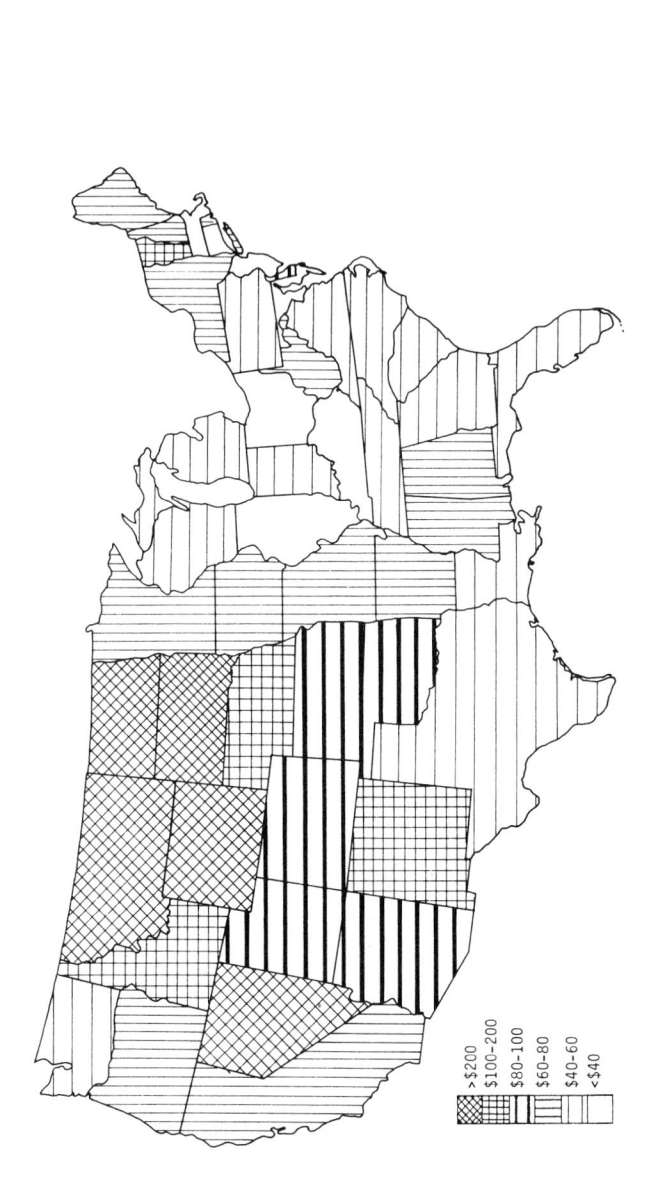

FIG. 15-7. Federal Expenditures for Primary, Secondary, Urban Extension and Urban (ABCD) Highway System 1965-1975: Per Capita of State Population (1970). Bundesausgaben vom primär, sekundär städtischer Erweiterung und innerstädtischen Strassensystem (ABCD) 1965-1975: Pro Kopf der Bundesstaatlichen Bevölkerung (1970).

Source: Clifford W. Woodward, Trends in Federal Domestic Transportation Programs, Revenues and Expenditures, Washington, D.C.: U.S. Department of Transportation, 1978, Appendix.

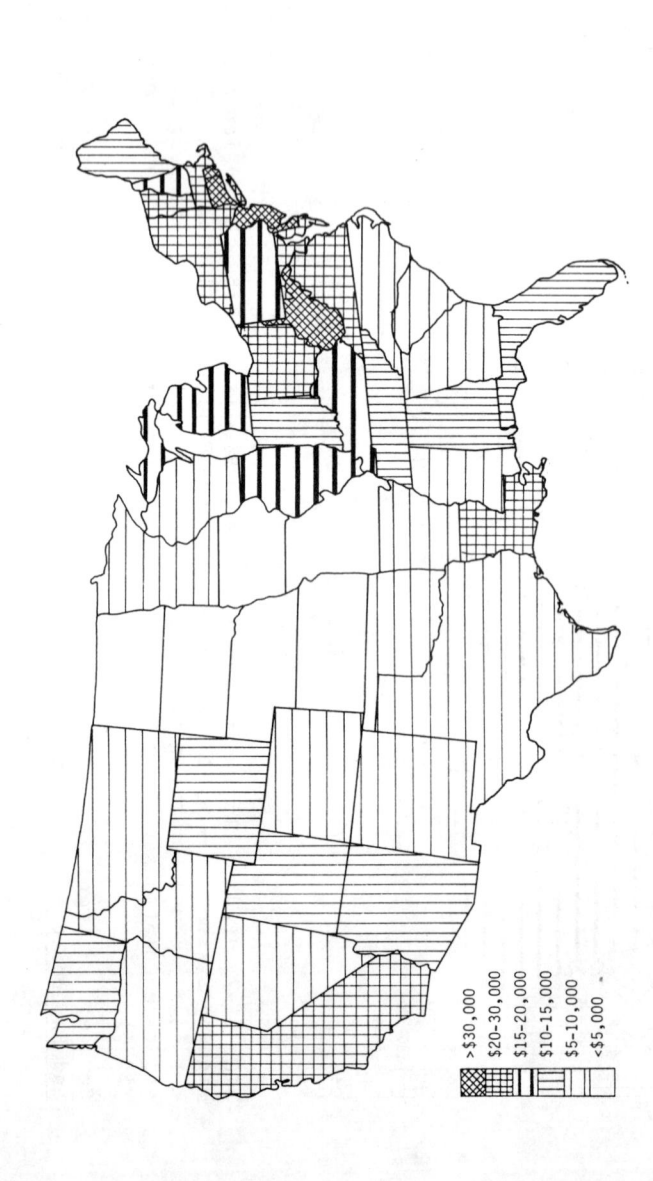

FIG 15-8. Federal Highway Expenditures 1965-1975, per Mile of Highway 1977. Bundesfernstrassen Ausgaben 1965-1975, pro Meile von Bundesstrassen 1977.

Source: Expenditure data, see Fig. 15-6; highway mileage: Federal Highway Administration, Highway Statistics, 1977, Washington, D.C.: U.S. Government Printing Office, 1978, Table M-12, p. 237.

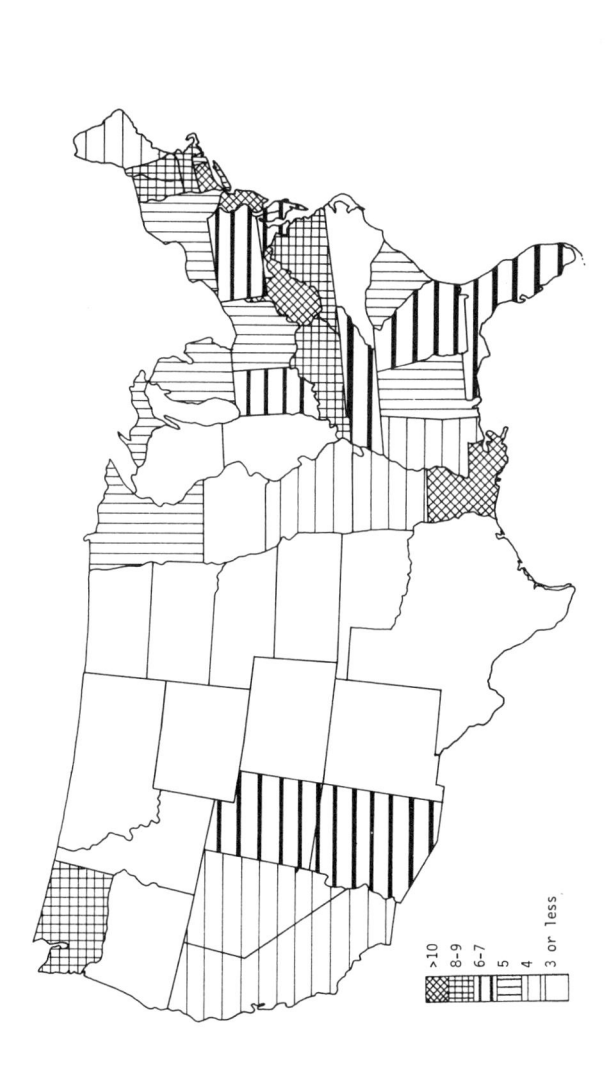

FIG. 15-9. Federal Highway Expenditures in Fiscal Year 1975 as a Ratio of Expenditures in Fiscal Year 1957.
Bundesfernstrassen Ausgaben im Fiskal Jahr 1975 als Ratio der Ausgaben im Fiskal Jahr 1957.

Source: Clifford W. Woodward, Trends in Federal Domestic Transportation Programs, Revenues and Expenditures, Washington, D.C.: U.S. Department of Transportation, 1978, Appendix.

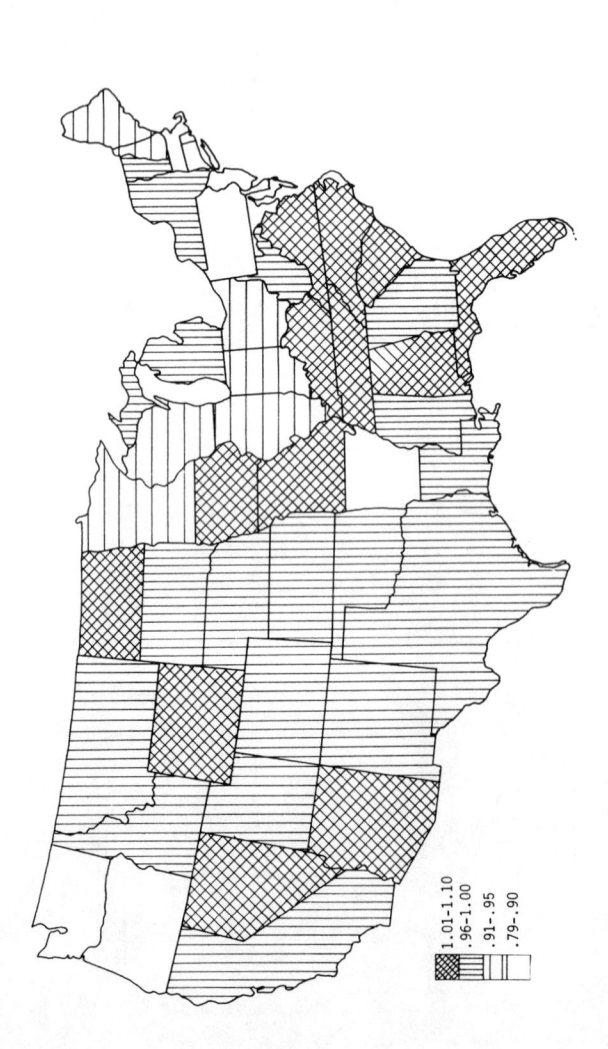

FIG. 15-10. Federal Highway Funds Committed to Interstate and ABCD Systems July 1, 1956, to December 31, 1977, as a Ratio of Apportionments from Highway Trust Fund, July 1, 1956, to August 21, 1977.
  Gesetzliche Verpflichtung der Bundesfernstrassen für zwischenstaatliche und ABCD Systems 1. Juli, 1956 bis 31 Dezember, 1977 als Ratio der Zuteilung vom Fernstrassen Trust Fund 1. Juli, 1956 bis 31. August 1977.

Source: Funds committed: U.S. Department of Transportation, News Release, March 6, 1978; Apportionments: Federal Highway Administration, Highway Statistics 1977, Washington, D.C.: U.S. Government Printing Office, 1978, Table FE-221, p. 42.

NOTES

1. Briggs, R., "The Impact of Federal Local Public Transportation Assistance Upon Travel Behavior," The Professional Geographer, Vol. 32, August 1980, pp. 316-25.

2. Comptroller General of the United States, Terms Used in the Budgetary Process (Washington, D.C.: U.S. General Accounting Office, 1977); Felrice, B., Financing Federal-Aid Highways--An Amplification (Washington, D.C., Federal Highway Administration, Highway Planning Technical Report No. 37, 1974).

3. For a more traditional, political-science approach to classifying grant-in-aid programs, see: Advisory Commission on Intergovernmental Relations, Improving Urban America: A Challenge to Federalism, Report No. M107 (Washington, D.C., 1976), pp. 83-86.

4. Smerk, G. M. Urban Mass Transportation: A Dozen Years of Federal Policy (Bloomington, Ind.: Indiana University Press, 1974).

5. This legislation, as amended through February 6, 1976, is usefully contained in: Urban Mass Transportation Administration, Urban Mass Transportation Assistance Act of 1964 and Related Laws as Amended Through February 6, 1976 (Washington, D.C.: U.S. Government Printing Office, 1976). All information in this section is from this source or from the public laws themselves, unless otherwise noted.

6. Figure for 1972. In this paper, all data on mass transit ridership levels in individual cities are from: U.S. Department of Transportation 1974 National Transportation Report: Urban Data Supplement (Washington, D.C.: U.S. Government Printing Office, 1976).

7. Federal Register, Vol. 40, January 13, 1975, Part I, p. 2545.

8. This is only a temporary expedient for fiscal years 1979 and 1980 awaiting the results of a study, called for by the act, of the most appropriate way of allocating bus transit monies.

9. Comptroller General of the United States, Hindrances to Coordinating Transportation of People Participating in Federally Funded Grant Programs (Washington, D.C.: U.S. General Accounting Office, 1977).

10. American Public Transit Association, '77-78 Transit Fact Book (Washington, D.C., 1978), p. 19.
11. Federal Highway Administration, America's Highways, 1776-1976: A History of the Federal Aid Program (Washington, D.C.: U.S. Government Printing Office, 1976).
12. The legislation with respect to highways is found in Title 23, United States Code. Useful summaries exist in the various chapter introductions in the annual publication Highway Statistics produced by the Federal Highway Administration. See also the reference in note 11 for a general history. The discussion in this section is drawn from these sources.
13. The primary, secondary, urban extension, and urban systems are often referred to as the ABCD system. Since the 1973 Federal Aid Highway Act, the urban extension portion of the primary system has been treated as part of the primary system, and the urban extension of the secondary system as been merged with the urban system. Consequently, there is no longer a separate "urban extension" system.
14. See, for example, Johnston, R. J., "The Allocation of Federal Money in the United States: Aggregate Analysis by Correlation," Policy and Politics 6 (1978), 279-297; Johnston, R. J., "Political Spending in the United States: analysis of political influences on the allocation of federal money to local environments," Environment and Planning A, Vol. 10 (1978), pp. 691-704.
15. Federal Highway Administration, Highway Statistics, 1977 and 1976 (Washington, D.C.: U.S. Government Printing Office), Tables HF-2 and FA-3, p. 120 and p. 52, respectively.
16. Smerk, G. M., "Update on Federal Mass Transportation Policy: The Surface Transportation Act of 1978," Transportation Journal 18 (1979), pp. 16-35.
17. San Juan, Puerto Rico, is excluded because of its cultural divergence from the continental United States. The U.S. Bureau of the Census' definition of the urbanized area in 1970 is used except for the data for unlinked passenger trips. This covers urbanized areas as they are expected to

exist in 1990 (U.S. Department of Transportation, 1976), and accounts for the absence of figures on expenditures per trip for San Jose and San Bernardino which, presumably, are incorporated in the San Francisco and Los Angeles areas. However, no compensating adjustments in the other variables have been made. The smallest place in the data set, the Toledo urbanized area, had a population of 487,789 in 1970.

18. Hilton, George W., Federal Transit Subsidies: The Urban Mass Transportation Assistance Program (Washington, D.C.: The America Enterprise Association, "Financing Public Transportation," Regional Plan News No. 98 [1976].

19. All of these have been claimed as benefits following from mass transit improvement. See Brock Adams, "Transportation and Energy; A New Policy for the 1980s," Transportation USA (Spring, 1978), pp. 2-4.

20. Briggs, "Impact of Federal Local Transportation," op. cit., (see note 1).

21. Ward, D., Cities and Immigrants (New York: Oxford University Press, 1971).

22. Weinstein, B. L., and R. E. Firestine, Regional Growth and Decline in the United States: The Rise of the Sunbelt and the Decline of the Northeast (New York: Praeger, 1978).

23. Beale, C. L., "The Recent Shift of United States Population to Nonmetropolitan Areas, 1970-1975," International Regional Science Review 2 (1977), 114-122.

24. Vining, D. R., and T. Kontuly, "Population Dispersal from Major Metropolitan Regions: An International Comparison," International Regional Science Review 3 (1978), 49-74.

25. Federal Highway Administration, Social and Economic Effects of Highways, 1974 and 1972 (Washington, D.C.: U.S. Dept. of Transportation, 1972 and 1974).

26. Humphrey, C. R., and R. R. Sell, "The Impact of Controlled Access Highways on Growth in Pennsylvanie Non-metropolitan Communities," Rural Sociology 40 (1975), 332-351; Fuguitt, G. U., and C. L. Beale, "Population Change in Non-metropolitan

Cities and Towns," Agricultural Economic Report No. 323, U.S. Dept. of Agriculture, 1976.

27. Federal Highway Administration, Social and Economic Effects of Highways, 1976 (Washington, D.C.: U.S. Dept. of Transportation, 1976), p. 75.

28. Hansen, N., The Future of Nonmetropolitan America (Lexington, Mass.: D. C. Heath, 1973), p. 26.

29. Wheat, L. F., "The Effect of Modern Highways on Urban Manufacturing Growth," Highway Research Record No. 277 (1979), pp. 9-24.

30. Bohm, R. A., and D. A. Patterson, "Interstate Highway Location and Country Population Growth," Urban Research Section, Oak Ridge National Laboratory, 1972.

31. Briggs, R., "The Impact of the Interstate Highway System on Nonmetropolitan Development," U.S. Department of Transportation, Office of University Research, Contract No. DOT-RC-92040, 1979-1980.

CHAPTER 16

FEDERAL AIR QUALITY LEGISLATION:
IMPLICATIONS FOR LAND USE

BUNDESGESETZE ZUR LUFTQUALITÄT: AUSWIRKUNGEN
AUF DIE LANDNUTZUNG

Ian R. Manners and Gundars Rudzitis

Abstract

The Clean Air Amendments of 1970 exemplified a trend toward a larger and stronger federal regulatory role with respect to pollution control. The difficulties inherent in such an approach have become apparent as the decade has progressed. Extensive litigation has proved both costly and time-consuming; deadlines and timetables have been repeatedly deferred. New issues, largely unrecognized when the Clean Air Act was signed into law, have arisen as the land use and growth implications of federal air quality regulations have become more clearly defined. Much of the debate has centered around what are by now familiar issues-the impact of clear air regulations on the nation's ability to develop alternative energy sources, the need to reconcile air quality standards with economic growth and regional development priorities. In exploring these issues the essay focuses on the enforcement and implications of the EPA's two most controversial programs-the prevention of significant deterioration of air quality in clean air areas and the emissions offset program for nonattainment areas. Neither program was anticipated in the 1970 Clean Air Amendments; both will have a major impact on patterns of economic growth and regional development.

Kurzfassung

Die 1970 verabschiedeten Ergänzungsgesetze zur Reinhaltung der Luft verdeutlichen den Trend zu einer grösseren und stärkeren Rolle der Bundesregierung in Hinsicht auf die Kontrolle der Umweltverschmutzung. Die in einem solchen Lösungsversuch innewohnenden Schwierigkeiten sind während des Fortganges dieses Jahrzehnts klar geworden. Zahlreiche Einsprüche erwiessen sich als teuer und zeitraubend, Termine

wurden wiederholt verschoben. Neue Probleme, die zur Zeit
der Verabschiedung Luftreinhaltungsgesetzes zum grössten
Teil noch nicht bekannt waren, sind aufgetreten, als die
Landnutzungs-und Entwicklungsauswirkungen der Bundesverordnungen für Luftqualität genau definiert wurden. Die Debatte
hat sich zum grössten Teil auf Probleme konzentriet, die
jetzt vertraut sind, zum Beispiel, die Wirkung der Luftrein-
haltung-Verordnung auf die Fähigkeit der Nation, alternative
Energiequellen zu entwickeln und die Notwendigkeit, den
Luftqualitätsstandard mit dem ökonomischen Wachstum und den
regionalen Entwicklungsprioritäten in Einklang zu bringen.
In der Erforschung dieser Probleme berücksichtigt der Aufsatz
besonders die Durchführung und Auswirkung zwei der strit-
tigsten Programme der ERP (des Ministeriums für Umweltschutz)
--die Verhinderung einer merklichen Verschlechterung der
Luftqualität in Gebieten reiner Luft und das Programm des
Emissionsausgleichs in belasteten Gebieten. Keines der
beiden Programme wurde in den 1970 verabschiedeten Zusatz-
anträgen vorausgesehen, beide werden einer grössere Wirkung
auf die Verteilung der wirtschaftlichen und regionalen
Entwicklung haben.

Federal Air Quality Legislation:
Implications For Land Use

The Clean Air Amendments of 1970 were widely acclaimed as a landmark in environmental legislation. Enacted at a time of intense public concern over environmental quality, the act committed the United States to an ambitious set of goals in the fight for "clean air." In particular, Congress provided for the establishment of ambient air quality standards for six major categories of pollutants-primary standards to protect public health and secondary standards to protect public welfare, including property, soils, biota and visibility (Table 16-1). The stated objective was to attain primary standards throughout the nation by 1975 and the more stringent secondary standards "within a reasonable period of time." In order to achieve these goals, the amendments outlined a pollution control strategy based on performance standards (incorporating the best available control technology) for all major new "stationary" sources such as power plants, smelters, and refineries; stringent emission standards for new "mobile" sources, i.e., automobiles and trucks; strict compliance schedules; and state implementation plans (1). In short, the 1970 Clean Air Amendments exemplified the trend toward a larger and stronger federal regulatory role with respect to pollution control.

A decade of experience has demonstrated many of the difficulties inherent in this approach to pollution control. From the outset, the emission standards, timetables, and regulations proposed by the Environmental Protection Agency (EPA) were subjected to repeated legal challenges by industry, by state and local governments, and by environmental

TABLE 16-1. National Ambient Air Quality Standards for Major Pollutants.[1]
Nationale Qualitätsanforderungen an den wichtigsten Arten der Verunreinigung.

Pollutant	Description	Primary Standard	Secondary Standard
Suspended Particulates	Solid and liquid particles in the atmosphere, including dust, smoke, mists, fumes & spray from many sources	75 ug/m^3, annual geometric mean; 260 ug/m^3, maximum 24-hour average	60 ug/m^3, annual geometric mean; 150 ug/m^3, maximum 24-hour average
Sulfur Dioxide[2]	Heavy pungent, colorless gas formed from combustion of coal, oil, & other	80 ug/m^3 (0.03 ppm), annual arithmetic mean; 365 ug/m^3 (0.14 ppm), maximum 24-hour average	1300 ug/m^3 (0.5 ppm), maximum 3-hour average
Carbon Monoxide	Invisible, odorless gas formed from combustion of gasoline, coal, & other; largest man-made fraction comes from automobiles	10 mg/m^3 (9 ppm), maximum 8-hour average; 40 mg/m^3 (35 ppm), maximum 1-hour average	Same as primary
Hydrocarbons	Reactive HC of olefin group & compounds of aromatic or benzene group, key ingredient in photochemical smog	160 ug/m^3 (0.24 ppm) maximum 3-hour average	
Ozone[3]	Hydrocarbons react with nitrogen oxides in sunlight to form photochemical oxidants including ozone	235 ug/m^3 (0.12 ppm) maximum 1-hour average	
Nitrogen Dioxide[4]	Brown, toxic gas formed from fuel combustion. Under certain conditions, it may be associated with ozone production	100 ug/m^3 (0.005 ppm), annual arithmetic mean	Same as primary

[1]The Clean Air Act Amendments of 1977 require that all health-related primary standards must be reviewed by EPA before December 21, 1980.

[2]The annual secondary sulfur dioxide standard (60 micrograms per cubic meter of 0.02 ppm), and the maximum 24 hour concentration of 260 micrograms per cubic meter (0.1 ppm) published as a guide to be used in assessing state implementation plans to achieve the annual standards, were revoked by the EPA in September, 1973.

[3]The ozone standard replaced the original photochemical oxidant standard of 0.08 ppm as of January 1979.

[4]The Clean Air Act Amendments of 1977 directed the EPA to develop a short-term standard for nitrogen oxides if required to protect public health.

groups. This tendency to rely upon litigation as a means of interpreting and enforcing the Clean Air Act has proved both costly and time-consuming. The failure to achieve the act's major objective (attainment of primary air quality standards) within the specified time period reinforced the view of many critics that too much was being attempted too quickly with too little regard to cost (2). Moreover, as the decade progressed new concerns, largely unrecognized or unanticipated when the 1970 amendments were signed into law, began to surface to further complicate the quest for "clean air." None of these new concerns has proved more pervasive or contentious than the implications of the Clean Air Act for regional development and land use planning.

At a time when "too much government" and "federal regulation" is acceptable political rhetoric, no subject is more volatile than land use regulation. And yet the measures being implemented by the EPA to achieve the goals of the Clean Air Act are forcing local governments and the general public to face up to the issue of land use planning, to recognize the linkages that exist between land use and air quality, and to question whether the Clean Air Act represents a desirable or appropriate instrument for land use planning. In order to explore this issue further, this essay will focus on the nature and implementation of EPA's nondegradation and emission offset regulations, since together these programs will have the most immediate and direct impact on patterns of industrial location and regional development.

CLEAN AIR AND NONATTAINMENT AREAS
The 1970 Clean Air Amendments did not allow for continued industrial growth in any air quality region that failed to

attain primary standards (Figure 16-1). Strictly interpreted, the act would have effectively prohibited both the expansion of existing plants and the location of new industries in nonattainment areas, even where the facilities were able to meet EPA's new source performance standards (NSPS). In order to resolve this problem (and calm political concerns over what was perceived as federal restrictions on regional growth), the EPA instituted a policy of "emissions offsetting" whereby new sources can be located in nonattainment areas provided it can be demonstrated that the contribution to the total pollutant load will be more than offset by reductions elsewhere within the region. EPA's prevention of significant deterioration (PSD) rules represent a complementary program for areas with air that is cleaner than required under secondary standards. By defining significant deterioration in terms of permissible increases in pollutant concentrations, the EPA has attempted to meet environmentalist desires for a minimum amount of air quality degradation without totally prohibiting economic growth in clean air areas.

In view of the controversy that continues to surround these programs it should be noted that both originated in the form of EPA rulemaking and are intended to facilitate and accommodate growth. Neither program was anticipated in the 1970 Clean Air Amendments; only in the 1977 Amendments to the Clean Air Act did they receive a clear and explicit legislative endorsement. In this respect the 1977 Amendments "did not strike out in bold, new directions" (3). Quite the contrary. Although the 1977 Amendments extended the deadlines for attaining national air quality and automobile emission standards, it essentially endorsed existing EPA programs and continued the same fundamental

approach to pollution control outlined in the 1970 Clean
Air Amendments.

THE "NO SIGNIFICANT DETERIORATION" ISSUE

It is eight years since the courts first ruled that the EPA
must protect air quality in clean air areas, yet preventing
significant deterioration (PSD) continues to be a controversial issue. As noted by the Council on Environmental
Quality (4):

> A nondegradation policy is not neutral between
> developed and nondeveloped areas. A literal
> nondegradation policy could severely curtail
> or even prevent growth in areas with clean
> air and require instead that growth be
> accommodated, if at all, in developed areas
> that may already have severe air quality problems.

From the outset, therefore, EPA's PSD regulations have
focused attention on the land use implications on the Clean
Air Act. Any PSD policy, stringently enforced, will not
only affect regional growth patterns and the siting of
major industrial facilities, but will place states in the
role of regulating land use through their air quality
responsibilities.

Sierra Club v. Ruckelshaus

Much of the controversy surrounding the significant deterioration issue (and many of the legal challenges) can be attributed to the origins of the nondegradation program. The
failure of the 1970 Amendments to specify protection for
those regions with air cleaner than required under national
standards was interpreted by some as an invitation to
pollute. In Sierra Club v. Ruckelshaus (5), however, the
U.S. District Court for the D.C. Circuit upheld the plain-

tiff's contention that any state implementation plan permitting the deterioration of air quality in clean air areas up to national standards was contrary to the intent of Congress as expressed in both the language and legislative history of the Clean Air Act. Under the terms of a preliminary injunction issued in May, 1972, the EPA was directed to disapprove any state plan that was deficient in this regard and promulgate its own regulations. This interpretation of the Clean Air Act and of EPA's responsibilities was upheld by the full court, and affirmed on appeal by both the Court of Appeals for the District of Columbia and the Supreme Court, the latter on the basis of a tie vote.

Thus the nondegradation program was actually initiated in response to a court order interpreting congressional intent. Arguably EPA's regulations lacked a statutory basis and involved a substantial element of policy making. EPA's own reluctance to implement any form of nondegradation policy was made clear in the notice of proposed rulemaking published in the Federal Register in July, 1973. In EPA's view, there had been "no definitive judicial resolution of the issue whether the Clean Air Act requires prevention of significant deterioration of air quality" (6). The agency remained convinced that other approaches, particularly the emission controls contained in the new source performance standards, would be more than adequate to prevent significant deterioration and that "it is not within the province of EPA. . . to impose limitations on the Nation's growth" (7). Accordingly, "the Administrator adheres to the view that Section 110 of the Clean Air Act requires EPA to approve State implementation plans that will attain and maintain the national ambient air quality standards and that the Act does not require EPA or the

States to prevent significant deterioration of air quality" (8).

Given the absence of any clearly defined congressional mandate and EPA's reluctant cooperation with the courts, a long and acrimonious debate over the need for and the impact of a PSD policy was inevitable.

The 1974 PSD Regulations

Although the preliminary injunction required the EPA to prepare regulations preventing significant air quality deterioration within six months, nearly two and a half years were to elapse before the EPA, again acting again under a court order, published final PSD regulations. These regulations defined significant deterioration in terms of permitted increases in sulfur dioxide and particulate emissions (Table 16-2). Three categories of clean air areas were defined within which the size of the increment would determine the amount of new growth and the degree of air quality degradation considered significant:

Class I. Areas in which practically any change in air quality would be considered significant (9).

Class II. Areas in which deterioration normally accompanying moderate well-controlled growth would be considered insignificant (10).

Class III. Areas in which deterioration up to the national secondary standards would be considered insignificant.

All clean air areas were initially designated Class II, but states were allowed to reclassify any area "to accommodate the social, economic, and environmental needs and desires of the public" (11).

In order to obtain a PSD permit, new or modified plants

TABLE 16-2. Prevention-of-Significant-Deterioration Regulations.
Verhinderung von signifikanten Luftverreinigungs Bestimmungen.

		1974 Regulations Maximum Allowable Increase (micrograms/cubic meter)			1978 Regulations Maximum Allowable Increase (micrograms/cubic meter)		
		Annual Mean	24-Hour Max	3-Hour Max	Annual Mean	24-Hour Max	3-Hour Max
(i)	Increments:						
	Particulates:						
	Class 1	5	10	—	5	10	—
	Class 2	10	30	—	19	37	—
	Class 3	60	150	—	37	75	—
	Sulphur Dioxide:						
	Class 1	2	5	25	2	5	25
	Class 2	15	100	700	20	91	512
	Class 3	60	260	1300	40	182	700
	Other Criteria						
	Pollutants:		Not Regulated		Regulations to be developed within two years.		
(ii)	Source Categories Subject to Preconstruction Review/ BACT:		18		28 plus any source with potential emissions of 250 tons or more per year		
(iii)	Baseline Year:		1974		1977 (less contributions from sources constructed since January 6, 1975)		
(iv)	Initial Designation:		Class II (Redesignation by State or Federal Land Manager)		Mandatory Class I Areas designated; others Class II but redesignation at discretion of state		
(v)	Visibility:		No protection		EPA directed to protect air quality related values in its PSD regulations and to develop a program to protect visibility in Class I areas within two years		

in eighteen major source categories had to demonstrate through a preconstruction review process that projected ground level concentrations of sulfur oxides and particulates resulting from their emissions would not violate permitted increments. Further, all new sources locating in clean air areas would be required to install the best available control technology (BACT) with respect to sulfur oxide and particulate emissions. Finally, the EPA indicated its intention of relying on diffusion models to predict the impact of new or modified emission sources on ambient air quality levels, and to monitor increment consumption.

Challenges to the 1974 PSD Regulations

Not surprisingly the regulations drew fire from all sides. Industrial groups (particularly power companies) sought to have the regulations set aside as an arbitrary and capricious exercise for which EPA had no statutory authority. Such groups, favoring less regulation, continued to maintain that existing programs provided adequate protection to clean air areas, that the regulations were the moral equivalent of land use controls prohibiting new industrial development, and that by establishing secondary standards to protect public welfare from a wide range of adverse effects Congress had already specified what it meant by "clean air." The EPA itself expressed similar reservations with regard to the conceptual basis of the PSD program:

> Pending the development of adequate scientific date on the kind and extent of adverse effects of air pollutant levels below the secondary standards, significant deterioration must necessarily be defined without a direct quantitative relationship to specific adverse effects on public health and welfare. (12)

From the conservationist viewpoint, EPA's final regulations

were deficient in several major respects: they failed to prevent the deterioration of air quality in clean air areas to national standards; they applied only to major sources (100 tons of annual emissions) of sulfur dioxide and particulates; and by selecting 1974 as the base year against which to measure increment consumption, the EPA tacitly accepted as a fait accompli all sources that had located in clean air areas since the court order.

Collectively these criticisms amounted to a fairly major indictment of the PSD regulations and of EPA's "responsiveness" to the court's directive. The most serious criticism related to the failure to prevent air quality deterioration to secondary standards. Indeed, despite the terms of the initial injunction, EPA's final regulations specifically authorized this outcome by allowing states to redesignate as Class III "areas experiencing rapid and major industrial or commercial expansion" (13). Moreover, as the EPA itself acknolwedged, since significant deterioration was defined in terms of increments, infringement of national standards could "also occur in Class I or II regions where the difference between existing air quality and the national standard is less than the prescribed air quality increment" (14).

Many of the criticisms can be attributed to the method of determining significant deterioration adopted by the EPA. From the outset the agency expressed serious misgivings with respect to both the data base and analytical procedures for determining significant deterioration. Air quality monitoring was concentrated in the heavily polluted urban areas; monitoring in relatively clean areas was not only limited but unreliable. "Vast numbers of additional monitors would be necessary to precisely define existing air quality, making a plan that is dependent on a knowledge of existing air quality virtually unworkable" (15). In these circumstances EPA argued that its determination of significant deterioration had to be based on preconstruction review of major new sources. Since pollutant concentrations in clean air areas would not be continuously monitored, there was no way of estimating or veryfying increment consumption except through diffusion modelling. Yet this approach in turm imposes certain constraints. Firstly, it is entirely dependent on the quality of the emissions data (to be provided by those seeking a PSD permit) and the accuracy of EPA's diffusion models. Secondly, it effectively restricts the PSD program to situations where air quality concentrations can reasonably be estimated using diffusion modelling, i.e., it rules out regulation of pollutants other than sulfur oxides and particulates since "existing analytical procedures are not adequate to determine the impact of individual sources on air quality concentrations of reactive pollutants" (16).

Underlying these criticisms of PSD regulations and methodologies was the conviction of many conservationists that EPA had allowed the court-mandated goal of protecting existing air quality to become subordinate to other "growth" priorities. Such critics pointed to EPA's dilatoriness in rule making (and then often only under the threat of a court order) and apparent willingness to compromise by narrowing the scope and weakening the regulatory provisions of the PSD program. Certainly in several significant respects-the addition of Class III areas, the deletion of requirements that BACT be applied to sources of pollutants other than particulates and sulfur oxides, deferral of the baseline year-the final regulations appear less restrictive than earlier EPA proposals. In these circumstances, it was even suggested that the EPA's strategy had been "to promulgate the least effective regulations which can withstand legal challenge" (17).

Certainly there would appear to be a strong prima facie case against the EPA. Yet in defense of EPA, the agency clearly did not act consistently to diminish the impact of the PSD program. The final regulations, for example, required preconstruction review of all new sources locating in clear air areas, a significant strengthening of the proposed rules which had exempted new sources in Class III areas. Moreover, as already noted, the agency was forced to define and implement a PSD program at a time when new national concerns, notably the oil embargo and recovery from economic recession, began to influence the debate. In this respect the so-called energy crisis provided both the catalyst and the rationale for concerted efforts to modify what were viewed as unnecessarily stringent, court-enforced interpretations of the Clean Air Act. In the immediate aftermath of the oil embargo, the Nixon administration submitted proposed amendments to the Clean Air Act that included elimination of the PSD program. While the EPA concurred in several of the suggested amendments, it strongly opposed the Federal Energy Office proposal to eliminate PSD. This opposition may be attributed in part to the personal commitment to the program of Russel Train, the new EPA administrator, and in part to the growing realization that other programs (notably the establishment of new source performance standards) were not only far behind schedule but by themselves inadequate to achieve the goals of the Clean Air Act (18). As a result of EPA's support of the PSD program, the Energy Supply and

Environmental Coordination Act of 1974 retained only the measures allowing for conversion of power plants to coal use and extension of automobile emission deadlines.

Efforts to eliminate the requirement for prevention of significant deterioration of air quality continued in 1974 and 1975. In the presidential message accompanying the proposed Energy Independence Act it was suggested that there might be more appropriate ways of dealing with the issues associated with significant deterioration than through the Clean Air Act. Although it quickly became apparent that legislating energy policy would be a complex, controversial and time-consuming business, the continued trade-offs between air quality and energy development insured that the issue would be addressed by the Ninety-fifth Congress.

The 1977 Clean Air Act Amendments

Far from eliminating the PSD program, Congress in the 1977 Clean Air Act Amendments reaffirmed the nation's commitment to a nondegradation policy and provided a clear and explicit statutory basis for the inclusion of PSD regulations in state implementation plans. In effect, Congress retained EPA's basic approach while expanding the scope of the program and tightening its regulatory provisions (Table 16-2). The most significant changes include:

(a) Mandatory Class I status for all international parks, all national wilderness areas and memorial areas exceeding 5,000 acres in size, and all national parks exceeding 6,000 acres in size.

(b) More restrictive air quality increments in Class III areas for sulfur oxides and particulates. Permitted increments in Class III areas are now set below secondary standards; under no circumstances are pollutant concentrations to be allowed to exceed secondary standards, thereby setting an overriding ceiling to any otherwise allowable increment.

(c) Expansion of the program to include all pollutants for which national standards have been established, EPA being directed to promulgate PSD regulations for all other criteria pollutants within two years.

(d) Expansion of the list of sources subject to preconstruction review and BACT requirements and inclusion of any new source with the potential to emit two hundred and fifty tons per year or more of any air pollutant.

(e) A requirement to protect visibility in Class I areas, the EPA being directed to identify appropriate remedial measures within two years (19).

In general, these changes appear to go a long way toward accommodating the criticisms raised by conservation groups of EPA's previous PSD regulations. According to the assistant administrator of the EPA, "The new provisions for the prevention of significant deterioration modify and substantially expand EPA's former regulations . . . (together with other amendments) they provide a strong mandate, clearly indicating that Congress does not intend that the nation's energy problems or economic problems be allowed to compromise environmental quality. Some people have referred to the legislation as a 'mid-course correction.' I believe that 'mid-course reaffirmation' is more appropriate" (20).

Already the new PSD program has been subjected to legal challenge. While these are no longer directed towards its statutory basis, new controversies have emerged with respect to the amended PSD regulations promulgated by EPA on June 19, 1978. Petitions have been filed in the U.S. Court of Appeals for the D.C. Circuit by over 150 individual companies, by the State of Texas, by nearly every major trade association, by the District of Columbia, and by three environmental groups. These petitions have been consolidated into a single case and oral arguments were heard in April, 1979. While EPA's regulations have again been challenged from both conservation and industrial "camps," the general thrust of the petition is that EPA's rule making was far more restrictive than intended by Congress (21).

Implementation of the PSD Program

The PSD controversy has revolved around what are by now familiar issues-the impact of EPA's regulations on the nation's ability to develop alternative energy sources (more specifically coal), the need to reconcile air quality goals with economic growth and regional development priorities, the intervention of the federal government in local decision making. As the program is implemented, these issues will become more clearly defined. In this process, individual "interpretation" of the regulations and shifting, multifaceted public attitudes toward environmental quality and economic growth will be key variables.

In this context PSD regulations appear to be sufficiently flexible to allow for the establishment of a western, coal-based power industry. EPA, for example, exempts emissions from power plants that switch from oil to coal from inclusion in increment consumption. Moreover, under the 1977 Amendments, any governor may consider granting a variance from Class I sulfur dioxide standards for up to eighteen days a year, a provision that was designed to meet the needs of the proposed 3,000-megawatt Intermontane Power Project in southern Utah (22). Similarly, EPA has reduced the impact of including surface mines in the PSD review process by excluding emissions of "fugitive dust" from increment consumption. In practice, as of mid-1979, PSD permits had been issued for some sixty utility boilers totalling 35,000 megawatts. Eight of these permits have been for power plants located within fifty miles of Class I areas. In addition, two new refineries with a total of 435,000 barrel/day capacity, plus numerous refinery expansions, have been approved for clean air areas.

There is little immediate evidence, therefore, that EPA is enforcing the regulations in such a way as to curtail essential growth or energy development. True, the EPA, given the strong congressional mandate, has significantly expanded the scope of the program. In an April, 1978, ruling, for example, EPA concluded that emissions from Exxon's offshore operations in the Santa Barbara Channel would have an adverse impact on air quality and would therefore be subject to the PSD provisions of the Clean Air Act (23). Exxon's proposal involved installing storage and treatment facilities on the platform (i.e., a modification of an existing source) and represented the first time EPA had applied any of the provisions of the Clean Air Act to the outer continental shelf area. It is also true that EPA has refused to issue PSD permits where it has been demonstrated that the permitted increments would be violated. The Indianapolis Power and Light Company was refused a PSD permit for its Patriot Generating Station since the company failed to demonstrate that the Class III three-hour sulfur dioxide increment would not be exceeded more than once a year as allowed under EPA regulations (24). Yet one can also

FEDERAL AIR QUALITY LEGISLATION

point to instances where the EPA appears to have leaned over backwards to accommodate industrial priorites, issuing PSD permits despite community and conservationist opposition. Under the 1974 PSD regulations, for example, the Northern Cheyennes successfully petitioned the U.S. Department of Interior for redesignation of their lands as Class I (25). Following approval of this request in 1977 (after three years' negotiation), EPA refused a PSD permit to the Montana Power Company for construction of two new 700-megawatt units at its Colstrip Power plant, some fifteen miles north of the Cheyennes' reservation. Early in 1978, however, EPA reversed itself, arguing, first, that the Montana Power Company's application could be considered under existing PSD regulations since the new provisions of the 1977 Clean Air Act Amendments would not take effect until March 1, 1978; and second, that revised data submitted by the company indicated that Class I increments would be violated only once a year as allowed under the 1974 PSD regulations.

While various interested parties representing both industrial and conservationist viewpoints can point to examples of what they perceive to be arbitrariness and bias in EPA decisions, the PSD program appears to have operated with little of the disruption feared by industry. Since it began in mid-1975 some 200 PSD permits have been approved by EPA; only two have been denied. There is no evidence that the preconstruction review and permitting process is creating substantial and costly delays. In Region VI, which has issued more PSD permits than any other region, the average processing time for permits has been less than five months from receipt of completed application. Thus industry's concern that allowing EPA up to one year to act on a permit application would result in substantial delay appears to be unfounded.

Unresolved Forward Planning Issues

While PSD regulations appear to be accommodating essential growth and development, there remain a number of unresolved issues. Most of these relate to (a) the phasing and allocation of permitted increments through time, (b) the options available to states when increments have been consumed, and (c) the adequacy of existing regulations in protecting air quality.

In the first instance, the EPA has already expressed its concern over multifacility sources that involve phased construction. Issuance of a PSD permit for the entire project would in effect reserve a significant proportion of the increment for a single source, thereby limiting other growth options. This issue has already surfaced in Texas in the context of an application by Vistron Corporation to construct a petroleum-based chemical complex in Calhoun County. Despite the corporation's claims that the proposed facilities were interdependent and "certain and well-defined" within the meaning of the regulations, the EPA granted a PSD permit for only the first phase of the complex. In support of its position, EPA noted testimony by the corporation at the public hearing that "certain units could be substituted based on marketing conditions, feedstock availability, changing technology, or future regulatory provisions," that the corporation had only secured a Texas Air Control Board permit for the first phase, and that subsequent phases would be subject to BACT review (26).

A second major issue concerns the situation and pressures that will confront states and communities when increments are consumed. As EPA notes, new growth could still occur since "States can expand the available PSD increment(s) by requiring emissions reductions from existing sources" (27). An alternative to an emissions offset approach would be redesignation from Class II to Class III. While such a situation has yet to arise, it could precipitate precisely the pressures which the PSD program was intended to avoid, i.e., create the opportunity for industry to play off one state against another by threatening to locate in a state with more lenient redesignation procedures. As Freeman points out, preventing such a situation was one of the objectives of federal intervention in air pollution control in the first place (28).

Finally, there is apprehension over the extent and character of air quality deterioration that will occur despite existing PSD regulations. In particular, it seems clear that neither Class I increments nor BACT requirements will be sufficient to prevent a further deterioration in visibility in some of the nation's most spectacular scenic areas (29). Already, emissions from the Navaho Power Plant near Page, Arizona, have on occasion filled the Grand Canyon with a layer of haze, reducing visibility to less than fifteen miles and obscuring the opposite canyon rim (30). Visibility is extremely sensitive to the presence in the atmosphere of fine particles, notably sulphate and nitrate compounds, emitted in gaseous form from power plants and smelters. Since these particles are only removed slowly from the atmosphere, visibility impairment in the form of haze is likely to extend for hundreds of miles beyond the actual emissions source. Implementation of the stringent controls and siting policies likely to be required to meet the visibility protection goals of the 1977 Amendments may well provide a major test of EPA's and the nation's commitment to protecting air quality in clean air areas.

THE "OFFSET" ISSUE

The 1970 Clean Air Act Amendments required compliance with ambient air quality standards by 1975. However, what if the standards were not met? The consequences of failing to meet the deadline were not spelled out in the act. Indeed, a strict interpretation of the law as written would have prevented new construction or expansion of old sources in areas that exceeded ambient air quality standards after 1975 (31). EPA initially reacted by prohibiting construction or modification of any facility which would interfere with attainment or maintenance of a national ambient standard (32). The significance of this was not lost on the established industrial areas of the United States. Future industrial growth was likely to be directed toward those areas where air pollution was not a problem. Some of the major urban areas (New York, Philadelphia, Cleveland, Chicago) were already experiencing problems of an eroding tax base and the vision of not being able to attract other industries because of air quality constraints was a haunting one.

A confrontation between the Clean Air Act's ambient standards and the pressures in metropolitan areas for continued urban-industrial growth was inevitable. It first arose in California where there were widespread post-deadline ambient standard violations. In response to several requests to build facilities in noncompliance areas, the California Air Resources Board adopted new source review laws which embodied the offset concept, and allowed for further growth under certain conditions (33).

Since the California confrontation was obviously not

going to be the only place where a conflict between the Clean Air Act and growth pressures would arise, EPA responded by adopting the emission offset approach as national policy (34). This policy was subsequently incorporated virtually unchanged into the 1977 Amendments (35).

The offset policy allows growth in nonattainment areas if the additional pollution from a new or modified source is more than offset by a reduction in emissions from existing sources. Theoretically, at least, air quality is to be actually enhanced by new growth. However, it has been argued that because of its vagueness on several critical issues the offset policy is in reality a tactical retreat, a step backward from the original intent of the Clean Air Act. Growth is now permitted in places where previously it was not until the air quality standards were met (36). If, indeed, the offset policy was a victory for continued industrial growth, it was one that was not warmly received by industry and the states. Prior to its incorporation in the 1977 Amendments there were four public hearings, and over 200 written comments received by EPA (37). The Texas Air Control Board initially refused to implement the policy, and even considered rejection of all applications for new construction permits. The controversial nature of the offset policy merits a closer examination of its elements.

The 1977 Clean Air Act Amendments

Under the 1977 Amendments, the emission offset requirement in nonattainment areas applies only to new or modified "major" stationary sources. Critics argue that this allows a significant number of polluters to escape review. A major source is defined as one having the potential to emit 100 tons per year of any criteria pollutant. Similarly, a modification is major if it increases potential emissions by 100 tons per year. The potential is based on uncontrolled emissions, i.e., the maximum capacity to emit a pollutant without any air pollution control equipment (38). This maximum capacity criteria offers several advantages if the firm's actual pollution is less than allowed. The firms can either trade-off "paper pollution" or increase their emissions and have more pollution to offset in the future. Moreover, in order to seek an offset "arrangement," any major new facilities (or expansion of existing plant) must demonstrate that it will control pollution to the Lowest Achievable Emissions Rate (LAER). The rationale is that any new pollution should be permitted only if it is held to the lowest possible level. In applying the LAER criterion considerations of cost will be given "far less weight" than under the BACT or the NSPS (39). Additionally, the owner of a major source must show that all other major sources owned, operated, or controlled in the state are either in compliance with the SIP or have an approved schedule for compliance.

The offset provisions which have generated the most debate are those requiring emissions reductions from existing sources to a level that not only assures reasonable progress towards the applicable ambient standard but achieves a "net air quality benefit in the affected area" (40). The required offsets may be proposed by the operator of the source, the local community of the state. For instance, if a community is trying to attract a growth-oriented industry it may commit itself to reducing emissions from existing sources to a greater level than the emissions from the new industry. The degree to which the offsets must be greater is not specified. The presumption is that they must simply be greater than one for one (41). The degree to which the offsets are actually significantly greater than one to one will determine whether reasonable progress means actual progress toward achieving the ambient standards. Additionally, there are several exemptions to the offset policy which may weaken its effectiveness. Switching from oil or gas to coal, for example, is generally not counted as a major plant modification. Its impact will be to raise pollution levels in the nonattainment area. The exemption of the increased coal-related sulfur dioxide, particulate, and NOx emissions from the offset provisions will put an added burden on other sources if reasonable progress is to be made toward attaining national standards (42). Exactly where the offsets will be secured could also pose some problems. No specific geographical limit is specified, so it is possible to get offsets from one facility which may in actuality not really contribute toward the reasonable progress goal.

Another controversial issue relates EPA's position on "banking" offsets. Originally, EPA did not allow for the banking or reserving of those leftover credits not required by a new source (43). For example, although a local community might have achieved greater emissions reductions than needed to allow a new industry in the nonattainment area, these leftover emissions reductions could not be saved for future use. Industry argued vehemently that excess reductions should be allowed since not to do so would discourage early clean-up of older and more polluting sources. In particular, it was argued that the steel industry might postpone the planned retirement of obsolete steel-making furnaces so that they could be used for offsets in the future (44). As will be discussed shortly, the EPA has modified its position to allow the use of banked emissions after June 30, 1979, in accordance with the SIP (45).

Other limitations worth mentioning briefly include intrapollutant and production curtailment emissions. Offsets may only be made against similar pollutants. Sulfur dioxide emission reduction may not be used to offset new or increased emissions of particulate matter. However, offsets obtained by shutting down or permanently cutting back production at an existing source are legitimate and may be used if certain conditions are met (46).

State Implementation Plan (SIP) Revisions

Under the 1977 Amendments, the use of offsets was only required until 1 July 1979 by which time all states were to have submitted revised implementation plans. The intention was to allow states some flexibility in deciding how they would attain the goals and timetables mandated in the 1977 Amendments. The revised SIP must impose controls on both new and existing sources such that primary air quality standards are met no later than December 31, 1982. Nonattainment areas unable to meet primary oxidant and/or carbon monoxide standards by 1982 have the possibility of an extension until 1987. Most states appear to have opted for an offset approach toward improving air quality in nonattainment areas.

In order to measure progress toward meeting the national standard, all SIPs must include a comprehensive up-to-date emissions inventory for each nonattainment area (47). The inventory must cover all pollutants for which NAAQS are exceeded. The function of the initial inventory is to provide a quantitative "starting point" for demonstrating reasonable further progress toward attainment. The inventory must identify and quantify all stationary sources which contribute to the nonattainment problem. To the extent that stationary sources outside the nonattainment area have a significant impact on the area, they must also be included in the inventory. Automotive emissions and nontraditional sources which contribute to the nonattainment problem must also be included. This inventory must be periodically revised in order to evaluate the amount of progress that has been made. It is clearly imperative that the initial inventory be accurate and comprehensive. If it is not, the effectiveness of the offset policy may be seriously weakened. If major sources are omitted at the outset, the "reasonable progress" calculations will be distorted. Conversely, if the original source inventory overestimates pollution, then more stringent controls than are actually necessary may be promulgated.

Once the emissions inventory is established, air quality simulation modelling will be used to determine the amount of reductions required to assure "reasonable further progress" toward meeting the 1982 deadline. The simulation models will also be used to estimate the impact of new sources on air quality, and to evaluate the net quality impact of source offsets.

The evaluation of reasonable further progress is a provision of the 1977 Act that was missing from the 1970 Amendments. Recall that the 1970 act set a 1975 goal but had no means of tracking progress. Apparently, Congress learned from that experience. Rather than just setting another deadline, it included a provision (Section 172(b)(3)) that all revised SIPs must demonstrate that reasonable further progress is being and will continue to be made between 1979 and the 1982 deadline.

The question arises as to what constitutes "reasonable further progress." It is defined as <u>annual</u> incremental emission reductions sufficient to provide for timely NAAQS attainment (48). The reductions are to be obtained through reasonably available control technology (RACT) (49). Unfortunately, the act doesn't define RACT. However, EPA has defined it as:

> the lowest emission limit that a particular source is capable of meeting by the application of control technology that is reasonably available considering technological and economic feasibility. (50)

Quite a mouthful. EPA has made it clear that RACT calls for "technology forcing" requirements going beyond off-the-shelf technological controls. The main criterion in applying RACT is that progress be made in attaining the standards.

The use of RACT for existing sources should decrease pollution levels, but the issue of growth still remains. The 1977 Amendments state unequivocally that reasonable further progress not be compromised as a result of emission from new or modified sources. Section 173 of the 1977 Amendments provides states with two ways of approving major construction in nonattainment areas without compromising progress. The states can adopt a modified version of the offset policy as a means of approving construction on a case-by-case basis. However, the conditions associated with the offsets are much more stringent than under the previous offset policy. Major new sources are now required to offset not only their own emissions on more than a one-to-one basis, but also those of all minor point sources which have come into the area since July 1, 1979. Minor point source offsets were not required under earlier policies. Furthermore, the required offsets must be quantitatively sufficient to allow for reasonable further progress.

There are therefore two issues: first, the reduction of emissions under the SIP which constitute reasonable further progress, and second, additional reductions which allow for new growth. Under the original policy EPA did not question whether a particular offset was sufficient to provide reasonable progress toward attainment (51). This is no longer true since offset approval is not contigent on unrelated SIP reductions. The offset emission reductions have to be accomplished before the new or modified sources begin operation and must be obtained from sources included in the emission inventory on which the SIP approval is based. In essence, actual emission levels after the new source begins operation must remain at or below what it would be under the reasonable further progress schedule.

The other option available to the state is what has been called a growth allowance. In effect, this growth allowance is built into the SIP. The SIP must identify and quantify the emissions which will be allowed from construction and operation of major new or modified stationary sources (52). Essentially, this is a nonpoint-source offset policy. The state in its SIP has to demonstrate that areawide reductions from existing inventoried sources will more than offset emissions from new and modified sources in the area. This areawide offset policy established an "allowance pool" from which new sources may draw. As this pool is depleted, growth will be curtailed.

The growth allowance is an example of the "banking" concept alluded to earlier. Under this option the state becomes the emissions bank. It is the existing sources which, as they become subject to tighter RACT controls under the SIP, become involuntary depositors in the bank. As these emission credits build up, new sources can draw upon them. Another complication is that the banked emissions can only be used if emission reductions have already occurred. Suppose, for example, that the SIP requires a ten-ton reduction in SO_2 emissions during 1979. Then, if a new ten-ton per year SO_2 source is to be approved in 1979, at least ten tons of emission reduction must have already occurred earlier in the year. No major growth can be allowed beyond that accommodated by the growth allowance available at the time the proposed source submits its application (53).

Impact on Nonattainment Areas

What will be the impact of the offset policy approach within the nonattainment areas? It will impact both existing and new sources. Existing sources can contribute to lowering areawide pollution by decreasing their own emission levels.

The potential for growth is greater for existing than for new plants. In the early years many existing plants may be able to significantly decrease emission by a combination of better operating procedures and improved maintenance. The control of fugitive dust arising from daily operation may alone make a significant contribution. However, while initially emissions reductions may be relatively easy, subsequent decreases will become more and more difficult.

The other option available to an existing firm is to shut down a plant rather than bear the control costs. If, for instance, in the case of a petrochemical plant, the old plant is "dirty," it may be shut down and replaced with a new one. Many existing firms may not have a major problem since they can provide their own offsets.

The real problem arises for new sources wishing to locate

in the nonattainment area. Since they have no plants in the area, they have to find offsets. Where do they find such offsets? They could buy them from another firm. Alternatively, they could purchase a "dirty" plant and shut it down to obtain the necessary offsets. Another option is to get a permit via a lobbying effort directed at the state agency. This would require some juggling of figures on paper to obtain an SIP which allows the plant to enter the nonattainment areas. Finally, the area may have a growth allowance which permits the plant to be built in the area. If it does not, the local community, state, or new source would have to show sufficient emission reduction to allow for the additional growth.

From an economic perspective the best solution to the above problem is quite straightforward. It has been proposed by economists for some time (54). Let the marketplace determine the value and, hence, price of a given offset unit. The new source desiring to enter the area has the responsibility of finding the necessary emission offset.

If new sources want to buy offsets, this will create the opportunity for existing sources to sell their offsets to these new sources. Hence, a classical trade situation arises. The existing source would be willing to sell its potential offsets by reducing its emissions, if the cost of doing so is less than what the new source is willing to pay for the offsets. On the other hand, the new source would be willing to buy the potential offsets if the price is less than the benefits it derives from locating in the nonattainment area.

The current offset type of policy is seen by many as a precursor to the increased use of economic incentives to pollution problems. However, what appears simple in theory may be difficult to implement. Unfamiliarity with market operations exists where the use of a public good is restricted by government action. The supply of pollution capacity in the air depends on governmental restriction. This in turn determines the scarcity value of the emission offsets. The scarcity is not natural or limited by resource utilization (at least in the short run). The strictness of enforcement will influence the market value of the offsets. The degree of enforcement in turn may depend on the political climate. This creates uncertainty in the offset market and explains the initial reluctance to commit offset rights to a marketplace. Early indications are that it is hard to buy offset rights. Sellers are not coming forward. As long as uncertainty reigns, offsets may not be available. The continuing pressure to provide variance and to relax current environmental regulations because of the "energy crisis" only adds to the uncertainty. If the market approach is to work, there will have to be more certainty and stability concerning the pollution rights marketplace. Another indication of a wait-and-see attitude toward an emissions offset market is the lack of air brokers. If a market were created in these rights, then the opportunity would exist for brokers to emerge as intermediaries to bring together buyers and sellers of rights. Currently, there is an understandable reluctance for the state agencies to fill the gap by playing such a role. Nevertheless, it may be too early to pass any judgment about the development of such a market.

OVERVIEW: POLICY ISSUES

It is easy to be critical of the federal PSD and offset programs. The regulations, complete with cryptic references to SIP's, NSPS, PSD, BACT, BPCT, RACT, and LAER raise the art of obscuratism to a new level. On a more serious note, any objective evaluation of these programs is impossible given the sensitivity of related issues. Thus the PSD and offset programs both exemplify the difficulty of reconciling air quality objectives with economic growth and regional development priorities that are themselves subject to continuing debate and redefinition in response to changing national circumstances. For all the rhetoric and argument over the PSD and offset programs, the basic questions remain unanswered. Do the benefits of preventing significant deterioration of air quality justify the costs of implementing such a policy? Is it possible to reconcile protection of air quality, particularly visibility, with development and use of domestic coal resources? Is enforcement of a nondegradation program actually impeding efforts to reduce the nation's dependency upon costly, imported hydrocarbons? Will growth restrictions in certain nonattainment areas contribute to increasing regional differentiation? Should land use decisions be made solely on the basis of air quality criteria? Given the complexity of the issues and the philosophical underpinnings of much of the argument, there can be no easy answers or simple judgments with respect to these questions. Whether the PSD or offset program has been "successful" or "unsuccessful," "necessary" or "unnecessary," cannot be divorced from ethical considerations. At best a few qualitative observations can be made with respect to the key issues that have surfaced as these programs have been formulated and implemented.

The Issue of New Growth and Industrial Location

The PSD and offset policies are clearly interrelated—both have spatial implications for future growth. Firms having difficulty in securing the necessary offsets to locate or expand in nonattainment areas will tend to "adjust" by moving to attainment areas. Indeed EPA has strongly supported a policy of industrial dispersal as the most effective way of achieving clean air standards in the nation's most polluted metropolitan regions. Yet PSD places an upper limit on the amount of new growth that can occur in the clean air areas. However, industry is in effect operating within a closed system (areas are either in the attainment category or nonattainment category), and growth will take place where resistance is least. This situation exacerbates tension between the cities and the suburban and rural communities as they compete for new industry with its promised benefits of jobs, tax revenues, and related real estate and commercial development. Despite increased awareness of the "costs" of such growth, "the promise of such benefits generates political support for business objectives from nonbusiness interests: workers want jobs, small businesses want increased local commercial activity and governments want more tax revenues" (55). Both the PSD and offset programs represent an attempt by EPA to facilitate and accommodate growth. Moreover, those who argue that it will be easier for future growth to occur in nonattainment areas (where paper offsets may well be available) overlook the opportunity for states to reclassify clean air areas. As Class II increments are consumed, areas may be redesignated as Class III. This automatically provides additional increment and allows for further growth. As Class III increments are consumed, the area in effect acquires a status similar to that of a nonattainment area with continued growth dependent upon the availability of offsets.

The Issue of Regional Development

Similar issues arise in the context of regional growth trends. Considerable attention has been paid to the shift of population and industry from the "Frostbelt" to the "Sunbelt," but the extent to which this trend has been diminished or intensified as a result of federal air quality regulations remains unclear (56). At the national level EPA has argued that its pollution control programs have had very little net impact on unemployment levels and that age and obsolesence have been more significant factors in plant closings than environmental regulations (57). Yet it acknowledges that the concentration of older, smaller, and marginally profitable facilities in the industrial towns of the Northeast will contribute to greater regional dislocation in areas already suffering high unemployment rates.

Consideration of the potential impact of environmental regulations on regional growth patterns cannot be divorced from differences in attitude (among both state and local officials) toward enforcement of the Clean Air Act. A key factor in the control strategy outlined in the 1970 Amendments was the perceived need for a set of national standards that would prevent interstate competition for investment and protect states from pressure through threatened relocation of facilities to states with less stringent environmental standards. The imposition of uniform standards and regulations, together with EPA's role in monitoring progress, represented an assertion of federal power. While retaining the basic regulatory approach, the 1977 Amendments confer much greater authority on state and local governments, particularly in such areas as the issuance of variances and the extension of compliance schedules. The emphasis appears to be on decentralization of environmental enforcement powers. This, however, brings us back full circle to the situation the 1970 law strived to avoid. In fact, even states which are more growth-oriented may in various indirect ways selectively enforce the law. The outcome may be a subtle form of competition for growth industries. For example, Texas and Louisiana have approximately the same number of sources in the petrochemical industry. However, Texas has over 500 employees in its Air Quality Control Board while Louisiana has around 40. Even with the best of intentions, there will be different levels of inventorying, monitoring, and enforcement between two states whose growth philosophies may not differ appreciatively.

The Issue of Modelling

Regional differences will be accentuated by the amount of growth allowed in various parts of the country. How much growth is permitted will depend upon the accuracy of EPA's pollutant dispersion models. One of the first cities likely to confront the dilemma of constraints on growth due to modelling of increment consumption (rather than monitoring of ambient air quality) is Houston.

While Houston is a nonattainment area with respect to carbon monoxides, hydrocarbons, oxidants, and nitrogen oxides, it is subject to PSD regulations with respect to sulfur dioxide. A recent study of Harris County sought to evaluate the expected air quality impact of existing and proposed sources of sulfur dioxide by (a) developing an emission inventory of SO_2 sources to enhance the available data base, and (b) analyzing the impact of proposed sources on SO_2 levels using the air quality dispersion models required by the PSD regulations, i.e., the approved EPA model. The results were, to say the least, disturbing: "The modelling shows that if all the permitted emissions were to occur . . . the increment of allowable increases in SO_2 would have been exceeded when the regulations went into effect on 19 June 1978, perhaps by as much as a factor of six. Additionally, these same projections would indicate that if all the permitted emissions were to occur, the NAAQS (National Ambient Air Quality Standards) would be exceeded by as much as a factor of two" (58). As the report notes, these results (obtained by using EPA's dispersion models) are in sharp conflict with monitored SO_2 levels which indicate that concentrations are only one-fourth of the standards for sulfur dioxide. "When comparing these monitoring data with the modelling of actual emissions in 1977, it indicates that modelling possibly over predicts ambient air quality by 50 percent of more" (57). Yet the PSD regulations are clear and unequivocal. Air quality analysis to determine existing air quality and future allowable increases in concentration is to be based on dispersion models. The permitting process is to be based on total allowable emissions rather than actual emissions; thus actual measured air quality is relegated to a secondary role. As the report concludes:

> Because the PSD regulations specify that regulatory permitting decisions are to be based upon modelling, the results of the present study indicate that there are potentially substantial problems ahead for the Houston area with respect to SO_2 emissions. Under the PSD regulations it will be extremely difficult to obtain a permit to build or modify an SO_2 source in the Houston area. In addition significant controls on SO_2 emissions may

be required for both existing and currently permitted (but not yet operating) new sources. Even if the sulfur content of fuel oil (source of approximately 60 percent of SO_2 emissions) were limited to as little as 0.5 percent, modelling results indicate that attainment of NAAQS would not occur. (60)

If modelling techniques bear little relationship to actual ambient air quality, do they have any role (let alone the primary role assigned them under PSD and offset regulations) in efforts to implement an effective and equitable air pollution control strategy?

The Issue of Equity

An increasingly important aspect of the fallout from environmental policy is its impact upon the distribution of income and well-being within society. More simply, who are the relative winners and losers? Who gets more than they pay for and who gets less?

It has been generally accepted that environmental policy is regressive (61). While the costs fall more heavily on the poor, there is a positive relationship between income and the perceived benefits from environmental improvements. As income increases, the demand for environmental quality increases at a proportionately greater rate. Consequently, the benefits derived by higher income groups are greater than those with lesser incomes.

Instead of examining the distribution of environmental costs and benefits by income class, another approach is to compare them across geographical locations. How are the net benefits from air improvements spread over the landscape? Is the pattern reasonably even or highly skewed? There has been limited research in this area, and the assumptions underlying the research are controversial.

FEDERAL AIR QUALITY LEGISLATION

Nevertheless, preliminary findings indicate that the spatial distribution of benefits is highly skewed. The major benefits accrue to only a few areas while the costs are borne by the entire population. Spatially, the dirtiest metropolitan areas in the Northwest and the North Central part of the United States derive the greatest net benefits. These are also the areas which tend to have large concentrations of low-income minority groups (62).

Whereas a few metropolitan nonattainment areas appear to derive the benefits from improvements in air quality, what are the implications on rural areas of PSD? How will net benefits be distributed? This is a difficult question to answer. However, if PSD is strictly implemented and the classification system is not abused, certain impacts will occur. The relatively clean rural areas contain many of the poorest of the poor. If growth is restricted in these areas, so is their potential for significant per capita income increases. This may lead to increased political resistance to the implementation of such policies. The importance of the often mentioned, but less often studied, redistributional impacts is that if they diverge too much from expectations, they may well influence the direction of future legislation.

The Issue of Uncertainty

Those who must formulate and implement environmental policy confront "a world of rapid scientific and technological advance, of equally rapid social and economic appraisal and reappraisal of resources" (63). Of necessity, any pollution control strategy must be sufficiently flexible to incorporate the most recent scientific evidence as to the generation, diffusion, and impact of air pollutants.

Thus, since the 1970 Amendments new concerns have emerged with respect to the effect on human health and welfare of extremely low concentrations of subtances not covered in the act. At the same time, technological capabilities have been expanded with all the attendant difficulties of identifying and evaluating the social costs and benefits. In such a situation, any approach to pollution control is likely to be an evolutionary process. Circumstances change; new coping strategies are required. This is likely to involve amendments to legislation or modifications in rule making. Yet uncertainty over future rules and regulations imposes an additional burden where industry would prefer a more stable investment climate in which the probable costs and benefits of pollution control can be estimated with greater confidence. Further uncertainty is created through protracted litigation. Even as this essay was being prepared, the opinion of the U.S. Court of Appeals in the case of the Alabama Power Co., et al. v. Douglas M. Costle, et al. significantly affected implementation of the PSD program by altering the definition of major sources subject to preconstruction review and rejecting EPA's interpretation of "potential to emit."

CONCLUSION

This essay has identified many of the problems that have emerged in efforts to control air pollution in the United States through government regulation. The failure to achieve the major goals of the Clean Air Act has led some to conclude that clean air is unattainable (64). Yet any overall assessment should not ignore the progress that has been achieved. EPA data show that both the severity of pollution in the nation's major cities and the number of days on which pollution levels adversely affect public health have steadily declined (65). Estimating the costs and benefits of pollution control is fraught with difficulty; yet at least one major study undertaken for the Council on Environmental Quality suggests that the nation is already enjoying net benefits of $5 billion a year, largely as a result of lower health costs (66). Undoubtedly the first reductions are likely to be the easiest to achieve. Nevertheless, they were made despite a sluggish economy and reluctant compliance. Moreover, as the decade progressed, there was growing recognition on the part of both local governments and the general public of the implications of the Clean Air Act for land use and industrial location. This may be attributed to specific programs implemented by the EPA (albeit often with reluctance and under court order), but it provided a test of the nation's commitment to protecting the health and welfare of all.

For example, in the EPA's own words, the transportation controls (including compulsory car pooling and restrictions on gasoline sales) proposed for the nation's most polluted cities "reached the most profound implication of the Clean Air Act for the average citizen-the impact of the law on his relation to his own automobile" (67). Similarly, PSD regulations were interpreted by many as effectively preventing future industrial, commercial, or residential development. As noted with concern by EPA, there now exists the widespread impression that the Clean Air Act has been responsible for preventing or restricting growth. Needless to say, any form of imposed no-growth policy or central government intervention in land use decisions that are traditionally viewed as being the responsibility of individuals or local communities, runs counter to deeply held values—and nowhere more so than in western and southwestern states where the PSD program is likely to have the greatest impact.

Whether Congress fully absorbed the land use implications of the Clean Air Act remains unclear. Certainly land use planning at the national level is not likely to become an accepted part of federal policy in the near future. In theory, at least, the PSD and offset policies could serve as the catalyst for integrated statewide planning designed to reconcile environmental/development priorities by identifying those areas in which growth could be accommodated with the least environmental or social disruption. In practice, it seems unlikely that many states will perceive, let alone take advantage of, the opportunities available to them for such systematic comprehensive planning. Yet reluctance to engage in integrated planning does not mean that state air pollution agencies will not continue to regulate land use. Quite the contrary. However, those land use decisions will be based on selective criteria and will lack a broader context.

FEDERAL AIR QUALITY LEGISLATION 521

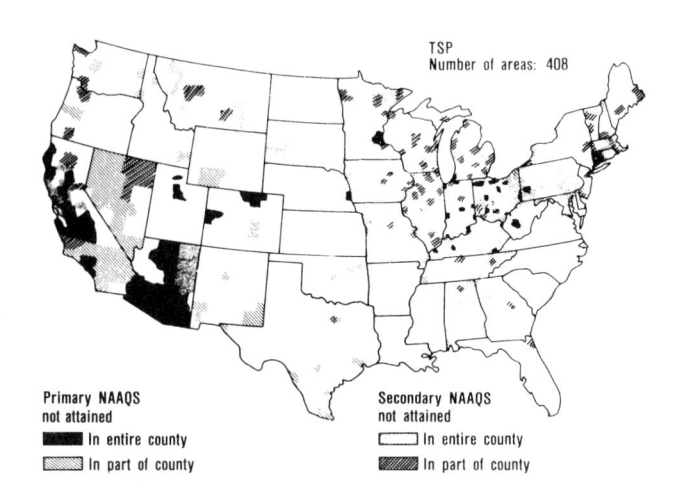

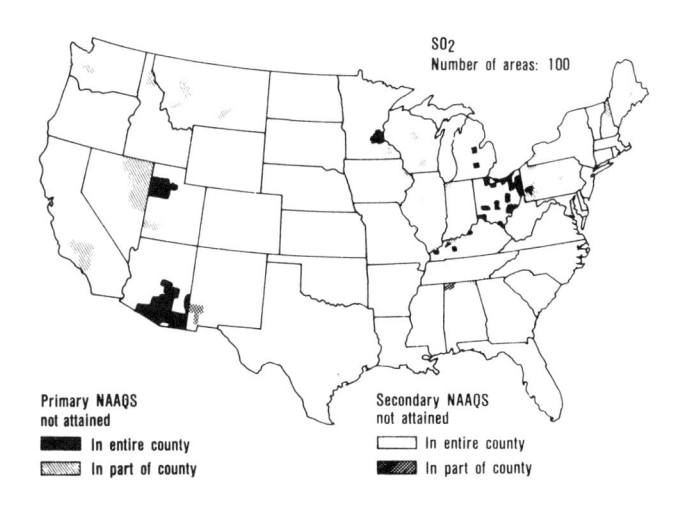

FIG. 16-1. Attainment and Nonattainment Areas for Particulate Matter and Sulfur Dioxide.
        Erwerbungs und Nichterwerbungsraum für besondere Zwecke und Sulfer Dioxide.

Source: Environmental Quality, The Ninth Annual Report, Council on Environmental Quality. Washington, D.C.: U.S. Government Printing Office, 1978.

NOTES

1. Although the EPA was given broad responsibility for implementing the Clean Air Act and for establishing emission standards and compliance schedules, Congress (perhaps to shield EPA from political pressures) specified the emission standards that were to be met by automobile manufacturers within a five year period. State implementation plans were required to document those measures that the state would utilize (in conjunction with federal abatement programs) to attain and maintain national air quality standards.

2. Although the EPA takes the position that there has been a substantial improvement in air quality since 1970, at the time of the mid-1975 deadline for attainment of primary standards, 156 of the nations' 247 air quality control regions failed to meet standards for at least one major pollutant.

3. Council on Environmental Quality, Environmental Quality-1977 (Washington, D.C.: U.S. Government Printing Office, 1977), p. 22.

4. "Environmental Trade-Offs and Other Choices," Resources 45 (1974), pp. 14-23.

5. For an excellent review of the issues raised in this case and subsequent EPA proposals see Disselhorst, T. M., "Sierra Club v. Ruckelshaus . . . On A Clear Day," Ecology Law Quarterly 4 (1975), 730-780, and Disselhorst, T. M., "The Clean Air Act and The Concept of Non-Degradation: Sierra Club v. Ruckelshaus," Ecology Law Quarterly 2 (1972), 801-835.

6. Federal Register, Vol. 38 (1973), p. 18986.

7. Federal Register, Vol. 38 (1973), 18987.

8. Federal Register, Vol. 38 (1973), p. 18986.

9. In EPA's judgment, the extremely small permissible increments for Class I areas represented "an extremely stringent deterioration criteria, and application of this increment would prohobit the introduction of even one small fossil fuelled power plant, municipal incinerator, medium apartment complex (assuming oil heating), or any other medium scale residential or commercial development using normal emission control techniques." Federal

Register, Vol. 38 (1973), p. 18998. As EPA noted, however, this did not preclude new development if current emissions could be reduced through improved control techniques.

10. While no indication is given in the 1974 Final Regulations of the type or amount of development that would be possible under Class II increments, the initial 1973 proposals suggested that increments of this size "would limit future development to the level of light industrial and residential complexes, or a very small amount of heavy industry such as stringently controlled power plants." Federal Register, Vol. 38 (1973), p. 18990. According to EPA data, a well-controlled, large (1000-1500 MW) coal-fired power plant could be located in Class II areas.

11. Federal Register, Vol. 39 (1974), p. 42510.

12. Federal Register, Vol. 38 (1973), p. 18987.

13. Federal Register, Vol. 39 (1974), p. 31004.

14. Federal Register, Vol. 39 (1974), p. 42510.

15. Federal Register, Vol. 39 (1974), p. 42510.

16. Federal Register, Vol. 39 (1974), p. 42511.

17. Disselhorst, op. cit., (note 5), p. 780.

18. Train, R. E., "Speaking Out at EPA," Science 184 (1974), 140.

19. There is a clear inconsistency here in the congressional approach since national secondary standards are intended to protect (among other things) visibility. If the present standard does not achieve this, the logical course of action should be to modify the standard for all parts of the nation, not just Class I clean air areas.

20. Hawkins, D.G., "The Clean Air Act of 1977-New Dimensions in Air Quality Management," Fourth Symposium on Flue Gas Desulfurization, Holywood, Florida, November 8-11, 1977.

21. Nickel, H. V., "Litigation on EPA's Prevention of Significant Deterioration PSD Regulations," paper prepared for Environmental Law Institute, State Bar of Texas and Travis County Bar Association, Austin, Texas, March 15-16, 1979.

22. An operator must first seek a variance from the federal land manager (for example, the Secretary of the Interior in the case of a national park). If refused, the operator may then take the issue to the state governor. In a classic "Catch 22" bureaucratic procedure, the governor may issue a variance if the federal land manager concurs. If a class I variance continues to be opposed be the federal land manager, the issue must be resolved by the president.

23. Federal Register, Vol. 43 (1978), p. 16393.

24. Federal Register, Vol. 43 (1978), p. 4772. Significantly, IPALCO (Indianapolis Power and Light Co.) submitted modelling data to EPA which indicated that the Class II increment would not be exceeded more than once. The State of Kentucky Division of Air Pollution Control, however, performed an additional analysis of IPALCO's data and concluded that 3-hour sulfur dioxide increments would be exceeded more frequently. Since IPALCO presented no information to refute the State's contention, EPA refused to issue a permit.

25. Parfit, M., "And the Skies Will be Cloudy All Day," New Times, May 15, 1978, pp. 49-54.

26. Texas Air Control Board, Approval of PSD permit No. PSD-TX-76, March 30, 1979.

27. Federal Register, Vol. 43 (1978), p. 26387.

28. Freeman, A. M., III, "Air and Water Pollution Policy," in Current Issues in U.S. Environmental Policy, ed. Paul R. Portney (Baltimore: Johns Hopkins University Press for Resources for the Future, 1978), p. 43.

29. Tundermann, D. W., "Protecting Visibility: The Key to Preventing Significant Deterioration in Western Air Quality," Natural Resources Lawyer 9 (1978), 373-383.

30. Council on Environmental Quality, Environmental Quality-1978, The Ninth Annual Report of the Council on Environmental Quality (Washington, D.C.: U.S. Council on Environmental Quality, op. cit., (note 4), p. 24.

31. Council on Environmental Quality, op. cit., (note 4), p. 24.

32. Raffle, B. I., "Prevnetion of Significant Deterioration and Non-Attainment under the Clean Air Act," Environmental Reporter 10 (1979), 1.
33. Raffle, op. cit., (note 32), p. 3.
34. Federal Register, Vol. 41 (1976), p. 53661.
35. Federal Register, op. cit., (note 34), p. 55558.
36. Walker, R., and M. Storper, "Erosion of the Clean Air Act of 1970: A Study in the Failure of Government Regulation and Planning," Boston College Environmental Affairs Law Review 7 (1978), 189-257.
37. Raffle, op. cit., (note 32), p. 6.
38. Federal Register, op. cit., (note 37), p. 3282.
39. Federal Register, op. cit., (note 34), p. 55526.
40. Federal Register, op. cit., (note 37), p. 3284.
41. Federal Register, op. cit., (note 37), p. 3285.
42. Raffle, op. cit., (note 32), p. 13.
43. Federal Register, op. cit., (note 34), p. 55529.
44. Raffle, op. cit., (note 32), p. 15.
45. Federal Register, op. cit., (note 37), p. 3280.
46. Federal Register, op. cit., (note 37), p. 3284.
47. P.L. 95-95, (1977), Sec. 172(b) (4), p. 95.
48. P.L. 95-95, op. cit., (note 47), Sec. 110 (a) (2)B, p. 18.
49. P.L. 95-95, op. cit., (note 47), Sec. 172 (b) (3), p. 95.
50. Raffle, op. cit., (note 32), p. 21.
51. Federal Register, op. cit., (note 37), p. 3285.
52. P.L. 95-95, op. cit., (note 47), Sec. 172(b) (5), p. 95.
53. Raffle, op. cit., (note 32), p. 24.
54. For example, see Baumol, W. J., and W. E. Oates, The Theory of Environmental Policy (Englewood Cliffs, New Jersey: Prentice-Hall, 1975); Dolan, E. G., TANSTAAFL, The Economic Strategy for Environmental Crisis (New York: Holt, Rinehart and Winston, 1971); Kneese, A. V., and C. L.

Schultze, *Pollution Prices and Public Policy* (Washington, D.C.: The Brookings Institution, 1975), and Seneca, J. J., and M. K. Taussig, *Environmental Economics* (Englewood Cliffs: Prentice Hall, 1974).

55. Walker and Storper, op. cit., (note 36), p. 248.
56. Perry, D. C., and Watkins, A., eds., *The Rise of the Sunbelt Cities*, (Beverly Hills: Sage Publications, 1977).
57. Council on Environmental Quality, op. cit., (note 30), pp. 431-432.
58. Environmental Research and Technology, Inc., *Evaluation of the Impact of the Federal Prevention of Significant Deterioration Regulations for Sulfur Dioxide in Houstin, Texas* (Houston, 1979), p. iii.
59. Environmental Research and Technology, Inc., op. cit., (note 58), p. iv.
60. Environmental Research and Technology, Inc., op. cit., (note 58), p. iv.
61. For example, see Cicchetti, C. J., and V. Smith, *The Costs of Congestion* (Cambridge, Mass: Ballinger, 1976); Dorfman, N. S., and A. Snow, "Who Will Pay for Pollution Control?" *National Tax Journal* 28 (1975) 101-115; Freeman, A. M., III, "Distribution of Environmental Quality," in *Environmental Quality Analysis*, ed. A. V. Kneese and B. T. Bower (Baltimore: The Johns Hopkins Press, 1972), pp. 243-280; and Harrison, D., Jr., *Who Pays for Clean Air?* (Cambridge, Mass: Ballinger, 1975).
62. Peskin, H. M., "Environmental Policy and the Distribution of Benefits and Costs," in Portney, P. R., ed. op. cit., (note 28), pp. 145-163.
63. O'Riordan, T., *Perspectives on Resource Management* (London: Pion, 1971), p. 109.
64. See, for example, Walker and Storper, op. cit., (note 36), pp. 240-257.
65. Council on Environmental Quality, op. cit., (note 30), pp. 4-14.
66. Council on Environmental Quality, op. cit., (note 30), pp. 418-421.

67. Statement by Robert W. Fri, Acting EPA Administrator, Transportation Control Press Conference, July 27, 1973.

CHAPTER 17

FEDERAL IMPACTS ON ENERGY DEVELOPMENT AND ENVIRONMENTAL
MANAGEMENT IN THE AMERICAN WEST

DER EINFLUSS DER BUNDESREGIERUNG AUF ENERGIEENTWICKLUNG
UND UMWELTBEWIRTSCHAFTUNG IM AMERIKANISCHEN WESTEN

Melvin G. Marcus

Abstract

Energy development and environmental management in the
United States are enmeshed in an intricate web of federal
statutes and regulations. This is especially true in the
American West where most of the land area is under federal
ownership and/or management. Federal policy is the stress
point about which conflicts emerge in this energy-rich
region. Such conflicts will increase as the American
thrust for energy independence encounters resistance from
federal forces of environmental protection. The impact of
several laws and promulgated regulations are considered
in this regard. Included are the Environmental Policy Act,
Clean Air Act and Amendments, Toxic Substances Control Act,
Hazardous Materials Transportation Act, Federal Mine Safety
and Health Act, Noise Control Act, Endangered Species Act,
Surface Mining Control and Reclamation Act, Federal Land
Management Policy Act, Wilderness Act, and Clean Water Act.

Kurzfassung

Energieentwicklung und Umwelterhaltung in den Vereinigten
Staaten sind verstrickt in ein Netz von Bundesverordnungen
und-vorschriften. Das gilt besonders im amerikanischen
Westen, wo die Landfläche zum grössten Teil im Besitz und/
oder unter Beaufsichtigung der Bundesregierung ist. Die
Bundespolitik ist der Spannungspunkt an dem sich Konflikte
in diesem energiereichen Gebiet zeigen. Solche Konflikte
werden verstärker auftreten, in dem Masse das amerikanische
Streben nach Energieunabhängigkeit dem Widerstand der Bundes-
interessen des Umweltschutzes begegnet. Die Wirkung mehrer
Gesetze und verkündeten Vorschriften werden in dieser Hinsicht berücksichtigt. Eingeschlossen werden das Environmental Policy Act (Umweltschutz-Gesetz), Clean Air Act (Luft-

einhaltungs-Gesetz) and Amendments (Zusatzanträge), Toxic Substance Control Act (Giftstoffkontroll-Gesetz), Hazardous Materials Transportation Act (Gesetz über den Transport gefährlicher Materialien), Federal Mine Safety and Health Act (Bundesgesetz zur Bergwerkssicherheit und-Gesundheit), Noise Control Act (Lärmkontroll-Gesetz), Endangered Species Act (Gesetz zum Schutz gefährdeter Arten), Surface Mining Control and Reclamation Act (Oberflächenabbaukontrolle und Reklamations-Gesetz), Federal Land Management Policy Act (Bundesgesetz zur Landbewirtschaftungspolitik), Wilderness Act (Naturpark-Gesetz), and Clean Water Act (Wasserreinhaltungs-Gesetz).

Federal Impacts on Energy Development and Environmental Management in the American West

Energy development and environmental management in the United States are enmeshed in an intricate net of federal statutes and regulations. This is especially true in the American West where a large proportion of the land area is under federal ownership and/or jurisdiction. The federal regulatory machinery has been developed in order to protect the environment and enhance the quality of life. Unfortunately, these admirable goals have been brought into ever-increasing conflict with regional and national demands for both economic growth and energy resources--a situation excerbated by inflationary energy costs and the uncertainty of foreign petroleum supplies. The unhappy result is that not only have the federal government and private sectors been pushed into an escalating adversary relationship, but departments of the federal government often find themselves with conflicting mandates.

The President and the Congress of the United States have declared energy independence as a major national goal, but they have yet to agree on the comprehensive policy and programs involved. Whatever path they follow, they must inevitably face the reality that energy development and environmental protection cannot be mutually accommodated unless major policy and regulation changes are forthcoming. The present stresses between advocates of energy development and forces of environmental protection leave no one satisfied and provide no coherency in the management of environment. It is the purpose of this essay to review the manner in which this situation has evolved and to describe the current circumstances of energy development and environmental management in the United States. Particular examples from the American West will be cited.

Although an attempt is made to present up-to-date regulatory information, this is an almost impossible task. New regulations are promulgated every few weeks, and landmark court decisions seem to appear several times a year. In these regards, this essay is out-of-date as it is written. In any event, the particulars are perhaps not as important as are the general conditions and trends which reflect the impact of broad-scale federal policy.

LAND POLICY

Land policy in the United States has transited several phases during the nation's short history. In the first years of the Republic, public domain land could be acquired by purchase. This era of sales quickly passed, however, and nineteenth-century American land policy was characterized by one of the greatest land giveaways in history. Land west of the Appalachians, and especially west of the Mississippi, was acquired in a multitude of ways--by grants to railroads, schools, veterans, and canal companies; by so-called reclamation of swamps and deserts; by legitimatized squatter's rights; and by the massive disposals of the Homestead Acts between 1862 and 1934. By the turn of the century, most useful agricultural land had moved into private hands.

A variety of national motives contributed to this extraordinary land policy. Significant among them was the drive to establish sovereignty over southern and western lands acquired by sales, treaty, military action, or exploration. The most effective means to lay claim to such land was to encourage its settlement. Further, the doctrine of

Manifest Destiny--fueled by a seemingly endless supply of immigrants ready to settle and exploit the waiting land--dominated this period of American history.

By 1900, it was becoming apparent that the best of the arable land had been taken up. Homesteaders were forced onto marginal land--where they usually failed, stripping fertility and initiating soil erosion in the process. The federal government began to reverse its policies, turning to restrictive and/or conservational land management practices in an effort to reduce wasteful exploitation. With passage of the Taylor Grazing Act in 1934, the federal government established clear control over the ownership and management of public domain lands. This closed out the Homestead Acts, and all public domain land was withdrawn pending classification. Although a few small land parcels were considered suitable for homesteading, the majority were organized under appropriate federal agencies, including the newly created Bureau of Land Management. The land, where feasible, was then leased in districts under conservational controls.

The land ownership patterns that emerged had the greatest impact in the western states where huge tracts of mountain, desert, and semiarid plateau lands were held in federal ownership. Additionally, large areas in the West had been established as Indian tribal lands and came under the management jurisdiction of the U.S. Bureau of Indian Affairs. Table 17-1 reveals the extraordinarily large federal holdings in the eleven westernmost states. In Arizona, for example, only 15 percent of the land area is privately owned; the rest is state or federal domain (1). The most dramatic case is Nevada, where federal holdings account for 89 percent of the land area.

TABLE 17-1. Federal Land Ownership in Eleven Western States.
Grundstückeigentum des Bundes in 11 Western Bundesstaaten.

State	Total Land (1,000 acres)	Federal Ownership or Jurisdiction (including Indian Lands) Area 1,000 acres	Percent	Federal Land (without Indian Lands) Area 1,000 acres	Percent	Indian Lands Area 1,000 acres	Percent
Arizona	72,688	52,155	71.8	32,118	44.2	20,037	27.6
California	100,207	46,776	46.7	46,228	46.1	547	0.5
Colorado	66,486	24,431	36.7	23,649	35.6	782	1.2
Idaho	52,933	34,550	65.3	33,722	63.7	828	1.6
Montana	93,271	32,908	35.3	27,628	29.6	5,280	5.7
Nevada	70,264	62,713	89.3	61,560	87.6	1,153	1.6
New Mexico	77,776	33,881	43.6	26,038	33.5	7,843	10.1
Oregon	61,599	33,077	53.7	32,316	52.5	761	1.2
Utah	52,697	36,593	69.4	34,316	65.1	2,277	4.3
Washington	42,694	14,929	35.0	12,421	29.1	2,508	5.9
Wyoming	62,343	32,215	51.7	30,327	48.6	1,888	3.0
Total	752,958	404,228	53.7	360,323	47.9	43,904	5.8

Source: United States Department of Commerce, Bureau of the Census, 1978. Statistical Abstract of the United States, 1978. Washington, D.C.: U.S. Government Printing Office.

The fact that land is federally owned and/or managed does not, of course, mean that it is unavailable for resource development. Given certain controls and regulations, grazing, forestry, mining, and recreation are all economic activities exercised on public domain land. To protect such land from uncontrolled exploitation, the federal government and its management agencies (e.g., the Forest Service, Bureau of Land Management, National Park Service, Bureau of Reclamation) have promulgated a complex hierarchy of rules and regulations for land use which requires leases, franchises, or permits. In the last decade, the number of these regulations has dramatically increased. Greater emphasis than ever has been placed on protective measures. These now include consideration of the impacts of environmentally degrading activities which take place on or affect private land as well, given the conditions (a) that the activity could impact federal land, (b) that federal funds are used, or (c) that federal licensing is required. Little escapes this net; this is especially true since the Clean Air Act and its amendments and regulations have been developed. It is not surprising that in the American West, where most energy development either takes place on federal land or not far from it, the battle lines between environmentalists and developers are being drawn.

EVOLUTION OF U.S. ENVIRONMENTAL POLICIES
The environmental concerns, which led to the current regulatory system, have evolved slowly in the United States. During the 1800s, two doctrines of nature and man's role therein were prevalent. Manifest Destiny, a justification of American expansionism, was popular during the last half of the century. Some Americans, however, adhered to a

different philosophy exemplified in the concept of the "balance of nature." This group denounced human greed for growth at the expense of the shrinking wilderness; support for their theme called for aesthetic preservation of nature's domain. Thus, the historical development of environmental movements in the United States is often seen as a confrontation between these two doctrines and their adherents.

The history of conservational, preservational, and environmental movements is comprehensively treated elsewhere (2, 3, 4, 5, 6). Only a brief reprise will be provided here as a backdrop to current policies and regulations.

There are many contradictions and ironies in the ways that Americans have used and perceived the natural landscape. If, on one hand, the early settlers were struck by the extraordinary beauty and bounty of the land, they set out to subdue and exploit it on the other. Or there is the irony that Stuhr (7, p. 69) points out: "People who had always been denied land and its resources were not, after settling in America, protectively appreciative of it." From the very beginning, the new Americans wanted to have their cake and to eat it, too; little has changed in this regard.

Inevitably, reactions to expansion and exploitation set in, and over the years environmentalism has waxed and waned in many guises; preservationism, conservation, resource management, ecology, and nature training, for example, are labels that have represented portions or the whole of the environmental spectrum. Three peak environmentalistic periods--the first two, which had strong identification with the political fortunes of Theodore Roosevelt and Franklin Roosevelt respectively, and the third, which was loosely associated with the consecutive administrations of Lyndon Johnson and Richard Nixon--are significant benchmarks in the

American attitude to environment and environmental education. Each of these is described in following paragraphs.

The First Environmental Period: Early Federal Efforts

The first major blossoming of environmental concern in the United States culminated in the conservation-oriented administration of Theodore Roosevelt. Before this time, however, the foundations of the conservation movement had been laid. The cornerstone was surely George Perkins Marsh's Man and Nature (1864), later retitled The Earth as Modified by Human Action. He has been fairly represented as:

> the first American to lay down for the populace the broad principles of conservation and to demonstrate, by examples from other countries, the direction in which America was headed by wantonly wasting her forests. These broad principles were based upon the doctrine of ecological balance. (3, p. 11)

If Marsh's work is in retrospect the cornerstone upon which the conservation movement was built, other voices were also heard and their influence felt. The transcendental writings of Henry David Thoreau, Ralph Waldo Emerson, and others--which expounded the benefits to be accrued from communion with the natural world--laid the philosophical groundwork whereby many Americans made at least the intellectual transition from a resource exploitation ethic to an aesthetic environmental ethic. The aesthetic approach, which also posited a preservational attitude, was further enhanced by the lectures and publications of environmental prophets such as naturalist John Muir, editor-conservationist Robert Underwood Johnson, and artist-writer George Catlin.

While the aesthetic conservationists tended to promote a back-to-nature wilderness philosophy, another group more immediately influenced American environment policies and actions. These were the scientist-conservationists and resource managers, who saw the role of nature in terms of its utility to man. Typical of these were politician-forester Gifford Pinchot, geologist-explorer John Wesley Powell, academic administrator and soil scientist Nathaniel Shaler, forester Carl Shurz, and wildlife champion George Bird Grinnell.

By the time Theodore Roosevelt entered office, a trend had already been set whereby the nation was gradually and slowly withdrawing from the tenets of Manifest Destiny. Roosevelt was much influenced by the pronouncements and recommendations of men such as Pinchot, Powell, Muir, and Grinnell. Some of the earlier environmentalists served in his administration; Pinchot was particularly influential. Roosevelt's tenure was characterized by an explosion of conservation actions, which included the organization of national and international conservation commissions and conferences and the passing of important legislation relating to wildlife, forests, and water. An outdoorsman and nature-lover, Roosevelt sympathized with the preservationists and set lands aside for national forests and wildlife refuges. On the other hand, he subscribed to utilitarian approaches, and much of his legislation was directed toward wise resource management.

Thus, through the medium of the presidency the United States experienced for the first time a period of national public awareness of major environmental problems and policies. This was the first focused input of the federal government into environmental and conservational affairs. The effort was not totally integrated; much energy and attention was given to specific facets of the environment, particularly forests, wildlife, fish, and water. In the long run, however, while the public was widely aware of these activities, the actions of both government and public groups represented primarily the support, advice, intent, and philosophies of a highly educated, elitist sector of the population.

The Second Environmental Period: Federal Expansion

A second crest of environmental and conservational activity arrived with the depression-years administration of Franklin Delano Roosevelt. His New Deal programs signaled the first major entry of the federal government into broad and multidisciplinary environmental planning at regional levels. Federal authority, regulations, and management peaked in a number of then-controversial projects such as the Tennessee Valley, Columbia River, and Missouri Valley projects. While Theodore Roosevelt's administration was characterized by attempts at preservation and some utilitarian conservation of a disappearing resource base, Franklin Roosevelt's administration directed its efforts more to problems of integrated and broad-scale resource management planning.

The New Deal's resource management programs were dramatic and innovative and probably could not have been initiated except for Roosevelt's landslide election mandates and the extreme unemployment of the 1930s; they also represented a wide swing of the pendulum to the relative environmental left after more than twenty years on the reactive right. Earlier, the antitrust and proenvironment policies of Theodore Roosevelt had come under attack in the later years of his administration. Subsequent administrations adhered to policies which were dedicated to the philosophies of free enterprise and individualism; by definition in the logic of the times, this meant that regulation of environment and resource management should be minimized. This laissez-faire attitude was further exacerbated by two factors: the rapid and often wasteful resource exploitation required by World War I, and a general public reaction against wartime restrictions and regulations in the postwar period. For example, Nash (8, p. 139) notes: "Riding to office on a wave of reaction to wartime restrictions, [President] Harding understood little of the necessity for conserving natural resources." Even considering the earlier Tea Pot Dome scandal, the subsequent Coolidge administration conducted a policy of unfettered private enterprise. The Coolidge-established Federal Oil Conservation Board, for example, concluded, in seven annual reports, that private companies, not the government, must bear the burden of wise conservation (3).

No single individual or event can be identified as the cornerstone to the subsequent conservational splurge of the 1930s; rather, it was an accumulation of events--such as the disastrous Johnstown, Pennsylvania, floods and the depletion of Pacific Coast fishery resources--which slowly made both public and government aware of a threatened environment. The convincing tracts of advocates such as soil scientist Hugh H. Bennett and conservationist-planner Benton MacKaye also gained increasing credibility with the decision makers. Thus, even before the spectacular programs of the New Deal, Herbert Hoover had begun to turn national policy toward a conservation ethic. Because he strongly believed in individualism, Hoover did not strive for stringent federal regulation of resources; rather, he urged cooperation among individuals and agencies involved in these problems.

The first two terms of Franklin Roosevelt's administration saw the initiation of huge national and regional projects designed to combine preservational and utilitarian conservation goals. If these programs were implemented to alleviate unemployment and regenerate a collapsed economy, they also led to tremendous progress in areas such as flood control, integrated resource management, development of recreational lands, soil conservation, and range management. As Nash (8, p. 147) states:

> During the 1930s no resource escaped consideration as a subject for conservation. More significant still is the fact that, although the approach was comprehensive, the record of achievement in the conservation of any single resource surpassed that of any previous administration.

The impact of the New Deal years on America's environmental policies, as well as its political and socioeconomic structure, has been lasting and controversial. Roosevelt's programs were advertised as "for the people," and claimed to protect and manage land for the public trust. Significant legislation included the Soil Conservation Act, the Taylor Grazing Act, the Omnibus Flood Control Act, and the Forest Service "U" Regulations (which applied wilderness preservation policies to the national forests), not to mention the establishment of major agencies and programs involved in river basin authorities, the Civilian Conservation Corps, the Neighborhood Youth Corps, the Works Progress Administration, and others.

These activities not only provided considerable progress in environmental management, but they also placed much greater control of environmental management and decision making in the hands of federal agencies. It was during this period that tremendous regulatory and administrative powers were given, for example, to the Department of the Interior, Department of Agriculture, Corps of Engineers, and the Bureau of Reclamation. Thus, the shift to more considered management and planning of environment was accompanied by the creation of a massive new federal bureaucracy in the environmental decision-making field.

The Third Environmental Period: Public Participation and Expanding Federalism

From past experience, it appears that environmental/conservational cycles in the United States run in periods of roughly a third of a century--twenty to twenty-five years of doldrums in which only a few voices are heard and recognized, followed by eight to ten years of frantic activity and commitment. This happened between the Roosevelt eras and again between 1941 and the late 1960s. It is tempting to draw conclusions about periodic impacts of successive generations in this regard, but this is undoubtedly a gross oversimplification.

In any event, another world war and the subsequent rebuilding period again coincided with the termination of an environmentalist period and was followed by a hiatus of activity. When finally a new environmental groundswell began to be felt in the mid-1960s, the causes and the manner of its emergence were quite different from those in the past. First, and perhaps most significant, the new movement had a larger and more diversified public clientele. The movement still relied on the highly educated and well-placed, but America's educated population base had also been expanding. Thus, the highly elitist nature of earlier movements was lessened, although not eliminated. Second, the new environmentalists/conservationists led, and not followed, the decision makers in the promulgation of national policies and the drive for new environmental legislation. Third, the efforts and energies of the movement were based in a youthful constituency that was both massive and vocal.

As in the past, however, the seeds had been planted by environmental prophets whose dire predictions began to converge with the escalating problems of modern society: population growth, pollution, high resource and energy consumption, denudation of land, and proliferation of endangered and threatened species. In the 1950s, this had been seen as an academic argument between "Optimists," such as Mather (9) and Holman (10), and "Pessimists," such as Osborn (11, 12) and Vogt (13). The first major benchmark in the new environmental movement, however, was probably Rachel Carson's influential work, Silent Spring (14). This book expanded the links between the use of chemicals on crops and insects and, through a hierarchal structure, the effect on human beings. The impact of her work was immense:

> the message of Silent Spring reverberated beyond the pesticide controversy. It was the first "ecological" book to reach a wide audience. In its pages man was shown not only to produce irreversible effects upon his environment, but to be subject to environmental effects as well. For the first time man was coming to see himself in the place of the buffalo, the fur seal, and the plume birds; the passenger pigeon presented itself to gloomier souls.
>
> "There is no question" a government expert on natural resources said, "that Silent Spring prompted the federal government to take action against water and air pollution--as well as against persistent pesticides--several years before it otherwise would have moved." (2, p. 315)

A number of phenomena occurred subsequently. Both academic and popular cultures rediscovered the balance-of-nature principle, particularly through the writing of Henry David Thoreau and Aldo Leopold. Organizations that had previously focused on small special interest memberships dramatically expanded their memberships and moved forcefully into the national arenas of public relations, legislative lobbying, and judicial advocacy. The Audubon Society, Sierra Club, and National Wildlife Federation are prominent examples. Finally, a new breed of scientific and/or social scientific writers engaged a popular readership. Most were pessimists to one degree or another, and soon the public was absorbing the crisis-laden sermons from the likes of Commoner (15), Paul and Anne Ehrlich (16, 17), Udall (18), and the Club of Rome (19).

The converging ideas and actions of the 1960s which became the new environmental movement cannot be elaborated in terms of simple cause and effect. The tenor and realities of American life in the time between publication of Silent Spring in 1962 and the first Earth Day (Ann Arbor, 1968) were extremely complex, and it is important to place the evolution of the new environmentalism in the context of other events taking place. This was a time of increasing internal furor over the American commitment in Vietnam, rising discontent and riots in urban ghettos, and emerging (and often radicalized) student power. All three of these issues were inextricably intertwined in a confused nation's attempt to reassess its goals and its actions.

Regardless of how one feels about the era and its issues, it was productive of new and powerful means of group communication and advocacy development. For the first time in many years in the United States, new kinds of forums evolved, and the immediacy of modern communications made them easily transferable to a broad population base. From the point of view of the developing environmentalism of the sixties, this meant that a new constituency was ready and primed to move into the arena. No longer would the cause of environmentalism and conservation have to rely primarily on an elitist core taken from high government, the affluent, and outdoors enthusiasts. In short, a stronger and broader populistic base was available.

As the most violent, or at least the most overt, disruptions of the 1960s began to recede (about 1968), environmentalism became a perfect focus for new constructive vectors. It satisfied the need to identify and criticize what was wrong--pollution, urban blight, insecticides, landscape degradation--while at the same time providing a positive outlet whereby the community-at-large could define, promote, and even initiate public policy. Thus, by early 1968, the already active and committed voices of environmentalism were beginning to be heard from loosely organized grass roots.

By 1969, government was beginning to respond with new legislation. Locally, this was often manifested in sign ordinances, returnable container laws, undeveloped space preserves, etc. Broader legislation began to appear at state levels, particularly relating to pollution, constraints on development, and protection of the public domain. The most far-reaching legislation, however, was at the federal level. The National Environmental Policy Act of 1969 (NEPA) (PL 91-190) is a landmark in this regard. The purposes of the act are:

> To declare a national policy which will encourage productive and enjoyable harmony between man and his environment; to promote efforts which will prevent or eliminate damage to the environment and biosphere and stimulate the health and welfare of man; to enrich the understanding of the ecological systems and natural resources important to the Nation; and to establish a Council on Environmental Quality. (PL 91-190)

Among major results of this legislation was the creation of the Environmental Protection Agency and the requirement for Environmental Impact Statements. The decade that followed has seen a proliferation of laws, and regulations, and court decisions--most of which favored the forces of tight environmental controls. It is these efforts and their significance to environmental management and energy development that will be addressed in the remainder of this essay.

ENVIRONMENTAL REGULATION IN THE 1970s

Volumes would be required to describe and explain the network of federal laws and regulations that dominate environmental management and energy development in the United States. In fact, the very instrument used by the government to promulgate, explain, and establish such regulations--the Federal Register--is in some danger of collapsing under its own weight (Table 17-2). It has roughly tripled from 20,036 pages to 71,100 pages during the 1970s; in 1977, it contained 65,603 pages. While it is true that only a portion of the Federal Register is devoted to environmental and energy-related issues, those areas were responsible for much of the increase. Indeed, many organizations have found it necessary to assign employees as full-time "watchdogs" of the Federal Register. This is practiced in such varied constituencies as utilities, industry, schools and universities, state and local governments, and agencies of the federal government itself.

A high proportion of environmental and/or energy-related regulations are based on federal laws passed during the 1970s; many laws of earlier vintage have also been amended in the environmental spirit of the last decade. A selection of such laws, which significantly influence environmental

TABLE 17-2. Number of Printed Pages in Federal Register.
Anzahl der gedruckten Seiten im Bundesregister (über Umweltbewirtschaftung und Energieentwicklung).

Year	Pages	Increase (pages)	Increase (%)
1967	21,050		
1968	20,050	(1,000)	(5)
1969	20,418	368	2
1970	20,036	(362)	(2)
1971	25,447	5,411	27
1972	28,924	3,477	14
1973	35,591	6,667	33
1974	45,422	9,831	22
1975	60,221	14,799	33
1976	57,072	(3,149)	(5)
1977	65,603	8,531	15
1978	61,100	(4,503)	(7)

Source: Arizona Public Service Company, Phoenix, Arizona.

management and energy development, are presented in Table 17-3. It must be understood that although the table identifies many key statutes, it only samples the full federal influence. For example, laws and regulations directly involved in nuclear energy development have not been included. The intent of Table 17-3, then, is to convey some sense of the array of federal inputs which come to bear on resource-related activities.

Actually, while regulations proliferated during the 1970s, the bloom of the last environmental movement faded quickly; most broad-based activity occurred in the years 1969 through 1972. The gasoline shortage of 1973 turned much of the public toward a syndrome protective of immediate personal desires and away from the enthusiastic (if short-lived) period of environmental altruism. Indeed, it is ironic that oil, which had provided two great rallying points in the environmental battles of the late 1960s and early 1970s-- the Alaska Pipeline and the Santa Barbara oil spills--had become the focus of disenchantment with environmentalism. People were not certain they wanted to protect environment so carefully as to interfere with their high energy consumption habits.

The momentum of the federal system, however, was not so easily deterred and new public laws were manifested in an expanding bureaucracy and proliferation of regulations. The machinery, once started, was not easily stopped. From the environmentalist's point of view, this is an important advantage of the federal regulatory system; that is, repeal of legislation occurs rarely and inertia tends to maintain and enhance the gains made during brief periods of public support. This principle holds true for all three historic groundswells of environmentalism in the United States.

Table 17-3. Selected Federal Laws which Significantly Influence Environmental Management and Energy Development.
Ausgewählte Bundesgesetze mit besonderem Einfluss auf Umweltbewirtschaftung und Energie Entwicklung.

Law and Administrating Agency	Date	Selected Aspects
National Environmental Policy Act (NEPA), P.L. 91-190; Environmental Protection Agency	1970	Established Council for Environmental Quality; led to Environmental Protection Agency and Environmental Impact Statements to accompany development in any way related to federal land, licensing, or financing.
Air Quality Act, P.L. 90-148 Clean Air Act, P.L. 91-604 Amendments, P.L. 93- 15 P.L. 93-319 P.L. 95- 95 P.L. 95-190; Environmental Protection Agency.	1967 1970 1973 1974 1977 1977	To protect and enhance the nation's air quality; sets standards for designated pollutants; establishes visibility standards; sets up PSD requirements.
Clean Water Act (CWA), P.L. 92-500 Amendments, 95-217, 95-576; Environmental Protection Agency.	1972 1977 1977	Establish national water quality standards and enforcement and research mechanics; focuses primarily on surface waters.

Safe Drinking Water Act (SDWA) P.L. 93-523 Amendments, 95-190; Environmental Protection Agency.	1974 1977	Establishes national primary drinking water standards, maintains enforcement umbrella over contamination problems; primarily focuses on groundwater.
Endangered Species Act, P.L. 93-740 Amendments, 16 U.S.C. 1532 Department of Interior Fish and Wildlife Service.	1973 1978	316A and B laws deal with impingement and entrapment vis-à-vis thermal pollution, water screens, etc.; the law generally deals with identification in and inventory of threatened and endangered flora and fauna, providing appropriate protective and mitigating measures.
Noise Control Act, P.L. 92-574; Environmental Protection Agency.	1972	Governs community noise standards and problems; affects operations of both fixed and mobile equipment.
Wilderness Act, P.L. 88-577; Forest Service Department of Agriculture.	1964	Established a National Wilderness System by withdrawal of wilderness areas with intent to preserve unimpaired; exceptions allowed for previous uses in some cases
Federal Land Management Policy Act (FLMPA), P.L. 94-579; Bureau of Land Management.	1976	Establishes review and inventory of all federal lands for determination of future use, jurisdiction, management, etc.; Sec. 603 requires Bureau of Land Management review all roadless areas of 5,000 acres or more to determine suitability for wilderness.

TABLE 17-3 (continued).

Construction Safety Act, P.L. 87-581; Amendments, P.L. 91-54; Department of Labor	1962 1969	Affects transmission line construction, operation and procedures.
Federal Mine Safety and Health Act (MSHA), P.L. 95-164 Amendments, P.L. 92-303, P.L. 95-239; Occupational Safety and Health Administration, Department of Labor	1972 1972 1977	Establishes operational, protective standards for health and safety in mining; amendments provide black-lung benefits.
Surface Mining and Control Act (SMCRA), 30 U.S.C. 1201 Exec Order; Department of Interior	1977	Section 710 gives complete authority to reservation tribes to promulgate regulations and rules; allows land reclamation costs to be passed on to consumer; regulates mineral exploration.
Resource Conservation and Recovery Act (RCRA), P.L. 94-580	1976	Defines hazardous waste and how best to dispose, store, and transport it.
Federal Insecticide, Fungicide, and Rodenticide Act (FIFRA), P.L. 92-516 Amendments, P.L. 94-140; Environmental Protection Agency.	1972 1975	Controls selection and application of chemicals.

Hazardous Materials Transportation Act, P.L. 93-633; Department of Transportation	1975	Mandates training of shippers, transporters, and receivers of hazardous materials; defines use of shipping documents, vehicles labels, containers, etc.
Toxic Substances Control Act (TSCA), P.L. 94-469; Environmental Protection Agency.	1976	"Cradle-to-grave" control of toxic chemicals in U.S.; affects marketing, distribution, and uses.

On the other hand, all laws, and not just environmental ones, are affected by such inertia. Thus, the creation of the Department of Energy and the national mandate for energy independence have created a situation whereby many goals of energy development must inevitably conflict with objectives of environmental protection.

Regulatory Impacts on Energy Development
The federal regulatory process affects all four phases of energy development: extraction of energy resources, transportation of energy resources, generation of power, and transmission of power. Each of these activities is influenced by several of the laws cited in Table 17-3, not to mention literally scores of other regulations at federal, state, and local levels. Industry has blamed the size and inertia of this regulatory system for the cancellations of several energy development projects. Two well publicized cases of cancellation in recent years are the SOHIO pipeline and the Kaiparowits generating system. Needless to say, the economic costs of environmental protection are a particular bone of contention in these regards. On the other hand, environmentalists claim that industry only drops those projects that would have been uneconomical anyway--that the energy industry can absorb environmental costs because its protects profits and passes the costs on to the consumer in any event.

To understand the web of regulations involved in energy development, let us view briefly some of the environmental requirements associated with the planning, construction, and operation of a coal-fired electric power-generating plant. Although this is a hypothetical case, the problems are exactly those encountered by utilities in the American West.

First, several years must be spent on a siting study in which efforts are made to optimize economics and minimize conflicts with environmental regulations. In effect, a siting study includes abbreviated versions of Environmental Impact Statements (EIS) for a number of potential sites. A major factor and current complication in site selection has been introduced by the withdrawal of land for wilderness evaluation under the Federal Land Management Policy Act (PL 94-579). This program, which is detailed in a later section of this essay, effectively blocks some 68 million acres of public domain from development in the short-range future.

Once a favored site has been selected, several procedures must be initiated. Perhaps the most difficult of these are the actions associated with the Clean Air Act (PL 91-604) and its various amendments. Air pollution travels great distances and, therefore, environmental protection must be considered for very large areas beyond the polluting source. The most stringent aspect of the Clean Air Act is the so-called PSD (Prevention of Serious Deterioration) component. Associated regulations require, among other things, a minimum one-year weather and ambient pollutant monitoring program (or an acceptable substitute) and "offset" trade-offs whereby existing pollutant sources must be removed in order for new ones to be introduced. This latter rule applies to areas where national ambient air quality standards are already exceeded or will be by the addition of the new source.

Regulations associated with the Clean Air Act and its amendments represent the single greatest area of confusion in the entire environmental protection area. They also highlight several of the basic problems which plague the resource management field. For example, the Clean Air Act gives to each state the responsibility for developing its own State Implementation Plan (SIP) for air quality management. Because the state plan must be approved by the Environmental Protection Agency and meet at least minimum national air quality standards, it is illusory to believe that environmental management has been returned to the state level. Instead, there is a further bureaucratic and technocratic layering of the system.

Another problem with air quality regulations is that it is sometimes impossible to figure out what is required; amazingly, the federal government expects people to guess in these instances. Two examples are the yet to be promulgated regulations for visibility and the prospect of minimum standards for hydrocarbon emissions. Finally, rules for TSP (total suspended particulates) are also a sore point in much of the American West, where ambient <u>natural</u> dust frequently exceeds the established standard during windy conditions. This illustrates a root problem in the environmental regulations field whereby rules and standards are established on a national basis and do not take into account regional variations of terrain, climate, and hydrography.

The siting of our hypothetical power plant will, of course, also require a full range of considerations under the aegis of an environmental impact assessment or statement. These include questions of endangered flora and fauna (PL 93-740), noise control (PL 92-574), clean water (PL 92-500), previously-mentioned aspects of the Clean Air Act and its amendments, and accommodation to cultural, ethnological, and archaeological sites and situations. There are additional ramifications. In the West, "once-through" water cooling systems are not possible because of short water supplies; ergo, brine concentrates in water that has been used several times and it is necessary to dispose of the brine in evaporation ponds. This, in turn, can lead to water pollution originating in the pond discharge; occasionally, this concentrates toxic substances and introduces a new environmental problem.

Similarly, in order to meet Clean Air Act requirements, "scrubbers" are used to reduce sulphur dioxide pollution. Large quantities of water are involved in the hydration of limestone in this process, and a scrubber sludge waste is produced, which is generally placed in standing ponds. Heavy metals and light radioactive substances (typical of coal seam sources) are concentrated in the sludge. Corrective measures must be taken to correct surface and ground water quality (PL 95-500; PL 95-190) and related laws such as the Resource Conservation and Recovery Act (PL 94-580) and the Toxic Substances Control Act (PL 94-469) become significant. Further, large surface areas are required for ponds and new questions of environmental site selection and protection are introduced. Here, then, is a classical case whereby protection against one kind of pollution (air) leads to another kind (water and land).

Lastly, even if our case example utility comes up with appropriate site plans and makes appropriate adjustments to compensate for or to eliminate environmentally damaging activities, they still may be moved back to the starting position. For example, this past summer (1979) the Eighth Circuit Court, in what is known as the Alabama Power Decision, overthrew the rules and regulations relating to the State Implementation Plans and their directions and coordination by the Environmental Protection Agency. Interestingly, the United States government was the defendant and both the utility industry and environmentalist groups were plaintiffs. One thought the regulations unreasonable; and others believed they were not strict enough. The net result is that a minimum of another twelve to eighteen months will be required to establish new regulations and ruling from the Environmental Protection Agency on SIPs. Meanwhile, all plans that have not already been licensed will be placed in a holding pattern with concomitant costs of delay and inflation.

While the above scenario represents only a portion of the impact of regulations on energy development, it does provide some flavor of the frustrations encountered by resource planners. Similar problems, with variations in the regulations, are encountered for other land uses on public domain. On the other hand, it is easy to be caught up by the perspective of environmental regulations seen through the eyes of the energy industry. One must remember that the record of that industry has not always been exemplary in these regards and that one of the reasons for the heavy regulatory counterattack was the industry's environmental behavior in the past. Indeed, environment needs its advocates. The major problem seems to be that a policy for rational use of the land has floundered in a morass of contradictory regulations and court decisions.

Case Example: The Federal Land Management Policy Act of 1976

The Federal Land Management Policy Act of 1976 (FLMPA) is another example of forces of environmentalism and resource development thrown into conflict. Section 603 of the FLMPA is rooted in the Wilderness Act of 1964 (PL 88-577). That act, which established the National Wilderness System, included provisions for ongoing review and inventory of both existing and potential wilderness areas. Despite the fact that these reviews presumably had been going on for the previous twelve years, the FLMPA required that the Department of Interior withdraw 68 million acres of federal land from development (an area roughly the size of Arizona) until it could be decided whether to give it wilderness status or not. This is being accomplished under RARE II, which stands for the second edition of the Roadless Area Review and Evaluation program. RARE II applies to all roadless areas of 5,000 acres or more; agricultural roads are not considered roads.

The implications of FLMPA and RARE II are immense--affecting the future of agriculture, forestry, mining, power generation, and recreation. As usual, the impact on energy and other resource development will be felt most heavily in the western states. The major advantage of RARE II is that it permits a revaluation of public domain lands in the context of current technology and knowledge, thereby enhancing opportunities to preserve and protect endangered natural areas and the flora and fauna that inhabit them. Further, the review process will undoubtedly temper the rush (by some) to extract energy resources in an environmentally unsound manner.

RARE II's principal disadvantage is that it involves an extraordinarily long review process that will not be completed until 1995 or later. The estimated FLMPA-RARE II timetable is schematically shown in Table 17-4. Clearly, some public domain lands will become available for use within a year or so, but any land with even slight potential as wilderness is likely to remain in the procedural pipeline through the 1980s. The economic and social costs of delay could be staggering, assuming continued inflation.

TABLE 17-4. Projected Flow Chart and Timetable for Implementation of RARE II, Federal and Policy Management Act of 1976.
Projektierte 'Flow' Tabelle und Zeittafel für die Verwirklichung von RARE II, Federal and Policy Management Act von 1976.

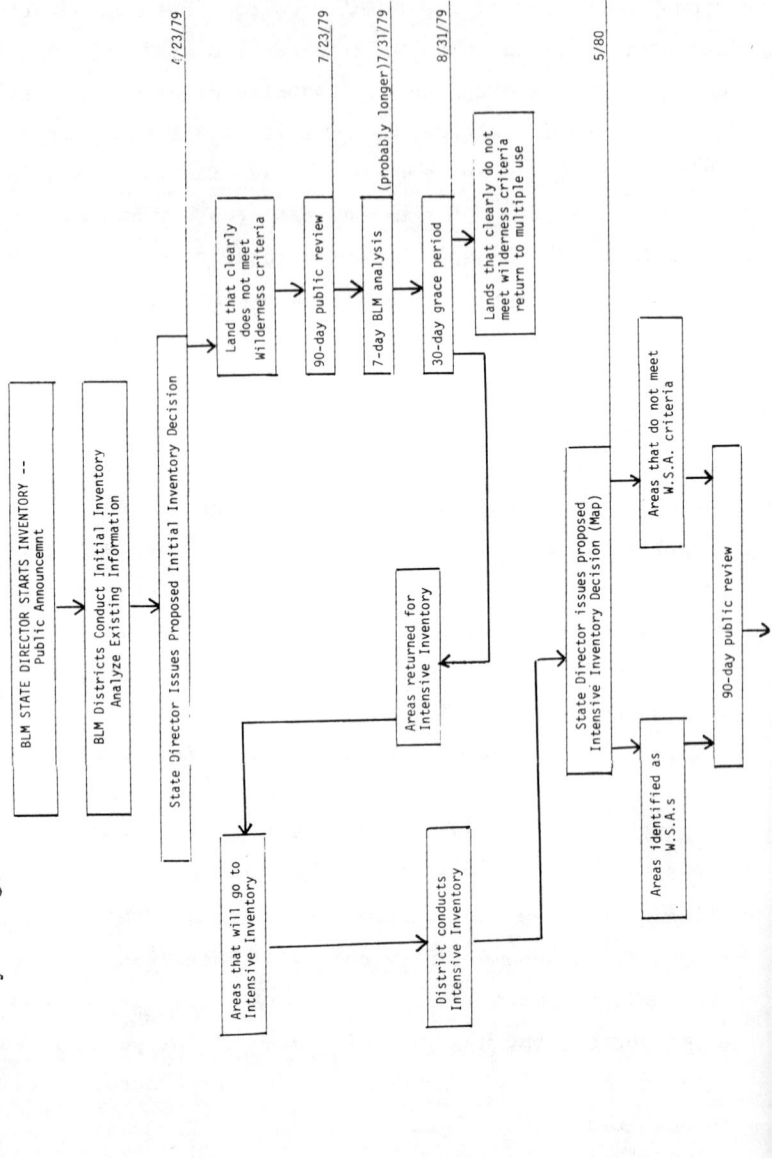

```
                    BLM STATE DIRECTOR STARTS INVENTORY --
                              Public Announcement
                                      │
                                      ▼
                    BLM Districts Conduct Initial Inventory
                         Analyze Existing Information
                                      │
                                      ▼
              State Director Issues Proposed Initial Inventory Decision     4/23/79
                                      │
                      ┌───────────────┼───────────────┐
                      ▼                               ▼
              Land that clearly                Areas that will go to
              does not meet                    Intensive Inventory
              wilderness criteria                      │
                      │                               ▼
                      ▼  7/23/79              District conducts
              90-day public review            Intensive Inventory
                      │                               │
                      ▼  (probably longer)7/31/79    ▼
              7-day BLM analysis              Areas returned for
                      │                       Intensive Inventory
                      ▼  8/31/79                      │
              30-day grace period                     ▼
                      │                       State Director issues proposed
                      ▼                       Intensive Inventory Decision (Map)
              Lands that clearly do not               │
              meet wilderness criteria        ┌───────┴───────┐
              return to multiple use          ▼               ▼
                                      Areas that do not    Areas identified
                                      meet W.S.A.          as W.S.A.s
                                      criteria
                                          │                   │
                                    5/80  ▼                   │
                                      90-day public review ◄──┘
                                          │
                                          ▼
```

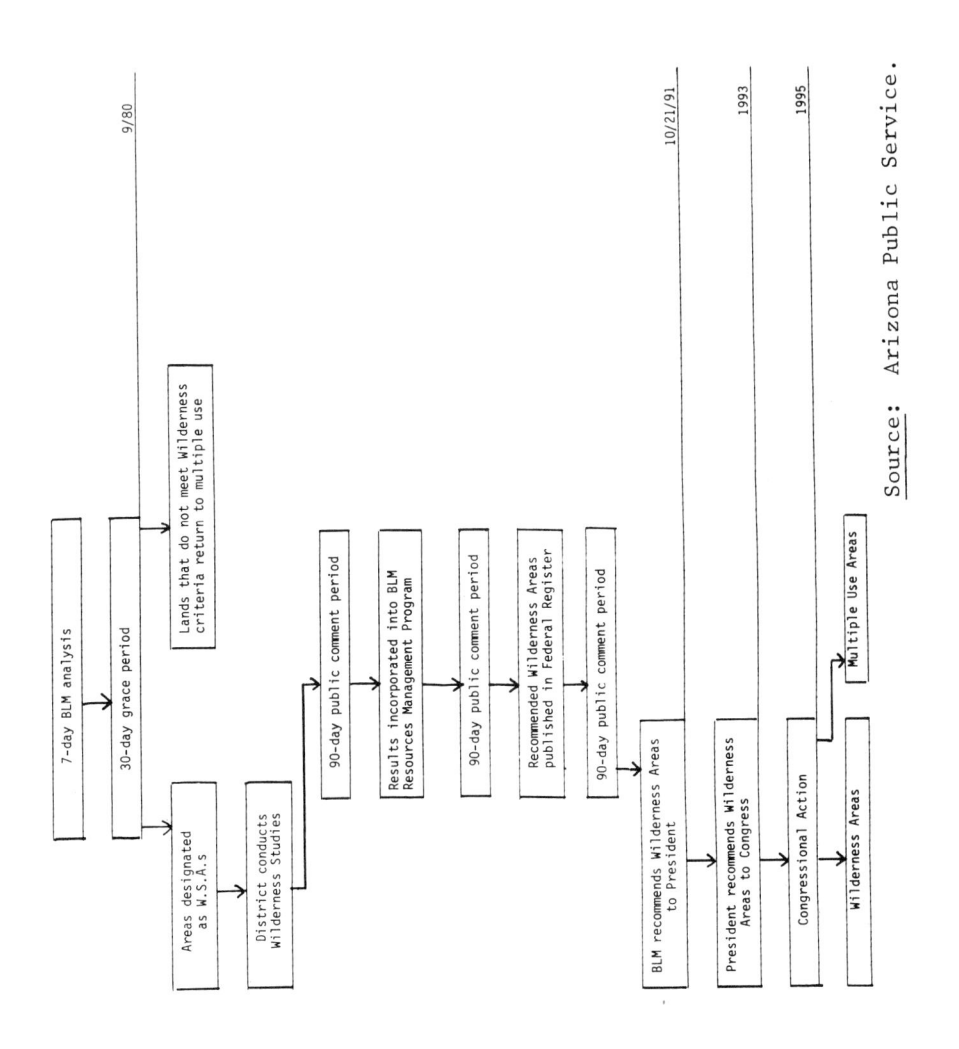

ENERGY DEVELOPMENT AND ENVIRONMENTAL MANAGEMENT   559

```
7-day BLM analysis
        |
        v
9/80 ──────────
30-day grace period ──> Lands that do not meet Wilderness
        |                criteria return to multiple use
        v
Areas designated as W.S.A.s
        |
        v
District conducts Wilderness Studies
        |
        v
90-day public comment period
        |
        v
Results incorporated into BLM Resources Management Program
        |
        v
90-day public comment period
        |
        v
Recommended Wilderness Areas published in Federal Register
        |
        v
90-day public comment period
        |
        v
10/21/91
BLM recommends Wilderness Areas to President
        |
        v
1993
President recommends Wilderness Areas to Congress
        |
        v
Congressional Action ──> Multiple Use Areas
        |
        v
1995
Wilderness Areas
```

Source: Arizona Public Service.

For example, utility companies are obligated to provide service within their franchise areas. With increasing populations in the American Southwest, there has been a concomitant rise in energy demand. Transmission lines are necessary to deliver this energy, but often these lines have been planned to cross areas withdrawn for wilderness studies. Utilities are faced with a delay of years until a wilderness decision is made; after waiting, the area may be withdrawn from use in any event. If industry accepts the delay, costs may soar; delays associated with the Sierra Pacific Power Company's proposed transmission line across northern Nevada have been estimated at $673,500 per month (20).

Meanwhile, public demand for energy continues. To avoid the delay, the utility may elect to realign the transmission line path. In the Sierra Pacific case, this meant a detour of 74 miles. As Metzger (20) states:

> Well, what does the extra 74 miles mean? An initial cost of $7.4 million for the hardware alone and more costs that go on for as long as the line is in existence--such as: transmission line losses, energy that would supply 1,600 homes each year, _every year_, if it weren't lost on these 74 extra miles and another $1.5 million, each year, to cover the extra capital costs.

Arizona Public Service similarly estimates the detour cost of a 500-KV transmission system at $300,000 per mile (21). Finally, one of the long-term implications of RARE II is that land designated as wilderness will also be designated Class I under the Clean Air Act Amendments' PSD and attainment requirement (discussed earlier). This will, in turn, impact on existing and proposed mining and power generation operations in areas adjacent to the wilderness. Given the stringent PSD expectation, it is predictable that such activities will be affected up to tens of miles distant.

Again it is seen that the national mandate for rapid energy resource development has been thrown into conflict with federal efforts to classify and manage land in a sound environmental manner.

CONCLUSION

The conclusions of this essay are inevitably statements of the obvious. Under present federal policies, laws, and regulations, a serious confrontation has been unintentionally encouraged between the forces of natural energy interdependence and those of environmental protection. Indeed, many persons find themselves favoring both these goals and confused as to how the two objectives can be achieved under present circumstances. Some of the major problems which hinder energy development in the context of rational environmental management are:

(a) Laws and regulations do not always clearly establish rules and criteria. As a result, resource users are forced to invest time and money in guesswork planning--only to be turned down and have to start all over again.

(b) Congress seldom in its laws spells out the details of its intent. It, therefore, becomes incumbent upon the assigned administering agency to promulgate regulations. It usually follows that the courts are asked to interpret both the agency's regulations and the intent of Congress. The entire process can delay decision making for as much as five to ten years.

(c) It follows from the above that ground rules are constantly changed either because of court decisions or the promulgation of new or "piggy-back" regulations. Late-developing research and technology often leads to the latter.

(d) Many national environmental standards and regulations have been established on a broad legal base and do not take into account geographical variations of terrain, climate, hydrography, or culture. Thus, rules that are eminently sensible in one location may make no sense whatsoever in another; water and dust are two examples of environmental elements in this class.

(e) Serious breakdowns in communications, policy, and management occur because there is a multiplicity of federal agencies and jurisdictions involved in land and energy management in the West. Sometimes the agencies have conflicting mandates; sometimes they seem to wear blinders and have little sense of the larger environmental picture.

(f) Almost every federal law relating to the environment creates state agencies to parallel the tasks administered by the federal agencies. Presumably, this is an effort to give the states leadership on environmental and energy policies and to appease those who fear that states' rights have been overly usurped by the federal government. In reality, because state policies and actions must be approved at the federal level, this only further layers an already complex bureaucracy.

(g) The federal government is the largest employer in the United States, and no small percentage of its work force is involved in land and energy management.

In other words, the federal system, like a dinosaur, is collapsing under its own weight. The wonder is that a system so large has managed to function as well as it has. Clearly, America's environmental laws and regulations have been created with the best of intentions and are needed to prevent improper exploitation of the environment. Unhappily, however, both the structure and magnitude of the federal management/regulatory system have tended to obscure these worthy intentions. This has led not only to unfavorable reactions from affected resource users, but has also been manifested in a move toward the reaffirmation of states' rights. The most dramatic example of this phenomenon to date is the so-called "Sagebrush Rebellion," whereby the state legislature of Nevada is attempting to "reclaim" federal land for the state.

If such actions and reactions are to be defused, major shifts in federal policy and structure (and even personnel) will be required, with concurrent adjustments at state and local levels. It is not likely that such major readjustments will occur. Rather, the system will tend to proceed on its own inertia and respond retroactively in crisis situations. This is not a hallmark of good environmental management or proper energy development, but it is unfortunately the way things will be for the next few years. This message of gloom should be tempered, however, by the recognition that environmental progress has occurred--that the three environmental groundswells of this century have each produced a net gain (Figure 17-1). To be sure, some of the gains have been lost in each instance, but the cumulative impact has been favorable to the cause of environmentalism. Perhaps the next groundswell will carry us toward a rational accommodation of the energy-environment conflict.

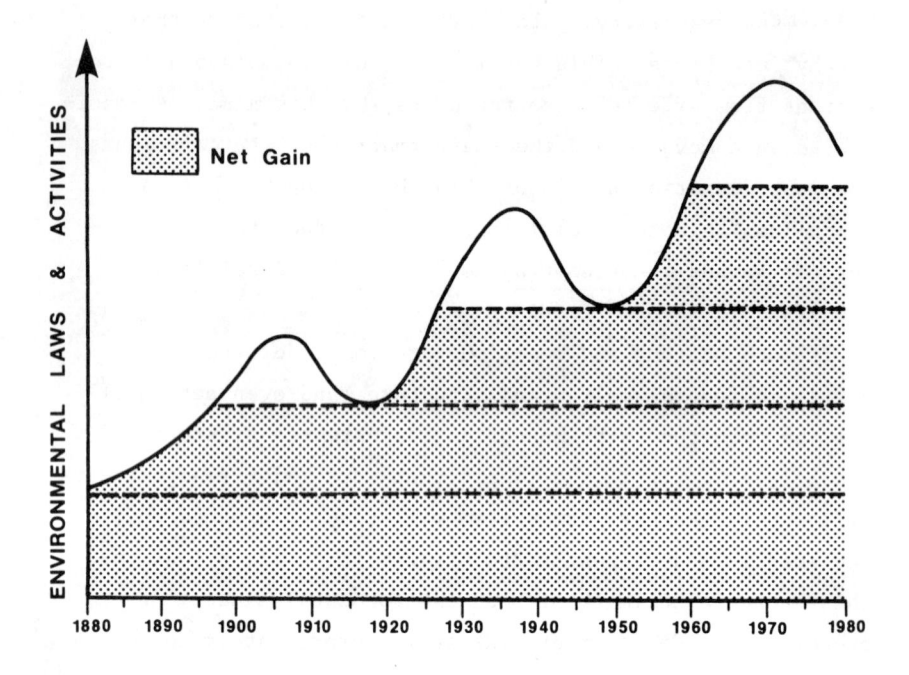

FIG. 17-1. Phases of Environmental Activity in the United States: 1880-1980.
Phasen der Umwelterhaltung in den Vereinigten Staaten 1880-1980.

NOTES

1. Valley National Bank of Arizona, *Arizona Statistical Review: 1978* (Phoenix: Valley National Bank of Arizona Economic Research Department, 1978).

2. Graham, F., Jr., *Man's Dominion: The Story of Conservation in America* (New York: M. Evans and Company, Inc., 1971).

3. Hawkes, H. B., "The Paradoxes of the Conservation Movement," *Twenty-Fourth Annual Frederick William Reynolds Lecture* 51, 11 (Salt Lake City: University of Utah Press, 1960), p. 35.

4. Manners, I. R., and M. W. Mikesell, eds., *Perspectives on Environment*, Commission on College Geography Publication No. 13 (Washington, D.C.: Association on American Geographers, 1974).

5. Mikesell, M. W., "Geography on the Study of Environment: An Assessment of Some Old and New Commitments," *Perspectives on Environment*, Commission on College Geography Publication No. 13 (1974), 1-23.

6. Nash, R., *Wilderness and the American Mind* (New Haven, Ct.: Yale University Press, 1967).

7. Stuhr, D. C., "The Heritage of Environmentalism," *The American Biology Teacher*, 35 (1973), 68-77.

8. Nash, R., *The American Environment: Readings in the History of Conservation* (Reading, Massachusetts: Addison-Wesley Publishing Company, Inc., 1968), p. 236.

9. Mather, K. F., *The Earth Beneath Us* (New York: Random House, 1945).

10. Holman, E., "Our Inexhaustible Resources," *Atlantic Monthly* 184 (1952), 29-32.

11. Osborn, F., *Our Plundered Planet* (Boston: Little, Brown and Company, 1948).

12. _____, *The Limits of the Earth* (Boston: Little, Brown and Company, 1953).

13. Vogt, W., *Road to Survival* (New York: William Sloane, 1948).

14. Carson, R., *Silent Spring* (Boston, Massachusetts: Houghton, Mifflin, 1962).

15. Commoner, B., *Science and Survival* (New York: Viking Press, 1967).
16. Ehrlich, P. R., *The Population Bomb* (Ballantine Books, 1968).
17. Ehrlich, P. R., and A. H. Ehrlich, *Population, Re-Sources, Environment* (San Francisco: Freeman, 1970).
18. Udall, S. L., *The Quiet Crisis* (New York: Holt, Rinehart and Winston, 1963).
19. Meadows, D. H., et al., *The Limits to Growth* (New York: Universe Books, 1972).
20. Metzger, H. P., "The Coercive Utopians: Their Hidden Agenda," *The Denver Post*, 30 April 1978.
21. Koch, D., personal communication, 10 August 1979.

CHAPTER 18

THE FEDERAL ROLE IN U.S. WILDLIFE CONSERVATION
WITH REFERENCE TO THE AMERICAN SOUTHWEST

DIE ROLLE DER BUNDESREGIERUNG IN DER WILDHEGE
IN DEN VEREINIGTEN STAATEN IM BEZUG AUF DEN
AMERIKANISCHEN SÜDWESTEN

Robin W. Doughty

Abstract

Through proprietary, legal, and fiscal controls the federal government influences wildlife-related activities across the nation. Several agencies have various degrees of commitment and authority over the preservation and conservation of native wildlife. In recent decades the federal agencies with most responsibility for wildlife have expanded their power and influence over state authorities involved with animal resources. Current moves by the U.S. government to promote research into nongame species, and to include nonconsumptive uses of wildlife into state programs reflect a departure from the traditional emphasis on material benefits from outdoor recreation. Decisions to study endangered animals, to establish reserves, and to manage closely game populations in the four-state area comprising the Southwest, a rich faunistic region, demonstrate efforts to develop joint planning and cooperation between state and federal wildlife-related departments.

Kurzfassung

Durch eigentumsrechtliche gesetzgeberische und fiskalische Kontrollen beeinflusst die Bundesregierung die die Wildtiere betreffenden Aktivitäten überall in der Nation. Mehrere Bundesbehörden haben in verschiedenen Grade Verpflichtungen und Macht bezüglich der Hege und Bewahrung der einheimischen Wildtiere. In den letzten Jahrzehnten haben jene Bundesbehörden mit der grössten Verantwortung für Wildtiere ihre Macht über und Einfluss auf die mit Wildtierangelegenheiten beschäftigten Behörden der Staaten vergrössert. Gegenwärtige Versuche der Bundesregierung, die Erforschung der nicht jagdbaren Arten zu fördern und eine nicht verbrauchs-orientierte

Nutzungen der Wildtiere in Programme der Staaten einzubeziehen, spiegeln eine Abweichung von dem traditionellen Nachdruck auf die materiellen Gewinne aus der Erholung im Freien (Jagd) wider. Die Beschlüsse, gefährdete Tiere zu studieren, Gehege einzurichten, und den Bestand der jagdbaren Tiere in den vier Staaten, die den mit Tieren stark bevölkerten Südwesten bilden, sorgfältig zu bewirtschaften, zeigen die Bemühungen auf, gemeinsame Planung und Arbeit zwischen den mit Wildtieren beschäftigten Staats-und Bundesbehörden zu entwickeln.

The Federal Role in U.S. Wildlife Conservation With Reference to the American Southwest

The federal government affects the conservation of American wildlife on a state level in three basic interrelated ways. First, a number of federal agencies, including the Departments of Agriculture, Interior, and Defense, own and operate large tracts of the nation's land which the government has subtracted frequently from the public domain. These and other agencies regulate land use practices on and access to sizable portions in a number of states, especially in the West, thereby affecting the wildlife resources.

Second, federal laws aimed at protecting wild animals and wildlife habitats date back to the turn of the present century. Congressional acts provide controls for the harvest of game and protect completely most migratory nongame species. Other laws seek to restore and rehabilitate selected species and to manage their populations, or provide the basis for state and local control of predatory or pestiferous animals.

International treaties and conventions also influence state and local wildlife policies by establishing agreements and directives for the conservation of migratory birds, fish, and marine mammals throughout North America's land area, offshore waters, and in the Western hemisphere.

The various U.S. laws to protect, manage, control, regulate, or restore wild animal populations provide a framework and serve as a benchmark for state legislation. Frequently, these laws contain provisions for research into the biology and ecology of selected animals, and establish a means for consultation and cooperation between federal and state wildlife agencies.

Congressional appropriations for wildlife research and management provide the third important method of conservation, particularly in state wildlife programs. Federal monies attached to specific legislation are apportioned frequently to the states on a matching basis. They may be used as "seed" funds for the establishment of wildlife programs, or revenues may be passed to the states as annual grants which have achieved over time an insulated or built-in permanence.

This essay examines the three methods of federal involvement in state initiatives for wildlife conservation--land ownership, legal powers, and program development. It discusses the status of key animals judged to have benefitted from legislation and appropriations. The chapter also described some of the problems that wildlife professionals face in current state management programs.

For logistical reasons and the constraints of space most discussion will be focused on the U.S. Southwest, particularly the State of Texas. The Lone Star State's diverse geography, varied biota, and a traditional interest in wildlife provide a good example of historic and contemporary interaction between federal and state wildlife authorities.

WILDLIFE ON FEDERAL LANDS

At one time the federal government held title to about four-fifths of the nation's surface area. Today, government agencies have jurisdiction over approximately one-third of the land area in the United States, in excess of 760 million acres.

Important Federal Landholders

The U.S. Department of Agriculture's Forest Service is a major landowner, particularly in the western states. What has become a national system of forests originated with the Forest Reserve Act of 1891 (Table 18-1). Timber is produced, managed, and harvested in national forests; stock grazing, outdoor recreation, and wildlife conservation are elements of a policy geared to "multiple uses" for forest areas. Since 1941, for example, hunting has taken place in national forests through agreements with individual states and in accordance with state regulations.

However, conflicts over use priorities and the desire for sustained yields from forest areas have plagued Service officialdom. Recent congressional laws such as the Sikes Act Extension (1974), which mandates federal agencies to coordinate programs on public lands and to consult with state authorities in drawing up comprehensive plans for respective holdings, have made the management of wild animals, especially endangered species and their habitats, a priority. Another recent act (the National Forest Management Act of 1976) sets out specific standards and guidelines, including provisions for public participation, in the development of forest area management plans. Thus, wildlife conservation is integral to planning objectives, and now funds from the sale of timber may be spent on habitat management in the National Forest system (1, pp. 142-161).

Like the Forest Service, the Bureau of Land Management (in the Department of the Interior), which has jurisdiction over 60 percent of all federal lands (about 20 percent of the land area in the U.S.), primarily in western states, has followed a similar multiple-use and sustained-yield policy in administering its extensive holdings (Table 18-1).

TABLE 18-1. Jurisdiction of Principal Federal Wildlife-Related Agencies.
Rechtsprechung der wichtigsten Bundesbehörden im Bereich des Wildlebens.

FEDERAL AGENCY	PERMANENT POSITIONS	ANNUAL APPROPRIATIONS FY 1977 ($MILLIONS)
U.S. Dept. Interior (1849): Bureau of Land Management (established 1946)	5,194	279 (66 for Renewable Resource Management)
Bureau of Reclamation (established 1902)	6,217	618 (4 for Recreational fish and Wildlife facilities)
Bureau of Outdoor Recreation (created 1962)	431	7
National Park Service (established 1916)	8,941	295 (284 for Park Management)
Fish and Wildlife Service (designated 1940)	4,710	148.5
U.S. Dept. Commerce: (designated 1913): National Oceanic and Atmospheric Administration (established 1970)	12,838	584.5 (77 for Ocean Fisheries and Marine Resources; 32 for Marine Ecosystem Analysis; 26.5 for Sea Grant)

JURISDICTION (MILLIONS OF ACRES)	REMARKS
470 (467 from public domain)	The nation's largest single manager of land and wild animal habitat (over 450 million acres of terrestrial habitat, 270,000 miles of stream and 5.2 million acres of lakes and reservoirs). The BLM manages range, wilderness and wildlife including 70,000 wild horses and burros on public lands. The Bureau protects 200 endangered plants, and 30 species of endangered fish and wildlife occurring on public lands.
7.5 (5.6 from public domain)	The Bureau plans, constructs and operates irrigation and municipal water supply facilities in 17 Western States. Fish and wildlife enhancement is one element in multi-purpose planning and development.
	The Bureau is concerned with nationwide outdoor planning and recreation benefits, including the preservation of resources which represent the nation's natural heritage. The agency administers the Land and Water Conservation Fund for recreational areas.
31 (25 from public domain)	The Park Service administers 294 units in 47 States for 260 million visitors per year: Wildlife is protected in National Parks.
34 27 from public domain)	The Division of Wildlife Resources administers 386 units and 7 wetland Management Districts in the National Wildlife Refuge System.
0.051	NOAA includes provisions for commercial and sport fishery programs, the conservation of endangered species, and for coastal zone management. Sea Grant provides matching funds for universities and industries to solve management and use related problems in marine resources.

TABLE 18-1 (continued).

FEDERAL AGENCY	PERMANENT POSITIONS	ANNUAL APPROPRIATIONS FY 1977 ($ MILLIONS)
U.S. Dept. Agriculture (1862): Forest Service (named 1905)	20,209	764.5 (350 for Forest Land Management; 82 for Forest Research)
Soil Conservation Service (established 1935)	13,772	223
Agricultural Stabilization and Conservation Service (established 1961)	2,369	157
Cooperative State Research Service (established 1953)	89	129
Agricultural Extension Service (established 1923)	181	242
U.S. Dept. Defense Corps of Engineers (established 1824)	28,690	
U.S. Environmental Protection Agency (established 1970)	9,779	

[1] See Table 18-2 for further details.

[2] For the Agricultural Research Service.

Source: The Budget of the United States, Fiscal Year 1979-- Appendix (Washington, D.C.: Government Printing Office, 1978).

JURISDICTION (MILLIONS OF ACRES)	REMARKS
188 (160 from public domain)	Forest Service administers 154 National Forests and 19 National Grassland units for multiple use and sustained yield principles. Upwards of 200 million visitors-days are spent on Forest Service lands where 11.4 million livestock units graze, and 10.5 billion board ft. of timber are harvested annually.
0.0015	The SCS administers 2,934 Conservation Districts to provide technical assistance for farmers and ranchers. Wildlife habitat improvements are included in conservation practices.
0.40[2]	The Service administers a conservation program and provides assistance for agricultural communities. It also maintains the Water Bank Program for the conservation of wetlands for migratory waterfowl. Water Bank agreements totaled 503,000 acres in 1978.
	The Service improves animal husbandry, agricultural and forestry research and provides grants for wildlife habitat related topics.
	The Service provides education and training in agriculture and related rural industries, including wildlife habitat management on private lands.
8 (1 from public domain)	Develops flood and beach erosion control and navigation improvement, providing for wildlife on lands adjacent to impoundments through mitigation.
0	Administers programs aimed at water and air polution abatement. Better quality wildlife habitat results from state-assisted pollution control programs.

Through written agreements with individual states the Bureau of Land Management (BLM) is responsible for the habitat (the states for the species) aspects in wildlife management. In recent years, the scope of BLM's authority has been limited by the National Environmental Policy Act (NEPA), which requires all federal agencies to prepare environmental impact statements for major federal actions. The Bureau's program has become subject to public scrutiny (expanded recently under the Federal Land Policy Act of 1976). And a new act directs that fees for grazing stock on BLM lands be placed in a fund for range improvement including the betterment of wildlife habitat. Wildlife is on an equal footing with timber, livestock grazing, and mining on public lands.

The BLM's Wildlife Porgram includes the restoration of impoverished habitat, management for threatened species, and the provision of wildlife values in the formulation of resource policy, in order to juxtapose the biological requirements of wild animals with the public's need for outdoor recreation. The Bureau's potential for enhancing the nation's wildlife is enormous because it administers 24.3 percent of the total area (approximately 174 million acres, a land area larger than the State of Texas) of 10 contiguous western states where there are 1.2 million deer, 190,000 antelope, 95,000 elk, 10,000 bighorn sheep, 4,300 bear, and other game animals. The BLM has jurisdiction over 17.3 percent of Arizona's acreage and 16.6 percent of New Mexico's, and is active in protecting and managing the habitats of several rare mammals and birds in both states (1, pp. 161-182; 2).

The U.S. Fish and Widlife Service's Wildlife Refuge System is a unique system of federally-owned lands set aisde specifically for wild animal conservation. In the mid-1970s there were 367 units in the National Wildlife Refuge (NWR) system comprising approximately 34 million acres (a little larger than New York State), similar in total area to the national forests (Tables 18-1 and 18-2). Refuge acreage has more than doubled in the past twenty years, and will more than double again (primarily from the addition of 50 million acres in Alaska) by 1981. The NWR system is provided for by laws and funding that go back fifty years, notably to the Migratory Bird Conservation Act of 1929 and the Migratory Bird Hunting Stamp Act of 1934, as amended, which provided respectively the necessary authorization and monies for the establishment and operation of wildlife and/ or waterfowl refuges.

President Theodore Roosevelt's Executive Order in March, 1903-whereby a breeding colony of brown pelicans on a three-acre island in the Indian River, Florida, was declared a preserve and given protection from plume hunters-set the precedent for a refuge program directed by the federal government for the public benefit. Roosevelt and subsequent U.S. presidents established new areas as federal refuges in the first two decades of the present century (Wichita Mountains Refuge, Oklahoma, for bison, longhorn cattle, and elk became the second one in 1905).

However, several federal laws enacted after 1918 (the year of the Migratory Bird Treaty Act which provided international protection but not habitat for many bird species) determined the basic objectives and direction for a national, unified program for refuge acquisition and management. The wildlife refuge concept blossomed in the late 1920s and 1930s when sportsmen and groups interested in conservation lobbied Congress and worked to restore populations of game mammals and birds, particularly waterfowl, numbers of which

TABLE 18-2. Holdings of the U.S. Department of Interior, Fish and Wildlife Service: Budget Appropriations, Fiscal Year 1977.
Besitz des U.S. Ministerium des Innern, Fisch und Wildleben Dienst: Haushaltungsbewilligungen, Fiskal Jahr 1977.

U.S. Fish and Wildlife Service	($million)	
Principal Activities:		
Habitat Preservation	24.9	Includes 260 pesticide monitoring sites, contaminants studies (144); licenses and permits (79,000); land and water resource investigations (850); technical assistance in coastal zone management (34).
Wildlife Resources	66.5	Includes 362 units totaling 8.54 million area for migratory birds, and 24 units of 23.9 million acres for other wildlife. Wetland Management Districts contain 1.54 million acres and produce about 2.8 million waterfowl. Refuge use by visitors totaled 55 million hours.
Fishery Resources	34.3	Includes 88 fish hatcheries, one spawning channel and 12 research laboratories, 19 biological stations, 81 research projects. Sixty million angler days were derived from 182 million fish produced, weighing 6.7 million lbs. in 1977.
Endangered Species	9.3	Includes the listing of threatened and endangered species, their protection, recovery and retention of critical habitat.
Administration	5.3	In FY 1977, 16,221 acres were acquired as Refuge area for migratory birds; an additional 54,220 acres were placed under assessment for waterfowl production.

Source: The Budget of the United States, Fiscal Year 1979-Appendix (Washington, D.C.: Government Printing Office, 1978).

had been hard-hit by drought, loss of habitat, and overhunting.

The Dust Bowl years stimulated the procurement of wetlands for migratory birds, and in 1934 the proceeds from hunting stamps were earmarked for refuge operations. Since 1958, these funds have been spent exclusively for refuge acquisition and for waterfowl production. However, revenue failed to keep pace with land costs; therefore, in 1961, under the Wetlands Loan Act, Congress authorized money for 2.5 million acres of wetland addition. The authorization ceiling is $200 million currently, and the repayment period of the interest-free loan has been extended.

Other products of the Depression Years were several big-game reserves and other large refuges for wildlife which were subtracted from the public domain in several western states. In 1939, for example, 1.5 million acres of the Sonoran desert wilderness in southwest Arizona were established as the Cabeza Prieta Game Range and the Kofa Game Range in order to protect desert bighorn sheep and pronghorn antelope (Figure 18-1). The two arid, desolate areas where summer temperatures top a searing 120° F., provide habitat for thirty-three species of mammals, among them the one hundred or so Sonoran pronghorn antelope which are found in their pure form in Cabeza Prieta (3). The Kofa Game Range holds the feral ass, whose protection under the Wild Horses and Burros Act (1971) caused controversy about the animal's alleged negative effects on the desert ecosystem, particularly on bighorn sheep.

The San Andreas Refuge in Dona Ana County, New Mexico, northeast of Las Cruces, is a similar rugged desert (Chihuahan) area consisting of 57,200 acres of former public domain which was set aside in 1941 for the preservation of desert bighorn sheep, mule deer, and other animals adapted to xeric environments (4, Appendix A).

After World War II, increased demand for outdoor recreation resulted in a review of refuge policy. Experts began to place greater emphasis on the amenities to be derived from wild animals, especially the conservation of nongame species and animals threatened with extinction.

Several federal measures for threatened species have proven important in management of the NWRs and deserve mention in this discussion of U.S. Fish and Wildlife Service jurisdiction. Elaboration on them is reserved for the section on federal legal policy. The Endangered Species Preservation Act of 1966 established a NWR "system" (from various administrative units), and instructed federal officials to devise a program to protect, restore, and to propagate rare and threatened native fish and wildlife. The act expanded the federal government's role from enforcing criminal laws to a policy of conservation and financial assistance aimed at the acquisition of habitat for vanishing species.

Also, attention was paid to endangered species under the Land and Water Conservation Act of 1965, as amended, which created a special Land and Water Fund from which critical habitat could be acquired for the NWR system (under section 5 of the updated 1973 Endangered Species Act; Appendix 18-1). The 1965 act authorizes appropriations to federal agencies, and to states on a matching basis, for outdoor recreation projects including the acquisition and development of parks, open space and lands adjacent to wildlife refuges, and holdings in the national forests and national parks. Monies generated under both the 1965 act (sources include oil and gas revenues from offshore oil facilities), and the earlier Wetlands Loan Act (1961) continue to be vital for habitat procurement. Under these laws over $1 billion has been granted for land acquisition to states, and almost as much to federal agencies.

The national park system, including wilderness areas, administered by the Department of the Interior, like the Fish and Wildlife Service, provides another important example of federal ownership and disposition of states' lands. The various uses made of large park acreages and the types of activities on them effect the character, structure, and populations of animal resources (Table 18-1). More than a dozen different types of units administered by the U.S. National Park Service (NPS) comprise an area of 31 million acres where the conservation of wild animals is recognized explicitly as an important goal. The Secretary of the Interior has used his authority to prohibit hunting in most parks; however, fishing is permitted. In some instances fish stocks are replenished in heavily used lake and streams.

The most important contribution to wildlife made by the NPS has been through the preservation of habitat. For example, grizzly bears remain in Yellowstone and Glacier National Parks because they are protected and their habitat is undeveloped. Likewise, in Florida's Everglades Park, several rare waterbird species survive because the NPS manages suitable nesting areas. Also, the 1964 Wilderness Act, by setting aside areas from development, has contributed directly to the preservation of animal habitat.

The federal government owns and directly affects the utilization of other lands. United States military authorities, for example, have jurisdiction over 30.7 million acres (roughly the area of Mississippi). Under the Sikes

Act (1960) the Secretary of Defense was authorized, in consultation with the heads of the federal agencies, to plan, develop, and maintain animal conservation on military areas. An amendment to the Act has provided for improvements to animal habitat; currently, many military reservations have management programs which are operated jointly with state wildlife departments.

Recent discussions about the outer continental shelf have extended federal jurisdiction over the nation's offshore waters to almost 200 miles. Regulations govern the harvest of commercial fisheries, and exploration for and extraction of marine and mineral (oil and gas) resources from subsurface waters and the seabed. The Outer Continental Shelf Act (1953) divided jurisdiction of the coastal shelf between the states, which were given control of the first three miles (for Texas, ten miles), and federal agencies, which were given authority over the remainder. The act instructed the Secretary of the Interior to provide for marine resource conservation through regulations that currently control oil and mineral extraction.

The Marine Mammal Act of 1972 established federal responsibility for conserving cetaceans, pinnipeds, sea otters, and polar bears, and included a moratorium on killing (section 1373 allows the taking of certain species) and importing them into the United States. Another 1972 act established a marine sanctuaries program for the preservation and restoration of marine animals. Finally, a recent 1976 act takes an affirmative stand on fishery resource utilization through specific regulations governing offtake.

Coastal and estuarine areas, vital for wildlife, also fall under the purview of the federal government. A compreprehensive inventory of these areas and a study of pollution abatement in coastal waters was begun thirteen years ago. In recent years laws have established the need to protect, conserve, and restore estuarine areas (the Estuary Protection Act, 1968), and have encouraged states to include wetlands in planning and management programs which federal agencies were prepared to fund (for example, the Coastal Zone Management Act, 1972). Grants have been made to acquire lands for beach access, island preservation, and for ecological and aesthetic benefits. Coordinated state and federal initiatives for coastal areas, including the preservation of their interesting, unique, and fragile biota, are made possible through an increasing federal concern for dwindling areas of undeveloped habitat (1, pp. 167-191; 5, 6).

Land Acquisition in Texas

The United States government claimed no land in Texas when it annexed the Republic in 1845 so that unappropriated lands were subject to disposition under state laws (7, pp. 18-19). As a consequence the federal government owns less than two percent of the Lone Star State's 171 million acres, the largest state in the Union outside Alaska. The largest federal land holders in Texas are the Department of Defense (with approximately 1.2 million acres) and the Department of the Interior (with approximately 1.1 million acres), whose principal components, the NPS and the Fish and Wildlife Service, have a special commitment to wildlife (Table 18-3).

There are ten U.S. Migratory Bird Refuges (mostly for waterfowl) which are habitat for several million ducks and geese which funnel down the central and Mississippi flyways to winter on coastal wetlands (Figure 18-1). The Aransas NWR was the first refuge, established in 1937 to protect

TABLE 18-3. Acreage Owned by the Federal Government - 1975.
Land im Eigentum der Bundesregierung - 1975.
(1,000s of acres)

Federal Agency	TEXAS Public Domain	TEXAS Acquired	ARIZONA Public Domain	ARIZONA Acquired	NEW MEXICO Public Domain	NEW MEXICO Acquired	OKLAHOMA Public Domain	OKLAHOMA Acquired
U.S. Dept. of Interior:								
Fish and Wildlife Service	0	157	877	0	16	300	78	2
Bureau Land Management	0	0	12,559	37	12,730	227	8	0
National Park Service	0	863	1,522	108	218	24	0	1
Bureau of Reclamation	0	77	986	73	80	118	0	70
U.S. Dept. of Agriculture:								
Forest Service	0	780	11,268	3	8,650	570	1	290
Department of Defense:								
Air Force	0	63	2,569	13	109	57	0	10
Army	0	373	935	61	2,200	158	51	76
Corps of Engineers	0	711	24	10	5	21	1	863
Total Federal Acreage	3,196(1.9%)		31,141(43%)		26,102(34%)		1,540(3.5%)	
Remainder	165,022		41,547		51,664		42,547	

Source: U.S. Bureau of Land Management, Public Land Statistics - 1976 (Washington, D.C.: Government Printing Office, 1977).

waterfowl. The whooping cranes, whose small flock of some fourteen birds was making its last stand in winter on the tidal marshes of the Blackjack Peninsula, Aransas County, wintered on this refuge. This large, conspicuous waterbird has become a symbol for conservation.

Today, the whooping crane exemplifies intensive and sustained efforts to rehabilitate endangered wildlife through programs for captive breeding, egg transplants, and the preservation and management of habitat. In 1977, the Aransas cranes numbered sixty-nine birds, a further nineteen birds were held in the Federal Patuxent Wildlife Research Center, Laurel, Maryland, and additional wild birds raised by sandhill crane "foster parents," migrate between Idaho and New Mexico (8).

Another important NWR, Santa Ana, contains more rare and threatened wildlife species than any other federal reserve. The 2,000-acre tract is a remnant of the Lower Rio Grande Valley's subtropical woodland, containing ebony, hackberry, ash, cactus, and chaparral which has been cleared for agriculture. Established in 1943, Santa Ana is regarded as the "gem" of the NWR System. It contains twenty-nine species of mammals, many of them unusual or rare, and lists 326 birds (many are migrants) or almost two-thirds of the species occurring west of the 100th meridian in the U.S. Its woodlands harbor a number of Mexican species on the northern extremities of their range.

Eleven Wildlife Management Areas totalling 190,000 acres (in 1976) comprise Texas' Wildlife Division's system of lands for wildlife conservation and research. All of the management units were purchased with federal appropriations. Approximately 22 percent of the acreage has been purchased since 1958; today Texas lags behind neighboring states in the amount of state land acquired for wildlife.

Oklahoma, for example, like Texas, has only a small portion of its land area (3.5 percent) owned by the federal government (Table 18-3). However, the Sooner State has set aside 57.6 percent more land for wildlife management than Texas, although the state is almost four times smaller. New Mexico is less than half the size of Texas; however, it has thirteen more state units for wildlife and 50,000 more acres in management areas or refuges. Moreover, the federal government owns roughly 34 percent of New Mexico's land, and the U.S. Fish and Wildlife Service's 316,000 acres (Table 18-3) is double the area that the agency controls in Texas.

Arizona has more units but a lower acreage for wildlife conservation than Texas; however, the federal government's 43 percent ownership of the entire state has resulted in very large tracts of land being established as refuges, game ranges, or forest areas (9, 10). The U.S. Fish and Wildlife Service, the Forest Service, and the National Park Service own 11.8 million more acres in Arizona than in Texas, an area almost 20 percent the size of West Germany.

FEDERAL LEGAL POLICY AND WILDLIFE CONSERVATION

The story of the exploitation of U.S. wildlife by commercial and sport interests has been told a number of times (11, 12, 13). The "War on Wildlife," as some have described it, was waged incessantly until, barely a century ago, the first organized demands for enforceable protective laws were voiced. Until the Revolution the essence of English wildlife law, whereby the authority to treat wild animals resided with the monarch, persisted in the United States. After independence, however, the states took the prerogatives of the British crown by determining the uses of wild animals. Indeed, the Supreme Court's decision, Geer v. Connecticut (1896), reaffirmed state sovereignty for wildlife by concluding that each state had the "right to control and regulate the common property in game . . . for the benefit of the people" (1, p. 18; 14).

The federal government's right to intervene in the interstate shipment of the nation's wildlife resource in violation of state law was established in 1900 by the Lacey Act (Appendix 18-1). Under the Lacey Act, Congress invoked powers to regulate interstate commerce (controls over foreign trade benefitted wild animals, too), by prohibiting shipments of game animals taken in contravention of state laws. The Lacey Act helped to support and enforce state laws for wild animals; also, it regulated the importation of injurious species into the United States.

The treaty-making power of the federal government was another means of establishing a precedent for wildlife regulations. A challenge to the constitutionality of a Congressional Migratory Bird Act (1913), which placed migratory game and insectivorous birds under the custody and jurisdiction of the federal government, was diverted when the Department of State concluded a wildlife treaty with Great Britain. This Migratory Bird Treaty Act of 1918 was judged to take precedence over the powers of individual states, and under its provisions federal agencies undertook to regulate the harvest of migratory bird species, and to end the commerce in waterfowl (15, 16). Most notable agreements between the U.S. and foreign countries and international organizations are listed in Appendix 18-1.

Federal laws which curbed the misuse of the nation's wildlife were based on the government's authority to regulate commerce, to make treaties with foreign nations, and also to control the taking of animals on federal lands such as parks, refuges, or forests; as early as 1894, for example, all hunting had been prohibited in Yellowstone National Park. These laws challenged the doctrine of state ownership and gradually eroded it.

Over the past eighty years federal legislation has moved from total protection for most animals to the establishment of laws and regulations for harvesting game mammals and birds on a sustainable basis. Through the imposition of closed seasons, bag limits, and a clarification of the concept of "game," including the methods by which hunters may kill animals, the phase of federal involvement with wildlife has shifted from preservation to management and refurbishment.

From the 1920s efforts to restore and rehabilitate the depleted stocks of native animals became important elements in congressional legislation. Acts which set aside refuges and habitat for wildlife helped to stabilize migratory waterfowl and in some cases built them up.

The tradition of managing game mammals and birds as a harvestable resource was determined largely by monies from hunting stamps used to fund provisions of the Migratory Bird Conservation Act of 1929. Amendments to the act established the practice of hunting on many wildlife refuges. Currently, as much as 40 percent of a federal refuge area may be opened for migratory bird hunting. Hunting regulations and public access to NWRs remain important, though controversial, land-use considerations in conservation thinking.

A number of wildlife groups, for example, are pressing for an overall decrease in consumptive uses of wildlife on refuges where a species-by-species approach to management has, in their opinion, tended to promote game animal research. These people prefer a policy of refurbishing, where possible, the preexisting plant and animal communities, and upgrading refuges which they believe are a low priority item in the U.S. Fish and Wildlife Service's program. They are urging federal wildlife officials to manage animals other than game species on NWRs and to curb what they consider to be unsportsman-like shooting practices on and around them (17, 18).

Federal officials are aware that almost one in two Americans (who are at least nine years old) engage in some wildlife-related activity every year. About one in five males hunt small game, turkey, ducks, doves, and geese in that order, and over one in three engages in recreational fishing. Taxes from the sale of hunting and fishing equipment have supported wildlife programs, including the purchase of habitat, for forty years. Many people engage in viewing wildlife, too, and demand for nonconsumptive uses of wildlife has grown enormously (19).

Fewer than 10 percent of the estimated 95 million Americans who participated annually in wildlife-related activities in 1975 hunted migratory birds, and the numbers of hunters on NWRs dropped slightly from 1970 to 1974. Fish and Wildlife Service projections for the mid-1980s show a further 10 percent decline in game mammal and bird hunting on refuges but an 11 percent increase in visitors wishing to observe wild animals, and a 16 percent growth in wildlife-related photography (9, 14).

Funds from hunting licenses combined with taxes on hunting and fishing equipment have supported research and management initiatives for wildlife in recent decades. Contemporary discussions focus on the need to increase and to diversify the sources from which revenues for wildlife, particularly nongame conservation, are drawn. Possible new sources include taxes on sport and outdoor recreational items other than hunting equipment, including skiing, camping, and backpacking items (20).

Current national and state laws are beginning to reflect this interest in nongame and the need to preserve and restore vanishing animals and plants. For example, provisions of the Endangered Species Conservation Act of December, 1969, expanded the 1966 act by requiring the Secretary of the Interior to draw up a list of endangered species and subspecies. The commercial exploitation and importation of endangered species was regulated, and a program for international cooperation through trade regulations was set in motion. Importantly, authorization was made for the acquisition of privately owned lands for the protection and rehabilitation of native wildlife with no commercial value within any state or area under the control of the U.S. Interior Department.

The 1973 Endangered Species Act replaced the 1969 act in toto and most of the provisions of the 1966 act. The important elements of the current act (the 1973 act as amended in 1978, Appendix 18-1) provide preventive rather than remedial assistance to dwindling fauna and flora because "threatened" species are added to the list of endangered species, so that a species may be protected before it becomes endangered. Also, the 1973 act provides economic assistance to states which develop an endangered species program (including plants) in accordance with provisions contained in the federal statute.

Recent interagency litigation over enforcement of the

1973 Endangered Species Act exemplified by the snail darter and the Tennessee Valley Authority's $120 million Tellico Dam project, and federal-state disagreements over the official status of several species, have given the federal government strong powers. The effect of the act has forced congressional review of major public works projects to see that the claims of the environment have been given due consideration. Some states, including Texas, are reluctant to enter into agreements with the Federal Office of Endangered Species in order to share in assistance for threatened species because of fiscal problems and possible unnecessary or inflexible constraints on conservation practices (21).

A number of federal laws since the 1930s have required that various economic activities involving planning and development include considerations for mitigating damage to wildlife. Also, federal pollution control legislation has sought to achieve a range of environmental objectives including, but not limited to, wildlife. The 1934 Fish and Wildlife Conservation Act was the first federal law to compel investigations to determine the effects of municipal and industrial effluents on wild animals. Regarded as hortatory and not mandatory, the forward-looking scope of the act was given substance only recently with the Water Pollution Control Act Amendments (1970), the Clean Air Act Amendments (1970), the National Environmental Policy Act (1969), and other statutes which transcend the narrower definition of "wildlife law." However, these broadly directed U.S. laws affect the wildlife resource on state lands throughout the nation because conservation is inextricably bound up with both environmental statutes (such as pollution and land use controls) and transportation and commerce (22, 23, Appendix 18-1).

Federal Laws and Wildlife in the Southwest

Texas' six-member Parks and Wildlife Commission is authorized currently by the state legislature to exercise regulatory control over all or part of the wildlife resources in 239 of 254 counties. This power includes the establishment of bag and possession limits, and appropriate seasons for native game animals and game birds, fur-bearing animals, and certain species which reside within the Lone Star State. However, the Wildlife Commission does not have overall jurisdiction for migratory game.

Under the powers of the Migratory Bird Treaty Act of 3 July 1918 the federal government in the person of the Secretary of the Interior establishes the framework for the killing and possession of migratory birds. Since 1918, the Secretary of the Interior has prohibited certain hunting practices such as the use of live decoys or setting out bait, and has placed limits on gun gauge and the number of shells a weapon can hold (24).

A list of ninety-seven species within five families (Anatidae or ducks, swans, and geese; Gruidae or cranes; Rallidae or railes, gallinules and coots; Scolopacidae or shorebirds; and Columbidae or pigeons and doves) are classified as migratory game birds. Texas sportsmen must adhere to the framework set annually by the federal government, and to specific season dates and bag limits chosen by state officials. Individual states may adopt more stringent regulations within the federal framework, but they may not establish more lenient ones (25).

Thirty-six species of native ducks, seven species of geese, and three swans comprise the migratory waterfowl in North America. In autumn, ducks and geese migrate from northern breeding grounds along four "flyways" (or routes that have administrative significance since 1948, more than biological exactitude) to wintering areas on coastal and interior wetlands in southern states. Texas is the terminus for many waterfowl utilizing the Central flyway which contains a varying but significant fraction of the 77-120 million ducks, and 4-6 million geese which migrate every year. Duck productivity varies with the abundance of surface water on northern prairies; goose numbers are affected by spring temperatures in northern Canada and Alaska (24).

Estimates of waterfowl productivity and overall numbers provide the basis for annual harvest regulations which are set for each flyway from exchanges of information between state agencies through the Flyway Councils, U.S. Fish and Wildlife Service representatives, and interested groups. Each Flyway Council is basically the organization of states sharing in the common waterfowl resource. Texas officials contribute to the formulation of policy and recommendations of the Central Flyway Council. Additionally, state personnel generate research data about the status of waterfowl from periodic bird surveys, banding returns, and hunter questionnaires. This degree of cooperation, collaboration, and coordination between states and federal wildlife biologists is important in establishing and adjusting regulations for waterfowl and other migratory game birds such as woodcock, doves, and sandhill cranes. Current plans envisage an annual harvest of 800,000 ducks and 280,000 geese by approximately 135,000 migratory bird hunters in Texas. Two state biologists are assigned full-time to direct the Wildlife Division's waterfowl program. The average annual harvest between 1961 and 1970 was in excess of 900,000 ducks, but only 146,000 geese. A "Goose Productivity Survey" is attempting to balance winter goose populations in Texas with habitat conditions on breeding grounds in successive summers (26, 27).

Also, the U.S. Fish and Wildlife Service is promoting federal-state cooperation in goose and other waterfowl management by seeking ways to share responsibilities for the preservation of high-quality wetland habitat. The Service's director estimated that 10 million acres of critical habitat remained unprotected in 1975, and expressed the intention of preserving one-fifth of this acreage by 1985. He hopes that many states, including Texas, will acquire wetlands in order to slow down economic activities which have caused the loss of approximately one-half of the nation's 127 million acres of pristine wetland.

Another federal statute with important and expanding significance to Texas and other states is the 1973 Endangered Species Act. In one sense the act ties the hands of state wildlife departments by making it unlawful for people subject to the jurisdiction of the U.S. to "take" any species listed federally as endangered. The act, however, opened up a program for expenditures from the Federal Land and Water Conservation Fund to acquire habitat for threatened and endangered wildlife. It instructed federal authorities not to modify or destroy habitat "critical" to the survival of vanishing species, and to date (May, 1979) officials have listed thirty-four "critical habitats" for listed species.

Under the 1973 act the Fish and Wildlife Service has entered into cooperative agreements with twenty-one states which are now eligible for financial assistance (up to two-thirds of the cost of their respective endangered species programs) if funds are available in return for meeting conservation criteria under the 1973 act. New Mexico, for example, signed a cooperative agreement with the U.S. Fish and Wildlife Service in 1977, thereby becoming eligible for federal matching funds for conserving endangered species. New Mexico employs four biologists in its Endangered Species Program which is surveying North America's most elusive and rare mammal, the black-footed ferret, and supporting research on the peregrine falcon. Under the State Act of February, 1974, New Mexico lists 104 species as endangered (including 12 on the federal list). The objective is to conserve the biological diversity of New Mexico's flora and fauna (28, p. 4; 29; 30).

Texas passed an Endangered Species Act in 1973 and has its own list of endangered species. The State Act charged the Parks and Wildlife Department with responsibility for conducting investigations on nongame and endangered species. Special wildlife investigations, including information and education, and investigations into the status of nongame animals, and projects for endangered mammals, bird, fish, reptile, and amphibian species, make up the state's program, which was budgeted for $11,204 in 1978. Recent surveys have included eagles and falcons, fish-eating bird rookeries on the Gulf coast, and the status of the red-cockaded woodpecker, Houston toad, and other animals.

Finances for the nongame animal studies are drawn from appropriations from the state's General Fund, not from sport license monies, which sustain efforts for game. Although Texas and Arizona appear to meet the requirements for concluding a cooperative agreement under Section 6 of the 1973 Federal Endangered Species Act, they have not sought to do so. Currently, revenues for state conservation agencies are static or are actually decreasing, and there is a marked lack of state funds to match available federal dollars.

FEDERALLY FUNDED PROGRAMS FOR WILD ANIMALS

Federal and state programs for wildlife date from the 1930s when the U.S. Congress established animal restoration measures and set aside special funds for them. The states are reimbursed by annual apportionments for a range of wildlife-related activities.

The most important of the conservation projects is the Pittman-Robertson Program (P-R) set up by the Federal Aid in Wildlife Restoration Act of 1937. The act provided the basis for the apportionment of monies to state-directed wildlife projects. Revenues are raised from an excise tax on sporting arms and ammunition (first imposed in 1932) which was earmarked for wildlife management, particularly for waterfowl, in 1936. In that year a White House-sponsored North American Wildlife Conference was held to assess the critical status of many game animals and their habitats. The International Association of Game, Fish, and Conservation Commissioners and a number of other groups interested in wildlife endorsed legislation which Key Pittman of Nevada introduced into the U.S. Senate, and Willis Robertson of Virginia introduced into the U.S. House of Representatives early in 1937. The Pittman-Robertson (P-R) Act, as it is called, received President Franklin D. Rossevelt's signature on 2 September 1937 (31).

Initially, some state legislatures were reluctant to pass "assent" legislation, incorporating the provisions of P-R, because the P-R Act was more than merely a conduit for tax revenues. It requested that states place their respective wildlife programs on a financially stable basis by including a provision against hunting license fees being used for other purposes than the administration of the state's Fish and Game Department. Also, projects from state agencies had to be approved by federal authorities (in this case the U.S. Fish and Wildlife Service). However, all states adopted the provisions of P-R, although it took some of them almost a decade to pass the requisite enabling legislation.

The specifications of P-R, and a more recent companion act for fisheries, the Dingell-Johnson Act of 1950 (D-J), are set out in Table 18-4. Funding formulas are based upon the number of hunting licenses sold and the geographic area of each state. Several amendments have modified P-R. One of them in 1946 established a ceiling for total funds not to exceed 5 percent, nor to be less than 0.5 percent, for any one state. Under this formula the larger states such as Texas would not receive disproportionately large appointments.

The mission of the P-R program is four-fold. First, P-R provides reimbursement funding to states for the protection and management of habitat. It is anticipated that 38 million acres of wildlife habitat will be under active management by 1985. Second, P-R funds states in meeting the public's demands for nonconsumptive and consumptive uses of wildlife. Third, the Program enables states agencies to survey, inventory, and research wildlife assets. Fourth, through hunter safety training programs, P-R assists states through reimbursements for "safe and ethical conduct in fish and wildlife recreation," thereby reducing hunting accidents and game law violations (1, p. 238; 32, p. 1-10; 33).

In absolute terms P-R makes a minute contribution to

TABLE 18-4. Funding Provisions of the Pittman-Robertson Program.
Mittelvorsorge für das Pittman-Robertson Programm.

	Federal Aid in Wildlife Restoration Program P-R Act	Federal Aid in Sport Fish Restoration Program D-J Act
Purpose	Conserve and manage wild birds and mammals	Conserve and manage fish
Funding source	Manufacturers' excise tax on sporting arms, ammunition. Sport guns 11 percent Hand guns 10 percent (1970) Archery equipment 11 percent (1972)	Manufacturer's excise tax on rods, reels, baits, etc. 10 percent.
Date	September 2, 1937	August 9, 1950
Initiation	FY 1939	FY 1951
Apportionment	Formula based on State area and the number of paid hunting licenses. Five (5) percent ceiling, or 0.5 percent minimum per State amendment 1946.	Formula based on State area (including coastal waters) and the number of paid fishing licenses. Maximum of 5 percnet, minimum of 1 percent to any State.
Availability	Annually, and the following F.Y.	Annually
Federal Funds	75 percent maximum	50 percent maximum, except for multi-State projects.
Total $ millions	736.97 (1939-1977)	227.79 (1951-1977)

Source: U.S. Fish and Wildlife Service, Federal Aid in Fish and Wildlife Restoration Manual. Rev. ed. (Washington, D.C.: Bureau of Sport Fisheries and Wildlife, 1973), mimeographed.

habitat retention and management. Of the estimated 1,785 million acres of big-game habitat in the nation, only 33.5 million acres (2 percent) are under the full or partial control of state wildlife agencies. P-R can do little to offset an estimated 200,000 acres of wetland loss each year, although the program has acquired 1.5 million acres of waterfowl habitat since its inception. However, P-R is vitally important in providing the means for states to conduct wildlife surveys and game animal research so that meaningful recommendations for hunting seasons and cropping limits can be established.

Over the past forty years federal influence over state wildlife programs through P-R funding has tended to diminish as amendments have broadened the scope of state activities under the conservation program. Now, funds may be used to aid a state's "comprehensive fish and wildlife resource management plan" (an amendment in 1970), rather than be expended piecemeal for individual restoration projects. Current interest in nongame wildlife conservation is siphoning off some P-R monies.

A Cooperative Federal and State Wildlife Research Units program was begun in 1935 to offset dwindling stocks of game mammals and birds in the United States. The program was the achievement of Jay N. "Ding" Darling, Chief of the Bureau of Biological Survey, who inaugurated it in order to train wildlife scientists through cooperative agreements with state land-grant colleges and conservation departments. The purpose was to staff game and fish agencies, to develop research information and programs in order to solve wildlife problems, and to educate the public about the value and needs of wildlife resources. The Cooperative Unit program was expanded in 1960 to authorize agreements with universities and colleges for training programs in wildlife and fishery resources. There are twenty Cooperative Wildlife Research Units and twenty-five Cooperative Fishery Units at twenty-six universities and colleges throughout the nation. Congressional appropriations provide funds annually for the Research Unit program in which eighteen states participate.

The Texas Cooperative Wildlife Research Unit was activated in 1935. Early Unit studies concentrated on the natural history of squirrels, the opossum, the armadillo, and Attwater's prairie chicken. Before it was discontinued in 1954 the Unit trained a number of personnel who have worked in the Texas Parks and Wildlife Department.

A Wildlife Unit opened in Arizona in 1951 (a Fisheries Unit followed in 1964), and biologists have researched the problems of waterfowl, the impact of logging on fish populations, and the ecology and distribution of the gray squirrel, bobcat, and the collared peccary.

The Oklahoma Unit is part of Oklahoma State University, Stillwater, and was established in 1948. Recent research includes the evaluation of wildlife habitat from ERTS satellite imagery, the manipulation of habitat for game mammals and birds, and the ecology of fish species in artificial lakes. New Mexico does not participate in the Cooperative Unit program (34, 35).

The nation's fishery resource has received federal support, and a number of programs have been set up to protect and conserve state fisheries. In 1976, there were ninety-four National Fish Hatcheries existing under the jurisdiction of the U.S. Fish and Wildlife Service. Records of hatchery outputs go back to a series of publications issued since 1872. The hatchery system produced salmon, trout, catfish, pike, bass, carp, and sunfish, in order to assist in meeting the demand for sport fishing while insuring the survival of the nation's fish resource. Primary obligations consist of stocking international waters, others owned by the federal government and managed by state agencies, waters under the jurisdiction of state agencies, and, finally, the stocking of private waters (36, 37).

The Grant-in-Aid for Fisheries Program, in the National Oceanic and Atmospheric Administration, Department of Commerce, is another important federally-directed program. It consists of grants to protect, develop, and enhance the nation's aquatic environment. Formerly with the U.S. Fish and Wildlife Service, Bureau of Commercial Fisheries, the program is authorized under two federal acts. The first is the 1964 Commercial Fisheries Research and Development Act (PL 88-309), as amended, which authorizes the Secretary of Commerce to cooperate with state agencies in carrying out research and development of commercial fisheries. Cost-sharing varies from 50 or 75 percent of federal funds in accordance with the nature of the projects. (The act was extended by Public Laws 92-590 and 95-53 to 30 June 1980). The second fisheries law is the 1965 Anadromous Fish Conservation Act (PL 89-304), as amended, which authorizes the Secretary of Commerce to enter into agreements with states or local interests in order to conserve anadromous fishery resources (38).

An interest in aquatic ecosystems and the natural communities they support has directed the research programs of several federal agencies toward the discovery of essential biological and ecological data that can be used by decision makers for environmentally sound resource management. One example is the National Wetlands Inventory Program, directed by the U.S. Fish and Wildlife Service, that seeks to "describe all wetlands on an individual and/or cumulative basis in terms of their ecological and physical characteristics, geographic location and natural resource values" (39). The listing of the nature, size, location, and function of all U.S. wetlands will aid federal and state agencies in assessing applications for wetland utilization and acquisition. Currently, the survey (an update of a 1954 inventory) is involved with classifying, mapping, and analyzing the resource values of wetlands for a three-year period terminating in 1980. Results will be placed in the hands of state and local agencies and the interested public.

Wetland conservation (primarily for migratory waterfowl reproduction) has continued under the U.S. Department of Agriculture's Water Bank Program funded by Congress in 1972. Some 2.25 million hunters make 75 percent of waterfowl kills in wetland habitat during winter months in the United States. About 5 million acres of the nation's wetlands are in public ownership, but 15 million acres remain vulnerable to drainage for agriculture, especially in the pothole country of Minnesota and North and South Dakota. The Water Bank aims at leasing (for a decade at a time) waterfowl production areas in the Plains States. Agreements tend to be fragile as there are more attractive economic options for owners of pothole country. Also, questions remain about the Water Bank's critical contribution to waterfowl productivity and the Department of Agriculture's long-term interests in administering the program (40).

Under a federally-funded Dredged Material Research Program, the U.S. Army Corps of Engineers has begun (in 1973) to seek ways of utilizing the 280 million cubic yards of dredge material extracted from waterways and port facilities at a cost of approximately $250 million annually. Marsh creation and management for selected plant species, the establishment of spoil islands as waterbird breeding sites, plus land improvement for agriculture, are experiments at habitat creation, restoration, and enhancement. Two of the twenty U.S. experimental sites are on the Texas Gulf Coast (41, 42).

PROGRAMS FOR WILD ANIMAL CONSERVATION IN TEXAS

The federally funded P-R program has been invaluable to Texas' conservation initiatives over the past forty years. In recent years (Table 18-5) the Lone Star State has received the largest apportionments of any state permitted by law. Hunting licenses have continued to sell well and attest to the avocation for outdoor recreation. However, Texas has not had a strong program of land acquisition; currently, the state has a low ranking in this regard. Funds have gone into the supervision, coordination, and supply of services related to the P-R program; toward the establishment of hunting regulations based on game surveys; and to research in key game species (such as the white-tailed deer, bighorn sheep, pronghorn antelope, turkey, and white-winged dove).

In the late 1930s P-R monies were used to determine the status of game animals throughout Texas. Biologists, trained frequently under another federal program, the Cooperative Research Unit Program at Texas A & M, confirmed that many species had declined numerically and had been extirpated from areas of former range. The white-tailed deer, for example, had disappeared from many places in East Texas. Pronghorn antelope numbers on the High Plains had not recovered from unregulated killing despite a closed

TABLE 18-5. Federal Aid to Texas' Wildlife 1970-1976.
Bundeshilfe für Texas Wildtiere 1970-1976.

Year	Texas Hunting Licenses Sold	U.S. Total (millions)	Texas' Share of U.S. Total (percentage)	U.S. Ranking	Texas Acreage for Wildlife Management Areas (Hunting)[1]	U.S. Ranking	Texas Acreage for Refuges (non-hunting)
1970	924,317	22	4.27	5	334,952	20	16,747
1971	966,163	22	4.35	5	312,140	22[a]	14,535
1972	1,010,794	23	4.41	5	304,663	23[a]	13,575
1973	1,078,110	23	4.63	4	310,187	21[b]	16,389
1974	1,105,905	25	4.35	5	257,184	21[b]	11,744
1975	1,125,158	26	4.34	5	186,002	32[b]	3,890
1976	1,126,509	25	4.47	4	186,002	35[b]	3,890

[a] of 49 states [d] of 42 states

[b] of 48 states [e] of 44 states

[c] of 43 states [f] of 45 states

[1] A Wildlife Management Area is land under lease, easement, agreement or ownership of a State Game and Fish Department wherein development, maintenance or management is carried out with Federal Aid funds. Hunting may be restricted and is controlled by State authorities.

[2] A Wildlife Refuge is land where no hunting is permitted.

Source: U.S. Fish and Wildlife Service, <u>Federal Aid in Fish and Wildlife Restoration-1970</u>, etc. (Washington, D.C.: Wildlife Management Institute, 1971), etc.

U.S. Ranking	U.S. Management Areas and Refuges (millions of acres)	Texas' Share of U.S. Total (percentage)	Texas P-R Apportionment ($ millions)	U.S. Total ($ millions)	Texas' Share of U.S. Total (percentage)	U.S. Ranking
9[c]	52	0.64	1.58	31.68	5.0	1 with Alaska
15[c]	37	0.89	1.54	30.80	5.0	1 with Alaska
18[d]	38	0.84	1.65	34.46	4.79	1
12[d]	33	0.99	1.98	41.05	4.82	1
17[e]	34	0.80	2.29	47.39	4.82	1
27[e]	35	0.55	2.58	53.47	4.83	1
30[f]	41	0.46	2.81	58.60	4.80	1

season imposed by the legislature in 1903. The eastern turkey, bobwhite quail, and Attwater's prairie chicken had also suffered major declines (43).

Accordingly, P-R funds were expended in an ambitious and largely successful program to restock game through trapping and transplation. Aransas NWR, the King Ranch in South Texas, and other areas supplied wild trapped white-tailed deer for transport to release points both inside and outside Texas. Since 1939, more than 5,000 antelopes have been relocated on suitable range, and huntable populations occur in four ecological areas--the Trans-Pecos, the Northwest Edwards Plateau, the Rolling Plains, and the High Plains. Other restocking schemes under the P-R program have included turkey, quail, javelina, and beaver (44). Wildlife specialists continue to provide broodstock of selected species to landowners for conservation purposes and have utilized P-R to introduce exotic game birds, principally ring-necked pheasants and partridges, and a foreign ungulate, the barbary sheep or aoudad (into Palo Duro Canyon in 1957) to areas where they will not compete directly with indigenous game.

Research conducted under P-R on the eight big game mammals and on the score or so of upland and migratory game birds (Table 18-6) has aimed at determining the population dynamics, interspecific relationships, and habitat requirements of various species in order to relate them to hunter recreation through the establishment of annual harvest regulations. The state's Wildlife Division has been reorganized around the species concept of management for the past five years, moving away from the single project and area orientation which marked earlier work under P-R.

The Lone Star State is a principal beneficiary of the

Federal Fish Hatchery Program dating back to the 1930s, because Texas has established many large impoundments geared to instate water delivery. Texas and Oklahoma are among nine states which contain more than 50 percent of the nation's reservoir surface area. Also, the state has benefitted substantially from another federal program, the Farm Pond Program. The number of farm ponds in the U.S. increased from an estimated 20,000 in 1934 to over 2 million by 1965 (45).

The state's Fishery Division has conducted surveys and research aimed at stocking the growing number of deep water and warm water impoundments with suitable sport fish species in order to support the growing army of anglers who purchase 1.5 million fishing licenses every year. In fiscal year 1975, Texas obtained 17.3 million (or 18,364 pounds) of fish representing twelve species from national hatcheries, and received $842,000 in federal apportionments under D-J for fishery restoration within the state. Also, Texas received $2.8 million, ranking tenth in the nation, under the 1964 Commercial Fisheries Act as grant-in-aid for coastal activities. Five projects are being completed currently under the aid program to conduct research and experimentation on bays and estuaries, including experiments in aquaculture, the raising of shrimp, oyster, and three fish species in artificial ponds.

Government involvement with the nation's wildlife resource has expanded constantly in recent decades to encompass legal, fiscal, and scientific provisions for the protection and management of wild animals. Federal agencies increasingly influence activities which disrupt or damage plant and animal assemblages in both the public and private sectors. Recent amendments to the 1973 Endangered Species

TABLE 18-6. Pittman-Robertson Funding for Game Animal Transplant and Restoration in Texas.
Pittman-Robertson Mittel für die Verpflanzung and Wiederherstellung von Wildtieren in Texas.

SPECIES	AREA	YEAR
Big Game		
Auodad Sheep	Introduced to Palo Duro Canyon	1957-58
Bighorn Sheep	Virtual extirpation in Trans-Pecos; introduced to Black Gap Management Area	1954-59 / 1977
White-tailed Deer	Restocked statewide	1938 to present
Mule Deer	Restocked in Panhandle	
Pronghorn Antelope	Restocked in four ecological areas of its former range in West, Central and North Texas	1939 onwards
Elk	Extirpated; Canadian Elk introduced in the Guadalupe Mountains.	1927
Javelina	Formerly north to Red River and east to Brazos River; limited restocking and exchanges for brookstock with other states	
Upland Game		
Turkey	Restocked east of 97th meridian; some propagation	1932 onwards
Bobwhite Quail	Restocked; some propagation statewide from a hatchery at Tyler from 1956-68	

PAST STATUS	PRESENT	REMARKS
44 introduced in 1958	1,400	Hunted since 1963
9 (alive in 1959) 6	about 40	Predation has been severe since 1970 when 68 captive sheep existed
much reduced	about 3.1 million	Aransas NWR and the King Ranch supplied broodstock
much reduced	154,000	Hunted
down to 2,407 (in 1924)	about 14,000	Hunted since 1944
44	718	Transplanted to other uplands in the Trans-Pecos; a few are hunted by permit
reduced	locally common in southern one-third of the state	145 transplanted since 1953; decline through brush clearance continues
	about 400,000 (6-8,000 of eastern race)	Eastern race extirpated by 1930, restocking continues
widespread, including East Texas	locally abundant, 5-6 million harvested annually	Stronghold in central and south Texas

TABLE 18-6 (continued).

Prairie Chickens (Lesser)	Native to the North Texas Plains	
Prairie Chicken (Attwater's)	Endemic to Gulf Coast Prairies (originally over approximately 6 million acres)	
Pheasant	Releases in Gulf Coast Prairie, Post Oak and Rolling Plains	1964 onwards
Chachalaca	Transplanted in Rio Grande Valley Counties	1959

Source: Texas Parks and Wildlife, Wildlife Division, 1978.

much reduced in High and Rolling Plains	about 16,000 in North Texas	Habitat destruction, pesticide and drought cause declines; some hunting
much reduced in the Coastal Plain (about 8,700 in 1937)	about 1,500	A 1,700-acre NWR established near Eagle Lake, Colorado Co., in 1972
31,434 released since 1964	27,800 harvested on High Plains (1977)	Hunting in coastal counties in 1977
more widespread in S. Texas; five counties received 228 birds from 1964-67	locally common in heavy brush in S. Texas	Brush control and intensive farming have reduced its range

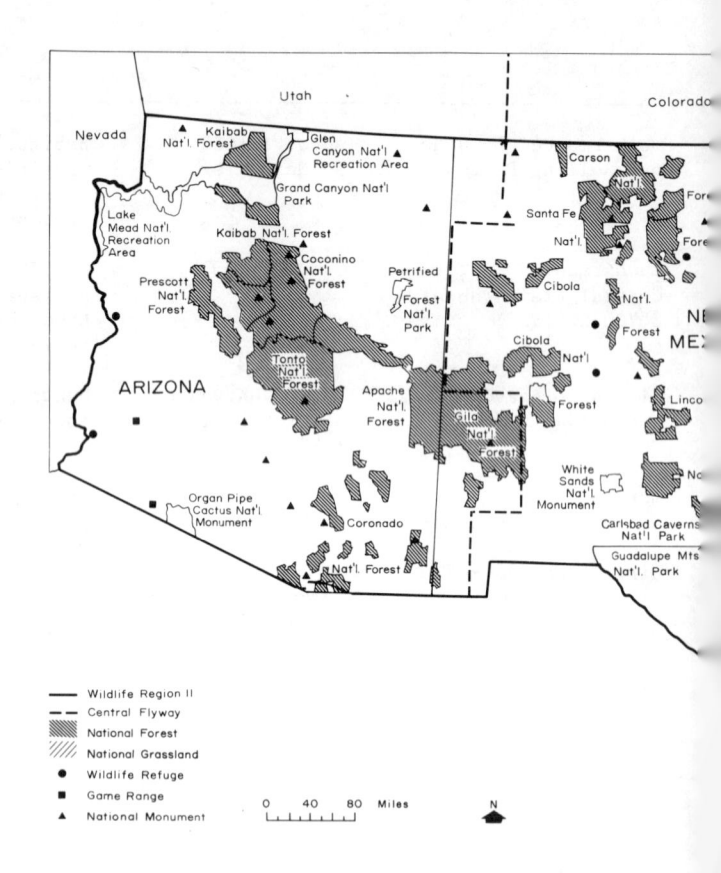

FIG. 18-1. Operation of the National Wildlife Refuge System in the Southwest, 1977.
	Tätigkeit zwecks Erhaltung des nationalen Wildbestandes im Südwesten, 1977.

Source: U.S. Fish and Wildlife Service, Department of the Interior, Operation of the National Wildlife Refuge System, 1977 and Michael Frome, National Park Guide, 1977.

U.S. WILDLIFE CONSERVATION

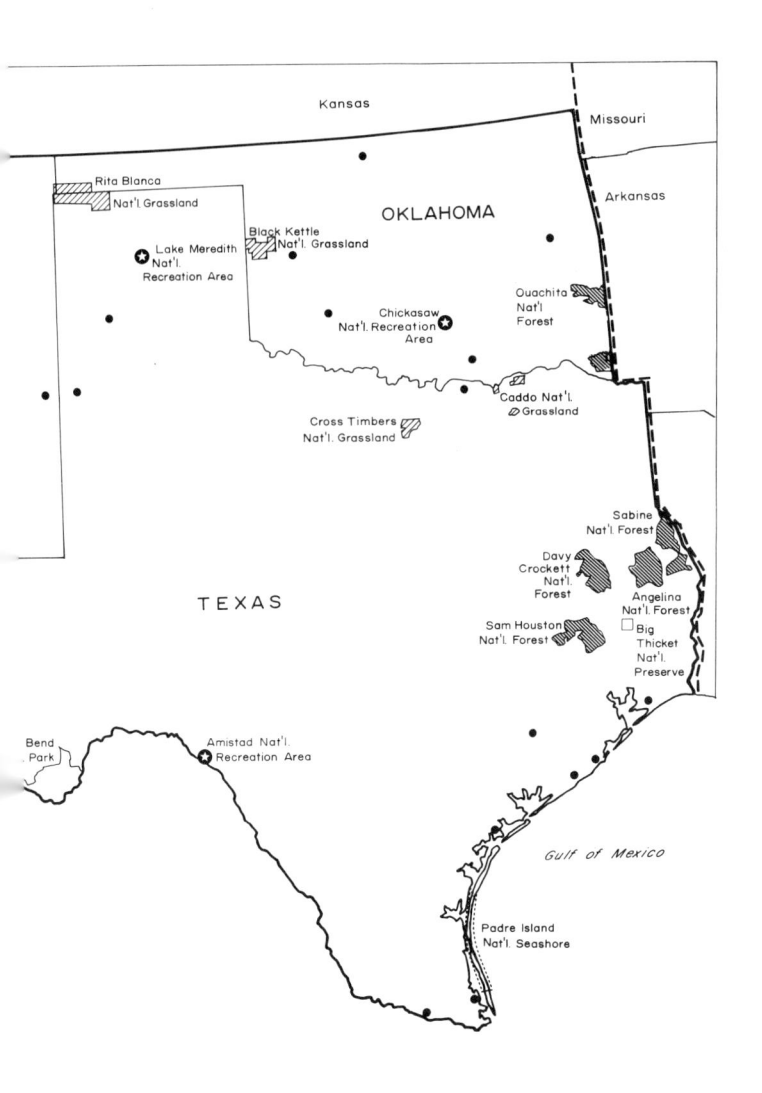

Kansas
Missouri
Rita Blanca Nat'l. Grassland
OKLAHOMA
Arkansas
Lake Meredith Nat'l. Recreation Area
Black Kettle Nat'l. Grassland
Ouachita Nat'l Forest
Chickasaw Nat'l. Recreation Area
Caddo Nat'l. Grassland
Cross Timbers Nat'l. Grassland
Sabine Nat'l. Forest
Davy Crockett Nat'l. Forest
Angelina Nat'l. Forest
TEXAS
Sam Houston Nat'l. Forest
Big Thicket Nat'l. Preserve
Bend Park
Amistad Nat'l. Recreation Area
Gulf of Mexico
Padre Island Nat'l. Seashore

Act, for example, have provided expertise for wildlife recovery programs in more than twenty states, and state agencies are finding cooperative agreements with federal departments a practical and useful means of implementing conservation.

Some persons believe, however, that federal strictures, including new international regulations aimed at controlling the harvest and trade in flora and fauna, have eroded states' rights. This trend to centralized oversight and control exemplifies to them an increasing insensitivity to local, specific problems best dealt with by regional or state entities, and a suffocating bureaucracy. Others argue that federal directives provide both the structure and guidelines for local flexibility and the critical financial backing for efficient comprehensive and progressive policies aimed at managing the nation's wild animal heritage.

APPENDIX 18-1 - IMPORTANT FEDERAL LAWS FOR WILDLIFE CONSERVATION

1896 U.S. Supreme Court in Geer v. Connecticut (161 U.S. 519) established rights to control and regulate the utilization of game animals. The decision remains the foundation of the much discussed state-ownership doctrine.

1900 Lacey Act (16 U.S.C. 667e and 701, 31 Stat. 187, 32 Stat. 285), as amended, specifies that the U.S. Department of Interior must adopt all measures for the "preservation, distribution, introduction, and restoration of game birds and other wild birds." The introduction of foreign animals may be regulated and prohibited if injurious to man, agriculture or other wildlife. Interstate transportation of wildlife and their parts, taken or possessed in violation of federal, state or foreign laws, is also prohibited.

1929 Migratory Bird Conservation Act (16 U.S.C. 715-715d; 45 Stat. 1222), as amended, establishes a program for refuge acquisition. Funds are provided for National Wildlife Refuges by the Migratory Bird Hunting Stamp Act of 1934 (see below).

1934 Migratory Bird Hunting and Conservation Stamp Act (16 U.S.C. 718-718h; 48 Stat. 452), as amended. The "Duck Stamp Act" requires waterfowl hunters sixteen years of age and older to possess a valid federal hunting stamp. Revenues from the sale of more than 60 million stamps sold in the past forty years worth $176 million, have been placed in a Migratory Bird Conservation Fund. They are appropriated for land acquisition for the National Wildlife Refuge System.

Fish and Wildlife Coordination Act (16 U.S.C. 661-666c; 48 Stat. 401), as amended, (in 1946, 1958, and 1965), assisted federal, state, and other agencies to protect, develop, and restore fish and wildlife on federal lands.

1937 Federal Aid in Wildlife Restoration Act (16 U.S.C. 669-669i; 50 Stat. 917), as amended. The act is called the Pittman-Robertson Act (P-R). See Table 18-5. Since 1938, the federal government has directed more than $650 million to states for wildlife restoration and hunter safety.

1950   Federal Aid in Fish Restoration Act (16 U.S.C. 777-777k; 64 Stat. 430) as amended, commonly referred to as the Dingell-Johnson Act (D-J). See Table 18-5. Approximately $183 million has been reimbursed for fish restoration by 1975.

1961   Wetlands Loan Act (16 U.S.C. 715k-3-715k-5; 75 Stat. 813), as amended, provides the means of accelerating acquisition of migratory waterfowl habitat. About $94 million has been appropriated for habitat acquisition (FY 1976).

1965   The Anadromous Fish Act (16 U.S.C. 757a-757f; 79 Stat. 1125), as amended - P.L. 89-304. Under the Act a combined federal-state program was initiated to build back and extend anadromous fishery resources through stream clearance, species transplants, fishway construction and other projects. This program has been most beneficial to Pacific Coast, Atlantic Coast, and the Great Lakes fisheries.

1965   Land and Water Conservation Fund Act (16 U.S.C. 460L-4-460L-11; 78 Stat. 897), as amended by PL 88-478. The act created a fund for outdoor recreation, including lands for the Wildlife Refuge System. Over $960 million have been spent for 1.7 million acres of park, forest, and wildlife areas, and $1.3 billion has been apportioned to states for an additional 1.5 million acres (1977). Each state must prepare a comprehensive outdoor recreation plan to be eligible for matching grants.

1966   Endangered Species Preservation Act (PL 89-669, 80 Stat. 926 repealed in 1973, see that act), directed the Secretary of the Interior to administer a program to conserve, restore and propagate certain species of native fish and wildlife threatened with extinction.

1968   Estuary Protection Act (16 U.S.C., 1221-1226; 82 Stat. 625), authorizes the Secretary of the Interior with cooperation from other agencies and states to study the nation's estuaries, and to agree to cost-sharing with states in order to manage local estuarine areas.

1972   Coastal Zone Management Act (16 U.S.C., 1451-1464; 86 Stat. 1280), as amended, assists states to develop land and water use programs for coastal areas. Texas initiated a program in 1974, and the <u>Resources of the Texas Coastal Region</u> (Austin:

U.S. WILDLIFE CONSERVATION

General Land Office, 1975) provides an inventory of major physical, biological, and cultural resources for twenty-seven coastal counties.

Marine Protection, Research and Sanctuaries Act (16 U.S.C. 1431-1434 etc., 86 Stat. 1052), as amended, provides authority for the Environmental Protection Agency to regulate the dumping of materials at sea; it authorizes the Secretary of Commerce to designate marine sanctuaries.

Marine Mammal Act (16 U.S.C. 1361 etc., 86 Stat. 1027), as amended, vests responsibility for the conservation for marine species, with the Department of the Interior, and made the Department of Commerce responsible for whales and seals.

1973 Endangered Species Act (16 U.S.C. 1531-1543; 87 Stat. 884), as amended, provides for the conservation of threatened and endangered species of fish, wildlife, and plants, by prohibiting the taking, possession, sale and transport of endangered species as listed. The act expands land acquisitions, and authorizes cooperative agreements with states operating an adequate program for threatened and endangered wildlife.

1976 Federal Land Policy and Management Act (43 U.S.C. 1701-1771; 90 Stat. 2743), an "Organic Act" for the BLM requiring that public lands be retained in federal ownership and managed for recreation, range, timber, minerals, watershed, and wildlife and fish uses. Under the act the BLM manages 20 percent of the nation's wildlife values in all land-use decisions.

Fishery Conservation and Management Act (16 U.S.C. 1801-1802 etc., 90 Stat. 331) establishes a 200-mile fishery conservation zone.

1978 The President signed "The Endangered Species Act Amendments of 1978" (PL 95-632) reauthorizing the 1973 Act. Amendments established a cabinet-level committee to consider possible exemptions from Section 7 of the 1973 Act.

INTERNATIONAL CONVENTIONS AND AGREEMENTS

1916-1918 Convention for the Protection of Migratory Birds between the U.S. and Great Britain on behalf of Canada led to the Migratory Bird Treaty Act of

1918 (U.S.C. 703-711; 40 Stat. 755), as amended. The convention developed guidelines for the regulation of hunting, and the shipment or export of migratory species. The convention is a most important historical landmark for the protection and management of birds in North America.

1936 A Convention for the Protection of Migratory Birds and Game mammals between the U.S. and Mexico (50 Stat. 1311; T.S. 912) as amended, established hunting seasons, refuges, and granted full protection to insectivorous bird species.

1972 Convention for the Protection of Migratory Birds and Birds in Danger of Extinction between the U.S. and Japan (25 U.S.T. 3329; T.I.A.S. 7990) protects species of migratory birds common to both nations.

1973 Convention on International Trade in Endangered Species of Fauna and Flora (T.I.A.S. 8249) established regulations to prevent the commercial exploitation of animals and plants listed in three appendices to the convention (updated in 1979).

1976 A Convention for the Conservation of Migratory Birds between the U.S. and U.S.S.R. provides protection for migratory species between the U.S. and Soviet Union.

NOTES

1. Environmental Law Institute, The Evolution of National Wildlife Law, prepared for the Council on Environmental Quality, (Washington, D.C.: U.S. Government Printing Office, 1977).

2. Olendorff, R., et. al., "The Bureau of Land Management Program, Wildlife Habitat Management Program with Special Emphasis on Nongame Bird Habitats," in Proceeding of the Symposium on Management of Forest and Range Habitats for Nongame Birds, Tucson, Arizona, May 6-9, 1975. Forest Service, General Technical Report WO-1 (Washington, D.C.: Forest Service, 1975), pp. 305-313; the ten states are Arizona, California, Colorado, Idaho, Montana, Nevada, New Mexico, Oregon, Utah and Wyoming.

3. Carr, J. N., "The Sonoran Pronghorn, An Endangered Species," in Symposium on Rare and Endangered Wildlife in the Southwestern United States, ed. William S. Huey (Santa Fe: New Mexico Department of Game and Fish, c. 1973), pp. 38-45.

4. U.S. Fish and Wildlife Service, Final Environmental Statement: Operation of the National Wildlife Refuge System (Washington, D.C.: U.S. Government Printing Office, 1976).

5. Pruitt, E. L., et. al., "The Coastal Zone," in Sourcebook on the Environment, ed. Kenneth A. Hammond, George Macinko, and Wilma B. Fairchild, (Chicago: University of Chicago Press, 1978), pp. 469-489.

6. U.S. Senate, Committee on Commerce, A Legislative History of the Fishery Conservation and Management Act of 1976 (Washington, D.C.: U.S. Government Printing Office, 1976).

7. Hibbard, B. H., A History of the Public Land Policies (Madison: University of Wisconsin Press, 1965 [1924]).

8. Zimmerman, D. R., "Endangered Bird Species: Habitat Manipulation Methods," Science 192 (1976), 876-879.

9. U.S. Fish and Wildlife Service, Federal Aid in Fish and Wildlife Restoration 1976 (Washington, D.C.: Wildlife Management Institute, 1977).

10. U.S. Bureau of Land Management, Public Land Statistics 1976 (Washington, D.C.: U.S. Government Printing Office, 1977).

11. Matthiessen, P., Wildlife in America (New York: Viking, 1959).
12. Graham, F., Man's Dominion, The Story of Conservation in America (New York: Evans, 1971).
13. Trefethen, J. D., An American Crusade for Wildlife (New York: Winchester Press, 1975).
14. National Research Council, Division of Biology and Agriculture, Committee on Agriculture land Use and Wildlife Resources, Land Use and Wildlife Resources (Washington, D.C.: National Academy of Sciences, 1970), pp. 226-255.
15. Phillips, J. C., Migratory Bird Protection in North America, Special Publication No. 4 (New York: American Committee for International Wildlife, 1934).
16. Hayden, S. S., The International Protection of Wildlife (New York: Columbia University Press, 1942).
17. Defenders of Wildlife, A Report on the National Wildlife Refuge System (Washington, D.C.: Defenders of Wildlife, 1977).
18. National Wildlife Refuge Study Task Force, Recommendations on the Management of the National Wildlife Refuge System (Washington, D.C.: U.S. Government Printing Office, 1978).
19. U.S. Fish and Wildlife Service, 1975 National Survey of Hunting, Fishing and Wildlife-Associated Recreation (Washington, D.C.: U.S. Fish and Wildlife, 1977).
20. Wildlife Management Institute, Current Investigations, Projected Needs and Potential New Sources of Income for Nongame Fish and Wildlife Programs in the United States (Washington, D.C.: Wildlife Management Institute, 1975).
21. Palmer, W. D., "Endangered Species Protection: A History of Congressional Action," Environmental Affairs 4 (Spring, 1975), 255-293.
22. Parenteau, P. A., "Unfulfilled Mitigation Requirements of the Fish and Wildlife Coordinational Act," Transactions of the North American Wildlife and Natural Resources Conference 42nd (1977), pp. 179-184.

23. Greene, A. F. C., "The Need for Cooperative Approaches to Fish and Wildlife Management Planning," Transactions of the 40th North American and Natural Resources Conference (1975), pp. 133-141.
24. U.S. Fish and Wildlife Service, Issuance of Annual Regulations Permitting the Sport Hunting of Migratory Birds, Draft Environmental Statement (Washington, D.C.: Fish and Wildlife Service, 1975).
25. U.S. Fish and Wildlife Service, Use of Steel Shot for Hunting Waterfowl in the United States, Final Environmental Statement (Washington, D.C.: Fish and Wildlife Service, 1976).
26. Texas Parks and Wildlife Department, Wildlife Division, "Wildlife Operational Plan, 1978-79," (Austin: Parks and Wildlife Commission, 1978), mimeographed, pp. 153-180.
27. Carney, S. M., and M. F. Sorenson, "Distribution in States and Counties of Waterfowl Species Harvested During 1961-70 Hunting Seasons," U.S. Fish and Wildlife Service, Special Scientific Report-Wildlife No. 187 (Washington, D.C.: U.S. Government Printing Office, 1975), pp. 44-45.
28. Editorial, "Black-footed Ferret, Peregrine Head, New Mexico's Agenda of Endangered Species Projects," Endangered Species Technical Bulletin 3:6 (June, 1978), 4-5.
29. Hubbard, J. P., et. al., Handbook of Species Endangered in New Mexico (Santa Fe: N.M. Dept. Game and Fish, 1978).
30. Huey, W. S., Symposium on Rare and Endangered Wildlife of the Southwestern United States, Albuquerque, Sept. 22-23, 1972 (Santa Fe: N.M. Dept. of Game and Fish, c. 1973).
31. U.S. Fish and Wildlife Service, 35 Years of Shared Wildlife Management (Washington, D.C.: U.S. Government Printing Office, 1975).
32. U.S. Fish and Wildlife Service, "Draft Environmental Impact Statement: Federal Aid in Fish and Wildlife Restoration Program," (Washington, D.C.: U.S. Fish and Wildlife Service, 1978), mimeograph.
33. U.S. Fish and Wildlife Service, Federal Aid in Fish and Wildlife Restoration Manual, Revised Edition (Washington, D.C.: U.S. Fish and Wildlife Service, 1973).

34. U.S. Fish and Wildlife Service, Thirty Years of Cooperative Wildlife Research Units: 1935-1965, Bureau of Sport Fisheries and Wildlife, Resource Publication 6 (Washington, D.C.: U.S. Government Printing Office, 1965).

35. Kennelly, J. K., and R. L. Applegate, eds., Cooperative Research Units: Fishery and Wildlife, Annual Report 1974-75 (Washington, D.C.: U.S. Fish and Wildlife Service, 1976).

36. U.S. Fish and Wildlife Service, Propagation and Distribution of Fish from National Fish Hatcheries for the Fiscal Year 1975 etc., Fish Distribution Report 10 (Washington, D.C.: U.S. Government Printing Office, 1976).

37. U.S. Department of Interior, Anadromous Fish Resources: Their Conservation, Development, Enhancement (Washington, D.C.: U.S. Government Printing Office, 1970).

38. U.S. Department of Commerce, National Oceanic and Atmospheric Administration, National Marine Fisheries Service, Grant-in-Aid for Fisheries: Program Activities 1977 (Washington, D.C.: U.S. Government Printing Office, 1977).

39. Montanari, J. H., and J. E. Townsend, "Status of the National Wetlands Survey," Transactions of the 42nd North American Wildlife and Natural Resources Conference (1977), pp. 66-72.

40. Womach, J., "National Evaluation of the Water Bank Program," Transactions of the 42nd North American Wildlife and Natural Resources Conference (1977), pp. 246-254.

41. Smith, H. K., "Habitat Development Aspects of the Dredged Material Research Program," Transactions of the 42nd North American Wildlife and Natural Resources Conference, (1977), pp. 93-101.

42. Parnell, J. F., and R. F. Soots (eds.) Proceedings of a Conference on Management of Dredge Islands in North Carolina Estuaries, Atlantic Beach, N.C., May, 1974 (Raleigh: North Carolina State University, Sea Grant Program, 1975).

43. Texas Game, Fish and Oyster Commission, Principal Game Birds and Mammals of Texas (Austin: Von Boeckmann-Jones, 1945).

44. Davis, W. B., The Mammals of Texas, Bulletin 41, Revised Edition (Austin: Texas Parks and Wildlife Department, 1974).

45. Swingle, H. S., "History of Warmwater Pond Culture in the United States," A Century of Fisheries in North America, ed. Norman G. Benson (Washington, D.C.: American Fisheries Society, 1970), pp. 95-105.

CHAPTER 19

REGIONAL DEVELOPMENT PROGRAMS AND THEIR EFFECTIVENESS
IN AREAS ALONG THE EASTERN BORDER
OF WEST GERMANY

REGIONALE ENTWICKLUNGSPROGRAMME UND IHRE WIRKSAMKEIT
IM BEREICH DES ZONENRANDGEBIETS DER
BUNDESREPUBLIK DEUTSCHLAND

Karl Lenz

Abstract

The Zonenrandgebiet is a strip of land approximately 40 km wide bordering the German Democratic Republic (GDR) and Czechslovakia. It takes up about one-fifth of the area of the Federal Republic, yet contains scarcely 4 percent of the inhabitants. The border was organized in 1945 between zones of occupation and was later, as a national border, heavily fortified by the GDR. The border region became peripheral both geographically and economically; the infrastructure was inadequate. Many localities had to reorient themselves toward the West, resulting in an exodus of working people.

In order to compensate for the economic and social disadvantage, the federal government and the states initiated special programs of development. They include the construction of apartments, schools, and recreational facilities, the promotion of industry, and the expansion of the transportation network. The exodus of the population was thus reduced. There is still a lack of attractive jobs, and the transportation system is still unsatisfactory. On the other hand, the disadvantaged position of the border region has been successfully compensated in large areas.

Kurzfassung

Das "Zonenrandgebiet" ist ein etwa 40 km breiter Gebietsstreifen entlang der Grenze zur Deutschen Demokratischen Republik und zur Tschechoslowakei. Es nimmt etwa 1/5 der Fläche der Bundesrepublik ein, besitzt jedoch nur knapp 4% der Einwohner. Die Grenze wurde 1945 zwischen den Besatzungszonen eingerichtet und später von der DDR als Staatsgrenze militärisch stark befestigt. Das Grenzgebiet geriet in eine

REGIONAL DEVELOPMENT PROGRAMS 625

geographische und ökonomische Randlage, die Infrastruktur war ungenügend. Viele Orte mußten sich nach Westen umorientieren. Eine Abwanderung von Erwerbspersonen war die Folge.

Um den ökonomischen und sozialen Nachteil auszugleichen, erließen Bund und Länder besondere Förderprogramme. Sie schließen den Bau von Wohnungen, Schulen und Freizeiteinrichtungen ein, die Ansiedlung von Industriebetrieben, eine Erweiterung des Verkehrsnetzes. Mit diesen Maßnahmen konnte die Abwanderung der Bevölkerung stark eingeschränkt werden, jedoch mangelt es noch an attraktiven Arbeitsplätzen und einer befriedigenden Verkehrsstruktur. In großen Bereichen ist es dagegen gelungen, die Nachteile des Grenzgebietes auszugleichen.

Regional Development Programs and Their Effectiveness
in Areas Along the Eastern Border
of West Germany

THE SITUATION BEFORE 1945

Before 1945 Germany was a unified economic area. Economic regions had evolved naturally and had become fairly fixed by the time of the formation of the German state in 1871. These regions were interdependent and had many strong connections with each other. A map of the distribution of industry in 1928 shows three large regions (Figure 19-1): (a) Western Germany including the Ruhr and the axis along the Rhine above Frankfurt; linked to this are the areas around Stuttgart and Munich in southern Germany; (b) Central Germany with centers in Saxony and Thuringia, particularly around Halle and Leipzig, and northerly offshoots leading up to Hannover; and (c) Eastern Germany with Berlin at its center, as well as Breslau and the Upper Silesian mining and industrial area in the east. Isolated industrial areas are to be found mainly in the ports of Hamburg and Bremen. It is obvious that these industrial areas were very closely linked: railroads, roads, and canals catered to the necessary flow of goods and people. The traffic flow took mainly a west-east course.

Just as Germany's industrial areas were connected, there were also numerous contacts between individual settlements. The village of Obersuhl can serve as an example (1). Obersuhl is in the province of Hessia and lies directly on the border with the neighboring eastern province of Thuringia. In 1939 the village had over 2,600 inhabitants, mainly workers employed in other towns who commuted daily. There were also farmers, both full-time and part-time, as well as a few businesses. For these commuters, the most important places of work before the war are shown in Figure 19-2. They were: Heringen (Hessia), 6 km from Obersuhl and attracting approximately 280 commuters; Gerstungen (Thuringia), 2.5 km, approximately 250 commuters; and Eisenach (Thuringia), 25 km, approximately 100 commuters. The neighboring towns of Gerstungen (2.5 km) and Berka (2 km) in Thuringia were central places for the population of Obersuhl where any necessary shopping could be done and where the services of doctors, pharmacists, banks, etc., were available. Eisenach (25 km) was a central place of a higher order with numerous businesses and other facilities such as theaters, high schools, hospitals, etc. (Figure 19-3). Apart from works and services, the inhabitants of Obersuhl had many personal contacts with the people in Thuringia. They resulted from marriages or from special contacts, i.e., through the church, sporting clubs, and other institutions. The orientation of the village of Obersuhl toward Thuringia affected the development of the road network. Most roads led to the places mentioned and were of good quality, whereas to the west the roads were few and of poor quality.

THE FORMATION OF THE BORDER BEFORE 1945 AND THE CONSEQUENCES FOR THE POPULATION AND THE ECONOMY

The contacts between the economic regions of Germany and, on a smaller scale, between individual villages and towns, were abruptly curtailed at the end of World War II by a border. The course of this border follows the old German provincial borders which had formed over the centuries and had been altered frequently. Wars, the sale of estates, marriages between princely houses, and other events meant that the borders were not straight and practical but rather distorted, enclosing certain settlements or running through the middle of others. In extreme cases even groups of houses were divided. But connections always existed, and the population could cross the border at any time. By the formation of the German _Reich_ in 1871 there were merely the boundaries of local government which people were hardly conscious of.

In 1945 these one-time provincial boundaries became the borders between the allied areas of occupation. Thus arose the _Zonengrenze_ (zonal border) between the eastern part of Germany occupied by the Soviets and the American- and British-occupied regions in the West. Until 1952 a certain exchange across the borders of these zones was still possible; workers drove from one part to another, farmers tilled their fields on the other side. The situation on the border changed in 1952 with the acceptance in the West of the Treaty of Germany. The German Democratic Republic (GDR) founded in 1949 set up the so-called "closed zone," and only illegal traffic thereafter was able to cross the border. Since 1961 there has been a military extension of the border, making escape from the GDR virtually impossible. Therefore, a one-time provincial boundary within Germany has become the border between two German nations. It is fortified and guarded by the GDR like no other border in the democratic world.

As a consequence of this border both the economy and the population of the area directly on the border were seriously hampered, especially when an area's traditional orientation, as in the case of Obersuhl, led across the border (2). The following main points are taken from the example of Obersuhl but also apply generally to other places in the border zone.

The population was at first hardest hit by the separation from friends and relatives on the other side of the border. Many lost their places of work. Contacts with familiar

REGIONAL DEVELOPMENT PROGRAMS 629

places, businesses, doctors, etc., had to be given up. The roads and railroads were cut (Figure 19-2). A reorientation was necessary, i.e., to places which would hardly have been visited before the war. The following places have now become important for Obersuhl (Figures 19-3 and 19-4):

<u>Heringen</u>, with its jobs in the potash mines; because of the necessary detour the distance increased from 6 km to over 25 km.

<u>Bebra</u> as a place of work, mainly at the freightyard, and as a shopping center, about 20 km away.

<u>Rotenburg</u> as a place of work and a shopping center, seat of the local administration (<u>Kreisverwaltung</u>) until 1976, over 28 km away.

<u>Bad Hersfeld</u> as a place of work and as a shopping center, with local administration, about 35 km away.

The enforced abandonment of the traditional connections and the reorientation to new centers naturally came hard for the people in places near the border. An even greater problem was that the distances were greater and the road network was in no way designed to serve the new centers. The transport system's lack of access westwards was true of many places on the border and greatly hindered their economic development so that an improvement of this situation was one of the first and most pressing tasks. Within the framework of the FRG the areas on the "zonal border" were now on the periphery. In general the distances to the traditional industrial areas of the Ruhr-Rhine-Neckar are relatively great, and there are few connections. Their position beyond the industrial conurbations necessarily hindered the economic expansion of these border areas.

A further factor which especially characterized the border region in the first two decades after 1945 was the emigration

of population. As the villages had suffered relatively
little damage in the war, after 1945 numerous refugees from
East Germany were at first housed there (3). The increased
population diminished rapidly again in the fifties and sixties when people could no longer find work in the area. The
resulting population decline could become dangerous especially as the quota of younger immigrants was very high. Altogether the economic situation of the border regions lagged
far behind that of the strongly expanding conurbations in
the Federal Republic. The disadvantages were expressed
especially in this loss of population.

DEVELOPMENT-AID PROGRAMS FOR THE BORDER REGION AND THEIR IMPACT

After the currency reform in 1948 and the foundation of the
Federal Republic of Germany in 1949 the special situation of
the border regions initiated numerous development-aid programs. They came at first from the federal states
bordering the "zonal boundary." Later the federal government also participated in the aid programs. In 1953 a
special area was delineated--the region along the borders
with the GDR and Czechoslovakia which consisted of areas
belonging to the four federal states (4). It stretches
along the border as a zonal strip an average of 40 km wide
(Figure 19-5). As far as the economy is concerned the area
is very heterogenous. It includes large urban industrial
conurbations such as Kiel, Lübeck, Braunschweig/Salzgitter,
and Kassel, as well as rural and extremely underdeveloped
areas such as Lüchow/Danneberg in Lower Saxony. The aim of
the aid programs decided upon and implemented by the federal
government and the states was to lessen the disadvantages
which exist for both the economy and the people. In the

Spatial Planning Act of 1965 a framework was formulated which would allow the economic productivity in this area to be strengthened and brought up to the same level as the other economic areas of Germany. Therefore, the economic disparities which caused the population to leave the border region are to be eliminated (5).

The aid program includes a series of measures which can be summarized as follows (6):

(a) The support of social facilities in the villages and towns through financial aid. Such facilities include nurseries, athletic fields, indoor and outdoor swimming pools, leisure centers, especially for young people, schools, and other centers of education. These facilities are intended to make life in the villages more attractive, particularly for young people.

(b) Building assistance. New construction and the repair and modernization of apartments and houses are encouraged and partly subsidized in order to make living in the border zone more attractive and to prevent migration.

(c) The extension of the transport network. This is a particularly important measure which is intended to make it possible for the inhabitants of the border region to get to their places of work and to the central places more quickly. A compact transport system is also important for businesses that already have to bear the high transport costs to distant markets.

(d) Encouraging the economy of the border region. Here, too, a catalog of relief measures is available. This includes, among other items, financial assistance in the establishment or expansion of firms, supplying industrial estates with energy and water, the construction of training and retraining centers, as well as a series of tax exemptions. These measures are intended to encourage productive firms to settle in greater numbers in the border region and to assist the expansion of firms already present.

As already stated, the catalog of aid measures is composed of aid supplied by the federal government and the affected states as well as from individual communities. Thus, the necessary financial assistance is shared by the three responsible bodies.

One may well ask whether any effects of the varied support and preference given to the border regions can be determined once the disadvantages of this area are removed. Without any doubt, one can ascertain that in most villages and towns of the border region considerable financial assistance has been available. Most settlements are now equipped with such facilities as gymnasiums, swimming pools, new schools, etc. Numerous new houses have also been built, and old buildings have been modernized. The settlements generally give an impression of being well cared-for. This superficial impression and the construction of leisure centers, which were hardly known in a German village before the war, should not disguise the fact that there are still problems in the border region.

Most important certainly is the strengthening of the economy and thereby the creation of jobs. Labor has been released by the trend in agriculture toward concentration and specialization. Young people, especially, look for well-paid jobs as well as good working conditions and holidays. In order to prevent their migration, attractive industries are to be settled. However, this is very difficult despite all kinds of inducements. The disadvantages of the border region have not yet been eradicated. These are principally the relatively long distances from consumer markets, the isolation from other industries and necessary services, the lack of skilled labor, and the relatively backward infrastructure. Although small and medium-sized firms, due to the development aid, have settled in the villages and towns of the border region, many could exist for only a short period and others have been unable to make any great expansion. They cannot offer attractive places of work, and wages are lower compared to industries in other areas. Recently, hardly any firms could be established in the smaller settlements. There has been a concentration of industrial plants in a few larger centers. Here there are fully equipped industrial plants, the transport situation is more favorable, and the necessary services such as banks, insurance firms, lawyers, etc., are available. There is also more attractive accommodation for management.

On the other hand, the workforce has farther to travel to reach these firms. The cost in time is too high, particularly when public transportation facilities must be used. These operate infrequently and have to make detours and pass through narrow village roads (7). A problem which has not yet been satisfactorily solved is the extension of roads to the larger industrial centers and the creation of public transport (bus lines) which can transport workers quickly to their firms. The time-consuming distances and the unfavorable transport situation together with relatively low wages are important factors for migration. The disparities within industrial conurbations are still too great. When asked, people wanting to migrate gave as their intended destinations the industrial conurbations, where much more money can be earned. Up to now it has not been possible to stop migration. However, the number of migrants has decreased (8).

SUMMARY

After the war the unified political and economic entity of Germany was dissected within a few years. The border divides two completely different economic areas in Germany and in Europe; the sphere of the COMECON in the East and the European Community in the West. The border region fell into a geographic and economic peripheral area. For a few years (up to 1952) some traffic across the border was still possible. In the Federal Republic the concept of a united Germany lives on and long influenced generous long-range planning in the border region.

The border region in the FRG quickly became economically disadvantaged compared with other areas. Many settlements were oriented eastwards before the war, so that the transport system was also laid out in that direction. A reorientation to the West, as well as the economic development of the border region, was not possible without external aid. The federal government and the individual state governments created laws and aid programs to further the development of the border region. They are mainly concerned with financially supporting economic expansion, the infrastructure, house construction, and other facilities. Up to now, large parts of the border region have been consolidated through this help, even though regional differences exist. Industries are settled in certain larger centers which must be easily reached from the surrounding villages. The transport system in many places can barely cope with the demands put upon it. It is also necessary to improve the quality of the transport network.

Although the initial heavy migration, particularly among young people, has decreased, it could not be stopped. As in other rural areas of the Federal Republic, too, there is a considerable lack of desired professional training, of corresponding jobs, and of good wages. The industrial conurbations will continue to be lures to migrants. On the whole it can be said that most inhabitants and especially the new generation has recovered from the shock which the people had to suffer through the creation of the border. The border was not accepted, of course, but it is realized that it must be lived with. The help of the various aid programs has gradually eliminated some of the economic and social disadvantages in most parts of the region. However, the process is not yet complete.

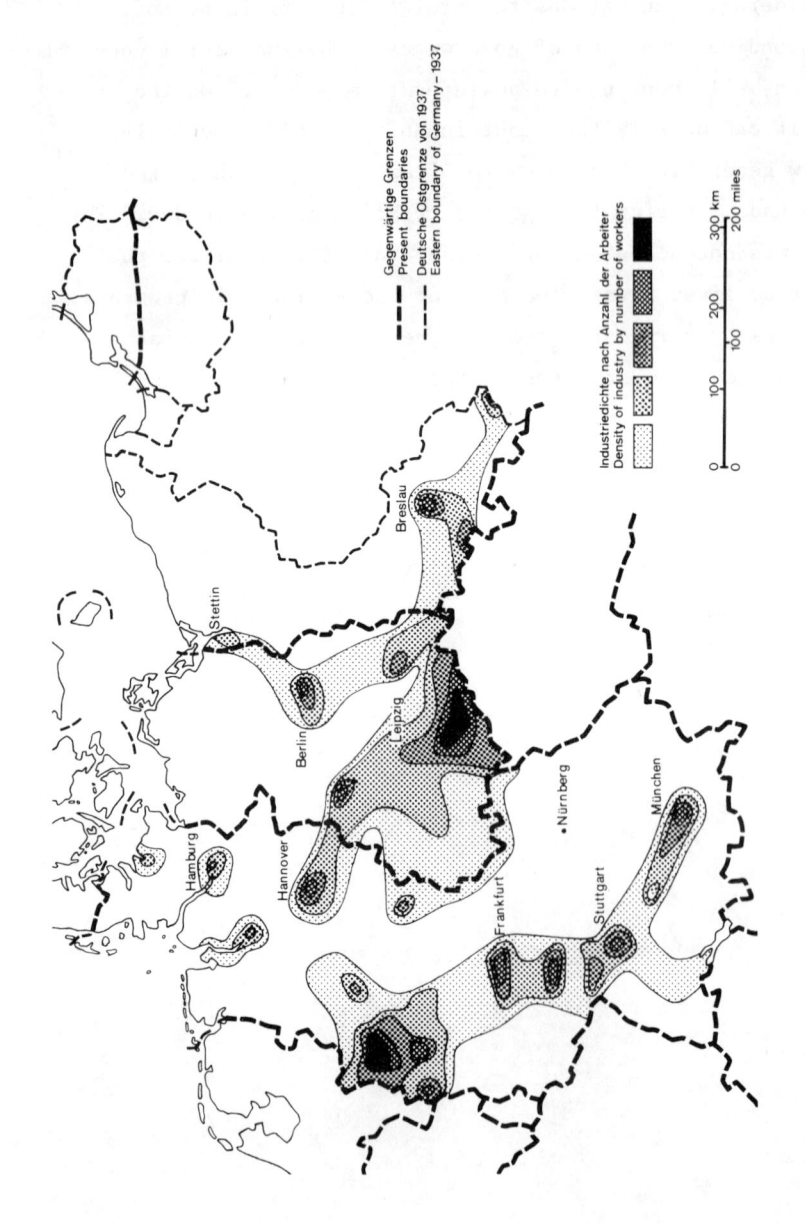

FIG. 19-1. Main Industrial Areas of Germany-1928.
Hauptindustriegebiete Deutschlands-1928.

REGIONAL DEVELOPMENT PROGRAMS

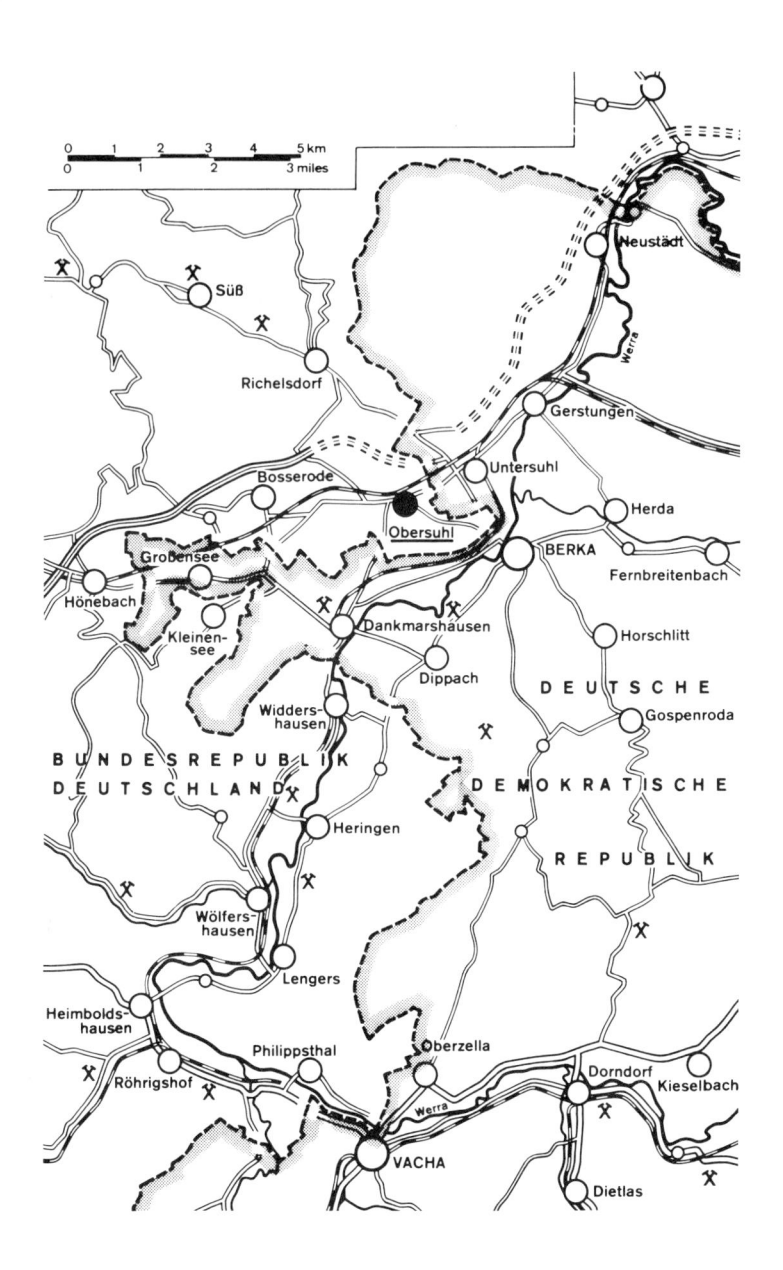

FIG. 19-2. Interrupted Lines of Transportation in the Border Region.

Unterbrochene Verkehrslinien im Grenzraum.

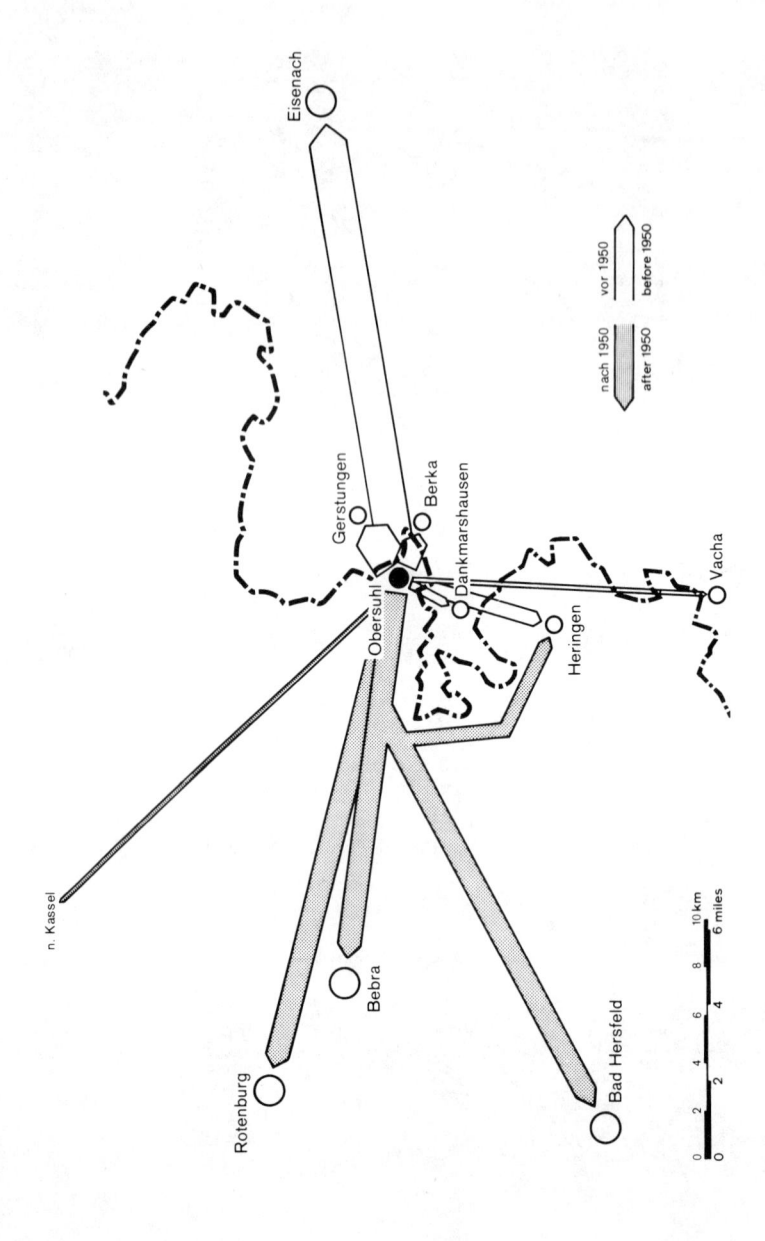

FIG. 19-3. General Orientation of Obersuhl Before and After 1950.
Allgemeine Orientierung von Obersuhl vor und nach 1950.

REGIONAL DEVELOPMENT PROGRAMS

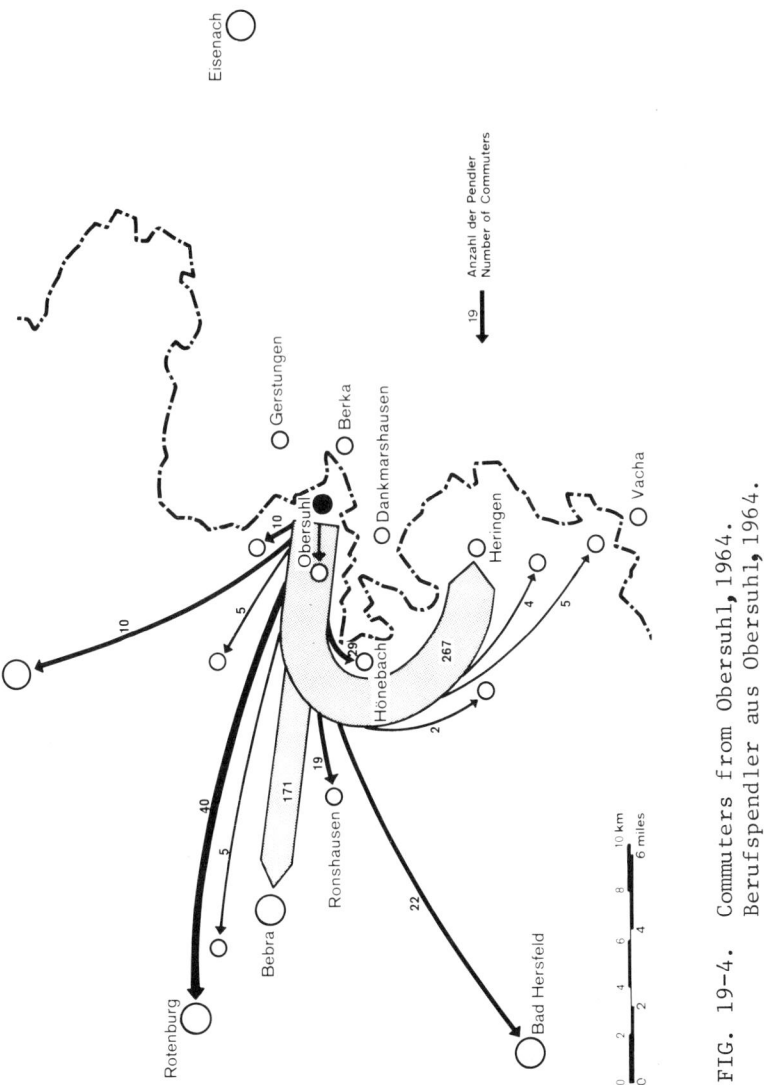

FIG. 19-4. Commuters from Obersuhl, 1964.
Berufspendler aus Obersuhl, 1964.

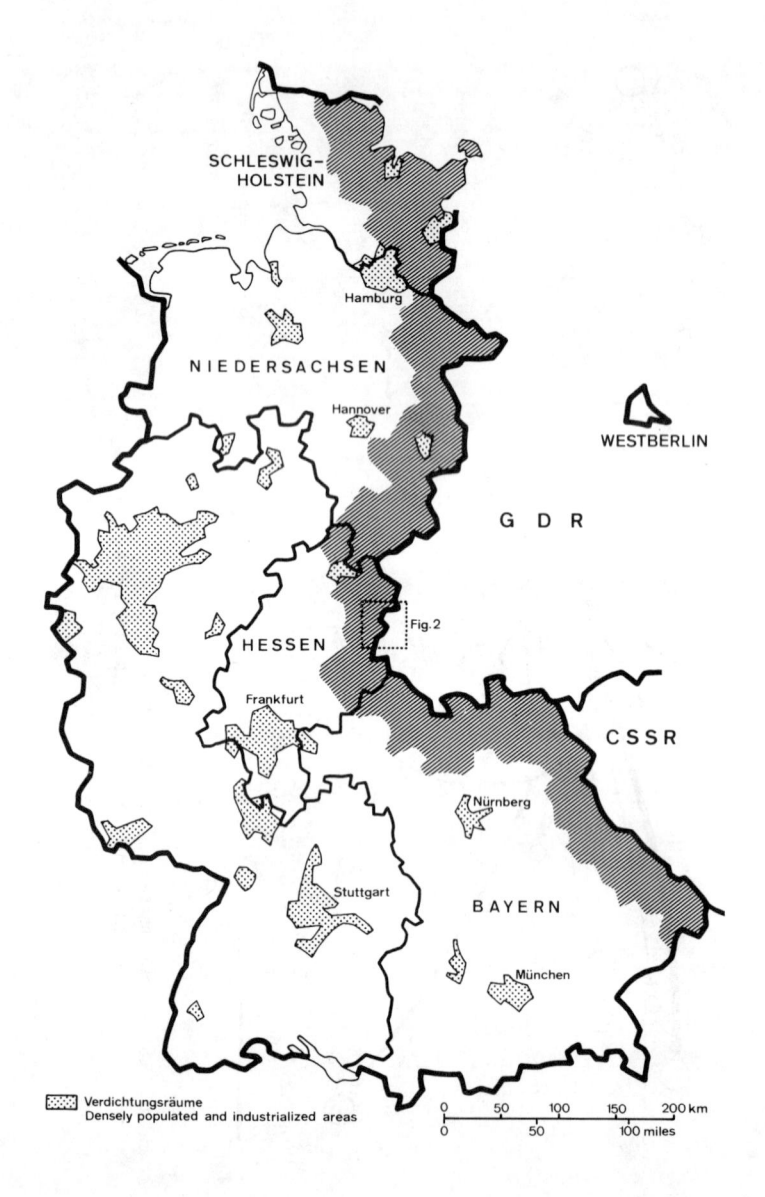

FIG. 19-5. The Eastern Border Region of the Federal Republic of Germany.
Das östliche Grenzgebiet der Bundesrepublik Deutschland.

NOTES

1. The statements concerning the region around Obersuhl are based upon personal observations and conversations with the mayor of the village and with numerous inhabitants. See also Roth, W., Dorf im Wandel (Frankfurt a.M.: Hassmüller, 1968); Brecht, W., "Die Problamtik der Entwicklung des Zonengrenzkreises Rotenburg," Heimatadressbuch Kreis Rotenburg (1964)" Struktur und Entwicklung von Wirtschaft und Bevölkerung im Raum Obersuhl. Gutachten der Hessischen Landesentwicklungs-und Treuhandgessellschaft MBH (March, 1971).

2. An assessment can only be made for the border regions within the Federal Republic of Germany. There is no information available about the border regions of the GDR.

3. The fluctuations in the population figures for Obersuhl are as follows:

   1939 - 2,626   1970 - 3,074
   1952 - 3,472   1978 - 3,051
   1961 - 3,240

4. These are from north to south, the federal states of Schleswig-Holstein, Lower Saxony, Hessen, and Bavaria. In the Zonenrandgebiet (eastern border region), including the Bavarian areas bordering on Czechoslovakia in 1971, were: 25 Stadtkreise (city with county functions), 79 Landkreise (counties. These are districts of which more than half are up to 40 kilometers distant from the border. The total eastern border region comprises about one-fifth of the area of the Federal Republic; with its 2.3 million inhabitants, it contains 8.8 percent of the total population of the FRG (61.5 million).

5. Raumordnungsgesetz von 1965, paragraph 2.4 Bundesgesetzblatt 1965, part I, p. 307.

6. Gesetz zur Förderung des Zonenrandgebietes vom 5 August 1971 (law to promote the peripheral zonal regions), Bundesgesetzblatt, part I, No. 77, p. 123 ff.

7. The journey from Obersuhl to Bad Hersfeld, with its sizable expansion of industry, takes one hour by bus. This time could be reduced by at least half.

8. Migration in Obersuhl as a percentage of the population:

   1950–1969: 21 percent
   1961–1969: 5 percent

CHAPTER 20

WEST BERLIN AND THE FEDERAL REPUBLIC OF GERMANY

BERLIN (WEST) UND DIE BUNDESREPUBLIK DEUTSCHLAND

Burkhard Hofmeister

Abstract

West Berlin's postwar history may be appropriately divided into three periods: the period before and after the erection of the Wall of 1961 and the Quadripartite Agreement of 1972. After the unemployment and the restrictions on inmigration of the 1950s, vacant positions had to be filled by people hired in West Germany and countries like Turkey, Yugoslavia, and Greece. Above-average percentages of retired people and people living on welfare still remained. The 1960s were characterized by the impacts of the Berlin Assistance Act of 1962 with the creation of a preferential taxation system, the granting of loans for various economic activities, and federal guarantees for transit shipments. The Quadripartite Agreement achieved a sounder basis for West Berlin's political status, thus improving the construction, maintenance, and use of transit routes, but it neither improved the geographical isolation effect for manufacturing industries nor the deficiencies of the service sector after the loss of the national capital functions and related activities. The FRG contributes 52 percent of West Berlin's annual budget. Of this, however, only 50 percent are subsidies in the strict sense, while 50 percent are regular payments like social security funds. In 1979 West Berlin received approximately DM 8.4 million from the FRG while it paid DM 7.6 billion of taxes to the FRG, so the balance does not look as bad as it is often anticipated.

Kurzfassung

Die Geschichte Berlins (West) nach dem Kriege kann in die Zeiträume vor und nach der Errichtung der Mauer im Jahre 1961, und die Zeitspanne nach dem 1972 in Kraft getretenen Vier-Mächte Abkommen geteilt werden. Nach der Arbeitslosigkeit und den Einschränkungen der Einwanderung der fünfziger Jahre mussten vakante Stellen durch Leute aus

Westdeutschland und Ländern wie der Türkei, Jugoslawien, und Griechenland besetzt werden. Es blieben noch überdurchschnittliche viele Rentner und Fürsorgeempfänger. Die sechziger Jahre wurden durch die Wirkungen des 1962 verabschiedeten Berlin-Hilfe-Gesetzes gekennzeichnet, das ein Vorzugssystem der Besteuerung schuf, und sowohl Kredite für verschiedene ökonomische Tätigkeiten als auch Bundesgarantien für den Transitverkehr bewilligte. Das Vier-Mächte Abkommen erreichte eine gesunde Basis für die politische Lage West Berlins, was den Bau, die Erhaltung, und die Benutzung der Verkehrswege verbesserte, aber es verbesserte weder die Wirkung der geographischen Absonderung auf die Industrieproduktion noch die Mängel in dem Dienstsektor nach dem Verlust der Hauptstadtfunktionen und der dazu gehörigen Aktivitäten. Zweiundfünfzig Prozent des Budgets Berlin (West) sind von der BRD erhaltene Zahlungen, unter denen jedoch nur 50 Prozent Subsidien im engen Sinn sind, während 50 Prozent normale Zahlungen wie Rentenversicherungsgelder sind. 1979 soll West Berlin DM 8.4 billion von der BRD erhalten, während es DM 7.6 billion für Steuern der BRD zahlen wird, so dass die Bilanz gar nicht so schlimm aussieht, wie es oft erwartet wird.

West Berlin and the Federal Republic of Germany

WEST BERLIN AND THE FRG AFTER THE
QUADRIPARTITE AGREEMENT

It seems appropriate to divide West Berlin's postwar history into three periods: the first lasting from the blockade in 1948-1949 to the construction of the Wall in 1961; the second from the erection of the Wall--creating the complete political partition of the former Greater Berlin and the isolation of the western sectors--to the implementation of the Quadripartite Agreement of 1972; and the third from this event to the present. We shall only consider the second and third periods in some detail and try to answer the question: What was the situation like prior to the Quadripartite Agreement and what changes have been brought about by the agreement and the consecutive treaties between the two German states?

Two issues seem to be of great importance for a full understanding of the political status of West Berlin. The relevant paragraph of Appendix II of the Quadripartite Agreement reads as follows: "The Governments of the French Republic, the United Kingdom and the United States of America declare that the ties between the western sectors of Berlin and the Federal Republic of Germany will be maintained and developed, taking into account that these sectors continue not to be a constituent part of the Federal Republic of Germany and not to be governed by it" (1).

This means that, on the one hand, the Western Allies maintained their position, in contrast to the Soviet government, that legal ties between West Berlin and the FRG did exist prior to the agreement and that these should continue to exist and even to be further developed; and that, on the other hand, under these conditions the demonstrative FRG presence in West Berlin would be less important and might very well be reduced. Thus, the Western position was upheld that West Berlin was considered a part of the area to which the judicial, financial, economic, and sociocultural systems of the FRG apply while usually the bills passed by the Bonn Parliament with certain exceptions are voted into law by the West Berlin House of Representatives; i.e., they do not apply automatically to West Berlin.

To mention the negative aspects of the Quadripartite Agreement first:

(a) The English and Russian texts of the agreement differ with regard to the decisive expression of the relations between West Berlin and the FRG. While the English text uses the word ties, the Russian word sviazy has more the meaning of technical or communication links, connection, or relationship, although according to a Russian dictionary it may also be used in the sense of ties of friendship.

(b) The Western Allies resumed responsibility for reducing FRG presence in West Berlin, which meant that the president of the FRG must not be elected in Berlin; that the Federal Assembly and the political parties represented in the Bonn Parliament ceased to have plenary sessions in the Reichstag building (only committees would be allowed to hold business meetings in Berlin); and that no more FRG offices would be admitted to West Berlin. The only attempt of this kind, namely, to establish the Federal Environmental Office in Berlin, was answered by heavy Soviet protests.

(c) No satisfactory solution was found for incorporating West Berlin into treaties negotiated between the FRG and any country belonging to the COMECON.

(d) No satisfactory solution was found for incorporating West Berlin participants in any international events--cultural, sports, or others--although the Soviets had agreed "to accept the right of the FRG to represent West Berlin in international organizations and agreements and to provide consular services for local residents." The Soviet point of view here is that everything not expressly permitted in the agreement is considered forbidden (1).

Now to the positive aspects of the agreement. The greatest achievements have been in the field of the technical links between the FRG and West Berlin. For the first time since 1948 the hitherto unclarified status of civilian surface traffic was settled within the framework of the agreement. This certainly is an important point.

Transit by train and car has improved; procedures at the borders have been simplified now and traffic has become more expeditious. This has led to shorter travel time, especially for the trains between Berlin and Hamburg, by opening up a more direct route instead of the Hamburg trains from the northwest encircling half the metropolitan region in order to enter West Berlin from Griebnitzsee in the southwest, which had been the only border crossing between Hamburg and the Federal Republic prior to the agreement. The most rapid train connection between Hamburg and Berlin took 5 hours and 26 minutes in 1969, 4 hours and 22 minutes in 1973, and 3 hours and 31 minutes in 1979. In the past only one station was available in the whole city of West Berlin, Zoologischer Garten in the heart of the city. In the meantime Wannsee Station for the trains to the west and south and Staaken Station for the trains to the northwest have been opened (Figure 20-1).

For travelers in motor vehicles the agreement made the provision "that these persons, their conveyance and personal baggage will not be subject to search, detention or exclusion" with the only exception that there would be "sufficient grounds for suspicion on misuse of the transit routes" (2). This made travel in private cars more expeditious and gave the travelers a feeling of greater security. Both modes of traffic, train and private car, increased while the number of air passengers temporarily declined from a peak of more than 5 million in 1970 to approximately 4 million in the mid-1970s.

As far as the transport of civilian goods in transit is concerned the agreement contains the provision that as many trucks as possible should be equipped with seals before departure so that cars could pass control without the usual inspection by East German authorities. For the use of the inland waterways between the FRG and Berlin, provisions were made for berths as resting places, supplying information on water levels and the operation of locks, and assistance of East German authorities in case of accidents.

One of the consecutive agreements between the two German states provided the renewal of the heavily used and considerably damaged surface of the Autobahn from West Berlin via Helmstedt to Hannover and Cologne. The FRG agreed to pay a very high amount for this construction work.

Another agreement provided for a new Autobahn link to be constructed between Berlin and the border crossing point on the route to Hamburg which thus far had been a regular state highway leading through a number of villages and towns making the trip to Hamburg by car rather time-consuming and even somewhat hazardous. The FRG will also finance this project.

A further agreement settled the reopening of the Teltow Canal leading through the southern boroughs of the city. The western and eastern entrances of the canal located on the territory of the GDR had been closed, and the portion of the canal belonging to the western sectors could only be reached by a big detour through the West Berlin canal system requiring delays of one and a half days in either direction.

The other two major achievements of the agreement are mentioned only briefly because they do not directly refer to the relations between the FRG and Berlin.

There has been a minor exchange of territory of mutual benefit to the GDR and West Berlin. Half of the area of the former dozen enclaves, two of which had been inhabited permanently and two of which had been used just by West Berlin residents for visits to their weekend homes, was traded for a corridor to Steinstücken, the access to the larger of these controlled by East German authorities. In a later agreement the area of two abandoned railroad stations was acquired partly through purchase at a high price and partly through an exchange for a new large railroad station in the south, a project which dates back to prewar times.

The accords enabled West Berlin to make some use of its natural hinterland located on the territory of the GDR. A number of telephone lines and other communication links between West Berlin and East Berlin and the GDR were brought into operation successively; West Berlin residents were allowed to apply for permits for a stay of up to thirty days a year for visits or merely as tourists, thus easing the situation in the overcrowded recreation areas within the city limits. They also could again make use of their leisure gardens, some 50,000 of which had been located on GDR territory. This was a great improvement since much of the leisure garden area in West Berlin proper had been absorbed for other purposes, such as the establishment of new industrial plants, housing projects, and road construction. The East German authorities in a consecutive agreement also permitted a large amount of West Berlin's garbage to be brought to garbage disposal sites on its territory, which also helped to ease the competition for the limited space within the city limits.

The agreement did not include anything about the air corridors between West Berlin and the GDR. The Western Allies, who had to decide on the use of the air corridors, were confronted with two incompatible goals. On the one hand, the strict refusal of landing permits to other than American, British, or French airlines favors the competitive position of East Berlin's Schoenefled Airport, which already enjoys the advantage of lower fares of the airlines of the COMECON countries, thus making air traffic through the corridors less and less profitable and also more vulnerable. On the other hand, the juridical foundation of the corridors prohibits an unrestricted opening to other airlines. Thus far, not even the German Airlines (Lufthansa) are allowed to operate between the FRG and West Berlin (Figure 20-1).

WEST BERLIN'S POPULATION: DEMOGRAPHIC
AND SOCIAL CHARACTERISTICS

The construction of the Berlin Wall in 1961 marked the turning point in West Berlin's population development. Throughout the 1950s decreasing unemployment restricted the movement of people who wanted to make West Berlin their permanent residence, and measures were taken to relocate refugees from the GDR to places in the FRG. After this influx had been stopped suddenly and almost completely by the erection of the

Wall, West Berlin reached full employment, and the situation was thus reversed. Vacant positions were filled by people hired in the FRG and in countries such as Turkey, Yugoslavia, and Greece. The number of foreign laborers mushroomed from 18,000 in 1968 to 82,000 in 1971. Of the 250,000 West German people taking a job in West Berlin in the decade 1961-1971 approximately 100,000 returned within less than two years, while most of the rest remained for good. Nonetheless, West Berlin's population has been declining constantly due mainly to its above-average percentage of retired people and consequent high death rates (20 percent), its above-average percentage of single-person households (44 percent as compared with 24 percent in the FRG), and its low birth rates (approximately 8 percent) and the drain of people who do not find adequate jobs in the city (3).

This age structure has also resulted in a very high percentage of people living on welfare. Approximately one-third of the purchasing power of West Berlin's population is related to some government source, and this in turn is one reason for the rather heavy subsidies from the Bonn government to West Berlin's annual budget. Moreover, the continuous though slow decrease in population has negative effects on consumer demands--retail sales as well as services. Slightly decreasing numbers of employees in these nonbasic functions could only be made up by an increasing number of available jobs in the production and interregional service sectors discussed below.

THE TWO SUPPORTS OF WEST BERLIN'S
ECONOMIC BASE

While the Quadripartite Agreement and its consecutive treaties provided a certain base for West Berlin's existence as

a political entity and for its relations with the FRG they
certainly could not improve the two major prerequisites for
a real sound economic base; i.e., they neither offered com-
pensations for the continuing geographical isolation and its
adverse effects on manufacturing nor for the lack of the
national capital functions and its negative effect on the
service sector of the economy. Let us take a closer look
at both economic factors.

MANUFACTURING: BRANCHES, EMPLOYMENT,
VALUE ADDED, EXPORT

In the course of reconstruction West Berlin regained Greater
Berlin's prewar rank as Germany's greatest industrial city
in terms of employees as well as value added. Generally
speaking, conditions for industrial development have been
rather favorable. Lacking raw materials in the vicinity,
the city never developed branches such as steel production
or heavy chemicals. Light industries prevail offering both
a high degree of refinement of the materials being processed
and a comparatively high percentage of female labor. Most
of the traditional branches may be traced back to Berlin's
particular location factors. The Department of Defense,
the Prussian Telegraph and Telephone Administration, and
the state-owned railroads as the major customers made Berlin
the leading production center for electrical equipment and
steam locomotives. The royal court and gentry encouraged
the founding of textile mills and garment shops, mainly by
French and Bohemian refugees, in the eighteenth century.
The local market eventually exceeded the 4 million mark in
the early 1940s. Small bakeries became large factories, and
little roadside pharmacies developed into world renowned
pharmaceutical enterprises with subsidiary companies in all

continents. Postwar preferential taxation stimulated tobacco processing in Berlin, and the output grew twenty-fold during the 1950s and once more quadrupled during the 1960s (4).

Certain branches, however, suffered from the postwar situation. Thus Frankfurt, Düsseldorf, Stuttgart, and Munich succeeded Berlin as the former German focal point of the printing and fashion industries. Certain factors have impeded further growth of West Berlin's industrial output. There have been limits set by the area available for the promotion of new industrial plants by the lack of skilled labor, and last but not least, by the lack of adequate housing for those willing to accept a position in the city (5).

One peculiar disadvantage, besides the geographical isolation and higher transportation costs, has been controls by East German authorities at border crossings and the highway fees for the use of the transit routes. The FRG has taken specific measures in support of transport by truck between it and West Berlin. One such measure is the resumption of the responsibility for the political risk involved in transit shipments. Another is the payment of subsidies to refund the highway fees. We shall return to this topic later.

Thus, if West Berlin has sometimes failed to attract still greater numbers of new industrial enterprises due to the lack of adequate sites, skilled labor, or even adequate housing for labor, expansion of the tertiary sector on a level proportionate to a metropolis of its size has proven even more difficult.

SERVICE FUNCTIONS IN THE FORMER
GERMAN CAPITAL

In 1939 Berlin had 574,000 people employed in manufacturing and 877,000 in the service sector. While the input of goods by far surpassed the output, this deficit was more than compensated for by the service sector. The interregional accomplishments of Berlin's services earned in 1939 approximately 50 percent of the city's income. By 1970, this had sharply dropped to a mere 6 percent (6). Although the present city administration, including the city-owned enterprises, had more employees than the prewar governments of the Reich of Prussia, and the city administration together, the loss of the government functions and in consequence the loss of the top positions in the bureaucratic hierarchy are reflected in the lower income level and lower purchasing power of West Berlin's population. Aside from the governments proper, many associated functions are lacking or have been more or less reduced, such as foreign diplomats and their staffs, the Post and Railroad Administrations, and many others. The lack of orders from former customers in the publishing and printing industries has been mentioned already.

Chances to promote commercial, scientific, and cultural activities in West Berlin are confronted with the limits set to the FRG presence. Since the implementation of the Quadripartite Agreement only two attempts have been made to establish new FRG institutions in West Berlin. One, the opening of the Federal Environmental Office, resulted in heavy Soviet protests. The second project, that of organizing the so-called Foundation of Prussian Cultural Institutions, comprising the former royal castles now mainly used as museums, the National Archives, the National Gallery, and some other buildings outside Berlin into a more comprehensive national foundation with West Berlin as its headquarters was abandoned after heavy disputes accompanied by Eastern attacks.

In the field of education West Berlin holds a very dominant position. Approximately 7 percent of the whole university enrollment of the Federal Republic including West Berlin has concentrated on the universities and colleges of West Berlin. The so-called "educational export," which is the amount of money invested in education on the university level for people not completing their studies, reached 55 percent at the end of the 1960s and has very likely increased in the last decade (7).

FEDERAL AIDS TO WEST BERLIN

Immediately after the blockade of 1948-1949 creating the ultimate partition of Greater Berlin it became obvious that the Western sectors could not survive without considerable assistance from outside in excess of expenditures which are borne by the Federal Republic and granted to each state or each eligible citizen of the Federal Republic. More assistance was designed specifically to help West Berlin and the West Berlin residents.

The various measures taken over the years cannot be treated here in any detail. Three examples, however, may summarize the efforts made since 1949 when West Berlin was included in the European Recovery Program.

(a) During the 1950s a number of programs were sponsored to create more jobs in the city, especially to induce investments in the manufacturing sector, to order all sorts of goods from Berlin producers, to speed up reconstruction, and to make the city attractive by such projects as the International Construction Exhibition of 1957. All these measures and financial help were combined in the Berlin Assistance Act of 1962 (Berlin-Hilfe-Gesetz BHG) and the Berlin Aid Act of 1970 (Berlin-Förderungs-Gesetz BFG), the latest of which was approved on 8 March 1979.

(b) When reviewing these assistance programs one may distinguish two periods: the first prior to the Wall (1961), the second after the Wall. Markets for products made in West Berlin were the major goals of the former period. An increase in investments, the creation of more jobs, and the hiring of more labor, as well as efforts to keep the existing labor force, were the major goals of the latter period.

(c) The diverse assistance programs may be grouped under three headings: the creation and augmentation of a preferential taxation system, the granting of loans for various economic activities in the city, and federal guarantees for transit shipment in the case of political or technical accidents--and, in consequence of this, damage or loss of freight or equipment--and federal refunds of fees for the use of the transit routes which have already been referred to.

This comprehensive body of financial assistance for West Berlin has consistently been brought up to date by amendments as a result of changes in the FRG or the GDR. To give just one example, a reduction of the value-added tax was granted to Berlin entrepreneurs for goods originating in their Berlin plants. Recent economic trends rendered this measure insufficient since it was found that in many cases Berlin entrepreneurs have certain goods processed in subsidiary plants located outside Berlin that they are nevertheless involved in concerning the planning and installation, or as consultants for the operation of their equipment. The most recent regulation honors such circumstances and enables the respective Berlin entrepreneurs also in these cases to profit from preferential taxation.

(d) As to passenger traffic between West Berlin and the FRG one special arrangement should be mentioned: the federal subsidies to air fares. Civil aviation through the three air corridors has always been subsidized by the Federal Republic. During the 1960s (1963-1971) the subsidies increased from DM 31 million to DM 84 million, or by approximately 175 percent, while the number of air passengers increased by only 75 percent, which means that subsidies made up for a higher percentage at the end of the decade while the fares had been almost stable or even declined somewhat. In 1970 one air passenger paid just DM 51 for a return flight to Hannover while the government paid another DM 45 to the airline. It must be added, however, that the route Berlin-Hannover was the most subsidized of all to enable all persons feeling a risk in surface travel to travel by air. By 1974 the fare to be paid by the air passenger had risen to DM 77, and it is now DM 127.

What has been the financial transfer from the FRG to West Berlin or vice versa as a result of all those measures? For a realistic view of the financial situation of West Berlin two circumstances must first be taken into consideration. First, of the annual amount transferred from the FRG in 1968, only 45 percent were direct subsidies of West Berlin's budget, the other 55 percent were payments the Federal Republic would have been obliged to make since they are comparable to payments to all the states for social security and other purposes. The peculiar age structure of the Berlin population mentioned earlier provides for less income from fees and above-average expenses for social security, but such payments must not be labelled subsidies in the strict sense of the word. Second, at no time since 1949 have internal revenues been comparable to those of Hamburg or other big cities. While during the 1950s tax revenues increased faster than expenditures so that West Berlin's financial situation had started to improve, the Wall caused a sudden setback, and the introduction of taxation preferences made tax revenues drop considerably (8).

A report published in 1970 arrived at the following figures. During the seventeen-year period 1951-1968 the capital transfer from the FRG to West Berlin had amounted to DM 74.8 billion, while West Berlin had paid DM 24.3 billion of taxes to the FRG, so that the deficit had been DM 50.5 billion, or an average of DM 3 billion per annum (3). During the 1970s the situation obviously improved. Estimates for 1979 were DM 8.4 billion of payments from the FRG to West Berlin vis-a-vis a transfer of tax revenues of DM 7.6 billion from West Berlin to the FRG, resulting in a deficit of only DM 8.4 billion. Those subsidies of the FRG, on the other hand, amounted to 52 percent of West Berlin's budget, the other 48 percent being evenly raised by tax revenues and other sources.

IMPACTS OF THE VARIOUS TAXATION PREFERENCES
What can be said about the effects of all those measures with regard to the viability and vivacity to West Berlin? As far as manufacturing is concerned the city administration promoted industrial plants producing exportable goods with an anticipated high demand which, e.g., required little space and labor, especially such industry as electronics, hydraulic and other precision instruments, and synthetics. The forty-eight plants founded between 1968 and 1972 on the former site of a municipal farm are precisely this type and

differ favorably from the West Berlin average as far as the investment and the output per employee are concerned (9). As a result of the emphasis on such plants and the modernization of those existing, the number of industrial employees has dropped following a similar development in the manufacturing plants of the FRG; West Berlin experienced a sharper drop. Manufacturing employment in West Berlin's plants dropped by 26 percent from 1970 to 1976, which was certainly due to the rationalization measures induced by the respective subsidies.

According to a recent investigation by the German Institute of Economic Research, West Berlin in 1977 received 58 percent of all region-oriented subsidies granted by the Federal Republic and the states. This resulted in a definite advantage for West Berlin in comparison with all other underdeveloped regions within the Federal Republic with regard to industrial location. The Bank for Industrial Loans (Industriekreditbank AG) stated that while by 1975 preferences balanced the locational disadvantages, they did not give Berlin a real lead by 1977. A comparison of two samples of West Berlin and West German middle-size plants showed that the subsidies did not just balance the locational disadvantages but caused an increase of their income value above the West German level (10).

However, such developments are always threatened by certain trends in the overall situation in West Berlin. For example, the price level of the real estate market and the construction business is approximately 25 percent above that in comparable cities of the FRG and may well counterbalance the advantages achieved by the preferential taxation system. Hardly anything can be said about the future contribution of the service sector to West Berlin's budget.

There have been efforts toward this end such as the newly opened Convention Hall with a capacity of 5,000, and this may very well help to realize the anticipated increase in income from interregional services.

As to real estate, the preferential taxation system initiated after the erection of the Wall caused a construction boom and a shortage of land. With considerable amounts of tax deductible money big office buildings and mixed-use projects were begun with the result that not all office and retail space by far could be sold or leased. The program of this kind of investment was abandoned in 1974. Although prices for lots in the first years after the erection of the Wall increased four-fold, it is typical for Berlin's situation that prices even in the most favorable locations never jumped to such extreme heights as they did in cities like Munich. On the other hand, competition for land, especially for housing, is higher than in other cities that are able to make ready use of the hinterland. This is why the level of rents is prohibitive for a larger proportion of the population, including newcomers from West Germany and from foreign countries.

The age, profession, and income structures of the population are not yet favorable. However, the trends for the near future are better than they would be without the subsidies. Thanks to the many younger West German and foreign laborers the percentage of persons gainfully employed has been slightly but continuously increasing, while the number of retired people has been dropping slightly, thus making for a better ratio between the labor force and those unemployed because of retirement. This also means that the number of women of child-bearing age is increasing slightly and that the number of children will increase again. A

slight rejuvenation is a signal for a slow improvement of
the whole situation, although it does not solve all problems.

CONCLUSION

This essay has emphasized the limitations to West Berlin's
growth and development. It has shown that neither the
Quadripartite Agreement nor the continuous and substantial
aid from the Federal Republic could possibly offset the two
negative factors inherent in Berlin's present situation:
first, that West Berlin has been separated from its political and economic hinterland by a distance of at least 200 km
of foreign territory; and second, that the city continues to
be sensitive and vulnerable to political as well as economic
changes in both the Western and Socialist worlds.

Taking into account the constraints of the secondary and
tertiary sectors of the economy indicated earlier, a decrease of West Berlin's population from the present 2 million
to approximately 1.75 million at the end of the 1980s has
been predicted. This population figure is considered to be
adequate with regard to the limited resources of the city
in terms of the number of jobs available, housing demands,
and area per capita needed for various purposes including
recreation. In other words, this lower figure reflects the
actual capacity of West Berlin in the long run.

The predicted shrinkage of the number of inhabitants is
expected to ease West Berlin's situation to a certain extent. One may assume that competition of various land uses
for the same area will diminish and unemployement figures
will decrease. This shrinkage will not achieve West Berlin's
independence from FGR subsidies as long as the two negative
factors, i.e., the city's geographical isolation and its
vulnerability, persists. However, West Berlin is a political
issue and must not be judged merely by economics.

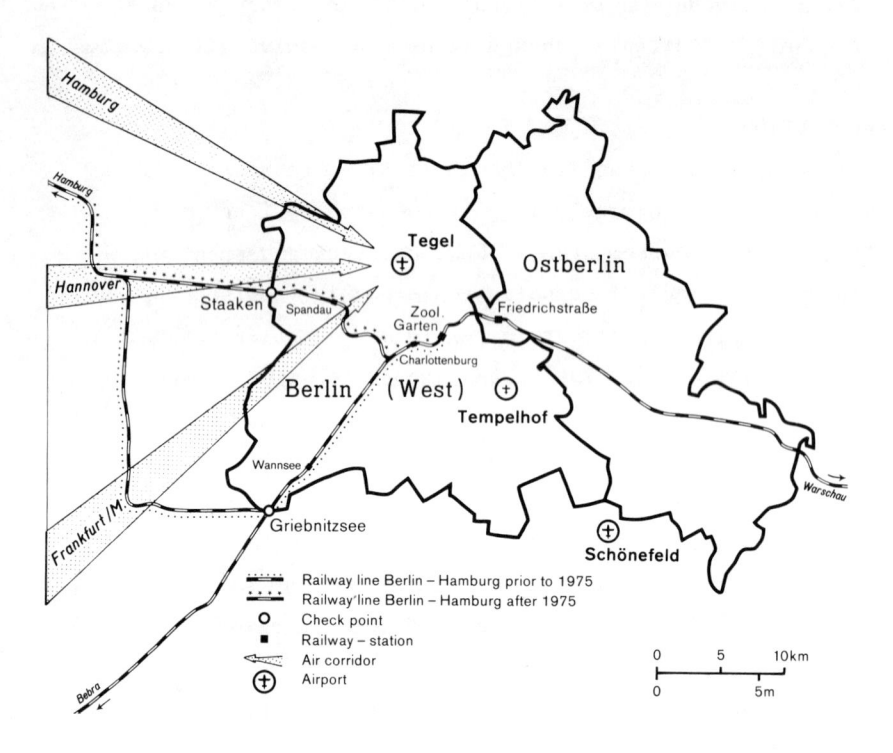

FIG. 20-1. Rail and Air Traffic Between West Berlin and the Federal Republic of Germany.
Eisenbahn, Luftverkehr zwischen West Berlin und der Bundesrepublik.

NOTES

1. Catudal, H. M., Jr., The Diplomacy of the Quadripartite Agreement on Berlin (Berlin: Berlin Verlag, 1978) p. 253 and p. 275.

2. Ibid., pp. 261-262.

3. Hofmeister, B., Berlin. Eine geographische Strukturanalyse der zwölf westlichen Bezirke (Darmstadt: Wissenschaftliche Buchgesellschaft, 1975) pp. 153-154.

4. Hofmeister, B., Berlin. Eine geographische Strukturanalyse der zwölf westlichen Bezirke (Darmstadt: Wissenschaftliche Buchgesellschaft, 1975) pp. 171-211; and Hofmeister, B., "Germany's industrial giant," The Geographical Magazine 50 (1978), 439-445.

5. Hofmeister, B., Berlin. Eine geographische Strukturanalyse der zwölf westlichen Bezirke (Darmstadt: Wissenschaftliche Buchgesellschaft, 1975) p. 113 and p. 159.

6. Hofmeister, B., Berlin. Eine geographische Strukturanalyse der zwölf westlichen Bezirke (Darmstadt: Wissenschaftliche Buchgesellschaft, 1975) pp. 168-171; and Hofmeister, B., "Germany's industrial giant," The Geographical Magazine 50 (1978), 439-445.

7. Studien zur Lage und Entwicklung Westberlins. Politik - Wirtschaft - Bildung. Gutachten erstattet von der Wissenschaftlichen Beratungskommission beim Senat von Berlin (Berlin, 1978).

8. Cornelsen, D., "Finanzhilfe für West-Berlin. Eine Untersuchung über Umfang und Bedeutung der finanziellen Verflechtung im öffentlichen Sektor zwischen West-Berlin und Westdeutschland," DIW Beitraege zur Strukturforschung, Vol. 12. (Berlin: Duncker and Humblot, 1970).

9. Hofmeister, B., "Germany's industrial giant," The Geographical Magazine 50 (1978), 439-445.

10. Industrie- und Handelskammer zu Berlin, ed., Jahresbericht, various years, and Die Berliner Wirtschaft, bi-weekly, various years.

REFERENCES

Ebel, G., and E. Elsner, "Die positiven Tendenzen im Personenverkehr von und nach Berlin (West) im Fremdenverkehr und im Beherbergungsgewerbe," Berliner Statistik, Monatschrift 9 (1979), pp. 256-266.

Hofmann, W., "West-Berlin--the isolated city in the twentieth century," Journal of Contemporary History 3 (1969), 77-93.

Lanzl, A., Raumgestaltung durch staatliche Planung in der Bundesrepublik Deutschland. Fragenkreise (Paderborn/Munich: Schoeningh and Beutenberg, 1976).

Senat von Berlin, ed., Die Lage der Berliner Wirtschaft und die Massnahmen zu ihrer Weiterentwicklung. 11. Bericht (Berlin, 1973).

CHAPTER 21

THE POSTWAR DEVELOPMENT OF COLOGNE: A CASE STUDY OF
THE IMPACT OF FEDERAL AND STATE AUTHORITIES AND
ASSISTANCE UPON A LARGE URBAN COMMUNITY

DIE NACHKRIEGSENTWICKLUNG VON KÖLN: EINE FALLSTUDIE
ÜBER DEN EINFLUSS UND DIE HILFE VON BUND UND
LAND AUF EINE GROSSE STADTGEMEINDE

Reinhart Zschocke

Abstract

In the FRG the municipalities are self-governing bodies as well as the smallest spatial administrative units directed by federal and state authorities. An important requirement for self-government is the power of the purse. This is especially important for planning projects, but the municipalities have only limited tax authority. Therefore, there is intergovernmental revenue from the state government available because the receipts from the municipalities are insufficient for fulfilling their functions.

It is impossible to understand the functions, structure, and pattern of Cologne without knowledge of the aid available from the federation and the states. For example, there is no school, museum, fire department, highway, or street with a through-traffic function, and hardly any bridge construction without this aid. This indicates a great influence on town planning by the state and limits the possibility of self-government in Cologne as a self-government city. On the other hand, the difference between rich and poor municipalities has been reduced by grants-in-aid. These grants, therefore, are the means by which the regional planning effort tries to prevent the occurrence of distressed regions.

Kurzfassung

Die Gemeinden der Bundesrepublik Deutschland sind sowohl Selbstverwaltungskörperschaften als auch unterste Verwaltungsbehörden des Staates. Wichtig für die Selbstverwaltung ist die Finanzhoheit, vor allem im Hinblick auf die Planung. Die Gemeinden können aber nur über

bestimmte Steuern verfügen. Daher erfolgen Finanzhilfen
des Landes, soweit die eigenen Mittel nicht für die
Erfüllung der Aufgaben ausreichen.

Man kann Funktion, Struktur und Aufriß der Stadt Köln
nicht ohne die Kenntnis der Hilfe von Bund und Land verstehen.
So wurden zum Beispiel keine Schulen, keine Museen, keine
Feuerwachen, keine Durchgangsstraßen, fast keine Brücken ohne
diese Hilfen gebaut. Dies bringt aber einen bedeutenden
Einfluß des Landes auf die Stadtplanung mit sich, wodurch
die Selbstverwaltung eingeengt wird. Andererseits wird
durch die Finanzhilfe der Unterschied zwischen reichen und
armen Gemeinden verringert. Diese Beihilfen sind damit auch
ein Mittel der Landesplanung zur Vermeidung von zurück-
gebliebenen Gebieten.

The Postwar Development of Cologne: A Case Study of the Impact of Federal and State Authorities and Assistance Upon a Large Urban Community

The municipal governments perform a dual function in the Federal Republic of Germany (FRG). On the one hand, they are governing bodies that work under the control of the elected municipal parliaments; on the other hand, the municipalities constitute the smallest spatial administrative units. In this second function they are subject to the direction of federal and state authorities. An important requirement for self-government is the power of the purse. This is especially important for planning projects. The municipalities have the right to control land use and to plan development projects within the framework of federal and state laws. Efficient planning, however, is only possible if the planning authority also has the financial means at its disposal for carrying out the plans. As it is, the municipalities have only very limited tax authority.

This essay intends to show how the urban development in Cologne since World War II has been influenced by the government of the Federal Republic of Germany, and of the State of North Rhine-Westphalia, of which Cologne is a part. Cologne is the largest city in the western part of the FRG. As of March, 1979, it had 978,481 inhabitants and is the fourth largest urban community after Berlin, Munich, and Hamburg. It is situated upon the broad, flat terraces on both sides of the Rhine River, about 50 meters above sea level. It is an important focal point of different transportation systems in the Rhineland and has good connections by rail, air, and highways to all countries in Western Europe. There are various types of industry in Cologne.

A refinery (Esso), a chemical plant, and an automobile factory (Ford) are situated in the north of the city, and in the south a refinery (Shell) and another chemical plant. A chemical plant is also to be located in the eastern part of the central urban area, as well as two plants for internal combustion engines and tractors. Besides these there are other industrial districts with small and medium-sized factories making various kinds of products, some known the world over like the famous "4711" eau de cologne. There are also large insurance companies, major bank branches, and other business and administrative offices. These business enterprises are important contributors to revenue, especially in the form of real estate tax and trade tax from corporate receipts and capital assets.

The main economic growth of Cologne took place during the nineteenth and twentieth centuries. For this reason municipal boundaries of the city have been extended several times, namely in 1888, 1910, 1914, 1922, and 1975 (Figure 21-1). The last expansion, especially, amounts to indirect aid to the community by the state. During the last decades many inhabitants and factories left Cologne and resettled in the outlying vicinity. This resulted in a loss of much tax revenue. The expansion of the city by annexation of adjacent communities brought them back into the fold.

The most important period in the recent history of Cologne was World War II. The life of the city suffered a severe setback because of the massive air raids. About one-third of the residential houses and more than half of all housing units were destroyed (Table 21-1). This setback, however, provided the occasion for a new type of federal and state aid, namely, aid for reconstruction. If anyone in the years following the war invested his or her money in the con-

TABLE 21-1. Residential Houses in Cologne.
           Ortsansässige Wohnungen in Köln.

Year	Residential Buildings		Housing Units
1939 (May)	59,000		252,373
1950 (Sept)	41,554		122,977
1956 (Sept)	54,559		198,396
1961 (June)	59,970		246,123
1968 (Oct)	70,036	89,770*	341,446
1975 (Dec)		98,760*	405,187
1977 (Dec)		100,431*	415,453

*Dates of 1975

Source: Statistiches Jahrbuch der Stadt Köln 63 (1977), p.83.

TABLE 21-2. Assessment of Taxes.
           Einschätzung der Steuern.

Bund (Federation) — Federal Republic of Germany

Main taxes: customs; tobacco tax; alcohol license tax; mineral oil tax and other sales and receipts taxes.

Land (State) — North Rhine-Westphalia

Main taxes: property tax; motor vehicle tax; beer tax; death and gift tax; lottery tax; fire protection tax (taken from fire insurances)

Kreis (counties)   Kreisfreie Stadt: Cologne
                    (self-governing towns)

Gemeinde (municipalities)

Main taxes: Trade tax from corporate receipts and capital assets; real estate tax; up to 1978: payroll tax struction of residential buildings, this investment was reduced from his or her income tax, and he or she saved money. Thus the construction of houses was stimulated. Even with these tax advantages it was fifteen years before the original number of buildings had been replaced. Besides the residential houses, many public buildings were also destroyed or damaged during the war. Nearly the whole downtown area as well as other parts of the town were in ruins. All bridges were destroyed, and most streets and highways were damaged. Without federal and state assistance it would have been impossible to rebuild the city.

REVENUES AVAILABLE TO COLOGNE

Earlier it was mentioned that states are subdivided into counties. The counties are subdivided into municipalities, and large cities like Cologne are self-governing cities, i.e., they are neither a part of a county, nor subdivided into municipalities. They have the same rights and duties as counties and municipalities.

Until 1970 the main taxes, owing to the municipalities and the self-governing towns, were the real estate tax (Grundsteuer) and the trade tax from corporate receipts and capital assets (Gewerbesteuer vom Ertrag und Kapital) (Table 21-2). Besides the taxes mentioned in Table 21-2 there are also taxable incomes for the federation, states, and municipalities: (a) Individual income tax and corporate income tax. Until 1970, these taxes were assessed as follows: 50 percent to the federation, and 50 percent to the states. Since 1970, the break-down has been 43 percent to the federation, 43 percent to the states, and 14 percent to the municipalities. (b) Value added tax: This tax is assessed by both the federation and states, and the percentage has varied over the years. (c) Trade tax from corporate receipts and capital assets. Until 1970, this tax was assessed only by municipalities. Since 1970, the federation and the states take their share, and the percentage is altered during the year.

Since 1970 the municipalities and self-governing cities have received a share (14 percent) of the individual income taxes (<u>Lohnsteuer</u> and <u>Einkommensteuer</u>) and the corporate income tax (<u>Körperschaftssteuer</u>). Besides these sources of revenue there is an intergovernmental revenue from the state government in case the receipts of the municipalities, counties, and cities are insufficient for the fulfillment of their functions. The state grants general financial allocations and grants for special purposes. To prevent rich municipalities from getting the same percentage of the general financial allocations as the poor ones, these allocations are given as standard allocations (<u>Schlüsselzuweisungen</u>), as grants from a compensation fund (<u>Ausgleichsstock</u>), and as reimbursements for performance of general government functions. The calculation of the standard allocation to a municipality is based on its average expenditure and its own tax resources. It is a very complicated calculation that has been altered several times over the years. Allowance is made for special burdens like those which result from the population having a high proportion of children, from war damages, etc. Payments from the compensation fund are made available in individual cases for extraordinary financial situations or specific tasks to be performed by municipalities, counties, and self-governing cities. Thus an equalization in the revenue is achieved that prevents the community from going bankrupt. The reimbursements for performance of functions and services are calculated in proportion to the number of inhabitants, or as compensation for financial losses incurred as a result of the war. The grants for special purposes are given as a percentage of the full costs. These percentages have been altered over the years; also, the types of projects for which subsidies are given vary. The following figures give an idea of the amounts paid by states and the federation: in 1950 Cologne received DM 52 million from taxes and DM 18 million standard financial allocations; in 1977 there were DM 1,372 billion from taxes and DM 108 million from standard allocations (Figures 21-2 and 21-3).

THE MUNICIPAL FUNCTIONS OF COLOGNE IN TERMS OF EXPENDITURE

The city provides many services; some of these are paid for by fees, others from tax revenue and grants-in-aid. Several functions like sewage and waste disposal, street cleaning, etc., are paid by fees. There is no subsidiary payment by the city. Public urban transportation (bus and streetcar service; subway) has high deficit spending. On the other hand, utility revenue produces profits. Therefore, the two municipal companies, the Kölner Verkehrsbetriebe (transportation) and the Gas-, Elektrizitäts- und Wasserwerke (water, natural gas, and electric utility), are combined as a corporation operating without deficit and making only small profits.

Education

In 1939 there were 204 school buildings. During the war 126 of them were destroyed, and only 78 remained, most of them damaged. In 1977 there were 331 public schools at different levels. The city was not able to construct school buildings from its own tax base. Therefore, 75 percent of the construction costs were paid by the state as grant-in-aid.

Since 1958 the salary of the teachers has been paid by the state; the teachers of the public schools became employees (Landesbeamte). Between 1958 and 1970 Cologne was obliged to reimburse the state for between 25 percent and 40 percent of these salaries. Since 1970 Cologne has not paid for its teachers. On the other hand, the city is responsible for all other expenses concerning the schools. In 1919 the University of Cologne was reorganized as a municipal university. The expenditure constantly increased after the war. As a result the city was unable to pay for it. Therefore, the university became a state university. Before 1964 the city still had to pay 50 percent of the expenditure except for the construction of buildings. Between 1964 and 1972 Cologne's share of the costs of the university hospital amounted to 20 percent. Since 1972 the city has had the advantage of having a university without having to pay for it.

Police and Fire Protection

Before 1954 the state granted 50 percent of the costs for the county police. In 1954 they became state police, and the police employees became state employees. For eleven years, from 1954 to 1965, the city had to bear part of the police costs. Since 1966 the city has made no contribution.

The city is responsible for fire protection. On the other hand, the fire protection tax is a state tax, paid by the fire insurance companies since 1939. Grants are given to the municipalities and cities for fire protection purposes out of the tax receipts.

Public Welfare

The counties and self-governing cities are responsible for the public welfare. There is an equalization in the support of and assistance to needy persons throughout the state. Standards are fixed by a commission. The Cologne City Council has the right to vary the payments to needy persons within those standards. It is useless to move to another county or city in order to get more support. The relief costs, resulting from war damages, have been reimbursed by the federation since 1955; before 1955, 85 percent of these costs were reimbursed by the state.

Construction and Maintenance of Streets, Highways, Bridges, and Subways

Grants-in-aid were given to the city to remove the war damages on streets and highways and to reconstruct the bridges. These grants until 1966 were given on the condition that the city bear at least 25 percent of the cost. Besides this, a special grant was given to maintain highways, roads, and streets with through-traffic functions, calculated on a per kilometer basis. In 1967 the calculation was altered. The state alloted 30 percent of the motor vehicle tax to the counties, municipalities, and self-governing cities as standard allocations for this purpose. In addition to these amounts, grants-in-aid were paid in individual cases of very expensive road construction projects. Between 1962 and 1978, DM 277,116,000 were paid, e.g., by the federation and the state. The total amount during this period was DM 538,459,000 (Table 21-3).

After World War II several routes of the subway were constructed; some are still under construction. The city never would have been able to construct this important trans-

TABLE 21-3. Total Expenditure and Grants-in-Aid from the Federation and State Concerning Highway and Street Construction.
Gesamtauslagen und Hilfe vom Bund and Ländern bezüglich Fernstrassen und städtische Strassen.

Year	Total Expenditure in thousand DM	Grants-in-Aid in thousand DM
1962	29,283	3,539
1963	29,321	18,654
1964	38,434	5,427
1965	29,197	16,800
1966	23,143	12,070
1967	23,985	12,214
1968	22,170	15,103
1969	22,313	21,232
1970	30,115	21,383
1971	32,367	16,265
1972	33,180	14,006
1973	30,597	18,296
1974	32,906	19,719
1975	38,297	21,183
1976	33,302	18,027
1977	41,114	23,987
1978	48,735	19,211

Source: Letter from the highway department (Strassenbauamt) in Cologne.

portation system without assistance from the federation and state. The city is also responsible for the four bridges across the Rhine River used by motor vehicles and streetcars. These bridges were constructed with grants-in-aid from the federation and state, for instance, the so-called Zoobrücke, which opened in 1966. The whole cost of this bridge was DM 115.7 million of which DM 70.7 million were granted by the federation and state.

Urban Renewal

Although large parts of Cologne were destroyed during the war, in some parts of the city not ruined by air raids many of the old houses that remained undamaged are substandard. A study made in 1972 delimited nineteen areas as urgently requiring urban renewal. A priority schedule was prepared. In four areas the situation was especially urgent, and high priority was given to their renewal. Under the 1971 law concerning town planning (Städtebauförderungsgesetz), one area in southern downtown Cologne, the Severins quarter, was approved for renewal by the state government. This means that grants-in-aid are paid by the federation and state, and an annual amount of DM 16 million has been allocated for the next fifteen years.

Besides the above-mentioned grants-in-aid, other construction projects are supported by the federation and the state, such as theaters, museums, homes for aged persons, etc. At least 239 projects scattered over the whole city were subsidized between 1964 and 1976 (Table 21-4). Other projects were supported in the years before and after this period.

TABLE 21-4. Number of Projects Subsidized by the Federation and the State Between 1964 and 1975.
Anzahl der Projekte die vom Bund und den Ländern zwischen 1965 und 1974 finanziell unterstützt wurden.

```
Schools: Elementary (Primerstufe-Grundschule).......................31
         Secondary (Sekundarstufe I-Volksschule,
                    Hauptschule, Realschule, Sonderschule)..........49
         High School (Sekundarstufe II-Gymnasium; Berufsschule,
                      Gesamtschule).....................................29
         School for Social Work (Werkschule).............................2
Home for aged persons......................................................5
Workshop for handicapped people............................................1
Kindergarten..............................................................70
Youth club.................................................................2
Hospital...................................................................5
Public health department...................................................1
Stadiums, athletic fields, swimming pools.................................24
Allotment garden areas.....................................................9
Museum.....................................................................5
Protected monuments........................................................2
Fire department............................................................4
```

Source: Bridge tally plans of the city of Cologne.

SUMMARY

It is impossible to understand the functions, structure, and pattern of Cologne without knowledge of the aid and assistance received from the federation and the state. There is no school, museum, fire department, highway, or street with through-traffic functions and hardly any bridge construction without the aid of the federation and state. This results in considerable influence by the state on town planning. All expensive projects are scrutinized, particularly in cases of grants-in-aid, by the federation or state. If not approved, they will not be carried out. For this reason the possibility of Cologne becoming a self-governing city has been limited.

In the city manager's opinion, municipalities, counties, and self-governing cities should receive a greater share of state and federal taxes, thus making grants-in-aid necessary. On the other hand, the difference between rich and poor municipalities and cities has been reduced by grants-in-aid. They are, therefore, instruments in the regional planning effort in the FRG to prevent the occurrence of distressed regions.

POSTWAR DEVELOPMENT OF COLOGNE 679

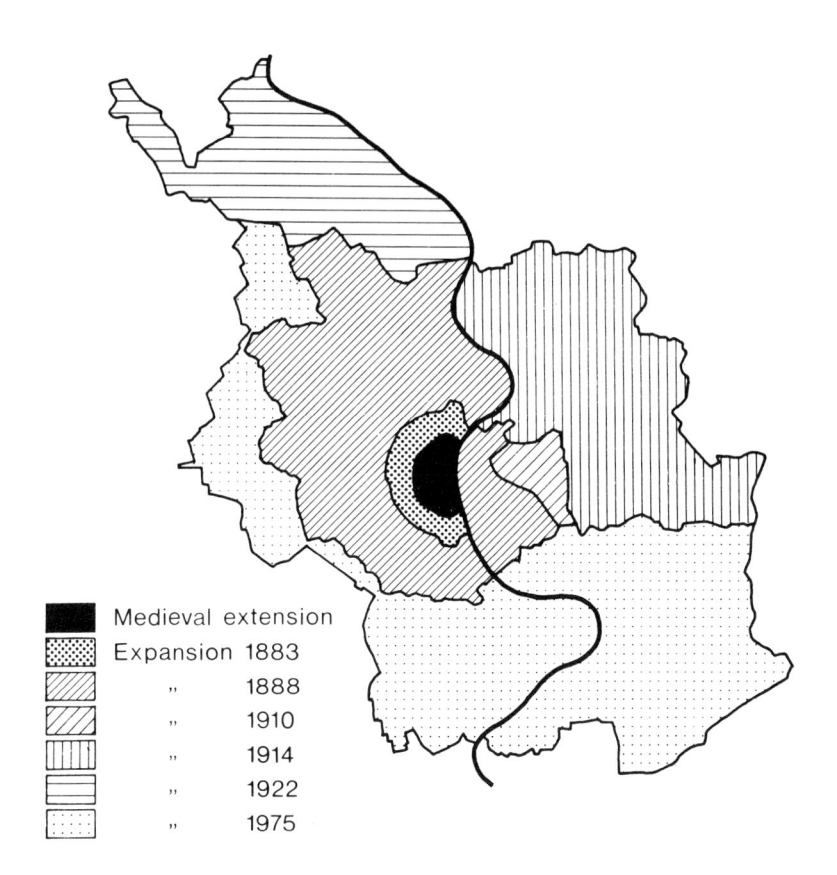

FIG. 21-1. Cologne, City Boundaries.
            Köln, Stadtgrenzen.

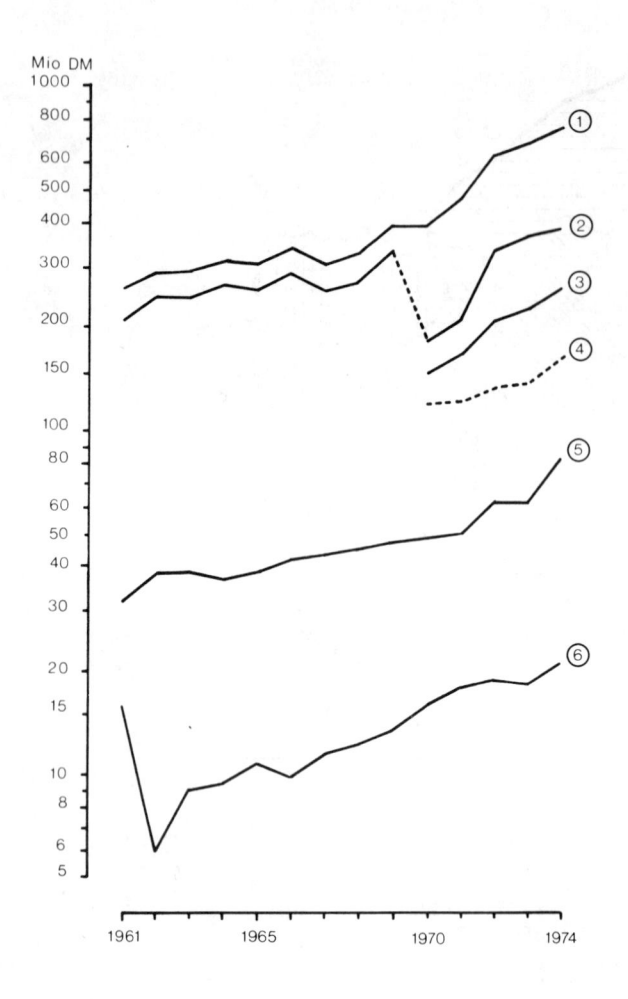

1) Steuern insgesamt/Total taxes. 2) Gewerbesteuer/Tax from corporate receipts and capital assets. 3) Gemeindeanteil Einkommensteuer/Municipal share of the individual income tax. 4) Gewerbesteuerumlage/Federal and State share of the Gewerbesteuer. 5) Grunsteuer/Real estate tax. 6) Sonstige Steuern/Other taxes.

FIG. 21-2. Tax Revenue, 1961-1974.
Steuer Einnahmen, 1961-1974.

Source: "Die Finanzwirtschaft der Stadt Köln im Spiegel der Statistik," Statistische Berichte 21 (Cologne 1975).

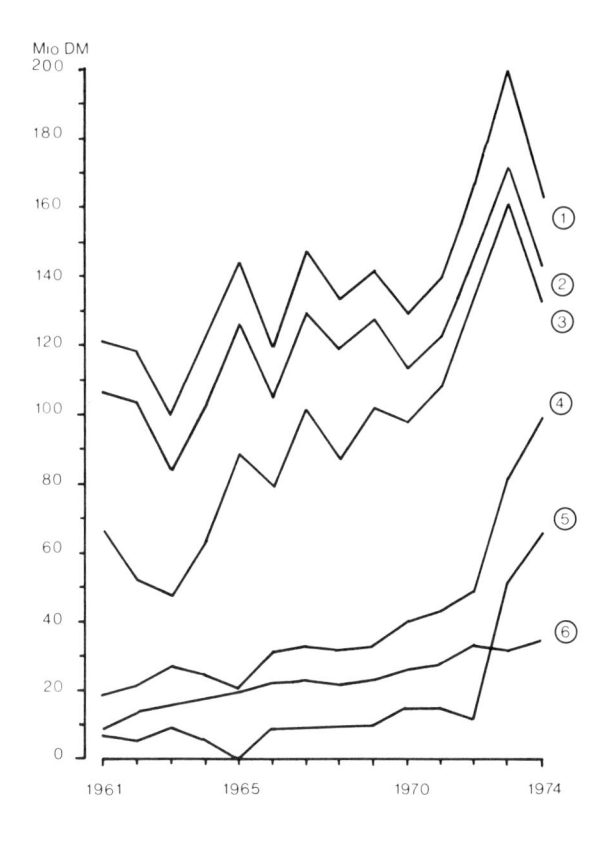

Grants for special purposes: 1) total, 2) from Bund/Land with reimbursements for war burdens (LAG), 3) from Bund/Land without Lag. 4) Total standard financial allocations. 5) Standard allocations. 6) Reimbursements for other functions and services.

FIG. 21-3. Standard Financial Allocation and Grants-in-Aid for Special Purposes: 1961-1974.
   Normale Finanzielle Zuteilung und Beihlife für Spezial Zwecke: 1961-1974.

Source: "Die Finanzwirtschaft der Stadt Köln im Spiegel der Statistik," Statistische Berichte 21 (Cologne, 1975).

REFERENCES

Die Finanzwirtschaft der Stadt Köln im Spiegel der Statistik, Statistische Berichte No. 21 (Cologne, September, 1975).

Finzel, K., "Die Entwicklung des Finanzhaushaltes der Stadt Köln in der Zeit 1950 bis 1969," Wirtschafts-und Sozialwissenschaftliche Dissertation, Freiburg/Switzerland (Cologne, 1974).

Gesetz-und Verordnungsblatt für das Land North Rhine-Westphalia, Vol 3 (1949); Vol. 32 (1978).

Haushaltunsplan der Stadt Köln, 1946-47 to 1948.

Statistisches Amt der Stadt Köln, ed., Statistisches Jahrbuch der Stadt Köln, Vol. 36 (1950) to Vol. 63 (1977).

CHAPTER 22

STATE GROWTH MANAGEMENT IN A FEDERAL SYSTEM:
THE EXAMPLE OF HAWAII

DIE STEUERUNG DES WACHSTUM EINES STAATES IN
EINEM BUNDESSYSTEM: DER FALL HAWAII

Willard T. Chow and Roland J. Fuchs

Abstract

Hawaii is acknowledged to be in the forefront of states attempting to manage their population and economic growth. Excessive rates of population growth and too extreme a concentration of population and development on the island of Oahu have been identified as key problems by state officials and planners. While difficulties in coping with these problems have occasionally been exacerbated by the unintended effects of state development policies, greater difficulties have been created by federal policies regarding immigration, support of agricultural and economic diversification, and the location within the state of federal activities and employment. State intervention measures--such as a general plan, strict land use controls, and dispersed infrastructure investment--have proven inadequate to counter the undesirable effects of federal policies.

Kurzfassung

Bei der Steuerung des Wachstumes kommt es nicht einfach auf die Annahme eines allgemeinen Plans, den einschränkenden Kontrollen der Landesnutzung und infrastrukturellen Stufenprogramme an. Sie schließt in sich auch die Beschränkung der Entscheidungen von Bundesbehörden ein, die nationale und nicht regionale Ziele verwirklichen wollen. Die Einwirkung der Bundesebene auf das Bevölkerungswachstum, die sektorale Ausweitung und die räumliche Entwicklung Hawaiis in den letzten zwei Jahrzehnten deckte sich nicht mit der Politik des Staates. Die Bemühungen des Staates, die Landwirtschaft zu erhalten, ihre ökonomische Basis mannigfaltiger zu machen und das Wachstum auf die Außeninseln umzuverteilen, müssen von der Bundesregierung in stärkerem Maße unterstützt werden. Im Hinblick auf die bestehenden Möglichkeiten in dem Planungsprozess wird sich die Lösung der Konflikte zwischen den Interessen des Bundessystems und denen eines Subsystems nicht leicht finden lassen.

State Growth Management in a Federal System: The Case of Hawaii

Federal programs have clearly had a decisive impact on regional growth patterns in the United States. Few would claim, however, that the effects of federal actions and inactions were explicitly intended, that federal programs have been systematically implemented to achieve national policies, or that there are indeed federal growth or settlement policies in which the national interest is well articulated. This essay presents a case for state (or subnational) growth management, describes state efforts in Hawaii to manage growth, identifies the conflicts and problems which Hawaii has encountered working in a federal context, and suggests some ways in which the federal system might be reformed to allow states to play a more active role in managing their population growth, decline, and redistribution.

Coping with the strains of immigration, outmigration, and population dispersal has become increasingly difficult in most states, where traditional local land use controls have proven ineffective. The Carter administration's new partnership nonetheless continues to stress the importance of federal efforts, relegating states to the backstage role of assisting urban areas with their problems (1). Yet federal efforts may be the cause of, not the solution to, local population problems. As Daniel L. Elazar has noted: "Today there is simply no justification for thinking that the states and localities, either in principle or in practice, are less able to do the job than the federal government" (2).

STATE VS. LOCAL GROWTH MANAGEMENT

Although most of the world's nations have already begun to implement population growth and distribution policies (3), the United States has yet to adopt, much less implement, such a policy. Regional development patterns remain the outcome of individual migratory and cultural predispositions, corporate decisions, and the inadvertent effects of public activities and programs (4, 5). The individual and collective interests of population movements clearly diverge (6).

Given the absence of population policies defining the role of federal agencies in closing these discrepancies, many local communities in the United States see little choice but to protect their own interests. Local growth management schemes have proliferated as towns in developing regions attempt to cope more effectively with growth that may or may not be in the national interest. The principal objections to such local growth management from a federal perspective are that it excludes the disadvantaged, infringes upon the "right to move," and unfairly shifts fiscal burdens to older central cities (7, 8, 9, 10).

Critics of local growth management continue to call for regional solutions, such as fair share housing quotas, metropolitan taxation and services, and councils of government, even though there is still little evidence that they indeed work (11, 12, 13). Regional remedies have rarely been successful because of legislative and constitutional obstacles inherent in the federal system (14, 15).

In view of the limited capacity of regional planning organizations to implement plans, the exclusionary tendencies of localities, and the lack of an explicit federal population growth policy, what can be done to deal with developmental spillovers and the divergence between the individual and collective effects of growth and mobility? Although the states seem more inclined than localities to adopt broad policies that transcend short-run parochial interests and better equipped than either federal agencies or regional organizations to implement those policies, the potential of states for managing growth has only recently been recognized. "As the residual repository of all governmental power in the federal system, the states have potentially a critical role to play in the government structure" (16).

According to a survey by the American Institute of Planners in 1975, virtually all states have adopted a broad range of individual land and resource management programs, but few deliberately use tax or utility rates to influence land use patterns (17). "Some 40 states now have some formal mechanism for dealing with growth policy issues, with the majority (27) having set up some unit in the executive branch charged with the development of a state growth policy" (18). Even in Texas, whose vast lands and faith in free enterprise welcome further growth, conflicts rage over where and how expansion should occur and water resources should be developed (19).

Managing growth presumes that public officials have the financial, political, and legal support to systematically implement, not just adopt, growth plans. Some states, as illustrated by the recent "Sagebrush Rebellion," claim they have too little control over development on federally controlled lands and waters (20). Others, acutely affected by federal energy, defense, or immigration policies, likewise feel they exert too little influence over developmental pressures. The quiet revolution in land use controls has seen more state governments exert authority over land use decisions having more than local impact (21, 22, 23). Those states which have the most to lose ecologically and economically from environmental deterioration (Florida, Colorado, Oregon, Hawaii, and Vermont) have apparently been the most active in formulating growth management policies (24).

Opposition to state growth management efforts springs from local as well as national sources. Advocates of home rule contend that decisions restricting the use of land must be made close to home by those most affected by the decision (25, 26). They argue that local government tends to be the most responsive and accountable in addressing citizen needs and providing services (27). Thus, few examples can be found of states actually taking back authority which they have delegated to local governments; in most cases states are simply restructuring the way in which local governments must make those decisions (28). Developers facing the permit explosion tend to regard state intervention as one more bureaucratic layer of controls that must be overcome, which ultimately raises the cost of development and presumably the cost of living in the state (29, 30).

Critics point out that coordinating state actions, decisions, and regulatory practices is difficult even where state growth policies have been adopted to guide these efforts. This is particularly the case in more populous states, such as California and New York, which provide subsidies but leave service delivery to local governments (31). More than 3,000 governments are found in each of nine states, with the average number of governmental units per state exceeding 1,500 (32). Getting counties, municipalities, townships, and special districts, not to mention state agencies, to comply with statewide policies will not be easy. It is understandable that few states have made much progress within the American federal system.

THE EXAMPLE OF HAWAII

Hawaii is probably one of the best examples of a state in which statewide population growth management is needed. It is also an example of progress deterred within a maze of federal constraints. Since the achievement of statehood twenty years ago, Hawaii has experienced a population growth rate averaging twice that of the national norm and annual rates exceeding the world average (33). As Governor George R. Ariyoshi noted in his 1977 State of the State address, "the problem of excessive population seems to be central to nearly every problem in our State.... We must shape our own future, not have it thrust upon us by forces over which we have little or no control" (34). Faced with rapid population growth in an island ecosystem, many state officials believe that current growth rates surpass the collective ability of Hawaii's people to rationally plan and guide it. Hawaii's de facto density, about 149 persons per square mile in 1976, is over twice the national average. Moreover, Hawaii's density has been increasing at a faster rate since 1960 than any of the fifteen most densely populated states, except Florida (35).

State officials now concede that innovations in state land use planning have not been adequate to cope with recent growth. In 1957 Hawaii was the first state to establish a planning office responsible for developing a general land use plan. This provided the conceptual foundation for the state's pioneering Land Use Law (Act 187), passed in 1961. While many doubt the wisdom of the Land Use Commission's decisions, particularly in terms of preserving prime agricultural land, "even critics agree that Hawaii's early start in statewide land use management has put it well ahead of other states in dealing with its land resource" (36). Rapid economic and population growth during the 1960s has continued, casting further doubt upon the ability of the commission to contain growth within existing urban districts where public facilities can accommodate it most efficiently (37, 38).

Efforts to formulate population policies in Hawaii are over a century old, dating back to missionary times when "rapid and uncontrolled population decline was recognized as the most pressing and intractable problem confronting the government and business community in Hawaii" (39). Since 1900, however, its population has been growing at an excessively high rate, reflecting patterns of high migration and fertility (40). Although concern about overpopulation, especially through heightened inmigration after statehood, was registered during the early 1970s (41, 42, 43) neither Governor John A. Burns nor Honolulu Mayor Frank F. Fasi saw reason to curb growth. According to Schmitt (44), "The Burns administration...remained cool to suggestions for population ceilings and migration limitations, and instead espoused a policy of population redistribution. Interviewed in 1971, the governor said that 'two of his major goals are to disperse population to better use the total geography of the state, and to maintain Hawaii's ethnic majority.'"

The Hawaii State Temporary Commission on Population Stabilization, created by Governor Burns in 1971, became the nation's first official body explicitly concerned with state population policy (45). Although many states have attempted to define population growth, decline, distribution, or composition problems, few have addressed their population problems so comprehensively or so vigorously. Even fewer states have made so many efforts to identify alternative strategies for managing population growth and to weigh the implications of those alternatives (46, 47, 48, 49).

However, Hawaii has become increasingly vulnerable to outside forces. State efforts to influence when, where, and how growth occurs and to mitigate its most adverse impacts are limited by federal constraints. In 1978 Hawaii was the first state in the country to adopt by law a state general plan (50). The state plan presumably will be the guide for coordinating decisions by the State Land Use Commission, the state legislature, state functional agencies, and Hawaii's four counties. Yet the state plan has no effect upon federal actions, rulings, and legislation. If Hawaii, renowned for its achievements in zoning, population growth policy, and statewide policy planning, has not been able to manage its growth within the federal system, then the prospects for other states with similar objectives may also be dim.

FEDERAL EFFECTS ON POPULATION AND ECONOMIC GROWTH

Although Hawaii's sensitivity to federal imperatives is by no means exceptional, its precarious social and ecological balance and limited resources make it especially vulnerable, particularly when growth is induced by federal policies and programs over which state and local officials exercise little political influence. Federal spending (civilian and defense) is the largest source of income to the state, amounting to slightly over 2.5 billion dollars in fiscal year 1978. A Tax Foundation of Hawaii study indicates that Hawaii received the equivalent of one dollar in federal expenditure for each 86 cents in taxes paid to the national treasury (51).

Of greater importance are the hundreds of federal policies, laws, and regulations that affect other sectors of the state economy. Federal airline regulations play a major role in the health of Hawaii's tourism; federal price supports hold virtual life-and-death power over the future of the sugar industry; and federal seed money will play a critical role in determining the success of new economic ventures, the most promising of which are aquaculture and energy development. Federal laws and programs also impinge on Hawaii's illicit industries, such as marijuana, which reportedly rivals the value of the sugar cane harvest in Hawaii county (52). Foreign tariffs have a pronounced effect on the viability of the state's other agricultural export industries, such as cut flowers, fruits, and nuts, which are expected to lead the way to agricultural diversification.

While federal regulations favor many firms, federal agencies provide many jobs and federal programs assist many industries in Hawaii, they do not necessarily favor the right firms, provide the right kinds of jobs, nor assist the right kinds of industries. The new state plan, for example, is aimed at attaining "a growing and diversified economic base that is not overly dependent on a few industries" (53). Federal programs are apparently unstable, insensitive to community needs, offer limited opportunities for employment and advancement for local residents, fail to patronize local producers, and are reluctant to return lands that are not required for national defense (54). Hawaii's search for greater self-sufficiency in agriculture has not been facilitated by federal officials who feel it should function as a strategic base, visitor center, and administrative headquarters, as the United States draws closer to Asia and the Pacific, and particularly to the People's Republic of China.

Immigration, which accounted for only 4.4 percent of the state's de facto population growth between 1960 and 1965, was responsible for 20.2 percent of the growth from 1970 to 1975 (55). Civilian fertility and rates of natural increase in

Hawaii, as in other states, have dropped since 1960. Immigrants from abroad have become an important component of population growth in the state, after changes in federal immigration laws raised the quota for immigrants from Asian countries in 1965. The percentage of Hawaii's population born in foreign countries climbed from 1.6 in 1853 to 58.9 in 1900, but dropped to 9.8 in 1970. The trend was reversed in 1975, when 12.7 percent of the population was born abroad. In contrast, the percent of state residents born on the U.S. mainland rose from 20.4 percent in 1960 to 23.2 percent in 1970, but dropped to 21.7 percent in 1975 in response to changing economic conditions in the state (56). These figures do not include Hawaii's illegal immigrants, estimated by the district director of the Immigration and Naturalization Service to number about 10,000 (57).

Relative to its population, Hawaii receives a disproportionately large number of immigrants, greater than four times the national average. It receives a larger number of immigrants per thousand residents than any other state (58). According to the Hawaii Health Surveillance Program Survey from July 1974 to July 1976, about four-fifths of the state's foreign born population live on Oahu (59). Foreign-born residents tended to be overrepresented in agriculture and manufacturing. The survey also indicated that one-tenth were members of the armed forces or their dependents. Accommodating such a large share of the nation's immigrants is an increasing burden, one which would be eased if more immigrants were required to settle in other states or if federal assistance to the state were increased.

Although the military component in Hawaii's population growth is small, its lagged and indirect effect on foreign immigration and the influx of retired military personnel to the islands may be sizeable. The impact is heightened by the relative insensitivity of both flows to variations in local employment opportunities. The likelihood of migration to an area is generally enchanced by previous experience there. Most of Hawaii's servicemen and servicewomen continue to be stationed on Oahu, where many retire to take advantage of benefits available on bases.

The visitor industry, as in the case of national defense, provides Hawaii with a large pool of resident candidates from which to draw since many visitors or their children eventually return to reside. Tourists, who comprise only 8.1 percent of Hawaii's de facto population growth from 1960 to 1965, were responsible for 25.9 percent of the increase from 1970 to 1975 (60). The average number of tourists has grown annually by 7,800 persons since 1970, so that about 100,000 visitors (equal to the present population of Maui and Kauai combined) use Hawaii's land and resources each day (61).

Another problem with continued reliance on mass tourism is that it tends to generate the "wrong" kind of migration. The expansion of tourism on the outer islands provided desperately needed jobs for local residents during the 1960s. Later, however, as the local pool of secondary workers was exhausted, continued growth of the industry attracted a large number of footloose inmigrants from the mainland, not from Oahu or other parts of Hawaii as state planners had hoped (62). Since most of these footloose inmigrants tend to be young, hypermobile, and prospective outmigrants, they have had an adverse impact on the continuity of acculturation and social stability of Hawaii's rural communities.

Although visitor spending contributed 2 billion dollars to the Hawaiian economy in 1978, the multipliers for tourism tend to be smaller than they are for agriculture or federal expenditures (63). Critics argue, therefore, that tourism is not as "propulsive" as other industries. However, it continues to receive the hearty support of most state officials, who have doggedly resisted attempts to establish even a small hotel room tax in Hawaii, one which would have negligible effect on visitor demand (64).

Many people in Hawaii believe that they have little choice but to rely on tourism, despite its drawbacks, for the new jobs that will be needed for the state's growing population (65). When one examines trends in the components of this growth, however, a different conclusion emerges. The bulk of that growth will stem not from natural increase but rather from current or former visitors and from foreign immigrants. If it were not for federally induced foreign immigration to Hawaii, fewer new jobs would be "needed," and thus resort expansion would not be necessary. Tourism is important because adequate federal support for agriculture and other alternative industries has not been forthcoming: federal support in fiscal year 1977 for agriculture and for natural resources, energy, and environment was much lower than one would expect in terms of the state's population in 1976 (66).

Systematic national development involves specialization, dependence, and extensive leakages from one part of the system to another. It does not involve diversification, import substitution, and containing the benefits of growth within one part of that system. Conflicts between federal and state interests over population growth and economic development cannot help but reflect inherent differences between what is good for the national system and what is good for a state subsystem.

Although the Department of Health, Education and Welfare was the largest source of the 400 million dollars in total federal grants to Hawaii in fiscal year 1977, HEW also received the greatest amount of Hawaii's federal taxes. The state contributed $1.36 for every dollar it received from this source in fiscal year 1978. In contrast, Hawaii's residents paid only 38 cents for every dollar they received from the Department of Defense (67). Lack of federal support from HEW to meet the needs of Hawaii's immigrants and inmigrants is especially aggravating to state officials, who wish to "encourage federal actions that will promote a more balanced distribution of immigrants among the states...[and] pursue an increase in federal assistance for states with a greater proportion of foreign immigrants relative to their state's population" (68).

FEDERAL IMPACT ON POLARIZATION

Economic problems in Hawaii stem not only from population growth and sectoral specialization; they are also rooted in the polarized nature of its settlement pattern. To what extent does the federal system affect these patterns? About 80 percent of Hawaii's million residents live on Oahu. Slightly less than half of these people reside in central Honolulu, the financial, industrial, commercial, educational, governmental, and communications center of the state, and the Pacific Basin.

The primacy or dominance of Oahu, however, has not always been the case, even in modern times (69). The population of Hawaii island was larger than Oahu's in 1778. Maui's population exceeded that of Oahu until the mid-1830s. Oahu's increasing percentage of the state's population between annexation in 1898 and 1970 was regarded by the Burns' administration as a persistent problem during the 1960s, as previously mentioned. Mechanization of plantation agriculture (sugar cane and pineapple) during the 1950s and 1960s reduced the prospect for employment programs on the outer islands. Rapidly expanding educational programs at the University of Hawaii and federal employment in Honolulu after statehood in 1959 prompted an increasing number of young people from the neighbor island counties to Oahu. Under the leadership of Governor Burns and neighbor island legislators, the state sought to raise the potential for economic growth on the outer islands through new infrastructural improvements, a statewide community college system, and developing land for new resorts (70). The resurgence of neighbor island populations since 1970 may thus be seen as a manifestation of their efforts (71).

Although state officials want to "encourage an increase in economic activities and employment opportunities on the neighbor islands," officials also want to be sure they are "consistent with community needs and desires" (72). To what extent has the federal system been responsive to Hawaii's desire to redistribute growth to the outer islands and to do so in compliance with local needs and desires? One would expect that, if this were indeed the case, it would be noticeable in changing patterns of federal spending, employment, housing, and land ownership by county. Comparisons between federal and state shifts would provide an empirical basis on which to evaluate their differential impact on polarized development in Hawaii.

Comparisons of the sources of labor and proprietor's income between 1970 and 1975 reveal that the increase in local income from federal civilian agencies was lower for the City and County of Honolulu than it was for any of the other three counties during the early 1970s (73). Although this pattern suggests that federal civilian spending was compatible with state "dispersal" policies, the difference between rates of growth in federal civilian income between Oahu and the neighbor island counties was not that great. In comparison increases in local income from federal military sources during the same period rose much more rapidly for Honolulu than for any of the other outer island counties. Defense spending helped to polarize development. Increases in local income from state and county government, however, showed a similar pattern with spending on Oahu growing faster than on the neighbor islands, even though the discrepancies are not as striking. Moreover, state spending also helped to polarize development during the early 1970s.

Changes in the sources of county revenues from 1960 to 1975 also reveal the extent of inconsistency between federal and state grants and statewide development objectives. Although income from federal grants has mushroomed for each county and the state, the increase has been most dramatic on the island of Oahu (74). State grants to counties favored the outer islands during the 1960s but dwindled during the early 1970s. In comparison, federal revenue sharing funds from fiscal year 1975 to 1978 have risen more rapidly for Kauai and Hawaii counties than they have for Honolulu, reflecting variations in county population growth. Federal categorical grants have thus had more of an adverse effect on dispersal objectives.

An overwhelming portion of those employed in federal civilian agencies worked on Oahu in 1977. Although the federal system is clearly a polarizing force in terms of jobs, the state system itself does not fare so well. The state capital is centered in downtown Honolulu, and 83 percent of those working in state agencies were located on Oahu in 1977 (76). State employees on the outer islands increased by 55 percent between 1968 and 1977, while state workers on Oahu rose by 75 percent.

Opposition by military officials to relocating the Army's 25th Infantry Division, or at least part of its operations, to the Pohakuloa Training Area on the Big Island of Hawaii is disconcerting to those who believe, based on an environmental impact statement prepared by the U.S. Army Support Command at Fort Shafter, that the Army's presence on Oahu has "some adverse" effects, which could be mitigated by such a move (77). According to the EIS, the Army occupies more than 15 percent of Oahu's land areas, limits public access to lands with potential recreational value, and degrades the environment, particularly through the use of high explosives in training exercises. The Big Island is much larger in size, less densely settled, and better suited to that kind of activity.

More than 99 percent of the military personnel and their dependents stationed in Hawaii in 1971 were based on Oahu (78). The number of military personnel and their dependents on Oahu rose from 1971 to 1978 by 14.5 percent and 1.6 percent, respectively. Although military spending for civilian employees, military salaries and allowances, and local purchases have benefitted Hawaii as a whole in the past, this does not mean that continued expansion will generate increasingly large net benefits in the future, nor that all communities will share equally in those benefits.

Continued concentration of military operations on highly

urbanized Oahu has already caused strain. Although only about 15 percent of federally owned land in Hawaii is located in urban areas (Figure 22-1), the acres of urban land owned and leased by the federal government have both risen during the past decade, while its rural holdings (owned and leased) have declined (79). The assessed value of tax exempt federal real property (assessed at 70 percent of market value) on Oahu in 1978 exceeded a billion dollars, ranking second only to that of state owned real property (80). The general plan for the City and County of Honolulu, moreover, specifies that future development is to be concentrated along the Ewa corridor, much of which is adjacent to Pearl Harbor. Many insist that nuclear weapons are being stored in Pearl Harbor, which new housing planned for the corridor will overlook.

Federal actions and inactions have thus played a pivotal role in reinforcing concentrated settlement and development patterns. They have done little to relieve the strains that result from concentration. The cost of housing is as high as, if not higher than, that of any other major city in the country. Yet federal mortgage lending agencies, such as the Federal Housing Administration and Veterans Administration, have been reluctant to adjust their standards to the situation. Funds from the Department of Transportation for a mass transit (rail) system in Honolulu and an interisland ferry system have likewise been difficult to acquire.

According to the Department of Defense land utilization study, 2,944 acres of military controlled land on Oahu, or about 3 percent of all its holdings on the island, are now available for release to civilian use (81). The parcels, however, do not include prime recreation sites at Fort DeRussy in Waikiki nor at Bellows Field in Waimanalo on the windward side of Oahu. In addition, the Department of

Defense wants to acquire 901 more acres, including 767 acres for its West Loch ammunition wharf in Pearl Harbor. Makua Valley on Oahu and the island of Kahoolawe, used as bombing ranges by the military but sought for protection, study, and reclamation by many of Hawaii's residents, were also not offered for release.

Past promises to release excess land have not been implemented. The FRESH (Facilities Requirements Evaluation, State of Hawaii) report, released by the Department of Defense in 1973, stated that 9,500 acres on Oahu would be released from military control (82). Because of objections by the House Armed Services Committee, headed by Representative Otis Pike, only 4,147 acres, most of it not worth much, have since been released. The FRESH report urged retention of Kahoolawe and Makua Valley for bombing and live fire exercises, but recommended that choice lands on much of Oahu be returned to meet the growing needs of local residents.

Clashes between local residents and military personnel have escalated in recent years over a widening range of issues. Do attacks against servicemen by local youths spring from personal differences over "girls," as some would have us believe? Do they stem from resentment against increasing federal abuse or misuse of Hawaiian lands and waters in an urbanizing region? Or are they indirect, poorly articulated, but deeply felt expressions of bitterness about the process by which differences between community and federal interests are supposed to be resolved?

CONCLUSION

While a number of mechanisms for addressing conflicts between federal and community development objectives already exist, they are ineffective, particularly in small but rapidly growing states such as Hawaii that have limited influence in Washington. This has been recognized by U.S. Senator Daniel K. Inouye, who has introduced legislation in Congress to establish a Temporary Federal Governmental Planning Commission in Hawaii (83). The proposed commission would be composed of federal, state, and county representatives and would consider federal land use plans and their impact on state and county plans. The commission would be charged with preparing a comprehensive federal land use plan which, if approved by Congress, would require compliance by federal agencies.

While such an innovation might conceivably remedy current land use conflicts, it would leave unaffected other federal policies guiding Hawaii's development in directions at variance with state and local plans. With the exception of Congressional intervention there would remain no mechanism for ensuring federal support of agricultural and economic diversification, controls on immigration, or the relocation of federal employment and activities to the outer islands. Growth management as Hawaii has learned so painfully is not simply a matter of adopting a state general plan and restrictive land use standards and controls. In a federal system it also requires the power to constrain the potent decisions of federal agencies.

STATE GROWTH MANAGEMENT: EXAMPLE HAWAII

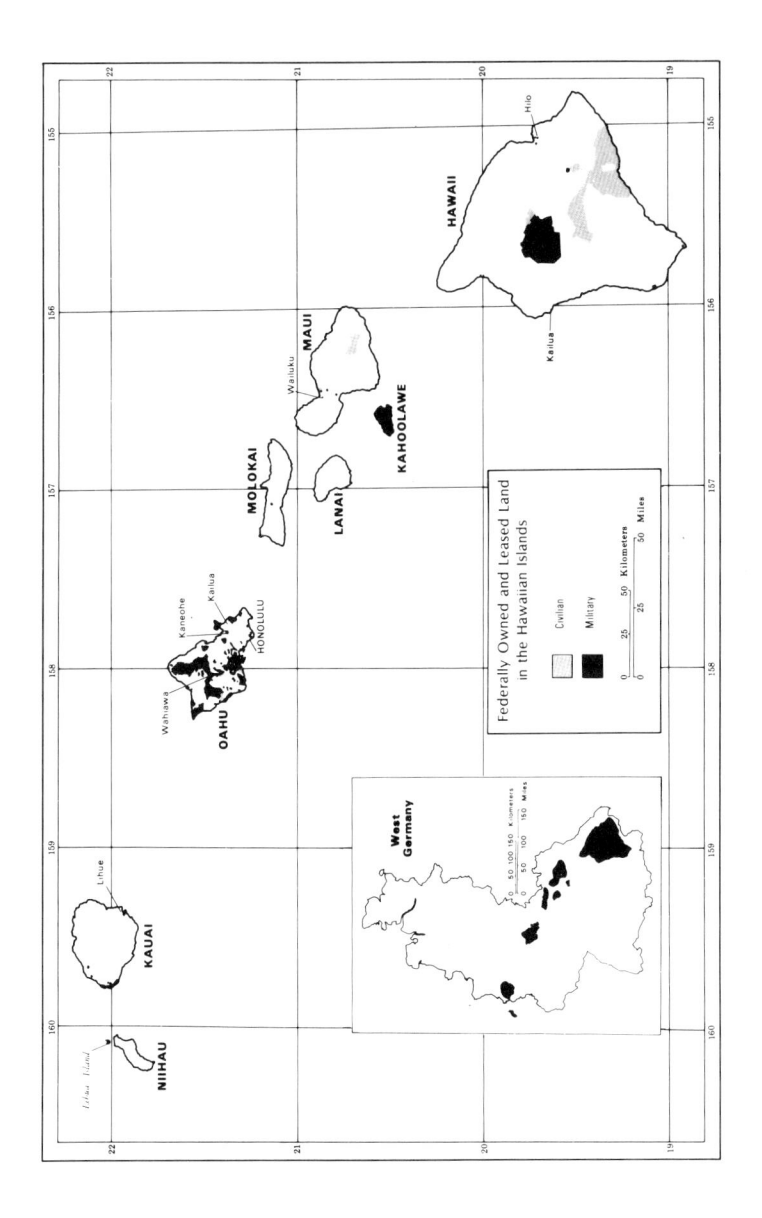

FIG. 22-1. Federally Owned and Leased Land in the Hawaiian Islands. Bundesbesitz und Pachtland in den Hawaiian Inseln.

NOTES

1. United States Department of Housing and Urban Development, The President's National Urban Policy Report (Washington, D.C.: HUD, 1978), p. 2.

2. Elazar, D., "The New Federalism: Can the States Be Trusted?" The Public Interest 35 (Spring, 1974), 89-102.

3. United Nations. 1974. Report of the United Nations World Population Conference (New York: United Nations) E/Conf/19.

4. Alonso, W., "Problems, Purposes and Implicit Policies for a National Strategy of Urbanization," in Research Reports, Vol. 5 Population Distribution and Policy, ed. Sara Mazie (Washington, D.C.: U.S. Commission on Population Growth and the American Future, 1972), pp. 635-647.

5. Morrison, P. A., "Toward a Policy Planner's View of the Urban Settlement System," Rand Corporation Report P-5357, 1975.

6. _____, "Population Movements: Where the Public Interest and Private Interests Conflict," Rand Corporation Report R-987-CPG, 1972 (prepared for the U.S. Commission on Population Growth and the American Future).

7. Godshalk, D. R., et al., Constitutional Issues of Growth Management (Chicago: The American Society of Planning Officials, 1977).

8. Scott, R., ed., Management and Control of Growth, Vol. I, Ch. 6-7 (Washington, D.C.: Urban Land Institute, 1975).

9. Urban Land Institute and National Committee Against Discrimination in Housing, Fair Housing and Exclusionary Land Use (Washington, D.C.: Urban Land Institute, 1974).

10. Babcock, R., and F. B. Bosselman, Exclusionary Zoning (New York: Praeger, 1973).

11. Mandelker, D. R., and D. C. Netsch, State and Local Government in a Federal System (Indianapolis: Bobbs-Merrill, 1977).

12. Glennon, R. C., "Regionalism Land Use Control: A Reality," Environmental Comment (March, 1978), p. 12.

13. Scott, op, cit., (note 8), Vol. III, Ch. 16.
14. Mark, S. M., "At What Level Should Decisions Be Made?" Environmental Comment (March, 1978), pp. 7-8.
15. Mandelker and Netsch, op. cit., (note 11), pp. 46-47.
16. Mandelker and Netsch, op. cit., (note 11), p. 27.
17. Malone, L., "State Land Use Planning: A Survey," State Planning Issues 2 (Winter, 1977), 7-11.
18. Silverman, J. A., "Growth Policy in the Federal System: The 1976 Report on National Growth and Development," Environmental Comment (July, 1978), pp. 2-3.
19. Williams, D. L., and J. B. Blackburn, Jr., "Managing Growth: Texas Style," Environmental Comment (July, 1978), pp. 2-3.
20. Nevada seems to be at the helm of the "Sagebrush Rebellion," having passed a bill claiming state sovereignty over federal land within its borders. Federally owned lands also exceed half the land in Alaska, Utah, Idaho, and Oregon.
21. Bosselman, F., and D. Callies, The Quiet Revolution in Land Use Control (Washington, D.C.: Council on Environmental Quality, 1971).
22. Whisler, M. W., "Population Policy Implementation: Local Growth Management Strategies," Population Policy Analysis, ed. Michael E. Kraft and Mark Schneider (Lexington: Lexington Books, 1978), pp. 181-193.
23. Widner, R. R., "State Growth and Federal Policies: A Reassessment of Responsibilities," State Government (Spring, 1974), reprinted in Management and Control of Growth, ed. R. W. Scott, 3 (Washington, D.C.: Urban Land Institute, 1975), pp. 403-409.
24. Haskell, E., and V. Price, State Environmental Management: Case Studies of Nine States (New York: Praeger, 1973).
25. Chapman, G. B., "Regionalism and Land Use Control," Environmental Comment (March, 1978), p. 8.

26. Jacobs, A., "Local Land Use Planning and the Impacts of Emerging State Involvement," in Land Use: Planning, Politics and Policies, ed. R. Cowart (Berkeley: University Extension Publications, 1976), pp. 6-16.
27. Mark, op. cit., (note 14), p. 7.
28. Malone, op, cit., (note 17), p. 7.
29. Bosselman, F., et. al., The Permit Explosion (Washington, D.C.: Urban Land Institute, 1976).
30. Scott, op. cit., (note 8), Vol. III, Ch. 19.
31. Mandelker and Netsch, op. cit., (note 11), pp. 29-38.
32. Patton, H. M., and W. Patton, "Harbingers of State Growth Policies," State Government (Spring, 1974), reprinted in Management and Control of Growth, ed. Randall W. Scott, Vol. 3 (Washington, D.C.: Urban Land Institute, 1975), pp. 318-327.
33. Growth Management Task Force, A Program for Selective Growth Management in Hawaii, State of Hawaii, 1978, p. 3
34. Anderson, A. R., "The Growth Issue in Hawaii: A Point of View," Growth Management Issues in Hawaii, Hawaii Institute for Management and Analysis in Government, Department of Budget and Finance, State of Hawaii, 1977, pp. 3-6.
35. Growth Management Task Force, op. cit., (note 33), p. 4.
36. Meyers, P., "Zoning Hawaii," Environmental Comment (July, 1976), p. 19.
37. Lowry, K., et al., "Analysis of Alternative Land Use Management Techniques for Hawaii," Growth Management Issues in Hawaii, Hawaii Institute for Management and Analysis in Government, Department of Budget and Finance, State of Hawaii, 1977, pp. 15-16.
38. Lowry, K., and M. McElroy, "State Land Use Control: Some Lessons of Experience," State Planning Issues, Vol. 1 (Spring, 1976), pp. 15-28.
39. Schmitt, R. C., "Population Policy in Hawaii," The Hawaiian Journal of History 8 (1974), 91.

40. Nordyke, E. C., The Peopling of Hawaii (Honolulu: University Press of Hawaii, 1970).

41. Pacific Urban Studies and Planning Program, Toward a Population Policy for Hawaii (Honolulu, University of Hawaii, 1970).

42. Babbie, E. R., The Maximillion Report (Honolulu, 1972).

43. Fisher, T., "Hawaii: Growing Pains in Paradise," Population Bulletin 29 (1973).

44. Schmitt, op. cit., (note 39), p. 104.

45. Schmitt, op. cit., (note 39), p. 90.

46. Department of Planning and Economic Development, State of Hawaii Growth Policies Plan (Honolulu: State of Hawaii, 1974).

47. Department of Budget and Finance, Growth Management Issues in Hawaii (Honolulu: Hawaii Institute for Management and Analysis in Government, 1977).

48. Kugisaki, C., Preserving the Quality of Life in Hawaii: A Strategy for Population Growth Control Report No. 2 (Honolulu: Legislative Reference Bureau, 1977).

49. Holstrom, J. R., et. al., "Growth Management and the Land Use Commission: Some Options for Change," Department of Budget and Finance, Land and Water Resource Management in Hawaii (Honolulu: Hawaii Institute for Management and Analysis in Government, 1979), pp. 5-68.

50. Department of Planning and Economic Development, The Hawaii State Plan (Honolulu: State of Hawaii, 1978).

51. Shimabukuro, B., "Study Breaks Down Federal Spending in Islands," Honolulu Star-Bulletin, 2 August 1979, p. B-3.

52. Police Chief Guy Paul has estimated that more than 250,000 pounds of marijuana are harvested per year on the island of Hawaii (quoted in a television interview, 19 June 1979). Assuming the dried product is 10 percent of the wet weight and the crop value is $1000 per pound, the harvest would be worth about 50 million dollars. If allowed to mature, the street

value could be worth up to ten times as much, according to Major Alika Parish, head of the Honolulu police vice division (Mary Adamski, "Police Sweeps Net $5.7 Million in Pot," Honolulu Star-Bulletin, 23 June 1979, p. A-2). The value of (unprocessed) sugar cane sales on the Big Island in 1977 was $51,900,000 (State of Hawaii, Data Book, 1978, p. 292). The current value of sugar cane harvested on the Big Island is less than 50 million dollars, since annual values have declined since 1974.

53. Department of Planning and Economic Development, op. cit., (note 46), p. 27.
54. Department of Planning and Economic Development, op. cit., (note 46), p. 29.
55. Kugisaki, op. cit., (note 48), p. 9.
56. Department of Health, "Immigration Trends in Hawaii," Population Report 10 (State of Hawaii, 1978), 8.
57. Schwenke, R., "10,000 Illegal Aliens in State," Honolulu Star-Bulletin, 9 March 1979, p. A-4.
58. Growth Management Task Force, op. cit., (note 33), p. 3.
59. Department of Health, op. cit., (note 56), p. 8.
60. Kugisaki, op. cit., (note 48), p. 9.
61. Nordyke, E. C., "Hawaii is Overcrowded," Honolulu Star-Bulletin, 1 August 1979, (letter to the editor) based on data from the Department of Planning and Economic Development, State of Hawaii.
62. Chow, W. T., and R. J. Fuchs, "Population Redistribution Policies in Hawaii," presented at the Annual Meeting of the Population Association of America, Philadelphia, April, 1979.
63. Chow, W. T., "Tourism and Regional Planning: The Legend of Hawaii," Proceedings of the Fifth Pacific Regional Science Conference, Vancouver, British Columbia (Bellington: Western Washington University, 1978).

64. Mak, J., and E. Nishimura, "The Economics of a Hotel Room Tax," prepared for the Department of Planning and Economic Development, State of Hawaii (August, 1977).

65. Office of Tourism, State Tourism Study: Proposal for a Hawaii Tourism Functional Plan (Honolulu: Department of Planning and Economic Development, State of Hawaii, 1978), p. 38.

66. Community Services Administration, Geographic Distribution of Federal Funds in Hawaii, FIXS-77-12 (Washington, D.C.: Community Services Administration, 1978), pp. 22-23.

67. Shimabukuro, op. cit., (note 51).

68. Department of Planning and Economic Development, op. cit., (note 46), p. 27.

69. Department of Research and Development, Data Book, County of Hawaii, Hilo, 1978, p. 1.

70. League of Women Voters, State Planning in Hawaii: A Primer (Honolulu: League of Women Voters, 1975), p. 11.

71. Chow and Fuchs, op. cit., (note 62).

72. Department of Planning and Economic Development, op. cit., (note 46).

73. Local Area Personal Income, 1970-75, Vol. 9, Far West Region, BEA-REM 77-11 (Washington, D.C.: Bureau of Economic Analysis, U.S. Department of Commerce, August, 1977).

74. Community Services Administration, op. cit., (note 66).

75. Tax Foundation of Hawaii, Government in Hawaii (Honolulu: Tax Foundation of Hawaii, 1976, 1979), Table 9.

76. Department of Planning and Economic Development, State of Hawaii, Data Book (Honolulu: State of Hawaii, 1979).

77. Scott, N. W., "Engineers Suggest Army Consider Leaving Oahu," Honolulu Star-Bulletin, 23 July 1979.

78. Department of Planning and Economic Development, op. cit., (note 46).

79. Department of Planning and Economic Development, op. cit., (note 46), p. 114.
80. Department of Planning and Economic Development, op. cit., (note 46), p. 148.
81. Morse, H., "Pentagon Identifies Land for Release," Honolulu Star-Bulletin, 20 June 1979, p. A-2.
82. Nelson, L., "Military's Land Needs Restudied," Honolulu Star-Bulletin, 19 March 1976, p. F-8.
83. Inouye, D. K., "Federal Lands in Hawaii," Honolulu Star-Bulletin, 5 June 1979, letter to the editor.

CHAPTER 23

REGIONAL DEVELOPMENT POLICIES BY THE FEDERAL STATE OF
SCHLESWIG-HOLSTEIN: THE PROGRAM NORTH

REGIONALE ENTWICKLUNGSPOLITIK DES LANDES
SCHLESWIG-HOLSTEIN: DAS PROGRAMM NORD

Karl Weigand

Abstract

The federal state of Schleswig-Holstein in 1953 inaugurated a reclamation project, the Programm Nord (Program North). The outstanding objectives to be achieved were as follows: to carry out long-term development measures in large areas; continuous financing with investment grants from the federal state; and authorization of an independent institution for executing the project. The peripheral border regions and the coastal districts with low population and unfavorable natural and economic conditions were recognized as areas for development. There were striking deficiencies in comparison with neighboring Denmark that caused political problems.

When the project was begun an inventory of existing conditions was made. This was followed by a critical analysis of the objectives of the project and its execution. Special attention was given to the integrative measures. They became a model for nationwide development planning in rural areas. Selected examples were used to show a remarkable flexibility in executing the project. The reclamation, primarily agrarian in the beginning, changed into a complex development program. This became most important for tourism, which plays a new and important role in a region that has no industrial plants of importance. The results after twenty-five years are positive. It can be shown that the living conditions have been improved equal to the standard that is taken for granted in other regions. In addition, the depressing discrepancy when compared with Denmark no longer exists.

Kurzfassung

Das Bundesland Schleswig-Holstein leitete 1954 ein "Landeskulturprogramm Nord" ein mit
- langfristigen und großflächigen Erschließungsmaßnahmen,
- kontinuierlichen Mittelzuwendungen mit Beteiligung des Bundes,
- übertragung der Erschließungsaufgaben an eine unabhängige Gesellschaft.

Erschließungsgebiete waren die periphere nordwestliche Grenzregion und dünn besiedelte Westküstenbereiche mit naturbedingten und ökonomischen Standortproblemen. Hinzu kamen augenfällige Benachteiligungen gegenüber dänischen Nachbargebieten, die auch zu politischen Problemen führten.

Diese Ausgangssituation wird erläutert, dann folgt eine kritische Analyse der Zielvorstellungen des Programmes und der praktischen Durchführung. Die integralen Maßnahmen werden besonders herausgestellt, als anerkanntes Vorbild für agrarstrukturelle Vorplanungen in der gesamten Bundesrepublik. Einzelbeispiele belegen eine bemerkenswerte Flexibilität in der Bewältigung besonderer Aufgaben. Aus dem anfangs vorwiegend agrarisch ausgerichteten Erschließungsprogramm wird zunehmend eine komplexe Förderung, die einer neuen für den industriearmen Raum bedeutungsvollen Fremdenverkehrsentwicklung zugute kommt. Die positive Bilanz nach 25 Jahren zeigt, daß es gelungen ist, die Lebensbedingungen dem allgemeinen Standard in anderen Regionen anzugleichen. Die ehemals bedrückende Diskrepanz gegenüber diesen Regionen und dem dänischen Nachbarn besteht nicht mehr.

Regional Development Policies by the Federal State of
Schleswig-Holstein: The Program North

The state of Schleswig-Holstein, located in the northernmost part of the Federal Republic of Germany, started a regional development program twenty-five years ago. Its aims and accomplishments received recognition in the Federal Republic of Germany (FRG) and in the European Community. In this essay the most important objectives will be presented, together with a critical analysis of its achievements.

AGRARIAN PROBLEM AREAS IN SCHLESWIG-HOLSTEIN AFTER WORLD WAR II

(a) Unfavorable natural conditions were found to exist. In contrast to the situation in the arable areas that have excellent soil in the eastern part of Schleswig-Holstein, farming in the northwest, within the region of the so-called "Atlantic climate wedge" on the Geest and Marshlands, suffered from various difficulties caused by nature. The proportion of marginal areas with only low yields made up more than 10 percent of the available arable land; 11 percent suffered from compacted soil (Ortsteinbildung), and 25 percent was threatened by wind erosion.

(b) The watershed between the North Sea and the Baltic lies so far to the east that the precipitation affecting more than two-thirds of the total area of the region was diverted into the North Sea through the low land lying at sea level or below. Natural draining is possible only at low tide. A permanent west wind, together with the high levels of the surrounding water and heavy rainfalls, increase the problems; we speak of Wasser-Hypothek (water mortgage). Large districts like the Gotteskoog (Gottes Polder) near the Danish border (made famous by the painter Emil Nolde who resided there) suffered permanently from floods. The large catchment area of the Eider-Treene rivers was another example of permanent flooding. Arable farming became hazardous and entailed high expenditure resulting in 80 percent of the area being covered by permanent grassland.

(c) The catastrophic flood in The Netherlands in 1949 drastically demonstrated that large parts of Schleswig-Holstein's west coast were insufficiently protected. If that great flood had struck Nordfriesland with the same force (as really happened in 1962), 27,000 hectares of marshland would have been flooded if the dike securing the area around Bongsiel had broken. The Hauke-Haien Polder, with an entirely new coastline, was built in the same place later on. As an immediate protection against the dangerous floods, higher dikes would have been needed, and at many places there existed no second-line dikes. In addition, the system of roads for protecting the dikes was not adequate. The natural draining of the tidal rivers, as mentioned before, caused more problems concerning the protection of the entire coastal area.

(d) The northwestern area of Schleswig-Holstein is also one of the economically underdeveloped areas in contrast to the eastern parts and the areas surrounding the metropolis of Hamburg. It is far away from potential centers, lacks industrial resources and sources of energy, and the coastline is unsuitable for harbors due to its shallow waters (Wattenmeer). Only 1.5 percent of the people in the border area were industrial workers in 1961. Many people make their living almost exclusively from farming, and the most important problem for them is the great distance from larger market places.

(e) An important reason for this economic weakness can be seen in the drawing of the boundary between Germany and Denmark in 1920. Since that time the development of the border regions has been intensive. The state of Denmark made every effort to give all possible aid to its newly integrated area of North Schleswig. The area that remained a part of Germany (South Schleswig) became extremely peripheral and was characterized by negligence, emigration, and stagnation in all fields of life. There is considerable data showing that the two parts of the country developed differently. Figure 23-1 shows a map of the road conditions in the areas north and south of the Danish-German border. It reveals most clearly a different structure a decade after the war, at a time when the influx of thousands of German refugees from the Baltic areas caused many additional problems for the poor German border region.

(f) Following the end of World War II, in 1945, there was a common political vacuum which was of special importance to the Danish minority party (Südschleswiger Wählerverband SSW) in the part of Schleswig south of the border. In 1947 this Danish party experienced an increase in public votes never known before (nearly 100,000 votes in the state election). Since 1920 the SSW had represented the political interests of the Danish minority group in Germany, as had the German minority party north of the border. The true number of minority members can be seen by the votes during the seventies when the Danes received approximately 20,000 votes, and the German votes amounted to only 7,000 in Denmark. The unusual increase in Danish votes, after 1947, reflected the feeling of the people that insufficient attention had been given to the social and economic situation in the border area, further encouraged by the direct Danish social welfare offered to German citizens. Following the improvements in the German economy, after 1948, the Danish party soon had a drastic setback in the number of its supporters. However, within the German "problem areas" in the northwestern part of the state a disproportionate amount of nonvoters (in the fifties) could be noticed, as was shown very clearly by G. Isbary in his 1960 study (1).

There is little sense in speculating about what might have happened, especially since Germany and Denmark, in 1955, acknowledged the state boundary of 1920. However, in discussing the Programm Nord (Program North), certain political facts should be pointed out to show that the state of Denmark was at that time accepted by a large segment of the population as a model for regional development. Danish activities in that field have a long record. In the nineteenth century on the Geest of Jutland, the Danish <u>Heidegesellschaft</u> (heath reclamation) became well known for its methods of recultivation of heath land. Danish afforestations and wind-protective hedges became models for Europe during the last 100 years. Therefore, after World War II many people thought it would be best to let the Danish do the reclamation of this depressed German area, just as they had done most successfully after 1920 in their district of Nordschleswig.

GENERAL AIMS, ORGANIZATION, AND FINANCING

On 24 February 1953, the government of the state of Schleswig-Holstein decided: "The reclamation of the distressed areas of Schleswig is a task to be carried out urgently in the state interest. In order to solve this problem a so-called Program North has been worked out" (2). It started at the border in the northwest. However, from the

very beginning, it was decided that the reclamation area
should be extended further to the south (3):

- 1953: First regional separation: 83,000 ha Geest and marshland located south of the border;
- 1957: Englargement to the catchment area of the Bongsiel River: 110,000 ha;
- 1960: An extension of the area to Ditmarschen to the Kiel Canal. Total area now: 542,000 ha, one-third of the total farm area of Schleswig-Holstein;
- 1972: New additions in the north and in the region of Rendsburg; total area of Program North now: 716,330 ha.

The first objective of the program, especially in the fifties, was to improve the agrostructural situation in this depressed area in order to create regions for employment in agriculture. At the same time the goal was to achieve a well rounded development in harmony with further development projects.

Outstanding characteristics of the major planning system included: (a) initial long-term measures in adjacent development areas; (b) establishment of a system of harmonious regions; (c) coordination of all measures with the planned coastal protection works at the border of the North Sea, which also had been planned on a large scale; and (d) maximum flexibility in the execution of special work. The projected close cooperation with the planned coastal protection works led to very pragmatic rules for the area to be developed. Its boundaries followed the catchment areas of the long tidal rivers. Only after 1972 were other districts outside of those catchment areas added (Figure 23-2).

In the beginning financing was achieved by investment grants from the federal state. The federation and state, in 1960, agreed on long-term continuous financing through the so-called "Special Funds North" in the proportion of two to one. The plan has always been that ultimately complete financing should be arranged before the project is begun. Since 1974 the financing for Program North has been part of the joint tasks of federation and state. The proportion of the state has been fixed at 40 percent. As can be seen from Table 23-1, these special funds demand additional funds from other sources which increase from year to year.

Special attention was given to a unique form of organization. In order to achieve the greatest possible freedom of decision, it was decided that the Program North, Ltd. should be established. Membership is made up of the state of Schleswig-Holstein and five participating local authorities as associates (the five counties with the Program North area). The object of the enterprise is "the fostering of the community through the total improvement of the underdeveloped areas, in particular the coordination of the planning and harmonization of all measures as well as the coordination of the financing and the cooperation of the management" (4). Of the capital stock belonging to the company, Schleswig-Holstein controls 50 percent and the five local participating authorities 10 percent each.

The division on land cultivation in the State Department of Agriculture is responsible for the general planning of cultivation. The head of the department is the state representative for Program North and managing director of the company. In addition, the program is run with the aid of the existing offices of the Ministry of Agriculture and of the Ministry of Trade and Traffic. The reason for this was that existing well departmentalized and experienced offices could best guarantee the smoothest execution of an integrated improvement scheme.

In conclusion, the neglected border area was a political challenge that the state wanted to solve with a well prepared regional development program. In addition, it was generally agreed that "reclamation objectives" were to avoid a political vacuum and finally strengthen the German culture within the border area. On this subject all German political parties agreed and, therefore, they unanimously accepted the prime objectives of Program North (although today one sometimes gets the impression that one or the other party may have forgotten these objectives).

CRITICAL ANALYSIS OF ACHIEVEMENTS TO 1979

The long-term run of the project gave it an exceptional regional importance. That the organization achieved continuous financing of such dimensions as shown earlier can be attributed to the representatives in charge. This is particularly noteworthy since Schleswig-Holstein, following the war, was considered to be the poverty region of the German Federation. To bring a program amounting to DM 2 million to a successful realization required enormous efforts and courage. This made it possible to carry out the project systematically in cooperation with the FRG within a quarter of a century. Table 23-1 shows the future funds already committed, and one can count on an extension of the plan for the next 10 years.

The so-called "integrative measures" became typical parts of the entire Program North. They were tested by Jens Iwersen in the Eider area before the war, and he then introduced them to the new program (5). He differentiated between descriptive planning and formative planning by using

TABLE 23-1. The Amount of Investments Sanctioned by the Federation and the State for the Special Funds North in the Main Fields Between 1953 and 1978 and for 1979.
Der Betrag der Investionen welcher der Bund und das Land erlaubt für den Spezialfund Nord in seinen Hauptteilen zwischen 1953 und 1978 und für 1979.

Main Fields	1953	1954	1955	1956	1957	1958	1959	1960	1961	1962
A. Land Allocation/Costs	0,807	7,188	8,245	10,992	11,863	10,786	14,766	15,180	22,763	32,63
B. Agricultural Engineering Measures	-	-	-	-	-	-	-	-	-	-
C. Afforestation	-	0,484	0,492	0,354	0,488	0,580	1,165	1,195	1.229	1,23
D. Water Control Measures	5,945	15,713	11,457	10,839	10,048	11,715	9,328	9,065	11,002	10,68
E_1 Water Supply	-	-	1,222	2,105	1,565	2,025	2,709	7,579	13,295	19,06
E_2 Sewage Disposal	-	-	-	-	-	-	-	-	-	-
F. Development Roads	1,340	1,695	4,531	7,284	6,022	6,730	6,143	5,187	6,671	7,82
G. Dune Strengthening	-	-	-	-	-	-	0,207	0,324	0,188	0,24
H. Protective Measures for Hallig Inhabitants	-	-	-	-	-	-	-	-	0,779	2,57
J. Infrastructural Measures according to the Principles of the Programme for Regional Development	-	-	-	-	-	-	-	-	-	-
K. Administrative Costs	-	-	-	-	0,006	0,040	0,006	0,160	0,22
Total	8,092	25,080	25,947	31,574	29,986	31,842	34,358	38,596	56,087	74,4

	1953-72	in %	1973	1974	1975	1976	1977	1978	1973-78	in
A + B	464,7	43,0	29,6	29,3	23,0	21,0	19,3	17,5	139,7	27,
C	10,9	1,0	0,3	0,4	0,3	0,2	0,3	0,3	1,8	0,
D	247,1	22,9	20,0	25,1	21,5	15,6	14,6	11,0	107,8	21,
E_1	151,6	14,0	19,1	22,5	16,9	12,5	18,9	17,7	107,6	21,
E_2	27,8	2,6	7,4	17,3	14,2	12,7	10,5	10,8	72,8	14,
F	155,5	14,4	9,9	14,5	6,3	7,7	13,5	15,1	67,0	13,
G	2,5	0,2	1968 completed		-	-	-	-	-
H	12,7	1,2	1967 completed		-	-	-	-	-
J	5,1	0,5	0,7	1,0	1,6	1,0	1,3	0,7	6,3	1,
K	1,8	0,2	0,1	0,2	0,2	0,2	0,1	0,1	0,8	0,
Total	1,079,6	100	87,1	110,1	84,0	70,8	78,4	73,2	503,7	10

Sources: Geschäftsberichte der "Programm Nord GmbH, Keil" and "25 Jahre Programm Nord-Gezielte Landentwicklung," Rendsburg 1979.

1963	1964	1965	1966	1967	1968	1969	1970	1971	1972
23,038	41,608	36,271	35,246	35,480	34,077	33,444	31,811	25,702	26,603
-	-	0,377	0,353	0.639	0.755	0.528	1,054	0,415	0,383
0,969	0,752	0,439	0,250	0,195	0,216	0,197	0,249	0,149	0,225
14,395	13,165	13,589	11,793	15,843	17,171	16,874	13,416	12,785	12,285
17,480	13,931	11,958	8,254	10,417	5,517	4,927	10,023	8,427	11,130
1,835	2,930	3,343	2,242	2,256	3,263	2,035	2,734	3,355	3,849
11,638	11,232	10,856	9,973	11,027	10,501	9,866	8,974	9,112	8,884
0,379	0,116	0,293	0,267	0,277	0,156	-	-	-	-
2,794	2,475	1,775	1,282	0,991	-	-	-	-	-
-	-	-	-	-	-	-	-	0,810	4,294
0,182	0,161	0,104	0,109	0,102	0,102	0,118	0,120	0,137	0,135
74,710	86,390	79,005	69,769	77,225	71,578	67,989	68,381	60,892	67,388

1953-78	in %	planned total investments
604,3	38,2	830,0
12,7	0,8	50,0
354,9	22.4	400,0
259,2	16,4	250,0
100,6	6,3	170,0
222,5	14,0	230,0
2,5	0,2	2,5
12,7	0,8	12,5
11,4	0,7	40,0
2,6	0,2	3,5
1,583,2	100	1,988,5

the phrase "stock-taking". Furthermore, he considered the permanent safeguarding of the sites as an urgent requirement. Consequently, his planning system is based on planning, executing, and safeguarding. The present manager of Program North described these methods in the following way:

> It is necessary to introduce the basic principle of an all-around view into the work of cultivation by not only harmonizing the physical, chemical, and biological measures in a meaningful way, but also by considering together water supply, road construction, land reallocation, soil improvement, afforestation and encouragement of trade and commerce. It is further objectionable to split up these goals into isolated measures, but also to look at it from the partial view of an area . . . . (6)

From this arose the pattern of procedure for the Program North, and basic principles were established for the general development planning in rural areas. Bothe (7) and Peters (8) stated that the Program North became the outstanding example for the Agrarstrukturelle Vorplanung (agrarian planing) within the entire FRG. The development planning in rural areas in which proposals are made for the improvement of production conditions and enterprise structures in agriculture and forestry and for the development proposals for recreation facilities, etc., form the basis for the replanning of rural areas.

In the first years the most important objectives of the development measures are easily discernable. From 1953 to 1972, 43 percent of the funds were exclusively spent for reallocation and another 30 percent for water control works. In the seventies there was a clear move toward granting funds for other infrastructural needs. Hence, only 27.7 percent of the money was spent for reallocation in the period from 1973 to 1979. Table 23-1 shows all investments during the past twenty-five years.

In Table 23-2 additional data are presented in order to show the immense amount of comprehensive measures undertaken in connection with reallocation and water control. There is no need to go into detail to stress the variety of agro-structural improvements achieved thus far. A few selected figures will show that all objectives planned were achieved, and in some cases they were surpassed:

(a) In 1949 only 15 percent of the farms exceeded 30 ha in the Program North area. In the other Landkreise (rural districts) the proportion was 20 percent. The proportion in 1978 rose to a level of 41.9 percent, which was 1.1 percent higher than that of other rural districts, which had 39.8 percent. In 1949, 46.1 percent of the cultivated land belonged to these farms in the Program North area and rose to 76.4 percent by 1978. The increase within the entire state rose from 53.6 to 78.1 percent. In other words, there is no difference today between the Program North area and the rest of the state. With a few exceptions the increase in the harvest also surpassed the state average, as the following selected figures show:

Increase of the harvest in the period from 1960-1977	Program North area	Schleswig-Holstein total area
winter wheat	56.5%	52.4%
winter rye	50.4%	46.1%
sugar beets	14.7%	13.7%

TABLE 23-2. Results of 25 Years of Land Reallocation and Water Control Conducted by the Programm Nord (Program North).
Ergebnisse von 25 Jahren der Land Zuteilung und Wasserkontrolle unter der Verwaltung des Programmes Nord.
(Selected data from various sources)

Land-reallocation

462 projects started, involving an area of 475,213 ha (64.5% of the Program North area).

In 416 cases, the reallocation was finished, and the land has passed into ownership, involving an area of 419,700 ha. There are only 90,000 ha left to be reallocated (12% of the originally planned area).

Within the scheme of reallocation

Farm road constructions	7,773 km
Creek and river constructions	2,580 km (open and with pipes)
New drainage areas	31,113 ha
Land improvement areas	10,245 ha
Wind-protective plantations	9,133 km
Afforestation areas	4,531 ha

Location of farmsteads outside the villages due to reallocation: 750 farmsteads

Water regulations - total areas: 150,000 ha

Water supply

Since 1953, 18 water supply districts were established, mainly in rural areas, and 29 water reservoirs have been built serving 476 communities with a population of approximately 550,000, 85% of the total population in the Program North area.

In Northfriesland, the area where the program was started, 90% of all communities have a central water supply system.

Within the same period of time the number of milk cows increased:

    in Schleswig-Holstein - total area   13.3%

    in the Program North area   30.8%

    and within the area of Nordfriesland   50.0%

This can be attributed to better land use for dairy production purposes by measures undertaken by the Program North.

(b) The integrative development measures as they emerged because of Program North became more than a simple improvement in the agrostructure. They exceeded by far the normal range of traditional reallocation measures. This factor should be stressed because critics of the program quite often speak only of agrarian economic improvements and look at the reallocation as an agrarian improvement measure. This criticism is easily rejected by pointing to the dimensions of the work done for water supply and sewage disposal which is of equal benefit to agrarian and nonagrarian people alike. In this connection it is necessary to stress particularly that while the Program North is an independent development program, it has always been in full harmony with all regional policies and special development plans introduced by the state of Schleswig-Holstein since 1968-1969. This is expressed plainly in the first regional development plan for the development of area IV (Regionalplan für den Planungsraum IV--Dithmarschen) which states: "The present aims of the Program North are identical with the official objectives of regional development plans" (9). The demands set forth in the Federal Regional Development Program concerning the joint tasks, Improvement of Regional Economic Structure (Raumordungsgesetz zur Gemeinschaftsaufgabe, Verbesserung der regionalen Wirtschaftsstruktur) will be completely achieved by the Trostran Nord. Therefore, that "the improvement measures (in the scheme of the Program North) have been tuned neither in their directions nor in the financing towards the comprehensive economic development," as claimed by Schmitt in 1979 (10), was not correct. As an excellent example of the infrastructural improvements mentioned, one could look again at the road construction. In comparison to the situation in 1954, when the program was begun, two selected typical neighboring areas north and south of the state boundary have been mapped (Figure 23-3). The examples show not only the thorough development of the communities with newly built roads, but the comparison also demonstrates that the earlier discrepancy with Denmark no longer exists. In contrast, the road system on the German side of the boundary is quite often more complete than on the other side of the border.

(c) Within the last twenty years the west coast region of Schleswig-Holstein has become a privileged recreation area for the entire Federal Republic. Not only have the excellent recreation facilities on the island of Sylt had a boom never known before, but the agrarian areas within the district of Program North have also profited from this development as well.

Research has shown the following interesting developments: tourism has been developed in the former truly agrarian region of Eiderstedt caused by the spillover from the famous spa St. Peter-Ording; there has been a fundamental change in the pure agrarian structure of the Halligen (a small island in the Wattenmeer) as a result of modern tourist discovery; and there has developed a special form of tourism known as "Holidays on the Farmsteads" (Ferien auf dem Bauernhof), especially within the region of Nordfriesland. In all of these areas there is no doubt that tourism has become a most important economic source of income, next to farming. However, a basic need for this type of development was a modern road system and an up-to-date water supply system which had been provided thus far primarily for agriculture only. It is acknowledged that the well developed farms, especially, have made the necessary economic improvements possible with the income received from tourism. It is also possible to prove these statements by the following examples.

The Program North contributed considerably to improving the growing tourism in the west coast areas, and in many respects even started it. This new development in the field of tourism should be stressed in particular because until now it has left its impact only on the establishment of new trade and industries on a smaller scale in the coastal region of Program North. It certainly can be considered as a success of infrastructural improvements executed by the program that the number of employees in industry rose 2.2 percent in the period from 1959 to 1977. There also was an increase in the residential population of 9.1 percent during the period from 1961 to 1978. Nevertheless, the Program North area is part of a German planning region which shows the least dense population. Although an increase from 89 to 96 inhabitants per square km could be registered, this is the lowest population density of all the states (the FRG average is 165 per square km). The ratio of employees in industry was only 46 per 1,000 inhabitants in the Program North area (the FRG average is 73).

Today agriculture is still a very important source of income in the Program North area; the gross domestic product (GNP) in the field of agriculture was 13.3 percent in 1974 (in Schleswig-Holstein as a whole, 7.1 percent). Only 17 percent of the people were employed in agriculture in 1970, as compared with 9 percent in the state.

Innovations in regard to industrial development are lacking, and perhaps this is not unexpected in a peripheral area. Since several military bases are located in the area, a considerable number of jobs could be offered. Tourism, with all its economic consequences, is being developed, but whether it will achieve a position of importance cannot possibly be judged at the moment.

An outstanding example of how living conditions of a certain region could be changed by the Program North (in close cooperation with the projects for coastal protection) is the recultivation and development of the Halligen. In this particular case one must give high credit to the managers responsible for carrying out all measures with great flexibility, so that the procedure of development was characterized by a minimum of preconceived administrative plan or thought. The data listed in Table 23-1 give very little explanation as to whether the plans have been executed with much red tape or by common sense. Or, to put it another way, does the state as the responsible organization permit sufficient flexibility in the performance of prescribed work?

In this short essay it is not possible to describe in detail how Halligen was developed. This was published in a separate study (11). But it should be pointed out that on those islands the entire traditional way of life had to be changed in less than one decade (from 1961 to 1968). One has to keep in mind that after the war outmigration from these islets reached its high point. Halligen, in the early sixties, still reminded one of the eighteenth or nineteenth century. Only sixteen farm buildings were built in the twentieth century of the 100 existing Hallig farmsteads;

forty-six of them were over 100 years old and twenty-eight even more than 200 years old. Most of them were not sufficiently protected against storm floods, and the Warften (artificial hills where farmsteads are located) were too small and too low. There were no paved roads, and on several islands electricity was not available. Water was supplied by old-fashioned Fethinge (artificial cisterns collecting the rain which ran down thatched roofs), and during the Great Flood of 1962, all cisterns were flooded once more by salt water, creating a very dangerous situation for the animals on the islands. By means of the comprehensive measures of Program North this situation has been drastically changed, and today life on the Halligen does not differ from life on the mainland. In addition, the new Mauke-Haien Polder made it possible to build new harbors for a new ferry line that was no longer dependent on the rhythm of the tide. This demonstrates how different projects were integrated most efficiently.

Earlier it was mentioned that Halligen became a spot for tourism during the past few years, and many Hallig farmers decided to engage in tourism, neglecting their traditional jobs, especially in view of the fact that farming on their islands no longer could compete with the more favorable conditions on the mainland. Therefore, new plans were designed by Program North to aid the Halligen a second time. During the past six years financial help has been given to the Hallig farmers to enable them to take cattle from the mainland for grazing during the summer time. Hallig agriculture thus was assisted in a way similar to what is done in the Alpine region. In addition, a new project of modernization of life in the village will be instigated on the larger islands of Hooge and Langeness. Once more it was demonstrated that Program North could help these islands by flexible measures meeting the needs of the present situation.

A critical analysis of the achievements of a development project such as the Program North has to meet certain standards. Accomplishments must be judged on their long-term impact. As an example, one can look at the first spectacular project of Program North, the new colonization of the Friedrich-Wilhelm-Lübke Polder located close to the Danish border south of Hindenburg Dam, which was constructed with a new dike in 1954 (12). The size of the new farmsteads in that polder was set at 24 hectares. The present view is that this is definitely too small for a modern farm providing the farmer with a sufficient base for living. However, many Danish farmsteads nearby (the so-called Husman farms) that were organized in the forties and fifties were only 12 hectares in size. In many respects the Lübke Polder farmstead size of 24 hectares at that time was considered too large, and the planners had to overcome considerable resistance in order to accomplish their project. In another publication it was shown that in the meantime the Lübke farmers have changed to modern management and production methods, and the average farm size had grown to 44.5 hectares by 1978 (Figure 23-4).

One should not judge the cost of this colonization by economic criteria only. In a time of high unemployment in the border area, the Lübke-Polder project offered jobs to approximately 1,300 persons in the period from 1953 to 1955-1956. One of the major tasks of the postwar period was the integration of the German refugees into the economy of the area. In the Lübke-Polder project, 50 percent of the farmsteads were given to refugees from eastern parts of

THE FEDERAL STATE OF SCHLESWIG-HOLSTEIN 731

Germany, and 50 percent to the people who had always lived in the region of Schleswig-Holstein.

The success of the planned integration was evident in that after twenty-five years only one farmer had left and that was because of illness. All the others still work on their farms, and in all cases it is apparent that the children are anxious to inherit the property.

When colonization began, a small school was built that was the pride of the settlement. The Program North was praised for its help. Only ten years later (in 1968) the school had to be closed due to a reorganization in the field of education. How did the people react, and could it be considered a typical fault in planning? Not a single farmer could be found who regretted the new development that their childred now had to attend a new comprehensive school outside the polder. On the contrary, they made the best of that new situation and, as a result of their initiative, a new kindergarten was established in the old school building. It is now attended by children from three communities.

In the same way one should be cautious about judging neglect in landscape conservation. Deficiencies in planning should not be concealed or excused. However, it would be unfair again to reproach the program for these shortcomings only. Comprehensive planning, including the whole range of land conservation measures, has become very popular only during the last ten years. This applies to planning projects in rural areas as well as in urban regions. There is no reason to argue that in the fifties or in the sixties different Program North areas with marginal soils should really have been afforested (e.g., as recreation forests for tourism) instead of put into soil improvements for the benefit of agriculture only. Some moors and heath areas, for example, could have been protected instead of put into cultivation. However, those views became popular in most recent times, and not only within the area of Program North. Therefore, one can appreciate the fact that the comprehensive concept incorporated into the Program North stressing long-term development programs was sufficiently flexible to acquire new conservation measures on a large scale during the last years. In addition, one should observe that the execution of each reallocation project has to be coordinated in terms of landscape conservation.

In this connection a new task should be pointed out--steps taken for a village renewal program initiated since 1977. This task is not really entirely new, and there have been many previous examples, i.e., the well known public competitions "Let's improve our village." Lately one has come to the conclusion that only when the total combined measures are executed at the same time can a structural renewal of those villages be achieved. So far only the physical aspect of the renewal had been stressed. Program North has taken on this new task with several model communities in the area, and another future task for the whole program may arise. The dimensions for this project may possibly reach the same importance as reallocation with all the impact this has had for decades.

CONCLUSION

In conclusion, the major objectives of Program North have been achieved. The distinct disparity in the development between the FRG and Denmark has been erased. Today a political vacuum no longer exists in the German border areas. Both national groups, south and north of the border, live in a peaceful neighborhood. Thanks to reclamation of the Program

North the border areas today are now in a position even to compete with their Danish neighbors. Land development measures were never considered as a short-sighted mobilization of reserves for food production on semicultivated wasteland. Thanks to the Land Reclamation and Development Company it has been possible to give Program North an increasingly comprehensive character. These integrative development measures became a model for many other rural development projects.

Primarily this program began as an agrarian development program. Today it is a complex concept for the entire area. Not only the farming community but the whole population has also profited from this development. Commerce, trade, and especially tourism are the most important beneficiaries next to agriculture.

It should not be assumed from the positive results mentioned that the coastal district in the west and the border region in the north have gained a lasting consolidation and that no further aid will be necessary. By mapping the population density in the entire region of the two federal states, Hamburg and Schleswig-Holstein, and the neighboring country, Denmark, it can be shown that both of the west coast regions north and south of the border reveal a striking difference as compared to the east coast of the peninsula of Jutland (Figure 23-5). There are many more economic activities in the east, and it is a logical consequence that the important interstate highway, which was built in 1963, should run through eastern Jutland and connect the two centers of Hamburg and Copenhagen by the shortest route. This highway successfully competes with the older northern route via Jutland. It can easily be seen that this contributed again to the previously described peripheral situation of the Program North area.

Much effort will still be necessary to maintain the advancements that have now been gained in that formerly depressed region where there is still a low population density. It is much appreciated that the entire regional development policy of the so-called Program North definitely will be continued by law for another ten years. Negotiations with Denmark would also be useful, since similar problems exist in this adjoining western region as indicated in Figure 23-5. The positive results achieved by the reclamation after twenty-five years ought to be a platform for future developments to be executed in Germany as well as within the framework of a joint task with Denmark, thus maintaining the accomplishments which have been achieved.

THE FEDERAL STATE OF SCHLESWIG-HOLSTEIN

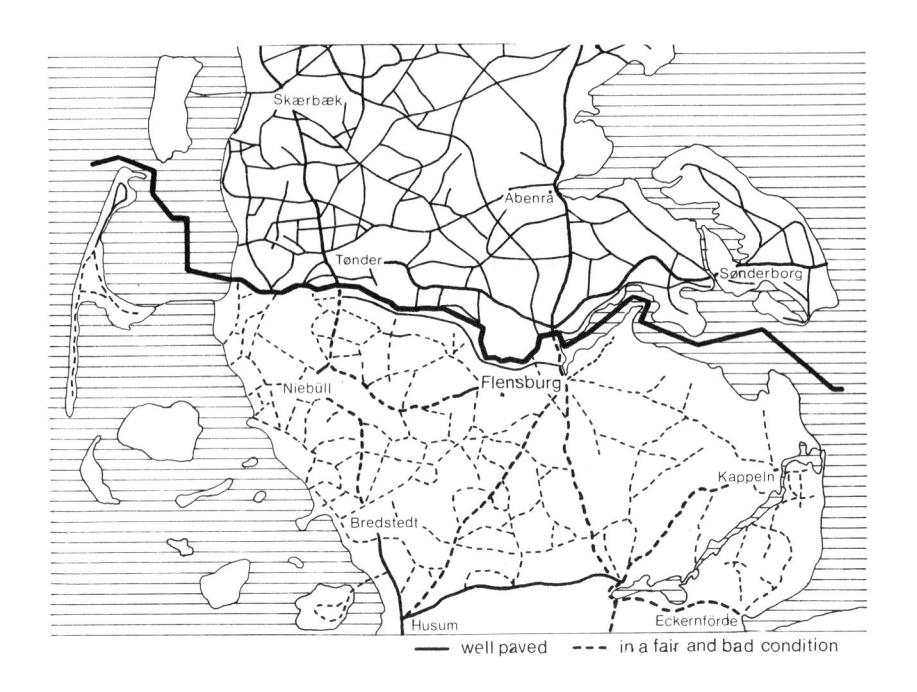

FIG. 23-1. Public Roads in the Regions North and South of the German-Danish Border, 1954.
Öffentliche Strassen in der Region Nord und Süd von der Deutsch-Dänischen Grenze in 1954.

Source: Weigan, K., Programm Nord, Wandel der Landschaft in Schleswig-Holstein, 2nd revised ed. (Kiel: Hirt, 1970); Weigand, K., and Riechen, G., "Strukturwandel der nordfriesischen Halligen mit besonderer Berücksichtigung der Hallig Hooge," in Beiträge zur Frühjahrstagung der Agrarsozialen Gesellschaft (1977), pp. 58-62.

FIG. 23-2. Program North Area, Location and Extension.
Programm Nord Region, Lage und Ausdehnung.

Source: Peters, J., 25 Jahre Programm Nord, Gezielte Landentwicklung (Flensburg: Programm-Nord GmbH., 1979), pp. 54-55.

THE FEDERAL STATE OF SCHLESWIG-HOLSTEIN

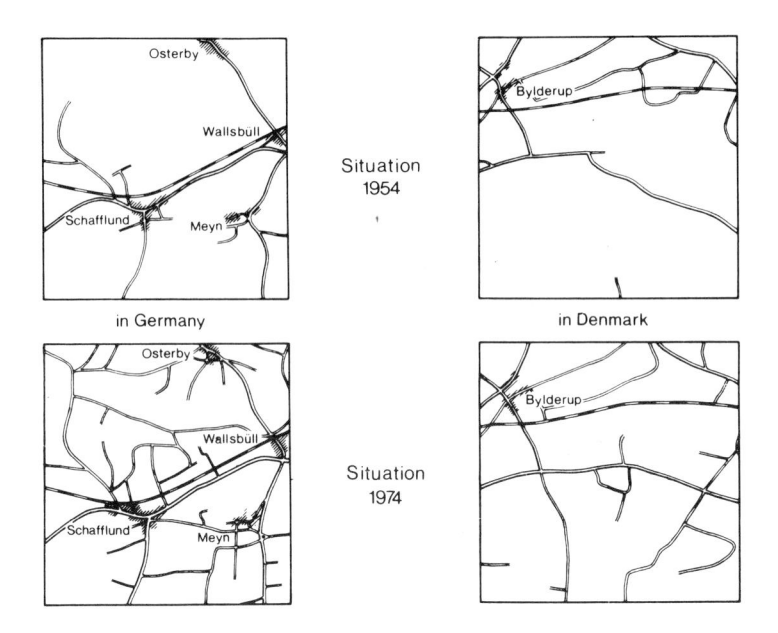

FIG. 23-3. Main Roads and Farm Roads in Two Selected Areas North and South of the German-Danish Border.
   Strassenzustand in zwei ausgewählten Regionen nördlich und südlich der Deutsch-Dänischen Grenze.

Source: Official Road Maps of Denmark and Schleswig-Holstein.

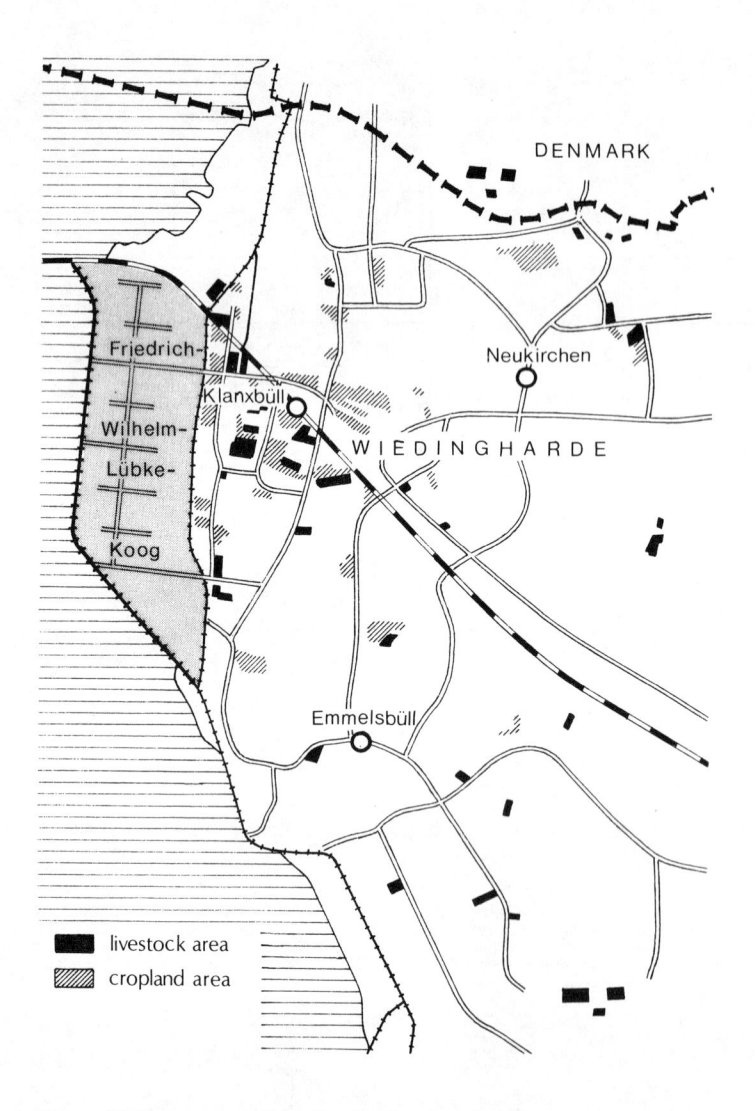

FIG. 23-4. Land Use in Adjoining Communities by Farmers of the Lübke-Koog.
    Landbenutzung in angrenzenden Gemeinden bei Bauern in der Lübke-Koog.

Source: Weigand, K., ed., Friedrich-Wilhelm-Lübke-Koog (Flensburg: Schlesiger Druck-und Verlagshaus Institut für Regionale Forschung und Informationen, 1979).

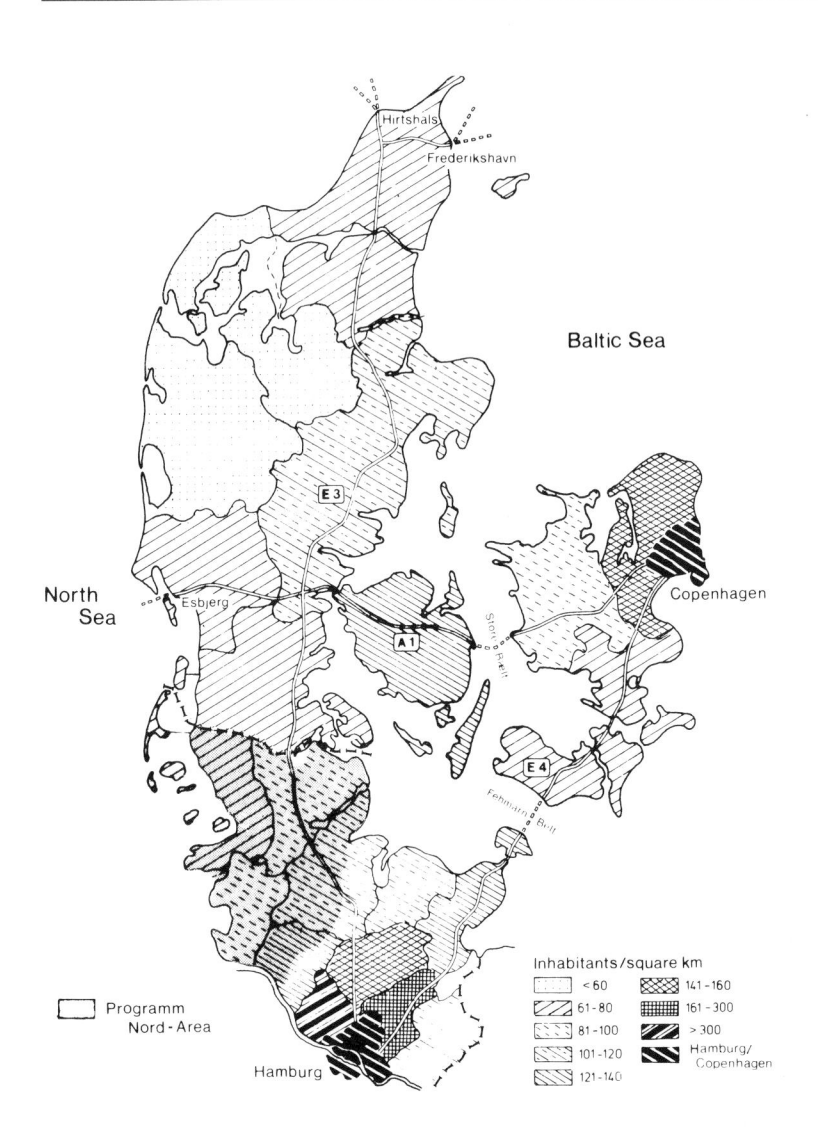

FIG. 23-5. Location of the German Development Region and Population Density in the Total Area: Hamburg, Schleswig-Holstein and Denmark.
　　　　　Dichte in der Gesamtregion Hamburg, Schleswig-Holstein und Dänemark.

Source: Weigand, K., Flensburg Atlas, 1978.

NOTES

1. Isbary, G., Problemgebiete im Spiegel politischer Wahlen am Beispel, Schleswigs, Heft 43 (Bad Godesberg: Bundesanstalt für Landeskunde und Raumforschung, 1960).

2. Bielfeld, C., Policies and Programs for Rural Areas Development. Comparative Analysis of Selected Rural Areas: The Wiedau-Bonsiel Region in the "Programm-Nord" Area of the Federal Republic of Germany, Vol. II (Paris: O.E.C.D., 1966), AGR/T (66), p. 16.

3. Jahresberichte der Schleswig-Holsteinischen Landgewinnungs-und -erschliessungsgesellschaft (Programm-Nord GmbH, 1954-1979).

4. Fröbe, A., Das Programm Nord, Bilanz 1953-1967 (Niebüll: Programm-Nord GmbH, 1968).

5. Reinersdorff, A. von., "Programme North," (Kiel: Programm-Nord GmbH, 1976).

6. ------, op. cit., (note 5).

7. Bothe, H. G., Vorplanung im Agrarbereich, Stand und Grundlagen ihrer Weiterentwicklung, Heft 149 Schriftenreihe der AID-Land und Hauswirtschaftliche Auswertungs-und Informationsdienst (1967).

8. Peters, J., 25 Jahre Programm Nord, Gezielte Landentwicklung (Rendsburg: Programm-Nord GmbH, 1979), pp. 54-55.

9. Innenminister des Landes Schleswig-Holstein, ed., Regionalplan für den Planungsraum IV (Kreis Dithmarschen und Steinburg) 1978.

10. Schmitt, G., Die Probleme traditioneller Landentwicklungspolitik, gezeigt am Beispiel des "Programm Nord", Band 54, Schriften des Vereins für Sozialpolitik (1970), p. 232.

11. Weigand, K., Programm Nord, Wandel der Landschaft in Schleswig-Holstein, 2nd revised ed. (Kiel: Hirt, 1970); and K. Weigand and G. Riecken, "Strukturwandel der nordfriesischen Halligen mit besonderer Berücksichtigung der Hallig Hooge," in Beiträge zur Frühjahrstagung der Agrarsozialen Gesellschaft (1977), 58-62.

12. Weigand, K., ed., Friedrich-Wilhelm-Lübke-Koog (Flensburg: Schlesiger Druck-und Verlagshaus Institut für Regionale Forschung und Informationen, 1979).

GLOSSARY

Arbeitsmarktregionen	labor market regions
Bauleitplan	development plan (collective term)
Bauleitplanung	town and country development plan
Bebauungsplan	local land use plan
Bund	federal government
Bundesbaugesetz	federal building law
Bundesfernstrassen (Autobahnen)	federal highways, long distance trunck roads
Bundesrat	Federal Council or Upper House (federal chamber of the states/Länder)
Bundesraumordnungsgesetz	Federal Regional (Spatial) Policy Act
Bundesraumordnungsprogramm	Federal Regional (Spatial) Planning Program (BROP) (national interregional plan)
Bundestag	Lower House
Entwicklungsachsen	growth axes
Entwicklungszentren	growth centers
Ergänzungsgebiet	neighboring municipalities
Gebietseinheiten	areal units, subarea
Gemeinden	municipalities
Gemeinschaftsaufgabe	joint task
Gemeinschaftssteuern	joint taxes
Gestaltungsmittel	constructive or formative instruments
Grundgesetz	Basic Law, the Constitution
Grünflächenkommission	commission for the preservation of verdure
Grundsatz der Politik	policy principles

Heidegesellschaft	a corporation for the reclamation of heath, thus making agriculture possible
Industriestandortpolitik	distribution of industry policy (industrial location policy)
Kernstadt, Kerngebiet	central city, central zone
Kreis	county
kreisfreie Städte	self-governing cities, towns
kommunale Entwicklungsplanung or Stadtentwicklungsplanung	town development planning
Land, Länder, Bundesland	state, states, federal state
Baden-Württemberg	Baden-Württemberg
Bayern	Bavaria
Bremen	Bremen
Hamburg	Hamburg
Hessen	Hessen
Niedersachsen	Lower Saxony
Nordrhein-Westfalen	North Rhine-Westphalia
Rheinland-Pfalz	Rhineland-Palatinate
Saarland	Saarland
Schleswig-Holstein	Schleswig-Holstein
Berlin	West Berlin
Landesbaubehörde	association of local planning authorities
Landesentwicklungsprogramm	regional development program of a state
Landesplanung	regional policy of a state
Landesplanungsgemeinschaft	authorities in North Rhine-Westphalia responsible for the preparation of regional plans
Landesplanungsgesetz	regional planning policy law
Landschaftsverbände	autonomous administrative units existing only in North Rhine-Westphalia since 1953, e.g., social service, road service

Landesraumordnungsplan	regional strategy of a state
Landesraumordnungsprogramm	state regional planning program
Landkreis	rural district
Landtag	parliament of a state
Ministerkonferenz für Raumordnung	ministerial standing conference for regional policy
Oberzentren	highest central places
Planungsregion	planning region
Politikverflechtung	political involvement, policy interdependence
Programm Nord	Program for Schleswig-Holstein North
Rahmengesetzgebung	framework legislation
Rahmenkompetenz	framework responsibility to issue legislation
Randzone	outer zone
raumbeanspruchend	land using (term for all planning and measures which place a demand on land resources)
Raum, räumlich, gebietlich	regional, spatial, areal
Raumordnung	regional policy (collective term)
Landesraumordnung	regional policy of a state
Raumplanung	physical planning
Raumordnungsklausel	regional planning clause
Raumordnungsverband	association of subregional planning authorities with specific responsibilities
Regierungsbezirk	government district
Regierungspräsident	intermediate authority on state level
Regionale Wirtschaftspolitik	regional economic policy
Regionalforschung	regional research
Regionalplan	subregional planning, regional planning

regionale Planungsgemeinschaft	standing conference for regional planning
Reichstelle für Raumordnung	supreme Reich agency for regional policy
Reichstag	pre-World War II parliament
Schwerpunktort	focal place
Siedlungsordnungsgesetz	registration of larger projects of housing construction
Siedlungsverband Ruhrkohlenbezirk	Ruhr Regional Planning Authority
Stadtregion	city region
Städtebauförderungsgesetz	Urban Renewal and Town Development Act
Stadtkreis	city with county functions
Stadtstaaten	city states (Hamburg and Bremen)
Standortplanung	locational policy
Strukturschwäche	structural weakness
Trendwende	turning point
Umweltpolitik	environmental policies
Verdichtung, Verballung	agglomeration
Verdichtungsgebiet, Ballungsgebiet	state of pronounced concentration of population, housing and employment in area
Verfassungsgericht	Constitutional court
verstädterte Zone	urbanized zone
Vorrangfunktion	areas with priority functions
Wirtschaftsplan	economic plan
Wirtschaftswunder	economic wonder
Wohnungsförderungsgesetz	housing development act
Wohnungssiedlungsgesetz	housing development act
Zonengrenze	zonal border, frontier border
Zonenrandgebiet	zonal peripheral regional (eastern border region)
Zwangsmittel	instruments of obligatory character

NOTES ON CONTRIBUTORS

The Federal Republic of Germany

DR. DIETRICH BARTELS, Professor of Geography at the University of Kiel, studied geography and economics and was awarded a degree as Diplom-Volkswirt (economics) before receiving his Ph.D. in Hamburg (1957). He habilitated at the University of Cologne (1968). Dr. Bartels taught at the Technical University of Karlsruhe before working in Kiel. His research interests are theory of spatial sciences, spatial economic theory and regional planning.

DR. KLAUS-ACHIM BOESLER is Professor and Director of the Economic Geography Institute of the University of Bonn. He received his Ph.D. (1959) and completed his habilitation at the Free University of Berlin (1966). From 1966 to 1972 he was Associate Professor at the Free University and since 1973 is Professor at the University of Bonn. His major research interests are in Political and Economic Geography, Spatial Sciences, and the regional geography of Europe.

DR. HELMUT BREUER, Professor of Geography and occupant of the chair for Geography and the Theory of Geography with special emphasis on the Rhineland, at the Technische Universität Aachen. He received his Ph.D. (1968) and completed his habilitation (1974) at the Technical University Aachen. His research specializes in the Northeastern part of the USA, Benelux countries, the Rhineland industrial and transportation geography, as well as theory of Geography.

DR. WERNER FRICKE, Professor and Head, Department of Geography, University of Heidelberg. He received his Ph.D. and habilitated at the University of Frankfurt (1967). Presently is a member of the seven man Administrative Board of the University of Heidelberg. He started research on rural social geography in Southern Germany and has published a number of studies on suburban population and housing development in the Rhine-Main and Rhine-Neckar regions. After 1961 he did field work in applied agricultural geography in Nigeria and was Senior Research Associate at Makerere University College, Kampala/Uganda in 1969, 1974 and 1978 working in the field of settlement structure and population geography of East Africa. He is editor of the Heidelberg Geographische Arbeiten.

DR. BURKHARD HOFMEISTER is Professor at the Technical University West Berlin. He received his Ph.D. and habilitated at the Free University Berlin (1958). He was a recipient of the Whitbeck Fellowship from the University of Wisconsin at Madison 1955/56 and was a graduate teaching assistant in the University of Utah at Salt Lake City 1956/57. He is president of the Gesellschaft für Erdkunde zu Berlin (Berlin Geographical Society).

DR. GEORG KLUCZKA is Professor of Applied Geography at the Free University Berlin. He received his Ph.D. (1966) from the University of Muenster and habilitated at the University of Cologne (1973). From 1965 to 1975 he served as advisor on spatial structure research at the Federal Research Institute for Planning at Bonn-Bad-Godesberg. From 1971 to 1975 he was also lecturer in applied geography at Cologne University. Since 1975 he has been at the Free University. His special research fields are in urban geography and infrastructure supply.

DR. KARL LENZZ, Professor and Head of the Department of Geography at John F. Kennedy Institute for North American Studies, Free University Berlin, received his Ph.D. from the

University of Greifswald and habilitated at the University
of Marburg. Research interests are in geography of settlements, economic geography, regional: United States and
Canada, West and East Germany.

*DR. PETER SCHÖLLER is Professor and Director of the Depart-
ment of Geography at the Ruhr-University Bochum. He studied
history and geology at the Universities of Berlin and Bonn
and received his Ph.D. from the University of Bonn (1951)
and habilitated at the University of Muenster (1959). He
held the position of director of the Westphalian Research
Institute, Muenster. His research field: Urban Studies,
Human and Political Geography; Regional Geography: Central
Europe and East Asia (Japan). Dr. Schöller was between
1969-1971 President of the Association of German Geographers
and is since 1977, President, National Committee for the
International Geographical Union.

DR. KARL WEIGAND is Director of the Research Institute for
Regional Geography at the Education University of Flensburg
(Pädagogische Hochschule) and Associate Professor at the
Geographical Seminar at the same institution. He received
his Ph.D. at the University of Frankfut (1955) and habili-
tated at the University Kiel (1970).

DR. REINHART ZSCHOCKE, Professor of Geography at the Technical University at Aachen. He obtained his Ph.D. (1958) and
habilitated (1967) from the University of Cologne. He
has been teaching since 1968 at the Geographical Institute
of the Technical University at Aachen. His main research
interests are connected with the urban and agrarian geography of Central Europe, especially the Rhineland and Historical Geography.

The United States

DR. JOHN S. ADAMS is Professor of Geography and Public Affairs and Director of the Hubert H. Humphrey Institute of Public Affairs, University of Minnesota. He received his Ph.D. in geography and economics from the University of Minnesota (1966). He directed the Comparative Metropolitan Atlas Project sponsored by the Association of American Geographers (1971-76) and was senior Fulbright-Hays lecturer at the Institut für Raumordnung at the Economic University in Vienna (1975-76).

DR. LEWIS M. ALEXANDER is Professor and Chairman, Department of Geography and Marine Affairs, University of Rhode Island. He received his Ph.D. from Clark University. Dr. Alexander was the Director of the Law of the Sea Institute (1966-73) and has been Director, Master of Marine Affairs Program, University of Rhode Island since 1969. He has been a consultant for the U.S. Department of State since 1963. His research is in Political and Marine Geography.

DR. RONALD BRIGGS is Associate Professor of Geography and Political Economy in the School of Social Sciences, Graduate Program in Political Economy. He holds a Ph.D. in geography from the Ohio State University (1972). He taught at the Department of Geography, University of Texas at Austin. Currently, he is working on research grants for the U.S. Department of Transportation on the impact of the interstate highway system on non-metropolitan growth and for the U.S. Administration on Aging on a reassessment of the transportation problems of the elderly.

DR. CLYDE E. BROWNING, Professor of Geography at the University of North Carolina at Chapel Hill, has a Ph.D. from the University of Washington (1958). Prior to his present post he was land use analyst for the Chicago Area Transportation Study and Professor of Real Estate and Land Use, the University of Oregon. His principal research interests are urban, quaternary economic geography and the South.

**DR. WILLARD TIM CHOW, Assistant Professor of Geography and Urban and Regional Planning at the University of Hawaii. He received his Ph.D. from the University of California, Berkeley (Economics and Geography) (1970). Dr. Chow taught at Laney College in Oakland and at San Francisco State University before joining the University of Hawaii in 1975. He has focused most of his research on the role of public policies in regional development, land use, and community revitalization.

DR. ROBIN DOUGHTY is Associate Professor of Geography at the University of Texas at Austin and holds a Ph.D. from the University of California at Berkeley (1971). He was a research associate in ecology at the Smithsonian Institution in Washington, D.C. He is interested in biogeography and the history of animal utilization.

**DR. ROLAND J. FUCHS, Professor and Chairman of the Department of Geography at the University of Hawaii at Manoa. He received his Ph.D. from Clark University (1950). His research centers on population distribution, regional development and urbanization policies in socialist and developing countries. Dr. Fuchs is Chairman of the U.S. National Committee of the International Geographical Union, and has been active in the American Association for the Advancement of Slavic Studies and the Pacific Science Association.

DR. PATRICIA GOBER, Associate Professor of Geography at Arizona State University. She obtained a Ph.D. from the Ohio State University in 1975. Her research interests include population, economic and urban geography with an emphasis on the interrelationship between migration and regional economic growth, the migratory behavior of elderly people and intra-urban variations in demographic characteristics.

DR. NILES HANSEN is Professor of Economics at the University of Texas at Austin. He received his Ph.D. from Indiana University (1963). From 1975 to 1977 he was on leave to carry out research on human settlement systems at the International Institute for Applied Systems Analysis, Laxenburg, Austria. He is author of numerous books and articles on regional development policies and has been a consultant to such organizations as the Ford Foundation, the World Bank and the United Nations.

DR. GÜNTER KRUMME is Professor of Geography at the University of Washington in Seattle. He holds a degree in Business Economics (dipl. oec. publ.) Munich and a Ph.D. in Geography from the University of Washington. His research interests and publications relate to spatial, regional and policy aspects of organizational behavior and industrial change. He is a corresponding member of the IGU Commission on Industrial Systems.

**DR. IAN R. MANNERS is an Associate Professor of Geography at the University of Texas at Austin. He holds a D. Phil. from Oxford University (1969). He has worked extensively in the Middle East on water resource management issues, acting as a consultant to governments of Jordan, Kuwait, and Saudi Arabia. He was Chairman of the Commission on College Geography's Panel on Environmental Education (1970-73) and co-editor of <u>Perspectives on Environment</u>, published by AAG.

DR. MELVIN G. MARCUS, Professor and Chairman of the Department of Geography at Arizona State University, received his Ph.D. from the University of Chicago (1963). He is a past-

NOTES ON CONTRIBUTORS 753

President of the Association of American Geographers and a member of the Executive Committee of the Governor's Commission on Arizona Environment. His research interests have been in physical geography, environmental science, and environmental education. He has done research and field work in alpine and polar environments. In recent years he has shifted some of his research efforts to urban and desert landscapes of the American Southwest. Dr. Marcus has served as Chairman of the Commission on College Geography. He has published extensively on his research in Alaska, the Yukon, New Zealand, Mexico, Turkey, and the United States.

DR. RUTHERFORD H. PLATT, Associate Professor of Geography and Planning Law at the University of Massachusetts, Amherst. He holds a Ph.D. and J.D. from the University of Chicago (1971). He is a member of the Illinois Bar and the American Bar Association as well as the Association of American Geographers. His principal research interests concern jurisdictional constraints in the management of land and water resources. He has served as consultant on floodplain management policy to the U.S. Army Corps of Engineers, the U.S. Water Resources Council, the U.S. Office of Technology Assessment, and the White House Domestic Policy Council.

DR. JOHN REES is Associate Professor of Geography and Political Economy and Acting Director of the Southwest Center for Economic and Community Development at the University of Texas at Dallas. He received his Ph.D. from the London School of Economics (1977). His research interests are manufacturing change and industrial location.

**DR. GUNDARS RUDZITIS, Assistant Professor of Geography at the University of Texas at Austin, received his Ph.D. from the University of Chicago (1977). He worked as a research analyst and program manager for the U.S. Navy. He has also acted as a consultant for the Environmental Protection Agency. His current research interests are in environmental impact assessment and related equity issues.

*in absentia
**joint authors

Editor and Project Director

DR. GEORGE W. HOFFMAN, Professor and Chairman, Department of Geography at the University of Texas at Austin received his Ph.D. from the University of Michigan (1950). He was chairman of the AAG Committee on International Cooperation (1974-79), is a member of the Board of Directors, its Executive Committee and chairman of the Program Committee of RFE-RL; a member of the Committee on Academic-Government Relations of the American Association for the Advancement of Slavic Studies (AAASS). He served as chairman and member of numerous AAASS Committees, was a member for many years of the American Council of Learned Societies Committee on Eastern Europe and the Joint Committee on Slavic Studies of the SSRC-ACLS, was a member of the first Academic Advisory Board, Kennan Institute for Advanced Russian Studies of the Woodrow Wilson International Center for Scholars (1975-1978) and served on many government and foundation advisory and review panels. He was twice Fulbright professor in the Federal Republic of Germany (Munich, Heidelberg) and traveled and lectured widely in both East and West Europe. His research interests are in Political Geography, History and Philosophy of Geography and various topics of economic development with emphasis on the countries of Eastern Europe. He is author of numerous books, scholarly articles and government reports.

LIBRARY OF DAVIDSON COLLEGE

Books on regular loan may be checked out for **two weeks**. Books must be presented at the Circulation Desk in order to be renewed.

A fine is charged after date due.

Special books are subject to special regulations at the discretion of the library staff.